D1706254

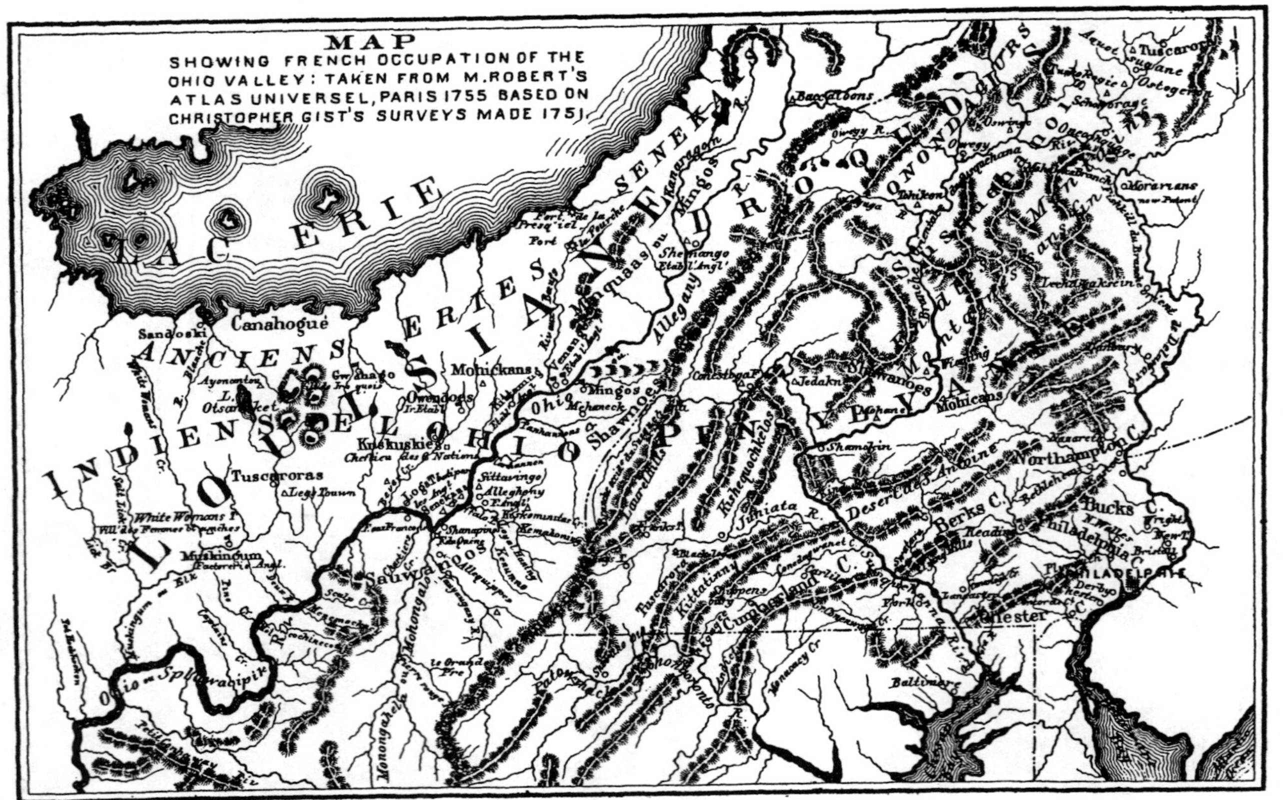

MAP
SHOWING FRENCH OCCUPATION OF THE OHIO VALLEY: TAKEN FROM M. ROBERT'S ATLAS UNIVERSEL, PARIS 1755 BASED ON CHRISTOPHER GIST'S SURVEYS MADE 1751.

VIRGINIA COURT RECORDS IN SOUTHWESTERN PENNSYLVANIA

Records of the District of West Augusta and Ohio and Yohogania Counties, Virginia

1775-1780

By

BOYD CRUMRINE

Consolidated Edition

With an Index by

INEZ WALDENMAIER

CLEARFIELD

Excerpted and Reprinted from
Annals of the Carnegie Museum,
Volumes I-III,
Pittsburgh, 1902-1905

Reprinted with an Added Foreword
and an Index, and Re-paged
Genealogical Publishing Co., Inc.
Baltimore, 1974, 1981

Reprinted for
Clearfield Company, Inc. by
Genealogical Publishing Co., Inc.
Baltimore, Maryland
1995, 1997, 2001

Library of Congress Catalogue Card Number 74-7238
International Standard Book Number: 0-8063-0624-6

Made in the United States of America

Reprinted from a volume in
the George Peabody Branch,
Enoch Pratt Free Library,
Baltimore, Maryland
1974

Made in the United States of America

FOREWORD

By an Act of 1776 the District of West Augusta, Virginia was divided into the counties of Ohio, Yohogania, and Monongalia—now constituting territory in both southwestern Pennsylvania and West Virginia—in consequence whereof many Virginia court records of great rarity and importance are today found in Pennsylvania and West Virginia, including a very large proportion of early land titles. The minute books of the old Virginia courts herein transcribed cover the District of West Augusta and Yohogania and Ohio Counties during the period when Virginia claimed and exercised jurisdiction over what are now the Pennsylvania counties of Washington, Greene, Fayette, Westmoreland, and Allegheny. Much of the area disputed between Virginia and Pennsylvania was ultimately placed in the jurisdiction of Pennsylvania, the rest stayed with Virginia until it was forged into part of the new state of West Virginia. The minute books of the Virginia courts held within the limits of southwestern Pennsylvania from 1775 to 1780, when the contest between the two states had temporarily abated, contain, in addition to land titles, transcripts of legal instruments of immense genealogical value such as deeds, mortgages, conveyances, probate records, administrations, contracts, suits, judgements, and oaths of allegiance—through which are identified thousands upon thousands of the early settlers of the Monongahela Valley.

When the border controversy was at length settled an Act was passed authorizing the clerk of Washington County, Pennsylvania to collect the probate registers, records of deeds, and records of court administrations from the clerks of the counties of Yohogania, Monongalia, and Ohio insofar as they related to the Pennsylvania territory then embraced by Westmoreland and Washington Counties. Those parts of Monongalia and Ohio Counties pushed out of Pennsylvania by the running of the new boundary lines were, of course, responsible for the custody of their own records. Everything else, though, including the records of the court held at Fort Dunmore in the District of West Augusta, became the official records of Washington County, Pennsylvania, and they are herein transcribed for the period 1775-1780—the period most likely to cause consternation to the genealogical researcher because of the legal chaos coincident to the border controversy.

The original minute books of West Augusta, including the court order books of Yohogania County, were transcribed by the historian Boyd Crumrine from the holdings of the Washington County Historical Society. (Those of the old court of Ohio County he transcribed from photostats of the records furnished him by the Clerk of the County Court in Wheeling, West Virginia; but those of the old court of Monongalia County were unfortunately destroyed by fire before any transcription was undertaken.) The Crumrine transcriptions were originally published in serial form in five separate parts in the first three volumes of the *Annals of the Carnegie Museum* (1902-1905), a periodical largely devoted to scientific subjects and one which would tend to throw even the most industrious genealogical researcher off the scent. The Genealogical Publishing Company is indeed fortunate to have discovered the existence of these important records in such an unexpected place and still more fortunate to have been permitted to join Inez Waldenmaier's *Index* to the body of the work, all of which, now fully excerpted, consolidated, and repaged, is available in this handy one-volume edition.

It will be noticed that the Waldenmaier *Index* refers only to full-name entries wherever such names occur in the text. Surnames appearing in the text without given names, particularly those cited in the various lists of suits, can be located easily enough by skimming the pages of the text. As the index entries correspond to the volumes and page numbers of the original publication, we have retained the old pagination. At the same time we have re-paged the text to lessen confusion with the original and to lend body to the reprint edition.

Genealogical Publishing Co., Inc.

TABLE OF CONTENTS

THE BOUNDARY CONTROVERSY BETWEEN PENNSYLVANIA AND VIRGINIA; 1748–1785.

A SKETCH,[1] BY BOYD CRUMRINE, OF WASHINGTON, PA.

It is proposed to publish in the ANNALS of the Carnegie Museum, the original minute books of the old Virginia Courts held within the limits of southwestern Pennsylvania, during the period when Virginia claimed and exercised jurisdiction over what is now Washington, Greene, Fayette, Westmoreland, and Allegheny Counties, Pennsylvania, and it is fit that these minutes should be preceded with a sketch of the boundary controversy between the two states, beginning as early as 1748, and terminating only by the final establishment of the western boundary line as it is to-day in 1785.

When this contest began our Western country was indeed a wilderness. Thomas Hutchins, an engineer with Bouquet's expedition in 1764, said of it in his "Topographical Description of Virginia, Pennsylvania, and Maryland," published in London in 1778: "The whole country abounds in Bears, Elks, Buffaloes, Deer, Turkies, etc., an unquestionable proof of the goodness of its Soil." In a foot-note, Hutchins quotes from Gordon, a still earlier explorer: "This country may, from a proper knowledge, be affirmed to be the most healthy, the most pleasant, the most commodious, and the most fertile spot of earth, known to European people." Francis Parkman, writing of the country west of the Alleghanies in 1760, says: "One vast and continuous forest shadowed the fertile soul, covering the lands as the grass covers a garden lawn, sweeping over hill and hollow in endless undulation, burying mountains in verdure, and mantling brooks and rivers from the light of day:"[2] Thus, more than a century ago, when our country was a wilderness, did it give promise of its future greatness.

[1] This sketch is founded upon an address delivered before the Western Pennsylvania Historical Society, in Allegheny City, in the spring of 1894.

[2] Conspiracy of Pontiac, 147.

THE FRENCH OCCUPATION.

But, before proceeding to discuss the special subject of this sketch, it should be noticed that, as the custom of nations with reference to new discoveries by their peoples went, the country west of the Alleghanies, prior to its actual occupation and settlement by Englishmen, was in the occupation and jurisdiction more or less rightful of France, known as the French Occupation; so that, had there not been a change of jurisdiction, we might have been a French people.

At one time in American history France claimed all the lands west of the Alleghanies by right of prior discovery; and the establishment of her power on the coasts of North America was coeval with the first colonies from England.[3] In 1682, the year in which William Penn first came to his new colony on the Delaware, Robert Cavalier, Sieur de la Salle, having passed with his expedition from the lakes into the Mississippi, proceeded in April to the mouth of that river, and in the name of Louis XIV. took possession of all the lands watered by the Mississippi and its tributaries, and named the country Louisiana.[4] In the library of Washington & Jefferson College is a very rare and valuable atlas, entitled "Atlas Universel," etc., published at Paris in 1755. The ninety-eighth map of the series shows a part of North America, embracing the course of the Ohio River, New England, New York, New Jersey, Pennsylvania, Maryland, Virginia, and Carolina. It represents the boundary line between Pennsylvania and Louisiana as being the most western ridge of the Alleghany mountains.

The map mentioned, purporting to have been based upon surveys made by Christopher Gist in 1751, is the oldest map of western Pennsylvania the writer has seen. On it is indicated "F. du Quesne," at the mouth of the "Monongahela ou Mohongalo." The river below Fort Duquesne is called the "Ohio ou Splawacipika"; above the fort it is called "Ohio ou Allegany." Several Indian villages are designated, and two English towns, or settlements, Kittanning and Venango. Lake Chatauqua is indicated, but without a name. It was called in early historical writings, "Jadague."

But there was an older map extant; for, at a meeting of the Provincial Council on August 4, 1731, there was produced a "Map of Louisiana, as inserted in a Book called a New General Atlas, published at London in the year 1721," when it was first observed how "exor-

[3] I. Bancroft, 17, 18. [4] II. Bancroft, 338.

bitant the French claims were on the Continent of America; that by the description in said Map they claimed a great part of Carolina and Virginia, and laid down the Susquehanna as a Boundary of Pennsylvania." It was also noted that, by the information of Indian traders west of the Alleghanies, the French were endeavoring to "gain over" the Indians to their interests.

Pennsylvania was thus warned as early as 1731 that a powerful continental nation, with which her parent kingdom was at peace, was threatening a foothold upon fertile lands within her own charter limits, undefined however until a later date. Disturbed for many years by a controversy with Lord Baltimore concerning her southern boundary, and also by disagreements between the proprietary Governors and Provincial Assemblies, as well as by continuously embarrassing relations as to her Indian affairs in her undoubted possessions and settlements east of the mountains, for many years she made no effort to repel the French intrusion. Not until Virginia, in 1748 and 1749, had taken the initiative in the establishment of the Ohio Company in the vicinity of the Pittsburgh of to-day, did Pennsylvania manifest an interest in the subject. Where her western boundary might lie she seemed to know little and care less. It was the Virginian occupation in the years mentioned, resulting in the French and Indian war, which brought to Pennsylvania a suggestion of watchfulness as to her western boundary.[5]

In 1748, Thomas Lee, of the King's Council in Virginia, formed the design of effecting settlements on the wild lands west of the Alleghanies, through the agency of a land corporation called the Ohio Company. Lawrence Washington and Augustine Washington, elder brothers of George Washington, were interested in the scheme. A grant was obtained from the English king of five hundred thousand acres of land, to be taken chiefly on the south side of the Ohio, between the Monongahela and Kanawha rivers. Two hundred thousand acres were to be selected immediately, and to be held for ten years free from quit-rents and taxes, on condition that the company should seat one hundred families on the lands within seven years, and build a fort and maintain a garrison sufficient to protect the settlements.

In 1751, Christopher Gist was sent out from Virginia as the agent of the Ohio company to explore the lands, and it was then doubtless

[5] Crumrine's History of Washington County, p. 140.

that he made the surveys, which, being published, formed the basis of the French map of 1757. In 1752, with Joshua Fry and two other commissioners representing Virginia, Mr. Gist attended a treaty with the Indians, with whom the French were tampering. This treaty was held at Logstown, eighteen miles or so below Pittsburgh, on the Ohio. Some years ago there was quite a discussion in the newspapers as to the location of Logstown, whether it was on the north or on the south side of the river. In fact there were two Logstowns, opposite each other; one on the north bank, occupied by white or half-breed traders, and the other on the south bank occupied by the Shawanese Indians.

It is manifest that one of the principal objects of the Ohio Company was to meet the French claim and occupation of lands upon the Ohio and Alleghany by actual settlements to be made by English colonists from Virginia. The headquarters of Leguardeur de St. Pierre, the French commandant, were at Venango; and in 1753, Governor Dinwiddie, then also one of the proprietors of the Ohio Company, sent George Washington, a youth of twenty-one years, to the French commandant, to ascertain the purpose of the threatened encroachment. It was on this journey that Washington stood on the "Point" at the confluence of our two rivers, which he reported in his Journal, as an eligible place for a fort.[6] In 1754, the erection of a fort at the place indicated was begun by Capt. William Trent in command of a body of Virginia militia. After its commencement, Captain Trent returned to Will's Creek (now Cumberland) leaving the construction of the fort to Ensign Edward Ward; but on April 17, 1754, a hostile force of about seven hundred French and Indians came down the Alleghany under the command of Capt. Contrecour, to whom Ensign Ward[7] with but thirty-three men, surrendered the unfinished fort. The fort was then completed by the French and named Fort DuQuesne, in honor of the Marquis DuQuesne, the French Governor General of Canada.

Thus were the French in the actual military occupation of the valley of the Ohio. Then followed the events of the so-called French and Indian war: the battle of Fort Necessity, at Great Meadows in what is now Fayette county, Washington's maiden engagement; and the surrender of the fort to the French on July 4, 1754; in the next year the battle of Braddock's Defeat, on July 9, 1755, resulting in the complete expulsion of the English from the waters of the Monon-

[6] The Olden Time, Vol. I., p. 12.

[7] Afterwards one of the Justices of the old Virginia Courts.

gahela and Ohio. All this contest between the French and Indians on the one side, and the English on the other, was brought about without the agency of Pennsylvania.

There followed a state of quiesence on the part of the French, themselves apparently satisfied with the fact of their possession; but not so was the state of the Indians. Secretly incited by the French, doubtless, the Indians carried their bloody incursions into the valleys east of the mountains, leaving desolation, death, and suffering on every side. But, in 1756, occurred the expedition of Col. James Armstrong from Fort Shirley, in what is now Huntingdon county, resulting in the destruction of the Indian towns at Kittanning; in 1758, Forbes's expedition, with Grant's defeat on Grant's Hill, Pittsburgh, on September 14, followed by the capture or rather the abandonment of Fort Duquesne on November 25th, and the erection of Fort Pitt (though not in the same location as Fort Duquesne), in 1759, by a force under the command of Gen. Stanwix.

It must be remembered that this expulsion of the French from the Ohio valley was not by the militia alone of either Pennsylvania or Virginia, but by royal forces sent over by the English government, aided by the militia from both colonies. And so the French occupation was terminated by the definitive treaty of peace between England and France, signed on February 10, 1763, and then passed from France all her possessions in America east of the Mississippi, including Canada.

THE VIRGINIA OCCUPATION.

The erection of the fort at the Point by Capt. Trent, in 1754, a trespass by Virginia upon the lands in the valley of Ohio, brought about the French and Indian war, resulting beneficially, however, in the loss to France of most of her American possessions and their acquisition by the English, and bringing directly to Pennsylvania a sharpened sense of the necessity for looking after her political interests west of the Alleghanies.

Now, what was the origin of this Virginia usurpation, for usurpation it was? How did it happen that Virginia claimed any of her territory within our western border? How did she come to claim jurisdiction over the great Northwestern Territory, the mother of magnificent states of the Union? The answers to these queries arise out of the following facts:

The charter granted by Charles II. to William Penn, for the province of Pennsylvania, was dated March 4, 1681. The grant was bounded on the east by the Delaware River, "unto the three and fortieth degree of Northern latitude, if the said river doth extend so far northward; . . . The said land to extend westward five degrees in longitude to be computed from the said eastern bounds; and the said lands to be bounded on the north by the beginning of the three and fortieth degree of northern latitude, and on the south by a circle drawn at twelve miles distance from New Castle northward and westward, unto the beginning of the fortieth degree of northern latitude, and then by a staight line westward to the limits of longitude above mentioned."

It thus is made plain, that Pennsylvania was a province of three degrees of latitude and five degrees of longitude, extending from the fortieth degree, *i. e.*, line 39°, to the beginning of the forty-third degree, *i. e.*, line 42°; and in the absence of an interference with any prior grant, doubtless no other position would ever have been entertained. But in 1632, forty-nine years before Penn's charter, Charles I. had granted a province to Lord Baltimore, named Maryland, under the terms of which charter a very interesting controversy arose between Penn and Lord Baltimore, whether Penn's charter carried him to the parallel 39°, as he claimed it did, or only to parallel 40°, as claimed by Lord Baltimore. But it was destined that our southern border should be neither at parallel 39°, nor at parallel 40°; although many were the contentions and strifes among settlers along the Maryland line, arising before this controversy was determined by the running of Mason and Dixon's line at 30°, 43′, 26″, in 1767, to a point two hundred and forty-four miles from the river Delaware, and within thirty-six miles of the whole distance to be run. This point was at the second crossing of Dunkard Creek, near the southern boundary of Greene county; and by that point passed the Warrior Branch of the old Catawba or Cherokee trail, along which traveled the war parties of the northern and southern Indians. Across it the Indian escort of the surveying party would not allow even an imaginary line to be drawn. Thus, at the beginning of 1768 the southwest corner of Pennsylvania had not been found and marked, and the western boundary, whether an irregular line or a meridian, was as yet unknown.

But how the controversy with Virginia came about has not yet appeared. For this we must go back to the Virginia charter, which antedated both that of Maryland and that of Pennsylvania.

The first charter or patent for the colony of Virginia was by Queen Elizabeth in 1583, and it had neither name nor bounds. The settlers under this patent, partly from misconduct and partly from the opposition of the Indians, and other calamities, abandoned their efforts and the patent became extinct. But in 1602 James I. succeeded Elizabeth, and in 1606 he issued a new patent incorporating two companies, called the South Virginia Company, and the North Virginia Company, afterwards called respectively the London Company and the Plymouth Company. Each was to be limited to a square of one hundred miles backward from the sea. The London Company, with which we are concerned, settled at Cape Henry, and hence the square of one hundred miles granted by that patent could not have extended to the eastern base of the Blue Ridge. But in 1609, the London Company received a new patent, with the boundaries of their grant enlarged by the following terms:

"All those lands . . . lying and being in that part of America called Virginia, from the point of land called Cape or Point Comfort, all along the sea-coast to the northward two hundred miles; and from the said Point or Cape Comfort all along the sea-coast to the southward two hundred miles; and all that space and circuit of lands lying from the sea-coast of the precinct aforesaid up into the land throughout, from sea to sea, west and northwest."

Observe the ambiguities in the terms of this grant, the chief of which is in the words "up into the land throughout, from sea to sea, west and northwest," as containing directions for the northern and southern boundaries. Shall the due west line be drawn from a point on the sea-coast two hundred miles north of Point Comfort, and the northwest line be drawn from a point on the sea-coast two hundred miles south of Point Comfort? If so, then the London Company was limited to a triangle which extended to no territory in our western border. Or, shall the west line be drawn from a point on the sea-coast two hundred miles south of Point Comfort, and the northwest line from a point on the sea-coast two hundred miles north of Point Comfort? This was the interpretation claimed by Virginia, and one will see that if it were correct, the northwest line would run through the heart of Pennsylvania, passing east out of Erie City; while, the southern boundary line, running due west, the two would never meet, and Virginia would have owned the greater part of the entire continent. But, without discussing further the propriety of either interpretation, let it be said that Virginia always, while yet a colony and after she became a state, referred chiefly to this charter of 1609 as authorizing her jurisdiction, not only over the Monongahela and Ohio valleys, but also as giving her an ownership over the entire Northwestern Territory.

This jurisdiction over the territory northwest of the Ohio River, Virginia refused to cede to the Confederacy of the United States, though her refusal endangered the confederation, until in 1781, when, no longer able to resist the influence of the other states, especially that of Maryland, she finally gave way so far as to abandon her claims over lands north and west of the Ohio River, on condition, however, that the United States would guarantee her rights to the south and east of the Ohio. This guaranty the Congress of the United States refused, and in 1784 the condition was withdrawn and the cession made absolute. But it is interesting to note that no sister state or government, nor the Congress of the Confederation, ever at any time recognized the right of Virginia to such jurisdiction. Only for the sake of perfecting the Union, such as it then was, was there any respect at all paid to her pretensions.

But, assuming that Virginia's interpretation of her charter provisions was the correct one, there was another fact which wholly ousted her claim to any lands which might eventually be found to fall within the boundaries of Penn's charter. In 1624, prior to the grant of Maryland to Lord Baltimore, as well as prior to the grant of Pennsylvania to William Penn, the charter to the London Company was dissolved in the English courts by a writ of quo warranto; and from a proprietary colony somewhat like that of Pennsylvania, Virginia from that time on was a Crown colony. The distinction between a colony and a province, such as was Pennsylvania, is well known. Whatever rights are secured to the proprietor of a province cannot be infringed or altered by the Crown, without the consent of the proprietor, nor abrogated unless by judgment of law founded upon some act of commission or omission working a forfeiture or dissolution. But a royal or crown colony is a mere creature of the royal will; its boundaries, all its machinery of government, may be modified, altered, or annulled at the royal pleasure and discretion. For this reason alone, therefore, Virginia having become a crown colony prior to the passing of Penn's charter, she could thereafter make no claim to any lands within the limits of Penn's charter, whatever interpretation was to be put upon the terms of her own charter provisions.

To explain the origin of Virginia's usurpation of territory upon the Monongahela and Ohio, the writer digressed from the building of Fort Pitt, near the mouth of the Monongahela, in 1759, followed by the cession of the French claims by the treaty of 1763. Soon after that treaty occurred what is known as the Conspiracy of Pontiac, in the summer of 1763. This was an effort set on foot in 1762, at Detroit, by that great chieftain Pontiac, who organized all the Indian tribes under a common purpose to drive the hated English entirely out of the country. It is said that, to raise means to supply his forces in their incursions eastward he issued promissory notes on birch bark, signed with the figure of an otter, and that, moreover, they were all subsequently redeemed by him. In the spring of 1763 Pontiac appeared with his savage forces in the neighborhood of Fort Pitt, moved across the mountains, and almost desolated the settlements on the east, even through the valley of the Susquehanna. During this Indian war, terminated by Bouquet's expedition, and the desperate battle of Bushy Run, on Turtle Creek, in Westmoreland county, on August 5, 1763, and the relief of Fort Pitt thereby, there was no opportunity for an immediate conflict of civil jurisdiction west of the Alleghanies. From 1764 to 1774, however, there was peace with the tribes, the pioneers being disturbed only at times by the occasional depredations of savages intent upon plunder rather than moved by the havoc of war. And George Washington, then a colonel, turned his attention to the acquisition of lands west of the mountains. In 1770, on October 17th, with Dr. Craik, who had been his companion in arms at the battle of Great Meadows and in Braddock's defeat, he arrived at Fort Pitt, and in his journal[8] he mentions his meeting at Semple's tavern, where he stopped, Dr. John Connolly, "nephew to Col. Croghan, a very sensible and intelligent man, who had traveled over a good deal of this western country, both by land and water." This Dr. John Connolly, thus introduced to us by no less a personage than Col. George Washington, was soon to play an important part in the civil history of the country west of the mountains; for he became the leader of the Virginia adherents in the contest to establish the Virginia jurisdiction along our rivers, and, as will be seen, a justice of one of her courts.

In 1772, John Murray, the fourth Earl of Dunmore, one of the Peers of Scotland, became Governor of Virginia; and early in 1773 he made a visit to Fort Pitt, where he met Dr. John Connolly, hereto-

[8] Olden Time, Vol. I., p. 416.

fore introduced to us by Col. Washington, who had dined with him at Semple's. Most probably Lord Dunmore, who was an intense loyalist, had early information of transactions presaging the rupture of the colonies from the mother country, and in the controversy instituted over the boundary question, as well as in his management of the Indian war of 1774, known as Dunmore's war, he was impelled in both to put the two colonies of Pennsylvania and Virginia in antagonism to each other. And it must be remembered that on February 26, 1773, Westmoreland county had been erected, covering all the territory of southwestern Pennsylvania, and the seat of justice was placed at Hanna's Town, about four miles from the present Greensburg. The establishment of government and courts of justice over this territory necessitated increased taxation upon the lands of the pioneers; and, as the greater number of them had come over the mountains from Maryland and Virginia, by way of Braddock's road, it was not a matter of very great difficulty to equal the number of patriotic Pennsylvanians by the number of Virginian partisans from our own settlers. It may be noted that Capt. William Crawford, he who was burned at the stake by the Indians at Sandusky in July, 1782, was a Pennsylvanian, being one of the justices of the peace, and justices of the county of Bedford, when first organized in 1771; but he afterwards espoused the cause of Virginia in the boundary controversy, and in 1775, when presiding judge of the Westmoreland county court, his judicial office was taken from him, as he had then accepted the appointment of justice under Lord Dunmore.

On January 1, 1774, Dr. John Connolly had posted a printed advertisement at Pittsburgh, and throughout the vicinity, announcing that Lord Dunmore, Governor of Virginia, had been pleased to nominate and appoint him "Captain, Commandant of the Militia of Pittsburgh and its Dependencies," and proposed "moving to the House of Burgesses the necessity of erecting a New County, to include Pittsburgh;" a Virginia county, of course. This official announcement created some consternation among the good people of the Pennsylvania jurisdiction. Arthur St. Clair, prothonotary of Westmoreland county, caused Dr. Connolly to be arrested, but the prisoner, after a few days confinement in the county jail at Hanna's Town, prevailed upon the sheriff to permit him to visit Pittsburgh, pledging his honor to return before the next court in April. He did return, but in a manner entirely unexpected. He returned with from one hundred and fifty to one hundred and eighty men, "with their colors flying, and Captains, &c., had their swords drawn." "The first thing they did was to place sentinels at the court-house door, and then Connolly sent a message that he would wait on the magistrates and communicate the reasons of his appearance:" so says the letter of Thomas Smith to Governor Penn, dated April 7, 1774. Connolly explained his appearance, saying among other things, "My orders from the Government of Virginia not being explicit, I have raised the Militia to support the Civil Authority of that Colony vested in me." The Pennsylvania Court at Hanna's Town rose the next day, April 8th, and Æneas Mackay, Devereux Smith, and Andrew McFarlane, three of the justices residing at Pittsburgh, returned to their homes at that place; and the next day, April 9th, all three were arrested upon the order of Dr. Connolly and sent under guard to Staunton jail, in the valley of old Virginia. Arriving at Williamsburg the prisoners met Lord Dunmore, who heard their story and told them "that Connolly was authorized by him as Governor of Virginia to prosecute the claim of that Colony to Pittsburgh and its Dependencies; and, as to taking of prisoners, he Connolly, only imitated the Pennsylvania officers in Respect to Connolly's imprisonment by them." Dunmore, moreover, released them, and permitted them to return to their homes.

Then followed a series of arrests and counter-arrests, long continued, resulting in riots and broils of intense passion. Every one who, under color of an office held under the laws of Pennsylvania, attempted any official act, was likely to be arrested and jailed by persons claiming to hold office under the government of Virginia. Likewise were Virginia officials liable to arrest and imprisonment by the Pennsylvania partisans.

It is impossible to go into any detail in narrating special instances of these extraordinary commotions among the pioneers of a wilderness, all of them occupying homes of rude construction, their roof-trees and firesides all the time to be guarded from the incursions of their savage Indian foes. This condition of things must be remembered in thinking of these scenes; and an illustration of the state of the times among our white fathers themselves may be found in extracts from a letter dated August 4, 1771, a little prior to the assumptions of John Connolly, written by George Wilson, residing on the Monongahela near the mouth of George's Creek, in what is now Fayette County. George Wilson was then one of the justices of the courts of Bedford county, which had been organized early in 1771; and was the great-grand-father of Hon. W. G. Hawkins, now one of the judges of the Orphans' Court of Allegheny county. That letter is a "quaint and curious volume of forgotten lore." The writer, stating that he had just returned home from court, relates that he found a paper being circulated among his neighbors pledging the subscribers to oppose "Every of Pen's Laws, as they called them, except felonious actions, at ye risk of Life & under ye penalty of fiftey pounds, to be Received or Leveyed By themselves off ye Estates of ye failure. The first of them I found hardy anuff to offer it in publick, I emediately ordered into Custody, on which a large number Ware assembled as Was supposed to Resque the Prisonar. . . . When their Forman saw that the Arms of his Contrie, that as he said He had thrown Himself into, would not Resque him By force, hee catched up his Rifle, Which Was Well loaded, jumped out of Dors & swore if any man Cam nigh him he would put what Was in his throo them. The Person that Had him in Custody Called for assistance in ye King's name, and in particular Commanded myself. I told him I was a Subject, & was not fit to Command if not willing to obey; on which I watched his eye until I saw a chance, Sprang in on him & Seized the Rifle by ye Muzzle, and held him So as he Could not Shoot me, until more help Gott in to my assistance, on which I Disarmed him & Broke his Rifle to peses. I Res'd a Sore Bruse on one of my arms By a punch of ye Gun in ye struggle; Then put him under a Strong Guard, Told them the laws of their Contrie was stronger than the Hardest Ruffin among them. I found it necessary on their Complyance & altering their Resolves, and his promising to Give himself no more trouble in the affair, as hee found that the people Ware not as hardy as hee Expected them to be, to Relece him on his promise of Good Be-haviour."

Correspondence between the Governor of Pennsylvania and Virginia occurring immediately after the arrest of Connolly and the Pennsylvania Justices, resulted in a meeting of Commissioners at Williamsburg, Va., on May 19, 1774, to endeavor to establish the boundary line. This meeting was fruitless; but it is interesting to note that the Pennsylvania commissioners proposed as our western boundary a line to be drawn from the western end of Mason and Dixon's line, to be extended its proper distance of five degrees of longitude, thence northward but parallel at all points with the meanderings of the Delaware River. This line would have left almost all of the present county of Washington, and corresponding portions of the counties north and south of it, in the "Pan-Handle" of Virginia. The proposition was rejected on the part of Virginia, her commissioners contending that under a proper construction of Penn's charter, the boundary line should run east of Pittsburgh.

Soon thereafter, in July, 1774, occurred what is called Dunmore's war, at the close of which Logan, the celebrated Indian Chief, made his supposed speech referring to the killing of his dusky family at the mouth of Yellow Creek below the present Steubenville: "Who is there to mourn for Logan?" Although this war was not of great magnitude, and was confined to what is now the state of Ohio, yet its approach so frightened the settlers of the Ohio and Monongahela valleys that it is said in a letter written by Valentine Crawford to Col. Geo. Washington, "There were more than one thousand people crossed the Monongahela in one day at three ferries that are not one mile apart.

Dunmore himself was with the white forces, chiefly adherents of the Virginia jurisdiction; and it is clear, as before intimated, that in the adjustment of the terms of peace, Dunmore, foreseeing the approaching revolution from the mother country, arranged such terms with the Indians as subsequently made them, or aided to make them, the allies of the British armies against our American patriots.

On his way down the river to the scene of the conflict, Lord Dunmore stopped at Fort Dunmore, as the fort at Pittsburgh had been baptized by Dr. Connolly, whence he issued his proclamation, this time personally and publicly asserting the claim of Virginia to all the territory west of the Laurel Hill mountains, and alleging instructions he had lately received from the English government to take it under his immediate control. A counter proclamation by Governor Penn followed on October 12, 1774, instructing the Pennsylvania magistrates to maintain the jurisdiction of Pennsylvania, nothwithstanding Dunmore's fulminations. Dunmore, on his return after the treaty of peace, which was made in the same month of October, stopped again at Pittsburgh, or at Fort Dunmore, as he called the place, when he was once more brought into personal contact with his adherents. He thence proceeded to Redstone, now Brownsville, where he had Thomas Scott arrested and brought before him for the offence of exercising the functions of a Pennsylvania magistrate. Thomas Scott was a distinguished man of that day and afterward. He became the first prothonotary of Washington county when organized, held many other important public positions, and was a member of the first Congress of the United States under the Constitution of 1787. On the hearing before Lord Dunmore, he was bound over to appear for trial at a court for Augusta county, Va., to be held at Fort Dunmore on December 20, 1774.

DISTRICT OF WEST AUGUSTA.

The Augusta county court was not opened, however, on December 20, 1774, but on December 12th. A writ had been issued by Dunmore, in the name of his British Majesty, adjourning the county court of Augusta county from Staunton, Va., to Fort Dunmore, accompanied with a new commission of the peace, embracing with the old justices of the parent county the names of such of the adherents in the Monongahela valley as were regarded as proper persons for Virginia magistrates.

The District was called the District of West Augusta, and in its territory now in Pennsylvania it was bounded on the east by the Laurel Hill mountains and extended along the east side of the Allegheny River some distance beyond the Kiskeminitas, embracing all of Westmoreland, Allegheny, Beaver, Washington, Greene, and Fayette counties.

The first term of this Virginia court was held at Fort Dunmore on February 21, 1775, when George Croghan, John Campbell, John Connolly, Thomas Smallman, Dorsey Pentecost, John Gibson, George Vallandigham and William Goe appeared, took the qualifying oaths, and occupied their seats as justices. George Croghan, settled about where Lawrenceville now is, at first a Virginia adherent, had become quite a Pennsylvanian during Dunmore's war, but he was now made the presiding justice of Dunmore's court, and this brought him back once more among the Virginia partisans. From this date there were not only two different sets of magistrates, with their subordinate officers, assessors, and commissioners, over the same people in the Monongahela valley, but within a few miles of each other there were established two different courts, one at Pittsburgh, the other at Hanna's Town, regularly or irregularly administering justice under the laws of two different governments.

On the next day after the first sitting of the court, to wit, on February 22, 1775, Robert Hanna and James Caveat, two of the Westmoreland county justices, were arrested for the performance of their duties as Pennsylvania magistrates, and confined at Pittsburgh for

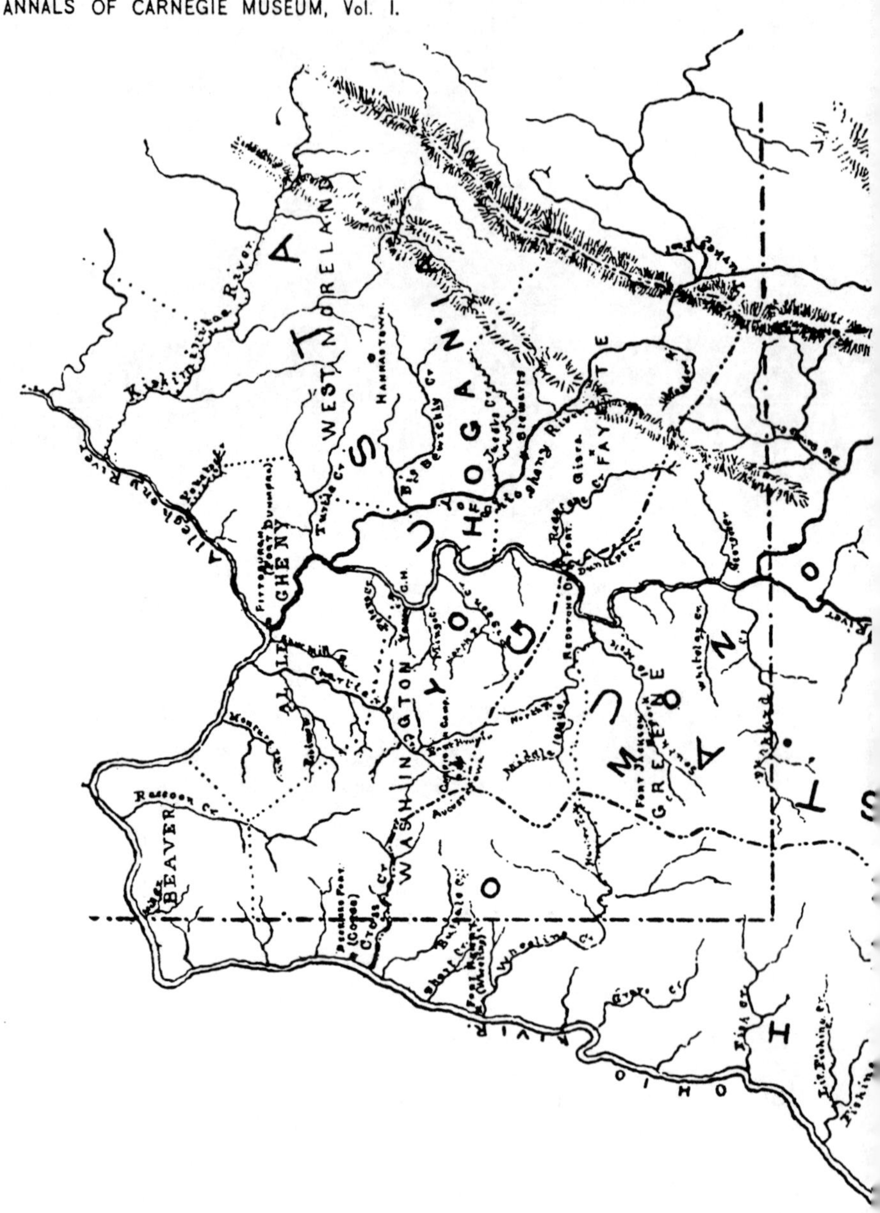
WESTMORELAND
ALLEGHENY
WASHINGTON
BEAVER
GREENE
FAYETTE
HANNASTOWN
Allegheny River
Kiskiminitas River
OHIO
RIVER

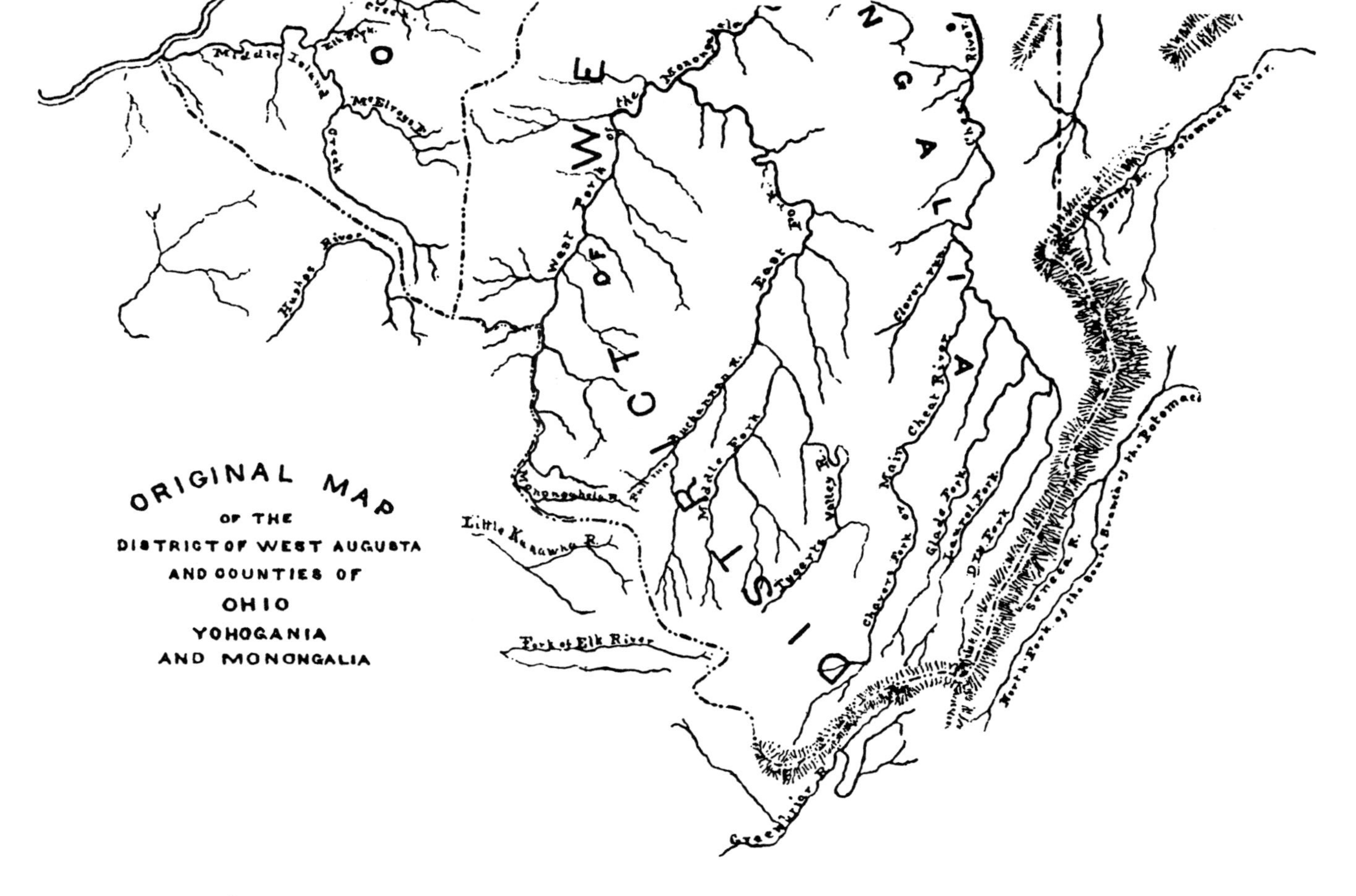

ORIGINAL MAP
OF THE
DISTRICT OF WEST AUGUSTA
AND COUNTIES OF
OHIO
YOHOGANIA
AND MONONGALIA

about three months, vainly endeavoring to obtain a release. The Governor and Council of Pennsylvania were probably engaged in the consideration of affairs of a most auspicious nature; but, in the latter part of June, 1775, the sheriff of Westmoreland county, aided by a posse of effective strength, proceeded to Pittsburgh and set the two justices at large, taking Dr. John Connolly with him to Hanna's town; and on the records of the Westmoreland county court, July Term, 1775, there is found an action of Capias in Case, indicating an arrest for damages, brought by "Robert Hanna, Esq. *v.* John Connolly."

THE REVOLUTION.

This case, however, was never brought to trial; for public affairs had taken on a new aspect. Our settlers for a time ceased to fight each other, but stood together expectant looking for a contest with the trained forces of the mother country. On April 19, 1775, Lexington and Concord became noted names of history. The astounding news from those villages had scarcely reached the Monongahela valley, when public meetings were held on the same day, to wit, May 16, 1775, both at Hanna's Town and Pittsburgh. At Hanna's Town the Pennsylvania adherents assembled; at Pittsburgh, the Virginia partisans. Each meeting passed a set of resolutions with equally forcible approval of the armed resistance to the invasion of American rights by the English government, and equally urging united action by force of arms successfully to sustain that resistance. We may call these sets of resolutions, adopted on the same day by the separate adherents of two colonial jurisdictions, the Monongahela Declaration of Independence. They antedate more than a year the Declaration of Independence adopted and read to the people at Philadelphia on July 4, 1776, and they antedate the celebrated Mecklenburg Resolutions of North Carolina by four days. All honor to the Monongahela valley!

A portion of the resolutions of the Westmoreland county meeting is worthy of being copied:

"Resolved, unanimously, That there is no reason to doubt but the same system of tyranny and oppression [referring to the oppressive measures of the British government] will (should it meet with success in Massachusetts Bay) be extended to other parts of America; it is therefore the indispensable duty of every American, of every man who has any public virtue or love for his country, or any bowells for posterity, by every means which God has put in his power, to resist and oppose the execution of it; that for us we will be ready to oppose it with our lives and fortunes."

The spirit of the Revolution being abroad, the Monongahela and Ohio are soon rid of both John Connolly and his illustrious chief, Lord Dunmore. Dunmore became alarmed for his own safety and removed his family aboard the "Fowey," a British man-of-war in the Chesapeake. Connolly, soon after his release by the Westmoreland authorities was sent to General Gage commanding the British forces at Boston. General Gage returned him to Lord Dunmore, who granted him a commission as lieutenant-colonel of a regiment to be raised in the "back parts" and Canada, which meant, to be composed of Indians. While on his way to Detroit with his commission and instructions, he was captured by the American forces at Hagerstown, Md., when he was turned over to Congress and held a prisoner until 1780–81, and was then exchanged. After the Revolution he seems to have settled in Canada; subsequently he published in London his "Narrative" of his life and public acts, a copy of which was purchased of late years for a large sum of money and is now in the library of the Historical Society of Pennsylvania at Philadelphia. It has been reprinted in the pages of the *Pennsylvania Magazine of History*. But the Virginians and Pennsylvanians on the Monongahela and Ohio fought side by side under the Stars and Stripes; for it will not do to suppose that only the people of the east fought with the British lion. At least two full Pennsylvania regiments were raised west of the mountains and served in the battles of the east, a fact to be remembered by the local historian.

DIVISION OF WEST AUGUSTA.

The Revolution after July 4, 1776, was a fact accomplished, though its success was still in the dark future. Pennsylvania from a province, and Virginia from a crown colony, had both become independent states in the new American confederacy. And in October, 1776, the District of West Augusta, by an enactment of the General Assembly of Virginia, was divided into three new counties, Ohio, Yohogania, and Monongalia. For a short while before this division, the courts of West Augusta were transferred to Augusta Town, a mile west of Washington, Pa. At that place the courts were held September 17, 18, and November 19, 20, 1776. The new division then took effect. All three of the new counties came together at Catfish

Camp, now Washington. The courts of Ohio county were held at Black's Cabin, on Short Creek, now West Liberty, West Virginia; those for Monongalia county on the farm of Theophilus Phillips about two miles above New Geneva, in what is now Fayette county; while the courts of Yohogania were held on the farm of Andrew Heath, a mile or so above West Elizabeth in what is now Allegheny county. The courts of this county continued to be held regularly for the dispatch of business, civil and criminal and there was much of it, until August 28, 1780, when it was "Ordered that Court adjourn till Court in course." There was no court in course, for an agreement had been entered into for the running of the boundary between the two states on a line that would blot out Yohogania county forever.

ADJUSTMENT OF THE BOUNDARY LINE.

As has been stated, during the War of the Revolution the Pennsylvania and Virginia adherents on the Monongahela and Ohio ceased to fight each other, and not only sent more than two regiments of yeomenry to join with the continentals in the battles in the east, but they were obliged at the same time to provide for the protection of their families from the hostile incursions of the savage allies of the British in the west. Yet the boundary controversy was not yet determined.

On December 18, 1776, both houses of the General Assembly of Virginia passed a resolution that it was expedient and wise to remove as much as possible all causes of future controversy; and "to quiet the minds of the people that may be affected thereby, and to take from our common enemies an opportunity of fomenting mutual distrust and jealousy, the commonwealth ought to offer such reasonable terms of accommodation, (even if the loss of some territory is incurred thereby), as may be cordially accepted by our sister State, and an end put to all future dispute by a firm and permanent agreement and settlement." The resolutions then proceeded to authorize the Virginia delegates in Congress to propose to Pennsylvania that a line be drawn from the Maryland corner on Mason and Dixon's line due north to parallel of latitude 40°, and thence the southern boundary of Pennsylvania was to be run full five degrees of longitude west from the Delaware River, and from the end of that line the western boundary should be run corresponding with the meanderings of the Delaware River on the eastern boundary. This line would have given to Virginia a large part of what is now Fayette county, all of Greene county, and quite a portion of Washington and of other counties to the north of it. Of course Pennsylvania could not accept this offer, though during 1777 and 1778 negotiations were made through the Virginia delegates; with such little interest, however, that the papers became lost.

It appears that early in 1779, just when is not now known, both States appointed commissioners to deal with the subject, and these commissioners — George Bryan, John Ewing and David Rittenhouse on the part of Pennsylvania, and Rev. James Madison, Rev. Robert Andrews and Thomas Lewis on the part of Virginia — met at Baltimore on August 27, 1779. The proceedings at this meeting were in writing, were reported to the Assemblies of the respective States, and may be found in Henning's Statutes of Virginia, Vol. X., p. 119. A final agreement was reached and put in writing on August 31, 1779. It was very simple in its terms, for a matter so long contested and of such magnitude. It was as follows:

"To extend Mason and Dixon's line due west five degrees of longitude, to be computed from the river Delaware, for the southern boundary of Pennsylvania; and that a meridian drawn from the western extremity thereof to the northern line of said State be the western line of said State forever."

This Baltimore agreement was ratified and finally confirmed by the Pennsylvania General Assembly on November 19, 1779. Virginia, however, held back, and whether from a dissatisfaction with the boundary as recommended by the commissioners or with an intention of benefiting her whilom adherents in the Monongahela valley, her Assembly had no action on the subject until the following summer. And what occurred in the meantime?

The General Assembly of Virginia, in May, 1779, passed an act "for the adjusting and settling titles of claimants to unpatented lands" upon the western waters, creating districts, with four commissioners to each, to hear proofs of settlement rights and grant certificates to claimants. The commissioners for Ohio, Monongalia and Yohogania counties were Francis Peyton, Philip Pendleton, Joseph Holmes and George Merriweather. All this before the Baltimore conference. But after the Baltimore agreement, and before its ratification by the General Assembly of Virginia, these commissioners met at Cox's Fort, in Washington county, near the Monongahela River, above Elizabeth, and at other points, and granted hundreds of certificates to claimants under Virginia settlement rights. These "Virginia Certificates," so-called, afterwards formed the basis of a very large portion of the land titles of Washington county. Gen. Washington's title to over a thousand acres in Mount Pleasant township, Washington county, was based upon Virginia certificates. This act of sovereignty, before Virginia's ratification of the Baltimore agreement, raised a storm of indignation among the Pennsylvania adherents, and again some forcible but polite correspondence and negotiations resulted. The two States seemed about to resort to arms again to bring about an adjustment. The end of the contest, however, approached gradually, and on July 1, 1780, the Senate of Virginia passed an act of the Lower House which confirmed the Baltimore agreement "on condition that the private property and rights of all persons acquired under, founded on, or recognized by the laws of either country previous to the date hereof, be saved and confirmed to them," etc.; and Pennsylvania was then prepared, for the sake of an end to the controversy, to yield even to the humiliating conditions proposed, and on September 23, 1780, her General Assembly, protesting against the conditions, accepted and fully ratified "the said recited conditions, and the Boundary Line formed thereupon."

RUNNING OF THE BOUNDARY LINE.

It only remained to run and mark the line on the ground. Washington county was erected by an act of assembly passed on March 28, 1781, embracing all the land lying south of the Monongahela, to the southern boundary. But on June 3, 1781, only a temporary line was run. Troubles had ensued resulting in "Obstructions" producing "Anarchy and Confusion." Such terms as "Villanous Banditti" were of frequent use on either side, and letters in the State Archives are full of them. There was still much anxiety for the final establishment of the two boundaries.

In the spring of 1782 occurred the Indian raids into Washington county, followed by the slaughter of the peaceful Moravian Indians in the Ohio towns by Col. David Williamson's command, and the Crawford expedition against the Sandusky Indians, resulting in the burning of Col. Wm. Crawford at the stake. The times were almost as cloudy as ever. But in 1783, the authorities of each state appointed four commissioners to run and mark the permanent boundary. Rev. John Ewing, David Rittenhouse, John Lukens and Thomas Hutchins were appointed by Pennsylvania. By Virginia, Rev. James Madison, Rev. Robert Andrews, John Page and Thomas Lewis were appointed. June 1, 1784, was the time set for beginning the work. An interesting report of the running of Mason and Dixon's line to the western extremity thereof, dated December 23, 1784, will be found in the Pennsylvania Archives, Vol. X., p. 375. The meridian line itself from the southwest corner of the state, was finally run and marked, by David Rittenhouse and Andrew Porter, on the part of Pennsylvania, and Andrew Ellicott and Joseph Neville on the part of Virginia, on August 23, 1785.[9] For the Pennsylvania commissioners and their assistants, in order to insure the prompt and effective performance of their work, there was made the liberal provision of sixty gallons of spirits, twenty gallons brandy, and forty gallons of Madeira wine. And thus was the matter ended.

The original record or minute book of the old Virginia court, held for the District of West Augusta, first at Fort Dunmore, at Pittsburgh, afterwards on the late Gabby farm about a mile southwest of what is now the Borough of Washington, will now be presented, to be followed in a subsequent issue by the records of the court for Yohogania county (after the division of the District of West Augusta into the three new Virginia counties), held on the farm then owned by Andrew Heath near what is now West Elizabeth, in Allegheny county.

These minute books belong to the Washington County Historical Society at Washington, Pa. Those of the old court of Monongalia county, held at the house of Theophilus Phillips on George's Creek, Fayette county, were destroyed on the burning of the court-house at Morgantown in 1796; while those of the old court of Ohio county should be found at Wheeling, W. Va.

Copies of the records as printed in these ANNALS will go into the hands of persons familiar with the local history of southwestern Pennsylvania, who are requested to aid in identifying and locating the individuals and places referred to in them, for future publication.

[9] Colonial Records, Vol. XIV., p. 655; Vol. XV., p. 38.

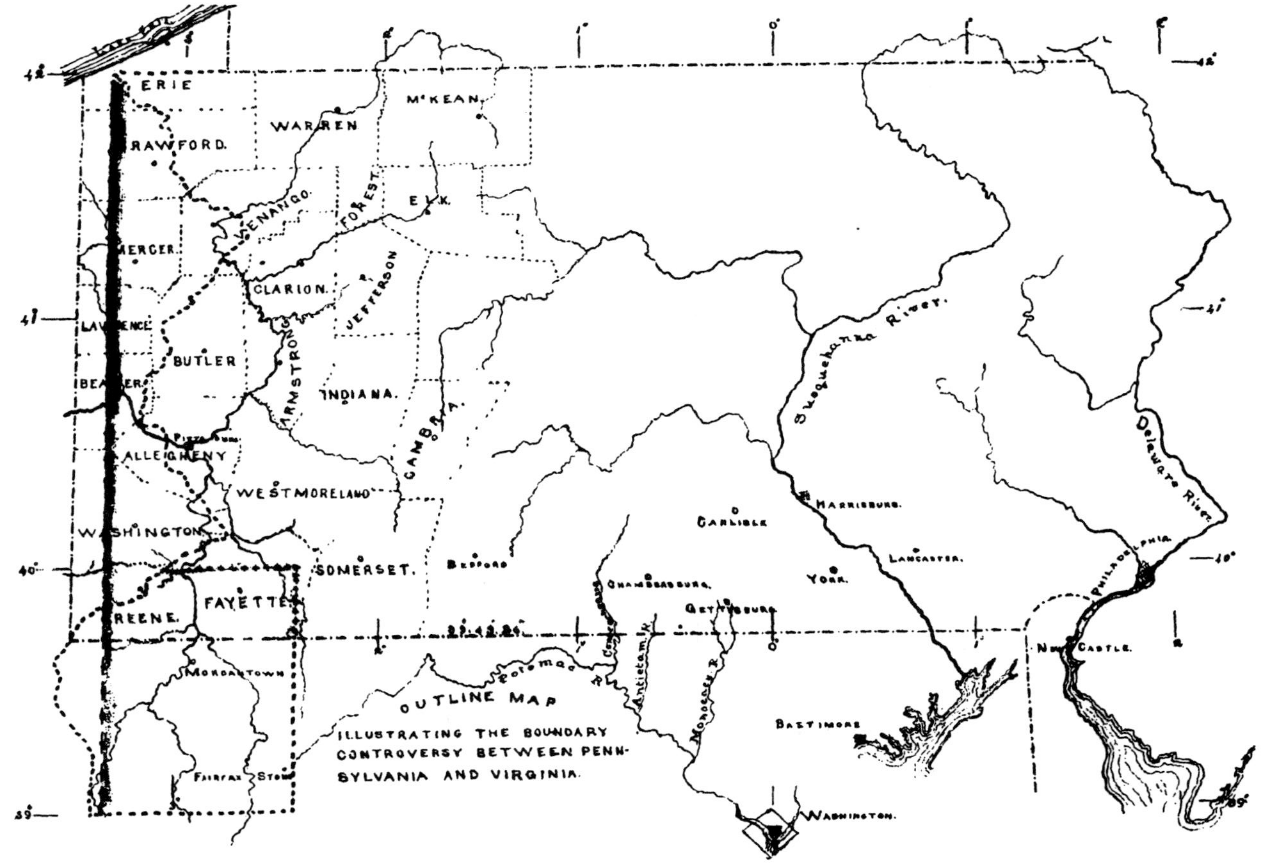
OUTLINE MAP
ILLUSTRATING THE BOUNDARY
CONTROVERSY BETWEEN PENN-
SYLVANIA AND VIRGINIA.
Delaware River
Susquehanna River
Potomac R.
Antietam R.
Monocacy R.
Philadelphia
New Castle
Lancaster
Harrisburg
York
Carlisle
Chambersburg
Gettysburg
Baltimore
Washington
Bedford
ERIE
CRAWFORD.
WARREN
McKEAN.
VENANGO.
FOREST.
ELK.
MERCER.
CLARION.
JEFFERSON
LAWRENCE
BUTLER
BEAVER.
ARMSTRONG
INDIANA.
CAMBRIA.
ALLEGHENY
WESTMORELAND
WASHINGTON.
SOMERSET.
FAYETTE
GREENE.
MORGANTOWN
FAIRFAX STONE
39° 43' 26"
42°
41°
40°
39°

XXI. MINUTE BOOK OF THE VIRGINIA COURT HELD AT FORT DUNMORE (PITTSBURGH) FOR THE DISTRICT OF WEST AUGUSTA, 1775–1776.

EDITED BY BOYD CRUMRINE, OF WASHINGTON, PA.

[NOTE: In copying these minutes no portions will be omitted, save certain lists, here and there, containing the names of cases called and unintelligible memoranda concerning them, with nothing to identify the parties, the causes of action, or the localities whence they came.]

[THE FORMAL ORGANIZATION OF THE COURT.]

(1)[10] HIS MAJESTIES Writ for adjorning the County Court of Augusta from the Town of Staunton to Fort Dunmore, and with a new Commission of the Peace and Dedimus and a Commission of Oyer and Terminer and Dedimus from under the hand of John, Earl of Dunmore, his Majesties Lieutenant and Governor in chief, bearing date the Sixth day of December One Thousand Seven Hundred and Seventy four, directed to

Silas Hart, James Lockhart, John Dickinson, John Christian, Daniel Smith, Archibald Alexander, John Poage, Felix Gilbert, Abraham Smith, Samuel McDowell, George Moffett, Sampson Mathews, Alexander McClenachan, William Bowyer, Matthew Harrison, George Mathews, Michael Bowyer, Alexander Robertson, John Gratton, John Hays, Thos. Hugart, James Craig, Elijah McClenachan, John Frogg, Jonah Davidson, William Tees, John Skidmore, George Croghan, John Campbell, John Connolly, Edward Ward, Thomas Smallman, Dawsey Penticost, John Gibson, William Crawford, John Stephenson, John McCullough, John Cannon, George Vallindigam, Silas Hedge, David Shepherd, and William Goe, Gentlemen,

being read, & thereupon, pursuant to the said Dedimus, the said George Croghan, John Campbell, John Connolly, John Gibson, George Vallandegham, William Goe, Gentlemen, took

[10] The figures to left of pages in brackets refer to the pages of the original MS. Editor Annals Carnegie Museum.

the Usual Oaths to his Majesties Person & Government, Subscribed the Abjuration Oath and test, and also took the Oaths of Justices of the Peace, and of Justices of the County Court in Chancery, and of Justices of Oyer & Terminer, all which Oaths were administered to them by Thomas Smallman and Dawsey Penticost, and then John Campbell and John Connolly administered all the aforesaid Oaths to the aforesaid Thomas Smallman and Dawsey Penticost, who took the same and subscribed the Abjuration Oath and Test, on which the Court being Constituted the following Members were Present, February 21st, 1775:

George Croghan, John Campbell, John Connolly, Thomas Smallman, Dawsey Penticost, John Gibson, George Vallandegham and William Goe, Gentlemen Justices—

(2) George Brent and George Rootes took the Usual Oaths to his Majesties Person and Government, Sub the Abjuration Oath and Test, and then took the Oaths of Attorneys.

Ord that John Campbell, George Redman, Thomas Redman, and Benja. Renoe, or any 3 of them, being first sworn, Veiw a Road from Fort Dunmore to Frederick Dunfields, and make a report of the Conveniences and Inconveniences to the next Court.

Joseph Hill is appointed a Constable in the room of Jacob Vanmetere, and that he be summoned to be sworn in the office.

On the Petition of James Johnston and others, It is Ord Edward Cook, Joseph Hill, Senr., Levy Stevens, Gilbert Simpson, Rich'd McMahon, John Decker, Paul Froman, and James Innes, they being first sworn, Veiw a Road from the Road from Thomas Gists to Fort Dunmore to Paul Fromans on Shirtees Creek, by James Devores Ferry, and make a report of the Conveniences and Inconveniences to the next Court.

William Elliott, being bound over to this Court by Tho: Smallman, Gent., for disturbing the minds of his Majes... Good people of this County, by demanding in an arbitrary and Illegal Manner of sundry Persons what Personal Estate they are possessed of, that the same may be tax'd according to the Laws of Pennsylvania, being called, appeared and on hearing the argument of the attorneys the Court are of opinion that he be Committed to the Goal of this County, and there remain until he Enter into recog. in the sum of £100, with 2 Srtys in the

Sum of 50 £ Each, for his good Behavior for the space of One Month; and thereupon the sd Wm. Elliott, with John Harvie and Chas Irons, ack'd themselves Indebted to our Sovereign Lord the King, the sd Elliott in the Sum of £100 and the sd. Harvie and Irons in the Sum of £50 Each, to be levied on their respective Goods and Chattels, Lands and Tenements, in Case the sd. Wm. Elliott is not of good Behaviour for the Space of one month.

(3) Ordered that the Court be Adjourned until to Morrow Morning 10 o'clock. GEO: CROGHAN.

At a Court con'd and held for Augusta County at Fort Dunmore February 22d, 1775,

Prest John Connolly, Thomas Smallman, Dorsey Pentecost, Wm Goe, Gentlemen, Justices.

John Canon, one of the Gent in the Commission of the peace, took the Usual Oaths to his Majesties person and Governt, Subscribed the Abjuration Oath and Test, and then took the Oath of a Justice of the peace, and of Justice of the County Court in Chancery, and of Justice of Oyer and Terminer

On the Complt of John McAnully ag'st his Master, Casper Reel, for beating and abuseing him, It is ordered that he be summoned to appear here the next Court, to answer the Complt, and with the Servt.

Prest, John Canon.

On the petition of Alexr. Duglas and others, It is Ord that Wm. Crawford, Providence Mounce, Ezekiel Hickman, Joseph Beeler, John Vanmetere, Morgan Morgan, Vincen Colvin, Henry Taylor, Van Swearengen, they being first sworn, Veiw a road from Providence Mounce's Mill, by Ausberger's Ferry, and from thence to Catfish Camp, and make a report of the Conveniences and Inconveniences to the next Court.

Ordered that Robert Henderson, Benja. Kuykendall, John Robinson, and James Sulivan, they being first sworn, Veiw a Road from Fort Dunmore to Beckets fort, and make a report of the Conven and Inconveniences to the next Court.

Prest., John Gibson.

(4) David Semple, Gent, is recommended to the Gentn appointed to exam Attos., that he is a Person of Probaty, Honesty, and Good Demeanor.

On the Motion of Henry Heath, It is ordered that Silas Dexter, Gabriel Cox, Rich'd McMahon, Benja. Sweet, Robt. Henderson, Veiw the most Conven Way from fort Dunmore to Henry Heaths, they being first sworn, and make a report of the Inconv and Conven to the next Court.

Admon of the Estate of Wm. Craig, dec'd, granted to Andrew Vaughan, a Creditor, he having comp'd with the Laws.

Ord. that Gabriel Cox, Rich'd McMahon, James Bruce, and Henry Heath, or any 3, app the Est.

Patrick McElroy took the Usual Oaths to his Majesties Person and Govern, Sub the Abjur Oath and Test, and then was sworn a Deputy Sheriff.

William Christy took the Usual Oaths to his Majesties Person and Govern, Sub the Abj Oaths and Test, which is Ordered to be Certified on his Commission of a Lieutenant of Pittsburg and its Dependencies of the Militia.

Simon Girty took the Usual Oaths to his Majesties Person and Govern, Sub the Abjuration Oath and test, which is Ord to be Certified on his Com of a Lieutent of the Militia of Pittsburg and its Dependencies.

Jacob Bousman took the Usual Oaths to his Majes Person and Govern, Sub the Abjur Oath and test, which is Ord to be Certified on his Comn of Ensign of the Militia of Pittsburg and its Dependencies.

Ord that Paul Froman, Thomas Cook, Josiah Crawford, Jacob Long, and Rich'd Crooks, they being first sworn, Veiw
(5) a road from Fort Dunmore to Paul Froman's and make a report of the Conveniences and Inconveniences thereof to the next Court.

Prest., John Campbell.

William vs. Bresser; deft moved for a ded. to take the deps. of Jacob Dorenin, a Wits who is agoing down the Ohio river, which was overuled.

Ab., John Connolly.

John Connolly took the Usual Oaths to his Majesties person and Govern, Sub the Ab Oath and test, which is Ord to be Certified on his commission of Major of the Millitia.

Prest., John Connolly.

Windle Ourey, being bound over to this Court for acting as an assessor under the Laws of Pennsylvania, appeared, and having made Confession to the Court, it is Ordered that he be discharged from his recog.

James Cumerford being bound over to this Court on Complt of John Gibson, Gent, being called and failing to appear the Prosecution is withdrawn.

Ord. that the Sheriff make use of the Room in the Fort now Used as a Guard Room as a Goal for this Part of the County, and also that John Campbell and Dorsey Penticost, Gent, with the Surv. lay of Prison Bounds for the same, Includ the ally of the fort and two rods wide to the town

Robert Hannah, being bound over to this Court for openly disturbed the peace by interrupting the execution of Legal Process by the officers of this Government, and did actually imprison a Certain Philip Baily in the discharge of his duty as a Consta, ag'st the Peace of our Sovereign Lord the King, being called, appeared and offered a Plea to the Jurisdiction of the Court, which Plea was Overuled; and It is ordered that he be Committed to the Goal of this County, and there to remain
(6) until he Enter into recog in the Sum of £1000 with 2 Secys. in the sum of £500 Each, to be levied of their respective Goods and Chattels, Lands and Tenemets, in case Robt. Hanah is not of Good Behaviour for a Year and a day, and also desit from acting as a Majestrate within the Colony of Virginia by any authority from the Province of Pennsylvania, and that he keep the peace to all his Majesties Leige Subjects in the Mean time.

James Caveat, Gent, being bound over to this Court for sundry times Malevolently opposed the authority of His Majesties officers of the Government of Virginia, and has rioutsly opposed the legal Establishment of his Majesties Laws in this County, Contrary to the peace of our Sovereign Lord the King, being called, appeared and offered a plea to the Jurisdiction of the Court, which was overuled; and it is ordered that he be Committed to the Goal of this County and thereto remain until he Enter into recog in the Sum of £1000 with two Secys in the Sum of £500 Each, to be levied of their respective Goods
(7) and Chattels, Lands and Tenements, in case James Caveat is not of Good Behaviour for a Year and a day, and also desist from acting as a Majestrate within the Colony of Virginia by

any authority derived from the Province of Pennsylvania, and that he keep the peace to all his Majesties Leige Subjects in the mean time.

Francis Brown took the Usual Oaths to his Majesties Person and Govern, Sub the Abjur Oath and test, and was Sworn as a deputy Sheriff, with the Consent of John Christian by a note from under his hand

James Smith being bound over to this Court for acting as a Commissioner under an authority derived from under the Province of Pennsylvania within the Colony of Virginia, being called appeared, and on being heard It is Ord that he Committed to the Goal of this County, and there to remain until he Enter into recog in the Sum of £100 with two Secys. in the Sum of £50 Each, to be levied of their respec Goods and Chattels, Lands and Tenements, in case he is not of Good Behaviour for a Year and a day, and also desist from acting as a Commissioner from under any authority derived from under the province of Pennsylvania within this Colony

Ord that Davd Steel, John Wals, Oliver Miller, and Nathan Couch, they being first sworn, Veiw a Road from Devor's ferry to the road that leads from fort Dunmore to Dunfeilds, to join Dunfeild's road on Shirtee's Creek near Ben Renoes, and make a report of the Conven and Inconven to the next Court

(8) Ord that the Sheriff Imploy a Workman to build a Ducking Stool at the Confluence of the OHio with the Monongohale and that the person Imployed bring in his Charge at the Laying of the Levy.

Bousman vs. McGoldrick, Joseph Chriswell Spbd.

Edward Armstrong, being bound over to this Court on the Complt of Frederick Ferrie, for Stealing a Hog the prop of the sd. Ferrie, on hearing the Wits and the parties by their Attos, and It is ordered that the Complt be dismised.

David Steel took the Usual Oaths to his Majesties Person and Govern, Sub the Ab Oath and test, which is Ord to be Cert on his Commission of Ensign of Pittsburgh and its Dependances.

Ord that Thos. Brown, Bazil Brown, Wm. Colvin, Reuben Camp, and Conrad Walter, they being first sworn, Veiw a Road from Old Redstone fort to Conrad Walkers, and make a report of the Conven and Inconv to the next Court

Ord that the Court be adjourned until to Morrow Morning 10 o'Clock. JNO. CONNOLLY.

At a Court Con'd and held for Augusta County February 23d, 1775 Prest, Jno. Campbell, Jno. Gibson, Thos Smallman Wm. Goe, Jno. Cannon.

James Berwick, Gent, is recommed to the Gentlemen to Examine Attos, as a person of Probaty, Honesty, and good Demeanor.

Andrew Ross, Gent, is recommended to the Gentlemen to Examine Attos, as a person of Probaty, Honesty, and Good Demeanor.

(9) On the Motion of Henry Heath, leave is granted him to keep a ferry on the Monongohala River at his own Plantation, and he provide a Boat for the sd ferry

On the Motion of Wm Lynn, leave is granted him to keep a ferry on Monongahale River, from his House over the River to the Land of Fras. Holls (?),[11] and that he provide Boats.

On the Motion of Mich'l Cresap, leave is granted him to keep a ferry on Monongohale River at Redstone fort to the Land of Indian Peter, and that he provide a Boat.

On the Motion of James Devore, leave is granted him to keep a ferry on Monongohale River, from his house over the river to the Mouth of Pidgeon Creek, and that he provide Boats.

Luke Joliff, being committed and brought before the Court for deserting from the Militia, and for takeing with a stand of arms, and for preventing the Indians for not delivering up Sund Prisoners, then in their custody; On hearing Sund Wits and the s'd Luke, the Court are of Opinion that he for the s'd offence receive for the s'd offence of deserting 500 Lashes with a Cat-o'nine tails on his bare back, well laid on, and it is said to the Sheriff that execution thereof be done at such times and in such number as not to endanger life or member.

[Here follows a long list of cases, seventy-four in number, indicating that the cases had been called and some order made in them. Only the surnames of the parties being given, with unintelligible memoranda which do not indicate the nature of the action, nor identify or localize the parties, this list is omitted.]

Ord that Edward Cook, Joseph Hill, Senr., Levy Stevens,

[11] Name illegible.—EDITOR.

Gilbert Simpson, Rich'd McMahon, John Decker, Paul Frooman, and James Innes, they being first sworn, Veiw a Road from Thos. Gists to Paul Froomans Mill on Shirtees Creek, and make a report of the Conven and Inconvenc to the next Court.

(12) Ord that Thomas Crooks, Wm. Bashears, Robt. Thornton, Thos. Egenton, and Philip Whittan, they being first sworn, Veiw a road from Redstone old fort to Shirtees Creek to Paul Froomans, and make a report of the Conv and Inconv to the Next Court.

[On the motion of Jacob Bousman, leave is granted him to keep a ferry across the Monongohale River, from his House to the Town oposite thereto, & that he provide & keep a suff numer of Boats for that Purpose.[12]]

John Campbell, Gent, with his Servt Michl Haney, came into Court, and the sd. John acknowledged that he had served the time mentioned in his Ind, which is Ord to be Certified.

Ord that Dav'd Steel, Thos. Bond, John Mckee, and Silas Dexter, they being first sworn, Veiw a road from the Mouth of the Yough River, at Mckee's ferry, to the Road from Devore's ferry to Renoe's near Sampson Beavers, and so On to Fromans Mill, and make a report of the Conv and Inconvenien to the next Court.

On the Motion of Dorsey Penticost, It is Ord that his Mark be recorded a Cross in the left Ear and his Brand D P.

Christopher Turby, John Carpenter, Joshua Wright, Joseph Hill, Snr, John Hawthorn, Emson Brumfield, Jno. Harden, Junr., John Pettyjohn, John Warick, James Booth, Reeson Virgin, Ezekial Rose, Wm. Hawkens, James Taylor, Nathl Blackmore, James Murdough, Jas. Young, Abraham Slover, Jno. Bell, John Dousman, Andrew Robinson, Nicholas Higarthy, Barney Wistner (?),[13] Jno. Castleman, Elias Myers, Wm. Teagard, Junr., Joseph Erwin, Jno. Nicholas, James Baird, Sam'l Hinly, Moses Smith, Terry Moore, Michl Martin, Rich'd Wells, and Garshom Hull, are app'd Constables, and It is Ord that they be summoned to be sworn before a Majestrate, or Attend at the next Court to be Sworn.

(13) John Campbell and Dorsey Penticost, the persons appointed

[12] This entry, placed in ( ), is erased in the original record.

[13] Name somewhat illegible.—EDITOR.

to lay off the Prison bounds, made a report, and Ord to be Recorded.

Ord that the Sheriff Summon a Grand jury for the Inquest of the body of this County, to appear here in May next.

On the Motion of Sam'l Semple, It is Ord that his Mark be recorded a Crop of the right Ear and a Nick in the Edge.

On the Motion of John Gibson, It is Ord that his Mark a Slit in the right and a Crop in the left Ear and brand I G.

Ordered that Alexander Mckee, James Innis, Thomas Galbreath, Wm. Harrison, Thomas Gaddis, Jno. Swearingen, Thomas Freeman, Benjamin Davis, Edward Cook, John Whitacre, Philip Ross, David Rogers, James Chew, David Scott, Chas. Wheeler, Thos. Crooks, Jno. Robertson, John Nevill, Michl Rough, Isaac Mason, Eli Coulter, Wm. Elliott, Henry Vanmetre, Geo Rodgers Clark, Rich'd Yates, John Irwine, Christopher House (?), and Joseph Beeler, are humbly recommended to his Excellency, the Governor, as proper persons sons to be added to the Commission of the Peace for this County.

Edward Armstrong and James Ryan was brought before the Court for fighting in the Court Yard and disturbing the Court; It is Ord that they be committed to the Goal of this County, and there to remain until they Each Enter into recog in the Sum of £10 with 2 Secys in the Sum of £5 Each, to be levied, and for their appearance at the Grandjury in May next, and that his Majesties deputy Atto prosecute them for the same: Sum Geo Ashton, John Collins, and Sam'l Mckinsie (?).[14]

(14) On the Motion of John Canon, It is Ord that his Mark be recorded, a Crop in the right Ear and half Crop in the left.

A Bill of Sale from James Cumberford to Geo Aston was prov'd by Valentine Thos. D'Alton, the Wit, and O R.

A Bill of Sale from Simon Butler to Geo Aston was prov'd by Valentine Thos. D'Alton, one of the Wits, and O R.

An Agreement between Cornelius Dougherty and Geo Aston was prov'd by Valentine Thos. D'Alton, one of the Wits, and O R.

Geo Aston took the Usual Oaths to his Majesties person and Government, Sub the Ab Oath and test, and Ord to be Cert'd on his Commission of Captain of the Militia.

[14] Spelling doubtful; word illegible.—EDITOR.

Licence to keep an ordinary is Granted to John Ormsby, he hav'g compld with the Law.

Licence to keep an Ordinary is Granted to Sam'l Ewalt, he hav'g Compld with the Law.

The Last Will and Test of Shedrich Muchmoor, dec'd, was proved by Valentine Thos. D'Alton and Wm. Plumer, two of the Wits, and O R, and On the Motion Mary Muchmoor the Widow, Admon with the Will Annexed is granted her, she hav'g Comp with the Law.

Ord that Benja Tomlinson, Joshua Baker, Jacob Cockran, and Jos Cockran, and any 3, app the Est of Shedrich Muchmoor, dec'd, and return the App to the next Court.

Jonathan Muchmoor of the age of 19 years Orph of Shedrich Muchmoor, dec'd, chose Thos. Smallman his Gaurd, who Compld with the Laws

(15) Ordered that the Court be adjorned until to Morrow Morning 10 o'Clock. JNO. CONNOLLY.

At a Court Con'd and held for Augusta County at Fort Dunmore Feby. 24th 1775,

Prest. John Campbell, Jno. Connolly, Thos. Smallman, John Gibson, Dorsey Penticost.

Ord that Providence Mounce, Wm. Crawford, Paul Froman, James Innis, or any three, being first sworn, Veiw the Most Conv way for a road from Mounce's Mill to Froomans Mill, and make a report of the Conv and Inconv to the next Court.

P. Jno. Cannon.

Licence to keep an Ordinary is granted to Frederick Feree, he hav'g Comp with the Law.

The same to Jacob Bousman, on the South side of the Monongohale River oppisite the Town.

On the Motion of Samuel Sinclair, who lives on the forks of the river Monongohale and Youghagano leave is granted him to keep a ferry over Each of the Rivers, and that he keep boats.

Licence to keep an Ordinary is granted to Sam'l Sample, he hav'g Comp with the Laws.

Wm Hawkins, Andrew Robertson, and Nicholas Hagerty, took the Usual Oaths to his Majesty's Person and Governm, Sub the Ab Oath and Test, and then took the Oaths of Constables.

Bertney Whitney took the Usual Oaths to his Majesties person and Govern, Sub the Ab Oath and Test, and then took the Oath of a Constable.

(16) Ord that Peter Elrod John Whitacer, Andrew McMeans, and Benja Davis, or any 3, they being first sworn, Veiw a Road from Fromans Road to Sam'l Sinclairs, the nearest and best way, and make a report of the Conv and Incon to the next Court.

Ord that Silas Dexter, Gabriel Cox, Rich'd McMahon, Benja Sweet, and Robt Henderson, or any 3, they being first sworn, veiw the nearest and best way from Sam'l Sinclairs to Fort Dunmore, and make a report of the Conven and Inconv to the next Court.

Ord that Chas Bruce, Geo Aston, Abraham Slover, and Josiah Osburn, or any 3 of them, being first sworn, Veiw the nearest and best way from Fort Dunmore to Chas. Bruces on Racoon Creek, and make a report of the conv and Inconv to the next Court.

His Majesties Writ for adjorning this Court from Fort Dunmore to the Town of Staunton being read, It is Ordered that the s'd Court be Adjorned Accordingly.

JNO. CONNOLLY.

His Majesties Writ for Adjorning the County Court of Augusta from Staunton to Fort Dunmore being read, this 16th May 1775,

Present Geo Croghan, Jno. Campbell, John Connolly, Thos. Smallman, John Gibson, John Cannon.

Edward Ward and John McColloch took the Usual Oaths to his Majesties Person and Govern, Sub the Ab Oath and Test, and then took the Oath of Justice of the peace, and of
(17) Justice of the County Court in Chancery, and of a Justice of Oyer and Terminer.

Henry Peyton took the Oath of an Atto and is admitted to Practice as such in this Court.

Small vs Gray, Nordica Mordica Spbd.

Shilling vs Young, Geo Corn Spbd.

Cresap vs Swearingam, Michl Tygert Spbd.

At a Cald Court held for the Examination of Thos Glenn, who stands Committed to the Goal of this County, charged with the Murder of his Servt Man Peter Eglington,

Prest. Geo Croghan, Jno Campbell, John Connolly, Edward Ward, Thos. Smallman, Jno. Gibson, Geo Vallandigham.

The above named Thos. Glenn was brought to the barr and upon Examination denied the fact wherewith he stands charged; whereupon several Witnesses were Sworn and Examined, and upon Consider at which the Court are of opinion that he is Guilty of the fact wherewith he stands Charged, and that he ought to be tried for the s'd Supposed fact at the General Court in October next, at the 6th day thereof, and in Order thereto he is remanded to the Goal of this County and thence to be removed to the Pub Goal in the City of Wmsburg.

Be it Remembered John McCollock, Moses Williamson, James Johnson, James Nowland, of this County, ackn'd themselves Indebted to our Sovereign Lord the King in the Sum of £100 Each, to be levied of their respective Goods and Chattels,
(18) Lands and Tenements, in Case they do not appear at the Capitol, in the City of Wmsburg, on the 6th day of the next General Court, and then and there give evidence ag'st Thos. Glenn for the Murder of his Servt Peter Eglington, and not depart without leave of the Court.

Then the Court did rise.

Spa. to Jos. Blackford,
for the Prisoner. Geo: Croghan,

Noble vs Chamberlain. Walter Briscoe Spbd.

Prest: Geo Croghan, John Connolly, Edward Ward, John Cannon, John McCulloch, John Gibson;

Michael Ginder and Geo Ginder Ack'd L & R to Nicholas Mace and O R.

The same to Francis Mcbride and O R.

The Commission for the private Examin of Cath, the Wife of Michl. Ginder, and Susanna, the wife of Geo Ginder, to a tract of land sold by their Husbands to Nicholas Mace, being ret. is O R.

The same to Fras. Mcbride and O R.

Susanna, the wife of Geo Ginder, came into Court, and relinq her right of Dower to 100 acres on the branches of Brooks Creek, formerly conveyed by her husband to Fra's Mcbride, and O Cd.

Benja Renoe, Geo Redman, and Thos. Redman, 3 of them,

persons appointed to Veiw a road from Fort Dunmore to Frederick Dunfields and make a report, and made their report; It is Ord that the Road be Established, and that Geo Redman, and Benja. Renoe be Surveyors thereof, and that the Tithables within 3 Miles on Each side work thereon.

(19) Wm. Crawford, one of the Gent in the Com of the Peace, took the Usual Oaths to his Majesties Person and Govern, Sub the Ab Oath and test, and then took the Oath of a Justice of the Peace, and of a Justice of the County Court in Chancery, and of a justice of Oyer and Terminer.

Pres, Wm. Crawford.

On the Petition of Maly Hayes, and others, It is Ord that Peter Elrod, John Whitacre, Andrew McMeans, Benja Davis, Silas Dexter, Gab'l Cox, Rich'd McMahon, Benja Sweet, and Robt. Henderson, or any 6 of them, being first sworn, Veiw a Road from Dorsey Penticost's, by Peter Barrackman's ferry, to fort Dunmore, and make a report of the Conven and Inconven to the next Court.

On the Motion Capt. Paul Froman, It is Ordered that John Decker, John Muns, James Innes, and Thomas Edgington, or any 3 of them, being first sworn, Veiw the most Conven Way from Froman's Mill on Shirtees Creek, to Fromans Mill on the East side of the Monongohale, and make a report of the Conven and Inconven to the next Court.

A Grandjury for the Inquest of the body of this County, to wit: Geo McColloch, foreman, Oliver Miller, Abraham Teagarden, John Swann, Jesse Pigman, Bazil Brown, Rich'd Waller, Jacob Vanmetre, Wm. Colvin, Josiah Wallace, Moses Williamson, John Deckar, Rich'd McMahon, Rich'd McGlaughlin, and Daniel Cannon, having received their charge retired.

(20) George Croghan Ackn'd a Barg and Sale and a receipt to Benjamin Tate and O R.

The same to Jacob Bousman and O R.

Teagarden vs Hammon James Crawford Spbd.

Cresap vs Peterson Indian Erasimes Backys Spbd.

vs Cox John Wall Spbd.

Woods vs Gray Wm. Cuningham Spbd.

Samples vs Fernsley Walter Grymes Spbd.

Cresap vs Vaughan John Gab'l Jones Spbd

Elliott vs Martin- Jacob Bousman Spbd.
Boly vs Springer John Springer Spbd
Hawkins vs Wheat James McConnel Spbd.
Cook vs McConnel Conrad Wheat Spbd.
Ab Geo Croghan
Williamson vs Mills Wm. Hawkins Spbd
Swagler vs Mills Wm. Hawkins Spbd
Bell vs Finn. James Crawford Spbd.
Vallandigham vs Crinnell.
Colvin vs Frederick Geo Wilson Spbd.
Boly vs Ross.
Wilcox vs Craighead James Sulivan Spbd.
Cook vs Froman. James Chambers Spbd
Boley vs Springer in Debt Paul Froman Spbd.
Penticost vs Briscoe Pat McElroy Spbd
Kuykendal vs Allenthrop Paul Froman Spbd.
Bond vs Mordica

On the Complt of James O'Neel against his Master, Patrick Fleming, for beating and abuseing him, It is Ord that his Master be Sum'd to appear here the next Court, to Ans the Complt, and that he in the mean time treat well and give Security for
(21) the same, himself in the sum of £30, and 1 Secy in the Sum of £15; and thereupon he with James Chambers his Secy Ack'd himself Indeb to our Sovereign Lord the King in the Sum of 30£, and Jas. Chambers, his Secy, also in the Sum of £15, to be levied of their respective Goods and Chattels, Lands and Tenements, in Case he doth not use his servt, James O'Neel, well til the next Court

On the Complt of John Connolly, Gent, ag'st Geo Wilson, Gent, as a disturber of the peace, on hearing the parties the Court are of Opinion that the Complt be dismissed,

Ord that Rich'd Heth (?),[15] Dav'd Steel, Thos Cook, Rich'd Crooks, and Paul Froman, or any 3 of them, being first [Sworn], Veiw a road from Fort Dunmore to Paul Fromans Mill on Shirtees Creek, and make a report of the Conv and Inconv to the next Court.

Ord that the Court be adjorned until to Morrow Morning 10 o'clock.

JOHN CAMPBELL.

[15] Spelling doubtful; illegible.—EDITOR.

At a Court Com'd and held for Augusta County May 17th, 1775,

Prest. Geo Croghan, Edward Ward, Thos. Smallman, John Gibson, John McCullough, Wm. Crawford.

Ord that John Vance, Providence Mounce, Edward Dial, and Wm. Mckee, or any 3 of them, being first sworn, Veiw the most Conven Way from Maj Crawford's to near the forks of Indian Creek, and make a report of the Conv and Inconv to the next Court.

(22) On the petition of Rezin Virgin and others, it is Ord that Philip Shute, Rich'd Waller, Abraham Teagarden, Wm. Teagarden, Geo Teabolt, and Rezin Virgin, or any 3 of them, being first sworn, Veiw a road from the foot of Laurel Hill, by Wm Teagarden's ferry, to the Mouth of Wheeling, and make a report of the Conven and Inconv to the next Court.

On the Motion of Dav'd Mckee, for leave to keep a ferry over the Monongohale and Youghogana, which Motion being opposed, on hearing the parties It is Consid that the ferry is Unnecessary; It is therefore Ord that the s'd Motion be rejected.

The persons app'd to Veiw a road from old Redstone fort to Conrad Walters, and made a report, It is Ord that the road be Established, and that Jacob Beason be Overseer from Conrad Walters to Jennings's run, and Robt. Jacman be Overseer from the East side of Jennings run to James Chamberlains Run, on the East side of the dividing Ridge, and that Philip Fouts be Overs from Chamberlains run to the River at old Redstone fort, and that the tithe's within 3 miles on Each side work thereon

Prest. John Cannon

John White, being bound over to this Court on the Comp of Thomas Christy, for stealing his swine, on hearing the witnesses the Court are of Opinion that he is guilty of the fact wherewith he stands Charged, and that he be Committed to the Goal of this County, there to remain until he Enter into recog in the Sum of £100 with two Securitys, in the Sum of £50 Each, for his good behavior, and for his personal appearance at the next Grand jury Court to be held here, and that his Majestys deputy Atto prefer a bill of Indict ag'st him.

Thomas Martin being bound over to this Court on the Complt of Archibald Hamilton for Burning his House in the Neighbourhood of Sandy Creek, whereby he has lost some of his Effects, being called, appeared, and on hearing the parties by their Atto and Sund Wits the Court are of Opinion that he is guilty of a High Misdemeanor; It is Ord that he be Committed to the Goal of this County for the s'd offence, and there to remain until he Enter into recog in the Sum of £100 with 2 Secys in the Sum of £50 Each, for his good behaviour for a Year and
(23) a day; and thereupon he with Jacob Bousman and Hugh O'Harro, his Secy, ack'd himself indeb to our Sovereign Lord the King in the Sum of £100, and the s'd Jacob Bousman and Hugh O'Harro Ack'd themselves Each Indeb to our Sovereign Lord the King in the sum of £50 Each, to be levied of their respec Goods and Chattels, Lands and Tenements, in case the s'd Thos. Martin is not of Good behaviour for a Year and day.

Peter McCartney Ack'd a Claim to 50 Acres of Land to John Campbell, Gent, and O R.

Cook vs Shilling, Peter Hillibrand Spbd.

On the Complt of Benjamin Kyser against Hugh Davidson for a forceable Entry made, being called, appeared, and on hearing the parties and the Wits the Court are of Opinion that he is Guilty, and that he be Committed to the Goal of this County, and there to remain until he Enter into recog in the Sum of £100, with 2 Secys in the Sum of £50 Each, and thereupon he with John Caveat and John Sampson his Secys Ack'd himself Indeb to our Sovereign Lord the King in the Sum of £100 and the s'd John Caveat and John Sampson Ack'd themselves Each to owe to our Sovereign Lord the King in the Sum of £50 Each to be levied of their respective Goods & Chattels, Lands & Tenements, in Case thes'd Hugh Davidson is not of Good Behaviour for a Year and a day.

Fred Ferree, being bound over to this Court on the Complt of Geo Phelps, for beating him, being called, appeared, and on hearing the parties & the Witnesses, the Court are of Opinion that the Complt be dismised.

(24) Stevens vs Shilling Peter Hillibrand Spbd
Mitchell vs Scott Michl Tygert Spbd & Imp P

McMichal vs French David Scott Spbd & Imp P

Russell vs Sessney David Steele SB & Impl B.

The Granjury for the Inquest of the body of this County returned, and haveing ret'd Several Indict true bills, It is Ord that the Kings Atto do pros them and that the Clk do Issue process on them Accord'gly; & also several bills of Indict being preferd & found Ignoramus, It is Ord that the same be dis'd.

Ord that the Court be Adjourned until to Morrow Morning 10 o'Clock

GEO: CROGHAN.

At a Court Con'd and held for Augusta County May 18th 1775.

Prest. Geo Croghan, John Campbell, John Gibson, Geo Vallandigham.

On the Petition of Charles Harrison and others, It is Ordered that Richard Walker, Charles Harrison, Daniel Cannon, and Isaac Pearce or any 3 of them being first sworn Veiw a road the nearest and best way to Veiw a Road from Thomas Gists house to Cap'n Fromans mill and make a report of the Conv and Inconv to the next Court.

Mitchell vs Val Crawford Wm. Crawford Spbd.

Nevell vs Gist. Wm. Crawford Spbd.

Speer vs Gist. Wm. Crawford Spbd.

P. Ed Ward, John Cannon, Wm Crawford, John McColloch.

Thomas Scott being bound over to this Court for his acting and doing Business as a Justice of the peace under Pennsylvania, in Contempt of the Earl of Dunmore's late Proclamation, as also to such other Misdemeanors as shall be then and
(25) there objected ag'st him, appeared, and On hearing him and the Wits the Court are of Opinion that he is Guilty, and it is Ord that he be Committed to the Goal of this County, and there to remain until he Enter into recog in the sum of £500, with 2 secys in the Sum of £250 Each, to be levied of their respective Goods and Chattels, Lands and Tenements, in Case Thomas Scott is not of Good Behaviour for a year and a day and, also desist from acting as a Majestrate within the Colony

of Virginia by any authority derived from the Provence of Pennsylvania, and that he keep the peace to all his Majesties Leige Subjects in the mean time.

George Croghan, Esqr. Ack'd a Deed of Bargain and Sale and a receipt thereon Endorsed to Bernad Gratz, and O R.

The same to Joseph Simon & O R.

The same to Bernard Gratz and O R.

The same to Bernard Gratz and O R

P. Thos. Smallman, Ab. Wm. Crawford.

Devorix Smith being bound over to this Court on the Complt of Susanna Styger, for asaulting, Beating & Wounding her, appeared, and on hearing the parties and the Witnesses the Court are of Opinion that the Complt be dismised with Costs

Susanna Sturgus being bound over to this Court on the Complt of Devereux Smith, for Insulting his wife and threatening her, on hearing the parties and Wits the Court are of Opinion that the Complt be dismised.

Mills vs Williamson — Pat McElroy Spbd.

Hawkins vs Hillibrand — Moses Williamson Spbd.

Cresap vs Teagarden — Wm & Geo Teagarden Spbd

vs French Moses Williamson Spbd

On the Complt of John McaNully ag'st his Master, Casper Reel, for beating & abuseing him, being Sum'd, appeared, and on hear'g the parties & the Wits the Court are of Opinion that the Complt is Groundless & be dismised, and It is Ord that the Sheriff take the Serv't and give him 25 Lashes well Laid on, and it is said to the Sheriff that Execution be done Immediately.

Casper Reel prod and made Oath to his Account of £2.16.0, his Expences in takeing up his Serv't, John McaNully, when run aw, and for 4 days absent time when run away; It is ord that he serve for the same accr to Law.

(26) Edward Armstrong being bound over to this Court on the Complt of John Miller, Senr., for takeing away a Plow & Irons with several other Utensels of Husbandry and Household furnitur, the property of the s'd John and the s'd Edward, appeared, and hearing the parties and the Wits the Court are of Opinion that he is Guilty of the facts wherewith he stands Charged, and that he be Committed to the Goal of this County, and there to remain until he Enter into recog in the Sum of £30, with 2

Secys in the Sum of £15 Each, to be levied in case he is not of Good behaviour for a Year and a day

The persons app'd to Veiw a Road from Shirtees Creek to Devor's ferry made their report; It is Ord that the Road be Established, and that David Steel and Jed Ashcraft be Overseers, and that the tith's within 3 miles on Each side work thereon.

Joseph Cisnea and Wm. Donnellsan being bound over to this Court, on the Complt of Thomas Russell for a forceable Entry & detainer, and no persons appearing It is Ord to be dis'd.

The Complt of John Quay ag'st Dav'd McClure, no persons appearing It is Ord to be dis'd.

The Complt of Adam Bell ag'st Stephen Bennett, no persons appearing it is Ord to be dis'd.

The Complt of John Boley ag'st John Springer, no persons appearing It is Ord to be dis'd.

The Complt of Wm. Thomas ag'st Chas. Froman, & no persons appearing It is Ord to be dis'd.

The Complt of Devereaux Smith ag'st Edward Thompson, no persons appearing It is Ord to be dis'd.

The Complt of John Boley ag'st Joseph Ross, no persons appearing, It is Ord to be dis'd.

Beeler vs Walls, John McNew Spbd.

(27) Edward Armstrong came into Court with Robt Strain and Philip Reely, his Secy, Ack'd himself Indeb to our Sover Lord the King in the Sum of £10 and the s'd Robt. Strain and Philip Reily Ack'd themselves Indeb to our Sover Lord the King in the Sum of £5 Each, to be levied & in case the s'd Edward Armstrong is not of good behaviour for a Year and day.

Clinton & Noble vs. Bearshers, Bazil Brown Spbd.

Walls vs Brown, Pat McElroy Spbd.

Ord that the Court be adjourned until to Morrow Morning 3 o'clock in the afternoon.

GEO: CROGHAN.

At a Court Continued and held for Augusta County May 19th, 1775,

Prest. John Gibson, Wm. Crawford, John McCullough, Edward Ward, John Cannon.

On the Motion of Benja Wells It is Ord that his Mark, a Crop and a Slit in the left Ear, be Recorded.

On the Motion of Valentine Crawford, It is Ord that his Mark, a Slit in the left Ear, a Crop and under keel in the Right Ear & O Recorded

Abt. John Gibson. Gt.

Admon of the Estate of Jacob Linnd, dec, is Granted to Thos. Smallman, Gent, and Jacob Bousman, they having with Secy. Entered into & Ack'd Bond accr. to Law.

Ord that Wm Christy, Ignace Lebath Sam'l Semple, and John Ormsby or any 3, app the Est.

Cresap vs Dowling, Josiah Wallace Spbd.

Grub vs Dowling, Josiah Wallace, Spbd.

Sinclair vs Usherwood, Jud accr, act & O Sale.

Ord that the Court be adjourned until to Morrow Morning 8 o'Clock EDWD. WARD

(28) At a Court Con'd and held for Augusta County, May 20th, 1775,

Prest. Geo. Croghan, Ed Ward, Thos. Smallman, John Gibson.

[Here follows a list of over one hundred and sixty cases, with only the surnames of the two parties and unintelligible memoranda.]

A Mortgage from Benjamin Taite to John Campbell, Gent, was produced and O R.

On the Complt of John Ross against his Master, Moses Holliday, for detaining him as a Servant Contrary to Law, it was objected to by the Master by his Atto that the Matter should not concern this Court, as the s'd Master had never been Summoned and had not any previous Notice thereof til he came to court; but the Court Overuld the Objection, it appearing to the Court that he was fully prepar'd, and on hear'g the Wits the Court are of Opinion that the Servt. be set at Liberty.

Ord that Thomas Silk be by the Church wardens of Augusta Parish bound to Jacob Bousman accr. to Law.

On the Motion of Thos. Glenn by his Atto, seting forth that he had been Committed to the Goal of this County on Suspetion of being Guilty of the Murder of his Servant, and that the proceedings of the Cald Court were Irregular, & by which he was Illegally Confined, and praying that the Court will take the same into Consideration; and the Court being of Opinion that the Allegations are true, It is Ordered that he be dis'd from his Imprisonment.

(33) P. John Campbell & Wm. Crawford.

Geo Croghan, Gent, Ack'd a Deed of Barg & Sale to Edward Ward and O R.

The same to the same and O R.

On the Motion of Jacob Bousman, leave is granted him to keep a ferry aCross the Monongohale River from his House to the Town opposite thereto, and that he provide and keep a Sufficient number of Boats for that purpose, in ferrying over the Militia on Muster days.

On the Motion of John Ormsby, for leave to keep a ferry aCross the Monongohale River from this Town to his Land opposite thereto, being opposed by Jacob Bousman, and Motion Overuled.

Alexander Ross, Gent, Ack'd 4 deeds of Surrender and Barg & Sale to Edward Ward, Gent, and O R.

John Ormsby Ack'd a Deed of Barg and Sale to Benja Johnston & O R.

The App of the Est of Shadrach Muchmore, dec'd, being returned, is O R.

On the petition of James Erwin, It is Ord that Robt. Mckee, John Hughes, John Cavet, & John Sampson, or any 3 of them, being first sworn, Veiw a Road from the Pennsylvania Road to the Mouth of Youghioghany at Mckee's ferry, and here to meet the road that comes from Fromans Mill, and make a report of the Conven and Inconven to the next Court.

On the Motion of John Jones, on behalf Christinee Baker, It is Ord that Jacob Knight be Summoned to appear here the next Court, to shew Cause why he detains Michael Infant her Son.

(34) R Dye vs Dye A C
R Beally vs Shawn A C
R Barrakman vs Shevely A C
B McElroy vs Templin Atta
Ha Perkins vs Calloway A C
B McElroy vs Templin Atta
B Downer vs Teagarden A C
B Thomas vs Lea A C

B Swagler vs Mills Spbl. & Imp Ha
B Swigart vs Mills Aj'd
B Virgin vs Carr A C
Sims Wilson vs Cochrane A C
J G J Mills vs Hunter & A C — Hunter and Hawkins.
B Bromfeild vs Cox Atta
R Colvin vs Johnson A C
B Bond vs Long Atta
B Tigard vs Dunnivan A C
B Cresap vs Sheerer AlSub
R Colwell vs Brewster A C
R Sommer vs Brewster A C
R Colvin vs Johnson A C
J G J Sheerer vs Miller A C
B Baker vs Hendricks A C
B Whitacre vs Dixon A C
Sims Wells vs Rearden & AlSub
R Ward vs Thorn Lease Entry and Ouster Conf N G aj'd S
Ha Rodgers vs Campbell dis'd Cds Roote
S Ormsby vs Bousman Lease Entry & ouster & Conf & N G J G J
Ha Jones vs Speers De. & N G aj'd R
B Hukman vs Brumfeild Do. & N G aj'd R
Ha Miller vs Humble. Do. & N. G J G J
R Ha Clark vs Teabolt Do & N G & J G J
B Eyler vs Adams Do & N G and R
R Whitacre vs Dixon C O
R Penticost vs Linn Entry & ouster & N G & j'd B
R vs Jones Do & N G ej'd Sims
R Coin vs Miller Do. & Do. Ha
Johnston vs Swearengen. Pat McElroy Secty Costs and Lease Entry & Ouster Confered & N G ej'd Ha
(39) R Ha Girty vs Hanna Lease Entry & Ouster Confered & N G Sims
B Geegheeghan and vs Smith Do Ha
B Enocks vs Teagarden Do Ha & R
B Clinton vs Mayo Do Sims
B Hawkins vs Humble Do R

B Nicholas vs Swarnck Do J G J

J G J Lapsley vs Reed Ind and Wt of Possession & Admon of the Estate of Arthur Donerly, dec'd, is granted to John Gibson, he hav'g Comp with the Law. Ord that Chas Bruce, Ab Slower, Geo Gibson & Michl. Thorn, or any 4 of them, App the Estate.

Robt Elliott, a Deed of Barg & Sale to Wm. Elliott, & O R.

Admon of the Estate of Wm Cockrine, dec'd, g'd to Benja Elliott, he hav'g Comp'd with the Law. Ord that Benja Tomlinson, Joseph Baker & John Hendrick & Jas. Mathews or any 3, App the Estate.

His Majesties Writ for Adjourning this Court to the Town of Staunton on the 3d Tuesday in June next was produced and read, and It is Ord that the Court be adjourned accordingly

JOHN CAMPBELL.

(40) At a Cald Court held at Fort Dunmore, May the 27th, 1775, for the Examination of Thomas Glenn, who stands committed to the Goal of this County for the Murder of his Servant Man, Peter Eglington,

Present, Geo Croghan, John Campbell, Edward Ward, Thomas Smallman.

The above Named Thomas Glenn was led to the barr, and upon examination denied the fact wherewith he stands charged; whereupon several Witnesses were sworn and Examined, upon Consideration of which the Court are of Opinion that he is not Guilty of the Murder wherewith he stands Charged, but that he is Guilty of beating his Servant Ill, and that he ought to be tried for the same at the next Grandjury Court to be held at this Place, and that he be Committed to the Goal of this County, and there to remain until he Enter into recog in the Sum of £1000, with 2 Secys in the Sum of 500£ Each, for his appear at the Grandjury Court and for his good behaviour in the mean time, and that his Majesties deputy atto prosecute him foı the same.

Then the Court did rise. GEO: CROGHAN.

At a Cald Court held for the Examination of James Clark, who stands committed for the Murder of Silas Tucker, an Infant son of Wm. Tucker, this 12th day of July, 1775:

Prest, Jno Campbell, Thos. Smallman, Ed Ward, Jno. Gibson.

The above named James Clark was led to the Barr, and upon Examination denied the fact wherewith he stands Charged; whereupon several Witnesses were sworn and Examined, and
(41) on Consideration of which the Court are of Opinion that he is not Guilty of the facts wherewith he stands Charged, and that for the s'd offence he be acquitted.

Then the Court did rise

JOHN CAMPBELL.

At a Cald Court held at Fort Dunmore for Augusta County, September 12th, 1775, for the Examination of Wm. Evans for the breaking open the Kitchen of James McCashlin.

Prest. John Campbell, Dorsey Penticost, Wm. Crawford, John McColloch, Wm. Goe.

The above named Wm. Evans was led to the Barr, and upon Examination denied the fact wherewith he stands Charged; whereupon several Witnesses were sworn and Exam'd, on Consideration of which the Court are of Opinion that he is not Guilty of the Burgaly, but that he is guilty of a Trespass; It is Ord that he be Committed to the Goal of this County, and there to remain until he enter into recog in the sum of £50, with 2 Secys in the Sum of 25 £ Each, for his App at the next Grandjury and for his Good behaviour, and the s'd Wm. Evans, with Geo Aston and Cornelius Conner, his Secys, Ack'd the s'd Evans in the Sum of 50 £ and Aston & Conner in the Sum of £ 25 Each, to be Levied, and in Case he do not Appear and for his good behaviour in the mean time, and that his Majesties dep Atto pros them for the same.

Then the Court did rise

JOHN CAMPBELL.

(42) At a Cald Court for the Examination of James Nowland this 12th Sepr. 1775, for the breaking open of James McCashlen's Kitchen:

Prest, John Campbell, Dorsey Penticost, Wm Geo, Wm. Crawford, John McColloch,

The above named James Nowland was led to the barr, and upon Examination denied the fact wherewith he stands charged;

whereupon several Wits were sworn and Exam'd, and on Consid of which the Court are of Opinion that he is not Guilty of the Burgarly, but that he is guilty of a Trespass; It is Ord that he be committed to the Goal of this County, and there to remain until he enter into recog in the Sum of £ 50, with 2 Secys in the Sum of 25 £ Each, and thereupon he with Geo Aston and John Conner his Secys, the s'd Nowlan in the Sum of £ 50 and the s'd Aston and Conner in the Sum of 25 £ Each, to be Levied, and in case they do not appear at the next Grandjury Court to be held here, and for his good behaviour in the mean time, and that his Majes. deputy Atto pros him for the same. Then the Court did rise

JOHN CAMPBELL.

His Majesties Writ for adjorning the Court from Staunton to Fort Dunmore being read this 19th September, 1775:

Pres't Geo. Croghan, Jno. Campbell,
Dorsey Penticost, Thos. Smallman.

David Shepperd took the Usual Oaths to his Majesties person and Gov, Sub the Ab Oath and test, and then took the Oath of a Justice of the Peace, and of a Justice of the County Court in Chancery, and of a Justice of Oyer & Terminer.

(43) Pres't Dav'd Shepperd, and absent John Campbell. Ord that the Sheriff contract with a Workman to repair this house ag'st to morrow, with a barr & seat for the Clk and Justices,

P. Wm. Crawford.

On the motion of Sam'l Sample, It is Ordered that his Serv't Woman, Betty McHolister, serve him 12 Mo; it App by Wits that she had a bastard, It is Ord that she Serve.

Ord that the Court be Adjorned until to Morrow Morning 10 o' Clock GEO: CROGHAN.

At a Court Con'd and held for Augusta County at Fort Dunmore, Sepr. 20th, 1775:

Present Geo Croghan, Thos. Smallman, Dorsey Penticost, Dav'd Shepperd, Gentn, Justices.

Drenning vs Bay, James Gray Spbd.

David Steel took the Usual Oaths to his Majesties Person and Government, Sub the Ab Oath and test, and then took the Oath of a deputy Sheriff.

A Deed from Mordicai M Mordicai to Joseph Simon was proved by Jno. Anderson, Robt. Campbell, 2 of the Wits, & O C'd.

McQuity vs Gray, Thos Bay, Spbd.

Caldwell vs Brouster }
Sommerall vs Brouster } James Gray, Spbd.

An Indenture from John McMillen to Wm. Parkinson was provd by Jno Gab'l Jones and Benja Davis, 2 of the Wits, and O R.

Cresap vs Taylor, James Brownlee Spbd.

Morrison vs Ross, Michl Tygert Spbd.

Gillfillan vs Tygert, Jos Ross Spbd.

(44) George Wilson, Gent, being bound over to this Court for being confederate with aiding advising and abeting certain disorderly persons, who, on the Morning of the 22d of June last, Violently seized and Carried away Maj John Connolly from this place, and also adviseing others not aid the Officers of Justice When called upon to apprehend the afores'd disturbers of the peace, being called and not appearing, It is Ord that he be prosecuted on his Recog.

Richmond vs Scott, Jno. Boly, Spbd.

Christian Perkey, being bound over to this Court on the Complt of Edward Rice for Break'g down his Saw Mill dam, being call'd, app'd and Several Wits were Sworn and Exam'd; on Consideration of which the Court are of Opin that he be Committed to the Goal of this County and there to remain until he enter into Secy in the Sum of £50, with 2 Secy in the Sum of £25 Each; and thereupon he with Wm. Crawford and Haden Wells his Secys Ack'd themselves, the s'd Perkey in the Sum of £50, and the s'd Crawford and Wells in the Sum of £25 Each, to be levied, and in case the s'd Perkey is not of Good behaviour and for a year and a day.

(45) Vallandigham vs Tygart Jos Ross Spbd.

Tidball vs Martin Abm. Vaughan Spbd.

Licence to keep an Ordinary is Granted to Mordicai Moses Mordicai, he hav'g Comp'd with the Law.

Waford vs Cox Abm. Teagarden and Christopher Swigart Spbd.

Brumfeild vs Cox Am. Teagarden and Christopher Swigart Spbd.

Bond vs Mordicai. 2 Suits Ignace Labat Spbd.

The Persons app'd to Veiw a road from the Confluence of Wheeling to the foot of Laurel Hill at Conrad Walters, made a rept that they had Veiwed the same and find that there may be had a good road from the Confluence of Wheeling to the Confluence of Ten Mile on the Monongahala, and from thence to the s'd Walters; It is Ord the s'd Road be Established, and that James McCoy be over from the foot of the Laurel Hill to Chas. Hickman; and John Craig from Hickman to Wm. Teagardens ferry on the Monongohala; and Ezekiel Ross from there to John Dickensons, Junr., Reason Virgin from there to Alexr Douglas; and John Mitchell from there to the Mouth of Wheeling; and that the Tithe's in 5 Miles on each side work thereon.

James Chambers, being bound over to this Court for Common Barratry and other Misdemeanors by him committed ag'st the Peace, on hear'g and Several Witnesses sworn the Court are Opinion that the Complt be dis'd.

Val Crawford is App'd Over of the Road from Sewickley Cr to Stewarts Crossing, and that the Tith's within 3 Miles on Each side work thereon.

Lyons vs Duncan. Jas. Hamilton and Chas. Reed Spbd.

Persons App'd to Veiw a road from Fort Pitt to Becketts fort, made a report; It is Ord that the s'd Road be Established, and Andrew Pearce be Over from Beckets fort to Jas. Wilsons; Cornelius Thompson from Wilsons to the River Monongohala; James Sullivan from there to the head of the Saw Mill run, and Bashar Frederick from there to Fort Pitt; and the Tith's within 5 Miles on Each side from Fort Pitt to the Monongahala, and the Tiths, within 3 Miles on each side from the River to Becketts fort, work thereon.

Dunlavy vs Russell. Dav'd Scott Spbd.

Cresap vs Elliott

Ord that the Court be Adj'd until to Morrow Morning 10 o'Clock. GEO: CROGHAN.

(46) At a Court Con'd and held for Augusta County, September 21st, 1775:

Pres't Geo Croghan, Jno Gibson, John Cannon, John McCulloch.

Admon Of the Estate of John Campbell, dec'd, is granted his father James Campbell, he hav'g Comp with the Law. Ord that Matthew Ritchey, Rich'd Boyer, Nath'l Tomlinson, and Sam'l Clem, or any 3, app the Est.

Admon of the Estate of Jonathan Johns, dec'd, is g'd to Dav'd Johns, he hav'g Comp'd with the Law. Ord that Philip Rodgers, Robt Ritchey, Jonathan Reese, and Zedeck Springer, or any 3, app the Est.

A Deed of Barg & Sale from James Brenton to Michael Cresap Senior was prov'd by John Jeremiah Jacobs one of the Wits & O R.

A Deed of Barg & Sale from Robt Denbow to Mich'l Cresap was prov'd by Geo. Brent one of the Wits & O R.

A Deed of Barg & Sale from John Corey to Mich'l Cresap, Senr., was prov'd by Jno. Jeremiah Jacob, the Wits, and O R.

Payton Rootes Sims & Jones

On the Complt of Wm. Freeman ag'st his Master, John Collins, for beating and abuseing him, and on hearing Several Wits & the Parties, the Court are of Opinion that he is Guilty of the above abuse, and that he be Committed to the Goal of this County, and there to remain until he Enter into Recog in
(47) the Sum of £20, with 2 Secys in the Sum of £10 Each, for his good behaviour towards his Servt for the Space of One Year, and that he pay Costs.

John Collins prod an Acc't ag'st his Serv't, Wm. Freeman, who run away for 86 days absent time; It is Ord that he serve him for the same Accr. to Law, and the Expence for takeing him up is Continued til the next Court

Elliott vs Girty }
Smith vs Girty } Simon Girty Spbd.

John Collins prod an Acc't ag'st his Serv't, Moses Abraham, when run away for 86 days absent time; It is Ord that he serve for the same Accr. to Law, and the Expence for takeing him up is Continued til the next Court.

Ord that the Court be Adjorned until to Morrow Morning 10 o'Clock GEO: CROGHAN.

At a Court Con'd and held for Augusta County at Fort Dunmore Sepr. 22d, 1775.

Pres't Geo Croghan, Jno. Cannon, Thos Smallman, John McColloch.

[48]

Ord that the Court be adjorned until to Morrow Morning 9 o'clock GEO: CROGHAN.

(48) At a Court Con'd and held for Augusta County, September 22d, 1775,

Pres't. John Campbell, Wm. Crawford, John Cannon, John McColloch, Dorsey Penticost,

[Here follows another list of cases, over five hundred in number, wherein only the surnames of the parties, plaintiff and defendant, are given, with occasionally some unimportant memoranda, thus: "Croghan v. Whittaker," or "Cresap vs Bowlin, Atta." If Christian names had been given, or the nature of the action shown, this list of cases would not have been omitted.]

(61) At a Court Con'd and held for Augusta County, Sepr 23d, 1775, P. Geo Croghan, Jno. Cannon, Jno. McColloch, Dorsey Penticost, Dav'd Shepperd.

Lynch vs Jones, Jno. McCallister Spbd.

[It appearing to the Court that Geo Brent & John Gab'l Jones, practising Attos of this court, have this day insulted this court in a very gross manner, by directing the under sheriff not to appear & open the court when commanded by the Justices, met upon the adjournment of yesterday, from which directions the sheriff hesitated some time in doing his duty, & did commit other Insults highly derogatory from the dignity & Authority of this Court: It is the Opinion of this court that the sd George Brent & Jno. Gab'l Jones be suspended from practising as Attos in this Court untill the Pleasure of the General Court is known in this behalf. It is therefore Ordered that the Clerk do Certify these proceedings to the honble the General Court & that the Atto Genl be sumd, John Walker, Gent, of Albemarle, Edward Winston of Bedford, Geo. Rootes of Frederick, & Chas. Sims of West Augusta, to attend there to prove the facts alleged agst the sd Brent & Jones; & It is Ord that they be committed to the Goal of this County, and there to remain until they Enter into recog in the sum of £200 Each, with 2 Secys Each in the sum of £100 Each.][16]

[16] The entry thus embraced in [] was at first made in the minute as given, but was afterwards erased by lines drawn over it.

(62) Pres't, Jno. Campbell, Thos. Smallman; Abs, Geo. Croghan, Pres't, Wm. Crawford. Ab. Jno. Gibson & D P.

A Deed from the Sacchems or Chiefs of the Six United Nations of Indians to Geo Croghan Esqr was produced to be proved, which was objected by Chas. Sims & H. Peyton on behalf of Jno. Gibson, alledging that it is upwards of two years since the Execution of the s'd deed, that there was not 3 Wits present to prove the same; which objection was overruled, and the said Deed was proved by the Oaths of Tho. & John Walker & Ord to lie for fur proof.

Geo. Croghan Esqr. Ack'd a Barg & Sale to Thos. Lawrence & O R.

Ab. John Campbell, & pres't Geo. Croghan.

Edward Armstrong, having forfeited his recog by assaulting Prudence Labat, It is Ord that a proces ag'st him, and his Secys, on the same, and that the Sheriff take him into Custody, and there to remain until he Enter into recog in the Sum of £50, with 2 Secys in the Sum of £25 Each, for his good behaviour.

P. Dorsey Penticost

The Persons App'd to Veiw a road from Providence Mounce's Mill, by Asburger's ferry, and from thence to Catfish Camp, made a report; It is Ord that the Road be Established, and that Ezekiel Hickman be Overseer from Mounces Mill to Christof Bealers ferry on Yougha; & Morgan Morgan from there to Asburger's ferry; & Benja. Fry from there to Pidgeon Cr; and Evan Williams from Pidgeon Cr. to the East fork of Churteers Cr; and Garret Vanemon from there to Catfish Camp, and the Tith's within 3 miles on Each side work thereon

(63) A Resolution of the Convention directing a Mode for the Proceedings of the Court of West Augusta was prod and read, and thesame being approved of, Ord that the Court for the future be regulated thereby and that the same be Rec'd.

Penticost vs Jones }
vs Linn } A Dedimus to take the deps. of Barnet Johnston a Witness in the Province of Maryland, to which Object was made for want of affidavit of his being out of the Colony or his being aged and Infirm, which was Overuled and dedimus ag'd.

Kuykendal vs Smith Abel Westfall Spbd.
Brent vs Beeler Dorsey Penticost, Spbd.
Hamilton vs Goe Pat McElroy Spbd.
Morgan vs Beavers Dav'd Steel Spbd.
Wm Harden vs. Glenn Alex'r Douglas Spbd.

P. Jno. Campbell, Wm. Crawford, John Cannon, John McColloch, Dorsey Penticost.

Ord Thos. Smallman, John Cannon, John Gibson, or any 2 of them, to provide a House at the Pub Expence for the Use of Holding the Court, and that the Sheriff Contract with Workmen to put the same in repair ag't the 3d Tuesday in Jan'y next.

Ord that the Sheriff, with the Consent of Thos. Smallman, John Cannon, and John Gibson, or any 3 of them, Contract for a house for Save keeping of his Prisoners, and make a return of the whole to the next Court, at the County Expence.

(64) Wm. Hawkins took the Usual Oaths to his Majesties Person and Government, Sub the Ab Oath and test, and then took the Oath of a deputy Sheriff.

His Majesties Writ for adjorning this Court to the Town of Staunton, on the third Tuesday in Nov'r next, being read, the Court was Accordingly adjorned. JOHN CAMPBELL.

At a Court held for Augusta County at Pittsburg, October the 17th, 1775, According to an Ordinance of the Convent. held at Richmond:

Present, Geo Croghan, Thos. Smallman, John Gibson, John McColloch.

On a Complt of Wm. Freeman ag'st his Master, John Collins, for abuseing him and beating him, is Continued until the next Court, and that the Sheriff take the Servant into his Custody and provide for him or hire him out until the next Court.

It appearing to this Court by Witness that an Agreem't between John Campbell and his Serv't, James Martin, that he had to serve from the 26th December 1774, One Year and 9 Months, It is Ord that he Serve the same Accordingly

Ab Jno. Gibson;

Pres't John Campbell.

John Hume being bound over to this Court, on the Complt of Francis Wilson, for a riot and Assault Battery committed on the s'd Wilson, being called and not appearing, It is Ord that the recog be prosecuted.

James Royal being bound over to the Court on the Complt of Fra's Wilson for Assault and Battery committed on the s'd Wilson, being called and not appear'g, It is Ord that the s'd recog be continued.

Ord that the Court be adjourned until the Court in Course

GEO: CROGHAN,

(65) At a Court held for Augusta County at Pittsburg, Nov'r 21st, 1775, According to an Ordinance of the Convention held at Richmond:

Pres't Geo Croghan, Edward Ward, Thos Smallman, John Cannon, Geo Vallandigham.

Samuel Hinch is appointed Surveyor of the Highway in the room of David Steel.

The persons App'd to Veiw a road from Capn Fromans to the Mouth of Yough, made their report: It is Ord that the s'd road be Established and that John Malony and Thos. Lapsley and Edward Sharp be Survey and that Tithables with 3 miles on Each side work thereon

John Bears is App'd a Consta, and It is Ord that he be Sum'd to be Sworn.

It Appearing to this Court by Wm. Wilson that John Collins had paid £7. 10s. for takeing up his Serv't Wm. Freeman, who run away, It is Ord that he Serve Acc'd to Law for the same.

The Complt of Wm Freeman ag'st his Master, John Collins, for abuseing and beating him and, It App'g to the Court to be 2d Complt, It is Ord the Sheriff sell him Acc'd to Law.

Ord that the Court be adjorned until the Court in Course

GEO: CROGHAN.

At a Court held for the Examination of Mr. Devereux Smith, at His House, by His Petition to the Justices, this 21st No-ember, 1775, for the Murder of Capn Geo Aston:

Pres't Geo Croghan, Thos. Smallman, John Cannon, Geo Vallandigham, Edward Ward.

(66) The above Devereux Smith was Examined, denied the fact wherewith he stands Charged, whereupon several Witnesses were sworn and Examined; on Consideration of which the Court are of Opinion that after hearing Smith by his Atto, that he is Guilty of the s'd fact wherewith he stands Charged, that he ought to be tried for the said fact at the General Court in April, on the 6th day thereof, and in Order thereto he is remanded to the Goal of this County and thence to be removed.

Be it Remembered that John Nevill, Thos. Herbert, James Nowlan, Simon Morgan, all of this County, came before our Justices and Acknowledged themselves Indebted to ours'd Lord the King in the Sum of 100 Pounds Each, to be Levied of Each of their respective Goods and Chattels, Lands and Tenements, and to ours'd Lord the King rendered upon Condition they do appear at the General Court in April next and there testify and Evidence ag'st Devereux Smith for the Murder of Geo Aston, and shall not depart with out leave of the s'd General Court

The Prisoner moved the Court that he might be admitted to Bail and It is Ordered that the Court be adjorned until to Morrow Morning at 7 o'clock, GEO: CROGHAN.

At a Cald Court Con'd and held for Augusta County for the Examination of Devereux Smith for the Murder of Capt Geo. Aston:

Pres't, Geo Croghan, Thos Smallman, John Cannon, Geo Vallandigham.

Upon a motion made by Mr. Devereux Smith by his attorney to be admitted to Bail for his appearance at the 6th day of the next General Court, the Court are of opinion that from the situation Mr. Smith is in & the circumstances attending the fact where-
(67) with he is charged, that he ought to be admitted to Bail, and that he Enter into recog on the Sum of 3000£, with 3 Securities in the Sum of £1500 Each, to be Levied, and thereupon the s'd Devereux Smith Ack'd himself in the Sum of £3000 and Robert Hanna, Aeneas McCay and Wm. Butler, his Secys, in the Sum of 1500£ Each, to be Levied of their respective goods and Chattels, Lands and Tenements, and to our s'd Lord the King rendered, upon Condition that Devereux Smith doth

personally appear on the 6th day of the next General Court, if he be able at that time to attend the s'd General Court, from the situation of his wound & state of health, if not at the succeeding Court for the Tryall of Criminals, and shall not depart upon his appearance without leave of said Court.

Then the Court did rise

GEO: CROGHAN.

At a Court held for Augusta County at Pittsburg, Jan'y 16th, 1776, According to an Ordinance of Convention held at Richmond:

Pres't, Edward Ward, Thos. Smallman, Geo Vallandigham, John McColloch, Wm. Goe.

Admon of the Estate of Alexr. Miller, dec'd, is granted to John Colhoon, Gent, he having Comp'd with the Law.

Ord that Geo Wilson, John Swearengen, John Harden, and Jos Caldwell, or any 3, App the Est.

Licence to keep an Ordin is Granted to David Duncan, he hav'g Comp with the Law.

The same to James McCashlon.

(68) Admon of the Est of Thos Elvey is Granted to Thomas Newberry, he hav'g Comp with the Law.

Ord Silas Hedge, Edward Robertson, Thomas McGuire, and John Carpenter, or any 3, App the Est.

Thomas Girty, being bound over to this Court on the Complt of Samuel Sample for Threatening to beat his wife Sarah Sample, and that he was afraid that the s'd Thos. Girty will beat or wound her, he being in fear of his Wife's Sarah's Life, being Called, appeared, and on hearing and Examining Several Witnesses the Court are of Opinion that on his makeing Concessions for his good behaviour towards her for the future be discharged.

A Mortgage from Andrew Robinson to Jacob Saylor was proved by James Berwick and John McCallister, two of the Wits, and Ordered to be Certified.

Joseph Hammet is App a Constab, and It is Ord that he be Sum'd to be sworn in.

Hugh Scott is Appointed a Consta, and it is Ord that he be Sum'd to be sworn in.

Ezekiel Dewitt is App'd a Consta, in the room of John Carpenter.

Ord that the Court be adjorned until to Morrow Morning 8 o'Clock.

EDW'D WARD.

At a Court Con'd and held for Augusta County at Pittsburgh, January 17th, 1775, According to an Ordinance of Convention held at Richmond:

Pres't Edward Ward, Dorsey Penticost, John Cannon, John McColloch, Geo Vallandigham, Wm Goe

(69) On the Motion of Rich Willis, it is Ord that his Mark be recorded, a Crop in the near Ear and a Swallow fork in the off Ear.

On the Motion of James Wright,, Ord that his Mark be recorded, a Swallow fork in the Off Ear.

On the Motion of Daniel Harris, It is Ord that his Mark, a Swallow fork in Each Ear.

On the Motion of Thos. Glenn, Ord that his Mark, a Crop in Each Ear and under slit in Each.

On the Motion of Thomas Crooks, Ord that his Mark, a Crop in the Near Ear.

On the Motion of Thos. Atkinson, Ord that his Mark, a Crop and Slit in the Crop in the right Ear, and the left Ear slit down and one half Cropt off.

P. Thos Smallman.

Thos. Atkinson, being bound over to this Court on the Complt of Fras. Maines, Appeared; no prosecutor appearing, It is Ord that he be dis'd.

Samuel Mcbride is app a Constable in the room of Razon Virgin, and It is Ord that he Summoned.

Francis Morrison Mark be record, a Crop in the near Ear and a hole in the off.

Wm Hawkins Mark be record, a Crop off the left and a slit in the right.

Pet Hillibrand Mark be record, a Crop in the left Ear and a Swallow fork and under slit in the right.

Or that the Court be adjorned until the Court in Course.

EDW'D WARD.

(70) At a Cald Court for West Augusta for the Examination of Edward Armstrong for Horse Stealing, this 19th January, 1776, one the Prop of Geo Sly and the other of Jas Royal.

Pres't, Edward Ward, John Cannon, Geo Vallandigham, Dorsey Penticost, Thos Smallman.

The above named Edward Armstrong was led to the barr, and upon Examination denied the fact wherewith he stands Charged; whereupon Several Witnesses were sworn and Examined; on Consideration of which the Court are of Opinion that there is not at this time Suff Evidence to prove the fact; It is Ord that he be discharged.

Then the Court did rise
EDW'D WARD.

His Majesties Writ for Adjorning the County Court of Augusta from Staunton to Fort Dunmore being read, this 16th April, 1776:

Pres't John Campbell, Dorsey Penticost, Thos Smallman, Jno. Cannon,

Admon of the Est of Jeremiah Woods, dec'd, granted to John Stevenson, who is married to the Widow, he hav'g Comp'd with the Law.

Ord that Benj. Kuykendal, James Sullivan, Rich'd McMahon, and Peter Barrakman, or any 3, app the Estate.

Ord that the Court be Adj'd until to Morrow Morning 9 o'Clock.

JOHN CAMPBELL.

(71) At a Court Con'd and held for Augusta County, April 17th, 1776.

Pres't John Campbell, Edward Ward, Dorsey Penticost, John McColloch, John Cannon.

The Last Will and Test of Larkin Pearpoint, dec'd, was prov'd by Isaac Lamaster and Calder Haymond, two of the Wits, and O R.

Daniel Leet prod a Commission from the Colledge of Wm. and Mary to be deputy Surveyor of this County under Thos. Lewis, Gent, he hav'g taken the Oath According to Law and Ent'd in Bond with Geo Rice and Geo McCormick his Sec'y.

John Harry is App Surveyor in the room of Edward Sharp

Ab Dorsey Penticost.

A Deed of Barg & Sale from John Pearce Sen'r to John and And'w Pearce was proved by Dorsey Penticost and Moses Coe, 2 of the Wits, and O C.

Pres D. P.

A Deed of Barg and Sale from Wm. Dunbar, by his Atto Alex'r Ross, to Chas. Sims, was prov'd by Caleb Graydon and Daniel Brown 2 of the Wits, and O C.

A Deed of Barg and Sale and rec't from Alex'r Ross to Chas. Sims was prov'd by Caleb Graydon and Dan'l Brown, 2 of the Wits, & O C.

A Deed of Barg and Sale from Alex'r Ross to Chas Sims was prov'd by Caleb Graydon and Dan'l Brown, 2 of the Wits, and O C'd.

A Power of Atto from Alex'r Ross, Atto for Wm. Dunbar, to Chas. Sims prov'd by Caleb Graydon & Dan'l Brown, 2 of the Wits, and O C'd

A Power of Atto from Alex'r Ross to Chas. Sims was prov'd by Caleb Graydon and Dan'l Brown, 2 of the Wits, and O C'd.

On the Motion of Christopher Carpenter, leave is granted him to keep a ferry near his house on the Monongahela for the Purpose of Setting over the Militia on Muster days

(72) Solomon Froman is app a Consta in the room of Nath'l Blackmore, and that he be Summoned before Mr. John Cannon to be Sworn into the said Office.

Admon of the Estate of John Edwards, dec'd, is granted to Benjamin Kuykendall (Jersey Ben), a C'r, he hav'g Comp'd with the Law.

Ord that Zadock Wright, Gab'l Cox, Benja Sweet, and Isaac Custard, or any 3, app the Est.

Robert Morely, Thos. Peake, & John Hatchway, being bound over to this Court on the Complt of Peter McCawley, and he being called and not appearing It is Ord that he be dis'd.

James Innis, John Munn, and Thos. Edginton, 3 of the persons appointed to Veiw a road from Froman's Mill on Shirte to Fromans Mill on the East side of the Monongohela; It is Ord that the s'd Road be Est, and that John Munn be Surv from Froman's Mill on Shirtee to the fork of the road to that goes to Henry Spears, and that Tobias Decker from thence to the Mill on the Monongohala, and that the tithe's within 3 Miles on Each side work thereon.

Wm Andreas is App a Consta in the room of Joseph Hill, Sen'r., and that he be Sum'd to be sworn before Dorsey Penticost.

Peter Hursh is App a Consta in the forks of Yough, and that he be Sum'd to be Sworn before D. Penticost.

Jonathan Paddock is App a Consta in the room of Wm. Teagarden, and that he be Sum'd to be Sworn before Wm. Goe.

Deed of Lease and Release of Trust from Wm. Trent, Rob't Callender, David Franks, Joseph Simon, Levy Andrew Levy, the s'd Wm. Trent, Dav'd Franks, Joseph Simons, and Levy And'w Levy in their own Right, and in Right of Philip Boyle,
(73) John Chevalier, Peter Chevalier, Jos Bollock, Peter Baynton, devesees of John Baynton' Share; Sam'l Wharton by his Attos Thos Wharton and the s'd Wm. Trent, Geo Morgan, Thos Smallman, and Geo Croghan, the afores'd Sam'l Wharton Trustee for and of John Welch's Share in thes'd Premises, by his Attos, Thos Wharton and Wm Trent, Edward Moran, Evan Shelley, Sam'l Postlethwaite, Jno Gibson, Edward Cole, Grantee or Ass'e of Rich'd Winstons Share, Dennis Crotan, Wm. Thompson, Rich'd Neave Grantee or Ass'e of Ab'm Mitchell's Share in the Premises, by Rich'd Neave, Junr, his Atto, James Dundas, Jno Ormsby by his Atto Thos Bond, Jr., Wm. Edgar by his Atto, the s'd Rob't Callender, Wm Franklin, Esqr., Jos Galloway, Esqr., and Thos Wharton, to Rich'd Bache, Owen Jones, Jun'r, and Isaac Wharton, was prov'd as to Wm. Trent, Rob't Callender, Dav'd Frank, Levy And'w Levy, Joseph Bollock, Peter Baynton, Thos Wharton, and the s'd Wm Trent, in two Places, for and on behalf of Sam'l Wharton in his own right, as Trustee of John Welch by George Morgan, Edwd Cole, Thos Bond, Jr., for and on behalf of his Constituent, John Ormsby, by the s'd Rob't Callender, for and in behalf of his Constituent Wm Edgar, by Dr. Benja. Franklin for his Constituent Wm. Franklin, Esqr, and by the s'd Thos Wharton by Jno Chevalier, Peter Chevalier, Rich' Bache, Owen Jones, Jun'r., Isaac Wharton by Rich'd Butler, Jos Westmore & Thos. Flinn, and prov'd as to Rich'd Neave by his Atto Rich'd Neave, Jr, Joseph Galloway, Jos Simon,

James Dundas, Wm. Thompson, Sam'l Postlethwaite by Jos Westmore, Chas. Matheson & Thomas Flinn, & as to John
(74) Gibson was prov'd by Joseph Westmore, Chas. Matheson, and Rich'd Butler, and O R. A Deed of Partition from and between the same Persons was proved as before and O R.

A Mortgage from Abraham Mitchell and Sarah his Wife to Rich'd Neave was prov'd by Jos Westmore, Chas. Matheson, and Thos. Flin, 3 of the Wits, and O R.

Philip Whitezell is App a Consta in the room of Andrew Robertson.

John Dousman is App a Consta in the Town of Pittsburg, and It is Ord that he be Sum'd.

Philip Whitezel Ap'd and took the Oaths and the Oath of a Constable.

Wm. Forsythe, being bound over on the Complt of Henry Woods, and thes'd Henry being called and failing to appear It is Ord to be dis'd

Licence to keep an Ord is Granted to Thos. Brown at his House at Redstone Fort, Bazel Brown hav'g on his hehalf Ent'd into Bond Accr. to Law.

Licence to keep an Ord is granted to John DeCamp, he hav'g Comp with the Law.

Hawkins vs Greathouse, Gar; Abraham Miller affirmed he has 1 Watch, and that he is Indebted to him also £8 Pennsylvania Money, for which he has Passed his Bond for, and that he has had no notice of any assignment; Acc't proved & Jud and O Sale and Ord Condem'd.

(75) Sam'l Griffith is App'd a Consta; It is Ord that he be Sum'd before Wm. Goe to be Sworn into the Office.

John Greathouse is App a Consta; It is Ord that he be Sum'd before Geo Vallandigham to be Sworn into the s'd Office.

Ord that the Court be Adj'd until to Morrow Morning 10 o'Clock JOHN CAMPBELL.

At a Court Con'd and held for Augusta County, April 18th 1776,

Pres't, John Campbell, Edward Ward, Dorsey Penticost, John Cannon.

A Deed from Alex'r Ross, Atto to Wm. Dunbarr to Chas. Simons, being form prov'd by Caleb Graydon and Chas. Sims, was fur prov'd by Jas Mckee, the other Wit, & O R.

A Deed from Alex'r Ross to Chas. Sims prov'd as above and O R.

A Deed from Alex'r Ross to Chas Sims prov'd as above & O R.

A Power of Atto from Alex'r Ross, Atto for Wm. Dunbar, to Chas Sims, prov'd as above, O R.

A Power of Atto, from Alex'r Ross to Chas Sims proved as above, O R.

Licence to keep an Ord is Granted to Jacob Winemiller, he hav'g Compl'd with the Law.

(76) On the Petition of James Mitchell & others seting forth that a Road is Established from Conrad Walters, by Wm. Teagarden's ferry, to the Mouth of Wheeling, which is very Inconveniant to your Petrs, & praying that a Review of the s'd Road be made, It is Ord that Ebenezer Zane, James McMahon, David Owens, Henry Vanmatre, Dav'd Evans, Geo. Cox, James McCoy, & John McClalan, or any 6 of them, being first Sworn, Veiw if the old Road Estab is Conv, if not make a report of the most Conv way, and the Inconv and Conv thereof, to the next Court; that the Surveyors desist from working on the road until the report is returned

Ord that the Sheriff Summon 24 Persons to serve as a Grand jury in May next

Ord that the Court be adjorned until the Court in Course

JOHN CAMPBELL.

At a Court held at Pittsburgh, for the District of West Augusta the Twentieth day of August, 1776:

Present, Edward Ward, Dorsey Penticost, John Gibson, David Sheperd, John Cannon, and William Goe, gent.

Dorsey Penticost and John Gibson, Gent, administered the Oath prescribed by an ordinance entitled "an ordinance to enable the present Magistrates & officers to continue the administration of Justice & for setling the General mode of Proceeding in criminal and other cases, till the same can be more amply provided for," to Edward Ward, Gent, and then the said Ed-

ward Ward administered the aforesaid oath to John Gibson, Dorsey Penticost, John Cannon, David Shepherd, and Wm. Goe, Gentn. David Shepherd, and John Cannon, Gent, are
(77) appointed to Contract with some person or persons to build a house 24 by 14 With a petition in the middle, to be Used for a Goal at Augusta Town.[17]

John Madison, Jun'r, Deputy Clerk, took the Oath appointed by an Ordinance of Convention.

Patrick McElroy, Deputy Sheriff, took the Aforesaid Oath.

Court Proclaimed.

McKinley vs Beal, Agreed, pd.

Samuel Newell and Michael Thorn, being bound over on the Complt of James Chambers, who being called and not appearing to prosecute It is Ord that they be discharged.

Dav'd Steel, a Deputy Sheriff, took the Oath appointed by an Ordinance of Convention.

Admon of the Estate of Joshua Hudson, dec'd, granted to his brother Wm. Hudson, he hav'g Comp with the Law.

Ordered that Robert Jones, John Jarrett, Henry Hall, and Aaron Jenkins, or any 3, App the Estate.

Ord that all the Constables be Summoned to be Sworn agreable to the Ordinance of Convention before the most Convenient Magistrate to them.

Edward Ward, Dorsey Penticost, and John Gibson, Gentn, are recommended as proper persons for his Excellency to choose one of them to Act as Sheriff for the Ensuing Year.

Alex'r McKee, Philip Ross, Benja Kuykendall, John Nevill, David Rodgers, Isaac Cox, Geo McCormick, Matthew Ritchey, Wm. Louther, John Evans, Jas. Chew, David Scott, John
(78) Harden, Sen'r, John Swearengen, Thomas Gaddis, James McCoy, Wm. Harrison, John DeCamp, Caleb Graydon, Henry Heath, Sam'l Newell, Thos Brown, James Hammond, Thos Freeman, Wm Moore, Joshua Wright, Rich'd Yeats, John McDowell, Erasmus Bokias, David Enocks, James Hopkins, Henry Enocks, Henry Vanmetree, Chas Dodd, Daniel Mcfarlane, John Mitchell, James Caldwell, John Walker, John Williamson, Sen'r, Wm. Scott, Thomas Polk, David Andrews, John Mc-

[17] This Augusta Town, was at Catfish-camp, afterward Washington, Washington Co., Pa.

37

Donald, Oliver Miller, Zachariah Spriggs, And'w Swearengen, Benja Fry, Jonathan Coburn, John Hamilton, and Jonas Freind, are recommended as proper persons to be added to the Commission of the Peace.

Moses Williamson, Jun'r, is App'd a Constable, and It is Ord that he be Sum'd to be Sworn into the office before Mr. David Shepherd.

Ord that the Court be adjorned until the third Tuesday in September next to Catfish Camp[18] Augusta Town

EDW. WARD.

At a Court held at Augusta Town for the district of West Augusta the [September] 17th 1776:

Pres't, Edward Ward, Dorsey Penticost, John Cannon, David Shepherd.

Pat McElroy, deputy Sheriff, protested against the Insuff of the Goal, & on his motion Ord to be Certified.

(79) Ord the Sheriff Summon 24 Freeholders to serve as a Grand-jury at this Court in November next.

Ord that the Court be adjorned until to Morrow Morning 6 o'Clock. EDW'D WARD.

At a Court Continued and held at Augusta Town, for the district of West Augusta, September the 18th, 1776:

Present, Edward Ward, Dorsey Penticost, John Cannon, David Shepherd, Gentlemen, Justices.

John McColloch, Gent, took the Oath appointed by Order of Convention as a Justice.

Present, John McColloch.

Wm. Hawkins, a deputy Sheriff, took the Oath appointed by Order of Convention as a deputy Sheriff.

David Rodgers, Isaac Cox, John McDowell, Richard Yeats, Wm. Scott, Dan'l Mcfarlen, John McDaniel, George McCormick, Philip Ross, James McMahon, Benja Kuykendall, Wm Lowther, John Evans, David Scott, John Harden, Senr., John Swearengen, Thos. Gaddis, Wm. Harrison, Sam'l Newell, Thos Brown, Thos Freeman, Joshua Wright, Erasmias Bochias,

[18] These words, "Catfish Camp," are erased in the original minutes, and Augusta Town substituted.

Henry Enocks, Henry Vanmetre, James Caldwell, John Williamson, Senr., Thos. Polke, Oliver Miller, Zachariah Spriggs, Benja Fry, Jonathan Coburn, John Hamilton, Zachariah Morgan, Benja Wilson, Wm. Hamen, Moses Thompson, Ephraim Ritchardson, James Walker, James Anderson, Alex'r Maxwell, Amaziah Davidson, Jacob Cook, Matthew Ritchey, Jacob Haymaker, Thomas Crooks, Thomas Waller, James Wherry, Ab'm Inloe, James Linley, And'w Swearengen, Wm. Rankin are recommended as Proper persons to be added to the Commission.

(80) Patrick McElroy is appointed to go Express from this Place to Wmsburgh for the Commission of the Peace. The Sheriffs Commission, and the Acts of Assembly and the Ordinances of Convention for the district of West Augusta

And'w Nangle and Rob't McKinley are appointed Constables in the Town of Pittsburgh, and that they be Summoned before Edward Ward, Gent, to be Sworn into the s'd Offices.

John Dousman, who was appointed a Consta in the Town of Pittsburgh and refusing to swear into the said Office, It is Ord that for the s'd Contempt he be fined £2.

Richard Yeats, John Campbell, & James McMahon are recommended as proper persons for Coroners.

Andrew Vaughan, on behalf of Jos. Horton, Moved for a Judg Ag'st John Christian, High Sheriff, for the Amount of an Exn recovered by Francis Brown, a deputy of the s'd Joseph Horton, against Adam Bell Pat McElroy, a deputy also, and who farmed the same of the s'd Christian, appeared and confessed a Judgment. Pat McElroy, a deputy Sheriff, on behalf of John Christian, moved for a Judgment ag'st Francis Brown, a deputy also, and Daniel Brown and Wm Christy his Sec'y, for the Amount of the Judg, and Costs obtained ag'st him by Jos. Horton, for the Amount of the Ex'n of the s'd Jos ag'st Adam Bell, received by the s'd Francis, and Judgment is granted

Ab Dorsey Penticost

(81) The Court on Considering the Ordinance of Convention for holding a Court in the district of West Augusta without Writ of adjournments from East Augusta, on the third Tuesday in every Month, at such place as they shall appoint, are of Opinion that

by such Ordinance they are a separate and distinct County and Court from that of East Augusta, and they do appoint Dorsey Penticost, Esqr., there Clerk for this Court, to which John Madison, Jun'r deputy Clerk, on behalf of John Madison, Clerk of the County, objected to the appointment, alledging that they had no right so to do till the division of the County, looking upon him as Clerk of East Augusta and the district of West Augusta till a division is made by an Ordinance of Convention.

Ord that John Madison, Jun'r deputy Clerk, in whose Custody the records of the adjorned Court for this district are, is ordered to deliver them to this Court on the 25th of October next.

Ordered that the Court be adjorned until the Court in Course. EDW'D WARD.

At a Court held for the district of West Augusta at Augusta Town, November 19, 1776:

Present, Edward Ward, John McColloch, John Cannon, William Goe, David Shepherd.

Thomas Glenn, who was bound by recog to Appear at the Grand jury Court, appeared, and was Ord to be prosecuted for beating his Serv't. No prosecutor or Witnesses appearing, it is ordered that he be discharged.

Ord that the Court be adjorned until to Morrow Morning 8 o'clock EDW'D WARD.

At a Court Cont'd and held for the district of West Augusta County, November the 20th, 1776:

Present, Edward Ward, John McColloch, John Cannon, David Shepherd,

Capt'n Wm. Christy prod a Com of Capt'n of a Comp'y of Militia, took the Oath required by Ordinance of Convention O C'd.

Leiut Jacob Bousman, the same

Ensign Hugh Smith.

[Here the minutes of this court end.]

MINUTE BOOK OF THE VIRGINIA COURT HELD FOR YOHOGANIA COUNTY, FIRST AT AUGUSTA TOWN (NOW WASHINGTON, PA.), AND AFTERWARDS ON THE ANDREW HEATH FARM NEAR WEST ELIZABETH; 1776–1780.

EDITED BY BOYD CRUMRINE, OF WASHINGTON, PA.

INTRODUCTORY.

The minutes of this court, as well as those of the old Fort Dunmore court printed with an introductory sketch in Vol. I., pp. 505–568 of these *Annals*, are preserved in several old manuscript volumes of unruled paper, legal-cap size. The entries in these order books were evidently written hastily by the official clerks during the sessions of the court, accounting for the misspelling of many proper names and other words, and for frequent illegibility. They may have been intended to be copied out at length in the more formal records of the court proceedings; but it is possible that, as the courts themselves as well as the Virginia territorial jurisdictions ceased to exist after the final running of the southern and western boundary lines, no other and more regular transcript of the orders was ever made, and that the records now published are the only ones in existence containing the judicial business of these ancient courts.

These records are accurately copied, when at all legible, as spelled and capitalized in the original; even the punctuation is unchanged except now and then when thought to be absolutely necessary for intelligibility. For it is believed that when the details of local history are given, for the subsequent use of the general historian, this literalness of transcription gives color and strength to local incidents. So when one meets in old records with the name James Swolevan, he is interested in determining that the name must have been that of plain James Sullivan. And shall we say that the name "Worshington" was not "Washington"?

Attention is called to the efforts made, as disclosed in the proceedings of the Court of Yohogania County now published, to have the oath of allegiance to the State of Virginia administered to all the inhabitants of the Monongahela and Ohio valleys, within the limits of the actually exercised jurisdiction of Westmoreland County, Pennsylvania.[1]

Why are the records of these old Virginia courts found in the vaults of the court-house of Washington County, Pennsylvania? A reply to this question may be made as follows:

On March 1, 1780, just before the final ratification by Pennsylvania and Virginia of the agreement at the Baltimore Conference, on the establishment of the boundary lines between the two states, and whilst all the territory of Washington, Allegheny, Fayette and Greene counties and of that part of Beaver county south of the Ohio River still formed part of Westmoreland County, erected in 1773, the legislature of Pennsylvania, "first of all the states," says III. Bryant's Hist. of U. S., 177, passed an act for the gradual emancipation of all the slaves within its jurisdiction.[2] And on March 21, 1781, Washington County was erected, the first new County out of old Westmoreland. Then on April 13, 1782, less than two years after the Virginia courts had ceased to be held within the limits of Pennsylvania, and still before the boundary lines had been actually run on the ground, an act was passed by the general assembly of Pennsylvania, entitled "An Act to redress certain grievances within the Counties of Westmoreland and Washington."[3] The preamble to this act recited:

"Whereas a number of the inhabitants of Westmoreland and Washington counties have represented to the General Assembly that they labor under many inconveniences by reason that Before the Boundary was agreed to between the States of Virginia and Pennsylvania, many of the inhabitants aforesaid, conceiving themselves under the jurisdiction of Virginia, which exercised judicial authority over them, had taken and subscribed the oath of Allegiance and Fidelity as prescribed by the laws and the usages of the said State, [and] are considered in many respects as not entitled to all the rights of free citizens of this State; and but for the reason above mentioned they have had no opportunity

[1] See the Order of Court on August 26, 1777, and 9 Henning's Statutes 281.

[2] See Act of March 1, 1780, II. Carey & Bioren, 246; I. Dall. L., 838; 1 Smith's L., 492.

[3] This act is not found at length in any of the editions of our Pennsylvania laws, but see it noted as obsolete in I. Dall. L., p. 55.

of entering or registering their slaves agreeable to the Act of Assembly of this State for the gradual Abolition of slavery; and that a number of the records and papers containing the proceedings of the late counties of Yohogania, Monongalia and Ohio are now in the hands of the late Clerks, who are not authorized to give exemplied copies thereof:"

Then followed enacting sections providing that all the inhabitants of Westmoreland and Washington counties, whose names should be found in the records thereinafter mentioned, having and producing to the clerks of the General Quarter Sessions of the said counties respectively "certified copies or certificates of their having taken the Oath of Allegiance and Fidelity to the State of Virginia before the said Boundary was agreed to, shall be and they are hereby declared to be to all intents and purposes free citizens of this state;" and further providing that all such inhabitants "who were on the 23rd day of Sept., 1780,[1] possessed of Negro or Mulatto slaves or servants until the age of thirty one years," might register such slaves or servants under said act for the gradual abolition of slavery, "on or before the 1st day of January next; and the said master or masters, owner or owners of such slaves or servants shall be entitled to his or their services as by the said act is directed, and the said slaves and servants shall be entitled to all benefits and immunities in the said act contained and expressed." Then followed the final section:

"*And be it further enacted by the authority aforesaid*, that the Clerks of the Orphans' Courts, the Registers of the probates of Wills and granting letters of administration, and the Recorders of Deeds, for the respective counties of Westmoreland and Washington aforesaid, shall be authorized and empowered to call on the late clerks of the said counties of Yohogania, Monongalia and Ohio, for all such papers and records in their custody or possession, which relate to or affect the taking of the oath or affirmation of Allegiance, the probates of wills, granting letters of administration, and the Recording of Deeds or other indentures of Bargain and Sale, of any of the inhabitants of the said counties of Westmoreland and Washington, and when they shall receive all or any part of the said papers and records as aforesaid they shall be lodged within their respective offices and become part of the records of said counties; and the said Clerks are hereby required

[1] The day of the final ratification by Pennsylvania of the final agreement for the boundary lines; VIII. Penna. Archives, 570.

and enjoined on demand as aforesaid to deliver up intire and indefaced all such papers and records as aforesaid, and in case they or either of them shall refuse or neglect to deliver up the papers and records in manner and form aforesaid, they or either of them so neglecting or refusing shall forfeit and pay the sum of five hundred pounds, to be recovered by action of debt in any court of Common Pleas within this Commonwealth, for the use of the same.

"Signed by order of the House,

"*Fred'k A. Muhlenburg, Speaker.*"

Monongalia and Ohio counties, Virginia, did not become extinct, but were pushed out of Pennsylvania by the boundary lines established, and carried their records with them. The records of the courts at Fort Dunmore and for Yohogania County, thus became a part of the official records of Washington County, Pennsylvania.

By reference to the record of the formal organization of the old Fort Dunmore court, Vol. I., p. 525 of these *Annals*, it is seen that that court was constituted under "His Majesties Writ," issued by Lord Dunmore, "for adjorning the County Court of Augusta from the Town of Staunton to Fort Dunmore, and with a new Commission of the Peace," which included George Croghan and fourteen others named after him, all of whom resided in the Monongahela and Ohio valleys, as "Gentlemen, Justices." The creation of that court was by the will of King George as expressed by his colonial representative, Lord Dunmore. But there came a time when His Majesty's writs by whomsoever issued were inoperative west of the Alleghenies, as well as east of them to the Atlantic; and, as noted briefly on p. 520, Vol. I. of these *Annals*, the legislature of Virginia, now become an independent commonwealth, in October, 1776, passed An Act for ascertaining the boundary between the County of Augusta and the District of West Augusta, and for dividing the said District into three district Counties.

This act, to be found at length by the reference in the note,[1] established the southern boundaries of the District of West Augusta, and proceeded:

"And to render the benefits of government and administration of justice more easy and convenient to the people of said District, Be it enacted, &c., That from and after the 8th day of November next en-

[1] Chapter XLV., 9 Henning's Statutes, 262. See our map of the District of West Augusta, facing p. 518, Vol. I. of these *Annals*.

suing all that part of said District lying within the following lines, to wit: Beginning at the mouth of Cross Creek, thence up the same to the head thereof, thence southeastwardly to the nearest part of the ridge which divides the waters of the Ohio from those of the Monongahela, thence along the said ridge to the line which divides the county of Augusta from the said District, thence with the said Boundary to the Ohio, thence up the same to the beginning, shall be one distinct county and be called and known by the name of *Ohio County*.

"And all that part of the said District lying to the northward of the following lines, viz: Beginning at the mouth of Cross Creek, and running up its several courses to the head thereof, thence southeastwardly to the nearest part of the aforesaid dividing ridge between the waters of the Monongahela and Ohio, thence along the said ridge to the head of Ten Mile Creek, thence east to the road leading from Catfish-Camp to Redstone Old Fort, thence along the said road to the Monongahela River to the said Fort, thence along Dunlap's old road to Braddock's road and with the same to the meridian of the head fountain of the Potowmack, shall be one other distinct county and shall be called and known by the name of *Yohogania County*.

"And all that part of the said District lying to the northward of the county of Augusta, to the westward of the meridian of the head fountain of the Potowmack, to the southward of the county of Yohogania, and to the eastward of the county of Ohio shall be one other distinct county, and shall be called and known by the name of the *County of Monongalia*.

"And for the administration of justice in the said counties of Ohio, Yohogania and Monongalia, after the same shall take place, Be it enacted, &c., That after the said 8th day of November, courts shall be constantly held every month by the Justices of the respective Counties, upon the days hereafter specified for each county respectively, that is to say: For the County of Ohio, on the first Monday, for the County of Monongalia on the second Monday, and for the County of Yohogania on the fourth Monday in every month, and in such manner as by the laws of this Commonwealth is provided for other Counties, and as shall be by their Commission directed."[1]

A subsequent section of this Virginia statute provided that the court of Yohogania County should have jurisdiction to hear and determine all actions and suits, both at law and in equity, which should be

[1] See Crumrine's "History of Washington County," p. 183 and notes.

"depending" before the Court of West Augusta at the time the said jurisdiction should take place. And it was further enacted,[1] that the landholders of the said counties, respectively, should meet on the 8th day of December next, those of the County of Yohogania "at the house of Andrew Heath, on the Monongahela"; those of the County of Monongalia "at the house of Jonathan Corbin [Coburn] in the said county"; and those of the County of Ohio "at the house of Ezekiel Dewit in the said County," then and there to choose the place of holding courts for their respective counties.

Jonathan Coburn lived about ten miles southeast of New Geneva, in what is now Fayette County, and the place chosen for holding the courts of Monongalia County was the plantation of Theophilus Philips, ahout two miles above New Geneva, on the upper Monongahela, and here the courts of that county were held until the establishment of the boundary line, when, to get them out of Pennsylvania, they were removed to the plantation of Zachwell Morgan, afterwards Morgantown; but the early records of this court were lost in the burning of the court-house at Morgantown in 1796. The place chosen by the landholders of Ohio County for the holding of the court for that county was Black's Cabin, on Short Creek, now West Liberty, West Va., and the first court held there was on January 6, 1777. There these courts continued to be held until 1797, when they were removed to Wheeling.

Whether the election required to be held on December 8, 1776, at the house of Andrew Heath (near what is now West Elizabeth, Allegheny County, Pa.), to choose a place for holding the court for Yohogania County, was held at the time and place appointed is not known; but, whatever the fact, there is now room for the belief, from a more careful study of the records of that court here produced, that, from its first session on December 23, 1776, until on August 25, 1777, when it was ordered "That the court be adjourned to the house now occupied by Andrew Heath," the court for Yohogania County continued to be held at Augusta Town, now Washington, Pa., and that it was then removed to its new and last place of holding on the Monongahela.

We now submit to the student of western Pennsylvania history a full verbatim transcript of the records of the long since extinct court of Yohogania County, to be illustrated hereafter, it is hoped, by a collection of explanatory notes, identifying persons and places mentioned.

[1] 2 Henning's Statutes, 264, 265.

Signatures of the Virginia Judges.

ORGANIZATION; FIRST DAY'S BUSINESS.

(1)[1] Yohogania County, Dec. 23, 1776.

In consequence of an Act of the General Assembly of Virginia putting off all that part of the District of West Augusta Northward of the following bounds or lines (viz:) Beginning at the mouth of Cross Creek, running up the several courses thereof to the head; Thence South-Easterly to the nearest part of the dividing ridge Between the Ohio and the Monongahela Rivers, Thence along the said Dividing Ridge to the head of Ten Mile creek, Thence East to the road leading from Catfish camp to Redstone Old Fort, Thence with the said road to the Monongahela River, Thence across the said River to the said Fort, Thence along Dunlap's old road to Braddock's Road, and with said road to the meridian of Potowmac River, — and a Commission of the Peace and a Commission of Oyer and Terminer, Directed to John Campbell, Edward Ward, Thomas Smallman, Dorsey Pentecost, John Gibson, William Crawford, John Stephenson, John Cannon, George Vallandingham, William Goe, John Neaville, Isaac Cox, John McDowell, Richard Yeates, John McDaniel, George McCormick, Philip Ross, Benjamin KirKindall, William Harrison, Samuel Newell, Thomas Brown, Thomas Freeman, John De Compt, Joshua Wright, Oliver Miller, Benjamin Frye, Matthew Richie, Andrew Swearingen, Jacob Haymaker, Benjamin Harrison, and Zachariah Connell; Also a Dedimus Potestatum, directed to William Goe, John Neaville and Isaac Cox, or any two of them, to administer the oath prescribed by law to John Campbell, Edward Ward, Thomas Smallman, Dorsey Pentecost, John Gibson, John Cannon and George Vallandingham, or any two of them, and they to administer the aforesaid oath to the aforesaid Justices.

Whereupon the aforesaid William Goe and Isaac Cox administered the aforesaid oath to the aforesaid Dorsey Pentecost, who thereupon did administer the aforesaid oath to the aforesaid Richard Yeates, George McCormick, Benjamin KirKindall, Samuel Newell, William Goe, Isaac Cox, Thomas Freeman, Joshua Wright, Oliver Miller, Benjamin Frye, Matthew Richie, Andrew Swearingen and John Cannon, as Justices of the Peace.

[1] The marginal figures in ( ) represent the original paging of these records.

The court then proceeded to the election of their clerk,
(2) whereupon the said Dorsey Pentecost Esquire was unanimously chosen and appointed their Clerk, and ordered to take charge of their rolls.

Dorsey Pentecost took the oath Prescribed by Law as Clerk of this court.

The court demanded the Records and Papers from John Madison, Junior, Deputy Clerk of East Augusta, in whose custody they are, Which he Peremptorily refused, Notwithstanding he confessed he had seen an Act of assembly directing him so to do.

Edward Ward, gentleman, came into court and prayed that the court would receive his reasons for refusing to act as Sheriff of this county, which was granted and were as follows:—That he cannot think of acting as Sheriff, or appointing any under Sheriffs, until the line Between the States of Virginia and Pennsylvania are fixed or limited, for on the North Eastern Bounds of this County There is still a Door open for dispute and Contintion, which has been heretofore the cause of Disturbing the Peace of the People Settled and claiming alternately The Jurisdiction of each Government, and before he can think of acting or any Person under him, he proposes praying the General Assembly to have a Temporary line fixed between them, or the limits of Pennsylvania run, or the Government of Virginia Peremptorily running the same, until which is done he cannot think of acting in any state or Government to Infringe on the reserved rights of his fellow subjects; he further assures that when Government has this done, he is ready to act with Cheerfulness, and if this Cannot be done he begs that the Court will Recommend some other gentleman to his Excellency to serve as sheriff,—and hopes the Court will acquiesce in Promoting the having the above bounds ascertained; and further offers to qualify into the Commission of the Peace.

The Court is of opinion that the said Edward Ward, gentleman, may be Permitted to Qualify into the Commission of the Peace, they being of opinion that he is no sheriff untill he
(3) enters into Bond before this Court, and comply with the Tinner of his Commission as Sheriff; Whereupon the said Edward

Ward came into Court and took the oath of a Justice of the Peace.

The Court is of opinion that Joshua Wright Gentleman is a proper person to be recommended to his Excellency the Governor to serve as Sheriff, the whole of the above gentlemen named in the Commission of the Peace who are qualified refusing to act in said office on account of the great difficulty they apprehend will attend the execution of said office until such time as a line is fixed Between this CommonWealth and the state of Pennsylvania.

Brice Virgin is appointed Constable to serve the Insuing year and that he be Summoned before Richard Yeates Gentleman to be qualified into said office.

Richard Elson is appointed constable to serve the Insuing year, and that he be summoned before Isaac Cox, Gentleman, to Qualify into said office.

William Lankford is appointed Constable to serve the Ensuing year and that he be summoned before Matthew Richie Gentleman to be Qualified into said office, as also

John Alexander is appointed Constable to serve the Ensuing year, and that he be summoned before Matthew Richie Gentleman to Qualify into said office.

Samuel Clerk is appointed Constable to serve the Ensuing year, and that he be summoned before William Goe, Gentleman to Qualify in said office.

Samuel Griffith is appointed Constable to serve the Ensuing year, and that he be summoned before William Goe Gentleman to qualify into said office.

Isaac Sparks is appointed Constable to serve the Ensuing year, and that he be summoned before Thomas Freeman, Gentleman to Qualify into said office.

Also John Brown, James Buorass, Matthew Hays, ——— Bradley is appointed Constables to serve the Ensuing year, and that they be summoned before Edward Ward, Gentleman to Qualify into said office.

William Gaston is appointed Constable to serve the Ensuing
(4) year, and that he be summoned before Andrew Swearingen, Gentleman to Qualify into said office.

Wm Hays is appointed Constable to serve the Ensuing year

and that he be Summoned before John Cannon, Gentleman to be Qualified into said office.

John Johnston is appointed Constable to serve the Ensuing year, and that he be summoned before Joshua Wright Gentleman to Qualify into said Office.

Josiah Orsborn and Philip Philips is appointed to Serve as Constables the Ensuing year, and that they be summoned before Samuel Newell Gentleman to Qualify into said office.

Andrew Dye & Peter Austurges is appointed Constables to Serve the Ensuing year, and that they be summoned before Benjamin Frye, Gentleman to Qualify into said Office.

John Beans is appointed Constable to serve the Ensuing year, and that he be summoned before Oliver Miller, Gentleman to Qualify into said office.

Ordered that Dorsey Penticost Esquire be recommended to his Excellency the Governor as a proper Person to have the Command of the Melitia of this County; and that John Cannon be a proper Person to be recommended as Colonel of the said Melitia; Isaac Cox be recommended as Leutenant Colonel of said Melitia, and Henry Taylor, Major of said Melitia.

Ordered that the Clerk forward a letter to his Excellency & Council, notifying the general dissatisfaction of the people of this County against the late Election[1] being held on the Sabath day, the short notice of the said election, and of the Inconveniency of the Bounds circumscribing the said County.

Whereas by an act of the General Assembly the Suits &c brought and Instituted in the Court of the District of West Augusta are directed to be determined in this Court, and the Papers and Records relative thereto are now in the hands of John Maddison, Junior, Deputy Clerk of East Augusta, who hath this day been Called upon to deliver the said Papers and records to this Court, which he, the said John Maddison, in
(5) contempt of the said Act and the demands of this Court refuses to deliver, to the manifest Injury of Individuals and evident hurt of the Publick: Ordered, therefore, that a Process be Issued to apprehend the said John Maddison and forthwith bring him before this Court to answer the above misdemeanor.

Court adjourned until Court in Course. Edwd Ward.

[1] This was perhaps the election held on December 8, to choose a place for holding the court.

Court met on Monday the 28th of April 1777, according to adjournment to Court in Course.

Present: Edward Ward, John Cannon, John McDowell, Richard Yeates, Benjamin Kirkindall, Joshua Wright, Oliver Miller and Andrew Swearingen, Gentlemen Justices.

On the Court's meeting and the Sheriff's Commission not coming to Mr. Joshua Wright, agreable to recommendation of the Court and notwithstanding Colonel Penticost's letter to Colonel Cannon, Insuring him he had a Sheriff's Commission for Mr. Wright, he refused to act Protempory. Therefore the Court was reduced to the necessity of appointing another, as there was an Election to be held for a Senitor and Delegates, and a Criminal to be tried and other Breeches of the Peice.

The question being first put to Mr. Joshua Wright, to be appointed Protempory, and he refused, notwithstanding his hearing of the Commission as aforesaid; but said if his commission had came to this Court he would have sworn into said Office.—The Question then being put to the rest of the Court, who would serve as Sheriff, and all refused to, Except Mr. William Harrison, who agreed to be appointed, and the Court unanimously agreed that the said Mr. Harrison be recommended as a proper Person for Sheriff and Mr. Joshua Wright concurd with the Court.

The Court is of the opinion that William Harrison, Samuel Newell and Thomas Freeman are proper persons to be recommended for Sheriffs the Insuing year.

William Harrison came into Court and took the oath as Sheriff.

(6) Court adjourned Tuesday 7 O'Clock.[9]

Court met according to adjournment.

Present: Edward Ward, John Cannon, John McDowell, Richard Yeates, Benjaman Kirkindall, Joshua Wright, Oliver Miller, Andrew Swearingen, Gentleman Justices.

Zacheriah Connell came into Court and took the oath of Justice of the Piece.

The Court Still Labouring under great difficulty for the want of a Clerk, as Colonel Dorsey Penticost our former Clerk lying

[9] 7 o'clock!

in Baltimore in the Small Pox. The Court then applied to Mr. James Innis, who the said Colonel Penticost had appointed to serve as Clerk in his absence, and when application was made to said Mr. Innis, he refused to attend the Court; his answer was that he only agread to attend the March Court — upon which the Court Choose Mr. Isaâc Cox for their Clerk who Came into Court and swore into said Office.

Zachariah Connell, William Lee and Andrew Heth came into Court and took the Oath of Captains of the Militia.

John Cannon Came into Court and took the Oath as Colonel of the Melitia.

Henry Taylor came into Court and took the oath of Major of the Melitia.

Joshua Wrlght was applied to by the Court to Swear into his Captain's commission, but he refused as he was a Leiutenant of a former Nominal Company.

John Meligan being charged with Felloniously Murdering William Guttery and being Convicted for the same, was brought into Court, and he acknowledged he was guilty of the Crime he stod charged with, and the Court is of Opinion that the said Crimminal for said fellony ought to be sent to the general Court for farther Trial.

John Melony and Samson Beavers, Securities for Joseph Ross, for his appearance at the Court, as by his recognizance appears, came into the Court and delivered said Ross to the Court, and after the Court had heared the Complaint, was fined twenty five Shellings for swearing four Blasfemous Oaths before John Cannon, one before John Johnston — and ordered that
(7) the said Ross give Security for his better Behavior For one year and one day.

John Melony came into Court and agreed to be security for Joseph Ross's keeping the Piece and better Behavior to the Subjects of the Common Wealth, and esspecially to Colonel John Cannon, whome he had threatened to abuse the first oppertunity. The said security bound in the sum of one Hundred pounds.

Upon the Petition of Benjaman Jones ordered that John Bennitt be summoned to Bring a Boy Claimed by the said Jones to the Next Court.

Samson Beavers come into Court and entered Security for the payment of twenty five Shellings at the laying of the Next Parrish Levey, it being Joseph Ross's fine for swearing.

Court is adjourned untill Wednesday 8 Oclock.

Court met according to adjournment.

Present: Edward Ward, John Cannon, Oliver Miller and Zacheriah Connell, Gentlemen Justices.

The Sheriff came into Court and gave Bond and Security for the true performance of the said office.

John Crow being charged with Breach of the piece, ordered that the said Crow give Security for his Better behavior towards all the Subjects of the Common Wealth, and Especially to Joseph Ross for a year and one day. Henry Taylor and James Austurges enter Security for the same, bound in the sum of one Hundred pounds.

Ordered that the Clerk furnish the Sheriff with all papers necessary for the Tryal of John Milligan at the General Court.

Ordered that the Clerk send down the recommendation for William Harrison to be Sheriff.

Ordered that the Clerk send down by Mr. William Harrison all proceedings of the Court relative to the appointment of the Sheriff and Clerk.

Patrick McGey, Thomas Smyth and James Furgurson being Convicted for Breaches of the piece — Ordered that the said Patrick McGey, Thomas Smyth and James Furgurson give Security to each other, for their better Behaviour for the Space of one year and one day, and also to all the Subjects of the Common Wealth.

Henry Taylor and John McGey enter Security for Patrick McGey and Thomas Smyth.

John Crow and David Williams enter Security for James Furgurson.

(8) Ordered that Patrick McGey and Thomas Smyth be fined the Sum of two pounds each, and that the Sheriff secure the same and pay it to James Furgurson.

Charles Harrison and William McKee is appointed Constables for the Ensuing year, and that they be Summoned before Zacheriah Connel Gentleman to swear into said office.

The Court adjourned to Court in Course.

At a Court Continued and held for Yohogania County May 26th, 1777.

Present: William Crawford, Benjaman Kirkindall, John McDaniel and Oliver Miller, Gentlemen Justices — The aforesaid William Crawford and John McDaniel being Previously sworn by the aforesaid Benjaman Kirkindall and Oliver Miller, Gentlemen Justices.

Colo Dorsey Penticost came into Court and beged that the Court would consider the Cause of his not attending their Court at their last meeting — he the said Pentecost, Convinced this Court that it was out of his power to attend, he being at that Time confined in the Small Pox — and prayed the Court to reestablish him in his Office as Clerk of their Court. Colonel Isaac Cox who was appointed Clerk of this Court to succeed him, acquiesing in Said Petition, on the Proviso that his Bonds given the Court for the due performance of his Office be given up or Confiscated; the Court is therefore of opinion that the Reasons Offered by the said Pentecost for his non-attendance at Last Court is satisfactory and the Court acquiesce with his and Colonel Cox's request. — And it is accordingly ordered that Colonel Cox's Bond be delivered him and he is hereby released therefrom and that the said Pentecost enter into Bond with this Court for the due performance of his Office, and to Take the Charge of the Rolls of this County as Clerk to this Court.

Colonel Isaac Cox took his seat in Court.

(9) Colonel William Crawford absent.

Thomas Cook came into Court and took the Oath of Captain of the Militia.

John Muchelhaney is appointed Constable to Serve the Ensuing year and that he be Summoned before Benjamin Kirkindall, Gentleman, to Qualify into said Office.

Benjamin Kirkindall (otherwise Called Jorsey Ben)[1] is appointed Constable to Serve the Ensuing year, and that he be Summoned before Oliver Miller, Gentleman, to Qualify into said Office.

Court adjourned untill Tomorrow 9 O'Clock.

ISAAC COX.

[1] Not the Gentleman Justice, but another Benjamin.

May the 27th 1777, Court met according to adjournment.

Present: Isaac Cox, William Crawford, Oliver Miller, John McDaniel, Benjamin Kirkindall and Benjaman Frye, Gentlemen Justices.

Upon the Petition of Benjaman Jones exhibited against a certain John Bennitt for unlawfully detaining his son Enoch Jones, an Infant.

Ordered that the Said John Bennitt deliver the said Boy Enoch Jones unto the said Benjaman Jones, with Such Household firniture as he may have, the property of the said Boy Enoch Jones, and the said Benjaman Jones pay the said John Bennitt the Sum of Six pounds on the delivery of the said Boy Enoch Jones, and that the said John Bennitt deliver unto the said Infant, Enoch Jones, when he arrives at the age of Twenty one years, one good Cow and Calf.

Michael Thorn and Joshua Meeks both come into Court and Took the oath of Captains of the Melitia.

Ordered — That Zacheriah Connell Gentleman, Take in the List of Tithables in the following Bounds, Viz: — Beginning at the head of Maryland and Extending along Bradock's Road To Thomas Gist, Thence with Froman's Road to Byer's Run,
(10) thence down the said Run to Yough River, Thence down the said River to the mouth of Swedley Creek, Thence with said Creek and the Northern bounds of the County to the Beginning.[1]

Ordered—That Edward Ward, Gentleman be appointed to Take in the List of Tithables within that part of the County Lying West of Swedley Creek East of the Alleghany River & North of the Monaungahela River.

Ordered — That William Goe Gentleman be appointed to take in the List of Tithables within the following Bounds, (Vizt) Beginning at William Castleman's on the head of Little Redstone Creek, Thence on a Strait line to the mouth of Worshington's Mill Run,[2] Thence down Yough River To its Junction with Monaungahela River, thence up the said River

[1] At this time there were no townships, in Yohogania County at least, created by statutory authority, as in Pennsylvania.

[2] Doubtless Washington's Mill Run.

Monaungahela to the mouth of Little Redstone Creek, Thence up the said Creek to the aforesaid Willam Castleman's.

Ordered — Thomas Freeman Gentleman be appointed to Take in the List of Tithables within the following bounds (Vizt): Within that part of the County Lying Between the Laurel Hill and the Monaungahela River, and between the line of this County and the Monaungahela County and the following Line. Vizt — Beginning at the House of Thomas Gist Esquire and extending Along Froman's Road to Byer's Run, Thence down said Run to Yough River, thence Down said River to the mouth of Worshington's Mill Run. Thence on a Strait-line to the House of William Castleman on the head of Little Redstone Creek, Thence down said Creek to its junction.

Ordered — That Benjaman Frye Gentleman, be appointed to Take in the List of Tythables, within the following Bounds, Vizt. Beginning at the mouth of Pigion Creek and running up the said Creek to its fountain, Thence a South Course to the South Line of the County, Thence with said Bounds to the Monaungahela River, Thence down the said River to the Beginning.

Ordered — That Benjaman Kirkindall, Gentleman be ap-
(11) pointed to Take in the List of Tithables within the following Bounds (Vizt) Beginning at the mouth of Pigeon Creek and extending up the same to its fountain, Thence a South line to the South bounds of the County, thence with said bounds to the Top of the dividing Ridge Between the waters of the Monaungahela River and Chirteers Creek, Thence along said Ridge to the head of Peter's Creek, Thence down the said Creek to the mouth, thence up the Monaungahela River to the Beginning.

Ordered — That Oliver Miller Gentleman be appointed to take in the List of Tithables within the following Bounds, Vizt. Beginning at the mouth of Peter's Creek and extending up the same to its fountain—thence on a Strait Line to Ezeel Johnston's on Churteer's Creek, thence down the same to its Junction with the Ohio, Thence up the Rivers Ohio and Monaungahela to the Beginning.

Ordered — That Richard Yeates Gentleman, be appointed to take in the list of Tithables within the following Bounds Vizt.

Beginning at the mouth of the East fork of Churteers Creek and Extending up the same to Ezekiel Johnston's, Thence on a Strait Line to the head of Peter's Creek, Thence along the dividing ridge between Churteer's Creek and the Monaungahela River to the South line of the County, Thence along said line to the middle or main fork of Churteer's Creek, Thence down said Creek to the place of Beginning.

Ordered — That Andrew Swearingen Gentleman be appointed to Take in the List of Tithables within the following bounds, (Vizt) Beginning at the mouth of the West fork of Churteer's Creek and Extending up the same to the Top of the deviding ridge Between Churteer's and Cross Creeks, Thence along said Ridge to the South Line of the County, thence along said Line to the Main fork of Churteer's Creek, Thence down the same to the Beginning.

Ordered — That John McDaniel Gentleman be appointed to take in the List of Tithables within the following Bounds, (Vizt) Beginning at the mouth of the West fork of Churteer's and extending up the Said Fork to the Top of the Dividing Ridge Between Churteer's Creek and Cross and Raccoon
(12) Creeks, Thence down the Said ridge to the head of Robertson's run, Thence down the said run to Churteer's Creek, thence up the said Creek to the Beginning.

Ordered — That Samuel Newell Gentleman be appointed to Take in the List of Tithables within the following Bounds, Vizt — Beginning at the mouth of Churteer's Creek and extending up the same to the mouth of Robertson's run, Thence up said run to Croghan's Line, Thence with said line to Raccon Creek, Thence down said Creek to the Ohio, Thence up said River to the Beginning.

Ordered — Matthew Richie Gentlemen be appointed to take in the List of Tithables within the following Bounds, Vizt.— Beginning on the Ohio at the mouth of Raccoon Creek, Extending down said River to the mouth of Indian Creek, Thence up the same to its fountain, Thence on a Strait Line to Thomas Rogeres on Raccoon Creek, Thence down the same to the Beginning.

Ordered — That Isaac Cox Gentleman be appointed to Take in the List of Tithables within the following Bounds, (Vizt) —

Beginning at the mouth of Cross Creek and extending up the same to the head, thence along the dividing ridge between Cross, Raccoon and Churteer's Creeks to Croghan's line, Thence with said line to Raccoon Creek, Thence up the same to Thomas Rogers's, Thence on a Strait line to the head of Indian Creek, Thence down the Same to Ohio River, Thence with the Said River to the Beginning.

An Execution Issued by Edward Ward Gentleman against Samuel Ewalt, ordenary keeper, for keeping a disorderly House. The Sheriff returns Executed and five pounds ready to render — Ordered That the Sheriff retain said money in his hands untill the Laying the next Levy.

Abraham Dale
vs — Debt — Alias Capias.
Richard Elson

[2 folios, 4 pages missing]

(17) The last Will and Testament of Jacob Lamb deceased was proved by the oaths of John Crow and John Wright to of the subscribing Witnesses. George Kintner came into Court and Took the oath of Executor of the Last Will and Testament of Jacob Lamb deceased, and entered into Bond for his performance according to Law with John Crow and John Wright his securities.

Upon the Representation of Alen Tharp and Wife, that a Certain Michael Humble did forcibly and with a Strong hand Carry away from them, the Complainants, five of their Children. Ordered — That the said Michael Humble forthwith deliver the said Children to the aforesaid Alen Tharp and Wife.

Ordered — That the Court be adjourned untill Tomorrow 7 Oclock in the forenoon. ISAAC COX.

June 25th 1777, Court met according to adjournment.

Present: John Campbell, Isaac Cox, Richard Yeates, Thomas Freeman, Oliver Miller and Zacheriah Connell, Gentlemen, Justices.

Ordered — That the Sheriff cause to be Erected a pair of Stocks, and a Whiping post in the Court-House yard by next Court.

Upon the information of Zacheriah Connell, Gentleman, That James Johnston did this day swear two profane oaths and two profane Cusses — Ordered, That the said James Johnston be fined Twenty Shillings, Currant money for the same.

Upon the information of Isaac Gox Gentleman that James Johnston did this day swear three profane Oaths and one profane Curse — ordered, That the said James Johnston be fined Twenty Shillings Currant money for the same.

(18) Upon the information of John Campbell Gentleman That James Johnston did this day swear four profane oaths, ordered — That the said James Johnston be fined one pound Currant money for the same.

Ordered — That Richard Yeates and Isaac Leet be appointed to meet two Gentlemen to be appointed by the Court of Monaungahela County, at the House of Captain Reason Vergin's on the forth day of August Next, to run the line agreable to Act of Assembly between this County and the said County of Monaungahela.

Ordered — That Richard Yeates and Isaac Leet be appointed to meet two Gentlemen to be appointed by the Court of Ohio County at the House of William Shearer's, on the head of Cross Creek, on the first day of August next to run the line between this County and the said County of Ohio agreeable to Act of Assembly.

Ordered — That the Court of Monaungahela be requested to appoint two gentlemen of their County to meet two Gentlemen already appointed by this Court at the House of Captain Reason Vergin's, on the forth day of August next, to run the line Between this County and the said County of Monaungahela, agreeable to act of assembly.

Ordered — That the Court of Ohio County be requested to appoint two Gentlemen of their County to meet two Gentlemen already appointed by this County at the House of William Shearer's, on the head of Cross Creek, on the first day of August next to run the Line between this County and the said County of Ohio agreeable to act of assembly.

Ordered — That Court be adjourned untill Court in Course.

ISAAC COX.

(19) At a Court Continued and held for Yohogania County August 25th 1777.

Present: Isaac Cox, Richard Yeates, Thomas Freeman, John McDowell and Zacheriah Connell Gentlemen Justices.

Ordered: That for Conveniency of Seting and Expediting Business, That the Court be adjourned to the House now occupied by Andrew Heath.[1] ISAAC COX.

At the House of Andrew Heath, Court met according to adjournment.

Present: John Campbell, Isaac Cox, Richard Yeates, Thomas Freeman, John Cannon, John McDowell, John McDaniel and William Goe, Gentlemen Justices.

The last Will and Testiment of Job Robins was proved by the oaths of Joseph Brown and Joseph Sprouce, the two Subscribing Witnesses and ordered to be recorded.

Benjaman Custard and Rebekah Robins came into Court and Took the oath of Executors of the Estate of Job Robins deceased and entered into Bond with Gabriel Cox and Zadock Wright their Securitys.—

Ordered — That David Cox, John Trumbo and Thomas Spencer or any two of them being first sworn do appraise the Estate of Job Robins deceased and Return the Inventory to next Court.

Bargain and Sale, Jonathan Plummer to Henry Heath, was acknowledged by the said Jonathan Plummer party thereto and ordered to be recorded.

Zachariah Connell Gent, Plaintiff
vs In Case
Samuel Wells, Defendant

(20) This day the plaintiff by his attorney, and Edmond Lindsey personally appeared in Court and undertook for the said Defendant, That in Case he shall be Cast in this Suit that he shall pay and satisfie the condemnation of the Court or render his Body to Prison in Execution for the same or that he the said Edmond Lindsey will do it for him, whereupon the said Defendant prays and hath leave to Imparle untill next Court and then to plead.

[1] Had the court theretofore been held at Augusta Town?

Jacob Bauseman produced a Commission as Captain of the Melitia which being read, The said Jacob Bauseman Came into Court and Took the Oath of Captain of the Melitia.

George Vallandingham, Gentleman named in the Commission of the piece Came into Court and took the Oath of Justice of the Piece.

Edward Ward, Gent., Plant
vs In Case
Joseph Wells, Defendant

This day came the plaintiff by his attorney, and Thomas Freeman Gentleman, personally appeared in Court and undertook for the Defendant that in Case shall be Cast in this Suit, that he shall pay and Satisfie the Condemnation of the Court or render his Body to Prison in Execution for the same, or that he, the said Thomas Freeman will do it for him, whereupon the said Defendant prays and hath leave to Imparl untill next Court and then to plead

Walter Buscoe Plaintiff
vs. In Case
Edward Todd, Defendant

(21) This day came the plaintiff by his attorney, and Joseph Wells Personally appeared in Court and undertook for the said defendant that in Case he shall be Cast in this Suit that he shall pay and Satisfie the Condemnation of the Court or render his Body to Prison in Execution for the Same or that he the said Joseph Wells do it for him. Whereupon the Defendant prays and hath leave to Imparle untill next Court and then to plead.

Isaac Leet Came into Court and Took the oath of Deputy Sheriff.

Ordered that John James Wood be appointed Constable to serve the Ensuing year and that he be sommened before William Goe, Gentleman, to Qualify into said Office.

Ordered — That Court be adjourned untill Tomorrow morning Six O'Clock.[1] JOHN CAMPBELL.

August 26th 1777. Court met according to adjournment.

Present: John Campbell, John McDowell, Isaac Cox,

[1] 6 o'clock!

Richard Yeates, John McDaniel, William Goe, Zacheriah Connell, George Vallandingham, Thomas Freeman and John Cannon, Gentlemen Justices.

David McClure by his attorney Complains that Sarah Bresling an Indented Servant was delivered of a Bastard Child within her said Time of Service and the said Sarah Bresling being Called Came into Court and Confessed to the Charge. It is thereupon Ordered by the Court that the said Sarah Bresling doth serve her said Master the Term of one whole Year from the tenth day of October Next (being the expiration of her service by Indenture) to reembурs her said Master for his Loss and Trouble for the same — or that she pay her Master the sum of one Thousand Pounds of Tobacco in Leu of said Service.

Bargain and Sale. Dorsey Pentecost to Samuel and Robert
(22) Purviance for Three Hundred and fifty two acres of Land
acknowledged by said Pentecost, party thereto and ordered to
be recorded.

Bargain and Sale from Dorsey Pentecost to Samuel and Robert Purviance, acknowledged by said Pentecost party thereto and ordered to be recorded for four hundred and Six acres of Land.

Bargain and Sale from Dorsey Pentecost to Samuel and Robert Purviance for three Hundred and Seven acres of Land. Acknowledged by said Pentecost, party thereto, and ordered to be recorded.

Bargain and Sale from Dorsey Pentecost to Samuel and Robert Purviance for one Hundred & Sixty three acres of Land. Acknowledged by said Pentecost, Party thereto and ordered to be recorded.

Bargain and Sale. Dorsey Pentecost to Jesse Hollingsworth for five Hundred and fifty one acres of Land, acknowledged by Said Pentecost, party thereto and ordered to be recorded.

Edward Ward, Gent, Plaintiff
against In Case
Richard Dunn, Defendant

This day came the Plaintiff by his attorney, and Patrick MuckElroy Personally appeared in Court and undertook for the said Defendant, that in Case he should by Cast in this Suit that he Shall pay and Satisfie the Condemnation of the Court or render his Body to Prison in Execution for the same, or that he, the said Patrick MuckElroy will do it for him, whereupon the said Defendant prays and hath Leave to Imparl untill next Court and then to plead.

Joseph Wells is appointed Constable to serve the Ensuing year. Whereupon the said Joseph Came into Court and Took the Oath of a Constable.

Oliver Miller Gentleman, Justice Present.

(23) Upon the Petition of Paul Froman, Setting forth that he is desirous of Building a Water Mill on Mingo Creek at the mouth Thereof; and praying an order to view and Condimn one Acre of Land on the opposite Side from said Froman's Land for that Purpose,

Ordered—That the Sheriff be Commanded to Sommon twelve Freeholders of his Vissinage to meet on the aforesaid land and they being first Sworn Shall diligintly View and Examine the said Land which shall be Effected or Laid under Water by the Building Said Mill with the Timber and other conveniences thereon, and that they report the same to Next Court with the True Value of said acre of Land Petitioned for and of the Damages done the Party holding the same.

William Brashers produced a Bond Payable from Thomas Hamilton to Andrew Swearingen for five hundred pounds Currant Money with a Condition to deliver to this Court the Body of a Certain Robert Hamilton, which he hath not fulfilled.

Ordered—That the said Bond be put in Suit against the said Thomas Hamilton.

Ordered: That the following Gentlemen be Appointed to make a Tour of the Different Districts hereafter mentioned, and Tender the Oath of Allegience and Fidelity to this Common Wealth to all free Male Inhabitants, agreable to an Act of Assembly Intitled an act to oblige all the free Male Inhabitants above a Certain age to give assurance of allegience to this state and for other purposes, Therein Mentioned.[1]

Ordered—That Matthew Richie, Gentleman, be appointed

[1] For the act itself see 9 Hening 281.

for the above purpose within the following Bounds, Vizt:— Beginning at the mouth of Cross Creek and up the same to the Dividing ridge Between said Creek, Raccoon and Churteer's Creeks; thence along said Ridge to Croghan's Line; thence with said Line to Raccoon Creek; thence up the same to Thomas Rogers's; thence on Strait Line to the head of Indian Creek; thence down the same to the Ohio; thence down the said River Ohio to the Beginning.

24) Ordered:—That Samuel Newell, Gentleman, be appointed for the above purpose within the following Bounds, Vizt:— Beginning at the mouth of Churteer's Creek, extending up the same to the mouth of Robertson's run; thence up the said Run to Croghan's Line; thence with said Line to Raccoon Creek; thence down Said Creek to the Ohio; thence up the same to the Beginning.

Ordered:—That John McDaniel, Gentleman, be appointed for the above purpose within the following Bounds, Viz: Beginning at the mouth of the West fork of Churteer's Creek, Extending up the said fork to the top of the dividing ridge, Between Churteer's Creek, Cross and Raccoon Creeks; thence along Said ridge to the head of Robertson's run; thence down said Run to the Churteer's Creek; thence up the said Creek to the Beginning.

Ordered:—That Andrew Swearingen, Gentleman, be appointed for the above purpose within the following Bounds, Vizt: Beginning at the mouth of the West fork of Churteer's Creek and Extending up the same to the Top of the dividing ridge Between Churteer's Creek and Cross Creek; thence along said Ridge to the South Bounds of the County; thence with said Bounds to the Main Fork of Churteer's Creek; thence down the same to the Beginning.

Ordered:—That Isaac Cox, Gentleman, be appointed for the above Purpose, within the following Bounds, Vizt: all that part of the County Lying west of Sweedly Creek, East of the Allegheny River, & North of the Monaungahela River.[1]

Ordered—That Oliver Miller, Gentleman, be appointed for The above purpose within the following Bounds, Vizt: Begin-

[1] This indicates that the jurisdiction claimed extended well up northeast of Pittsbura

ning at the mouth of Peters Creek and extending up the same to the head, thence a Strait Line to Ezekeel Johnston's on Churteer's Creek, thence down the same to the mouth; Thence up the Ohio and the Monaungahela River to the Beginning.

Ordered: — That Benjaman Kirkindall, Gentleman, be appointed for the above purpose within the following Bounds,
(25) Vizt: — Beginning at the mouth of Pigeon Creek, Extending up the same to the head, Thence a South Line to the South Bounds of the County, thence with said Bounds to the Top of the dividing ridge between the waters of the Monaungahela River and Churteer's Creek, Thence along said ridge to the head of Peters Creek, thence down the same to the Monaunghela River, thence up the same to the Beginning.

Ordered: — That William Goe and Thomas Freeman, Gentlemen, be appointed for the above purpose within the following Bounds, Vizt: — Beginning at the mouth of Little Redstone Creek and Extending up the same to the House of William Castlemans, Thence on a Strait line to the mouth of Worshington's Mill run, thence up Yough River to the mouth of Byer's run, Thence up said Run to Froman's Road; Thence along said road to Thomas Gist, Esquire, Thence along Laurel Hill to Dunlap's old road, Thence with said road to the Monaungahela River, Thence with said River to the Beginning.

Ordered: — That Zacheriah Connell, Gentleman, be appointed for the above purpose within the following Bounds, Vizt: Beginning at the head of Maryland and extending along Bradock's Road to Thomas Gists, Esquires; Thence with Froman's Road to head of Byer's Run; Thence down said Run to Yough River; Thence down the same to mouth of Sweedley Creek; Thence with said Creek and North Bounds of the County to the Beginning.

Ordered: — That Benjaman Frye, Gentleman, be appointed for the above purpose within the following Bounds, Vizt: Beginning at the Mouth of Little Redstone Creek extending up the same to the House of William Castleman; Thence on a Strait Line to the mouth of Warshington's mill run; Thence down the river Yough to the Monaungahela; Thence up the same to the Beginning.

Ordered: — That Richard Yeates, Gentleman, be appointed

for the above purpose within the following Bounds, Vizt: Beginning at the mouth of Pigeon Creek and Extending up the same to its fountain; Thence South to the South Bounds of the County; thence with said bounds to the Monaungahela River; Thence down said River to the Beginning.

(26) Ordered:—That John Inks [illegible], Benjamin Wells, John White, Jun, Henry Boyles, Samuel Clerk, Samuel Griffith, William McKee, John Brown, Isaac Sparks, Peter Austerges, John James Wood, and Brice Vergin, be appointed Constables to serve the Ensueing year, and that they be Sommoned to attend Next Court (or the Nearest Justice) to Qualify into said Office.

Ordered:—That the Sheriff Call on Mr. John Anderson, of Pittsburg, or any other person, for the papers and records belonging to the District of West Augusta, and that the said Sheriff give the said Mr. John Anderson, or any other person who may deliver the said Records, a Receipt for the same; and that he deliver the said Papers and Records to the Clerk of this Court, who is also ordered to give the said Sheriff a Receipt for said delivery.

Robert Hamilton, a prisoner in the Sheriffs Custody, came into Court and in the grocest and most Impolite Manner Insulted the Court, and Richard Yeates, Gentleman, in particular: Ordered, That the Sheriff confine the feet of the said Robert Hamilton in the lower rails of the fence for the space of five minutes.

Ordered:—That any prisoner or prisoners the Sheriff have, Shall be Confined in the guard or some other room in Fort pitt, with the acquiesance of General Hand, untill such Time as a proper goal can be provided for the County.

Ordered:—That Isaac Cox, Oliver Miller and Benjaman Kirkindall, be appointed, or any two of them, to Contract with a proper person or Persons, to Build a Goal and Court house in the following manner, and at the following place, Vizt: The Goal and Court House are to be Included in one whole and Intire Building, of round sound Oak, to go Twenty four feet Long and Sixteen feet wide; two Story high; The lower Story to be eight feet high, Petitioned in the Middle;

with Squared hewed Logs with Locks, and bears to the door and Windows, according to law, which Shall be the Goal.
(27) The upper Story to be five feet high in the Sides, with a good Cabbin Roof, with Convenient seats for the Court & Bar, and a Clerk's Table, to remain in one room, with a pair of Stairs on the outside to Assend up to said Room, which Shall be place for holding Court; with two floors to be laid with strong hewed logs; the whole to be Compleat and finished in one month from the date hereof. The said Building to be Erected on the plantation of Andrew Heath at Such Convenient place as the said Isaac Cox, Oliver Miller & Benjaman Kirkindall, Gentlemen, or any two of them shall think Proper.

Ordered—That John McDowell, Gentleman, be appointed to Take a Tour within the following Bounds, and Tender the oath of allegience and Fidelity to the State, to all free male Inhabitants within the same, above sixteen years of age, agreeable to act of Assembly: Beginning at the mouth of the East fork of Churteer's Creek and Extending up the same to Ezekil Johnston's; Thence on a Strait Line to the head of Peter's Creek; Thence on the Top of the Deviding Ridge Between the Monaungahela River and Churteer's Creek to the South Bounds of the County; Thence with said Bounds to the Main fork of Churteers Creek Thence with said Creek to the Beginning.

Ordered—That the Court be adjourned to 6 Oclock Tomorrow Morning.

JOHN CAMPBELL.

August 27th Court met according to adjournment.

Present: John Campbell, Richard Yeates, William Goe, George Vallandingham, John McDowell, Isaac Cox, Thomas Freeman, Oliver Miller, Zacheriah Connel, John Cannon & John McDaniel, Gentlemen Justices.

(28) Alexander Bowling against William Poston. Pluries Capias.

Alexander Bowling against Francis Morrison. In Case. Plur. Capias.

Christian Summitt against John Golliher and wife. In Slander, Plurious Capias.

Thomas Rankin against Jeremiah Standsburry. In Case, Alias Capias.

David Day against Jacob Hedricks. In Case. Alias Capias.

John Lydea against Joseph Cox. In Case. Alias Capias.

Matthew Dale against Richard Elson. In Case, Alias Capias.

Benjaman Jones against Patrick McDaniel. In Case. Plurious Capias.

William McMahan against John Greathouse. In Case, Plu. Cap.

Daniel Swigert against Benjaman Newgent. Atteachment, Continued for want of Prosecution.

Peter Reasoner against Davis Ruth. In Case. Alias Capias.

—— Shillings against Spencer Collins. In Case. Alias Cap.

Dorsey Pentecost against Christopher McDaniel. Debt. Alias Cap.

Burr Harrison against William Williams. In Case. The Sheriff Returning agreed, Ordered that the Suit be Demised.

Joseph Lindsey
vs. In case
George Long The Sheriff having Returned that the Defendant is not in his Bailliwick, Ordered That This Suit be dismissed.

Zacheriah Connell against Abraham Vaughan. In Case. Ali. Cap.

Richard McMahan against John Trumbo. In Case. The Sheriff returning Executed and agreed and the Plaintiff not appearing, though Solemnly Called, Ordered to be dismissed for Non Procedendo.

Zacheriah Connell against Providence Mounce. In Slander. The Sheriff Returns Executed. Ordered that said Suit be Continued.

Zacheriah Connell
against In Slander.
John Lindsey The Sheriff returns Executed, Ordered that Said Suit be Continued.

Ignaw Labat
against In Case.
John Bradley The Sheriff returns agreed, Ordered that this Suit be dismissed.

(29) Hugh Sterling against Mordicai Richards. In Assault. Alias Capias.

Ignaw Labat, Plaintiff
against In Debt.
Thomas Girty Defendant The Sheriff returns that the Defendant Is not with in his Bailliwick. Ordered that the Suit be Dismissed.

David Wilson against Henry Bowling. In Case. Alias Capias.

Alexander Sumrall Jun
and Thomas Jack Plaintiffs
against In Case
Walter Summerall, Defendant Alias Capias.

John Worshington against James Poor. Ejectment. Ordered to be Continued.

John Spivey against Samuel Beeler. In Case. Alias Capias.

Richard Yeates, Plaintiff
against In Case
Brice Virgin, Defendant ordered to be Dismissed at Plaintiff's request.

Richard Waller Plaintiff
against In Debt
John Earskin, Defendant The Sheriff returns agreed Ordered that This Suit be Dismissed.

Dorsey Pentecost, Plaintiff
against In Debt
James Poor Defendant upon the Petition of the Plaintiff Seting forth that the Defendant Stands Justly Indebted to him four pounds Ten Shillings Courant Money refuseth payment.

The said James being Solemnly Called & failing to appear the Plaintiff produced a Note of hand Bearing Interest from the fifteenth day of December 1774, four pounds Ten Shillings with Credit on said Note for Two pounds Three Shillings and six pence. It is Considered by the Court that Plaintiff recover against the said James the Defendant for two pounds six Shillings and six pence with Interest from the said fifteenth day of December untill paid, with his Costs about this Suit in that behalf Expended.

Ordered — That Execution be Staid on this Judgment untill next October Court.

(30) Ordered — That the following Gentlemen be recommended to his Excellency the Governor as proper persons to be added to the Commission of the piece, Vizt, Isaac Leet, Senior, Joseph Beeler, Sen. John Carmichael, James Rogers, Isaac Meason, James McLane, James Blackstone, Joseph Becket and Joseph Vance, Gentleman.

Ordered: — That the Majestrates appointed to make the Tour of the County and Tender the oath of allegience and Fidelity, Shall also Take in the Numbers in Each Family within their Respective districts, In order to enable the justices to make an Equal distribution of the salt, and make return to October Court.

Zacheriah Connell against Abraham Vaughan. In Case. Ali. Cap.

Ordered — That Isaac Cox Gentleman be recommended to his Excellincy the Governor as a proper person to Serve as Leiutenant Colonel of the Militia of this County, In the Stead of Thomas Brown Gentleman who hath refused to Serve.

Ordered — That Court be adjourned Till Court in Course &c.

JOHN CAMPBELL.

At a Court continued and held by Adjornment September 22d 1777.

Present: Isaac Cox, William Goe, Oliver Miller, Joshua Wright, Gentlemen Justices.

Ordered that Isabel Pegg be appointed Administratrix of all the Goods, Chattles and Credits of the Estate of Garret New Gill deceased. She complying with the Law. Whereupon the said Isabel Pegg with James Wright her Surety, Came into Court and Entered into Bond for the Performance of the Said Administration. Isabel Pegg came into Court and took the Oath of Administratrix of the Estate of Garrett New Gill, deceased.

(31) Ordered that John Wall, Benjaman Collends & John Cox or any two of them being first Sworn do appraise all the Estate of Garret Newgil decd and make return to the Next Court.

A Bargain and Sale from Gabriel Cox to James Swolevan of three hundred Acres of Land acknowledged by the said Gabriel party thereto and ordered to be recorded.

William Taylor produced a Licence appointing him to preach the Gospel after the Manner of his Sect; which being read, the said William Taylor came into Court and took the Oath of fidelity and Allegience to this Commonwealth.

John Gibson came into Court and took the Oath of Ensign of Militia.

John Campbell Gent took his seat in Court.

Alex Sumrall & Thos Jack

Walter Sumrall

This day came the Plff, and William Anderson personally appeared in Court and undertook for Said Deft that in Case he shall be cast in this Suit he shall pay & Satisfy the Condemnation of the Court or render his body to prison in Execution for the same or that he the said William Anderson will do it for him. Whereupon the Deft prays and hath leave to imparl untill the next Court and then to plead.

Ordered that the Court be adjourned to tomorrow at 7 oClock.

JOHN CAMPBELL.

(32) September 23d 1777. The Court met pursuant to adjournment.

Present: John Campbell, Isaac Cox, William Goe, Oliver Miller, Gentlemen, Justices.

The last will and Testament of Johathan Reed was proved by the Oaths of Noah Flehearty and Hugh McCreedy, two of the subscribing witnesses and ordered to be recorded.

John Cannon, Joshua Wright & Matthew Richey Gentlemen Came into Court and took their Seats.

Robert Bowers being charged with a breach of an act of the Common wealth intitled an Act for the punishment of certain Offences being Called, pleads Not Guilty. Then came a Jury, to wit. James Swolevan, James Wall, Charles Bruce, James Campbell, William Marshall, Joseph Becket, John Crow, Zadock Wright, Edward Cook, Gabriel Cox, Andrew Heath and John Douglass, and being sworn say that the said Robert Bowers shall suffer One year's Imprisonment.

David England, being charged with a breach of an act of Assembly of this Commonwealth, intitled an Act for the punishment of Certain Offences, Came into Court and Confessed the Charge. Then came a Jury, to wit James Swolevan, James Wall, Charles Bruce, James Campbell, William Marshall, Joseph Becket, John Crow, Zadock Wright, Edward Cook, Joseph Bealer, Andrew Heath & John Douglass, and being sworn say that they find forty Shillings.

(33) John Teague and George Corn are allowed two days attendance each as Witnesses in behalf of the Common Wealth against David English.

Joseph Beeler Gent. is appointed Administrator of all the Goods, Chattles and Credits of the Estate of John Hutcheson, deceased, he complying with the Law. — Whereupon the Said Joseph Beeler with Christopher Beeler Came into Court and entered into Bond for the due performance of his said Administration.

Joseph Beeler Came into Court and took the Oath of Administrator of Joseph Hutcheson deceased.

Ordered — That Richard Antis, William Powell and James Burns or any two of them they being first sword to apprais the Estate of John Hutcheson deceased and Make Return to Next Court.

Benjamin Kirkindall Gent Justice Took his Seat in Court.

Andrew Swearingen
Thomas Hambleton This day came the Plff, and Robert Hamilton personally appeared in Court and undertook for the Defendant that in Case he Shall be Cast in this Suit he Shall

pay and Satisfy the Condemnation of the Court or render his Body to Prison in execution for the same, or that he, the said Robert Hamilton will do it for him. Whereupon the said Deft prays and hath leave to imparl untill next Court and then to plead.

William Brashiers

Robert Hambleton This day came the Plff, and Thomas Hambleton personally appeared in Court and undertook for the Defendant that in Case he shall be Cast in this Suit he Shall pay and Satisfy the Condemnation of the Court or render his Body to Prison in Execution for the Same or that the said Thomas Hambleton will do it for him. Whereupon the Deft prays and hath leave to imparl untill next Court and then to plead.

(34) Moses Davison Stands charged with Hog stealing. Ordered that the said Moses Davison be bound over to Next Grand Jury Court with one Security in the Sum of £25 each.

Whereupon the said Moses Davison and William Colvin his Surety Came into Court and Entered Bail as aforesaid.

Sarah Reed, Joseph Becket and Edward Cook, Executors of the last will and Testament of Jonathan Reed deceased with Joseph Beeler Christopher Beeler and Paul Froman, their securities came into Court and entered into Bond for the true performance of the said Executorship. Whereupon the said Sarah Reed Joseph Becket and Edward Cook took the Oath of Executrix and Executors of the last will and Testament of said Jonathan Reed Decd.

Ordered that Benjaman Davis Samuel Burns John Wright and Dorsey Pentecost or any two or more of them, being first sworn to appraise the Estate of Jonathan Reed deceased and make Return to Next Court.

Joseph Allen being Charged with a Breach of an act of Assembly of this Common Wealth intitled an act for the Punishment of Certain Offences being Calld Came into Court and pleads Not Guilty—Then came a Jury, to wit: James Swolevan, James Wall, Charles Bruce, James Campbell, William Marshall, Andrew Heth, John Crow, Joseph Becket, Zadock Wright, Joseph Beeler, Edward Cook and John Douglass, and saith that the said Joseph Allen is Not Guilty.

(35) Eliezer Brown being Charged with a Breach of an Act of Assembly of this Common Wealth intitled an act for the punishment of certain Offences—being Called comes before the Court and pleads, Not Guilty. Whereupon came a Jury, to wit: James Swolevan, James Wall, Charles Bruce, James Campbell, William Marshall, Andrew Heath, John Crow, Joseph Becket, Zadock Wright, Joseph Beeler, Edward Cook and John Douglass, who upon their Oaths say that the said Eliezer Brown is Not Guilty.

Thomas Estill, being charged with a Breach of the Act of Assembly of this Commonwealth, intitled an act for the punishment of Certain Offences, who being Called upon Comes into Court and pleads Not Guilty; Whereupon, a Jury being Sworn, to wit: James Swolevan, James Wall, Charles Bruce, James Campbell, William Marshall, Andrew Heath, John Crow, Joseph Becket, Zadock Wright, Joseph Beeler, Edward Cook, and John Douglass, do say they find for the Commonwealth Twenty Pounds Current Money.

Philip Tabor, Charged with being guilty of a Breach of an Act of Assembly of this Common Wealth intitled an act for the punishment of Certain Offences, being called comes into Court and pleads Not Guilty. Whereupon Come a Jury to wit, James Swolevan, James Wall, Charles Bruce, James Campbell, William Marshall, Andrew Heth, John Crow, Joseph Becket, Zadock Wright, Joseph Beeler, Edward Cook & John Douglass, who upon their Oaths do say the Said Philip Tabor is Not Guilty.

(36) Upon the Petition of Adam Wickerham setting forth that he is desirous of Building a Water Mill on Mingo Creek about three quarters of a Mile from the mouth and that he owns all the Lands that will be effected or overflowed by the building of the said Mill. It is therefore Considered by the Court that the Said Adam Wickerham have leave to build and compleat a mill at the place aforesaid.

Upon the Petition of Paul Froman setting forth that he is desirous of building a Water Mill on Mingo Creek at the mouth thereof and praying an Order to view and Condemn one acre of Land on the opposite side of the Creek to said Froman's Land for that purpose.

Ordered that the Sheriff be Commanded to Summon twelve good and lawful freeholders of the vicinage to meet on the premises aforesaid and being first sworn shall diligently view and examine the said Lands which may be affected or laid under water by the Building Said Mill with the Timber and other Conveniences thereof, and that they report the same to next Court under their hands and Seals with the true value of the one acre of Land Petitioned for and of the damage done to the party holding the Same.

Ordered that John Campbell, Gent., be requested to furnish the wife of Lemuel Davis, a poor Soldier now in the Continental service from this State, for the Support of herself and three Children, the Sum of four pounds per Month, to Commence from the said Lemuel Davis's March from this County.

Ordered that the provision made for the Children of Edward McCawley, by a former Order of this Court, Shall commence
(37) from the time of his March from this Country, and that the funeral Charges of one of the said Children since dead be paid by the said Mr. Campbell, and that this Court do draw on the Treasury of this Commonwealth for the payment of the Same.

A letter from General Hand addressed to Col. Campbell questing that Capt. Alexander McKee's Parole given to the Committee of West Augusta be given up to him, the said General Hand, in order to enable him to put Capt. McKee on a New Parole, as he finds it necessary to remove said Alexander McKee. Ordered that the said Parole be given up to General Hand and that he deposit a Copy of the New Parole to be taken from the said Capt. McKee in Lieu thereof, Certified by the said General Hand.

Ordered that a Dedimus be issued to take the Evidence in behalf of the Common Wealth, against John Beall, as well on behalf of said John Beall as on the Common Wealth.

Sarah Norris

Attachment

Charles Norris

These parties came into Court and request that this Action may be referred to Michael Rawlins, Thomas Keith and Andrew Swearingen Gent. It is therefore accordingly ordered by the

Court that the said Suit be referred to the said Michael Rawlins, Thos Keith and Andrew Swearingen or any two of them, they being first sworn diligently examine the Case and make return in writing to next Court, of their Judgment which Shall be considered the Judgment of the Court.

Ordered that the Court be adjourned to 7 oClock tomorrow morning.

JOHN CAMPBELL.

(38) The Court met according to Court in Course at the house of Mr. Andrew Heath Octo 27th 1777.

Present: John Campbell, Isaac Cox, Joshua Wright, Richard Yeates, Gentlemen Justices.

Ordered that the Court be adjourned to the new Court House.[1]

JOHN CAMPBELL.

The Court met at the Court House pursuant to adjournment.

Present: John Campbell, Isaac Cox, Richard Yeates, Joshua Wright, Benj Kerkendal, Andrew Swearingen, Samuel Newell, Gent. Justices.

A Bargain and Sale from Michael Kintner and Catherine his wife to Daniel Dozier for 200 acres of Land, acknowledged by said Michael Kintner and Catherine his wife and ordered to be recorded.

Jacob Feagley
v
Hugh Brawdy This day came the Plaintif, and James Wright personally appeared in Court and undertook for the said Defendant that in Case he shall be Cast in this Suit, he shall pay and Satisfy the Condemnation of the Court or render his Body to Prison in execution for the same or that he the said James Wright will do it for him, whereupon the said Defendant prays and hath leave to imparl untill next Court and then to plead.

(39) Peter Resner
v
Daviss Ruth This day came the Plaintiff, & David Leffergy personally appeared in Court and under took for the said De-

[1] Ordered on August 26th, to be built in one month.

fendant that in Case he shall be Cast in this Suit he shall Satisfy the condemnation of the Court or render his body to prison in Execution for the same, or he the said David Leffurgy will do it for him, whereupon the Said Defendant pleads and hath leave to imparl untill next Court and then to plead.

Ordered, that Jno Campbell, Gent., be requested to furnish the Wife of Richard Jaines, a poor Soldier in the Continental Service from this State, with the sum of four pounds per month, for the Support of herself and three Children, and this Court do draw on the Treasurer of this Common Wealth for the payment of the Same.—The same to commence one month prior to this date.

John Campbell, gent. absent.

Ordered that Mrs. Knox, the wife of ——— Knox, a poor Soldier in the Continental Service from this State, be allowed the Sum of three pounds per month, for the Support of herself and three Children, to commence from the date hereof, and that this Court do draw on the Treasurer of this Common Wealth for the payment of the Same.

Ordered that Mary Douthard, the wife of Thomas Douthard, a poor Soldier from this State in the service of the United States, be allowed four pounds per month, for the Support of herself and Six Children, to commence one Month prior to this date, and that this Court draw on the Treasurer of this Commonwealth for the Same.

(40) Ordered, that the wife of Abram Ritchey, a poor Soldier in the Continental Service from this State, be allowed three pounds per month for her Support and three Children, and that the Court do draw on the Treasurer of this Commonwealth for the payment of the same

Ordered that the sum of Two pounds per month be allowed the wife of William Ritchie, a poor Soldier now in the Continental Service from this State for the Support of herself and two Children, and that this Court draw on the Treasurer of this Commonwealth for the payment thereof.

A Deed of Partition, John Connolly to John Campbell Gent bearing date the Sixth day of February, one Thousand seven hundred and seventy-six, proved by the Oath of Thomas Flinn one of the Subscribing Witnesses and that he saw Joseph Westmore, Charles Matheson, and James Millegan Sign their names thereto as Witnesses.

Ordered that the Court be adjourned to tomorrow morning at eight O'Clock.

ISAAC COX.

(41) The Court met according to adjournment.

President: John Campbell, Richard Yeates, Andrew Sweringen, Samuel Newell, Gentlemen Justices.

Ordered, that the Inhabitants of this County have leave to Inoculate for the Small Pox, at their own houses or such other convenient Places as they may think proper.

Zelphia McClean
v
Thomas Palmer This day came the Plaintiff, and John Palmer personally appeared in Court and undertook for the Defendant that in Case he shall be Cast in this Suit he shall Satisfy the Condemnation of the Court or render his body to prison in execution for the Same or that he the said John Palmer will do it for him. Whereupon the said Deft prays and hath leave to imparl untill next Court and then to plead.

On the Petition of Sarah Sample setting forth that Ann McClean hath detained a Servant Girl, Ann Brook, to the great Damage of the said Petitioner. Ordered that a Subpona do issue to summon the said Ann to the next Court.

Alexander Bowlin
v In Case
William Poston Upon the testimony of Isaac Leet and the Debt being under fifty dollars and the said Defendant being in the Continental Service, Ordered that this Suit be dismissed at Plff's Cost.

(42) Benjn Kerkendal and Isaac Cox Gent Present. John Campbell, Gent. absent.

The Commonwealth
v Recognizance on Assault on Mary McCallister.
David Duncan

On hearing the Evidence, Ordered that the said David Duncan be bound over to answer the said Complaint of Elizabeth

McCallister in behalf of the Commonwealth exhibited against him, whereupon the said David with Zadock Wright his Security came into Court and acknowledged to be indebted to Patrick Henry Esq Gov &c for the use of the State to be levied &c the sum of £25 each conditioned for the personal appearance of the said David at the next Grand Jury Court to be held for this County &c

Joshua Wright, John Campbell Gent. Present.

On the Recognizance of James Fleming and John Gibson (packhorse man) the parties not appearing being Solemny called Ordered the same to be put in Suit.

Isaac Leet, Deputy Sheriff, in behalf of the high Sheriff of the County, entered his protest against the Goal of this County, he conceiving the same not sufficient to confine Prisoners.

Ordered that the Sheriff pay Colo Isaac Cox the sum of Thirty pounds to be applied towards the pay for building the Court house and Goal, and Andrew Heth pay five pounds now retained in his hands for Samuel Ewalts, fine for keeping a disorderly house to the said Sheriff.

Ordered that Ann Brook a Servant to Sarah Sample be and
(43) remain with her mother Ann McClain untill next Court.

Ordered that the Court be adjourned to tomorrow morning at 8 O'Clock.

JOHN CAMPBELL.

The Court met in pursuant to adjournment Oct 29th 1777.

Present: John Campbell, Isaac Cox, Samuel Newell, Richare Yeates, Andw Swearigen, Gentlemen Justices.

Ordered that the Sheriff do Summon a Grand Jury to attend next Court.

Zacheriah Connell, Gent.
Nathaniel Brown

Then came the Plff, and Richard Yeates Gent personally appeared in Court and undertook for the said Defendant that in Case he shall be Cast in this Suit He shall pay and satisfy the Condemnation of the Court or render his Body to Prison in Execution for the Same or the said Richard Yeates will do it for him. Whereupon the said Defendant prays and hath leave to imparl till next Court and then to plead &c

The Commonwealth
v
Jacob Judy

The Prosecution not appearing Ordered to be dismissed.

Upon the Petition of David Day against Jacob Hendricks on Request of the Parties Ordered that this Suit and all other Suits now depending in this Court between the said Parties be referred to John Smith, William Campbell and William Vance, they being first sworn and make return to next Court.

(44) The Commonwealth
v
David Stone & Jas Davis

In Breach of the peace.
James Fleming Prosr

Then came the parties and upon hearing their Allegations, Ordered to be dismissed at the Plff's Cost.

The Commonwealth
v
John Bradley

In Assault & Battery
David Irwin Pros.

Ordered that the Prosecutor David Irwin and the Deft John Bradley give Security for their good behavior towards all the good Subjects of this Commonwealth till the next Grand Jury Court. Whereupon the said David Irwin with David Stone his Security and John Bradley with James Scott his Security acknowledged to owe to Patrick Henry Esq Gov & the sum of £20 each to be levied &c conditioned as per the order of the Court and that they dot depart the Court without leave &c

Alexander Bowling
v
Francis Morrison

Then came the Plff, and James Scott personally appeared in Court and undertook for said Defendant that if he Shall be Cast in this Suit he shall pay the Condemnation of the Court or render his body to Prison in execution for the same, or he, the said James Scott will do it for him, whereupon the said Deft. prays and has leave to imparl untill next Court and then to plead, &c.

The Last will & Testament of Joseph Kirkwood deceased was proved by the Oaths of Nicholas Little and Geo Gillespie two of the Subscribing Witnesses and ordered to be recordered.

(45) James Allison and Margaret Kirkwood came into Court and took the Oath of Executor and Executrix of the Estate of

Joseph Kirkwood, deceased, whereupon the said James Allison and Margaret Kirkwood with George Gillespie and John McDowell, their Sureties come into Court and enter into Bond for the due performance of their said trust.

Ordered that Nicholas Little, Patrick McCollock and Patrick Scott or any two of them, being first sworn do apprais the Estate of Joseph Kirkwood deceased, and make return to next Court.

John Campbell, Gent. Absent.

John Ramage with William Ramage his Security come into Court and acknowledged to be indebted £500 conditioned for the appearance of the said John Ramage at a Court to be held the 5th day of November next for the Examination of the said John Ramage.

Ordered that the Treasurer of this Commonwealth pay to Colo John Campbell, the sum of ninety eight pounds current money to reimburse him, the said Colo Campbell, for money already furnished the wives and Children of poor Soldiers from this County, now in the Continental Service & for the farther Support for three months next ensuing, and that the Clerk draw on the treasury in favor of said Campbell, for the aforesaid sum of £98 0 0 Current money.

William McMachen
v In Case
John Greathouse Then came the parties and at the request of the Plff Ordered that this Suit be dismissed.

John Campbell Gent. Prest.

(46) Bazil Brown
v
Robert Hamilton Then came the Plff, and Thomas Hamilton personally appeared Court and undertook for Sd Deft, that in Case he should be Cast in this Action, he Shod pay and Satisfy the Condemnation of the Court or render his Body to prison in Execution for the same or he the said Thomas Hamilton will do it for him, Whereupon the said Defendant prays and has leave to imparl untill next Court and then to plead.

Ordered that this Court be adjourned to tomorrow morning at 8 oClock. JOHN CAMPBELL.

October 30th 1777 The Court met Pursuant to Adjournment.

Present: John Campbell, Isaac Cox, Andw Sweringen, Richd Yeates, Gentlemen Justices.

Ordered that the Clerk issue a Summons for Christian Brooks, Daniel Rysher and Michael Rysher to appear before the next Court to be held for this County to give Testimony against Conrad Winmiller in behalf of the Common Wealth.

Joshah Wright Gent. Present.

Ordered, that Isaac Cox, Oliver Miller and Benjamin Keykendal, Gent, or any two of them, be appointed to contract with a proper person or persons to build a sufficient Stone
(47) Chimney in the Court house and Goal, to be carried up in the middle of the Building, with three fire places, one in each room of the Goal, and one in the part where the Court is held; and to have the Court Rooms chunked and plastered; also a good loft of Clap boards, with a window in each Glebe, and four pains of Glass of ten Inches by eight, and the Goal rooms to be plastered.

Thomas Rankins v Jeremiah Stransbury, Case, Agreed.
David Day v. Jacob Hendricks. Ass & Bat. refer'd
John Lydia v Joseph Cox — Slander — Plu. Cap.
Abraham Dale v. Richard Elson — Trespass. — Agreed
Benj Jones v Patrick McDonald. — Ass & Bat. — Plu Cap
Balser Shilling v Spencer Collins — Trespass. Plu Cap.
Dorsey Pentecost v Chris McDonald — Case Plu Cap.
Zacheriah Connell. v Abraham Vaughan. Debt. Plu Cap.
Hugh Serling v Mordecai Richards — Ass & Bat Plu Cap
David Willson v Henry Boling — Debt — Plu. Cap.
John Spivy v Samuel Beeler. Trespass Plu. Cap.
John Gallahar & wife v Christian Summon. Slander. Al Cap.
John Smith v Sarah Dye — Debt — Cont'd
Charles Reno v Lewis Clock — Case — Agreed.
Robert McKeey v Moses Davison Case Cont'd

View of the Jury upon the Petition of Paul Froman returned by the Sheriff and ordered to be recorded

Ordered that the Court be adjourned to the Court in Course.

JOHN CAMPBELL.

(48) At a Court continued and held for Yohogania county — December 22 1777

Present: Isaac Cox, John McDowell, Richard Yeates, Olliver Miller, Gentlemen Justices.

Inventory of Jonathan Reed deceased returned by the appraisers and ordered to be recorded —

An Attachment, being obtained by Daniel Swigart against Benjamin Newgent, the Constable (John Johnston) having returned that he had executed the said attachment, on one horse, nine head of hogs, and a quantity of Rie in the Sheaf, and the said Benjn Newgent being Solemnly Called and not appearing to replevy the said attached Effects.— The said Daniel Swigart produced an account against the said Benjamin for £24 5 9 Pennsylvania Currency which he proved according to law. It is ordered by the Court that the said Daniel Swigart Plff. recover against the said Benjamin Defendant for Nineteen pounds eight Shillings and Seven pence farthing Current Money of the value of £24 5 9 Pennsylvania Currency Ordered that the Sheriff make sale of the aforesaid Attached Effects and Satisfy the Said Daniel Plff the Judgment and make return thereof.

John Crow took the Oath of Capt of Militia.

Maybury Evans produced a Commission from his Excy the Governor appointing him Lieut of the Militia of this County which being read the said Mayburry came into Court and took the oath of Lieut of Militia.

Ben Keykendal, Gent, Absent.

(49) Patrick Lafferty came into Court and took the Oath of Ensign of the Militia.

Daniel Williams came into Court and enters himself Defendant in the stead of Casual Ejector in an Ejectment at the Suit of Isaac Vance and Enters &c

Isaac Cox, Gent Absent.

Isaac Cox Gent, having obtained an attachment against the Estate of Richard Richardson for two pounds two Shillings and eight pence, and the Sheriff returns that he has levied the said attachment on a trowel & hammer, and the said Richard Richardson being solemnly called and failing to appear and the said Isaac Plaintiff proved the said account, it is considered by the Court that the said Isaac Plaintiff recover against the said Richard Defendant the said sum of two pounds two Shillings and eight pence. Ordered that the Sheriff make sale of the aforesaid attached effects to Satisfy the said Judgment and make return thereof.

Ordered on Motion of John Crow, his mark a Crop in the Left Ear and a Swallow fork in the right, be recorded.

Ordered that the Ear mark of Jacob Shillings a half Crop in the left Ear and a Crop and a half Crop in the right Ear be recorded.

Ordered that the mark of Richard Yeates a Crop and under keel in the left ear and two slits in the right year be recorded.

Ordered that the Ear mark of Olliver Miller, Gent a hole in the left year and two Slits in the right ear be recorded.

Ordered that the Court be adjourned to tomorrow morning at 9 oClock.

ISAAC COX.

(50) Dec 23d 1777. The Court met according to adjournment. Present: John McDowell, Isaac Cox, Richd Yeates, Oliver Miller, Gentlemen Justices.

The mark of Mayberry Evans a Swallow fork in the right ear and a Slit in the left. on motion of said Mayberry Ordered to be recorded.

The mark of Richard Evans, a Swallow fork in the right ear and a Crop in the left ordered to be recorded.

The Ear Mark of William Anderson two under half Crops on motion ordered to be recorded.

The Mark of Michael Teggert a crop and three Slitts in the left Ear, on motion of said Michael ordered to be recorded.

Bill of Sale Alexander Young to Joseph Wherry for 300 Acres of Land acknowledged by said Young party thereto ordered to be recorded.

On the Complaint of James Murphy and wife that a certain Jacob Jones hath for some time past forcibly detained George Alervine, the son of the wife of the said James Murphy to the great damage of the said James and Wife and against the peace and dignity of the Common Wealth. Ordered that the Said

Jacob Jones forthwith deliver the said George Alervine to the said James Murphy and wife.

Charles Morris
v In Debt
Thomas Rouse On Motion of Plff Ordered that this Suit be dismissed.

(51) On the Petition of Andrew Heath &c, Ordered, that Robert Henderson, Zadock Wright, John Robertson, John Crow, Thomas Applegate and Andrew Dye, view a road, the nearest and best way from Pittsburg to Andrew Heaths ferry on the Monongahela River, and from thence to Becket's fort.

Upon the motion of Andrew Heath, ordered that he have leave to keep a ferry at his house across the Mongahala River.

Benn Kekendal Wilm Goe, Gent present.

On the Information of Oliver Miller Gent. that William Dunaghgan did on this day swear two prophane Oaths Ordered, that the said William William Dunaghgan be fined 10s for the same.

Oliver Miller Gentleman returns five Shillings received from Martin Owens for Swearing. Ordered that the Sheriff receive the same.

Isaac Leet returns that he hath received five Shillings from James Johnston for prophane swearing. Ordered that the Said Isaac Leet, Sheriff retain the same in his hands.

Thomas Dickenson came into Court and enters himself Defendant in an Action of Ejectment at the Suit of James Roberts.

Inventory of the Estate of Garret Newgill deceased returned by the appraisers & ordered to be recorded.

Bargain and Sale. Paul Froman to Dorsey Pentecost for fourteen hundred acres of Land in this County was proved by the Oaths of James Allison, Isaac Leet, John Crow & John McDowell Gent. also the receipt thereunto annexed was proved by the oaths of the said John McDowell and John Crow, the Subscribing Witnesses to the Said Bargain & Sale & Receipt as aforesaid & ordered to be recorded

(52) Bill of Sale. Isaac Cox to James Allison for one one thousand acres of Land in the County of Kentucke, acknowledged

by the said Isaac Cox party thereto and ordered to be recorded.

David McClure v Patrick McElroy. Then came David McClure The Plaintiff, and John Crow personally appeared in Court and undertook for the said Defendant that in Case he shall be Cast in this Action he shall pay and Satisfy the Condemnation of the Court or render his Body to prison in execution for the same or he the said John Crow will do it for him. Whereupon the Defendant prays and has leave to imparl untill next Court and then to plead.

Upon the motion of Oliver Miller Gent on behalf of Catherine Dabler a servant to William Anderson that a certain Peter Brandon of the town of Pittsburgh now unjustly detains an Infant Girl born of the Body of the said Catherine. Ordered that the said Peter Brandon deliver the said Infant to the said William Anderson, it is also ordered to bring the said Infant before the next Court and that a Summons do issue to Cause the said Peter Brandon then to attend to Shew Cause wherefore he detains said Infant.

Ordered, that the Sheriff collect from every Tythable person within this County, the sum of three Shillings as County Levies, and that he account with the Treasury of the Common Wealth for the same.

(53) Ordered that the Sheriff pay John Campbell Gent out of the County Collection, the sum of Eleven Shillings and one penny for holding an Inquisition on the body of John Kelso.

Ordered that the Sheriff of this County pay John Bradley out of the County Collection the sum of four Shillings and two pence, for summoning an Inquisition on the body of John Kelso.

Ordered, that the Sheriff pay out of the County Collection to Richard Yeates, the sum of six pounds for laying two floors in a Goal formerly built for this district.[1]

Ordered that the Sheriff pay out of the County Collection to Dorsey Pentecost the sum of Sixty four Pounds ten Shillings and Six pence for Record Books, County Seal, and other papers for the Clerk's office of this County.

[1] Doubtless this "Goal formerly built for this district," was the jail on the late Wm. Gabby farm, at Augusta Town, about half a mile west of Washington.

Zadock Wright produced a commission from his Excellency appointing him Captain of the Militia which being read, the said Zadock Wright came into Court and took the Oath of Capt of the Militia.

The Ordinary Keepers within this County are allowed to sell at the following rates

one half pint wiskey.........One Shilling
The same into Tody.........One Shilling Six pence
A larger or lesser Quantity in the same proportion.
Beer per Quart.........One Shilling
For a hot Breakfast. ....One Shilling & Six pence
For a Cold Do.........One Shilling
For a Dinner.........Two Shillings
Lodging with Clean Sheets pr Night.........Six pence
Stablidge for one horse 24 hours
with good hay or fodder.........Two Shillings
Pasturage for Do.........do.........One Shilling
Oats or Corn per Quart.........Three pence
Supper.........One Shilling & Six pence

(54) Ordered that the above rates commence the fifteenth day of January next and not before.

Ordered that this Court be adjourned to tomorrow morning at 7 oClock WILLIAM GOE

The Court met according to Adjournment December 24th 1777.

Present: Isaac Cox, John McDowell, Richard Yeates, Benjamin Keykendal, Gent. Justices.

Ordered that the Clerk set up a Copy of the Rates of Sale for ordinary Keepers within the County at different public places so as to make it as public as possible.

William Goe and Oliver Miller Gent present

Attachment being obtained by John Campbell and Joseph Simon against the Estate of George Croghan for eight hundred and eighty eight pounds Pennsylvania Currency and the Sheriff of this County having returned that he had levied the said attachment in the hands of William Christy, Frederick Ferry, Geo Litenberger, Colo Archibald Steel, & David Duncan, and attached All the Effects in the hands of the said Garnishees,

and the said George Croghan being Solemnly Called and failing to appear to replevy what effects they have in their hands,
the said George Croghan and Robert Campbell factor for the
said John Campbell, and Joseph Simon Came into Court and
produced an account against the said George Croghan for
eight hundred and eighty-eight pounds, due upon Bonds for
the payment of four hundred and forty four Pounds Pennsyl-
(55) vania Currency which was proved by the said Robert Campbell. It is considered by the Court that the said John Campbell and Joseph Simon do recover Judgement against said
George Defendant for the sum of four hundred and forty four
Pounds Pennsylvania Currency of the Value of three hundred
and fifty five pounds and four Shillings Virginia Money, with
Interest from the 18th day of May 1775 untill paid and his
Cost about this Suit in that behalf expended.

Ordered that the said William Christy, Frederick Farrey, George Littenberger, Archibald Steel and David Duncan be summoned to attend the next Court, to shew what effects they have in their hands the property of said George Croghan and that the Sheriff make Sale for an towards Satisfaction of this Judgement and make Return thereof.

Mortgage from John Bowley to John Campbell Esqr bearing date the 14th day of November 1777 for a certain Quantity of Land &c on Shirteer's Creek was proved by the oath of Robert Campbell and Andrew Heath, two of the Subscribing Witnesses and ordered to be recorded.

Ordered, that the recommendation for Militia Officers of the 5th & 6th November last, by the Justices of this County, be confirmed as the Opinion of this Court, and they do hereby Confirm the proceedings of the said Justices respecting the Same, as the distressed Situation of this County demanded the particular attention of the said Justices at that time.

Ordered, that Gabriel Cox be recommended to his Excellency the Governor as a proper person to serve as Major of this County in the stead of Henry Taylor who has resigned his Commission.

Ordered that the Sheriff William Harrison retain in his
(56) hands the sum of Seventeen pounds Seven Shillings part of the
County Collection for Conveying John Millegan a Criminal
to the Public Goal and other contingencies.

Ordered that the Sheriff Collect from Joseph Ross the sum of Twenty Shillings which was adjudged his fine for swearing last April term.

Ordered that the Sheriff deliver Colo Isaac Cox the sum of Eighteen pounds to pay Paul Mathews due him as a Ballance for building the Court house and Goal.

Upon the motion of William Harrison, Gent, ordered that the Clerk issue a Summons to Call John Stephenson, Thomas Gist, Joseph Beeler and Edmund Rice before the Court, to testify and the truth say what they know respecting the marriage of Catherine Harrison with Isaac Mason, on the part of the said Catherine.[1]

Masterson Clark obtained Judgment against Joshua Baker for Thirty one pounds Pennsylvania Currency. John James Wood Constable returns he has attached a Black horse and one Cow, and the Sd Joshua failing to appear to replevy the said attached Effects the Plff produced a Note of hand against the said Joshua Defendant for Thirty one pounds Pennsa Currency with Credit on the Back for three pounds two Shillings and six pence like Currency. It is Considered by the Court that the said Masterson Plff recover against the said Joshua Deft the sum of Twenty two pounds Six Shillings Current Money and his Costs about this Suit expended. Ordered that the Sheriff make Sale of the Attached Effects or as much thereof as will be of value Sufficient to Satisfy this Judgment and make return to next Court.

(57) John Campbell and Joseph Simon obtained an Attachment against the Estate of Andrew Scott for four pounds Pennsylvania Currency, who is said to be so absconded that the Ordinary process of Law cannot be Served and the Sheriff having returned that he had levied the said attachment in the hands of Mathew Ritchey and the said Scott failing to appear and replevy though solemnly called and the said Campbell and Simon produced a proved account for the aforesaid four pounds Pennsa Currency, Ordered that the Sheriff make Sale of so much of the Estate of the said Andrew Scott, now in the hands of the said Garnishee as will be sufficient to Satisfy the said Plff for this Judgment of three pounds four Shillings and his Cost in this behalf expended.

[1] See the record of this matter made April 28, 1778, post.

David Ritchey and James Wright produced Commissions from his Excellency the Governor appointing them Captains of the Militia which being read as usual, the said David Ritchie and James Wright came into Court and took the Oaths of Captains of Militia.

John Lydea v Joseph Cox Case, Pl C.

Benjamin Jones v Patrick McDaniel Assault, P. C.

Paulser Shillings v Spencer Collens Trespass, P. C.

Dorsey Pentecost v Christopher McDonald Case, P. C.

Zachariah Connell v Abraham Vaughan Debt, P. C.

David Wilson v Henry Bowling Case, P. C.

John Spivy v Samuel Beeler Case, P. C.

Jno Gallaher & uxr v Christian Summet Slander, P. C.

John Smith v Sarah Dye Debt, Cont'd
Wm Harrison Special Bail.

Joseph Lindsey v Geo Long Debt, Al Cap

Thomas Gist v Henry Boyles Case. A. C.

— Same — v Richard Waller. Case, A. C.

Same v John Hall, Slander, A. C.

(58) Hugh Brady v Jacob Feagley Case, Al Cap.

Richd Swipicks v Jacob Jones, Case, A. C.

Paul Froman v Robert McCrowry Debt, A: C:

Francis Morrison v Daniel Swigart, Debt A: C:

Henry Martin v Sam Patterson & D. Rennels, Debt, A: C:

John Lawrence v Thos Rogers Case, A: C:

Charles Norris v Thomas Rouse Case, dismissed

George Sekley v John Ramage, Case, A: C:

Susannah Sekley v Robert McKinley Case. A: C:

Eli Williams v Philip Taylor Case, A: C:

Thos Freeman, Gent, v Jno James & Saml Lynch, Case, A: C:

Jacob Bausema v James Bradley Case, A: C

Elizabeth Burriss v Naomi Tampman Case, A: C:

Mary Burriss v Jno Johnson, M. Humble & Al, Case. A: C:

James Johnston v Godfrey Waggoner — Case, A: C:

Ordered that the Sheriff detain the Sum of six pounds out of the County Collection for his Public Services as by Law allowed.

Ordered that the Sheriff pay the Clerk of the Court the Sum of Six pounds for his Public Service as by Law allowed.

Ordered that the Court be adjourned till the Court in Course.

ISAAC COX.

At a Court continued and held for Yohogania County March 23d 1778.

Present: Isaac Cox, Joshua Wright Thomas Freeman, Benjamin Fry, Gentlemen Justices.

Ordered that Mary Mills be appointed Administratrix of John Mills deceased, she complying with the Law. Whereupon the said Mary Mills came into Court and took the Oath of Administratrix of the Estate of John Mills deceased.

Mary Mills with Joshua Wright and James McMahon came into Court and entered into Bond for her performance as Administratrix of the Estate of John Mills deceased.

Zacheriah Connell and Joshua Wright Gent Present.

Ordered that James Wright, John Wall and John Cox or any two of them being first sworn do appraise the estate of John Mills deceased and make return to this Court.

Ordered that Joseph Tomlinson be appointed administrator of the Estate of Saml Tomlinson deceased he complying with the Law. Whereupon the said Joseph Tomlinson, came into Court and took the Oath of Administrator of the Goods, Chattles and Credits of the deceased and Entered into Bond with John Wall and William Bruce his Securities.

Ordered that Isaac Williams, George Corn, and Robert Jackman or any two of them being first sworn do appraise such of the Estate of Saml Tomlinson deceased as may be found in this County, and that John Mitchell, David Shepeard, James Garri-
(60) son and Yeates Conwell, or any three of them, they being first sworn do appraise such of the said Estate as may be found in Ohio County and make Return to next Court.

Joseph Wherry
v
John White

Then Came the Plaintiff and James Patterson personally appeared in Court and undertook for the Defendant that in Case he Shall be Cast in this Suit he Shall pay and Satisfy the Condemnation of the

Court or render himself to prison in Execution for the same or he the said James Patterson will do it for him. Whereupon the said Defendant prays and has leave to imparl untill next Court and then to plead, &c

The last Will and Testament of John Vance deceased was proved by the Oaths of William Crawford and Samuel Hicks two of the Subscribing Witnesses and ordered to be recorded. Whereupon Margaret Vance and Edward Doyle came into Court and took the oath of Executor and Executrix of the Estate of the Said John deceased, and Entered into Bond accordingly.

Ordered that Edward Rice William McKee, Edmund Lindsey and James Blackson or any three of them they being first sworn do appraise the Estate of John Vance and make return to next Court.

Oliver Miller and William Crawford Gent Present.

John Stephenson Gent. named in the Commission of the peace came into Court and took the Oath of Justice of the peace, aforesaid.

Archibald Hall
v
Thomas Bonfield

Then came the Plaintiff, and Bazil Brown Personally appeared in Court and
(61) undertook for the Defendant that in Case he shall be cast in this suit he Shall pay and Satisfy the Condemnation of the Court or render his body to prison in Execution for the same, or he the said Bazil Brown would do it for him.

Whereupon the said Defendant prays and has leave to imparl untill nixt Court, when he is to plead, &c.

Joseph Cox
v
John Williams

Then came the Plaintiff, and Thos Bondfield personally appeard in Court and undertook for said Defendant that in Case he was cast in this suit, he should pay and Satisfy the Condemnation of the Court or render his Body to Prison in execution for the same, or the said Thomas Bondfield would do it for him. Whereupon the Defendant prays and has leave to imparl untill next Court when he is to plead

Joseph Cox
v
Theodore Davis

Then came the Plff, and Francis Hull personally appeard in Court and undertook for said Defendant that in Case he was Cast in this Suit he should pay and Satisfy the Condemnation of the Court or render his body to prison in execution for the same, or that he, the said Francis Hull would do it for him. Whereupon the said Defendant prays and has leave to imparl untill next Court when he is to plead.

Sale of the Estate of Garret Newgel deceased returned by the Administratrix and ordered to be recorded.

Thomas Freeman, Gent, produced a Commission from his Excellency the Governor, appointing him Captain of the Militia which being read, the said Thomas came into Court and took the Oath of Captain of the Militia.

Thomas Prather, Levingston Thomas, & Nicholas Christ, produced Commissions from his Excellency the Governor appointing them Lieutenants in the Militia of this County, which being read, the said Thomas Prather, Levingston Thomas, and Nicholas Christ came into Court and took the Oath of Lieutenants of Militia.

Luke Decker and John Johnson produced Commissions from his Excellency the Governor appointing them Ensigns in the Militia, for this County, which being read the said Luke Decker and John Johnson came into Court and took Oath of Ensigns of the Militia.

Thomas Cook
v
Levingston Thomas

Then came the Plaintiff, and John Wall personally appeared and undertook that in Case the Defendant shall be Cast in this Suit, he shall satisfy the Condemnation of the Court or render his Body to the Prison of this County in Execution of the same, or he the said John Wall will do it for him. Whereupon the said Defendant prays and has liberty to imparl untill next Court and then to plead.

John Decamp Gent named in the Commission of the peace came into Court and took the Oath of Justice of the peace.

Bargain and Sale from Samuel Heth to Patrick McElroy for 300 acres of Land, acknowledged by said Heath and ordered to be recorded.

Upon the Petition of John Rattan, Ordered that Peter Resner, George Berkhimer, Nicholas Christ and David Ritchie,
(63) view a Road, the nearest and the best way from the house of Edward Cook crossing the Monongahela river at the house of John Rattan to Zebulon Collins on the Road leading from Perkersons to Thos Egertons, they being first sworn and make Return to next Court.

Richard Yeates and Benj Kirkendal Gent. Present.

Upon the information of Joseph Beeler Gent. that a certain Samuel Wells and Johanna Farrow doth at this time and hath for some time past beat wounded and evilly treated Ann the wife of the aforesaid Samuel. Ordered that the Clerk issue a Subpona to Call the said Samuel Wells and Johana Farrow before the next Court to be held for this County to answer to the above charge and that Joseph Davis and Hannah his wife, John Crawford and Effee his wife, John Minter, Moses White, and Edmond Lindsey be subponed as Witnesses.

Ordered that the Court be adjourned to tomorrow morning at 7 oClock.

W. CRAWFORD.

March 24th 1778, the Court met pursuant to adjournment.

Present: John Campbell, Isaac Cox, Richard Yeates, Joshua Wright, Wm Crawford, Oliver Miller, Zacheriah Connell, John Decamp, Benjn Fry, Thos Freeman, Gentlemen Justices.

Lease Charles Norris to William Nation for two hundred acres of Land acknowledged by said Norris party thereto and ordered to be recorded.

The last Will and Testament of William Chaplin deceased was proved by Charles Bilderback and William Nation two of the subscribing Witnesses and Ordered to be recorded.

(64) Benj Kirkindal present.

Upon the motion of James Wherry in behalf of Joseph Wherry Plff against John White Deft Ordered that a Dedimus be issued to take the Examination of Thomas McDowell, Mathew Wilson, and William Wilson, Inhabitants of Cumberland County in the State of Pennsylvania without being directed to any Particular Majistrates of the Said County.

John Campbell Gentlemen objects to the above Order.

John Stephenson Gent present.

Upon motion of John Jackson, Ordered that his mark, a Crop and slit in the near Ear and under slit in the right Ear be recorded.

Upon motion of George Rowler, Ordered that his Mark, two Swallow forks in the left Ear and two half pennys in the Right be recorded.

Ordered that Lettice Griffeth be appointed Administratrix of the Estate of Edwd Griffeth deceased she complying with the Law. Whereupon the said Letice came into Court with John Wall and James Wright her Security and entered into bond and took the Oath accordingly.

Ordered that William Rice John Smith Nathaniel Brown and Henry Daniel do appraise all the Goods, Chattles and Credits of Edward Griffeth and make return to next Court.

James McGoldreck, being charged with pulling down and demolishing a Block house erected by Orders of General Hand for the preservation of the Inhabitants at Pittsburg, and the said James being brought into Court Confessed the Charge: Ordered, that the said James be held in One hundred pounds, with two Securities of fifty pounds each, for the appearance of the said James before the next Grand Jury Court, otherwise to remain in Custody by the Sheriff.

(65) John Campbell William Crawford John Decamp Jno McDowell, Benjamin Fry and Benjn Kirkindal Gent, Absent

George Vallandingham Gent, Present.

Bill of Sale. Susannah Nugent to Mordecai Richards proved by the Oaths of Michael Teggart, and Richard Richards, two of the Subscribing Witnesses and ordered to be recorded.

Richard Yeates Gent objects to this Order.

Bargain and Sale. Thomas Marshall to James Parker for a certain tract of Land on the waters of Chirteers. Acknowledged by said Marshall party thereto, and ordered to be recorded.

Bargain and Sale. William Poston to James Ellis for a Survey proved by the Oath of Benjamin Collins one of the

Subscribing witnesses. Ordered that a Dedimus do issue to take the Examination of Catherine Collins a Subscribing Witness to the above Bill of Sale.

Daniel Jacobs came into Court and took the Oath of Lieutenant of the Militia.

Michael Martain produced a Commission from his Excellency the Governor appointing him Lieutenant of Militia which being read as usual the said Michael came into Court and took the Oath of Lieut of the Militia.

Michael Martain enters himself Defendant in an Action of Ejectment at the Suit of the Lesse of John Washington, in the room of the Casual Ejector.

James McGoldreck with Michael Tygert and Robert Henderson his Suretys, the said James in the sum of £100 and the said Sureties in £50 each, for the appearance of the said James before the next Grand Jury Court.

Bargain and Sale James Roberts to Thomas Dickerson acknowledged by said Roberts and ordered to be recorded.

(66) Enoch Springer and Cornelius Manning being summoned as Garnishees at the Suit of William Dunnaighan against Benjamin Newgent came into Court and deposed that the said Springer hath four pounds two shillings Pennsylvania Currency, and the said Manning five pounds five shillings and nine Pence, like money and no more of the Estate of the said Benjamin.

View of a road from the Court house to Pittsburg, returned by Zadock Wright and Robert Henderson, viewers; passing by Zadock Wright's fields on Peters Creek, thence along the dividing Ridge passing the Widow Lapsleys, thence along the Old Road to Stewart's, thence along the old road to Jacob Bousman's; Ordered to be Confirmed.

Ordered that Zadock Wright be appointed Overseer of the Road from the Court house to Martha Lapsley's; Robert Henderson, Overseer of the Road from Martha Lapsley's to Jacob Judy's; and Sebastian Frederick, Overseer of the Road from Jacob Judy's to Jacob Bousman's; and that the Tythable Inhabitants within three miles on each side of said Road work on and keep it in repair together with the Inhabitants of the town of Pittsburg.

William Brashiers
v
Robert Hamilton

In Case. Then came the Plff, Robert Hamilton having been Called failed to appear. Then came a Jury to wit. Gabriel Cox John Hogland, James Wright, Nicholas Christ, Banjamin Vannatre, Jacob Bauseman, William Christy, Pearce Noland, Benjamin Collens, Patrick McElroy, Zadock Wright and David Ritchie, who say they find for Plff Two hundred pounds damages with Costs of Suit.

Bargain and Sale. Isaac Cox to John McDowell for one
(67) thousand Acres of Land in Kentucke County, acknowledged by the said Cox and ordered to be recorded.

William Goe Gent. Present.

Bargain and Sale. Isaac Cox to Garrat Vineman for five hundred acres of Land in Kentucke County, acknowledged by said Cox and ordered to be recorded.

Bill of Sale. John Campbell to Ignace Labat for a house and Lot in the town of Pittsburg, acknowledged by said Campbell and ordered to be recorded.

Elizabeth Burris
v
Nahomy Tapman

Then Came the Plaintiff, and John Lydia Personally appeared in Court and undertook for the Defendant that in Case he shall be cast in this Suit she shall Satisfy and pay the Condemnation of the Court or render her body to prison in Execution for the same or he the said John Lydia would do it for her. Whereupon the said Nahomy prays and has leave to imparl untill next Court and then to plead.

Mary Ferry and Samuel Ewalt are appointed Administrator and Administratrix of the Estate of Frederick Ferry deceased they complying with the law. Whereupon the said Samuel and Mary came into Court and took the Oath and Entered into Bond accordingly. Ordered that David Duncan, John Ormsby, and Willm Christy and John Anderson or any three of them being first sworn appraise the Estate of Frederick Ferry deceased and make Return to next Court.

John Lydia
v
Joseph Cox

Then came the Plff, and and John Douglass personally appeared in Court and undertook for

the Defendant that in Case he should be Cast in this Suit he should Satisfy & pay the Condemnation of the Court or surrender his body to the Prison in Execution for the same or that he the said John Douglass would do it for him. Whereupon
(68) the said Deft prays and has leave to impарl untill Next Court and then to plead.

James Murphy
v
Jacob Jones

Then came the Plff, and John Wall personally appeared in Court and undertook for the Defendant that in Case he Shall be Cast in this Action he shall Satisfy the Condemnation of the Court or render his body to prison in Execution for the same or that he the said John Wall will do it for him. Whereupon the said Defendant prays and has leave to imparl untill next Court and then to plead.

John Whitaker, a minister of the Gospel, came into Court and took the Oath of Allegience & fidelity, as directed by an act of General Assembly, intituled an Act to Oblige the free male Inhabitants of this State, above a certain Age, to give Assurance of Allegience to the same and for other purposes.

Bargain and Sale. Thomas Cook & Michael Thomas to John McMullen for three hundred and thirteen Acres of Land acknowledged by said Cook and Michael Thomas and ordered to be recorded.

Bargain and Sale. Thomas Egerton to John McDowell, proved by the Oath of Isaac Leet, James Bradford and James Allison and Ordered to be recorded.

The last Will and Testament of James Pearce decd was proved by the Oath of James Wall, Joseph Warner and Walter Wall, Subscribing Witnesses thereto and ordered to be recorded

Bazil Brown In Case
v
Robert Hamilton

Then Came the Plaintiff and then came also a Jury, to wit Gabriel Cox John Hogland, James Wright,
(69) Nicholas Christ, Benjamin Vannatre, Jacob Bousman, William Christy, Pearce Nowland, Patrick McElroy, Zadock Wright, David Ritchie and John Wall, who being sworn say they find for the Plff thirty pounds damages with Costs of Suit.

David Duncan a Garnishee in behalf of John Campbell against George Croghan, came into Court and says on Oath that he hath in his hands One hundred and Seventy nine Bushells and three pecks of Corn for which he has agreed to pay one Dollar per Bushell and no more of the Estate of the said George in his hands.

William Dunaughagain having obtained an Attachment against the Estate of Benjamin Nugent for three hundred and forty seven Pounds ten shillings Pennsylvania Money and the Sheriff having returned that he had levied the Said Attachment in the hands of Enoch Springer and Cornelius Manning and snmmoned them as Garnishees who this day came into Court and say that they have Nine pounds, fifteen Shillings and nine pence Pennsylvania Currency in their hands and no more of the Estate of the said Benjamin in their hands and the said Benjamin failing to appear and replevy the said Attached Effects tho Solemnly Called the said William produced a Bond against the said Benjamin for the aforesaid Sum of three hundred and forty seven pounds ten shillings Current Money of Pennsylvania. It is considered by the Court that the sd William recover against the said Benjamin the sum of two hundred and seventy eight pounds Current Money with Interest from the first day of October 1777 untill paid with Costs. Ordered that the Sheriff Collect the said money from the said Garnishees and pay it towards Satisfying this Judgment and make return of his proceeding to this Court.

Ordered that a Dedimus issue for the Examination of Eleanor Ackerson witness between John Lydia and Joseph Cox

(70) Ordered that Casper Sickler be allowed two days attendance as a Witness attending Court in the suit of William Brasheers v Robert Hamilton.

Ordered that Thomas Talbert be allowed twelve days as a witness in said Suit.

Ordered that a Dedimus issue for the Examination of John Crow a Witness in the Suit of Hugh Braudy against Jacob Feagley

Upon the motion of Thomas Applegate on behalf of Catherine Dablin now a Servant to the said Thomas that a certain Peter Brandon of the town of Pittsburg now unjustly detains an

Infant Girl born of the body of the said Catherine. Ordered that the said Peter Brandon deliver the said Infant Girl to the said Thomas Appelgate who is ordered to bring the Said Infant Girl here before the next Court to be held for this County.

Mathew Ritchey Gent Present.

Ordered that a Dedimus issue for the Examination of Casper Sickley a Witness in Behalf of William Brashiers against Robert Hamilton.

Upon Motion of Thomas Hamilton in behalf of Robert Hamilton praying a New Tryal and farther Hearing in the Suit of William Brashiers against Robert Hamilton. It is the Opinion of the Court that the Said Suit be reheard

William Brashiers
v
Robert Hamilton

Then came the Plaintiff, and personally appeared Thomas Hamilton and under took for the Defendant that in Case he shall be cast in this Suit he shall Sstisfy and pay the Condemnation of the Court or render his body to prison in Execution for the same or he the said
(71) Thomas would do it for him, Whereupon the Defendant prays and has leave to imparl till next Court and then to plead.

Ordered that the Court be adjourned to tomorrow morning 7 oClock.

JOHN CANON.

March 25th 1778 — The Court met Pursuant to adjournment.

Present: John Campbell, William Crawford, Richard Yeates, John Decamp, John Stephenson, Joshua Wright, John McDowell, Zacheriah Connell, Gentlemen Justices.

Upon the motion of Thomas Hamilton in behalf of Robert Hamilton praying a new Tryal and farther hearing of the suit of Bazil Brown it is the Opinion of the Court that the Said Suit be reheard.

Bazil Brown
v
Robert Hamilton

Then came the Plaintiff, and Thomas Hamilton personally appeared in Court and under took for the said Defendant that in Case he shall be cast in this Suit he shall pay and satisfy the Condemnation of the Court and Costs of Suit or render his body to prison in

Execution for the same or that he the said Thos Hamilton would do it for him. Whereupon the said Defendant prays and has leave to imparl untill next Court and then to plead.

Ordered that a Dedimus do issue to take the Examination of Casper Sickler a witness in behalf of Bazil Brown against Robert Hamilton.

Present: Isaac Cox, Wm Goe Oliver Miller Mathew Ritchey Saml Newell Thos Freeman, Benjn Kerkendal, John Cannon, & George Valandingham, Gent Justices.

(72) Ordered that John Stephenson and Isaac Cox be recommended as proper persons to serve as Colonels of the Militia, Joseph Beeler and George Valandingham as Lieutenant Colonels and William Harrison and Gabriel Cox as Majors of Militia.

William Christy came into Court being summoned as Garnishee in behalf of John Campbell and Joseph Simon against George Croghan ; being sworn, saith that he hath two pair of Geers, one old ax, one old Spade, one pitch Fork one small box of Iron and an old Lanthorn, and no more of the Estate of said George in his hands.

John Stephenson & Isaac Cox produced Commissions from his Excellency the Governor appointing them Colonels of the Militia which being read the said John and Isaac came into Court and took the Oath of Colonels of Militia.

John Campbell, William Crawford Zachy Connell, John Cannon, John Stephenson, John Decamp, Gent. absent.

Gabriel Cox produced a Commission from his Excellency the Governor, for appointing him Major of Militia, which being read the said Gabriel came into Court and swore into said Commission

George Vallandingham produced a Commission from the Governor appointing him Lieut. Colonel of the Militia, which being read the said George Vallandingham came into Court & Swore to his Commission

Charles Reed came into Court and produced a Commission from his Excellency the Governor appointing him Lieutenant of Militia, which being read the said Charles came into Court and Swore to said Commission.

David Lefergee produced a Commission from his Excellency
(73) the Governor appointing him Ensign of the Militia Whereupon the said David came into Court and Swore to his Commission.

Edmund Baxter produced a Commission from his Excellency the Governor appointing him Captain of the Militia. Whereupon the said Edmund came into Court and swore into his Commission.

Samuel Smith produced a Commission from his Excellency the Governor, which being read the said Samuel came into Court and Swore into his Commission.

Upon the Petition of Samuel Cook, setting forth that he is desirous of building a Water Mill on Brushy Run, a Branch of Chirteers Creek[1] and praying for an Order for the Condemnation of one acre of Land on the opposite side of said Run to said Cooks Land: Ordered that the Sheriff summon a Jury of Twelve Free holders of the Vicinage, to meet on the Said Land petitioned for and they being first sworn shall diligently view the said Lands and Lands adjacent thereto on both sides of the Run together with the Timber and other conveniences thereon, with the true value of the Acre, and of the damages done to the party holding the same, and report the same to the next Court under their hands and seals

Ordered that a Dedimus issue to take the Examination of Hatton Wells in behalf of Zacheriah Connell against Samuel Wells.

Oliver Miller Gent returned ten Shillings received from Thomas Pritchard & Philip Dougherty for swearing two profane Oaths Ordered that the Sheriff receive the said Money and account with the Court at the laying of the levy.

Bargain and Sale, from John Harry to Robert Henderson for a tract of Land acknowledged by the said Harry and ordered to be recorded.

John Greathouse is appointed Administrator of Daniel Great-
(74) house deceased he complying with the Law, Whereupon the said John Came into Court with Thos Cook and Samuel Smith his Securities, entered into Bond and Oath accordingly.

Ordered that Nathaniel Tomblinson Benjamin Tomblinson, John Baxter and Edmund Baxter or any three of them appraise the Estate of Daniel Greathouse deceased and make report to next Court.

[1] Can this be the Brush Run emptying into Chartiers Creek within a mile below Canonsburgh ?

Enoch Springer is appointed Administrator of the Estate of Lemuel Davis, he complying with the Law. Whereupon the said Enoch with John Springer his Security came into Court and entered into Bond and Oath accordingly

Ordered that Benjamin Reno, Christopher Miller Thomas Redman & Samuel Rice or any three of them, they being first sworn to appraise the Estate of Lemuel Davis deceased, and make report to next Court.

William Christy is appointed Administrator of the Estate of Francis Brown deceased, he complying with the Law. Whereupon the said Christy came into Court with Samuel Evalt his Security and entered into bond and oath accordingly

Ordered that Jacob Bousman, Samuel Evalt, David Duncan and John Ormsby or any three of them being first sworn to appraise all the goods Chattles and Credits of Francis Brown deceased and make Return to next Court.

On motion of Charles Reed, Ordered that his Mark a Crop in the left Ear and a Crop and Slit in the right Ear be recorded.

On Motion of John Hall, Ordered that his Mark, a slit in the left Ear and a Crop in the right Ear be recorded

(75) Upon Motion of Thomas Applegate, Ordered that his Mark a Crop and hole in the near Ear be recorded.

Thomas Gist
v
Richard Waller

Then came the Plff, and Isaac Pearce personally appeared in Court and undertook for the defendant that in Case he shall be cast in this Suit he shall pay and Satisfy the Condemnation of the Court or render his body to prison in Execution for the Same, or that he the said Isaac Pearce would do it for him. Whereupon the Defendant prays and has leave to imparl untill next Court and then to plead.

The Commonwealth
v
Jacob Shilling (a criminal) being charged with a dissafection to the Common Wealth.

Then came the Defendant, who pleads, Not Guilty: Whereupon Came a Jury, to wit: Patrick McElroy, Bazil Brown,

Benjamin Vanatre, John Custard, James Ellison, Pierce Noland, William Marshall, Sen; William Marshall Jun, John Munn, John Greathouse, Robert Henderson & John Morrison; who say that the Prisoner is Not Guilty.

Inventory of the Estate of Jeremiah Wood, deceased, returned by the appraisers & ordered to be recorded.

Thomas Gist
v
John Hall

Then came the Plaintiff, and Isaac Pearce personally appeared in Court and undertook for the Defendant, that in Case he shall be cast in this Suit he shall satisfy and pay the Condemnation of the Court or render his body to prison in Execution for the same or that he the said Isaac Pearce would do it for him. Whereupon the Defendant prays and has leave to imparl untill next Court and then to plead.

Charles Bilderback produced a Commission from his Excel-
(76) lency the Governor, appointing him Ensign of the Militia. Whereupon the said Charles came into Court and swore into said Commission.

Isaac Pearce produced a Commission from his Excellency the Governor appointing him Captain of the Militia. Whereupon the said Isaac Came into Court and Swore to said Commission

Josiah Springer produced a Commission from his Excellency the Governor appointing him Captain of the Militia. Whereupon the said Josiah came into Court and swore to said Commission.

George Redman produced a Commission from his Excellency the Governor, appointing him Lieutenant of Militia. Whereupon the Sd George came into Court and swore to said Commission.

Elijah Pearce produced a Commission from his Excellency the Governor, appointing him Lieutenant of Militia. Whereupon the said Elijah came into Court and Swore to said Commission.

Richard Waller produced a Commission from his Excellency the Governor, appointing him Lieutenant of Militia. Whereupon the said Richard came into Court and Swore to said Commission.

Ordered that a Bill of Indictment be preferred to the Grand Jury against John Nelson, for assalting John Johnston Constable in the Execution of his Office.

Ordered that a Bill of Indictment be preferred to the Grand Jury against Henry Newkirk Isaac Newkirk ——— Carter, John Williams John Hull Thomas Reed and Henry Hull, for refusing to assist the Constable in the Execution of his Office when assaulted in the same.

Bill of Sale. James Vanatre to Henry Morrison, proved by the Oaths of John Munn & John Morrison the two Subscribing witnesses and Ordered to be recorded.

(77)

Robert McKey

v

Moses Davison Case Ordered to be dismissed at the Plaintiffs Request.

Upon the motion of Thomas Cook, Ordered That he have leave to keep a Ordinary at his dwelling House the ensuing year, he complying with the Law.

On motion of Jacob Bousman Ordered that he have leave to keep an Ordinary at his Dwelling house, opposite the town of Pittsburgh, for the ensuing year, he complying with the Law.

Upon the motion of John Munn ordered that he have leave to keep an Ordinary at his Dwelling house, the ensuing year, he complying with the Law.

Jacob Shilling came into Court & Swore the peace against John Nelson, who is ordered to give Security for his peaceable deportment and good demeanor for one year, next ensuing, the said John Nelson held in fifty pounds, and Chrisley Crawbill his Security in fifty pounds.

Upon motion of William Christy Ordered that he have leave to keep an Ordinary at his Dwelling house in the town of Pittsburgh, the ensuing year, he complying with the Law.

Upon the motion of Josiah Snowden, Ordered that his mark a Crop and Slit in the left Ear and an Under an uper Slit in the right ear be recorded.

Ordered that Jonathan Rogers, Thomas Wilson, David Phillips William Nemons, George Gillespie John White Junr, Benjamin Wells, Moses Bradley, Nicholas Harrison, Jonathan

Philips, Bazil Weeks, John Hull and Benjamin Vanatre be appointed Constables the ensuing year and that they be summoned to next Court to qualify into said Office.

(78) William Bruce and Thomas Pollock produced Commissions from his Excellency the Governor which being read the said William and Thomas came into Court and swore to said Commissions.

Ordered that the Court be adjourned to tomorrow at 7 oClock.

JOHN CANON.

March 26th 1778, the Court met according to adjournment.

Present: John Cannon, Richard Yeates, Joshua Wright, Samuel Newell, William Crawford, Gentlemen Justices.

Upon the Petition of John Johnston; Ordered that Gabriel Cox, James Wright, Nathaniel Blackmore, and Paul Froman, or any three of them, they being first sworn view a road the nearest and the best way from the Court house to Pentecost's Mills[1] on Chirteers Creek and make Return to Next Court.

Benjamin Jones v Patrick McDonald, Assault. P. C.

Paulser Shilling v Spencer Collins, Trespass P. C.

Dorsey Pentecost

v

Christopher McDonald The Defendant being arrested and failing to appear, tho' Solemnly called, On motion of the Plaintiff It is ordered that unless the Defendant shall appear at the next Court and answer the plaintiffs Action that Judgment shall be then given against the said Defendant and his Appearance Bail for the Damages in the Declaration mentioned & Costs

(79) Zachariah Connell v Abraham Vaughan Debt P. C.

David Wilson v Henry Bowling Debt P. C.

John Spivy v Samuel Beeler. Trespass P. C.

John Gallaher & wife v Christian Sumitt Slander P. C.

Joseph Lindsey v George Lang Debt P. C.

Richard Swipicks v Jacob Jones. Case P. C.

Paul Froman v Robert McCrowdy Debt P. C.

Frances Morrison v Daniel Swigart Debt P. C.

Henry Martin v Samuel Patterson Debt — Agreed.

[1] Now, or late Beck's Mills, or Linden, North Strabane tp.

John Lawrence
v
Thomas Rogers The Defendant being arrested and failing to appear tho Solemnly Called, On Motion of the Plaintff It is Ordered that unless the Defendant shall appear at the next Court and answer the Plaintiffs Action that Judgment shall then be given against the said Defendant his appearance Bail for the Damages in the Declaration mentioned and Costs.

George Sekley v John Ramage Case, P. C.
Susannah Sekley v Robert McKindley Case, P. C.
Eli Williams v Philip Tabor Debt Agreed
Thomas Freeman v Jno James & Saml Lynch Case, P. C.
Jacob Bousman v John Bradley Case. P. C.

Mary Burris v John Johnston — Michael Humble — Abraham Jones — } Case P C

James Johnston v Godfrey Wagoner Case P. C.
Jacob Shilling v Henry Newkirk Case A. C.
Same v Same Debt A: C:
James Dunaghagan v James Gray Case A: C:
Paul Froman v John Dean Case A: C
Thomas Cook v Richard Dickerson Case A: C
William Thompson v John Fife Senr Assault A: C
James Miller v Jacob Peatt Case Agreed.

Francis Reno produced a Commission from his Excellency the Governor appointing him Lieutenant of the Militia which being read the said Francis Came into Court and swore into said Commission

(80) Maybary Evans produced a Commission from his Excellency the Governor appointing him Captain of the Militia which being read, the said Maybury came into Court and Swore to his Commission

George Waddle produced a Commission from his Excellency the Governor, appointing him Ensign of the Militia which being read the said George came into Court and Swore to his Commission.

Joseph Vance and David Cox produced Commissions from his Excellency the Governor appointing them Lieutenants in the Militia which being read the said Joseph and David came into Court and Swore to said Commissions.

Ordered, that the Wife of Robert Crawford a poor Soldier now in the Continental service, be allowed the sum of four pounds per month for the support of herself and three Children; and that this Court do draw on the Treasurer of this Common Wealth for the same.

Ordered, that Sarah Stewart, the wife of ——— Stewart, a poor soldier in the Continental service, be allowed the sum of three pounds per month, for the support of herself and two Children, to commence the 25th day of January last, and that this Court do draw on the Treasurer of this Common Wealth for the same.

Ordered that Colo John Campbell pay unto Richard Yeates Gent. the money now in his hands allowed to Mrs Nox for her and Childrens Support by a former Order of this Court and this Court and the said Mr. Yeates is requested to deliver the said money to said Mrs Nox.

(81) Ordered that Colo John Campbell pay to Benjamin Fry Gentleman the money now in his hand allowed the wives of William and Abraham Ritchey for their and Children's Support by a former Order of this Court and the said Fry is requested to pay said money to said women.

Joshua Wright, Gent, absent.

John Campbell produced an Indenture from John Milligan and Martha Milligan, binding Wm Milligan to Robert Campbell untill he arrives to the age of Twenty one years and prays the Consent of the Court to said Indenture which is accordingly consented to.

Ordered that John Minter, Maybery Evans, Nathan Ellis, Edward Kemp, Josiah Record, and James Scott be recommended to his Excellency as proper persons to serve as Captains of Militia and John Mason, James Hopkins Samuel Newell, John Chamberline Willm McCarmick Richard Crooks Nathl Blackmore Francis Reno, Robert Henderson, Thomas Lapsley, Willm Everard George Long Thomas Reed John White Junr & James Wherry as Lieutenants of Militia and Robert Newell, Michael Tygert Lewis Reno, George Wadale George Christ, Isaac McMichael William Murley, Edmund Riggs Samuel Johnston & Samuel Alexander as Ensigns of Militia.

Josiah Records produced a Commission from his Excellency the Governor appointing him Captain of the Militia which was read and sworn to accordingly.

(82) George Long produced a Commission from his Excellency the Governor appointing him Lieutenant of Militia which was read and sworn to accordingly.

Samuel Newell produced a Commission from his Excellency the Governor appointing him Lieutenant of Militia which was read and sworn to accordingly.

Upon the Motion of Zadock Wright Ordered that his Mark an under bit in the right ear and crop and slit in the left ear be recorded.

Ordered that the Effects of George Croghan in the hands of David Duncan and William Christy by them returned as Garnishees at the Suit of John Campbell and Joseph Simon against said Croghan be secured by the Sheriff for further proceedings thereof, and that an attachment issue against George Lightenberger who was summoned Garnishee in behalf of the Plaintiffs in said Suit and failed to appear to declare how much and what of the Estate of the said George was in his hands.

Ordered that the Court be adjourned to the Court in Course.

W. CRAWFORD.

(*To be continued.*)

MINUTE BOOK OF VIRGINIA COURT HELD FOR YOHOGANIA COUNTY, FIRST AT AUGUSTA TOWN (NOW WASHINGTON, PA.), AND AFTERWARDS ON THE ANDREW HEATH FARM NEAR WEST ELIZABETH; 1776–1780.[1]

EDITED BY BOYD CRUMRINE, OF WASHINGTON, PA.

INTRODUCTORY.

It will have been observed that the organization of the Virginia court at Fort Dunmore (now Pittsburgh) for the District of West Augusta, was on February 21, 1775: Vol. I., p. 525, of these *Annals;* that the last sessions of that court were held at Augusta Town (or Catfish Camp, now Washington), on November 20, 1776: *Idem*, p. 568; that in the meantime the Monongahela Declaration of Independence had been promulgated at two points in the Monongahela Valley, on the same day, to wit, May 16, 1775, more than one year antedating the Declaration of Independence read to the assembled people from the southern front of the State House at Philadelphia, on July 4, 1776: *Idem*, p. 519; and that in October, 1776, the legislature of Virginia, now a sovereign state of the new American confederation, divided the District of West Augusta into three new counties, Ohio, Yohogania and Monongalia, all shown, with reasonable accuracy, as it is believed, on the map in Vol. I. of these *Annals*, facing p. 518.

The sessions of the court for Yohogania County were held first at Augusta Town (Catfish Camp, now Washington) from December 23, 1776, until August 25, 1777: these *Annals*, Vol. II., p. 91: and from the latter date until the Virginia jurisdiction was wholly ousted, on the farm of Andrew Heath (then in old Washington County), West of the Monongahela River, and near the present dividing line between Washington and Allegheny counties. A portion of the Order Book (usually called the Minute Book in our courts) of the Yohogania

[1] Continued from pp. 71–140, this volume.

County court has already been given, and the following is a continuation thereof.

WHAT WAS PENNSYLVANIA DOING?

It has already been noted, perhaps, that a large amount of business of almost every nature and kind was transacted in these Virginia courts, and it would appear that a large majority of the inhabitants of the Monongahela Valley submitted their persons and property to the laws and courts of Virginia; indeed, it is undoubted that many landholders under Pennsylvania titles, and perhaps Pennsylvania sympathy, were suitors in these courts. Why was this? Doubtless it was because, the Revolution being on, and other causes existing, the power of the laws of Pennsylvania was not strongly felt west of the Allegheny Mountains.

Note the following facts:

Bedford County, the seventh Pennsylvania county established, was formed from Cumberland County, on March 9, 1771, and extended "Westward to the Western Boundaries of the Province," which boundaries, however, were not defined. The first term of court for that county was held at Bedford, about a hundred miles east of Pittsburgh, on April 16, 1771, and George Wilson, Esq., living near the mouth of George's Creek in what is now southern Fayette County, was of the justices, as were also Colonel (then Captain) William Crawford, living on the Youghiogheny River nearly opposite what is now Connellsville, Fayette County, Thomas Gist, son of Christopher Gist, settled near Mount Braddock in the same county, and Dorsey Pentecost, then living on his "plantation" called "Greenaway" in the "Forks of the Yough" settlement.

Now, Westmoreland County, Pennsylvania, was formed on January 26, 1773, from Bedford County, and embraced all the lands west of "the Laurel Hill," to "the limits of the Province." Old Westmoreland was thus organized two years before the Virginia Court at Fort Dunmore, and its first Court of Quarter Sessions, then the principal court of every county, was held at Hanna's Town, about three miles northeast of what is now Greensburg, on April 6, 1773. This Court of Quarter Sessions was the first court of justice ever held by English-speaking people west of the Allegheny Mountains, and it was held "Before William Crawford, Esq., and his associate Justices."

On January 25, 1775, about one month before the organization of the Virginia court at Fort Dunmore, the following entry was made upon the minutes of the Supreme Executive Council:

"At a Council held at Philadelphia, 25th January, 1775, . . . Captain St. Clair appearing at the Board and representing that William Crawford, Esquire, President of the Court in Westmoreland County, hath lately joined with the Government of Virginia in opposing the jurisdiction of Pennsylvania in the County, the Board advised the Governor to supersede him in his office as Justice of the Peace and common Pleas. A Supersedeas was accordingly ordered to be issued:" *X. Col. Records*, 228.

Others of the Justices of the Westmoreland County court were Arthur St. Clair, afterward a Major-general in the Revolution; Thomas Gist, above mentioned, Alexander McKee, afterwards with Simon Girty and Matthew Elliot, a deserter to the British Indians; Robert Hanna, William Louchry, George Wilson, above mentioned, Eneas McKay, Joseph Spear, Alexander McClean and James Caveat.

The early courts of Westmoreland County appear by their records to have been regularly held from April 6, 1773, to the second Tuesday of April, 1776. Observe that this last date was but a short time before the meeting of the Provincial Conference at Carpenter's Hall, Philadelphia, resulting in the great Declaration of Independence by the American colonies. At this session there were orders made relating to township lines, roads, and recognizances in criminal cases; and then there was an interregnum, and there are no records of any court held for Westmoreland County afterward until January 6, 1778. But the court for Yohogania County continued right along in a varied and extensive business, as will appear from the transcript of its records now publishing.

THE NATURE OF THE BUSINESS TRANSACTED.

It would seem that the transactions of these Virginia Courts were not confined to merely business matters. Witness the fact that at the session of the Yohogania County court held on September 22, 1777, "William Taylor produced a Licence appointing him to preach the Gospel after the Manner of his Sect; which being read, the said William Taylor came [—into Court and took the Oath of fidelity and Allegiance to this Commonwealth:" *Annals*, Vol. II., p. 102. Who was this William Taylor, and what was his "Sect"? And note that at the session of the same Court held on March 24, 1778, "John

Whitaker, a minister of the Gospel, came into Court and took the Oath of Allegiance and fidelty, as directed by an act of General Assembly, intitled an Act to Oblige the free male inhabitants of this State, above a certain Age, to give Assurance of Allegiance to the same and for other purposes:" These *Annals*, Vol. II., p. 129. Was this the eccentric Deacon Whiteakre who once prayed publicly to God, before his Methodist congregation, that he might be supplied with a new horse and soon received one?

Attention is called also to the records made in relation to the care of the families of soldiers from the Monongahela Valley in the War of the Revolution. These records are frequent but exasperatingly brief.

Our Pennsylvania histories show that at least two Pennsylvania regiments, fully organized, marched eastward to take part in the battles of the Revolution, but the records now published disclose that at least three regiments, organized as Virginia Voluntaries, the 5th, 12th and 13th Regiments, were composed more or less of men living in the Valley of the Monongahela. Verily the Revolutionary history of that valley is as yet unwritten.

The Early Currency.

We find in these records that the currency of the early days was in Pounds, Shillings, and Pence. And it will be noted that in the early causes in these courts, a recognizance of bail for an appearance at court was required in say £25, or in £100; while in 1780, at the end of the existence of this court in Pennsylvania, some such recognizances were in £5,000 or more, amounting, as we would now translate the English £, to about $25,000. Wherefore, an explanatory note on this early currency and its depreciation may not be out of place.

Before and during the Articles of Confederation of 1776, and until the adoption of the Constitution of the United States in 1787, there was no supreme national authority, and therefore no national currency based upon a recognized unit. In every State there were at least two units of value, the State pound and the Spanish milled dollar. Our people having been under the English government adopted the English pound, shilling, and penny, as the *name* of its currency or money of account, yet the trade with the Spanish colonies in America and the West Indies brought into the country as its only coined money the Spanish dollar and its subdivisions. Thus the Dollar of the early day was not the "Dollar of our Daddies," but the "Spanish Milled Dollar."

But each state in the thirteen composing the confederacy had its own pound. In Georgia, the pound in silver contained 1547 grains; in Virginia, Massachusetts, Rhode Island, Connecticut and New Hampshire, 1289 grains; in New Jersey, Delaware, Pennsylvania and Maryland, 1031¼ grains, while in New York and North Carolina it reached the minimum of 996 grains. These State pounds, and their divisions into shillings and pence, had no actual existence; they were used only in keeping accounts, but when debts were to be paid and received they were turned into dollars and their divisions, halves, quarters, eighths, and sixteenths, each represented by a silver coin. Thus it was that in New England and Virginia, six shillings, or seventy-two pence, made a dollar; in New York and North Carolina eight shillings, or ninety-six pence; in New Jersey, Pennsylvania, Delaware and Maryland, seven shillings and six pence, or ninety pence, and in South Carolina and Georgia four shillings and eight pence, or fifty-six pence. And hence, though accounts were kept in pounds, shillings, and pence in all the states, yet to pay or receive a debt in the coin dollars in circulation, eight shillings were required in New York, for instance, six shillings in Virginia and seven shillings and six pence in Pennsylvania. See McMaster's "History of the People of the U. S.," Vol. I., p. 23.

Observe: If 7s. 6d. in Pennsylvania currency made one dollar (Spanish) then 20 shillings (or one pound) would be worth $2.66⅔, a little more than one half the English pound sterling. And if six shillings in Virginia currency made a dollar, then the Virginia pound was worth $3.33.

"Fifty years ago the silver pieces which passed from hand to hand under the name of small change was largely made up of foreign coins. They had been in circulation long before the War for Independence, had seen much service and were none the better for the wear and tear they had sustained. The two commonest were the eighth and the sixteenth of the Spanish milled dollar, and these, taking the country through, passed under seven names. In New York and North Carolina, where eight shillings made a dollar, the eighth was a shilling (twelve pence), and went by that name. From New Jersey to Maryland (including Pennsylvania) the same coin was nearly equaled by eleven pence, and was there called the eleven-penny bit, or the levy, but became for a like reason nine pence in New England. In the same way the sixteenth of a dollar was called six-pence in New York;

five-penny bit or the fip in Pennsylvania, and four-pence in New England (and Virginia): McMaster's History, Vol. I., p. 189.

Now, as to the depreciation of this early currency:

It will be remembered, as already stated, that prior to the adoption of the Constitution of the United States in 1787, no paper money or currency was issued either by the United Colonies, or by any of the colonies separately, payable in their own coin, for they had none. True, the confederacy, and as well some of the colonies or separate states, perhaps, sometimes issued notes or bills of credit payable in "dollars" or parts thereof, but the coin meant was the Spanish coin. Usually, however, notes and bonds were issued payable in pounds, shillings, and pence, but, there being no pounds, shillings, and pence existing in coin, when debts were to be paid in coin the pounds, etc., were turned into dollars and their subdivisions, and all accounts were kept in pounds, shillings, and pence. Hence, the constant issue by the United Colonies during the War of the Revolution of paper money irredeemable according to its terms, resulted in an immense depreciation, which was one of the greatest sources of evil to the young nation.

The extent and the causes of this depreciation of the currency during the Revolution is best shown by the paper of Albert Gallatin on "The Currency and Banking System of the United States," first published in 1831, and contained in "The Writings of Albert Gallatin," edited by Henry Adams, Vol. III., p. 260, as follows:

"The paper money issued by Congress during the war of the American independence experienced no sensible depreciation before the year 1776, and so long as the amount did not exceed nine millions of dollars. A paper currency equal in value to that sum in gold or silver could therefore be sustained so long as confidence was preserved. The issues were gradually increased during the ensuing years, and in April, 1778, amounted to thirty millions. A depreciation was the natural consequence; but had the value of the paper depended solely on its amount, the whole quantity in circulation would have still been equal in value to nine millions, and the depreciation should not have been more than 3⅓ to 1; instead of which it was then at the rate of six dollars in paper for one silver dollar, and the whole amount of the paper in circulation was worth only five millions in silver. It is obvious that the difference was due to lessened confidence. The capture of Burgoyne's army was followed by the alliance with France, and her becoming a party to the war against England. The result of the war was no longer considered as doubtful, and sanguine expectations were formed of its speedy termination. The paper accordingly rose in value; and in June, 1778, although the issues had been increased to more than forty-five millions, the depreciation was at the rate of only four to one. From the end of April of that year to the month of February, 1779, although the issues had been increased from thirty-five to one hundred and fifteen millions, the average value in silver of the whole amount of paper in circulation exceeded ten millions, and it was at one time nearly thirteen millions, or considerably more than that which could be sustained at the outset of the hostilities. But when it was discovered that the war would be of longer continuance, confidence in the redemption of a paper money, daily increasing in amount, was again suddenly lessened. The depreciation increased from the rate of 6 to that of 30 to 1 in nine months. The average value in silver of the whole amount of paper in circulation from April to September, 1779, was about six millions, and it sunk below five during the end of the year. The total amount of the paper was at that time two hundred millions; and although no further issues took place, and a portion was absorbed by the loan offices and by taxes, the depreciation still increased, and was at the end of the year 1780 at the rate of 80 dollars in paper to 1 in silver. The value in silver of the paper currency was then less than two millions and a half of dollars; and when Congress, in March following, acknowledged the depreciation, and offered to exchange the old for new paper at the rate of 40 for 1, the old sunk in one day to nothing, and the new shared the same fate."

These observations will explain many entries in the records now following that would otherwise be somewhat unintelligible:

VOLUME II. OF THE RECORDS.

(1) At a Court Continued and held for Yohogania County, April 27th, 1778.

Present: William Crawford, John Stephenson, Joshua Wright & Isaac Cox, Gentlemen Justices present.

View of the road from the Court House to Pentecost's Mills on Churteers Creek returned by the Viewers and Ordered to be confirmed, Running from said Court House to Spencer's point, Thence near Richardson's School House, Thence through Gabriel Coxes Lane, Thence crossing Peters Creek near to

John Coxe's — Benjaman Colling's, Thence to Joshua Wright's, Thence to William Stephenson's, Thence to Thomas Cooks, Thence to said mills. Ordered that Gabriel Cox be appointed Overseer of the Road from the Court House to Peters Creek near John Coxe's, James Wright Overseer of the Road from Peters Creek near John Coxes to opposite Henry Johnstons, and Nathaniel Blackmore Overseer of the road from Henry Johnstons to Pentecosts Mills on Churteers Creek and that the Tithables within three miles of said road (except on the East Side of the Monaungohela River) work on Cut open and keep said road in repair.

John McDowell and John Cannon Gentlemen Justices Present.

Upon the Complaint of Cornelias Crow an Indented Servant that John Harry his Late Master lately told said Servant that he had Sold him to a Certain Thomas Cuningham to be forced into the Armies of the United States as a Soldier, and that he has for some Time and doth at this Time suffer for Necessary Cloathing, and uppon the view of the Court the Complaint respecting the Cloathing is justly founded.

Ordered that the sd Cornelias Crow be and remain a Servant, and that the said John Harry or Thomas Cunningham that claims property in said Servant be and appear before the next Court held for this County to Answer the Complaint of said Cornelias Crow.

(2) Robert McGlaughlin and James McLean produced commissions from his Excellency the Governor appointing them Lieutenants of the Militia which being read, the said Robert and James came into Court and swore into said Office.

Ordered that this Court be adjourned untill Tomorrow Morning 8 O Clock. W. CRAWFORD.

April 28th Court met according to adjournment.

Present, Isaac Cox, John Cannon, William Goe, Andrew Swearengen, John McDowell, and George McCarmick, Gentlemen Justices, Present.

Andrew Swearengen and David Andrew produced Commissions from his Excellency the Governor appointing Them Captains of the Militia, which being read, the said David and Andrew came into Coart and Swore into said Commissions.

Nathaniel Blackmore came into Court produced a Commission appointing him a Lieutenant of the Militia, which was read and Sworn to accordingly.

[Bill of sale from John Stueart to Jacob Bouseman for Three Hundred Acres.][1]

Power of Attorney John Stueart to Jacob Bouseman be as proved by the Oath of John McCollister, one of the Subscribing Witnesses.

Mortgage John Stueart to Jacob Bouseman for Three Hundred Acres of Land on Yohogania River was proved by the Oath of Jacob Leoport, one of the Subscribing Witnesses.

(3) Upon the motion of Jacob Bouseman ordered that his Mark Two Crops and Two Slits be recorded.

Thomas Gist came into Court and being Sworn on the Holy evangelist of Almighty God, Sayeth that in the year of our Lord one Thousand Seven Hundred and Seventy two, in the month of April to the best of his recollection, in the presence of Joseph Beeler, John Stephenson and Edward Rice, he Solemnized the wrights of Matromony between Isaac Meason and Catherine Harrison, according to the rights and ceremonies of the Church of England, he the s[d] Seponent then being a Majistrate in the State of Pennsylvania, and that he was under an Oath not to Devulge said marriage Except Legally called for that purpose.

John Stephenson and Joseph Beeler came into Court and being Sworn on the Holy Evangelist of Almighty God, Sayeth that they ware present at the Marriage of Isaac Meason with Catherine Harrison in the year one Thousand Seven Hundred and Seventy two in the Month of April to the best of their recollection, and was under a promise not to devulge the said Marriage Unless Legally called, or Death of either of the parties, and the said Joseph farther Sayeth that there was a preëngagement between the said Isaac and Catherine that upon the devulging the said Marriage contrary to the will of the sd Isaac then that said parties should be absolved from any obligation to each other as man and wife.

Indenture from Martha Daviss to Isaac Cox acknowledged by said Martha and ordered to be Recorded.

[1] The part in brackets erased in the original.

Bargain and Sale Thomas Bay to James Marshall for four Hundred Acres of Land acknowledged by said Bay and Ordered to be Recorded.

Bargain and Sale Thomas Bay to George Marken [or Marten, *Editor*] for Two Hundred Acres of Land acknowledged by said Bay and Ordered to be recorded.

(4) Bargain and Sale Ezekiel Johnston to Joseph Beeler Jun[r] proved by the oath of Dorsey Pentecost and Joseph Beeler Sen[r] two of the Subscribing Witnesses.

Joseph Beeler produced to this Court a Commission from his Excellency the Governour appointing him Colonel of the Militia was red & Sworn to in open Coart.

Nathan Ellis produced to this Coart a Commission from his Excellency the Governour appointing him Captain of the Militia which was red & Sworn to in open Coart.

W[m] Harrison took the oath of Major of the Militia in open Coart.

Richard Crooks took the oath of Lieutenant of the Militia in open Coart.

Michael Tigert took the oath of Ensign of the Militia in open Coart.

Ordered that Sarah Shirly be admitted to administer on the estate of James Shirly Deceased, she Complying with the Law, Whereupon the sd. Sarah came into Coart with her Securities & entered into Bond accordingly.

Ordered that Ignatius Lebat Sam'l Sample Sam'l Evalt & David Dunkin or any three of them Being first sworn do appraise the s[d] Estate & make Report to next Coart.

James Gray Enters himself special Bail in a suit wherein Jno. Pearce is plaintiff & Jno. Raredon Defendant.

Jno. Raredon Enters himself special Bail in Case wherein W[m] Danningin is plaintiff & and James Gray Defendant.

Ordered that Mary Lindsey the wife of William Lindsey a poor Soldier in the Continental service be allowed Six pounds per month for the support of herself and Six children to commence the first day of January Last.

Ordered that Eloner Lindsey the wife of Ezekial Lindsey be allowed the sum of five pounds pr. month for the support of herself and five children.

(5) Ordered that Jane Dunn the wife of Thomas Dunn a poor Soldier in the Continental Service be allowed the sum of four pounds pr month for the support of herself and four children.

Ordered that two children of Peter McCorkeys a soldier in the Continental Service be allowed the sum of two pounds pr month for their Subsistence.

Ordered that Elizabeth Depugh the wife of John Depugh be allowed the sum of three pounds pr Month for the support of herself and Three Children.

Ordered that the wife of Jeremiah McCarty be allowed the sum of three pounds pr Month for the support of herself and three children.

Ordered that the wife of William Nau a poor Soldier who died in the Continental Service be allowed the sum of six pounds pr month for herself and Six children to commence the first day of January until his Death.

Ordered that the wife of James Behan be allowed the sum of three pounds pr month for the support of herself and three children.

Ordered that the sum of two pounds pr month be allowed the wife of Richard Wade for the support of herself and two children to Commence the first day of this month.

Ordered that the wife of David Smith be allowed the Sum of three pounds for the support of herself and three children.

Ordered that Susannah Decompt and Christopher Hayes be appointed Administrator and Administratrix of the Estate of John Decomp Deceased they complying with the Law. Whereupon the said Susannah and Christopher came into Court and Entered into Bond oath accordingly.

Ordered that Joseph Beeler, James Blackstone, Edward Cook, and Benjamin Davis or any three of them they being first sworn do appraise the Estate of John Decomp Deceased and make return to next Court.

(6) Daniel Brooks is appointed Administrator of the Estate of Nathan Hammond Deceased he complying with the Law, Whereupon the said Daniel came into court entered into Bond and oath accordingly. Ordered that Joseph Parkerson, Thomas Parkerson, James Innis & David Richie any three of them

they being first sworn do appraise the Estate of Nathan Hammon Deceased and make return to next Court.

Ordered that Isaac Cox be appointed Administrator of the Estate of Samuel Richardson deceased he complying with the Law, whereupon the said Isaac came into Court and intered into Bond and oath accordingly. Ordered that Abraham Vannatree, Edmund Pollack, Richard Elson and Edward Wiggins or any three of them they being first sworn do appraise the Estate of Samuel Richardson, Deceased and make return to next Court.

Bargain and Sale John Pearce to James Patterson for three Hundred and Eighteen Acres of Land Acknowledged by the said Pearce and Ordered to be Recorded.

Ordered that George McCarmeck John Cannon & John Stephenson Gent. be recommended to his Excellency the Governor as proper persons to serve as Sheriff for this County, the Ensuing year.

Ordered that an Attachment Issue against Philip Whitsel and the papers and records belonging to the District of West Augusta, which by Act of Assembly are to be Inyrold amongst the Records of this County, and the said records so attached have before this Court for farther Proceedings.

Bargain and Sale Matthew Rogers to John White for an Improvement of Land on Churteers Creek Acknowledged by said Rogers and Ordered to be Recorded.

(8)[1] Ordered that Court be adjourned Until Tomorrow Morning 8 oClock. JOHN CANON.

Court met according to adjournment April 29th, 1778.

Present William Goe, Isaac Cox, Andrew Swearengen & Joshua Wright Gentlemen Present.

George McCarmick [2] is appointed Sheriff Protempore to serve one month he complying with the Law. Whereupon the said George with Samuel Beeler and Dorsey Pentecost his Securities come into Court entered into Bond and oath accordingly.

Ordered that Benjaman Collins have Leave to keep a publick Ordinary at his Dwiling House he complying with the Law.

[1] Paging of original followed, though erroneous.

[2] This name erased in the original.

Whereupon the said Benjaman came into Court entered in Bond accordingly.

Appraisement of the Estate of Job. Robins returned by the Appraisers and ordered to be recorded.

Benjamin Custard and John Wall Enter Special Bail for Michael Humble and John Johnston at the suit of Mary Burriss.

Upon the motion of John Wall ordered that his Mark a Crop in the right Ear and a hole in the Left be recorded.

Upon the motion of George McCarmick his mark a Crop in the right Ear and half Crop in the Left ordered to be recorded.

Upon the Motion of Benjaman Custard his mark a Cropt and slit in the right Ear and a Slit in the Left Ordered to be recorded.

The Ear mark of Thomas Cherry a crop in the right Ear ordered to be recorded.

(9) Samuel Newell, Gentleman Present.

Samuel Beeler being bound in recognizance and charged with Hogstealing which being called personally appeared and pleads not guilty. Ordered to be continued at Defendant's Request.

Benjaman Jones vs. Patrick McDonald. Plu. Cap.

Paulser Shilling vs. Spencer Collins. Tresp. Plu. Cap.

Ordered that a Dedimus Issue to Take the Examination Anne Taylor and Margaret Conner, a witness In behalf of Joseph Cox against John Williams, Theodorus Davis, and Mary Hazle.

Dorsey Pentecost vs Christopher McDonald In. Cas. Contd.

Zachariah Connell vs Abraham Vaughan In Debt. Plu. Cap.

David Wilson vs Henry Bowling In Debt. Plu. Cap.

John Livy vs Samuel Beeler I. Tresp. P. Cap.

John Gallehar vs Christian Summet In Slan. P. Cap.

Hugh Sterling came into Court and Took the Oath of a Deputy Sheriff.

Joseph Lindsey against George Long In Debt Plu Cap.

Richard Swissichs agt. Jacob Jones In Case. Plu. Cap.

Paul Froman against Robert McCrowry In Debt Plu Cap.

Francis Morrison agt. Daniel Swigert In Debt Plu. Cap.

George Schley against John Rammage In Case Plu. Cap.

Susannah Schley against Robert McKendley In Case Plu. Cap.

Thomas Freeman agt. John Jones and Samuel Lyneet In Case Plu Cap.

Jacob Bouseman agt. James Bradley In Case Plu. Cap.

Mary Burriss agt Michael Humble & John Johnston In Case Sp. B.

Jacob Johnston against Godfrey Waggonier In Case Plu. Cap.

Jacob Shillings against Henry Newkirk In Case Plu. Cap.

The Same against the same In Debt. Plu Cap.

William Dunnanghgain against James Gray In Debt Sp. Bail.

Paul Froman against John Dean In Case Plu. Cap.

Thomas Cook against Richard Dickerson In Case. Plu Cap.

John Pearce Sen. against Aron Carter In Case Al. Cap.

Thomas Wells against Paulcer Shillings In Case A Cap.

(10) James Murphy

against In Case

Jacob Jones Then came the parties and then also came a Jury To wit. James Wright, John Wall, Benjaman Custard, Benjaman Collings, Robert Craighead, David McKee, Enoch Springer, Michael Humble, Matthew Rogers, Joseph Cox, Patrick Jourden & John Johnston, who find for the plaintiff L 16. 15 6. & Costs.

David McClure

against In Debt.

Patrick McElroy, Assine. Upon the motion of the Plaintiff Judgmt was Confesed by the Difind in a letter to the clerk. It is Considered by the Court That the plantiff recover against the Defendant upon Bond Eighty pounds with Interest from the Sixth day of April 1777, untill paid and his Costs.

John Brown against John Crow. In Asst. Dismd. at Plantiffs Request.

John Pearce Senr. against John Reredon. Slep. Bail.

Joseph Pearce against Arnold Evins Al Cap.

Andrew Swearingen

against In Case

Robert Hamelton Ordered to be Dismissed at Plantiff's request, Defendant paying Costs.

Andrew Steel against Joeseph Ralston. In Case Al Cap.

William Braden against James Vannatree In Case Al Cap.

Obidiah Stout against Thomas Thompson and wife In Slan. Al Cap.

Richard McMahan against James Bruce In Case Agreed.

William Thompson against John Fife Sen. In Asst. Plu Cap.

Cloe Riggs against Ebenezer Corn In Case Al Cap.

Moses Thompson agt William Carpenter In Debt. Al Cap.

Dorsey Pentecost against Jacob Long In Debt Al Cap.

William Brashers against Robert Hamelton In Case Al Cap.

(11) John Nelson against Jacob Shilling In Case C. O.

John White against Ezekil Johnston In Case Al Cap.

William Bruce against Archibald Frome In Case. C. O.

John Springer against Henry Kearsey In Asst. Al Cap.

Nicholas Dawson against Francis Kirkpatrick In Sl. Al Cap.

William Thompson agt. John Fife Sen. In Tresp. Al Cap.

John Campbell agt William Patterson. In Trespass C. O.

Jacob Shillings vs John Wilson In Trespass C. O.

William How vs. William Genoway, Ebenezer Corn & George Corn Jun. In Trespass Al Cap.

Paul Froman vs James Boyers In Tresp. Al. Cap.

Michael Myors vs Philip Hooper In Trespass. Al Cap.

John Mitchel vs. Philip Hooper. In Case. Al Cap.

Mordeca Richards vs Joseph Ross In Slan. Al Cap.

John Springer vs. James Dunnaughan In Trespass. Al Cap.

John Crow vs John Brown In Slr. agreed.

Joseph Baker vs John Springer In Debt Al Cap.

Daniel Byers vs James Patterson In Case C. O.

Benjaman Fullum vs William Johnston, John McCornish. In Asst. Al Cap.

Benjaman Fullum vs William Johnston & John McCornish. In Case. Al Cap.

David Andrew vs W[m] Johnston In Tresp. Al Cap.

James Johnston agt. Godfrey Waggoner In Case Al Cap.

Jacob Shilling vs Samuel Fortner In Tresp. Al Cap.

Mary Burriss vs David Williams In Case. Al Cap.

Upon the Motion of Andrew Sweargen ordered that his Ear Mar a Crop in the Left Ear and a hole in the Right be recorded.

Upon the Motion of Thomas Hamelton ordered that his Ear mark a Crop slit and a bit in the right Ear be recorded.

Upon the motion of Joshua Wright ordered that his Mark a Swolefork in the Left Ear be Recorded.

(12) Ordered that Isaac Cox Gentleman contract with some Proper Person or Persons to build a pair of Stocks, whiping Post and pillory, in the Court house yard, and also a compleat Bar, and other work in the Inside of the Court House as he may thing proper for the conveniency of the Court and Bar, the whole to be compleat by next Court.

George McCarmick Gentleman high Sheriff Protest against the Strength & sufficiency of the Goal.

Ordered that the Sheriff summon a Grand Jury to attend the next Court.

Ordered that William Price, Thomas Rogers, and Isaac Wells be appointed Constables to serve the ensuing year, and that they be Summoned to attend the next Court to Qualify into said Office.

Isaac Cox having obtained an Atteachment against the Estate of Samuel McCored Thomas Apple garnishee being sworn sayeth that he hath about five acres of winter grain and no more of the Estate of the sd. Samuel in his hands. and the said Samuel being called and failing to appear and replevy the said atteached effects though Solemnly called, the Plantiff produced his acct. of five pounds, Ten Shillings and four pence & swore to the Justness thereof. Judgment for the afores[d]. sum of five pounds Ten shillings, and four pence, with Costs Ordered that the Sheriff make Sale of the Atteached Effects.

Ordered that Court be adjourned to Court in Course.

WILLIAM GOE.

(13) At a Court continued and held for Yohogania County May the 25th. 1778.

Present George Vallandingham, John McDonald, Samuel Newell, Benjamin Kirkendall, Gentlemen Justices.

Upon the Motion of William Brur Ordered that his Ear mark a Crop in the near Ear, and under bit in the off Ear be recorded.

Bargain and Sale Ezekil Johnston to Joseph Beeler Jun. was proved by the oath of Joseph Beckett one of the subscribing witnesses, and ordered to be recorded as Dorsey Pentecos and Joseph Beeler Sen., at a former Court was Sworn to the Execution of said Bargain and Sale and Subscribing Witnesses Thereto.

Administration of the Estate of Conrad Swessicks deceased is granted to Margaret Swessicks She having Complied with the Law.

Andrew Pearce and Sarah Pearce took the oath of Executrix & Ex.[or] of the Estate of James Pearce Deceased, and complied with the Law.

Ordered that Zadock Wright, W.[m] Brice, Gabriel Cox and William Frye or any three of them they being first Sworn do appraise the goods chattles and credits and Slaves if any of the Estate of Conrad Swessicks deceased and make return to next Court.

Administration of the Estate of Benjaman Bruer deceased is granted to Mary Bruer she having complied with the Law.

(14) Ordered that Joseph Beeler Sen, Christopher Hays John Mellender & John Morecroft or any three of them they being first sworn do appraise the goods chattles Credits and slaves if any of the Estate of Benjaman Brewer deceased and make return to next Court.

Benjamin Frye Gentleman Present.

Administration of the Estate of Jonathan Higgs deceased is granted to Catharine Higgs she having complied with the Law. Ordered that Joseph Beeler Sen. Christopher Hays John Millinger and John Morecroft or any three of them they being first Sworn, do appraise the Estate of Jonathan Higgs deceased and make return to next Court.

Mesheck Carter enters Special Bail for Daniel Williams at the suit of Isaac Vance.

Bargain and Sale James Patterson to John Strauthers for Six Hundred acres of Land acknowledged by the said Patterson and Ordered to be recorded.

Hugh Brawday enters Special Bail for Jas. Boyer at the Suit of Paul Froman.

Elijah Hart Took the oath of Lieutenant of the Militia for this County in open Coart.

Elijah Hart and Walter Sparks came into Court and took the oath of Allegience and Fidelity.

Administration of the Estate of Archibald McNeal deceased is granted to William Filds, he having complied with the Law. Ordered that Thos. Applegate William Crow, Andrew Pearce and Walter Wall or any three of them they being first Sworn do appraise the Estate of Archibald McNeal deceased and make return to next Court.

(15) Benjamin Jones v Patrick McDonald. Plu Cap.

Zacheriah Connell v Samuel Wells. Contd.

v Providence Maunce. Contd

John Worshington v Michael Morton. Eject, Contd.

Edward Ward v Richard Dunn. Contd.

v Joseph Wells Contd

Walter Briscoe v Edward Todd Contd.

Zachariah Connell v John Lindsey Contd.

Peter Reasoner v Davis Ruth Contd.

John Springer Plantiff
v
Henry Kearsey Defendt. Upon motion of the parties ordered to be refered to John Hull, Henry Taylor & George Vallandingham.

Valentine Shuster enters Special Bail for John Eliott at the suit of Philip Hooper.

William Collings enters Special Bail for Michael Myers at the suit of Philip Hooper.

William Collings enters Special Bail for George Myers at the suit of Philip Hooppr.

William Collings enters Special Bail for Michael Thomas and Zebuland Collings at the suit of Philip Hooper.

View of a Road from the House of Edward Cook Crossing the Monaungohela River at the House of John Ratton's, Thence to or Near the plantation of John Hop deceased, Thence to Luther Colvin's on Pigeon Creek, Thence the nearest and best way to the Road Leading from Parkersons to Zebuland Collings. Ordered to be Confirmed, and that the Tithables within three miles on each side work on and keep said Road in Repair.

John Decker, John Hull, Samuel Johnston, Jacob Johnston, Samuel Frye and Henry Newkirk came into Court and Took the oth of Feledity.

(16) Peter Reasoner is appointed Surveyor of the Road from Edward Cook's to John Rattons ferry.

Nicholas Christ is appointed Surveyor of the Road from John Rattons ferry to Pigeon Creek, near the House of Luther Colvins.

John Decker is appointed Surveyor of the road from Pigeon Creek near the House of Luther Colvins to the road Leading to Parkersons to Zebulon Collinings.

Then came a Grand Jury or Inquest of the Body of this County, vizt. John Decker, John White, Gabriel Cox, Jacob Bouseman, Henry Newkirk, Jacob Johnston, John Springer, Nicholas Christ, James Wright, Samuel Johnston, John Hull, Samuel Frye, David Andrew, Joseph Brown & James Patterson, who being Sworn received their Charge and Retired to their chamber.

Bargain and Sale Jasper Cawther and Catherine his wife to
(17) David Andrew for a Tract of Land on the waters of Millers Run proved by the oath of Samuel McBride and James Scott the two Subscribing witnesses & Ordered to be Certified.

Edward Kemp enters Special Bail for Spencer Collings at the suit of Paulcer Shilling.

Joseph Beeler Jun. came into Court and Took the oath of Deputy Sheriff of this County.

Bargain and Sale William Wilson to Jeremiah Ellis for One Hundred and five Acres of Land. Acknowledged by said Willson and Ordered to be record.

John Riggs enters Special Bail for Nathan Ellis at the suit of Tacitus Gillord.

Henry Kearsey and James Munn enters Special Bail for William Johnston at the suits of Benjaman Fullum and David Andrews.

Henry Kearsey and James Munn enters Special Bail for Robert Johnston at the suit of Benjaman Fullum.

John Gutteridge produced a Commission from his Excellency the Governor appointing him Lieutenant of the Militia, which was read, and Sworn to accordingly.

License is granted to Joseph Nicholas to keep an Ordinary at his Dweling House in the Town of Pittsburgh the Ensuing year he having Complied with the Law.

William Christie enters Special Bail for Robert McKindley at the suit of Susannah Schley.

(17) Upon the motion of Tobias Decker Ordered that his mark a Crop in the Left ear, and Swolofork in the right be recorded.

License is granted Richard McMahan to keep an Ordinary at his Dweling House in this County he having Complied with the Law.

George Christ produced a Commission from his Excellency the Governor appointing him Ensign of the Militia which was read as usual, & Sworn to, in Open Court.

Inventory of the Estate of Francis Brown deceased returned by the appraisers and ordered to be recorded.

Benjamin Vannatree enters Special Bail for James Vannatree at the Suit of William Braden.

Ordered that Isaac Cox and Benjamin Kirkendall, Gentlemen Bind Andrew Brooks an Orphan to Friend Cox, according to law.

Ordered that the Clerk draw on the Treasury of this Common Welth for the sum of Sixteen pounds for the support of Anne Jones the wife of Richd. Jones a poor Soldier in the Continental Service.

Ordered that Court be adjourned Untill Tomorrow Morning 7 OClock. WILLIAM GOE.

(20) Court met According to adjournment May 26, 1778.

A new Commission of the pice, and Commission of Oyor and Terminer, directed to, John Campbell, Edward Ward, Thomas Smallman, Dorsey Pentecost, John Gibson, William Crawford, John Stephenson, John Cannon, George Vallandingham, William Goe, John Neavill, Isaac Cox, John McDowell, Richard Yeates, John McDonald, George McCormick, Philip Ross, Benjaman Kirkendall, William Harrison, Samuel Newell, Thomas Brown, Thomas Freeman, John Decomp, Joshua Wright, Oliver Miller, Benjaman Frye, Matthew Richie, Jacob Haymaker, Andrew Swearingen, Benjaman Harrison, Zachariah Connell, Isaac Leet Senr. Joseph Beeler Senr. John Carmichael, James Rogers, Isaac Meason, James McLane, James Blackstone, Joseph Beckett and Joseph Vance, Gentlemen, which being read as usual, the said William Goe, Thomas Freeman, Andrew Swearengen, John McDonald, Benjaman Frye and George Vallandingham, Took the usual oaths of Justices of the Peace and Justices of Oyer and Terminer.

The Court being Constituted, Took their seats and proceeded to Business.

Anthony Dunleaver: . Special Bail for Joseph Ross at the suits of Mordaca Richard and Margarett Brownfield.

Tacitus Gillord Esquire came into Court and Produced a pasport from the Board of War and Disered that the same may be Entered on the minutes of this Court as a Testimoneal of his Allegience and Fidelity to the United States of America whi is granted and is as follows.

War Office York Town
October 15th 1777.

(21) Tacitus Gillard Esq. Late an Inhabitant of the State of South Carolinia being on his way to Florida or some of the Countries or places on this side Thereof, or adjacent Thereto, where he proposes to form a Settlement, and having applied for a pasport to enable him to go and Travel through the parts of the Country, in allegience to and in Amity with the united States of America, and having produced Testimonials of his having Taken the Oaths of allegience and Fidelity, to the said States, These are to permitt the said Tacitus Gillard, Esqr. freely to pass with his famely, Servants, Attendance, and Effects Down the River Ohio, and all persons, are Desired not to molest the said Tacitus Gallord Esqr. his Family, servants and Effects on any account or pretense whatsoever.

By order of the Board of War.

RICHD. PETERS *Secy.*

To all Continental Officers and others whom it may Concern.

Richard McMahon enters Special Bail for Jacob Long, Junr. at the suit of Benjaman Caster.

License is granted Robert Henderson to keep an Ordinary at his Dwiling House he having complied with the Law.

Andrew Swearenghen Gentleman Absent.

Administration of the Estate of Joseph Brashers deceased is granted to William Brashers he having complied with the Law.

Ordered that Bazel Brown, Thomas Brow, Hugh Laughlin and John Laughlin, do appraise the Goods, Chattles, and Credits and Slaves if any of the Estate of Joseph Brashers Deceased.

Andrew Swearengen Gentleman Present.

(22) Administration of the Estate of James Louden deceased is granted to Robert Louden he having complied with the Law. Ordered that Ralph Cherry, Edward Doyale, Edmond Lindsey and Isaac Meason or any Three of them they being first sworn do appraise the goods, chattles, credits and Slaves if any of the Estate of James Loudon deceased and make returns to next Court.

Isaac Cox and Benjaman Kirkendal Gentleman named in the Commission of the peace come into Court and Took the oaths of Justices, and Justices of Oyer and Terminer.

Edward Kemp produced a Commission appointing him Captain of the Militia, which was read and sworn to accordingly.

Upon the petition of David Philips and Others Ordered that John Jones, Robert Henderson, and John Wall they being first sworn do view a road from McKees ferry on the Monaungahela River to Pentecost's Mills on Churteers, and make report of the Conveniency and Inconveniency thereof to the Next Court.

Upon the Petition of David Philips Ordered that William Frye, Jacob Barrachman, and Jacob Shilty make a review of the road from Peters Creek to Robert Hendersons and make report of the conveniences and Inconveniences of the nearest and best way, to next Court.

Samuel Newell gentleman named in the Commission of the piece come into Court and Took the Oaths of Justices of the pece and Justices of Oyer and Terminer.

Resolved as a Rule that this Court will attend on the Business of this County and proceed to give Judgmt and Determine Causes, in the months of March, May, August and November, and that In the Intermediate Courts the Justices will hold Court for proving of Wills, deeds, &c. &c. &c.

(23) Upon the motion of George Schley ordered that his Mark a Crop in the right Ear be recorded.

Naturalization of George Schley was read and on the motion of the said George Ordered to be recorded.

James Kirkindall enters Special Bail for Samuel Dunn at the suit of Samuel Holms.

Ordered that the Sheriff make sale of Cornelius Crow an Indented Servant belonging to John Harry, and pay the money arising from such sale to the said Harry.

Upon the Petition of William Anderson Leave is granted him to keep a ferry from his own Land on the South Easterly side of the Monaungohela River to the Lands of Andrew Heath on the Opposite. And that the said Anderson shall receive Nine pence for Man and Horse, four pence half penny for every Head of neat Cattle, and the same for a foot person, furthermore to ferry over the Militia on publick Muster days at the rate of four dollars pr day.

Upon the motion of Godfrey Waggoner ordered that his ear mark a hole in the left ear & a slitt in the right be Recorded.

Jacob Feagly
v in Case
Hugh Brawdy Then came the defendt. & pleads the general Issue. Then came a Jury viz. Joseph Skelton, William Taylor, Ezekiel Johnston, Friend Cox, David Phillips, Alexander Douglas, John Wall, George Long, Thos. Lapsy, Michael Humble, Saml. Dunn & John Cox, who sayeth that the Defendant hath not paid the Dett as in pleading he hath allegd. Judgment for £. 7 : 8 : 9 Int 7 S. 6 and Costs.

(24) Upon the Petition of Elizabeth McMahon against Peter Ebrod. It is considered by the Court that the Plaintiff recover against the Defendant three pounds and three pence with Interest from the 13th day of May 1763 untill paid.

Leave is granted Samuel Ewalt to keep an Ordinary at his Dweling House in the Town of Pittsburgh he having Complied with the Law.

The Deppotion of James Elliott and John Barr Taken before John Campbell Esq. upon the Motion of James Swolevan in behalf of David Dunkin. Ordered to be recorded.

Jacob Decker
v Petition. Ordered to be Dismissed at
Joseph Hill Sen Plaintiffs Costs.

Upon the petition of Hugh Sterling against Anthony Dunleavey. It is considered by the Court that the Plantiff Recover against the Defendant the sum of three pounds four shillings, and Costs.

Tacitus Gallard Plantiff
v In Trover
Nathan Ellis Defendt. Then come the parties and agreed to Leave their Contro̊versy to the Judgment of the Justices Sitting, without the formality of a Jury. Whereupon Judgment is given the Plantiff for One hundred and forty five Bushells of Corn and Costs, upon Tacitus Gilliard's demand of the Corn & Tender of a Coppy of this Judgment.

Bazil Brown
v In Case Contd. premtory order. Rule
Robert Hamilon of Trial next Court.

(25) Alexander Sumral & Thomas Jock v Walter Sumral, Contd.

Upon the motion of Tacitus Gillard Ordered that the Sheriff summon John McCullum be Sommoned to attend this Court Tomorrow by two OClock after noon to prosecute his action against said Gillord.

William Marley producd to this Court a Commission from his Excellency the governour appointing him Ensign of the Militia which was read & swore to accordingly.

James Fasithe was Brought into Court and Stands Charged with Disaffection to the State, who pleads not Guilty, whereopon come the same Jury as before, who say that the sd. James Fasith shall pay a fine of Twenty dollars and Suffer forty Eight hours Confinement in the Common Goal, and before he be Discharged therefrom give such Security as the Court Shall think fit.

Edward Kemp enters Special Bail for Samuel Fortner at the suit of Jacob Shilling.

Jacob Johnston enters special Bail for Henry Newkirk at the suit of Jacob Shilling.

Upon the motion of Abraham Fry by Benjamin his son ordered that Abrahams ear mark an under Bit out of the under side of each ear be Recorded.

William Boshears produced to this Court a Commission from his Excellency the Governour appointing him Lieutenant of the Militia which was red and sworn to accordingly.

Wm. Downs enters Special Bail for Philip Hooper at the suit of Michael Myers.

Wm. Downs enters Special Bail for Philip Hooper at the suit of John Mitchell.

(26) Benjamin Vinater enters Special Bail for Godfrey Waggoner at the suit of James Johnston.

Upon the Complaint of John Campbell Gentleman that Samuel St. Clair & Joseph Erwin have Intentionally raised Sedition & mutinous Disturbances in the militia. Ordered that the said Samuel and Joseph be held in five hundred pounds Bail each, with two sureties for each in the sum of Two hundred & fifty pounds each. Whereupon the said Samuel St. Clair Came into Court with John Gorley and Michael Humble his securities and did Acknowledge to ow to Patrick Henry Esq. Governor or Chief Majestrate of the Common Welth or his Successor in Office the sd. Samuel in five Hundred pounds, and the said Suretys in Two Hundred & Fifty pounds each, to be levied on their respective goods and Chattles Lands & Tenements, on the Condition that the said Samuel be of his Good Demeaner Towards all within this Common Wealth, and Towards all the Good Subjects of the same for one year and a Day. Joseph Irwin, with Thomas Lapsley and John Gorley his sureties enter into recognezonce as Aforesaid.

Thomas Lapsley and Robert Henderson produced Commissions from the Governor appointing them Lut's of the Militia which was read and Sworn to Accordingly.

Ordered that Court be adjourned untill Tomorrow Morning 7 oClock. GEORGE VALLANDIGHAM.

(27) May the 27th, 1778. Court met according to adjournm't.

President William Goe, George Vallandham Samuel Newell, John McDonald, Gentlemen, Present.

On the motion of Henry Taylor Ordered that his mark a Crop in the Left Ear and Two Slitts in the right ear be recorded.

Thomas Freeman Gentleman Present.

James Ravenscroft P.
v Hog Stealing.
Samuel Beeler D.

Then came the parties and then came also a Jury, Towit: Joseph Shelton, Edward Kemp, Uriah Johnston, Ezekiel

Johnston, Alexander Duglass, Thomas Lapsley, George Long, William Marshall, Nathan Ellis, James Wright, Benjaman Collings, Benjaman Cox, which being Elected and Sworn Sayeth that the said Samuel is gelty. Ordered That the said Samuel be fined Ten pounds Current money, and four Hundred pounds of Tobacco. The Tob'o be paid to James Ravenscroft being Owner and Informer. Ordered that Thomas Moore be all'd five Days attendance as a witness in the above suit. John Hull the same, Charles Philis the Same.

(28) Joshua Wright Gentleman named in the Commission of the peace and Commission of Oyer and Terminer came into Court and took the oaths of Justice of the piece, and Justices of Oyer and Terminer.

David Philips v Joseph Killpatrick, Thomas Miller and Allexander Miller. Ordered to be Dismissed at Plaintiffs Request.

Joseph Killpatrick v David Philips ordered to be dismissed at Plantiffs request and Costs.

The Grand Jury having found a Bill against James McGoldreck for puling down a Block House belonging to the Town of Pittsburg, the said James being Called plead not guilty, then come the said Jury as before, and being Elected & Sworn sayeth that the said James is Gilty. Ordered, be fined Ten pounds Curr't. money.

Zacheriah Connell v Nathaniel Brown Ag'd.

Alexander Bowling v Francis Morrison Cont'd.

Christian Summitt v John Gallehor & wife Cont'd

Hugh Sterling v Mordecai Richards Cont'd.

Benjamin Wells v Hugh Newell Cont'd.

Isaac Vance v Daniel Williams Ej. Cont'd.

Hugh Brawdy v Jacob Feagley Cont'd.

William Brasher v Robert Hamelton Cont'd.

John Smith v Sarah Dye Dismiss. p. Dead.

Thomas Cook v James Ferrell Ejmt. Cont'd.

Joseph Cox v John Williams, Theodorus Daviss & wife & Mary Hazle Cont'd & P. R.

Joseph Cox v John Williams and Theodorus Daviss C. P. R.

John Lydea v Joseph Cox Cot'd.

Dorsey Pentecost v Christopher McDonald, Cont'd.

Oliver Miller Gentleman named in the Commission of the piece, came into Court and Took the oath of Justices of the pice, and Justice of Oyer & Terminer.

(29) William Christy & Joseph Nichols enter themselves as Sureties for Jacob Bousman's punctually & faithfully keeping proper & suitable Boats & hands for ferrying the Inhabitants across the River at his ferry Backwards & forwards, in the penal sum of five hundred pounds.

Rodrick Frazer and John Ferry appointed Constables to Serve the Ensuing year, and that they be summoned before some one Justice for this County and Qualify into said Office.

Thomas Gist v Richard Waller Cont'd.

v John Hall Cont'd.

v Henry Boyles Cont'd.

John Lawrence v Thomas Rogers Cont'd

Thomas Cooke v Levington Thomas, Cont'd.

Elizabeth Burriss v Naomi Tropman Con.

Leave is granted William Anderson to keep an Ordinary at his Duiling House in this County, he having Complied with the Law.

Archibald Hull v Thomas Bondfield Cont'd.

Joseph Wherry v John White Contd. at plaintiffs Costs.

Ordered that a Dedimus Issue to take the Examination of Matthew Rogers & Ezekil Johnston, Witness in behalf of John White at the suit of Joseph Wherry.

Mary Burriss v John Johnston & Michael Humble. Cont'd P. R.

William Dunnanghgain v James Gray. Cont'd.

John Peare Senr. v John Keredin. P. Dead. Dismiss'd.

John Nelson v Jacob Shilling Cont'd.

Jacob Shilling v John Nelson Contd.

Daniel Byers v James Patterson. Contd.

William Brue v Archibald Frome Dismissd at plantiffs request.

(30) John McDonald having obtained an Atteach. against Nathanie Patten, and the Constable having returned that he had Leveyed said Atteachment in the hands of Andrew Link and William Willson, and Sommoned them as Garneshees. Ordered that the sd. Link & Wilson be forced before the next Court to Shew

how much & what they have in their hands of the Estate of sd. Patten.

Upon the Motion of William Marshall Ordered that his marke a Crop in the left ear and Crop and slit in the right ear be recorded.

John McCullum v Isaac Gallard
v Tacitus Gallard In Case.

This day come the parties and agreed to submit their Controversy to the Justices now sitting, and after hearing the Allegations and Defence are of Opinion that the Defendants have paid the Debt in the Declaration mentioned, and ordered to be Dismissed.

Upon the motion of John Trumbo Ordered that his mark a Crop and upper bill in the near Ear, and his Brand I^{o}T be recorded.

Benjaman Jones v Patrick McDonald. P. C.
Zacheriah Connell v. Abraham Vaughan. P. C.
David Willson v. Henry Bowling Agrd.
John Sperry v Samuel Beeler C. O.
John Gallehan & wife v. Christian Summitt P. C.
Joseph Lindsey v. George Long. C. O.
Richard Swessichs v Jacob Jones P. C.
Paul Froman v Robert McCrowry P. C.
Francis Morrison v David Swigert C. O.
George Schley v John Rammage agd.
Susannah Schley v Robert McKindley S. R.
Thomas Freeman v John Linch.
v Samuel Lynch.
v James Lynch. } Dismissed at Plantiff's Request.
(31) Jacob Bousman v Jos. Bradley. Agreed.
Froman v Dean Plu Cap.
Cook v Dickerson P. Cap.
John Pearce Senr. v Aron Carter In Case p. Dead. D.
v the same same Order.
Thomas Wells v Paulcer Shillings C. O.
Joseph Pearce v Arnold Evins P. Cap.
Andrew Steel v Joseph Rolstone P. C.
Stout v Thompson & wife agreed.

Wm. Thompson v John Fife Sen. agrd.
Cloe Riggs v Ebenezer Corn P. C.
Moses Thompson v William Carpenter P. Cap.
Dorsey Pentecost v Jacob Long C. O.
William Brashers v Robert Hamelton. P. C.
John White v Ezekiel Johnston P. C.
Nicholas Dawson v Francis Kirkpatrick P. C.
William Thompson v John Fife Sen. agreed.
John Campbell v William Patterson P. C.
William How v William Geneway }
v Ebenezer Corn } P C
v George Corn Ju. }
John Springer v James Dunnaughhow. agreed.

Joseph Barker v John Springer. The plantiff Living out of the Country. the Defendt. dem'd. security for costs, which was not Complied with and Ordered to be Dismissed.

Benjaman Fullum v John McCornish. P. Cap.
the same Plu
Mary Burriss v David Williams. P. C.
James Patterson v Aaron Carter agreed
James Murphy v Mordacai Richard P. C.
Paul Froman v William Stephens P C
Mary Burriss v Abraham Jones P. C.

(32) Sam Johnston & Isaac McMichel produc'd. Commissions from his Excellency the Governour appointing them Ensigns of the Militia which ware red & swore to accordingly.

John Chamberlain produced to this Court a Commission from his Excellency the Governour appointing him Lieutenant of Militia which was red & swore to accordingly.

James Faisaithe come into Court with Mabary Evins and James Holliday, and did acknowledge to owe to Patrick Henry Esq. Governor and Chief Majestrate of this Common Wealth or his Successor in Office in the Sum of Twenty pounds. the said Fasithe and his Sureties in the sum of Ten pounds each, to be Levied on his goods and chattles Lands and Tenements for the use of the said Patrick Henry or his Successor in Office if default is made in this Condition, that the said James Fasithe shall be of good Demeaner to this Common wealth, and all the

Leage People Thereof for the Term of one year and one Day Ensuing the date hereof.

Ordered that John Wall, James Wright, Andrew Vaughan and Benjaman Collings or any three of them being first Sworn do appraise the goods Chattles and Credits and Slaves if any of the Estate of Samuel Richardson deceased, and make return to Next Court.

John G. Masterson is Recommended to his Excellency the Governor as a proper person to serve as Lieutenant of the Melitia.

John Daniel is recommended to his Excellency the governor as a proper person to Serve as Ensign of the Melitia.

(33) Upon the motion of Joseph Philis Ordered that his mark a crop and slit in the right ear, and a Swollow fork and half penny one left Ear be recorded.

Upon the motion of Henry Hoglond ordered that his mark a Crop and under slit in the Left ear, and an under bit in the right ear, be recorded.

Upon the motion of John McDonald Ordered that his mark a Swallow fork in the Left ear and Swallow fork and under bit in the right Ear be recorded.

Bazel Stotner is appointed Consta to serve the Ensuing and that he be Sommoned before William Goe Gentleman to Qualify into said Office.

Upon the Motion of Thomas Moore Ordered that his make a Cropt and Slit in the right ear and two slits in the Left, be recorded.

Henry Boyles, Thomas Philip & Jacob Knap, are appointed Constables the Ensuing year, and that they be Sommoned to appear before some one Justice of this County and Qualify into said Commission.

Ordered that Isaac Cox, Thomas Freeman & Andrew Swearingen Gentlemen distribute the Cards Consigned for this County upon proper & suitable Sertoficates to them produced, and that two thirds be delivered Isaac Cox and Andrew Swearengen, and one third to Thos. Freeman Gentleman.

Ordered that the Gentlemen named in the Commission of peace for this County yet Remaining unqualify'd be Summoned to next Court to qualify accordingly.

John Campbell Gentleman named in the Commission of the peace & Commission of Oir & Terminer Came into Court & took the oath of Justice of the peace & Justice of Oir & Terminer accordingly.

(34) Ordered that Court be adjourned untill Court in Course.

GEORGE VALLANDINGHAM.

(35) At a Court continued and held for Yohogania County June the 22nd. 1778.

Present Isaa. Cox, Benjaman Kirkindall, Benjamin Frye, Samuel Newell, Gentlemen Justices.

Inventory of the Estate of Conrod Swessicks deceased, returned by the appraisers and Ordered to be Recorded.

Joseph Beeler and Joseph Beckett Gentlemen named in the Commission of the Pice and Commission of Oyer and Terminer came into Court and took the Oath of Justice of the piece and Justice and Justices of Oyer and Terminer.

James Brue v. Benjaman Patton. Rich'd McMahon S P

Andrew Steel P.
v In Case
Joseph Rolston Jr. Then come the parties and agreed to Submit their Controversy to the Justices now sitting. Jud'm't. for 24 L. Cur. Money & Costs.

Bargain and Sale Gasper Carther to David Andrews, for Tract of Land was proved by the oath of David Welch one of the Subscribing Witnesses thereto and Ordered to be recorded. Samuel McBride, & James Scott witness Thereto was attested at a former Court, to the Execution of 1st Bargain and Sale.

Charles Masterson, John Daviss, Jonah Potter & Shadrach Carter, William Masterson & Joseph Hart took the Oath of Allegience and Fidelity.

Reuben Case and John Guttery being bound in recognizance, and stands charged with Secreting abeting and . . . abeting the Secreting Theophilus Case a Continental Soldier. Ordered to be Dismissed.

James Richards v Mordeca Richards, John McCormick S. B.

Benjaman Fullum v John McCornish, Mordeca Richards S. B.

Mary Burriss v David Williams, Saml. Devoir S. B.

David Williams took the oath of Allegiance and Fidelity to the State.

Paul Froman, Plant.
v In Case.
William Stevens Defd. At Request of Parties Ordered to be Refered to John McDowell, James Allison, Thomas Egerton, Jacob Long, Leverton Thomas, John Cox and John Wall and return this Judgment to next Court.

Bargain and Sale Paul Froman to Joseph Beckett for a Survey of Land on the Monaungahela River including Froman's old mill. Acknowledged by said Froman and Ordered to be Recorded.

Edward Hughy produced a License from the Presbytry of London Derry in the kingdom of Ireland to Preach the Gospel of Jesus Christ, which was Read. Whereupon the said Edward came into Court and Took the Oath of Allegiance and Fidelity to this Common Wealth.

William How v. George Corn Jur, William Jencons, George Corn Sr. S. B.

Upon the Petition of Paul Froman Ordered that Nicholas De Pugh, John Lovejoy, Robert McGee, and James Colvin or any three of them View a Road the nearest and best way from Devoir's Ferry to Pentecost's Mills on Charteers passing by Fromans Mill on Mingo Creek and report the Conveniences and Inconveniences to Next Court.

(37) Licese is Granted Jacob Judy to keep an Ordenary at his Duiling House he having Complied with the Law.

B. Frye Abst.

James Boyer v Paul Froman, Benjaman Frye S. B.

B. Frye Gent. Prest.

Henry Newkirk v Jacob Shilling, John Williams S. B.

Paul From v Robert McCrowry, Michael Powers. S. B.

Assignment of a Bill of Sale. Andrew Devoir Frederick Cooper. Acknowledged by Samuel Devoir one of the Assinees on sd Bill of Sale. Ordered to be Recorded.

License is granted David Dunking to keep an Ordenary at his House in the Town of Pitts Burgh he having Complied with the Law.

Writ of Adquidomcen[1] is granted Paul From to condemn an Acre of Land to Build a Mill on a Branch of Mingo Creek.

William Johnston enters himself Defendant at the suit of Timmothy Turnout Lessee of David Andrews against Sawney Saphead.

License is granted Francis Kelder to keep an Ordinary at his Dweling House He having Complied with the Law.

Richard Yeats Gentleman Named in the Commission of the peace and Commission of Oyer and Terminer came into Court and Took the Oth of Justice of the peace and Justice of Oyer and Terminer.

James Hogland Produced a Commission from his Excellency the Governor appointing him Lieut. of the Militia, which was read and sworn to Accordingly.

(38) John Hogland v Matthew Loghlin, Mastick Carter S. B.

v George Riggle, Shadreck Carter S. B.

Walter McFarlin v Samuel Beeler, Geo. McCarmick S. B.

Thomas Smallman Gentleman Named in the Commission of the Peace and Commissioner of Oyer and Terminer, came into Court and took the Oath of a Justice of Peace and Justice of Oyer and Terminer.

Daviss Ruth enters himself Defendant at the suit of Timmothy Turnout Lessee of John Decker, against Sawney Saphead.

James Matthew v William Hibbitt, Anthony Corker S. B.

Administration of the Estate of Dennis Stephens dec'd. is granted to Daviss Ruth he having complied with the Law.

Ordered that David Richie, Luther Colvin, Nicholas Depugh, & John Miller or Any three of them being first Sworn do appraise the goods, chattles, Credits and Slaves if any of the Estate of Dennis Stephens deceased and make return to next Court.

Leave is granted John Reredin to keep an Ordinary at his dweling House in this County he having Complied with the Law.

Upon the Petition of John Miller seting forth that William Cills is aged and Infirm and Not able to maen himself, Ordered that Thomas Smallman Gentleman agree with some proper person to support and maintain the said William Cills, and

[1] So written, but possibly intended for "ad damnum inquirendum."

that such person bring in his account at the Laying of the next Levy.

William Deal is appointed Constable in place of Malechias Hays.

Whereas George McCarmick Gentleman was at a former Court appointed Sheriff for this County, for one month, and at the same Time recommended the said George McCarmick to his Excellency the Governor as a proper person to Serve as Sheriff for this County by the Ensuing year, and no Commis-
(39) sion as yet arrived for the said Sheriff, and his pro Tempory appointed being now Expired, the County is without a Sheriff. Ordered that the said George McCarmick Gentleman be appointed Sheriff for this County for and During the Term of one Month next Ensuing he complying with the Law.

John Gibson Gentleman named in the Commission of the pice and Commission of Oyer and Terminer come into Court and Took the Oath of Justice of the piece and Justice of Oyer and Terminer.

Zacheriah Connel v Abraham Vaughan, Mordeca Richards S. B.

John Campbell Gentleman Present.

Ordered that William Deal be fined Ten Shillings for Refusing to Serve as Constable.

Ordered William Evins be appointed Constable the Ensuing Year, and that he be Sommoned before the nearest Justice to Qualify into said Office.

A Request from the Court of Ohio [County] to call on the Commissioners for adjusting the Boundery Line between this County and the sd. County of Ohio. This court are of Opinion that the sd. Request is highly reasonable. It is Therefore Ordered that the Commissioners on the part of this County doth proceed to finish the Business to which they have been appointed and make report to next Court.

Thomas Bay produced a Commission from the Governor appointing him Lieut. of the Militia which was read and Sworn to Accordingly.

John Campbell Abst.

(40) License is granted to James McClellen to keep an Ordinary in the Town of Pittsburgh he having Complied with the Law.

Ordered that William Masterson, Charles Masterson, John

Guttery, Mesheck Caster and Richd. Hoopkins, who is Guilty of a Briech of the peace in the presence of the Court, be and remain in the Custody of the Sheriff and be brought before the Court Tomorrey at seven oclock.

Ordered that Court be adjourned untill tomorning 7 oclock.

THO. SMALLMAN.

June 23. 1778. Court met according to adjournment.

Isaac Cox, Thomas Smallman, Benjaman Frye, Joseph Beckett, Samuel Newell, Joseph Beeler, Gentlemen Present.

Walter Grayham having obtained an Attach. against the Estate of Robert Strain who is said to be so Absconded that the Ordinary process of Law cannot be Served upon him for Nine pounds & Six pence Pennsylvania Curr'y. and the Constable having returned that by Virtue of sd. Att'mt. he has atteach'd one Cow, and no more of the Estate of the sd. Robert, and the sd. Robt. failing to app.r. and Repevy the sd. Att'd. Effects, though Solemly called, the sd. Walter produced a Note against the sd. Robert for thirteen pounds P. V. Currency. It is Therefore Considered that the Plaintiff Recovered against the Deft Seven pounds, Twelve shilling, & five pence Cur. money of the Value of the afo'sd. nine pounds and Six pence P V Currency. Ordered that the Sheriff make Sale of the Att'd. Effects, and satisfy the plant. this Judgmt with Costs, and make return to Court.

(41) Upon the Petition of Richard Yeates Ordered that Henry Taylor, James Allison, James Patterson, William Brashers, or any three of them being first Sworn View a Road from Catfish camp to Pentecosts Mills and make report of the Conveniency an Inconveniency to next Court.

Samuel Newell Gent. Ab't.

Administration of the Estate of Thomis Lewis deceased is granted Robert Newell he having complied with the Law.

Ordered that David Vance, David McCaw, James Tucker, and George Vance or any three of them being first Sworn appr. the Estate of Thomas Lewis deceased and make return to next Court.

Upon the Petition of Anthony Dunleavey ordered that Robert Henderson, Georg Redman, Richard Crooks and William Anderson or any three of them being first Sworn View a Road from Pittsburgh to Pentecosts mills on Churtees and make report of the Conveniency and Inconveniency to Next Court.

William Crawford, John Stephenson and William Harrison Gentlemen Named in the Commission of the pece and Commission of Oyer and Terminer come into Court and Took the Oath of Justice of the pice and Justice of Oyer and Terminer.

John Campbell and John Gibson Gent. Pt.

George McCarmeck Gentlemen came into Court and Took the Oath of his high Sheriff for this County for the Term of one Month.

Hugh Sterling come into Court and Took the Oath of Deputy Sheriff for this County for the Term of one month.

(42) Hugh Ohara with James McCleland & Walter Graham his Securities came into Court and acknowledged themselves to be indebted to Patrick Henry Esqr. Governor &c that is to say the said Hugh Ohara in the sum of £100 and the said James McCleland and Walter Graham in £50 each to be levied upon their respective Goods & Chattells lands and Tenements for the use of this State upon condition that the said Hugh Ohara shall personally appear before the Justices of this County at the next August Court then and there to answer to such Matters and things as shall be objected against him touching his being Accissary to the desertion of two Soldiers and not to depart the Court without leave, &c.

Margaret Brannon with Henry Heth Gent. her Security came into Court and acknowledged to be indebted to Patrick Henry Esq[r]. Governor &c. in the sum of £30 conditioned for the personal appearance of Margaret Brannon at the next august Court then and there to prosecute the above Hugh Ohara and not depart the Court without leave &c.

Malachia Hays v William Deal, Hugh Ohara Sp. Bl.

John Minter Gent. took the Oath of Capt. of the Militia & William McCormick Lieut.

Robert Newell is recommended a Lieut. of Militia and took the oath accordingly.

Richard Swisicks v Jacob Jones
Jas. Keykendal S. B.

Benjamin Vanatre v Jas. Keykendal
Jacob Jones S. B.

(43) John Ormsby obtained license to keep an Ordinary in the Town of Pittsburgh he having complied with the Law &c.

Mary Irwin obtained License to keep an Ordinary at Pittsburgh she having complied with the Law.

Joseph Vance came into Court and took the Oath of Captain of the Militia to which he is recommended.

Ignace Labat obtained License to keep an Ordinary at Pittsburgh he having complied with the Law.

Joseph Glass is recommended as Lieut. of the Militia and John Rankins Ensign.

William Masterson, Charles Masterson, Richd. Hopkins, John Guthery & Meshech Carter who were yesterday committed to the Sheriff s Custody being brought before this Court, it is the opinion of the Court they be fined viz. William Masterson & Richard Hopkins 40 S. each and that Richd. Hopkins be fined in the additional sum of 5 S. for drunkenness and that John Guthery & Meshech Carter be discharged, the Court do further adjudge that Charles Masterson be fined 20 S. for rioting and the further sum of 10 S. for swearing two profane Oaths.

Absent Isaac Cox.

Saml. Wall v John McCallister, Richd. McMahon S. B.

Absent Majr. Smallman & John Gibson Gentlemen.

Ignace Labat and John Irwin appeared in Court charged that they on the night of the 14th of April last did encourage a number of prisoners then in Confinement for disobedience of Orders, refusing their duty as Militia and Mutiny to break their Arrest and for opposing the officer in the Apprehending of them, it is the opinion of the Court that they be bound
(44) over to the next Grand Jury Court. Whereupon the said John Irwin with John Gibson & Thos. Smallman his Sureties acknowledged to be indebted to Patrick Henry Esqr. Govr. &c. that is to say the said John Irwin in £ 100 and the said John Gibson and Thos. Smallman in £ 50 each conditioned for the personal appearance of the said John Irwin at the next Grand Jury Court, and in the meantime be of good behaviour and not to depart the Court without leave &c.

Absent John Campbell, Gent.

It is also the Judgment of the Court that Ignace Labat be likewise bound over to the next grand Jury Court, whereupon the said Ignace Labat with John Gibson & Thomas Smallman Gent. his Securities acknowledged to owe to Patrick Henry Esq. Governor &c. the following sums, viz. Ignace Labat the sum of £100 and the said John Gibson and Thos. Smallman the sum of £50 each to be levied &c. upon condition that the said Ignace Labat shall personally appear at the next Grand Jury Court to answer the above Complaint and that in the meantime he be of good behaviour and not to depart the Court without leave &c.

Present Isaac Cox Gent. & John Campbell Gent.

On motion of James McMichael Ordered that his Ear-mark a Crop and a Slit in each Ear be recorded.

Joseph Beeler Jun. came into Court and Took the oath of Deputy Sheriff.

Petition & Summons John Allen Thorp against Thomas Applegate; Ordered to be Dismissed at Plantiffs Costs.

Andrew Dodge obtained License to keep an Ordinary at his Dwelling house on the Road from Devoir ferry to Shirtee's Creek, he having complied with the Law &c.

Ordered that William Crawford Gent. be appointed a Commissioner with Richard Yates & Isaac Leet for adjusting and settling the Boundary Line between this County and the County of Ohio.

(45) Thomas Lapsley a Lieut. in the Militia came into Court and informs them he is in dayly fears on acco'nt of being apprehended by the Millitary Law and desires the protection of this Court on a Matter which from the testimony of the Evidence now aduced appears an Affair of Slander. the said Mr. Lapsley now surrenders himself to this Court. Whereupon Proclamation being made that if any person could ought say against the said Thos. Lapsley they might then be heard, but none appearing the Court are of Opinion the said Mr. Lapsley be and he is hereby discharged.

Ordered that the wife of George Frederick Kiper a Soldier in the Continental Service be allowed the sum of Four pounds per month for the support of herself and three children.

Ordered that Three pounds per Month be Allowed to the three Children of John Evans a soldier of Capt. Heths Company in the Contl. Service.

Ordered that Court be adjourned until Tomorrow morning 6 oclock. THO. SMALLMAN.

June 24th, 1778. The Court met pursuant to their adjournment.

William Crawford, Thomas Smallman John Stephenson, William Harrison, Joseph Bealer, Gentlemen Present.

(46) Ordered that Colo. John Stephenson and Colo. Isaac Cox do call on Thomas Brown and receive from him the Cotton and Wool Cards sent up to this County, one half of which are to be distributed in the Battalion of Colo. Stephenson and the other in that of Colo. Cox. These Gentlemen to whom this charge is intrusted are to conduct themselves agreeable to the Governors Letter to the Justices of this County on the 26th Novr. last, provided that if there are more Women in either Battalion Colo. Stephenson & Colo. Cox are to supply each other according to the number of persons who may have a right to obtain the same.

Ordered that the Sum of 40 S. per month be allowed to the widow of James Shirley killed in the Service, then a Soldier in the 13th Virginia Regiment in the Service of the United States, for the support and maintenance of herself and Child, the same to commence from the 25th March last.

Ordered that Christiana Churchill the wife of Charles Churchill, now in the 12th Virginia Regiment in the Continental Service be allowed Three pounds per month for the Support of herself and two Children.

Ordered that Hannah Burns the wife of Matthew Burns late of the 11th Virginia Regt. deceased then in the Continental Service be allowed the Sum of 40 S per month for the Support and maintenance of herself and one Child.

Ordered that Mary the wife of John Overlin a Soldier in the Service of the United States and now in the 13th Virg'a. Regiment be allowed £ 5 per month for the support and Maintenance of herself & four Children.

(47) Ordered that Bridgit Blackston the Widow of Prideaux Blackston a Soldier in the 13th V. Regt. deceased then in the Continental Service be allowed £ 3 per month for the Sustenance and support of herself and two Children.

Ordered that the Support of the Wives of Soldiers and Widows of Soldiers deceased with their Children unless particularly ascertained from some particular date, such Support shall commence from the 25 March last. And that Colo. Campbell be requested to supply such distressed families agreable to the order of this Court, and the Clerk of this Court is to draw upon the Tresurer of this Common Wealth in favor of the said Colo. Campbell for the purposes aforesaid to the 25th September next, it is further the opinion of the Court that Colo. Campbell advance to such distressed families the Allowance granted by this Court to the 25th July and to retain the Ballance in his hand subject to the farther Order of this Court.

On the Petition of Colo. John Campbell setting forth that he is desirous of building a Mill on Charties Creek — that the Land on both sides of the Creek where he intends to build his dam in his own property, but he is apprehensive that some lands the property of some persons to him unknown at the mouth of Robinson's Run may be flooded by the Back Water of his Dam. Ordered that the Sheriff summon 12 freeholders of the vicinage to meet on the Land so said to be affected by the back water from his said Dam, and such Jury are to value
(48) the Damages and report the same to next Court under their hands and Seals.

Ordered that the following Gentlemen be appointed to receive the lists of Tythables within the following districts viz: — John Campbell Gent for the district of Capt Lee & Capt Bousman. Benjamin Keykendal Gent. for the districts of Capt. Evans & Capt Z. Wright. Joshua Wright Gent. for the districts of Capt. Jas. Wright & Capt. Cook. Benjn. Fry Gent. in the districts of Capt. David Ritchey, Capt. Ellis, & Capt. Kemp. John McDaniel Gent. for the district of Capt. David Andrews, Capt. Records & Capt. Nicholas Dawson. George Valandingham Gent. for the districts of Lieut. Newill. Andrew Swearingen Gent. for the districts of Capt. Vance, Lieut. Bay and Capt. Matthew Ritchey. Richd. Yates Gent for the Districts of Capt. A. Swearingens, and the district late Major Taylors. Isaac Cox Gent for Capt. Baxters district. Thos. Freman Gent for his own district & Capt. Ford's. William Harrison Gent for the district of Capt. Pearce. William Goe

(49) Gent. for Capt. Springer's district. Joseph Becket Gent. for Capt. Crows district and John Stephenson Gent. for the district of Capt. Minter.

Samuel Devoir is appointed Constable the Ensuing year, and that he be Sommoned before the nearest Justice and Qualify.

Inventory of the Estate of John Vance Deceased returned by the Appraisers and Ordered to be recorded.

Peter Stasey is appointed Constable for the Ensuing year who is to be Sommoned before the nearest Majistrate to Qualify in sd Office.

Ordered that William Crawford & David Shepeard Gent. do lay out the Prison bounds for this County agreable to Law and report to this Court.

The said William Crawford and David Shepherd Report as follows. Beginning at a Large Black Oak Standing Easterly from the Court House and Marked with Six Notches, and Extending Thence Southerly by a Line of Marked Trees to a White Oak Marked with Six Notches, Thence Westerly by a line of Marked Trees to White Oak Near and Including a Spring, Thence Northerly by a Line of Marked Trees Including the House of Paul Matthews to a White Oak, Thence by a Line of Marked Trees to the Beginning, which is ordered to be recorded.

Upon the motion of George McCarmeck Ordered that his mark a Lower half Crop on the Left Ear and Crop on the Right Ear be recorded.

(50) Upon the motion of George McCarmeck in behalf of Thomas Cherry Ordered that his ear mark a Crop in the Right ear be recorded.

Ab't. John Stephenson Gent.

Upon the motion of John Stephenson Gent. Ordered that his mark a Crop and hole in the Left ear a Slitt in the right Ear be recorded, and his Brand a figure of 3 on the near Shoulder and figure of 7 on the near Buttock be recorded.

Upon the motion of Thomas Spencer Ordered that his mark a Upper half Crop in the Left Ear and Under half Crop on the right Ear be recorded.

Upon the motion of John Campbell Gent. Ordered that his

Ear mark an under half Squear in Each Ear be recorded, and his Brand I C On the near shoulder be recorded.

Upon the motion of Joseph Beeler Gent. Ordered that his mark a Slit in the Left ear and a hole in the right Ear be recorded, and his Brand Thus J. B. on the near shoulder be also recorded.

Upon the motion of Henry Heath Gentleman Ordered that his Mark a upper half penny in the Left Ear and upper half penny in the Right Ear be recorded, and his Brand an H on the Near Shoulder be recorded.

Upon the motion of William Harrison Ordered that His mark a Swollow fork in Each Ear be recorded.

Upon the motion of Dorsey Pentecost Ordered that his mark a Crop in the Left Ear and Crop and Slit in the right Ear be recorded.

Ordered that Court be adjourned to Court in Course.

THO. SMALLMAN.

(51) At a Court Continued and held for Yohogania County July 27th, 1778.

Present Isaac Cox, Benjaman Kirkendall, Joseph Becket, Joshua Wright, Gentlemen Justices.

James Rogers Gent. named in the Commission of the peace and Commission of Oyer & Terminer came into Court and swore to the Same.

Joseph Cox v John Beetsman, John Williams S. B.

James Vanatre v William Braden, Thomas Bamfield S. B.

James Vanatre v Joseph Perkeson, William Fry S. B.

William Caldwell v William Fry, Thos. Lapsley S. B.

William Caldwell v Peter Reasner, Thomas Lapsley S. B.

Two deeds of Surrender William Fry to Adam Wickerham acknowledged by said Fry party thereto and ordered to be recorded, and two Assignments thereon from said Wickerham to Nicholas Depugh was also acknowledged by said Wickerham and likewise ordered to be recorded.

Thomas Lapsley who stands bound by Recognizance taken before John Gibson, John Stephenson & Wm. Harrison Gent. to this Court personally appeared and no evidences appearing to prosecute Ordered the said Thos. Lapsley be discharged from his Recognizance.

(52) Recognizance of John Springer was produced in Court but neither party appearing Ordered to be continued over to next Court.

Robert Henderson v John Kinkead, Benjn. Kirkendal Gent. S. B.

John McCullom v Isaac Galliard, Common Order against Deft. & app. Bail.

Report of the Commissioners for settling and adjusting the Line between this County and that of the Monongahela County returned by the said Commissioners and Considid with by the Commissioners on the part of the said County of Monaungala, is Ordered to be confirmed, as the Bounds between this County and the said County of Monaungahela and Ordered to be recorded.

John McAnulty
v
John Armstrong

Petition. Ordered to be Dismissed at Plantiff's Request.

Dorsey Pentecost clerk of this Court informed the Court on Oath that at a Court held for this County April 28th last Martha Davis acknowledged two Indentures to Isaac Cox Gent but through the hurry of Business the Letter S. was left out. It appears to the Court that the Indenture was executed by said Martha and by her acknowledged and it is ordered to be recorded.

Bill of Sale William Portor to James Ellis with the Return of Isaac Cox and Joshua Wright Gent of the Examination of Catherine Collins an absent witness Ordered to be recorded.

(53) Ordered that the Award of George Valandingham, Henry Taylor and John Hull in the Action between John Springer and Henry Kearsey be set aside the proceedings of the said arbitrators appearing to be illegal.

Paul Froman
v
William Stephens

In Case

Award returned and confirmed by the Court for the sum of four Hundred Eighty pounds Eight Shillings and his Costs about this Suit in that behalf Expended.

Ordered that Francis Reno be recommended to his Excellency the Governor as a Proper Person to serve as Captain in the Militia in the Room of William Lee now in the Continental Service.

Ordered that Jane the wife of Greenberry Stors a poor Soldier in the Continental Service from this State be allowed the sum of two pounds pr. month for the support of herself and one child to Commence the first day of May last, and that this Court draw on the Treasurer of this Common Wealth for the Same up to the 25th day of Sept. next.

Recognizance of Christian Lestnett and wife, Christian Lestnett Jun. Frederick Lestnett, Francis Lestnett and Stoffel Lestnett was Return and no prosecutors appearing Order to be Continued.

(54) View and Report of the road from Devoir's ferry to Pentecosts mills on Churteers Creek returned by the Viewers, Ordered to be set aside.

Ordered that Court be adjourned untill Court in Course.

ISAAC COX.

At a Court Continued and held for Yohogania County August 24th 1778.

Present Isaac Cox, Joshua Wright, Richard Yeates, James Rogers, Gent. Justices.

Ordered that Letters of Administration be granted to Elizabeth Ketchum and William Ketchum the Widow and bro'r of Samuel Ketchum decd. they having complied with the Law. Whereupon the said Eliza. and William came into Court and entered into Bond and Oath accordingly.

Oliver Miller & Andrew Swerengen Gent. Present. Joseph Beeler Gent. Prest. Joseph Becket Gent. Prest. Saml. Newell, Gent. Prest.

Joseph Beeler Gent
v Isaac Pearce S. B.
Ebenezer Walker.

Benjn. Kekendal Gent. Prest.

John Daniel produced a Commission from his Excellency the Govr. as Ens'n of Militia which being read the said John Daniel swore to the same.

John Masterson came into Court and took the Oath of Lieut. of the Militia he having produced his Excellency the Gov'rs. Commission.

(55) Richard Elson produced a Commission from his Excellency the Governor appointing him Ensign of the Militia, which being read the said Richd. swore to the same.

Saml. Newell Gent. Absent.

Administration of the Estate of John McCoy deceased is granted to Margaret McCoy his widow she having complied with the law. Ordered that Philip Philips, Jonathan Philips, John Nicholas & John Philips or any three of them being first sworn do appraise the Estate of John McCoy decd. and make return to next Court.

Ordered that Andrew Pearce, Richd. Johnston, James Wall and Richd. Sparks or any three of them being first Sworn do appraise the Estate of Samuel Ketchum decd. and make return to next Court.

Administration on the Estate of Thomas Brasher decd. is granted to Robert Brasher his Bro'r. he having complied with the Law. Ordered that Robt. Jackman Basil Stoker, Jeremiah Riggs & William Jackman or any three of them being first Sworn appraise the Estate of Thos. Brasher decd. and make return to next Court.

Patrick Jordan acknowledged two deeds of Bargain and Sale to Charles Norris which are ordered to be recorded.

John Gibson Gent came into Court and acknowledged a deed of Surrender to Matthias Slough Esq. 1000 Acres of Land on the Ohio which is ordered to be recorded.

(56) Thos. Freeman Gent. Present.

Ann Brook being bound over to answer the Stealing two pounds of Coffee from Sarah Sample appeared before the Court when no evidence appearing, Ordered that the same be dismissed.

John Logan enters himself Deft in an Action of Ejectment at the Suit of Walter Graham.

William McMahon produced a Commission from his Ex'cy the Governor appointing him Lieut. of Militia & took the Oath to the Same.

John Hall
v John Williams S. B.
Joseph Wells

Report of the County Line returned by Richd. Yeates, Wm.

Scott, Jas. McMechen & Isaac Leet Junr. read in Court and Ordered to be recorded.

License is granted to John Bradley to keep an Ordinary at his Dwelling house at Pittsburg he having Complied with the Law.

John Hall
v Nichs. Dawson S. B.
Joseph Waller

Ordered that the Court be adjourned to 7 o'Clock tomorrow morning. RICHARD YEATES.

(57) Court met Pursuant to adjournment August 25th. 1778.

Present William Goe, Richard Yeates, Samuel Newell, Oliver Miller, James Rogers, Joseph Beckett.

Deed of Surrender John Bull to Nicholas Peese acknowledged by the said Bool and Ordered to be Recorded.

Deed of Surrender Paul Froman to Adam Wickerham acknowledged by said Froman party thereto and Ordered to be recorded.

Deed of Surrender. James Fergurson to Adam Wickerham Acknowledged by said Furgerson party thereto and Ordered to be Recorded.

Deed of Surrender John Bolley to Michael Teggart acknowledged by said Bolley and ordered to be recorded.

Administration on the Estate of John Walker is granted to Gabriel Walker he having complied with the law. Ordered that James Ewen, John Bale, Alexr. McCandless and Thomas Redman or any three of them being first sworn do appraise the Goods Chattles and Effects and Slaves if any of the Estate of John Walker decd. and make return to next Court.

Inventory of the Estate of Edward Griffeth decd. retd. by the appraisers and ordered to be recorded.

Nicholas Dawson
v Saml. Holmes S. B.
Fra's. Kirkpatrick

(58) Present Andw. Swerengen and Benjn. Kekendal Gents.

Administration of the Estate of William McCoy decd. is granted to Philip Philips he having complied with the law.

Ordered that Jediah Ashcraft, Wm. Hinch Isham Barnet and Benjamin Sweet or any three of them being first sworn do appraise the Estate of William McCoy decd. and make return to next Court.

Administration of the Estate of William Lindsey decd. is granted to Michael Teggart he having complied with the Law. Ordered that Tobias Mattocks, Joseph Ross, Saml. Brice, & Thos. Bond or any three of them being first Sworn do appraise the Estate of Wm. Lindsey and make return to next Court.

Deed of Bargain & Sale and Receipt annexed from James Patterson to David McCrowry acknowledged by said James Party thereto and ordered to be recorded.

Deed of Surrender William Stephens to Andrew Devoier was proved by the Oath of Saml. Thompson and John Duke and Ordered to be certified.

Tobias Woods.
v
John McKee Maybery Evans S. B.

Daniel Swigert
v
James Murphy Michael Teggert S. B.

Thos. Freeman Gent. Absent.

An Indenture Jane Armstrong to Valentine Thomas D'Alton acknowledged by said Jane and ordered to be recorded.

Ordered that Jane Armstrong the wife of Geo. Armstrong a deceased Soldier then in the Service be allowed for the support of herself and four Children five pounds per month to the 6th
(59) of July from 6th April and Three per month from said 6th July. Ordered that the Clerk do draw on the Treasurer for the same.

Mortgage John Steward to Jacob Bousman was proved by the oath of James Berwick the other evidences having heretofore proved the same. Ordered to be recorded.

On the Petition of James Johnson & others Ordered that Andrew Pearce son of James, James Wall, John Crow & Rich'd. Johnson or any three of them they being first sworn view a Road out of the Road leading from Gists to Devoirs ferry near And'w. Dye's passing thro' the forks to the Monongahela opposite the mouth of Mingo Creek thence Crossing the River the nearest and best way to the Mill Froman is now building near the mouth of Mingo Creek.

Review of a Road from Peters Creek to the house of Robert Henderson beginning at the lower end of Zadock Wrights field from thence following the Ridge to Jacob Barrackmans land leaving him on the right hand and from thence to Martha Lapsleys Land leaving her to the right hand from thence to Robert Hendersons. returned by the reviewers & ordered to be confirmed.

Ordered that William Bruce be appointed Surveyor of the Road leading from Raredon's ford passing by Kekendals Mill to the house of Robert Henderson and that the Tythables within three miles of each side said Road work on the Same.

(60) Ordered that Robert Craighead be appointed Surveyor of the Road from the top of the Ridge near James Wilson decd. to Raredons on the Monongahela and that the Tythables on both sides said Road work on the same within three miles thereof.

Ordered that Andrew Dye be appointed Surveyor of the Road from the House of Leonard Extine to the top of the Ridge near the house of James Wilson and that the Tythables between the two Rivers not exceeding three miles work on the Same.

Ordered that the Wife of William Shaw a poor Soldier be allowed three pounds per month for the Subsistance of her three Children from this date, and the Clerk to draw on the Treasurer for the Same.

Deed of Surrender Henry Taylor Gent to David Ridle acknowledged by said Taylor and ordered to be recorded.

Administration of Estate of Samuel Duncan Decd. is granted to David Duncan he having complied with the Law. Ordered that John Ormsby, Samuel Sample, Samuel Evalt and William Christy or any three of them being first sworn do appraise the personal Estate and Slaves if any of Samuel Duncan deceased, and make return to next Court.

Joseph Beeler Gent. Present.

Benjamin Vanatre Enters himself Defendt. in an Action of Ejectment at the suit of Henry Morrison.

(61) John McDaniel Gent Present.

Bill of Sale Sarah Reed to Robert Blackley and John Reed for a negro named Pompey Approved by the oath of Joseph

Becket one of the Subscribing Witnesses and ordered to be certified.

George Lightenberger being summoned as a Garnishee in an Atta'm't. against Geo. Croghan at the suit of Simon & Campbell appeared before the Court and saith he hath one Wheat Fan the property of the said George in his possession and no more.

Henry Morrison.
v Benjn. Vanatre S. B.
James Vanatree

On the Petition of David Williams & others Ordered that Abraham Miller, Henry Millier, Henry Newkirk and William Murley or any three of them being first sworn Do view a Road from Paul Fromans Mill on Mingo Creek to the Road leading from Pentecosts Mills to the Court House and make Return to next Court of the Conveniences and Inconveniences thereof &c.

On motion of Paul Froman Ordered that his Mark a Crop in the right ear be recorded.

On motion of David Williams Ordered that his Mark a Crop off each Ear and a half penny in the under side of the right ear be recorded, and his Brand D W be also recorded.

On motion of Isaac Springer Ordered that his Mark a Crop in the near Ear and a Nick and a Slit in the off Ear be recorded.

(62) On Motion of Robert Little Ordered that his Mark a half Crop in the Left Ear and an under bit in the right Ear be recorded.

On Motion of William Downs Ordered that his Mark a Crop off each Ear and a Slit in each Ear be recorded.

Benja. Jones
v
Patrick McDaniel William Deal S. B.

Deed of Surrender Henry Wood to Conrad Loutherback acknowledged by said Henry Party thereto and ordered to be recorded.

Two deeds of Surrender, Sampson Beaver to Thomas Cook acknowledged by said Sampson Party thereto and ordered to be recorded.

Ordered that Isaac Taylor be allowed the Sum of 94 Dollars for the Carriage of the Cards allotted to this County from Williamsburg and that Colo. Cox and Colo. Stephenson do account with said Mr. Taylor for the Same as sold.

Ordered that the Subsistence granted to the Wife and Six Children of William Shaw a poor Soldier who died in the Continental Service be extended to the 25th Sept. next. Vide, April 28th, 1778.

James Scott produced a Commission from his Excellency the Governor appointing him Captain of Militia which was read & sworn to accordingly.

James Wherry Produced a Commission from his Excellency the Governor appointing him Lieut. of the Militia which was read & sworn to Accordingly.

(63) George Vallandingham Gent. Present.

Ordered that the sum of Twenty Shillings p. month be allowed the wife of Daniel McCay, a poor Soldier in the Continental Service for her support.

Deed of Surrender John Hodglond to James Rogers acknowledged by said Hoglond party thereto and ordered to be recorded.

Deed of Surrender Isaac Cox, to John Decker Acknowledged by said Cox and Ordered to be recorded.

Ordered that Thomas Bay be recommened to his Excellency the Governor as a proper person to Serve as Captain in the Melitia.

Thomas Bay produced a Commission from his Excellency the Governor Appointing him Captain in the Melitia which was read and Sworn to Accordingly.

Thomas Reed produced a Commission from the Governor appointing him a Lieutenant in the Militia which was read & Sworn to accordingly.

Richard Yeates, Absent.

Hugh McDonald produced a Duplicate of an Indenture Binding him the sd. Hugh a Servant for the Term of three and a half years, bearing Date the Twenty Ninth day of June 1775, which is not yet expired yet the said Hugh claim freedom from a Bargain between his late Master William Powel, & a former Master who sold the sd. Hugh to the said Powel, and from the Evidence aduced to this Court, it appears that the sd. Hugh McDonald is a free Person.

(64) Hugh Brawdy
v In Trespass.
Jacob Feagley. Then came the parties and requested that This Suit should be refered. Ordered that The said Suit be refered to John Decker, William Taylor Morris Brady, John Corn & Vinson Colvin, and that they do return their Opinion to Next Court.

Ordered that Peter Rowleter be recommended to the Governor as a proper person to Serve as Captain in the Melitia, and James Miligan as Ensign.

Inventory of the estate of Samuel Richardson Returned by the Appraisers and Ordered to be Recorded.

William Renno a Minister of the Gospel come into Court and Took the oath of Allegience and Fidelity to this State.

Inventory of the estate of Archibald McNeal returned by the appraisers and Ordered to be Recorded.

Deed of Surrender John Hill to John Cannon acknowledged by sd. Hill and Ordered to be recorded.

Joseph Cox
v In Case.
John Williams At request of Parties Ordered That this
Bright Daviss & Suit be Refered to Henry Taylor, John
Mary Hoyle Duglass, Nicholass Little, John Ackerson, William Colvin, & John Lydea, and that they Return their Opinion to Next Court.

(65) Joseph Cox
v In Case
John Williams & At Request of parties Ordered That this
Theodorus Daviss suit be refered to Henry Taylor, John Duglass, Nicholass Little, John Ackerson, William Colvin, and John Lydea, and make report to Next Court.

Ordered that Philip Ross be recommended to the Governor as a proper person to serve as Captain in the Melitia.

Philip Ross Produced a Commission from the Governor appointing him Captain in the Melitia which was read & sworn to accordingly.

Lewis Renno produced a Commission from the Governor appointing him Ensign of the Militia which was read & sworn to accordingly.

Joseph Alexander came into Court and took the Oath of Ensign of Militia agreably to his Commission read in Court.

Ordered that Saml. Newell Gent. do wait on Colo. Campbell for the Acts of Assimbly.

(66) On Motion of Jonathan Martin Ordered that his Mark a Slit in both ears be recorded.

On Motion of Samuel Dunn Ordered that his Mark two under half Crops in both Ears be recorded.

Ordered that Theophelus Case be appointed Constable to Serve the Ensuing year, and that he be Sommoned before James Rogers to Qualify into said Commission.

Ordered that Court be adjourned to Six Oclock tomorrow morning. BENJA. KUYKENDAL.

Court met Pursuant to adjournment, August 26th, 1778.

Present. Samuel Newell, James Rogers, John McDonald, Isaac Cox, William Goe, Oliver Miller, Gentlemen Justices.

Christian Summitt
v In case.
John Gollehair & wife. Ordered to be Dismissed at Plantiffs Request.

Benjn. Kekendal, Present.

The Last will and Testament of James Freeman was proved by the Oaths of John Thompson & Gilbert Cammeron the Two Subscribing Witnesses and Ordered to be recorded.

(67) James Johnston
v In Case.
Godfrey Waggoneer At Request of Parties Ordered That this suit be refered to John Crow, Henry Miller, Nicholas Christ & John Decker, and that they report their Opinion to Next Court.

John McDonald Took the Oath of Executor of the Last Will and Testament of James Freeman Deceased.

John Cannon and Matthew Richie Gentlemen named in the Commission of the Piece and Commission of Oyer and Terminer, Came into Court and Took the Oath of Justice of the Peece and Justices of Oyer and Terminer.

George McCarmick Gentleman produced a Commission from the Governor appointing him Sheriff for this County which was read, the Court demanded the sd. George McCarmick Gent. to enter into Bond according to Law, and Qualify into said Commission which he refused alleging that he was a Captain in the 13th Virginia Redgment in the Continental Service, and Contrary to his Expectation the General refused to permit him to resign his said Melitary Commission and that his serving as Sheriff was Incompatible with his duty in the Military department, it is the Opinion of the Court that the reasons are satisfactory.

Ordered that Matthew Ritchie, Joseph Beckett & James Rogers Gentl. be recommended to his Excellency the Governor as proper persons for his Excellency to Commission one as Sheriff to serve the Ensuing year.

(68) Matthew Ritchey Gent came into Court and took the Oath of High Sheriff for the Term of one month.

Joseph Ford produced a Commission from his Excellency the Governor appointing him Captain of the Melitia, which was read and Sworn to According.

Ordered that the Clerk forwared the following Letter to his Excellency the Governor.

Sir

Permit the Justices of the County Court of Yohogania to address your Excellency, in Answer to Your Letter of the 2nd of May Last. We feal as we hope we ought for the Governours attention to the affairs of this County. The reasons of the Courts passing over the Colonel, Lieutenant Colonel, and Major, (which your Excellency formerly Commissioned) in their Late recommendation, was, that the Colonel and Major Informed the Court, or some Members thereof, that they had signified their resignation to your Excellency and their reasons for so doing, and that the Causes was not removed and refused to be recommended we have Only heard that your Excellency Commissioned Mr. Thomas Brown as Lieutenant Colonel, and that the said Mr. Brown refused Serving, as he was not recom-

mended by the Court. This we believe to be the State respecting the Lieutenant Colonel as a Commission did not Come up to Isaac Cox who was recommended as Lieutenant Colonel at the Time the Colonel was recommended. We also found the County Lieutenant furnished with Blank Commissions which he filled up to the field and others Officers on the spot. Our Delegates not attending the last Cession, We have had no Convenient Conveyance to your Excellency, otherwise we should
(69) have answered your Letter Earlier, and which for the above reason has had no bad effect, the officers all being Commissioned by the County Lieutenant and Qualified before the arrival of your Excellency's Letter. We are to acknowledge the receipt of the Captains and Subaltrons Commissions which we delivered to the County Lieutenant, who detained Captain James Scott and Subaltrons Commissions untill yesterday, which was then Delivered and Sworn to.

Matthew Ritchie Gentleman high Sheriff Protest against the sufficiency of the Goal to retain Prisoners.

Ordered That John Cannon and Richard Yeates Gentlemen, Inspect the Clerks Office of this County, and report to next Court the Condition in which they find the Papers and Records.

Ordered that Mary the wife of Alexander McAdams a poor Soldier in the Continental Service be allowed 20 S. p. month, for her Support, to Commence the 25th of May last, and be Continued to the 25th of September next.

John Spivy, Plaintiff
v Case.
Samuel Beeler Def'd. At Request of Parties Ordered That this Suit be refered to Samuel Johnston, James Scott, David Andrey and George Long, and that they report their Opinion to the Next Court.

(70) Ordered that Jedeah Ashcroft be appointed Constable the Ensuing year and that he be Sommoned before Oliver Miller Gentl. to Qualify into said Office.

Ordered that Court be adjourned untill Court in Course.

JOHN CANON.

At a Court Continued and held for Yohogania County September the 28th, 1778.

Present Isaac Cox, Benjaman Frye, Joshua Wright, Joseph Beckett, Gentleman Justices.

Administration of the Estate of Thomas Cook deceased is granted to Anne Cook widow of sd. Deceased she having complied with the Law.

Ordered that Nathaniel Blackmore, John Munn, John McDowel and James Allison or any three of them being first Sworn do appraise the personal Estate and Slaves if Any of Thomas Cook deceased, and make return to Next Court.

Administration of the Estate of Archibald Wilson deceased is granted to Elizabeth Wilson his widow she having Complied with the Law.

Ordered that Thomas Jackson, Andrew Pow,[1] John Rogers & Michael Dellow Sen. or any three of them being first Sworn do Appraise the Personal Estate and Slaves if any of Archibald Wilson deceased and make return to next Court.

Andrew Pow Produced a Commission from his Excellency the Governor Appointing him Lieut. of the Melitia which was read and Sworn to accordingly.

(71) George Brent & Phil Pendleton Sworn Atto.

John White Ju. Took the Oath of Lieut. of Melitia.

Deed Pool Andrew McMeans to Thomas Applegate was acknowledged by sd. McMeans party thereto and Ordered to be recorded.

Hugh Brawdy Plaintiff
v
Jacob Feagley Defendt. Award returned & Judgment.

James Johnston v Godfrey Wagoneer. Award returned & Judmt.

On the motion of John Johnston, Ordered that his mark a Swolefork in each ear be recorded.

Samuel Newel Gentlement Present.

View of a Road from the Road leading from Gist to Devoirs Ferry Crossing the River opposite the mouth of Mingo Creek from thence to Fromans Mill on a Branch of sd. Creek, Returned by the Viewers, Ordered to be set aside. Ordered that Michael Humble, Daniel Applegate, James Colven & Hugh

[1] This was undoubtedly the celebrated Andrew Poe, Indian fighter.

Brawdy or any three of them being first Sworn review said Road; and make return to next Court, sd Road.

Ordered that an order for a View of a Road from Fromans Mill to the road Leading from the Court House to Pentecosts Mill be set aside.

Ordered that Henry Newkirk, John Lewis, John Morrison, and Henry Morrison, or any three of them being first Sworn view a road the Nearest and Best way from Fromans Mill on Mingo Creek into the Road leading from the Court House to Pentecosts Mills between the Plantations of Joshua Wright and John Johnston and make report of the Conveniency and Inconveniency to Next Court.

(72) Isaac Cox Gentlemen. Absent.

Ordered that the administration of the Estate of Daniel Greathouse deceased formerly granted to John Greathouse be revoked and that the same be granted to Mary Greathouse the widow of the said Deceased, she having complied with the Law. Ordered that Edmond Polk, James Campbell Richard Boyce, & Richard Elson or any three of them being first Sworn do appraise the Personal Estate and Slaves if any of the Estate of Daniel Greathouse deceased and make return to Next Court.

Ordered that Court be adjourned untill Tomorrow morning 7 oclock. SAMUEL NEWELL.

At a Court Continued and held for Yohogania County September 29th, 1778.

Present Isaac Cox Samuel Newell Benjaman Frye Oliver Miller Joseph Becket Gentlemen Justices.

Atteachments.

Clerk v Poston Contd.

O'hara v Brandon, Cont'd.

Cumings v Lindsey Cont'd.

Grayham v Strain Contd.

Issues.

Cox v Williams &c. Contd.

Lydea v Cox Contd.

References.

Connel v Vaughan Abates P. Dead.

v Wells Contd.

Washington v Martin Contd.
Ward v Dunn Contd
(73) Ward v Wells Contd.
Priscoe v Todd Contd.
Connel v Lindsey Contd.
Reasoner v Ruth Contd.
Brown v Hamelton Contd.
Summervill v Summervill Contd.
Bowling v Morrison Contd.
Summitt v Gollihar and wife Dismd. & P.
Stirling v Richards. Contd.
Wells v Newell Contd.
Vance v Williams Contd.
Brashers v Hamelton Contd.
Cook v Ferrell Abates by Plantiffs Death.
Gist v Waller Contd.
v Hull Contd.
v Boyles Contd.
Cook v Thomas Abates by P. Death.
Burriss v Tropman Contd.
Hull v Bandfeeld. Contd
Wherry v White Sen. Contd. at Issue.
Burriss v Johnston &c. Contd.
Dunnaughagain v Gray. Contd.
Byers v Patterson. Agreed.
Pentecost v McDonald. Agreed.
Shilling v Collingo. Contd.
Schley v McKindley Contd.
Shilling v Newkirk Contd.
v the same Contd.
Wills v Shilling. Agreed
Braydon v Vannatree Contd.
Cox v Williams &c Contd
Pentecost v Long. Agreed.
Myers v Hooper Contd.
Mitchell v the same Contd.
Richards v Ross Contd.
Fullum v Johnston &c. Contd.
v the same Contd.

v McCornish. Contd.

(74) Andrews v Johnston &c Contd.

Shilling v Fortner Contd

Hooper v Myers Contd

v George Miers Contd.

Brounfield v Ross. Contd

Holms v Dunn Contd.

Kaster v Long Ju. Contd.

Fullum v Johnston. Contd.

Hooper v Thomas &c. Contd.

Vance v Williams. Contd.

Fullum v Johnston. Contd.

Springer v Kersey S. Imprl.

Swissecks v Jones Contd.

Froman v McCroury Contd.

Decker v Ruth Contd

Pearce v Evins. Contd.

Murphey v Richards Contd.

Hays v Deale Contd.

Bruce v Pelton Contd.

Ewalt v McCallister Contd.

Hoglaland v Riggle. Contd.

v Laughlin. Contd.

Swessicks v Swessicks. Contd

Newkirk v Shillings Contd.

McFarling v Beeler. Contd.

Andrews v Johnston Cont.

Matthews v Hibbitt Contd.

How v Geneway &c. Contd.

Cox v Britzman Contd.

Vannatree v Braydon Contd.

v Perkerson Contd.

Colwell v Frye &c Contd.

Henderson v Kincaid. Contd.

Vannatree v Kuykenkall Contd.

Burriss v Williams Contd.

Jones v McDonald Contd.

Dawson v Kirkpatrick Contd

Morrison v Vannatree Contd.

(75) Hall v Wells Contd.
Grayham v Logan Contd.
Beeler v Walker Contd.
Woods v McKee Contd.
Morrison v Surgest Contd.
Froman v Boyce Contd.

Common Orders.

Lindsey v Long Contd.
Spivy v Beeler Judgt. Wt. Enqy.
Nelson v Shilling Judgmt. Wt. Enqy.
Shilling v Nelson. Jugt. Wt. Enqy.
Lawrence v Rogers. Judgt. Wt. Enqy.

Appearances.

Colwell v Wray. A C
Mattocks v Brown. A C
Williams v Garby Agreed.
Deal v Hays Contd.
Crooks v Hogland Contd.
Patterson v McCornish Contd.
v Emberson Agreed.
McKay v Davidson } Contd.
v the same }
Brown v Mattocks A C
Morrison v Vannatree Contd.
Bouseman v McGoldrick Contd.
Myers v Hooper Dismised P R.
Willson v Richards Contd.
Ralston v Lowry Contd.
Pearce v Evins. Contd.
Commingo v Boggs A. C.
Kinkaid v Henderson &c. Contd
v Henderson. Contd.
Martin v Shillings Discont.
McDonald v Slover A. C.
Hogland v McNew Alia.
(76) Springer vs. Listenet & ux. Agd.
Same vs. Same Agd.

Lochran vs. Brown Alias.

Lydia vs Collins Alias

Colwell vs Thorn Alias.

vs. Hoaghland. Alias.

Witzle vs McIlwaine. Alias.

Winebiddle vs. Valentine. Alias.

Pearce vs Evans Alias

Lebat vs Smith & ux Alias

Allason vs Douglas Discontd.

Lintenberger vs Oldcraft. Alias

Lindsey vs Hamilton Alias.

vs Smith Alias.

Wells, Infant &c. vs. Blackstone. Alias.

McIlwaine vs Witzle & ux Alias

Valaudingham vs Walker Alias

Wagoner vs Rape Alias.

Barrackman vs Woods Alias.

vs Harry Alias.

Miller vs Mitchell Alias

vs Same Alias

Harrison vs Hall Alias.

Beans vs Johnston Alias.

Witzle vs Crawford Alias

Brashers Admr. vs Colvin Alias.

vs Brasheirs Alias.

McCullum vs Brazier & Adm. Alias

Burns vs Loutherback Alias.

Sumrell &c vs Sumrell Alias.

Colwell vs Young & al Alias.

Listenet Inf. &c. vs Springer Alias.

Gallahier & ux vs Summitt Contd.

Froman vs Dean Contd.

Cook vs Dickenson. abates by Pltff's Death.

Riggs vs Corn Plurias

Thompson vs Carpenter Agd.

Brashairs vs. Hamilton Discontd. P. No Int.

White vs. Johnston Contd

Campble vs Patterson Plurias.

(77) Miller v McGowen. D. Contd.

Burris v Jones Discontd.
Colwell v Mills Plurias
Wallace v Dunkin Contd.
Schley v McKindley Alias.
Boyce v Froman &c. Contd.
Tygert v Bowley Contd.
v Chamberlain }
v Davidson } Contd.
Swigert v Murphey Contd.
Davis v Pelton Contd.
McCullum v Gilyard Contd.
Lessee Clerk v Again Contd.
Springer v Lestnett. Contd.
How v Geneway Plurias.

Petitions

Todd v Shearer A. S.
Hufman v Williams A. S.
Timmons v Gaffney A. S.
Wright Asse. v Dunleavy Contd.
Morgan v Stalsman A. S.
Dunleavy v Frye Contd.
Swigert v Ross A. S.
Baggs v Commingo A. S.
Devoir v Anderson. Contd.
Whitzle v Valentine A. S.

District Causes.

Miller v Humble Ejmt. Contd.
Pentecost v Jones &c. Contd.
v Linn. Contd.
Johnston v Swearengen. Contd.
Brounlee v Dugloss Contd.
Brent v Scott } Dis. Contd.
v the same } "
v the same } "

(78) Last Will and Testement of Abraham Vaughan deceased was proved by the Oaths of Thomas Gist & Edward Hattfield Subscribing Witnesses & O R.

Richard Vaughan, & Andrew Pow Sworn Executors of the Last Will and Testement of Abraham Vaughan deceas'd. Ordered that Stephen Ritchards, Adam Pow, Thomas Jackson & Joseph Jackson, being first Sworn do appraise the Estate of Abram Vaughan deceased and make return to next Court.

Ordered that the Tithables within five miles of the South side of the road of which Nicholas Christ is Surveyor work on and keep said Road in Repair.

License is granted James Johnston to Keep an Ordinary at the Court House of this County, he having Complied.

Benjaman Kerkindall Present.

Robert Louden is appointed Guardian Elizabeth Loudoun, Thomas Loudoun, Easther Loudoun, Catherine Loudown, John Loudun, James Louden, Mary Loudown, Orphans to James Lowden deceased, he having Complied with the Law.

Ordered that Matthew Ritchie Gentleman be appointed Sheriff for the Ensuing Month and that he be sworn accordingly.

Matthew Ritchie Gent. Sworn Sheriff for one month.

Ordered that the Sheriff Sommon a Grand Jury to attend next November Court.

David Philips is appointed Constable the Ensuing year and that he be sommoned before Oliver Miller Gentl. to Qualify into said Office.

(78) Ordered that Nicholas Depugh, Benjaman Kaster be appointed Constables the Ensuing year, and that they be Sommoned to Swear into Said Office.

Ordered that Atteachment Issue against Samuel Devoir for not Taking on himself the Office of Constable.

Edward Ward Gent. named in the Commission of the piece and Commission of Oyer and Terminer come into Court and Took the Oath of Justices of Piece and Justice of Oyer and Terminer.

Ordered that Anne McClain be sommoned to shew cause why her Daughter Anne Jefferess, Should not be Bound to Samuel Semple, agreable to the Tenner of a Contract Between the said Ann and Sarah Semple wife of the said Samuel in the year 1770.

Simmon & Campbell
v Atteachment.
Croghan —— Ordered that Judgment be set aside
Garnishee and redocked.

David Dunking having formerly declared, that he had in his hands one hundred Seventy Nine and three forth Dollars the Property of the Defdt. William Christie, two pair of Geers, one old Ax, one old Spade, a pitchfork, a Small Box of Iron & on old Lanthern. George Lentinburgher That he had a Wheat fan, the property of the Defdt. Money condemned in the hands of Garneshee. Judjm't according to former Judgment, and Order of Sale.

Bill of Sale Sarah Reed to Robert Blakely and John Reed was proved by the oath of Edwd. Cook one of the Subscribing Witnesses & O. R.

(79) Edward Ward Gentleman Present.

Joseph Brouster & Jacob Bouseman & Malechia Hays come into Court and did acknowledge to Owe to Patrick Henry Esq. Gov. or Chief Majestrate of this Commonwealth or his Successor in Office Vizt. the said Joseph Brouster in the sum of five hundred pounds, and the said Jacob Bouseman and Malichi Hays in the Sum of two Hundred and fifty pounds each, to be levied on their respective goods & Chattles Lands and Tenements, Conditioned for the Personal Appearance of the said Joseph Brouster at the Next Grand Jury Court to be held for this County and then and there answer to Such Objections as shall be alledged against him Touching his being concerned in the Late Conspiracy for Taking the Garrison of Pitt, and not depart the Court without Leave otherwise to remain in full force & Virtue.

Ordered that the allowance made to the wife of Daniel McKay a poor Soldier Shall commence the 25th of May Last and Continue to the 25th of the Present Month.

Ordered that Colo. John Campbell pay to the respective Soldiers wives & widows the money remaining in his hands due them up to the 25th of the Present Month.

Ordered that the Clerk perfer a Petition to the Assembly seting forth, that the Court Conceives the Laying a County Levy to defray the Necessary Expence of the County, in the administration of Justice, will from the Peticulear Situation of the County be attended with difficulty, and praying that it may be Enacted to enable the Court to receive and apply the fines, accruing in the County towards Lessing the County Levy.

Ordered that Court be adjourned untill Court in Course.

BENJA. KUYKENDALL.

(81) At a Court Continued and held for Yohogania County October the 26th, 1778.

Present. Edward Ward Benjaman Kuykendall, Oliver Miller William Harrison, Samuel Newell. Gentlemen Justices.

Archibald Hull v Thomas Bonfied. At Request of party ordered to be refered to George Cox & John Jackson, Jas. Innis & John Decker.

Richard Beall Sworn Lieut. of Melitia.

Inventory of the Estate of Benjaman Bruer deceas'd. Returned by the Appraisers and Ordered to be Recorded.

Inventory of the Estate of Jonathan Higgs deceased Returned by the appraisers and Ordered to be Rec'd.

Matthew Richie is appointed Sheriff for one month who was sworn accordingly.

John Southerlin Sworn Deputy Sheriff for one month.

The last will and Testament of John Pearce deceased was proved by the Oath of Moses Cox and Dorsey Pentecost two of the Subscribing Witnesses, and Ordered to be Recorded.

Inventory of the Estate of Samuel Ketcham deceased, returned by the appraisers and Ordered to be Recorded.

Ordered that Court be adjourned untill Tomorrow Morning 7 Oclock

EDWD. WARD.

(82) At a Court Continued and held for Yohogania County October 27th, 1778.

Present Edward Ward Benjaman Kuykendall, Oliver Miller, Samuel Newell, William Harrison, James Rogers Gentlemen Justices.

Ordered that the Ordinary Keepers within this County be allowed to sell at the following rates —

Whiskie by the half pint.............................. 2S.
The same made into Toddy.......................... 2S. 6.

for a Greater or Lesser Quantity in the same proportion ....

Beer p Quart.. 1S6

the same proportion for a Larger or Lesser Quantity..

for a hot Breakfast.................................... 3S

for a Cold ditto..................................... 2S6

for a Dinner.. 4S.

for a Supper.. 3S.

for Lodging with Clean Sheats........................ 1S6

Stablage with good hay or fodder...................... 5S.

Corn p. Quart 9d

Oats p. Quart.. 6d

Inventory of the Estate of Daniel Greathouse deceased Returned by the administrator and Ordered to be recorded.

Richard Crooks and Nathaniel Brackmore is Recommended to the Governor as proper persons to Serve as Captains of the Melitia.

(83) James Burriss & John Roadharmill be recommended to the Governour as proper Persons to Serve as Lieutenants of the Melitia.

James Guffee is recommended to the Governour as Proper Person to Serve as Ensign of the Melitia.

Michael Tygert, Samuel McAdams, John Shannon, James Morrison Ju. & Francis Morrison is recommended to the Governour as proper persons to Serve as Lieutenants of Melitia.

Jacob Long Jun. & Moses Cooe are Recommended to the Governour as proper Persons to Serve as Ensigns of the Melitia.

On the Motion of Colo. John Campbelle License is granted him to Build and Compleat a Water Mill on Campbell's Run emtying into Churtees Creek on the West side, a short distance below Robertson's Run.[1] It being made appear in this Court that the Building Said Mill will effect the property of no Person, the Lands on both sides being the Property of the said Campbell.

Ordered that Court be adjourned to Court in Course.

EDWD. WARD.

[1] Now Known as Robinson's Run, emptying into the Chartiers at the Borough of Carnegie.

(84) At a Court held for Yohogania County November the 23rd. 1778.

Present Edward Ward, Isaac Cox, Joshua Wright, & James Rogers, Gentlemen Justices.

Ordered that Colo. John Campbell have leave to Build a Mill on Churteers Creek near the mouth of Robertson's Run. It appearing by the Return of a Jury for that Purpose that It will effect no Person, and that the said Report be recorded.

Nicholas Dawson Sworn Captain of the Militia.

Deed poll Wm. Price to William Harrison acknowledged by the sd. Price party thereto and Ordered to be recorded.

Deed poll Daniel Casity to Edward Griffith Proved by William Price one of the Subscribing Witness. Ordered to Lie for farther Proof.

Deed Poll William Shannon to James Miller acknowledged by said Shannon and Ordered to be recorded.

Ordered that Samuel Johnston, Ritchard Boyce, James Campbell, Alexander McKendless, Peter Rowleter, William Christie, John Ormsby, Natheniel Tumbleson, Edmond Polke, Richard Wells, Joseph Noble, James Allison, Laurence Crow, Nicholass
(85) Little & Susbalze Bently, be fined agreeable to Law for non attendance as Grand-Jury Men.

John Lydea v Wm. Collings & Zebulon Collins. Spl. Bail.

Ordered that the Court be adjourned untill Tomorrow Morning 9 oclock. EDWD. WARD.

At a Court Continued and held for Yohogania County November 24th 1778.

Present: Edward Ward Isaac Cox, Samuel Newell, Oliver Miller, Gentlemen Justices.

Administration of the Estate Geo. Rineheart is granted to Mark Iler he having Complied with the Law.

Ordered that Richard Waller, Joseph Waller, Edward Hatfield & Augustus More or any three of them being Sworn do appraise the Estate of Geo. Rineheart deceased and Make report to Next Court.

Archibald Hull agt. Thomas Bondfield, Awd. Returned and Judgment.

License is granted John Collings to keep a Ordinary at his House he having Complied with the Law.

Administration of the Estate of John Green deceased is granted to William Colvin he having complied with the Law.

(86) Ordered that Thomas Brown, Bazel Brown, Benjamin Brashers & Otho Brashers do appraise the above Estate and make report to next Court.

Administrater of the Estate of John McClery is granted to William McClery he having complied with the Law. Ordered that John Reed, Robert Thompson, Joseph McGarman & Mabary Evins or any three of them being first Sworn do appraise the above Estate and make report to next Court.

Inventory of the Estate of John Mills deceased returned by the appraisers and Ordered to be recorded.

Joseph Brown v Tobias Mallocks, Samuel Dunn. Sp. Bail.

Samuel Holcross v Samuel Dunn. Tobias Mallocks Spl. Bail.

Com. Wealth
v for Disaffection to the State.
Joseph Brouster. The said Brouster being brought into Court and nothing appearing against him Ordered to be Discharged.

Deed Poll Walter Grayham to Thomas Christie was proved by the Oath of Jacob Bouseman one of the Subscribing Witnesses, and Ordered to Lie for farther proof.

Inventory of the Estate of John McCay deceased returned and ordered to be recorded.

Joshua Wright Genl. Present.

John Hall being bound in recognizance who being called failing to appear. Ordered that a Scerafacis Issue.

License is granted to John Roberts to keep an Ordinary at his House he having Complied With the Law.

(87) Ordered that Edward Hatfield, Christopher Price, John Beason and Henry Beason or any three of them being first Sworn do appraise the Estate of Abraham Vaughan deceased, and make return to next Court.

Lapsley vs Reed. Ordered that a Commission Issue to Take Deppositions in said Suit.

Edwd. Ward. Genl. Absent.

Ward v Thorn. Ordered that a Commission Issue to Take Deppositions in said Suit.

Ruburn vs. Laferty. No Inhabitant. Dism'd.

Ordered that the Administraters of the Estate of Frederick Farree be Sommoned to render acct. of said Estate to next Court.

Attachments

Ohara vs Brannon. Contd.
Cummings vs Lindsey. Contd.
Grayham vs Strain Abates. Def. Dead.

Issues.

Cox vs Williams Contd def.
Lydia vs Cox. Contd Ptf.
Wherry vs White. Contd PLf.
Miller vs Humble Contd PLf.
Pentecost vs Jones Contd Deft.
Johnston vs Swearengen Contd.
Brounlee vs. Douglas. Contd.

References.

Connell vs Weils Contd.
Washington vs Martin C. O. Eject.
Ward vs Dunn dism. by PLf.
vs Wells Contd.
Briscoe vs Todd Contd.
Connell vs Lindsey. Contd.
Reasner vs Ruth. Contd.
Broun vs Hambleton. Contd.
(88) Sumrell vs Sumrell, Contd
Bowling vs Morrison. Contd.
Sterling vs Richards Contd.
Wells vs Newell. Contd.
Vance vs Williams C. O. Eject.
Basheirs vs Hambleton Contd.
Guest vs Waller. Contd.
vs Hull Contd.
vs Boyles Do.
Burris vs Trapman. Contd.
vs Johnston Contd.
Donnagen vs Gray Contd.

Shilling vs Collins. Contd.
Sly vs McKinley. Contd.
Shilling vs Newkirk N. G. Agd.
vs Same Owe Nothing. Agd.
Braden vs Vanatre. Contd.
Cox vs Williams Contd Def.
Myers vs Hooper N. G. with Leave. Agd.
Mitchell vs Same N. G. do.
Richards vs Ross. Contd.
Fullum vs Johnston & at Contd. def.
vs Same Do.
vs Jno. McCornish Do.
Andrews vs Same Contd Def.
Shilling vs Faukner. N. G. with Leave Agd.
Hooper vs Myers N. G. with Leave. Agd.
vs G. Myers Do.
Brounfield vs Ross Contd
Custard vs Long Contd
Hooper vs Myers N. G. With Leave Agd.
Vance vs Williams. Contd Def.
Fullum vs Johnston N. G. w. Leave Agd.
Springer vs Kerny N. G. with Leave Agd.
Swassicks vs Jones Contd
Froman vs McCrory Judg. by Nihil dicet.
Decker vs Ruth Contd
Pearce vs Evans Contd.

(89) [Patrick Clerk having Obtained an Attachment against the Estate of William Poston for £4.18.4 Penn'a Currency who is said to be so obsconded that the Ordenary Process of Law cannot be served upon him, and the Sheriff returned that he had levied the said Attachment in the hands of Anthony Corkhern, and that the said Anthony confes'd that he had £16.10 Penn'a. Currency, Proprty of Plantiff, and the Plantiff produced a proved account agt. the sd Defendant for £4.18.4 Pennsylvania Currency. It is considered by the Court that the Plantiff recd. agt. the Defdt. £.3.18.6. with costs. Ordered that the Money be Cond. in the hands of Garneshee.][1]

[1] Erased in the original.

Murphy vs Richards. Contd.
Hay vs Dean do
Bruce vs Felton do
Evalt vs McCallister do
Hoagland vs Riggle do
vs Lauglin do
Swassick Adr. vs Swassicks. do Eject.
Newkirk vs Shilling. Conditions perfd. Contd.
Mcfarland vs Beelor. Contd.
Andrew vs Johnson. Contd.
Matthews vs Hibett. Contd.
Howe vs Jenniway. Contd.
Cox vs Bretsman. Contd.
Vanatre vs Braden. Contd.
vs Parkison. Contd.
Colwell vs Fry C. O.
Henderson vs Kinkade. C. O.
Vanatre vs Kuykendal. Contd.
Burriss vs Williams. Contd.
Jones vs McDonald. do
Dawson vs Kirkpatrick. Contd.
Morrison vs Vanatre. C. O.
Hall vs Wells &c. Contd.
(90) Grayham vs Logan Contd.
Beeler vs Walker. Contd.
Woods vs McKey. Con'd.
Morrison vs Swygart. Contd.
Froman vs Boyer C. O.
Deal vs Hays. Contd Plf.
Crookes vs Hougland. Contd.
Patterson vs McCornish. Contd.
Morrison vs Vanatre. C. O. Eject.
Bousman vs McGoldrick C. O.
Myers vs Hooper. C. Rule. N. G.
Willson vs Richards N. G.
Rolstone vs Lowry. Contd.
Pearce vs Evans. Contd
Gallahar vs Summitt. discontd.
Froman vs Deane. C. O.

White, Sen. vs. Johnson. C. O.
Wallice vs Duncan. Contd.
Sly vs M^c^Kenly. Contd.
Boyce v Froman &c. Contd. Ptff.
Tygart vs Boley. Contd.
vs Chamberlane. Contd.
vs Davis. Contd.
Swygart vs Murphy. C. O.
Devoir vs Pelton. Contd.
M^c^Cullum vs Galliard. Dism. with Costs.
Clark vs Again Contd.
Springer vs Listenett. Contd.
M^c^Coy vs Davison. Contd.
vs Same do

C. Orders.

Lindsey vs Long
Spivy vs Beelor. Contd.
Nelson vs. Shilling. Contd
Shilling vs. Nelson do.
Lawrence vs Rogers do.

(91) Ordered that a request be made to the Court of Monaungohela to appoint Two Gentlemen to meet Rich'd. Yeates and Isaac Leet Jun. appointed by this Court as Commissioners to ascertain Dunlaps old road from Redstone old Fort to Bradocks road as the Boundry Line between this County and the sd County of Monaungohela agreable to Act of Assembly.

Alias Capias.

Colwell v Wray. Plu. Cap.
Mallocks vs Brown Contd.
Brown vs Mallocks Contd.
Kinkaid vs Robert Henderson. Contd.
Cumings vs Baggs. Contd
Kinkaid v Henderson Contd.
McDonald v Slover Contd.
Hazle v McNew Contd.
Laughlin v Brown Contd.
Colwell v Thorn Plu Cap.
v Hogland Con.

Whitzle v McIlwane Contd.
Winebiddle v Valentine Contd.
Pearce v Evins Contd.
Labatt v Smith Contd.
Lentenburger vs Oldcrof. Contd.
Lindsey v Hamilton Contd.
v Smith Contd.
Wells Inf. v Blackson Contd.
McInwane v Whitzle Contd.
Valaninghan v Walker Contd.
Wagoneer v Rape Contd.
Barrackman vs Woods Contd.
v Havig Contd.
Miller v Mitchell Contd.
v the same Contd.
(92) Harrison v Hall Contd.
Beans vs Johnston Contd.
Whitzle vs Crawford. Contd.
Brashers adm. vs Colvin C. O.
v Brashers C. O.
McCullum vs Brashers. Contd.
Burns &c v Loutherback Contd.
Sumrall &c v Sumrall Contd.
Colwell v Young N. G.
Lestnett Inf &c. v Springer Contd.
Riggs v Corn Contd.
Campbell v Patterson. Contd.
Schley v McKindley. Contd.
How v Geneway. Contd.
Colwell v Mills. Contd.

Appearances.

Henderson v Walson Dis. by Plantiff.
Collings vs Vannatree. Contd.
Williams, Ass. vs Anderson Contd.
Tharp v Gray Contd.
v Matthews Contd.
Frye v Richie. Contd.
Murphey v Jourden. Contd.
v the same Contd.

Heath v Bruce Impl.
Brooks Adm. v Roberts. Contd.
Smith v Gibson Alias Cap.
Henry v Slone C. O.
Miller v Humble Alias Cap.
Henderson v Johnston Send out another Ejmt.
Froman v Boyce. Ejmt. Send out a new Process.
Johnston v Stephens Contd.
v the same Contd.
Reed v the same Contd.
Wright v Heart. Contd.
Boothe v Shuster Dism. by Plff.
(93) Kearns vs Loggan. Alias Cap.
Springer vs Walker. Alias Cap.
Hamelton vs Norris
vs Brashers.
vs Brashers Sen. } Ejm. Issue New Process.
Gallihair vs Tracy. Disctd.
M^c^Carmeck vs Willson. Contd.
Munn vs Crawford. Contd.
M^c^Mahen vs Matthews. Alis Cap.
vs Honks Alias Cap.

Ordered that Colo. Isaac Cox be Impowered to acct with all person that hath Negociated any Business relative to this County's Salt, Lodged with Israel Thompson of Louden County, and that he receive the remainder of said Salt, and Transport it to this County, and Issue the same to the Inhabitants to whome it is due, at Six pounds, Ten Shillings pr. Bushell, and that the profits thereon shall be his full satisfaction for his said Services and that the said Colo. Cox shall also pay all demands on said salt Either for the original purchase or otherwise.

Ordered that Philip Pendleton be allowed one Hundred pounds pr annum for his Services as the State Attorney.

The Court then proceeded to lay the County Levy.

Dr. the County of Yohogania.

To Philip Pendleton as States Attorny £100.
To Richard Yeates for Rûnning County Line 31

	To Isaac Leet Jun. Do.	36
	To Dorsey Pentecorst for Attending pr. Acct.	14.18
		£181.18
	Levy Continued.	
(94)	Dr. Brought Over	£181.18
	Cr. By 910 Tithables @ 12 S. Each	546.—
		364.2
	Dr. to the Sheriff for collecting £546 at 6 pr C.	32.15.2
		£331. 6.2
	To the sheriff for Extra Services 1200 & Tob'o.	7.10
	Depositum in Sheriffs hands	£333.16.10.

Ordered that the sheriff Collect from every Tithable person within this County the sum of Twelve Shillings each as a County Levy, and that he pay the above Charges to the different persons to whome they are due, and that he account for the above Collections.

Ordered that Benjaman Kuykindall, and Samuel Newell Gentlemen, Contract with a proper person or persons To Junk and Daub the Coort house, and provide Locks and Bars for the Doors of the Goal, and to Build an addition to the Ednd of the Court House and Goal Sixteen feet squear one Story High with good Sufficient Logs and a good Cabbin Roof, with a good outside wooden Chimney, with Convenient Seats for the Court, and bar, with a Sheriffs Box &c. with a good Iron pipe stove for the Goal Room, and that they have a pair of stocks, whiping post and Pilliory Erected In the Court yard, and that the whole be Compleated as soon as Possible.

Ordered that Henry Taylor, James Allison, James Patterson and William Brashers be atteached for Contempt in Neglecting to make report of the Conveniency and Inconveniency of a Road from Catfish Campt to Pentecosts Mills, agreable to a former Order of Court.

(95) Ordered that Court be adjourned untill Tomorrow morning 9 oClock. EDW^D. WARD.

At a Court Continued and held for Yohogania County November 25th, 1778.

Present, Edward Ward. Isaac Cox, Joshua Wright Richard Yeates and Samuel Newell Gentlemen Justices.

Atteachments from the District Dockett.

Anderson vs McLean. Contd.
McMahon vs Myers. Contd.
Campbell vs Street. Contd.
Morgain vs Connolly Contd.
Dunking & Wilson vs Linn Contd.
Price vs Linn Contd.
Hawkins vs Greathouse Abates by Def. Death.
Hull vs Linn. Contd.

New Atteachments.

Pillon vs Smith Contd.
Hammill vs Hanks Contd.
Duglas vs Hill Discontd.
Vergin vs Carr Abates by Def. Death.
Perkerson vs Duglass Discontd.
Decker vs Hanks. Contd.
Bowling vs Rutter. Contd
(96) Conee vs Casteel Contd.
Robertson vs Frenuty Contd.
Smallman vs McConnell Contd.
Thomas vs Kilgore Discontd.
Perkerson vs Edwards Contd.
Ormsby vs Dunn Contd.
Harrison vs Wallace Discontd.
Ogle vs McSwan Contd.

Issues.

Spear vs Jones Contd.
Decamb vs Nicholas. Abates by Plant. Death.
vs the same Do.
McCawley vs Jones Contd.
Campbell vs McKay. Abates by Defd. Death.
Spears vs Winemiller Contd.
Semple vs Collings Contd.

Colings vs Sample Contd.
Bouseman vs McGoldrick Contd.
Hawkins vs Wheet Contd.
Rowly vs Springer Contd.
Ward vs Thorn Contd.
Jones vs Spear Contd.
Heckman vs Brounfeld Do.
Pentecost vs Linn. Contd.
Corn vs Miller Contd.
Pentecost vs Briscoe. Contd.
McGinnis vs Gibson Contd
Hite vs Core Abates by Plat. Death.
Parker vs Barrackman Contd.
Shilling vs Taylor Contd.
Hawkins Ass. vs Clark Contd.
Hawkins vs Kuykendall Contd.
McLouney Adm. vs Thomas Contd.
v Smith Contd.
97) Eaton vs Cannon Contd.
vs McClelland. Contd.
Bond vs Mordacai Contd.
v the same Contd.
McDonald v Scott
vs Caveatt } Contd.
v Hannah
Brawdy Ass vs Trench Contd.
Grubb vs Dooling Contd
Vallandingham vs Teegarden Contd.
Thomas vs Hannah &c Contd.
v Hannah. Contd
v Caveatt Contd.
Haney vs McKay Contd.
Chambers vs Spear &c Contd.
vs Thorn Contd.
Ward vs Thorn Contd.
McLingt vs Knight Contd.
Wood vs Gray Contd.
Martin vs Duglass Contd.
Beeler vs Wells Discontd.

Cook vs Froman Contd.
v Shilling Contd.
vs McConnell Contd.
vs Robertson Contd.
Crow vs Williams Contd.
Same v the same Contd.
Same vs the same Contd.
Sample vs McKinzey Contd.
Heckman vs Dunkfield Contd.
Rogers vs McKay. Abates by Defds. Death.
Wilson vs Hannah Contd.
Colvin vs Frederick Contd.
(98) Holliday vs Hawkins Contd.
Bowley vs Springer Contd.
v Springer Contd.
Cresep v Dooling
v Peters
v Teegarden } Abates by Plant. Death.
v French
Bealle v Finn &c } Contd.
v McMahon } Contd.
Barrackman vs Mutzs Contd.
Armstron vs Ownigs &c. Contd.
Hamelton vs Dunfield Contd.
Hand vs Whitaker Contd.
Harrison vs Paul. Abates by Defds. Death.
Neavill vs Gist Contd.
Riley vs Hanna Contd.
Cresip adm. vs Tegarden Abates by Plant. Death.
Teagarden vs Hammon Contd.
Cresip vs Swearengen Contd.
Phelps vs McKay. Abates by Defd. Death.
v Sample. Contd
Campbell vs Bealle Contd
Paul vs Smith Contd.
McElroy vs Templin. Contd.
v the same Contd.
Kuykendall vs Ross Contd.

Referances Not at Issue.

Frye vs Tilton Contd
v the same Contd.
Chamberlain vs Hanthorn Contd.
the same Heckman } Abates by
the same } Defds. Death.
Ward vs Owings Jun. Disctd. Defd. paying cost.
Spear vs Heckman. Abates by Defds. Death.
vs Proctor Contd
vs Humble. Abates by Defds Death.
(99) Spear vs Gist Contd.
Croghan vs Waugh Contd.
Steenburgan vs Warbill. Abates by Defd. Death.
Newell vs Robertson Contd.
Kuykendal vs Hawkings Contd.
Small vs Teagarden Abates by Def. Death.
Sample & ux vs McKay. Abates by Def. Death.
Shilling v Young Contd.
v the same Contd
v Dement Contd.
vs Proctor Contd.
Newell vs Wiseman Contd.
Noble vs Chamberlain Contd
v Shay &c Contd.
Shilling vs. Martin Contd.
Hawkins Ass. vs Hilderbrand Contd.
Hawkins v the same Contd.
v Tonee Contd.
v Hanks Contd.
v White Contd.
Hardin vs Hawkins Contd.
Wm. Hardin vs Glen Abates Defd. Dead.
Spears vs Crawford Abates by Defd. Death.
v R. McMachen. Contd.
Wickweze, Ass. v Harrison Contd.
Prather vs Beaty Contd.
Wells vs Brown Contd.
Blackburn Ass. vs Peake Contd.
Brashers vs Swearengen Contd.

Vallandingham vs Chiswell Contd.
Chambers vs Amberson Contd.
Conrod vs Carter Contd.
Vannatree vs Kinkaid Dis Contd.
Heair vs McConnell. Contd.
Pentecost vs Trader Discontd.
Wood vs Griffith Contd
(100) Miseley vs Housesenger Contd.
Mitchell vs Scott. Contd.
Rogers vs Proctor Contd.
Avery vs Brown Contd.
Clinton & Noble vs Brashers Contd.
Baker vs Harges. Contd.
Wagler vs Warner Contd.
McGrue vs M:cConnell Contd.
vs Phelps. Contd
Glenn vs Henton. Abated. Plantiff Dead.
Holliday vs Belleywiss. Con.
Boley vs Ross. Contd.
vs the same Contd.
vs the same Contd
Bouseman vs Douseman Contd.
v the same Contd.
v McLean Contd.
Kuykindall vs Dunn Contd.
vs Hawkins
v Roberts
v Smith
v Vannatree } Contd.
McMahan v Irwin Contd
McKendless v McCornish. Contd
Taylor vs Irwin Contd.
Deining vs Lane Contd.
Moor vs Richman Contd.
Smallman vs Slover Contd
Deck vs Swearengen Continued.
Vergin v Moore Contd.
Barker vs Jourden Contd
Waller vs Meeks Contd

Cresip vs Bowling vs Wright vs Hedges vs Hanks vs Reasoner	Abates by Plat. Death.

Armstrong vs Rammage Contd.
Reasoner vs Heckman. Abates. Def. Dead.
Bedford Ass. vs Hill Contd.
Wilcox vs Creghead Contd
Barrackman vs Shousely. Contd.
Bealle vs Shawon Contd.
Keller vs Jones. Contd.
(101) Reasoner vs Shearer Contd.
Brent vs Beeler. Contd.
Ramsey vs Chambers Contd.
v the same Contd.
Stephens vs Berwick Contd.
Heath vs Farrer Contd.
Perkie vs Colloway Contd.
Cresip vs Shearer Contd
Hughes vs Thomas Contd.
Stephens vs Shilling Contd
Dye vs Dye Contd.
Downer vs Teegarden Contd.
Thomas vs Lee Contd.
Swagler vs Mills. Abates by Defd's. Death.
Virgin vs Carr. Abates by Defd's. Death.
Wilson vs Cockran. Contd.
Mills vs Hunter. Abates by Plant. Death.
Brounfield vs Cox. Contd.
Bond vs Long. Contd.
Tygert vs Dunnaughagain. Contd.
Colwell vs Brouster. Contd.
Sumrall vs. the same. Contd.
Shearer vs Miller Contd.
Baker vs Hendericks. Contd.
Whitaker vs Dickson Contd.
Wills vs Raredin Contd.
Whitzle vs Shearer Contd.

Stevens vs Stout. Contd.
Gallehan vs Dowling. Contd.
McMullen & ux vs Dixerson Contd.
Jas. McMullen vs the same Contd.
Moore vs Virgin Contd.
vs Jer. [?] Virgin Contd.
Dodd vs Virgin Ctd.
vs Virgin. Contd.
Bayars vs Philips Contd.
Campbell vs Brounfield Contd.
(102) Harrison vs Corn Contd.
Warvill vs Parmour Contd.
Jones vs Clark Contd.
Phelps vs McGrue Contd.
Simmings vs Daughan Contd.
Small vs Gray Contd.
McMichael vs French Contd.
Pursell vs Gibson. Contd.
Railouson vs St Clair. Abates by Plantif Death.
Couswell vs Dunn. Contd.
Barr vs Clerk Contd.
Halfpenny vs Wetzel. Contd.
Hill vs Corn } Abates by Defds. Death.
vs The same }
Thomas vs Merchant Contd.
Farree vs Kincaid. Abates by Plaintiff's Death.
Park vs Cockron Contd.
Ireland vs Wilson. Contd.
Collings vs Brody Contd.
Black vs Dunleavey Contd.
Vaughan vs McMahan Contd.
Stephenson vs Roads Contd
Tedball vs Stoner Contd.
Anderson vs Denney Contd.
Stephenson vs Barnett Contd.
McClellan vs Gray Contd.
Schely vs Smith. Contd.
Young vs Jackman Contd.
Linn vs Tilton. Contd.

Martin vs Johnston Contd.
Chambers vs McLean Contd.
Jones vs St. Clair. Abates by Pl. Death.
Reese vs Haymaker Contd.
Altman vs Hanna & Irwin Contd.
Cox vs Decker Contd.
Furgurson vs Carrol Contd.
Martin vs Glass Contd.
v Hamelton Contd.
Black vs Chamberlain Contd.
Mordecai vs Bond } Contd
v Knight }

(103). Black vs Jolley Contd
v Hanna. Contd.

Deed poll from Daniel Cassity to Lettis Griffith was proved by the oaths of Rich'd. Yeates and Daniel Curry two of the Subscribing witnesses and Ordered to be recorded.

George McCormick Gent. named in the Commission of the Piece and Commission of Oyer and Terminer sworn to said Commissions.

Tygert vs Burns wontd.
v Jefferess Contd.
Vaughan vs Elson Agreed.
Winebiddle vs French Contd.
Yough vs McCullough. Contd.
Grater vs Crawford. Abates by Defds. Death.
Swigert vs Clemens } Abates by
vs Robertson
vs Cox
vs Walker } Pl. Death.
vs Lucas
vs Scott
vs Cox
vs Fisher }
Morrison vs Ross Contd.
Brounfield vs Smith Contd.
Hunter vs Jones. Contd.
Caswell vs Dunn Contd.
Wallace vs Moredock Contd.

Faset vs Meeks Contd
Campbell, Ass. vs Dunn Contd.
Ridgley vs Linn. Contd.
Morecroft vs Doling Contd.
Fleman vs Gibson Contd.
Dunfield vs Hickman
vs Russell
v Ross
vs Lindsey
vs Fositt
vs Peershover } Contd.
Steel vs Johnston Contd.
v the same Contd.
Downer vs Morrison Contd.
(104) Woods vs McGlaughlin Contd.
Styger vs Smith Contd.
Elliott & ux. vs Martin. Contd.
vs Collings Contd.
Lynch, Infd. vs Laughlin Contd.
Semple vs Ferns, &c. Contd.
Williamson, Ass. v Mills. Abates by Pf. Death.
Gray vs Harrison Contd.
Croghan v Bowley
v McCollister
v Bouseman
v McKee
v Kuyendall.
v Ritchman
v Whitaker
v Whitaker
v Whitaker
v Kuyendall
v Frederick
v Rowleter
v Mc.Clean
v Bouseman
v Grimes
v Mc.Grue
v Trupe

v Switzwiks
v Meeks } Contd.
vs M^c^Manemy
v Druming
v Campbell
v Myers
v Gibson
v Weddle Sen.
v Beard.
v Mitchell
v Miller
v Ornsby
v Renno
v Elliott
v Price
v Lowden
v St. Clair
v R. Lowden.

(105) George Croghan v William Ramage. } Contd.
v Henry. Contd.
v McCartney
v Thompson.
v Ross.
v Ross.
v Whitzle.
v Hunter
v Gibson. } Continued.
v Grant
v Springer
v Conner
v Keezer
v Royall
v Davidson
v Elrod
v M^c^Connell

Sinkler vs Labatt. Contd
Ornsby v Bouseman. Contd.
Miller vs Humble Contd.
Clerk vs Tibott. Contd

Eagle vs Adams Contd.
Whitaker vs Dickson Contd.
Gerty vs Hanna. Contd.
Gaughagain vs Smith Contd.
Enock vs Teegarden Contd.
Clinton vs Mays Contd.
Hawkins vs Humble Contd.
Nicholass vs Swissicks Contd.

Swigert vs Hatfield
vs Case
vs Erskins
v Smith
v the same
v Daviss
v Sills
vs Crosby } Abates by Plt. Death.

Fife vs Holliday
v Fife
v Churchell } Contd.

(106) Fife v Fife Contd.

Hite v Morgan Contd
v White Contd.
v Evins. Contd.
v Mynett. Contd.
v Tearabaugh Contd.
v the same Contd.

Hite v McCabe &c. Abates by Plat. Death.

Bruin v Fife
v the s me
v W. Fife
v the same } Contd.

Dealton v Gruver
v Matthias Stoner } Contd.

Hales v Roach Contd.

Morgan v Nicholas
v Bond
vs Chamberlain
v Beavers } Contd.

Morgan v Wyer
v the same } Contd.

Kuykendall vs Pearceful
v Pancake } Contd.
v Douthard

Williams v Vannatree } Contd.
v Crow

Price v Linn
v Weddle } Contd.
v Hanks

Gray v Peters } Contd.
v Patten

Tygert vs Donnavan
v Craven
v Vanatree } Contd.
v Craven
v Oglin

St. Clair vs Sill Cont.
v Reuboarn. Abates by Def. Death.

(107) Mc.Cullogh vs McCormick Continued.
v Douthard. Contd.

Elliott vs Gerty Contd.
vs Brown. Abates by Deft. Death.

Jones vs Wilson. Abates by Parties Death.

Hawkins v Bell
v the same
v the same } Contd.
v Gray
v Perkerson

Semple v E. Thompson Contd.

Crisep, Ass. v Dunfield. Ab. by Pl's. Death.

Mic'l. Crisep vs Elliott } Abs. by Pl. Death.
v Taylor

Robertson vs Crow Contd.

Shilling vs Newkirk Contd.

Rogers vs Williams
vs Parr } Contd.
v Tumbleson

Zane v Hawkins } Contd.
v Drenning

Zane, Ass. v. Holdman Contd.

Castleman vs Taboe Contd.
Elliott Adm. vs Harges Contd.
McMullin vs Dickerson Contd.
Ross, Ass. v Cleman Contd.
Atkenson v Mairs Discontd.
Daviss v Dunn. Contd.
Lyon v Dunkan Contd.
Heizer vs Bruce Contd.
Glaswell vs Kizeer Contd.
McGlaughlin vs Young Contd.
Anderson vs Reese Contd.
Dunleavy, Ass. vs Frerell Contd.
Hammon v Teegarden Contd.
Armstrong vs Oharra Contd.
Thomas, Ass. vs Stark Contd.
(108) Ward vs Springsteen Contd.
vs the same. Contd.
v Labatt. Dismiss. by Plantiff.
Jones vs Evins. Contd.
v the same
v Mc. Goldrick } Contd.
v the same
Ogle v Wilson. Contd.
v the same. Contd.
Labatt v Rammage Contd.
v Aston. Abates by Plfs. Death.
Hamelton v Aston Abs. Plfs. Death.
Hamelton v Goe Contd.
Cleldenery vs Logan Contd.
Nevill, Ass. vs Holliday. Contd.
N. Nezer vs Davidson Contd.
Kelso vs Pigget Contd.
Allison v Lyon
v Duglass } Contd.
Hilderbrand vs Hawkins
Ass. v Hanks } Contd.
the same
Wallace vs Briscoe Contd.
v the same Contd.

Swearengen vs Spencer Contd.
v the same Contd.
Smith vs Smallman Contd.
v Sly, & u. Contd
Martin v Elliott Contd
Brasher vs Cossick Contd
Jones vs Ormsback. Contd.
Waferds Exr. vs Cox &c. Contd.
Heath vs Parks. Contd.
Hawkins vs McCarty Contd.
Rootes vs Coock. Contd.
Spencer vs Swearingen Contd
Brent vs Jones
Colwell, Ass. vs Linn Contd.
(109) Kid —— v McConnel. Contd
Theobald v Martin. Abs. by P. Death.
Lynch vs Jones Contd.
v Berwick Contd.
Mitchell v Zane, Contd.
Drening vs Boys Contd.
Braden v Elliott Contd
Johnston v Stell Contd.
Crooks vs Hilderbrand Contd.
Holliday, Ass. vs Wortherington Contd.
Hamelton vs Martin. Con.
Berwick v Atkinson Contd
Gilfillin, Ass. v Tygert Contd
McQuitly vs Gray. Contd
Mc.Collister vs Scott. Contd
Bowler vs Tygert Contd
Robertson vs McGoldrick Contd.
Mc.Elroy vs McMachen Contd
Atkinson vs White Contd.
Dunleavy vs Russell. Dismsd. by Plantiff.
Schley vs Smith. Contd.
Ferrell, Ass. vs Carr &c. Abs. by D. Death.
Price vs Crawford. Contd.
Wheat vs Kermicheall Contd.
Scott vs Vallandingham Contd.

Campbell vs Hanks. Contd.
Holliday vs Scott & ux Contd.
McCarty vs Craighead Contd.
Lyons vs Hamblebeerer Contd.
Frazier vs Chambers Contd.
Miller vs Hill Contd.
Kearns vs McQuing Contd.
Boyce v Thomas Contd.
Wright vs Springston Contd.
Davidson vs Hanks Contd.
Wothwall v Dristnell Contd.
(110) Clark vs Hawkins Contd.
Smith & Duglass vs Girty. Contd.
Dillo vs Perky Contd.
McManamy v Oharra Contd.
Beckman v Scott. Contd.
Ferrell v Daugherty. Contd.
Tharp v Collings. Contd.
Armstrong vs Oharra Contd.
Bouseman v Ornsby. Contd.
Thomas vs Elliott Adm. Contd.
Christie v White. Contd.
Richards v Aston. Abates by D. Death.
Brinkers Exr. vs Hardin Adm. Contd.
Daviss & Co.'y. vs. Young. Contd.
Elevy vs Dunn Contd.
Lyons vs Downes. Contd
Mitchell vs. Wade Contd.
Willson vs McGinniss Contd
Downard vs Vaughan. Abates Defend. Dead.
Coleman vs Gauze. Contd.
Wallias v. Meek. Discontd.
Johnston v Stephens Contd.
Wilson vs Hannon Contd
Mitchell vs Zane Contd
Williams vs Presser Contd
Kurtz v Jones Contd.

Croghan vs Henry
v Springer
v Ross
v Powell } Contd.

Hite vs Dodson Contd

Thompson vs Williams Contd.

New Petitions

Sells vs Irwin. Contd.

Campbell vs McKay. Abs. by Defds. Death.

Shilling v Blackman. Contd.

v Delaney Do.

Roach v Shaner Do

Christie, Ass. v Irwin. Do.

v Jackman Do.

Hite v Cox. Abates by Plant. Death.

Bell vs Huston. Discontd.

Parker, Ass. vs Daviss Contd.

Whitzle, Ass. vs Ryebolt. Contd.

Stone vs Crawford Extr. Do.

Wood vs Griffith Con.

Hamilton v Hawkins. Do.

Seman v Miller &c. Do.

v the same Do.

Cook v Berwick
v Heartt
v Johnston
v Dobbins
v Barker } Contd.

Vannatree vs Pelton &c Contd.

McKenzey vs Semple Cont.

Ryan v Clerk Do.

McDonald v Grimes Do.

Deale vs Grove Do.

Tennell, Ass. vs Marshell —

Colvin vs Ryley Contd.

Wells vs Johnston. Contd

Redford, Ass. vs. Hill Do.

Ryan vs Caswell Do.

[224]

v Shaner Do.
Brent v Teegarden Do.
Owry vs Fisher Do.
v Miller Do.
v Maurer Do.
(112) Farree v Duck Contd.
v Sinnett. Contd
Pigman v Seaton Contd
Stebbs v Templeton Do.
v Daviss Do.
v Accord Do.
v Carter Do.
v Edwd. Doolin Do.
Caswell, Ass. v Girty. }
v the same } Contd.
v the same }
v the same }
Caswell v Scott. Contd
Clinton vs Cuningham Contd
v Donne Do.
Weckwire v Downer Do.
Holliday v Jones Do.
v the same Do.
v the same Do
Wells v Zane Do.
Hawkins v Bodkin Do.
Watson v Kuyendall Do.
Hawkins v Coffee Do.
Little vs Brounfield Do
Virgin vs Colvin Do.
Paul vs West Do.
Day vs Christie. Do.
Taylor vs Byerly. Do.
Humble vs Clerk Do.
v Burns Do.
Devoir vs Scott Do.
Jones v McDowell Do.
Fowler v Brown Do.
Wall vs Doolin Do

Waddle, Ass. v Arle Do.
Farree vs McCatney Do.
v Carrell Do.
v Macken Do.
(113) Frederick Farree, Ass. v Kinkaid Contd.
Brent vs Simpson Contd.
Cresip v Colwell Abs. by Plaf. Death.
v Philips Do.
Swigert v Sinkman [?]
v Corree
v Beeler } Abates by Plan. Death.
v Myers
v Myers
McClelan vs Small Contd.
v the same Do.
Daviss, Ass. vs. Downer Do.
Devoir v Warner Do.
v Hanks Do.
Decks v Groggs Do.
Harden Ju. v Kinkaid Do.
Miller, Ass. v Custard Do.
Ryan vs Ross Do.
Tennal, Ass. v. Marshall Do.
Maxwell vs Ashcroft Do.
Killay v Cox Do.
Walls v Zane Do.
Kuykendall v Dunn Do.
Cuningham v Bruce Do.
Jollery v Barker Contd.
Moore v Churchell Do.
Schane, Ass. v Stephens Do.
Jackson v Clerk Do.
Bowley v Swigert Do.
v Russell Do.
McGrue v Ward. Do.
Morrison v Armstrong Do.
Gather v Swearingen Do.
Ross v Dunfield. Do.
Jacobs v Brasheers Do

Lennett v Aston. Abates by D. Death.
Dean v M^{c}.Namay Do.
Loughlin v the same Do.
(114) Rowleter v Labatt Contd.
Steel v Moncck Do.
Jackson v Clerk Do.
Hall v Redman Do.
Mordecai v Kuykendall Do.
Decmp v Freshwater. Abates by Pl. Death.
Thomas v Lambert. Contd.
M^{c}.Collister v Black Do.
Savage v Teegarden Do.
Finn v Williams Do.
Adams v Horn Do.
Lain v Peyton Do.
Walliace v Meek. Disctd.
House v Mayhon Contd.
Virgin v Moore Do.
Collings v Dolton Do.
—— Ass. v Clerk Do.
Adams vs Huston Do.
Cleldening vs Caarmichell Do.
Hanthorn, Ass. v Martin Do.
Semple v Owery Do.
Hamelton v Hawkins Do.
Rouse vs [?] Do.
Crawford v Aston. Abates by D. Death.
Johnston v Watson Contd.
Morgan v Wheeler Do.
Steel v Thomas Do.
Ewalt v Ross Do.
Daugherty v Aston. Abates by Def. Death.
McGloughen vs Irwin Contd.
Pearce vs Cherry Do.
Semple v Carrell Do.
Moore v Ritchnin Do.
Daugherty v Blacke Do.
Devoir v Tygert. Do.
(115) Tygert v Lindsey Contd.

v the same Contd.
v the same Do.
Stewart v Scott. Do.
Theobald v McCoy. Abates by Partys Death
Holliday v Zane. Contd.
v Wortherington Contd.
Simmon & Campbell v Gaughagain Contd.
Kuykendall v Kuykendall Do.
v Holliday Do.
v Heath Do.
v McGuire Do.
v Hogland Do.

Vallandingham v Springer
v Clemans
v Meeks
v Hartley
v Lindsey
v D. Lindsey
} Contd.

Farree v Linn, Sen. Do.
Downard v Parr. Abates by Defds. Death.
Maxwell v Thompson Contd.
Reed v Clerk Do.
Dealton v Shannon Do.
Clinton & Noble v Dooland Do.

New Petitions.

Smallman v McDorend
v Gaunseley
v Scott
} Contd.

Swigert v Higinbottom
v Newland
v Scott
v Pelegon
v Cox
v Castle
} Abates by Pl. Death.

(116) Daugherthey v White
v Philip
v Brownfield
v Bailey
Ass'ee. v McGinn
} Contd.

Ross vs Swift Do.
v Black Contd.
McClure v Lynch
v White } Contd.
v McCarty
Hawkins v Labatt Cont.
Bruce v Aston. Abates by D. Death.
Clerk, Ass. v Downer. Contd.
Irelawin v Ferree Do.
Holms v Huston Do.
Lynch, Ass. v Ornsbey. Do.
Anderson v Girty. Do.
Finn v Williams Do.
Kendall v Brounfield Do.
Parr v Korn Do.
Garrey v McCollogh Do.
McCullum v Edwards Do.
Christie v Alexander. Do.
Spear v McDoran Do.
Fitzgerreled v Ryley Do.

(117) A Commission from his Ex. the Gov. appointing Matthew Ritchie Sheriff of this County was read, Whereupon the said Matthew Ritchie Informed the Court that he had Taken every Method in his Power to Procure deputys to assist him in the Exn. of his Office, but from the present State of the fees, Together with the Contested Boundry of the County, and the small Emoluments Arising to the Sheriff of this County, although he has offered the whole to any Person who would act as Deputy, he has not been able to procure one, and Therefore refused to Act or Qualify into his Comm. Whereupon Geo. McCormick Gent. is recommend to his Excellency as a proper Person to Serve as Sheriff of this County. Ordered that the Clerk Transmit a Copy of this Recommendation to his Exc. as soon as Posible, with an Apolighy for the frequent application the Court are under the Disagreable Necessity of Making for Sheriffs Commissions, and also inform his Exc. that a Commission appointing the said Geo. Mc.Corm. Sheriff, was issued some Time ago, but the said Mc.Cormick was then an

Officer in the Continental Service, and Contrary to his Expectation the Genl. would not at that Time Suffer him to resign, and consequently could not Serve, but Since has been permitted to resign and is now clear of the Army, and now assures the Court that he will Except of the Office and have the Duty Done.

Geo. McCormick Gent. is appointed Sheriff for one Month. Entered into Bond, Sworn accordingly.

(118) Ordered that the Sheriff pay out of the Depositum in his hands in the State of the County Levy, the following sums.

To Wm. Nemmons as pr. Genl. [?]	£6.12
To. for Express	6. 0
To the Sheriff for three Called Courts. 600 lbs. Tob'o.	3.15
To Executing a Negro man belong'g. to J. DeComp	1. 7.6.

Ordered that the Clerk send the recommendation of the Sheriff to the Governour by Express for the said Sheriffs Commission for which he shall be allowed Eighteen pounds.

Deed poll William Price to Andrew Robetson was acknowledged by the said Price party thereto, and ordered to be recorded.

Two Deed polls Christopher McDonald to Robert McGee was acknowledged by the said Christopher party thereto and Ordered to be Recorded.

George McCormick Gent. high Sheriff come into Court and protested against the Insufficiency of the Goal to Secure Prisoners.

Thomas Applegate is Appointed Surveyor of the Road from his House to William Andersons on the Monaungohela, and that the Inhabitents within three miles on Each side of said Road, work on, Cut open and keep said road in repair.

Ordered that Court be adjoorned to Court in Course.

EDWD. WARD.

(119) At a Court continued and held for Yohogania County, the 25 Jany. 1779.

Present Benja. Kuykendall, Saml. Newell, Joshua Wright, Oliver Miller, Gent. Justices.

Ralph Bowker took the Oath of a Deputy Clerk for the County of Yohogania.

George McCormick Gent. took the Oath of High Shff. for the space of one month.

Hugh Sterling a Deputy Shff. for the space of one month for the County of Yohogania came into Court and made Affirmation according to Law.

Paul Mathews came into Court & took the Oath of a Goaler according to Law for one month.

Ordered that this Court be adjourned till Court in Course.

BENJA. KUYKENDALL.

(120) At a Court Continued and held for Yohogania County, March 22nd. 1779.

Present, Joshua Wright, Benjaman Kuykindall, Oliver Miller, Joseph Beckett, & Joseph Beeler, Gentlemen Justices.

Deed Poll George McCormick to Henry Renkin & Alex. McBride, also the Rec't. thereunto annexed was acknowledged by the said McCormick a party thereto, and O. R.

Saml. Irwin Swore in Attorney.

Inventory of the Estate of John McClery deceased returned. Ordered to be Recorded.

The last Will & Testament of James Devoir decd. was proved by Nicholas Depugh Tobias Decker & Daniel Depugh Jun. Witnesses thereto, & O. R.

John Devoir Sworn Ex. of the last Will & Testament of James Devoir, decd.

Ordered that Nicholas Depugh, Daniel Depugh, Jonh Decker & John Crow or any three of them being first Sworn do appraise the Est. of Jas. Devoir, & make return to next Court.

Deed Poll. Danl. Deshay to John Miller proved by Nichs. Depugh Danl. Depugh & Tobias Decker Witnesses & O. R.

Deed Poll, Peter Swath to Danl. Depugh acknowledged and O. R.

The last Will & Testament of Cathr. Lamb proved by Peter Swath & Henry Devoir two of the Witnesses thereto & O. R. Peter Black, John Devoir, John Lyda & Michael Myers appointed to appraise sd. Est. and make a return thereof to next Court.

(121) Samuel Frye is appointed Constable in the room of Nichs. Depugh.

Isaac Vance v Danl. Williams. Eject.

Order for Survey & Jury of View.

John Morrison is appointed Constable in the room of Benja. Vannater.

Ordered that this Court be adjourned till 7 O'clock Tomorrow morning. BENJA. KUYKENDALL.

Court met according to adjournmet March 23rd. 1779.

Present, Edward Ward, John Cannon, Richard Yeates, Joshua Wright, Oliver Miller, Gentlemen Justices.

Deed Edward Ward to George Ross the Elder, and George Ross the younger with the recept anaxed was acknowledged by the sd. Ward. O. R.

Deed Edward Ward to John Campbell was acknowled & O. R.

Deed John Campbell Gent. to Joseph Simon acknowleded. O. R.

Deed Joseph Simon & wife to John Campbell Gent. proved as Directed by Act of Assembly & O. R.

(122) Deed Christopher Miller to Joseph Simon & John Campbell, proved according to Act of Assembly & O. R.

John Corbley Jacob Vanater Abraham Vanmater Isaac Dye, John Eastwood, Abraham Holt, John Holt, Robert Tyler, having produced recommendations from the County Court of Monongehala to pass unmolested to the Falls of Ohio which was read and approved of.

Present Thomas Smallman & Thomas Freeman & William Harrison Gent. Justices.

Richd. Yeates Gent. Absent.

Administration of the Est. of John Murphy is granted to Van Swearengen he having comply'd with the Law.

Admn. of the Est. of Henry Brindley is granted to Van Swearengen he having complied with the Law.

Ordered that Nathl. Brown Isaac Israels Thomas Edginton Nicholas Vinamon any three of them do appraise the Estates of John Murphy & Henry Brindley, decd.

John Springer v Henry Kearsy.

Left to the award of John Cannon, Joshua Wright Geo. Valandingham, Gabl. Cox & Jno. McDonald Gent.

Benja. Kuykendall Gent present.

(123) Deed Poll Valentine Thomas Dolton to Edwd. Ward was proved by the oath of Thomas Smallman, William Christie, & Jacob Bouseman Witness thereto and O. R.

Deed poll Wm. Brashers to Van Swearingen was acknowleded and O. R.

Samuel Newel Gent. Present.

The administration of the Estate of Thomas Cook formaly granted to Anne Cook ordered to be set aside, and that the said Administration be granted to the said Anne Cook and Gabriel Cox they having Complied with the Law.

Charles Records with Henry Kearsey his Securt. came into Court and enter'd. into Recog. for the Personal appearance of sd. Records at the Next Grand Jur. Cour. held in £ 100 Each.

William Goe. Gent. Pt.

George Valandingham Pt.

Inventory of the Est. of Jas. Loudon decd. retd. & O. R.

Deed Poll Wm. Coventry to Jno. Miller Ackd. & O. R.

Adam Patterson v Wm. Tidball Benja. Swat Spl. Bl.

Sale of the Est. of Fredk. Farree decd. retd. and O. R.

Sheshbazzer Bentley v Camp. Agreed.

v Vititoe
v Eglin
v Warren } Ordered that a Didimus Issue to examine Wit.

(124) Spears v McMahan. Ordered that a didimus Issue to take deposition in sd. Cause.

Ordered that the Recommendation of George McCormick as Shff. be sent to the Gov. and the Com'n. brought up at the expence of the Co'ty.

George McCormick Sworn Shff for one Month.

Benja. Vanater and Jno. Lamon sworn Deputy Shffs for one month.

Wm. Bennett appointed Constable in the room of David Philips.

Tobias Matlocks appointed Consta. in the Room of Jno. Hull.

John Dean & John Hoglin his Securt'y held in £100 each for the sd. Deans appr. at next May Co't.

Ordered that Thos. Ashbrook Joseph Snowden James Bradford & Thos. Edginton or any three of them do view a Road the nearest and best way from Catfishes Camp to Pentecost's Mills and make a return to the next Court.

Isaac Walker and Gabl. Walker his Secut'y held in £100 each for the appr. of the sd Isaac the next G. J. Ct. and that Thomas Townsly be committed to the care of Gabl. Walker till May Court.

Ordered that Moses Bradley be summ'd to appear at the next Ct. to answer the complt. of Jno. Golahar for not doing his duty as a Constable.

Pentecost v Lynn. Ordered that a Didimus Issue to Examine Parties Wit's. and that the same be tried at Sept. Court.

George M^c.Cormick Gent. Protests against the Sufficiency of the Goal.

Deed Poll Jno. Dunn to Geo. Wallace proved by the Oaths of Joseph Skelton & Hugh Oharra. Ord'd. to by for further proof.

(125) Ordered that Court be adjourned till tomorrow morning 8 O'Clock. EDWD. WARD.

Court met according to adjournment March 24th. 1779.

Present Edwd. Ward Wm. Gowe, George Valandigham, Richd. Yeates, Thomas Freeman & Wm. Harrson. Gent. Justices.

Hugh Ohara vs Peter Brandon } Atta. Contd. at Def. Costs.

Thomas Smallman & Benja Kuykendall Gent. Joshua Wright, Present.

Brashears v Hamelton. Then came a Jury, Towit. Jos. Skelton, Jacob Bousman Saml. Ewalt David Day Jno. Hougland Jas. Munn Sheshbazzer Bentley, John Campbell John Farree James Burris William Colvin Thomas Gist, Verd't. for Plt. & Judgt. £ 500.

The fine imposed upon Jos. Noble for not appear'g. as a Grand Jury Man is omitted.

Shuster v Lyda Agreed.

Deed Poll Peter Brandon to Hugh Oharra was proved by the Oath of William Christie a Wit. Ordered to ly for further proof.

Ordered that the Allowance Allo'd Jane Armstrong the wife of ——— Armstrong a Soldier in the Contin. Service be contd. to the Date Hereof.

(126) Admn. of the Est. of the late Colo. White Eyes is granted to Thos. Smallman he having complied with the Law.

Jos. Skelton David Duncan Wm. Christie & Saml. Ewalt appointed appraisers to said Est.

Appraismt. & Sale of John Green's Est. retd. & O. R.

Administration of the Est. of Benja. Tate decd. is granted to Jacob Bousman he having complied with the Law. Wm. Christie, Jos. Skelton David Duncan & John Ornsby appoint'd apprais'rs of sd. Est.

Deed Poll Jas. Burris to Hugh Ohara acknd, also the Asst from Ohara to James McLeland & Wm. Redick acknowledged & O. R.

Pentecost v. Jones & Mayes [?]. Ordered that a Jury be Summ'd of view attend upon the Land and that the Survr. and Shff attend likewise.

Oliver Miller returns the following fines:

Robt. McGee for Drunkenness 5 S.

Jno. Hall 5 S. Wm. Brashers 15 S. George Sickman 20 S. & James Bruce 20 S. for prophane Swearing. Clerk Rec'd. the Money.

Ordered that the Ferries on the Monongehala River be allowed 2s. 6 for a man & the same for a Horse.

Ordered that Paul Mathews be allowed 75. 5. 10 for furnishing Prisoners & find'g Irons for Criminals.

Ord'd that Jno. Ornsby Esq. be appointed to keep a ferry Over the River Monongehala from the Toun of Pittsburgh to the opposite Shore and that he be allowed 2s. 6 for a man & the same for a horse and that he keep one good Boat and Suf-
(127) ficient hands to work her and that he give Bond agreable to Law, at the next Court.

Brashers v Colvin. Thos. Freeman S. B.

John Hogland v Geo. Riggle & Matthew Loghlin. Ordered that Didamus Issue for Examine of Witness.

Ordered that Court adjourn untill Tomorrow Morning 8 oClock.

EDWD. WARD.

Court met according to adjournment 25 March 1779.

Present Richd. Yeates, Thos. Smallman Joshua Wright, Benja. Kuykendall, Thos. Freeman Gent. Justices.

Ordered that Wm. Spurgen Thos. Cushman Thos. Moore Zebulun Hog be appointed to appraise the Est. of Danl. Greathouse's decd. & make retn. to next Court.

Assingmt. of two Deeds Poll Jas. Ellis to Saml. Irwin Ackd. & O. R.

(128) Attachments.

Patrick Clerk v William Paxton. D. N. ap.
Oharra v Brandon Contd. Pl. Costs.
Cumings v Lindsey D. N. ap.
Cox v Nelson. Contd.
Graybill v Hall D. N. apl.
Ritchie v Hall Contd.
Depugh v Hardin Contd.

Issues.

Cox v Williams Contd.
Lydea v Cox Contd
Wherry v White Contd
Miller v Humble Contd.
Pentecost v Jones C. O.
Johnston v Swearengen Contd.
Brownlee v Duglass Contd
Shilling v Newkirk Contd.
Same v the same Contd.
Myers v Hooper. Contd.
Mitchell v same Contd.
Shilling v Fortner Contd.
Hooper v G. Myers Contd.
v same Contd. v Thos. & ux Contd.
Fullum v Johnston Contd.
Springer v Kearsey Contd.
Spear v Jones Contd
McCauley v Jones Discon'd. N. P.
Campbell v McCoy Ab. Dt. Dead.
Spear v Winemiller Contd.
Semple v Collings Disd. N. Apr.
Collings v Semple D'd. N. Apr.
Bouseman v McGoldrick Contd
Ward v Thorn &c. Contd

Jones v Speers Dis'd. N. Ap.
Hickman v Brownfield Disc'd.
Pentecost v Linn Contd.
Corn v Miller dism'd.
(129) Pentecost v Briscoe Contd.
McGinnis v Gibson discont'd.
Shilling v Taylor Contd.
Hawkins, Ass. v Clerk Contd.
same v Kuykindall, Contd.
Malone v Thomas. discontd.
same, Admr. v Smith. discontd.
Eaton v Kennon Contd.
Same v McClellen Contd.
Bonce v Mordacai Contd.
Same v the same Contd.
McDonald v Scott discontd.
Same v Cavitt Do.
Same v Hanna Do.
Brawdy, Ass. v French Contd.
Grubb v Dawling Contd.
Vallandingham v Tygert Contd.
Thomas v Hanna &c. discontd.
Same v Same Do.
Same v Caveat Do.
Haney v McCay. Abates by Defds. Death.
Chambers v McFarlane & ux. discontd.
v Michael Thorn Do.
Ward v Thorn &c. Contd.
Woods v Gray disctd.
Beeler v Wells. Contd.
Cook v Paul Froman Contd.
Same v Shilling Contd.
Same, Ass. v McClellen Do.
McManamy v Robertson Contd.
Crow v Williams discontd.
Crow & ux v Same } discontd.
Do v Do }
Semple, McKinzie Contd.
Hickman v Dunfield discontd.

Wilson v Hanna Do.
Colvin v Frederick Do.
Holliday, Ass. v Hawkins Contd.
Cressip v Dooling A.P.D.
Same v Peters Do.
Same v French Do.
(130) Beall v Finn &c.
Beall, 3^{d} Assinee. v McMachen } Contd.
Hamelton, Ass. v Dunfield
Harrison v Paul A.D.D.
Neavill v Gist Contd.
Ryley v Hanna discontd.
Cressip, Adm. v Teagarden A.P.D.
Teagarden v Hammond discontd.
Cresip v Swearengen Contd.
Felps v Semple Discontd.
Campbell v Beall Contd.
Paul v Smith discontd.

Common Orders.

Warshington v Pearceall Contd.
Vance v McNew Contd
Colwell v Frye &c. Impl.
Henderson v Kinkaid Contd.
Morrison v Vannatree Contd.
Same v Benjaman Vannatree. Contd.
Bouseman v McGoldrick Contd.
Froman v Dean Impl.
White, Sen. v Johnstown Judgt W. E.
Swigert v Murphey Judgt. W. E.
Brashers, Adm. v Colvin Plea No dem'd. Contd.
Same same v Brashers. Judgt. W. E.
McCullum v Brashers, Adm. discontd.
Whitacker v Dixon discontd.
Croghan v McConnell
v Elrod.
v Davidson
v Royall
v Kysor
v Connor } Contd. Plt.

v Grant
v Gibson
v Hunter
v Witzel
v Ross

(131) George Croghan v Wm. Thompson.
v McCartney } Contd. Plt.
v Ramage

Elliott v Collins Contd.

Ferguson v Carroll discontd.

Cox v Dicker discontd.

Duncan & Barr v Clarke &c. discontd.

Liming v Douging Do.

Carswell v Dunn Do.

Croghan v Ross
v Springer } contd.
v Henry

Wickwire, Assee. v Harrison discontd.

Hawkins, Asse. v Hanks contd.
v Zane contd.

Deeck, Assee. v Swearengen discontd.

Kuykendall v Roberts A. P. D.

Holladay v Bell & ux. discontd.

Chambers v Emberson discontd.

Vallandigham v Chriswell Do.

Writs of Enquiry.

Hawkins v Wheat contd.

Nelson v Shilling contd.

Shilling v Nelson contd.

Spivy v Beeler contd.

Laurence v Rogers discontd.

Lindsay v Long discontd.

Kuykendall v Ross A. P. D.

McElroy v Templin
v the same } contd.

Hand v Whitaker contd.

Armstrong v Owens & ux. discontd.

(132) Barrackman v Mutz discontd.

Boley v Springer contd

v John Springer contd.
Martin v Douglas discontd.
McClingh v Knight Do.
Parker v Barrackman Do.
Boley v Springer contd.
Reference.
Ward v Wells Judgt. W. E.
Briscoe v Todd contd.
Connell v Mounce & ux. contd.
Reasner v Ruth contd.
Brown v Hamilton Judgt. contd.
Sumrall & ux v Sumrall agreed.
Boling v Morrison contd.
Sterling v Richards contd.
Wells v Newell contd.
Gist v Waller contd.
v Hall contd.
v Boyles Do.
Burris v Trapman Do.
Burriss v. Johnston & ux. Do.
Dunaughagan v Gray Judgt. Exn. Issued.
Shilling v Collins agreed.
Schley v McKindley contd.
Braden v Vannater contd.
Cox v Davis & ux Judgt. W. E.
Richards v Ross contd.
Fullum v Johnston N. G. w. leave & I'd.
(133) Benjamin Fullum v Johnston & ux
v McComish } N. G. w. Leave & I'd.
Andrew v Johnston & x.
v the same
Brownfield v Ross contd.
Holmes v Dunn agreed.
Custard v Long contd.
Vance v Williams Judgt. & W. E.
Swassicks v Jones contd.
Decker v Ruth N. G. & I'd.
Pearse v Evans contd.
Murphy v Richards contd.

Hayes v Deale contd.
Bruce v Pelton discontd. Plt.
Ewalt v McCollister contd.
Hougland v Riggle agreed.
v Loughlin contd.
Swissicks v Swissicks contd.
Newkirk v Shilling contd.
McFarlane v Beeler contd.
Andrew v Johnston contd.
Mathews v Marshall & ux. contd.
Howe v Genoway & ux. discontd.
Cox v Britsman contd.
Vannater v Bradon contd.
v Parkerson Do.
Vanater v Kuykendall Dis Contd.
Burris v Williams Contd.
Jones v McDonald Do.
Dawson v Kirkpatrick Do.
Hall v Wells & x. Do.
(134) Grimes v Logan contd.
Beeler v Walker Do.
Woods v McKee Do.
Morrison v Surgart Do.
Froman v Boyce Condition perfd. & Contd.
Deale v Hayes Contd.
Crookes v Hougland Contd.
Patterson v McCornish Discontd.
Ralston v Lowry Judgt. W. E.
Pearse v Evans contd.
Wallace v Duncan Do.
Tigart v Boley Do.
v Chamberlain Do
Tigart v Davis Do.
Devoir v Pelton A P. D.
Clarke v Again Issue I'd.
Springer v Listnett. Agreed.
McKy v Davidson } Contd.
v The same } Contd.
Mattocks v Brown Do.

Brown v Mattocks Do.
Lyda v Collins Do.
Caldwell v Houglin Do.
Witzle v McElwaine Do.
Caldwell v Corn Do.
Henry v Sloane Judgt. & W. E.
Heath v Bruce N. G. w. Leave.
Fry v Tilton } Judgt. & W. E.
v The same }
Chamberlain v Henthorn. contd.
v Hickman A. D. D.
(135) Spear v Proctor contd
v Gist contd.
Croghan v Waugh Do.
Newell v Robertson Do.
Kuykendall v Hawkins Do.
Shilling v Young } contd.
v The same }
v Demink }
v Proctor }
Nevill v Wisemen Do.
Noble v Chamberlaine. Judgt. for Want Plea.
v Key & x. Jt. W. E.
Shilling v Martin contd.
Hawkins, Ass'ee. v Hillibrand Judgt. for want of Plea.
Ass'ee. v The same Do.
v White Do.
Hardin v Hawkins discontd.
Spears v McMahan contd.
Prather v Beaty. Judgt. Ex. if Bd. found. Iss'd.
Wells v Brown agreed.
Blackburn, Ass'ee. v Peak. contd.
Brashers v. Swearengen discontd.
Schley v Smith contd.
Conrod v Carter Do.
Hiser v McConnel Discontd.
Wood v Griffith contd.
Misely v Housinger discontd.
Mitchell v Scott Do.

Rogers v. Proctor contd.
Oury v Brown Discontd.
Clinton & Noble v Brashers contd.
Baker, Ass'ee. v Hargis. Discontd. Pl. out of Country.
(136) Waggoner v Warner contd.
McGrew v McConnel Do.
The same v Philips Do.
Glenn v Hinton. Abates by P. death.
Bowley v Ross }
The same v the same } Agreed.
The same v the same }
Bouseman v Douseman Judgt.
Same v the same Do.
Same v John McClean Do.
Kuykendall v Dunn. Abates by P. Death.
v William Hawkins. Abs. by P. D.
v Benjaman Vannatree. Abates by P. Death.
McMahen v Irwin contd.
McCandish, Ass. v McComish. Do.
Taylor v Irwin discontd.
Drinning v Zane discontd.
Moore v Ritchman contd.
Smallman v Slover contd.
Virgin v Moore Do.
Barker v Jourden Do.
Wallace v Meek Dis'd.
Armstrong v Rammage contd.
Redford, Assine v Hill Do.
Wilcox v Craighead Do.
Barrackman v Shivily Do.
Beall Jun. v Shawn Judgt.
Keller v Jones A. D. D.
Reasoner v Shearer contd.
Brent v Beeler Judgt.
Ramsey v Chambers }
The same v the Same } contd.
Stephens v Berwick discontd.
Heath v Farree contd.
Parkin v Colloway Do.

T. Cresip v Shearer Do.
(137) Hughs v Thomas contd.
Stephens v Shilling Do.
Dye v Dye discontd.
Downer v Teagarden contd.
Thomas v Lee contd.
Wilson v Cockburn. Do.
Brownfield v Cox Do.
Bonce v Long Do.
Tygert v Dunnovan Do.
Colwell v Brouster Do.
Summerall v Brouster Do.
Shearer v Miller Do.
Baker v Hendricks. Do.
Whittaker v Dixson Do.
Wells v Reredon & ux. Do.
Whitzel v Shearer Do.
Gollehar v Docking Do.
Stephens v Stout Do.
McMullin & ux v Dickerson Do.
The same v the Same Do.
Moore v Virgin & ux Do.
Same v R. Virgin Do.
Moore v Virgin Do.
Boyce v Philips Do.
Campbell v Brownfield. Do.
Harrison v Sheerr Do.
Vowill v Pennum contd.
Jones v Clerk & x contd.
Phelps v McGrew Do.
McMichiel v French Do.
Purcel v Gibson Do.
Half Penny v Whitzel Do.
Thomas v Morght & x contd.
Park v Cockron A. P. D.
Ireland v Wilson. Do.
(138) Collings v Brady contd.
Black, Ass'ee. v Dunleavy Do.
Vaughan v McMahen Do.

Stephenson v Read & x Do.
Small v Gray. Do.
Tedball, Ass'e. v Shaner. Do.
Anderson, Ass v. Hughy Do.
Stephenson v Barnitt Do.
McClellan v Guy Do.
Shley v Smith Do.
Young v Jackman Do.
Lynn v Tilton Do.
Martin v Johnston Do.
Chamberlain v McLean Do.
Ruse v Haymaker Do.
Altman v Hanna & x. Contd.
Martin v Glass & x contd.
v Hamilton Do.
Black v Chamberlain Do.
Mordacai v Bond Discontd.
v Nigh Do.
Black v Jolly } discontd.
Black v Hannah }
Tygert v Barns contd.
The Same vs Jeffery Do.
Winebiddle v French Do.
Young v McCullogh Do.
Morrison v Ross Do.
Brownfield v Smith Do.
Hunter, Ass. v Jones Do.
Caswell v Dunn Do.
Wallace v Murdock Do.
Fosset v Meeks Do.
Campbell, Ass. v Dunn Do.
Ridgley & Cop'y. v Lynn Do.
Morecroft v Cooling Do.
Fleming v Gibson Do.
(139) Dunfield v Hickman }
v Ross }
v John Rossell } contd.
v Lindsey }
v Fossit }
v Pearcifull }

Stelt v Johnston
v Richd. Johnston } Do.
Downer v Morrison Do.
Woods v McGlashen Do.
Stiger v Smith Do.
Eliott & Cop'y. v Martin Do.
Lynch, Infd. v Loughlin Do.
Semple v Ferns &c. Do.
Gray v Harrison Do.
Croghan v Bowly
v McCallister
v Bouseman &c.
v McKee.
v Kuykindall A. D. D.
v Ritchman
v Whittaker
v Abr. Whittaker
v Jas. Whittaker
v Benj. Kuykindall
v Frederick
v Rowleter } Contd.
v McLean
v Bouseman
v Grimes
v McGrew.
v Troop
v Swissicks
v Meekes
v McManamy
v Drummond.
v Campbell.

(140) Geo. Croghan v Eleazer & James Myers.
v Gibson
v Weddle, Senr.
v James Beard
v Abr. Mitchell
v Miller
v Armstrong } contd.
v Renno

v Elliott
v Price
v Louden
v St. Clair
v Robt. Louden

St. Clair v Labatt contd.
Clerk v Teebolt Do.
Iler v Adams Do.
Girty v Hannah Discontd.
Gaughagain v Smith Contd.
Enoch v Teegarden Do.
Clinton v Mayes Do.
Hawkins v Humble Do.
Fife v Holliday Discontd.

Fife v Fife
Fife v Churchwell
v Fife } Contd.

Hite v Morgan
v White
v Evins
v Myrnett
v Deavebaugh
v the same } contd.

Bryan Bruin v Wm. Fife
v the same
v the same
v the same } Do.

Dolton v Gruver discontd.
Same, Ass'ee. v Shaner Do.
Hales v Roach contd.

(141) Morgan v Nicholas
v Bond
v Chamberlain
v Beavers } contd.

M. Morgan v Wyer
Same v the same } discontd.

Kuykendall v Pearcifull. Abates by P. Death.
v Pancate same.
v Douthwait same.

Williams v Vannatree agd.
v Crow discontd.
Price v Lynn contd.
v Weddle Do.
v Hanks Do.
Gray v Poston Do.
v same Do.
Tygert v Dunnavan
v Craven
v Vannatree } Do.
v Elisha Craven
v Hogland
St. Clair v Sills Do.
McCullogh v McCormick & ca. } P. D.
v Douthwait
Eliott v Girty Contd.
Hawkins v Beall
Same v the same } discontd.
v Same
v Patrick Gary. Abates. D. Dead.
v Perkerson. contd.
Semple v Thompson discontd.
Robertson v Crow contd.
Shilling v Newkirk Do.
Rogers v Williams &c
v Parr } Do.
v Tumbleston
Zane v Hawkins Discontd.
Zane v Drening Do.
Zane, Ass'e v Holdman contd.
(142) Castleman v Tabor contd.
Elliott, Adm. v Hargis
McMullin v Dickerson } D. contd.
Ross, Assinee v Clemons
Devoir v Dunn A. P. D.
Lyon v Dunking contd.
Hozier v Bruce Do
Glassell v Kizer Do.
Glassell v Young Do.

Anderson v Rees Do.
Dunleavy, Ass'e. v Ferrell Do.
Hammond v Teegarden Discontd.
Armstrong v Oharra contd.
Thomas, Ass. v Stack Do.
Ward v String Steel }
v Same } Do.
Jones v Evins }
v the same } Do.
v McGoldrick }
v the same } Do.
Ogle v Wilson Do.
v the same Do.
Labatt v Rammage Do.
Hamelton &ca. v Goe Do.
Cleldening v Logan Do.
Nevill v Holliday Do.
Kizer v Davidson Do.
Kelso &c. v Pigiott Do.
Allen v Logan &c Do
v Duglass Do.
Hilderbrand v Hawkins Do.
Same, Assin'e v Hanks }
v Do. } discontd.
Wallias v Briscoe Do.
v Same Do.
Swearengen v Spencer }
v the same } do.
(143) Smith v Smallman contd.
v George Schley & ca. discontd.
Martin v Elliott contd.
Brachen v Casat Do.
Jones v Ormsback Do.
Crawford, Exr. v Cox Do
Heath v Parker Discontd by Plt.
Heuthorn v McCarty Do.
Roots v Cook contd.
Spencer v Swearengen Discontd.
Brent v Jones contd.

Colwell, Assinee v Lynn Do.
Kidd v McConnell Do.
Lynch v Jones Do.
v Berwick Do.
Mitchel v Zane Discontd.
Drenning v Bay contd.
Braden v Elliott &c. Do.
Cook v Hilderbrand Do.
Johnston v Steel Do.
Holliday, Ass. v Wortherington. Discontd. Plt. & Judgt. for costs.
Hamelton v Martin contd.
Berwick v Atkinson Do.
Gilfillen, Ass. v Tygart Do.
McQuitty v Gray Do
McCollister v Scott Do.
Bowley v Tygert Do.
Robertson v McGoldrick Do.
McIlroy v McMahen Do.
Atkinson v. White Do.
Price v Crawford Do.
Wheat v Kermichael Do.
Scott v Vallandingham Do.
Campbell v Hanks Do.
(144) Holliday & Co'p. v Stout contd.
McCarty v Craighead Do.
Lyons v Humble Do.
Frazier v Chambers Do.
Miller v Hill Do.
Coins v McQuin & ca. Do.
Boyd v Thomas Do.
Wright v Springstone Do.
Davidson v Hanks Do.
Walker v Dresnett Do.
Clerk v Hawkins Do.
Smith &c v Girty Do.
Dillo v Perkie Do.
McManamy v Oharro Do.
Richman v Scott Do.

Ferrell v Daugherty Do.
Alen Tharp v Collings Do.
Ormsbrey v Oharra Do.
Bouseman v Ornsby Do.
Thomas v Elliott Adr. Do.
Christie v White Do.
Brinkers, Ex. v Hardin Adr. Do.
Daviss Jun. & Co'p v Young Do.
Elvy v Dunn Do.
Lyon v Downer Do
Mitchell v Wade Do.
Wilson v McGinnis Do.
Coleman v Gause Discontd.
Johnston v Stephens contd.
Wilson v Cannon Do.
Mitchel v Zane Discontd.
Williams v Pressor Contd.
Croghan v Powell Do.
Hite v Dodson Do.
Thornton, Ass v Williams Do.
Ornsby v Bouseman Do.
Dunlavy v Roberts Do.

(145) Petitions.

Sills	v Irwin
Shilling	v Blackman
	v Delaney
Roatch	v Shaner
Christie, Ass'e.	v Irwin
	v Jackman
Parker, Assn'e	v Davis
Witzel	v Rybolt
Sloane	v Mitchell
Wood	v Griffith
Hamilton	v Hawkins
Seaman	v Miller &c.
	v the same.
Cook	v Berwick
	v Hart
	v Johnston

v Dobbins
v Barker — contd.
Vannater v Pelton &c
McKinzie v Semple
Ryan v Parke
McDonald v Grimes
Deale v Grove
Fennel, Ass'e. v Marshall
Collins v Reiley
Wills v Johnston
Redford v Hill
Ryan v Carswell
v Shaner
Brent v Teagarden
Owens v Fisher
v Miller
v Maurer
Todd v Sheaner
Huffman v Williams agreed
146) Timmons v Gafney
Wright, Assne. v Dunlavy
Morgan v Saltsman
Dunlavy v Frye
Swigart v Ross — discontd A. P. D.
Bags v Cummins
Devoir v Anderson
Witzle v Valentine
Marshall v Brookes
Spurgen v Patrick
Farree v Duck A. P. D.
v Sinnett Do.
Pigman, Ass'e. v Laton contd.
Cresap & Stibs v Templin Judgt.
v Davis Do.
v Acord Do.
v Carter Do.
Chriswell, Ass'e. v Girty Contd.
Ass'e. v The same Do.
Ass'e. v the same Do.

Ass'e. v the same Do.
v Scott Do.
Clinton v Cuningham Do.
v Donne Do.
Wickwire v Downer Do.
Holladay v Jones
v the same
v the same } A. D. D.
Wills v Zane contd.
Hawkins v Bodkin Do.
Walter v Kuykendall A. D. D.
Hawkins v Coffee contd.
Tittle v Brownfield Judgt.
Virgin v Colvin Contd.
Paul v West Do.
Day v Christy Do.
Taylor v Byerly Do.
(147) Humble v Clarke
v Burns } Contd.
Devoir v Scott P. D.
Jones v McDowell contd.
Fowler v Brown Do.
Wall v Dowlin Do. Judgt.
Weddel v Arle contd.
Farree v McCartney
v Carroll
v McMahan
Ass'ee. v Kincaid } A. P. D.
Brent v Simpson Judgt.
McLeland v Small contd.
v the same Do.
Davis Ass'ee. v Downer Do.
v Warren Do.
Devoir v Hanks A. P. D.
Dix v Grogs contd.
Hardin, Jun. v Kincaid Do.
Miller, Assee. v Custard Do.
Ryan v Pross. Do.
Fennel Ass'e. v Mitchall Do.

Maxwell v Ashcroft Do.
Kelly v Cox Discontd.
Wells v Zane Do.
Kuykendall v Dunn A. P. D.
Cunningham v Bruce Contd.
Jolly v Barker Do.
Moor v Churchill Do.
Shaner Ass'e v Stephens Do.
Jackson v Clark Do.
Boley v Swigart } Do.
v Russell }
McGrew v Ward Do.
Morrison v Armstrong Do.
Mitchell & Grather v Swearengen Do.
Ross v Dunfield Do.
(148) Jacobs v Brashears Judgt.
Dean v McManamy contd.
Listnett v Same Do.
Ralston v Labatt Do.
Steel v Merrick Do.
Jackman v Clark Do.
Hall v Redman Do.
Mordecai v Kuykendall A. D. D.
McCallister v Black contd.
Savage v Teagarden Do.
Finn v Williams Do.
Adams v Hall Do.
Lain v Peaton Do
Wallace v Meek Do.
House v Mahon Do
Virgin v Moore Do.
Adams v Huston Do.
Clendenin v Carmichael &c. Do.
Henthorn, Ass'e. v Martin Do
Semple v Owens Do.
Hamilton v Hawkins Do.
Ross v Fransway Do.
Johnston v Watson Do.
Morgan v Weeler Do.

Steel v Thomas Do.
Ewalt v Ross Discontd.
McGlashen v Irwin contd.
Pearse v Chery Do.
Semple v Carrol Do.
Moor v Richmond Do
Dougherty v Black Do.
Devoir v Tigart A. P. D.
Tigart v Lindsey Contd.
v Same Do.
v Same Do.
Stewart v Scott Do
Holladay v Zane Judgt.
(149) Holladay v Worshington Discontd.
Simon & Campbell v Gahagan contd
Kuykendall v Kuykendall
v Holladay
v Heath A P. D.
v McGuire
v Hougland
Valandigham v Springer contd.
v Clements Do.
v Meeks Do.
v Harley Do.
v Lindsay Do.
v David Lindsay Do.
Farree v Linn, Sen. Do.
Maxwell v Thompson Do.
Reed v Clarke. Do.
Dalton v Shaner Do.
Clinton & Noble v Douland Judgt
Smallman v McDoran
v Gonsley Judgt
v Scott
Dougherty v White
v Philips
v Brownfield discontd.
v Beaty
Assn'e v McKean

Ross v Swift Contd.
v Black Do.
McLure v Lynch
v White } discontd.
v McCarty
Hawkins v Labatt Contd.
Clark, Assn'e. v Downer Do.
Eilewine v Farree A. D. D.
Lynch, Assn'e v Ormsby Judgt.
Anderson v Girty Judgt.
Finn v Williams A. P. D.
Kendall v Brownfield contd.
Karr v Karr Judgt.
(150) Gary v McCullock contd.
McCullum v Edwards Do.
Christy v Alexander Do.
Spear v McDoran Do.
Fitzgerrald v Reily Do.
Cox v Boling Do.
Halfpenny v Dennis Do.
Waddell, Assne. v Brown Do.
Ass'e. v Arnold Do.
Shaner v Ross Do.
v Plummer Do.
Flinder v Morshow Do.
Elliott v Small Do.
v Same Do.
v Sinnett Do.
Wm. Elliott v Winemiller Do.
Elliott &c. v D'Alton Do.
v Rogers Do.
v Frederick Do.
v Armstrong Do.
v Same Do.
Swearengen v Taylor Jugt.
Wells v. Gaughagan contd.
Ewalt, Ass'e. v Armstrong Do.
Brounfield v Hustage Do.
McMichael v French Do.

Barker v Knight Do.
Tilton ass'e. v Bell Do
Brinkers Exrs. v Elvy
v Bruce
v Beeler
v Davis } Do.
v Spineer
v Moyer
v Vantrees
Hite v Postlewait
v Wilson } Do.
v Carter
(151) Harden, the younger v Myers contd.
Cook v Dobins Do.
Parkerson v Byrns Do.
Russel v Groghagan Do
Collins v Dobson
Ass'e. v Clark } Do.
Lyons v Buther &c Do.
Maddison, Jun. v Stirling Do.
McMahan v Prickett Do.
Taylor v Hanks Do.
Cox v McMahan Do.
Polke v Inks Do.
Miller v Armstrong Do.
Thomas v Lambert Do.
Knight v Plummer Do.
King v Hansell Do.
McCashlin v Evans Do.
Holms v Huston Do.
McCallister v Corn Do.
Decker v Wilson Do.

New Petitions.

Springer v Listnett dismd.
Isaac Springer v the same Do.
Stevenson v Nicholas contd.
Beeler v Burns Do.
Springer v Patrick Do.
McGaughan v White Do.

Alias Capias.

Kincaid v Henderson
v Same.
McDonald v Slover
Hazle v McNew & ux
Laughlin v Brown
Caldwell v Thorn
Winebidle v Valentine
Pearse v Evans.
Labatt v Smith & ux.
(152) Lintenburgher v Oldcraft
Lindsay v Hamilton
v Smith
Wills, minor v Blackstone.
McElwane v Witzle & ux
Valandigham v Walker.
Wagoner v Rape.
Barrackman v Woods.
v Harry.
Miller v Mitchel
v same
Harrison v Hall
Beans v Johnston.
Witzle v Crawford
Burns & Al. v Loutherback
Sumrull & al v Sumrall
Listnett, Minor v Springer. Agreed.
Schley v McKindley
Howe v Genoway
Smith v Gibson
Miller v Humble
Kearns v Logan
Springer v Waller
McMahan v Mathews
v Hanks

Pluries Caps.

Rigs v Corn
Caldwell v Mills
Campbell v Patterson

Cummins v Baggs
Caldwell v Wray
v Thorn

Appearances.

Richards v Boley C. O.
Black v McCullum discontd.
Minor v Blazier A. C.
(153) Beaver v Mayhall A. C.
McCormick v Hollis A. C.
Riggle v Dodd C. O.
Christie v Heath N. G. & I'd.
Admn. v Same Do.
Patterson v Tidball Spl. Bl. Impl.
Beaver, Ass'e. v Cook, Ex. Impl.
Norris v Vineyard & ux A. C.
Beeler, Sen. v Inks Impl.
Crawford v Hamilton Do.
B. I. Day v Dean Spl. Bl.
Bruce v Hougland agreed.
Lyda v Richards A. C.
Elliott v McIntosh }
v same } C. O. Dept.
Bradley v Boley C. O.
McGlaughlin v Woods A. C.
Winebiddle v Valentine P. Cap.
Curry v Wells C. O.
Ellis v Marshall & ux. A. C.
Boling v Dowlin A. by Retn.
v Norris A. C.
Fife v Tigart & A. C. A. C.
v Same A. C.
Evans v Judy A. C.
v Same. A. C.
Brewer v Stacy. Discontd.
Bentley v Camp A. C.
v Vitito A. C.
v Eglin A. C.
v Warren A. C.

Brashears v Hamilton Dismd. p. Order.
McDowell v McComish Defendt. G. B. Issue.
Workman, Asse. v Saltsman A. C.
Springer v Rogers Agd.
McComish v Springer A. C.
Brice v same Do.
Henderson v Evans C. O.
Johnston v Springer A. C.
(154) Johnston v Mills A. C.
Ritchie v Thornbery A. C.
Reno v Walker Do.
v Isaac Walker Do.
Clark v Parkerson Do.
v Boley Do.
Shuster v Lyda Agd.
Hufman v Leatherman A. C.
Innis v Sawins A. C.
v same A. C.
Rogers v Murphy A. C.
v Maning A. C.
Swearingen v Dougherty A. C.
Kearsy v Springer Refered.
Collins v Vanater Agreed.
Williams, Ass'e, v Anderson A. C.
Tharp v Gray A. C.
Frye v Ritchie A. C.
Murphy v Jourdan A. C.
v same A. C.
Brooks, Admr. v Roberts A. C.
Johnston v Stephens }
v same } discontd.
Read v same }
Wright v Hart A. C.
McCormick v Wilson A. C.
Munn v Crawford Do.
Cox v Anderson Contd.
Forester v Murphy C. O.
McLeland v Beeler A. C.
Froman v Boyce Boyce. Deft. G. R. Issues.

McAdams v Devoir A. Eject.
Henderson v Johnston Discontd.
Steel v Hamilton Al Eject.
Hamilton v Brashear. Swearengen Deft. G. R. Issues.
Bond v Evins Al.
Valandigham v Walker A. C.
Norris v Embly &c. Do.
Whitesides v Girty C. O.
Singers v McCullock C. O.
(155) Henderson v Johnston Discontd.
Shirley v Thompson C. O.
McLeland v Irwin. Irwin Deft. G. R. & Issue.
Madison v Barr. Deft. G. R. & Issue.
Hamilton v Norris. Jno. Norris Deft. G. R. & Issue.
Bruce v McMichael. Henry Heath Deft. G. R. & Issue.
Campbell v Thompson. Wm. Vance. Deft. contd.
Atkinson v Mathews C. O.
Smallman v Such C. O.
Brown & Brashers v Hamilton A. C.

Grand Jury Presentmts

Commonwealth v Persons.
v Davis
v Fleming
v Campbell
v Lynn
v McDonald.
v McMahan
v Christie
v Boling
v McKindley
v Roberts negro
v McAdams
v Ohara
v the Court discontd.
v Hinch
v Caston
v Lindsay
v Mary Lindsay
v Pearcifull

} contd.

v Newkirk
v Carter.
v Hoagland
v Hull
v Williams
v Henry Hull

(156) Recognizances.

Common Wealth v Smith
v Springer & u.
v Steel
v Black
v Listnett
v Beall
v Bradley
v Winemiller
v Chambers
v Duncan
v Davidson
v Listnett &c. } contd.
v McLean
v Ormsby
v Irwin
v Schley
v Hall &c
v Day
v Brawdy
v Dean
v Carr &c.
v Ross &c.
v Little &c

Ordered that Benja. Vanater be allowed L 200 for his Expence & Services in going to Wms.burg for Shfs. Commission and other necessaries for the use of the Co't, to be paid out of depositum in the Shfs. hands if so much remain and if not the bal. to be Levied at the laying of the next Co'ty Levy.

(157) Isaac Taylor is allowed twenty two Dollars for bringing up the Acts of Assembly. Ordered that the Shff be directed to pay it.

Ordered that this Court be adjourned till Court in Course.

RICHARD YEATES.

At a Court continued and held for Yohogania County April 26[t.] 1779.

Present John Cannon, Joshua Wright Isaac Cox Benjaman Kuykendall Gent. Justices.

Two Deed Poll John Miller to Peter Casnor. Ackd. & O. R.

Deed Poll Nevill to Pentecost. Ackd. & O. R.

Luther Colvin is appointed Surveyor of the Road from Pigeon Creek into the Road Leading from Perkerson to Zebuland Colvinings.

Joseph Beckett Gent. Present.

Ordered that Isaac Cox Gent pay to the Clerk his proportion of the money arising from the Sale of the Cards Sent to this Co'ty. for the use of the Soldiers wives and that he transmit it by the first opportunity to the Treasury.

(158) Administration of the Estate of Jacob Shadaker. decd. is granted Ezekiel Painther he having comply'd with the Law.

Ordered that Bazil Brown Otho Brashears Andrew Lynn & Thos. Brown be appointed to appraise the above Est.

Ordered that Court be adjourned till Tomorrow 9 OClock.

JOHN CANON.

Court met according to adjournment April 27th, 1779.

Present Edward Ward William Gowe Oliver Miller Joshua Wright John Canon Gent. Justices.

Deed Poll Froman to Pentecost. Ackd & O. R.

On Motion of Wm. Vance Ordered that his mark crop & slit in the left Ear and Slit in the Right with his Brand W. V. be Recorded.

Assignt. of a Warrant for 50 acres of Land Peter McCartney to John Campbell Esq. prov'd by Edwd. Ward and Andrew Heath two of the subscribing Witnesses thereto. Ord'd to lye for further proof.

George McCormick Sworn Shff for one month.

Deed G. Crohan to Edwd. Milne with the probat thereto annexed admitted to Record.

John Dousman Sworn D. Shff. for one month.

View of a Road from Fromans Mill into the Road leading from Pentecost's Mills to the Court House retd. and O. R.

Ordered that Hugh Brodie be appointed Surveyor of the said Road and that the Tithables within three miles do cut open & keep sd. Road in repair.

(159) Ordered that William Dawlin an Infant be Bound to Danl. Thompson untill he arrives at the age of twenty one years and that the sd. Danl. teach the said Orphan or cause him to be taught to read the Engl. language and teach him the Art and mystery of Farming, and also teach him or cause him to be taught Arithmetic as far as the Rule of 3.

Richd. Swartick v Jacob Jones. discontd.

On the Petn. of Andrew Heath and others Ordered that Thos. Applegate Richd. Sparkes Jas. & Walker Wall or any three of them do view a Road from Wm. Andersons to Thos. Applegates and make retn. to next Court.

Ordered that Richd. Sparks Jas Wall & Walter Wall & Andrew Pearse Jun. do view a Road from the new store on Monongehala to the dividing Ridge Road near Jas. Wilsons & leading to Colo. Cooks.

Benjaman Kuykendal & Joseph Becket. G. P.

Patrick Clark v Thos. Perkerson. John Simon. S. Bl.

Zadock Wright v Elzat Hart. John Johnston S. Bl.

Inventory of Abraham Vaughan returned & Ordered to be Recorded.

John Lyda v Mordecai Richards. Enoch Springer S. Bl.

Jacob Bousman being appointed by an Act of Assembly to keep a Ferry from his Lands over the River Monongehala to the opposite Shore, and whereas the sd Jacob at the last May Court entered into a recog'ze. instead of bond, Ordered that sd Recog.ce. be set aside and that the said Jacob continue to keep the said Ferry agreable to said act, and enter into Bond accord'g. to Law at the Next Court.

John James Wood sworn D. Shff. for one month.

Ordered that Hannah Frazier Orphan of John Frazer be bound to Wm. Anderson according to Law, and that she be taught to read the English language and also the Art & mystery of a Mantua Maker.

(160) Jacob Shilling v Henry Newkirk.

Then came a Jury towit: Andrew Heath John Johnston Wm. Anderson Mordecai Richards Thos Hamilton John Guthridge, Henry Hougland Andrew Vaughan Jas. Bruce John White James Patterson Andrew Powe.

Articles between Elijah Hart and Elenor Frazier Ackd. O. R.

Elizabeth Devior widow of Jas. Devoir came into Court and refused the provision made for her by her said husbands Will.

Articles between Elenor Frather Dinah Anderson Ackd. O. R.

Deed pool James Bruce to Wm. Marshall A'd. O. R.

Inventory and Sale of Lemin Davis's Est. retnd. & O. R.

Jas. Innis, Henry Taylor, James Scott on Millers Run, John Reed, of Millers Run, Wm. Campbell, Jas. Eager, Wm. McComes, John Duglass, William Bruce, James Marshall, Wm. Parker, & Hezekiah Magruder are recommended to his Excellency the Governor as proper persons to be added to the Commission of the Piece.

James Boyace v Paul Froman. Id. & Ord. Survey.

Laughlin v Hogland Order Survey.

Ordered that Court be adjourned untill Tomorrow Morning 9 OClock.

JOHN CANON.

Court met according to adjournment

Pres't. Benja. Kuykendall, Oliver Miller, Benja. Fry, Joseph Beckett, Gent Justices. Joshua Wright, Gent. Pres't.

(161) Issues to April Court 1779.

Joseph Cox	v John Williams &c.
John Lyd	v Joseph Cox
Joseph Wherry	v John White Sen.
Abraham Miller	v Mich'l. Humble.
Pentecost	v Jones &c. Judgt.
Johnston	v Swearengen
Brownlee	v Douglas
Shilling	v Newkirk
Same	v Same
Myers	v Hooper
Mitchel	v same
Shilling	v Fortner
Hooper	v Myers

		v G. Myers	contd.
	Hoper	v Thomas &c.	
	Fullum	v Johnston.	
	Springer	v Kearsy.	
	Spear	v Jones.	
	Spear	v Winemiller.	
	Bousman	v McGoldrick	
	Ward	v Thorn	
	Ward	v Thorn	
	Pentecost	v Lynn	
	Same	v Briscoe	
	Shilling	v Taylor.	
	Hawkins, Ass'e.	v Clarke	
	Same	v Kuykendall	
	Eaton	v Kennon	
	Same	v McCleland.	
	Bond	v Mordicai	
	Same	v Same	
	Brodie, Ass'e.	v French.	
	Grub	v Dowlin	
(162)	Vallaudigham	v Tyart	
	Ward	v Thorn &c	
	Beeler	v Wells	contd.
	Cook	v Froman	
	Same	v Shilling	
	Same, Ass'e.	v McConnell	
	McManomy	v Robertson	
	Semple	v McKinzie	
	Holladay Ass'e.	v Hawkins	
	Beall &c	v Finn	
	Same	v McMahan	
	Hamilton, Asse.	v Dunfield	
	Nevill	v Gist	
	Cresop	v Swearengen.	
	Campbell	v Bell	
	Fullum	v Johnston &c.	
	Same	v Same	
	Same	v McComish	
	Andrew	v Johnston, &c.	

v the same
Decker v Ruth
Clarke v Again
Heath v Bruce
Burris v Trapman

Common Orders.

Washington v Martin { John Pearsall, Deft. G. R. Issue. I'd.
Vance v McNew Judgt. W E.
Caldwell v Fry &c. N. G. w. leave. Issue.
Henderson v Kincaid discontd.
v Johnston Ord'd. Redocketed.
Morrison v Vannater contd.
v Benja Vannater. contd
Bouseman v McGoldrick contd.
Hollady v Jones O. to be recdock'd.
(163) Froman v Dean Judgt. W. E.
Croghan v McConnel
v Elrod
v Davidson
v Royall
v Keizer
v Conner
v Grant
v Gibson } discontd.
v Hunter
v Whitsel
v Ross
v Thompson
v McCartney
v Ramage
Wm. & Benja Elliotts v Collins discontd.
Crogan v Ross
v Springer } discontd.
v Henry Do.
Hawkins, Ass'e. v Hanks Judgt. W. E.
v Zane Judgt. W. E.
Richards v Bowley Do.
Richards v Dodds Do.

Elliott v McIntosh }
v same } contd.

Bradley v Boleye contd.

Curry v Wells Impl.

Henderson v Evans }
v same } discontd.

Forrester v Murphy Judgt. Ex.

Singers v McCullock Judgt. Issue. Ex.

Shirley v Thompson Contd.

Atkerson v Mathews Do.

(164) Smallman v Such contd.

Whitesides v Girty Judgt. W. E.

Writs of Enquiry.

Hawkins	v Wheat	contd.
Nelson	v Shilling	
Shilling	v Nelson	
Spivy	v Beeler Judgt. L. 135, 15	
McElroy	v Templin	
	v same	
Hand	v Whitaker	
Boley	v Springer	
	v Jno. Springer	
	v same	
Ward	v Wells	
Cox	v Williams	
Vance	v Williams	
Ralston	v Lowry	
Henry	v Sloan	
Fry	v Felton	
	v same	
White	v Johston	
Swigart	v Murphy	
Brashears, Admr.	v Brashears	
Noble	v Key	

Alias Cap.

McCormick v Hollis P. C.

Norris v Vineyard & ux P. C.

Lyda v Richards Spl. Bl. Dist'd by Agmt.

McGlaughlin v Woods P. C.

Fife, Sen. v Tigart P.

v same &c P.

(165) Evans v Judy P. C.

v same

Bentley v Camp

v Vititoe

v Englin P. C.

v Warren

Workman, Ass'e. v Warren C. O.

Johnston v Springer P. C.

Johnston v Mills

Ritchie v Thornburg

Reno v Walker P. C.

v Isaac Walker

Clarke v Parkerson. Spl. Bl. Ind. N. D. Judgt. W. E.

v Boley P. C.

Hufman v Leatherman

Williams Ass'e. v Anderson Impl.

Tharp v Gray discontd.

Fry v Ritchie Agreed.

Murphy v Jourdan

v same P. C.

Brooks, Admr. v Roberts

Wright v Hart Spl. Bl. Implr.

McCormick v Wilson P. C.

Munn v Crawford

McCleland v Beeler Implr. P. B.

Norris v Embly P. C.

Ross v Manning P. C.

Boling v Norris

Beavers v Mayhall discontd. N. Ap.

Minor, Ass'e. v [illegible]

Brien v Springer P. C.

McComish v same

Henderson v Evans

Molton v Seaburn C. O.

McAdams v Devoir. Andrew Devoir, Deft. C. R. & Issue.

Steel v Hamilton P. C.

(166) Pleuries Cap's.

	McMahan	v Hanks	P. C.
		v Mathews	
	Kearns	v Logan	
	Miller	v Humble	
	Springer	v Walker	
	Smith	v Gibson, Colo.	P. C.
	Howe	v Genoway	
	Schley	v McKindley	
	Sumral	v Sumral	
	Burns	v Loutherback	
	Whitsel	v Crawford	
	Beans	v Johnston	
	Harrison	v Hall	
	Miller	v Mitchel	
		v same	
	Barrackman	v Harry	
		v Woods	
	Wagoner	v Rape. agreed.	
	Vallandigham	v Walker	
	McElwain	v Whitsel & ux.	
	Wells, a minor	v Blackstone	
	Lindsay	v Smith	
		v Hamilton	
	Lentenburgher	v Holdcroft	
	Labat	v Smith	
	Pearce	v Evans	
	Winebiddle	v Valentine	
	Laughlin	v Brown	
	Hazle	v McNew	
	McDonald	v Slover	
	Caldwell	v Thorn	
(167)	Kincaid	v Henderson	P. C.
		v the same	
	Riggs	v Corn	
	Caldwell	v Mills	
	Campbell	v Patterson	
	Cummins	v Baggs	
	Caldwell	v Wray	

Appearances.

Innis v Sawins C. O.
v same C. O. } not to be sent.
Rogers v Murphy A. C.
v Manning A. C.
Swearingen v Dougherty A. C.
Boyer v Froman Impl.
Mooney v Records Impl.
Gibson v Meek A. C.
Bromfield v Astergus No. Int. discontd.
Gist, Asse. v Alexander A. C.
McGlaughlin v Piggot A. C.
McCoy v Rearden agreed.
Caldwell v Tigart A. C.
Ward v Phelps A. C.
Allen v Boner A. C.
Hall v Lynch A. C.
v Fossett A. C
(168) Hall v Shearrer A. C.
v Hatfield A. C.
Protsman v Hill C. O.
Heath v Stokes A. C.
Chambers v Wallace A. C.
Campbell v McKee. Ordered Sp. be published & G'd.
McCrory v McCrory discontd.
Innis v Scott. Hugh Scott, deft. O. R. & Issue.
Hughes v McElry A. C.
Waller v Hatfield Agd.
Williams v Carter
v Brotsman
v Stocker
v Stone } contd.
Brady v Williams. Jno. Wms. Deft. O. R. Issue.
Hamilton v Swearengen A. C.
McMahan v Tumbleston A. C.
Campbell &c v Ward &c A. C.
Boyer v Froman
v Froman
v Graham & ux

v same
v same
v same
v same
v Atkins } Implr.

Gist v Cornwall A. C.

Boyce v Froman Implr.

Saml. Brewer v Peter Macy A. C.

Prottsman v Hill Implr.

(169) Power of Atto. Jacob Shilling to Geo. McCormick ackd. and O. R.

Ordered that James Gray be sum'd. to answer the informa tion of the States Atto. for ferrying over the River Monongehala & rec'd. 3 S. for the same cont'y to Law the following person at the following times.

Joseph Skelton & one horse March 27th, 1779.

James Bevard at the same time.

Danl. McClintock & one horse. 29th March 1779. 29 Pack Horses 27th March and took Rec't. for the same of David Kennedy. H. M.

Richd. Sparks & one horse 27th March.

Kuykendall v Hawkins N. G. & I'd.

Ordered that the Shff. Summon a Grand Jury.

John Gowe is appointed Const. in the room of John James Wood.

Andrew Pearce Jun. appointed Constl. Ord'd. that he take the Oath according to Law.

Ordered that Court be adj'd. till Court in course.

BENJA. KUYKENDALL.

(170) At a Court Continued and held for Yohogania County May 24th, 1779.

Present Isaac Cox, William Gow, Joseph Beeler, Joseph Beckett.

George McCormick Sworn Shff.

Benjamin Vannater & John James Wood Sworn Deputy Sheriffs.

Andrew Scott Sworn Atto. at Law.

Deed Poll Dorsey Pentecost to Benjamin Mills two lots of Ground in the Town Louisburg, Ackd. O. R.

Deed Dorsey Pentecost to Jno: Canon Saml. McCullough Andrew Robinson & Ebenezer Zane Ackd. & O. R.

Deed James Astergus to Morgan Deshay proved by Nicholas Depue one of the subscribing Wit's. Ordered to ly for further proof.

Ordered that Danl. Applegate James Colvin, Hugh Braady & Joseph Lemin do view the most convenient way for a Road from Andrew Dye's to the Monongehala opposite the mouth of Mingo Creek, from thence to Fromans Mill, and make rep[r]. &c.

Joseph Kilpatrick is recommended as a proper person to act as Ensign of the Militia.

Edwd. Ward and Benjamin Kuykendall Gent. present.

Power of Atto. Paul Froman to John McGee prov'd. by Isaac Cox and Benjamin Vannater & O. R.

Robert Johnston took the oath of allegiance & fidelity as prescribed by Law.

Two deeds Patrick Jourdan to John Fife proved by Dorsey Pentecost and Ralph Bowker two of the Wit's. Ordered to ly for further proof.

(171) Isaac Cox Gent. is allowed ten P. c't. as Adm. of the Est of Saml. Richardson decd. on the amt. of the value of sd. Est.

Saml. Newel Gent. Prest.

Ordered that George Depue orphan of John Depue be bound to John Kincaid until he arrives to the age of twenty one years and that the said John Kincaid do teach or cause him to be taught to read the Bible, write and Cyphert he five Common Rules of Arithmetic.

Ordered that William Depue Orphan of John Depue be bound to John Read according to Law and that the sd. Jno. Read do teach or cause him to be taught to read & write and to cypher the five Common rules of Arithmetic.

Ordered that John Depue orphan of Jno. Depue be bound to Wm. Read according to Law and that the sd. Wm. do teach him or cause to be taught to read the Bible write and to cypher the five common Rules of Arithmetick.

Vincent Colvin took the Oath of Allegiance and fidelity as prescribed by Law.

William Rankin took the oath of allegiance and fidelity according to Law.

Then came a Grand Jury (towit) Charles Morgan Joseph Brown Jno. White Nicholas Dawson Richd. Boyce James Patterson David Ritchie Sampson Beavers Isaac Vance Nathl. Brown John Embly Wm. Renkins Vincent Colvin Sheshbazzer Bentley Michael Tigart Samuel Dunn Josiah Crawford Andrew Vaughan & Robt. Ramsay.

(172) Two Indentures Conrod Wrightner to John & Margt. Read prov'd & O. R.

Licence is granted to Francis Morrison to keep an Ordinary at his house he having complied with the Law.

Present Richd. Yeates Gent.

Licence is granted to James McGaldrick he to keep an Ordinary at his house he having complied with the Law.

On the motion of Nicholas Pease setting forth that he is desirous of erecting a Gristmill On Shirtees Creek on which he has lands on both sides but that he cannot do it without condemning an Acre the property of Joseph Edginton & Isaac Kenny, Ordered that the Sheriff do summon a Jury to attend on the premises to lay of and value the sd. Acre of Land and make their report to next Court.

Francis Morrison Sworn Lt. of the Militia. Com^n^. Read.

Ordered that the Road from Thomas Applegates to Will'm. Andersons as returned by the viewers keeping along as the road is already opened, be confirmed. Thomas Applegate is appointed overseer of sd. Road and that the Tithables within three miles do cut open and keep sd. Road in repair.

Nichs. Depue v Duncan Hardin, Atta. prov'd. Judgt. & O. Sale.

Ordered that the wives of Greenbury Shous, Lem'l. Davis and John Depue poor soldiers in the Continental Service be allowed twelve pounds each.

(173) Ordered that Matthew Hindman's two children a soldier in the Continental Service be allowed twenty Shill's p. month each to commence from the first day of March last past and to be cont'd until March next.

Ordered that Eliza. Davis wife of Jonathan Davis a soldier in the Cont. Service be allowed eighteen pounds.

Ordered that Court be adjourned till tomorrow 8 OClock.

EDWD: WARD

Court met according to adjournment May 25th, 1779.

Present Edward Ward Richard Yeates Benjaman Frye Benjaman Kuykendall, Isaac Cox Thomas Smallman Oliver Miller Gentlemen Justices

Licence is granted to Willis Persons to keep an Ordinary at his house he having complied with the Law.

Licence is granted to James Fleming to keep an Ordinary at his house he having complied with the Law.

Present Sam'l. Newell & Joseph Beckett, Gent.

Abst. Thos Smallman. Prest. Joseph Beeler Gent.

Elizabeth Henry
v
Sloan } Wm. Long undertook for the Defendant that the Plt. should not be removed out of the County or sold untill the trial of this Cause.

(174) Ordered that a ferry be kept on the opposite side of the River from Fort Pitt to Jacob Bousmans and that Jacob Bousman is appointed to keep the same he giving Bond with Security according to Act of Assembly, and that he keep one hand and Boat at his own House and a Boat and one hand on the Pittsburgh Side constantly to attend and that in four months from this Date he has a third Boat built and ready to attend on either Side of the River.

Deed Ignace Labat to Jas. Chambers proved by Henry Heth & Jacob Bousman two of the Subscribing Wit's. Ordered to lie for further proof.

Ordered that Samuel Newell be appointed to keep a ferry over the River Monongehala from the new store to the opposite Shore and that he keep one good Boat with Sufficient hands to work her and that he give Bond with Security according to Law at the next Court.

Present Thos. Smallman Gent.

Wm. Henry Spears v Joseph Jones. Then came a Jury towit. Gabl. Cox John Decker Wm. Long Benja. Collins John Crow Henry Hougland Uriah Johnston Andrew Devoir James Wright John Springer Joseph Wherry Jno. Wall. Judgt. for Plaintiff nine hundred pounds damages.

And'w. Pearce Thomas Applegate and Andrew Dye his Security entered into Recog'ze. sd. Pearce in one thous'd.

pounds and his Securities in five hundred pounds each for his appearance at the next Court.

Thomas Crooks Sworn Capt. of the Militia. Com. read.

Michael Tegart sworn Lt. of Militia. Comn. Read.

Deed Saml. McAdams to Dorsey Pentecost Ackd. & O. R.

Deed Danl. Byers & David Miller to Dorsey Pentecost. Ackd. & O. R.

Deed Jas. Miller to Dorsey Pentecost Ackd. & O. R.

(175) Deed Thomas Miller to Dorsey Pentecost Ackd. & O. R.

Saml. McAdams Sworn Lieutenant of the Militia. Com. Read.

Ordered that Andrew Devoir be appointed Surveyor of the Road lead'g from the Ct. House to Pentecosts Mill from the top of the Ridge between the waters of Peters Creek and Shirtee opposite to the house of Henry Johnston.

Inventory of the Est. of Jas. Louden ret'd. & O. R.

Ordered that Jno. Decker Vincent Colvin Joseph Perkinson and Joseph Beckett or any three of them being first Sworn do lay of and assign unto Eliz[a]. Devoir widow & Relict of James Devoir decd. her dower in the Lands Slaves & Personal Est. whereof James Devoir decd. died seized and make report to next Court.

Deed Moses Holladay to Saml. Irwin Ackd. & O. R.

Elizabeth Burris v Naomi Trapman. Then came a Jury towit. William Price David Andrews Mordecai Richards Hugh Sterling Abraham Miller Richard Crooks Henry Miller William Crow Richard Vaughan Bazil Brown Thomas Lapsley & Robert Lowdon. Verd't. & Judgt for Plaintiff.

Mich'l. Tygert & Christopher McDonald being bound in Recog. appeared. Ord. to be Discharged.

Jacob Long sworn Ensign of the Militia. Com. Read.

Joseph Beeler v Benja. Wills. Then came a Jury (towit) Thomas Bond Samuel M[c]Adams Samuel Devoir Nicholas Christ John Johnston And'w. Dye Henry Spears John Bradley Nathl. Blackmore Wm. Fry John Hougland & Jacob Long. Ve't. for Plt. L 33.16 Debt one penny.

(176) John Spivy v Samuel Beeler. Then came a Jury (towit) Gabl. Cox John Decker William Long Benjamin Collins John Crowe Henry Hougland Uriah Johnston Andrew Devoir

James Wright Jno. Springer Joseph Wherry & John Wall. Verdt. & Judgt. for Plt. L. 135.15. Issue Ex^{n}.

John Springer v Thos. Waller, referred to Geo. Vallandigham John McDonald Joshua Wright Jno. Canon Henry Taylor.

Ordered that Lemuel Davis and John Davis orphans of Lemuel Davis be bound to Isaac Cox according to law, the sd. Isaac Cox to teach or cause them to be taught to read write Cypher the five Com. Rules of Arithmetic.

Deed Patrick McCarmick to Moses Andrews proved Joseph Brown & Thos. Bond. Ord. to ly for further proof

The Grand Jury having found several Bills of Indt. ordered that the Persons be summoned.

Charles Richards v Jno. Boley. Michl Tigert Spl. Bl.

Assigm't. Bill of Sale Sampson Beavers to Antho. Dunlavy. Ackd. & O. R.

Ordered that Court be adjourned till tomorrow 8 OClock.

EDWD. WARD.

Court met according to adjournment May 26th, 1779.

Present Edward Ward Isaac Cox Jno. Stevenson William Harrison Joseph Beeler William Crawford Gentlemen Justices.

(177) Edward Ward Isaac Cox John Stevenson Willian Harrison, William Crawford & Joseph Beeler Gent. took the Oath of Justices in Chancery.

Richie v Hall. Atta. Judgt. & P. S.

On the motion of Bazil Brown setting forth that he is desirous of erecting a Gristmill on Big Redstone Creek, Ordered that the Shff. do Summon twelve men of his vicinage to attend on the premises to lay of and value one Acre of Land on the opposite side of his Land, and value the damage done to the party holding the same, and make return to the next Court.

Joseph Kirkpatrick Sworn Ensign. Com. Read.

Joseph Beeler Jun. is recommended to his Excell'y the Governor as a proper person to serve as Ensign of the Militia.

Hooper v Thomas. Then came a Jury (towit) David Ritchie Henry Miller David Day Gab'l. Walker Isaac Walker John Crow David Andrew Abraham Miller Peter Rittenhouse Paul Humble Tobias Decker & Hugh Brodie, Verd'ct for plaintiff. Judgmt. for L 80. John Berry Mary Perry & Susanna Perry. 4 days attendance in above suit.

Tobias Decker took the Oath of Allegiance and fidelity according to Law.

Prest. Saml. Newell & Benja. Fry Gent.

Absent Edwd. Ward Gent.

Jane Perry being bound in Recognizance appeared agreeable thereto and under protestation of Innocence Submits herself to the Court. On hear'g the Testimony ordered that the Deft. be fined five pounds.

Uriah Johnston Took Oath of Allegience and Fidelity.

(178) Deed Saml. Stockwell to Ezekiel Hopkins Ack'd. & O. R.

Benjaman Frye Gentleman Took the oath of Justice in Chancery.

Com. Wealth v Hugh Brodie. N. G & I. Join. & a Jury (towit) Gabl. Cox David Ritchie Henry Miller Gabriel Walker Isaac Walker John Crow David Andrew Abraham Miller Peter Rittenhouse Paul Humble Tobias Decker John Deane. Verdi't. Def'd. not Guilty.

Jane Ferrel held in L 50 and Joseph Skelton & Saml Irwin in L 25 each conditioned for her keeping the Peace towards the good People of the C. W. & peticular to Eli Collins till next Court.

Paul Matthews sworn Goaylor.

George McCormick Gent. protests agt. the Sufficiency of the Goal.

On the motion of Mary Lypolt the wife of George Lypolt, by her attorney, Seting forth that she cannot live with her Husband an acct. of Ill Treatment, Ordered that the said George Lypolt be summoned to appear at the next Court to
(179) show cause if any why part of his Estate should not be applied for her seperate maintainence.

Campbell v Ward, Bousman & McGoldrick, Injun. Ordered that the Common Wealth Writ of Injunct. do Issue ag. the Defendants comm'g to stay Waste.

Ordered that Court be adjourned till tomorrow 8 O'Clock.

ISAAC COX.

(180) At a Court Continued and held for Yohogania County, May 27th, 1779.

Present Edward Ward William Crawford Benjaman Frye William Harrison John Stephenson John Cannon Gent Present.

Pluries Caps.

McCormick v Hollis P. C.
Norris v Vineyard & Ux Impl.
McGlaughlin v Woods P. C.
Fife Sen : v Tigart Sp. Bl.
v the same Spl. Bl. Jno. Boley.
Evans v Judy agreed.
v the same agreed
Bentley v Camp agreed.
v Vititor P. C.
v Englin Impl.
Workman, Asse v Saltsman[1] P. C.
Johnston v Springer C. O.
Johnston v Mills C. O.
Ritchie v Thornbury P. C.
Reno v Walker P. C.
v Walker P. C.
Clark v Bowley Impl.
Hufman v Leatherman Impl.
Fry v Ritchie agreed.
Murphy v Jourdan Abates by retn
Brooks, Adm. v Roberts Impl.
McCormick v Wilson agreed.
Munn v Crawford Impl.
Norris v Embly P. C.
(181) Ross v Manning P. C.
Boling v Norris Impl.
Minor, Asse. v Blazier P. C.
Brier v Springer Agreed & Settled.
McComish v Springer P. C.
Henderson v Evans P. C.
Steel v Hamilton P. C.
McMahan v Hanks P. C.
Kearns v Logan. P. C.
Miller v Humble Impl.
Springer v Waller referred.
Smith v Gibson P. C.
New v Genoway P. C.
Schley v McKindley discd.

Sumral v Sumral &c agreed.
Burns v Loutherback P. C.
Whitzel v Crawford P. C.
Beans v Johnston P. C.
Harrison v Hall P. C.
Miller v Mitchel P. C.
v The same P. C.
Barrackman v Harry P. C.
v Ross P. C.
Vallandigham v Walker P. C.
McElwaine v Whitzel & ux. dis'd. n. ap.
Wills v Blackstone P. C.
Lindsay v Smith P. C.
v Hamilton P. C.
Lintenberger v Holdcroft P. C.
Labat v Smith P. C.
Pearce v Evans P. C.
Winebiddle v Valentine agreed.
Laughlin v Brown P. C.
Hazle v McNew Abates by Pt. Marriage.
McDonald v Slover P. C.
(182) Caldwell v Thorn P. C.
Kincaid v Henderson &c. P. C.
v The same &c P. C.
Riggs v Corn discontd.
Caldwell v Mills P. C.
Campbell v Patterson P. C.
Cummins v Baggs P. C.
Caldwell v Wray P. C.
v Thorn P. C.
Wagoner v Rape agreed.

Alias Caps.

Gibson v Meek P. C.
Gist, Asse. v Alexander P. C.
McGlaughlin v Piggot P. C.
Caldwell v Walgomot &c C. O.
Curry v Wills C. O.
Ward v Phelps Impl.

U. States v Matthew Boner discontd.
Hall v Lynch P. C.
v Fossett P. C.
v Shearer P. C.
v Hatfield P. C.
Heath v Stokes P. C.
Chambers v Wallace P. C.
Gist v Cornwall Jr. P. C.
Forrester v Murphy P. C.
Mitchel v Pelton P. C.
Spears v Johnston Settled. Shff.
Waller v Springer C. O.
Miller v Pelton P. C.

(183) Appearances.

Nevill v Black C. O.
v Thompson C. O.
v Tharp C. O.
Stitt & ux v Williams A. C.
Crowe v Pearse A. C.
Henderson v Douglas A. C.
Wilson v Lynch &c A. C.
Evans v Russell A C.
Stewart v Crawford G. R. Issue.
v Harrison Do.
Shilling v Hinch A C.
Casner v McIntire A C
Innis v Spencer A C
Asse. v Hougland C. O.
Gilliland v Lynn Impl.
Shilling v Newkirk Impl.
Pentecost v Jones C. O.
Boley v Jourdan Abates by retn.
Stocker v Acklin A. C
Day v Stanbury C. O.
Cook v Mayes A. C.
Bay v Jackson A. C.
Alexander v Steen A C.
Dunagan v Boyce Impl.

Riddeck v Ross A C.
Wright v Beavers A C.
Mitchel v Boley A C.
McCollister v Corn Impl.
McGruders v Lynn. A. C. discontd. Plt. Cost.
Hamilton v Swearengen C. O.
Campbel v Ward &c. G. R. Issue.
Bond v Ervin A C
Waller v Hatfield A C
(184) McDowell v McComish A C
Boley v Or. disd.
Hughes v McElry A C
McMahan v Tumbleston A C
Henderson v Johnston C O
Ellis v Marshall A C
Brown & Brashears v Hamilton A C
Holladay v Matthews C. O.
Riggle v Dye. Andrew Pearce Spl. Bl. Judgt. by N. Dicit & W. E.
Embly v Crowe Impl.
Reed v Springer C. O.
Hougland v Lock discontd. no appear.
Boley v Manning A. C.
v The same A C
Penticost v Stephens discontd.
Brewer & ux v Stacey A C
Craven v Pearce Sen. A C
Cook v Beckett A C
Smallman v Guffee agreed.
Spears v Beckett Ex. &c. A C
Dye v Allen Tharp A C
Nicholas v Conn A C
Johnston v Alentharp A.
Matthews v Ellis A.
Nicholas v Day. Moses Holladay Sp. Bl. Impl.

(185) Chancery.

Crisop v Shearer B & Time
Simon v McKee &c. contd till publication.
Wills v Rearden contd.

Sci. Fac.

Lapsley v Read Oyer.

Brashears v Hamilton. Surrender of the Principal & I'd.

Baz'l. Brown v The same Do.

Ordered that Thomas Gist Thomas Warren Jno. Irwin of Pittsburg Matthew Richie & Dorsey Pentecost be appointed Comrs. agreeable to Act of Assembly as Judges of Counterfeit Money.

Ordered that John Allen Tharp & wife be sum'd. to appear at next Court to show cause if any why Elinor Humble orphan of Martin Humble should not be bound to Susanna Johnston, and the meantime the sd. Orphan remain with the sd. Johnston.

Henry Morrison v Benjamin Vannater. G. R. Issue.

George McCormick took the Oath of Allegience and fidelity as prescribed by Law.

Ralph Bowker took the Oath of Allegience and Fidelity.

Dorsey Pentecost Sworn Judge of Counterfeit money agreeable to Act of Assembly.

Day v Wilson Petn. C. O.

(186) Present Joseph Beeler & Joseph Beckett Gent.

Ordered that Thos. Tounsley an Orphan be contd. with Gabl. Walker agreeable to a former Order.

Ordered that Eve Sheek wife of a poor Soldier be allow L 18 for support of her self & two Children.

Order that the wife Abraham Ritchie be allowed be allowed the same that she was the last year to commence from the end of the last years allowance.

Wm. Downs being Sworn a Juryman on the Issue Join'd between John Decker Plaintiff and Davis Ruth Deft. absconded the Jury without bringing a Verdict. Ordered that he be fined twenty pounds.

Ordered that Court be adjourned till Court in Course.

EDWD. WARD.

(187) At a Court Continued and held for Yohogania County June the 28th, 1779.

Present William Goe Olliver Miller Joshua Wright Benjamin Kuykendall, Gentlemen Justices.

William Murley being recommended to his Excellency the

Governor as a proper person Ordered that he be appointed to serve as Lt. of the Militia in this Cot'y.

John Vannater appointed to serve as Ensign in the Militia for this County.

Present Samuel Newell Gentleman. Appraisement of the Estate Devoir decd retnd. by the Exr. and O. R.

Holladay v Brodie lef to the award of Wm. Marshall Jeremiah Johnston John Lemen & Wm. Anderson and their determination to be the award of this Court. Verd't. and Judgt. for plt. L 45. 15 s.

James Campbell sum'd. as a Grand Juryman and failing to appear on hearing his objections Ordered that the Sum's. be set aside.

Present Edward Ward Gent.

Charles Records appointed Surveyor of the Road whereof Andrew Devoir was formerly appointed.

Kinkead v Henderson. Saml. ——— Spl. Bl.

Ordered that Thomas Tounsley Orphan lately an apprentice to Isaac Walker be bound to Wm. Wm. Lee who is to teach him the Art and mystery of a blacksmith and also to teach or cause him to be taught to Read Write and Cypher the five common rules of Arithmetic.

(188) Day v Wilson. In Petn. dism'd.

John Reed being served with a Scire fac's. at the suit of Martha Lapsley, for a Judgment obtained against him by the said Martha on a declaration of Ejectment In May 1775, came into Court produced Mr. Benja. Kuykendall as Evidence that he had fee'd an Atto. and that he neglecting his duty the first Court Judgt. was obtained against him, unpresidented the Court are of oppinion that the matter in dispute be deferred till the next September Court and that the parties attend With their Wit's. at that time to have a decisive hearing.

Inquisition held on the Body of——— a Negro the property of James Hopkins from under the Hand & Seal of Wm. Goe Esqr. and the Jurors thereunto annexed was returned and O. R.

Ordered that Exn. agt. Wm. Downs for not appearing as a Juryman be deferred till next Court.

Ordered that the Common allowance be made for the children of Robert Crawford and Nich's. Hagarty poor Soldiers in the Continental Service to commence from the 25th of September last.

Ordered that the Common allowance be given the Wife and Children of Thomas Southwait a poor soldier in the Continental Service to commence from the 25 of Sept. last.

Ordered that Jacob Bousman be appointed Surveyor of the Road from his house to the Widow Stewarts, Robert Henderson from thence to where the Road from the Widow Lapsleys & Jno Read's forks, Jno. Read from thence to Benja. Kuykendall's Mill, Thomas Lapsley from the forks of the Road to the Court House, and that the Inhabitants within three miles do keep sd. Road in repair.

(189) Berry v Crawford, C. O.

Ordered that this Court be adjourned till Court in Course.

WILLIAM GOE.

At a Court Continued and held for Yohogania County July 26th, 1779.

Present Isaac Cox Joseph Beckett Joshua Wright Benjamin Fry Gent. Justices.

John Cox appointed Surveyor of the Road in the room of James Wright.

Henderson v Douglass. Hugh Sterling Spl. Bl.

Wright v Beavers. D. Steel Spl. Bl.

Brodie v Same Do. Do.

Heth v Stokes Do. Do.

Boley v Orr. Sampson Beavers. Do.

Dye v Tharp David Williams Spl. Bl.

George Lypolt Ad. v Mary Lypolt Att. Jno. Prothman Spl. Bl.

Stocker v Acklin Hugh Brodie Spl. Bl.

Zadock Wright appointed Surveyor of the Road from opposite Elijah Harts to the Ct. House.

Ordered that the fine imposed on Wm. Downs for not appearing as a Jury man, Jno. Decker v David Ruth, be remitted, he having given the Court satisfactory reasons for his non attendance.

(190) Berry v Andw. Crawford & Asse.— Bl. Judgt. L. 30. & costs.

Ordered that Court be adjourned till Court in Course.

ISAAC COX.

At a Court Continued and held for Yohogania County August 23d, 1779.

Edward Ward Isaac Cox Saml. Newell Joseph Beckett John McDonald Benja. Kuykendall Gent. Justices.

Wm. Murly Sworn Lt. Comn. Read.

Jno. Vannater Sworn Ensign. Comn. Read.

Deed Jediah Johnson to John Douglass Ackd & O. R.

Deed Jediah Johnson to Andrew Devoir Ackd. & O. R.

Springer v Waller. Henry Kersy Spl. Bl.

Deed Thos. Spencer to Saml. Heth Ackd. & O. R.

Deed Benjamin Vannater to Robt. Bowers Ackd. & O. R.

James McCullough v Jno. Taylor. Thos. Pritchard, Spl. Bl.

Release Saml. McAdams to Andrew Devore ackd. & O. R.

Andw. Devoir v Jediah Johnson. Agreed.

Thomas Parkeson v John Megee Non Suit.

Do. Do. Do.

(191) Andrew Heth Sworn Goaler for one month.

Geo. Vallandigham v Gabl. Walker. Ordered that Didimus Issue for the Exn. of John and Francis Reno.

Absent Isaac Cox.

David Steel v James Hamilton, John McComish Spl. Bl.

Lindsay v the same. Benja. Vannater Spl. Bl.

Acct. preferred by Saml. Newell & Benjn. Kuykendall L 472 for building the Ct. House and repairing the old Gl. approved of by the Court, Ordered that the Sheriff pay the same.

Deed Isaac Cox to Andrew Nigh Ackd. & O. R.

Ordered that this Court be adjourned till Court in Course.

EDWD. WARD.

At a Court held for the Examination of John Bryan who stands charged with felloniously stealing a horse the property of George Shannon.

Present Isaac Cox Benja. Kuykendall Oliver Miller Joseph Beckett Joshua Wright Samuel Newell.

The prisoner being set to the barr and it being demanded of him whether he was Guilty or not Guilty, answered Not Guilty. Whereupon Sundry Witnesses were examined, on consideration whereof and the circumstances it is the opinion of the Court that he is not guilty but that he is a person of bad character, and therefore that he give Security for his good behaviour for three years himself L 1000 and his two Securities L 500 each.

(192) At a Court held for Yohogania County September 27th, 1779.

Present Isaac Cox John Canon Joseph Beckett John Freeman Joshua Wright Oliver Miller Richard Yeates Gentlemen Justices.

Power of Atto. David Cox to Friend Cox. ackd. & O. R.

David Levinston ———— acknowledge themselves indebted &c the said David in the sum of L 400 and the said ———— in the sum of L 200 each, Cond'd. for the personal appearance of the sd. David at the next G. Jury Ct. to answer a charge exhibited agt. him for stealing a saddle the property of Robt. Henderson &c.

Administration of the Est. of Saml. Griffith decd. is granted to Elizabeth Griffith she having complied with the Law.

Ordered that Thomas Prather, John Purdie Robert McKie & Rich. Noble or any three of them are appointed to praise the sd. Est.

Ordered that Alexander Ewing an Infant and Orphan of Willm. Ewing decd. aged nine years old be bound to Thomas McMullin according to law, and that the said Thos. do give the said Alexander a new Bible and L 10 at the Exp'n. of his time.

Robt. McGlaughlin &c. v Tobias Woods, Mabara Evans Spl. Bl.

(193) Ordered that William Hammond an Infant and Orphan of John Hammond decd be bound to Joseph Scott according to Law, and to find him one Ax one Grubbing Hoe and one Bible at the expiration of his time.

Ordered that Sarah Hammond aged seven years be bound Infant and Orphan of John Hommond decd be bound to Joseph Scott according to Law and the said John to give her one Cow and Calf one Spining Wheel and Bible at the expiration of her time.

Ordered that this Court be adjourned till tomorrow 8 o'clock.

ISAAC COX.

Court met according to adjournment Sept. 28th, 1779.

Present Wm. Harrison Thomas Freeman Oliver Miller Richard Yeates Gent. Justices.

Administration of the Estate Timothy Hays is granted to Augustine Moore he having complied with the Law.

Ordered that Philip Shute Thomas Rodgers Richd. Waller & Saml. McLain do appraise the sd. Est.

Administration of the Est. of Wm. Noland is granted to Augustin Moore he having complyed with the Law.

Ordered that Philip Shute Thomas Rodgers Richd. Waller & Saml. McLain do appraise the said Est.

(194) An Order of Monongehala Court for appointing a Committee of three to draw up a remonstr. to the Genl. Assembly of Virg'a. praying a repeal of the Law for opening a Land Office & appointing Commrs. to take in entries of Land on the West of the Laurell Hill, was laid before the Court at the request of the Court of Monongehala; upon seriously consider'g the same & the consequences of repealing those Laws, Ord'd. that the sd. Ct. of Monongalia be informed that this Court cannot by any means concur with the sd. Ct. in wishing those Laws to be repealed as they cannot but consider them as exceeding well adapted to the Local circumstances & Situation of the People of this County: so far from wishing a repeal of those Laws this Court are determined to take every Method in their power to prevent it.

Present Isaac Cox, Gent. & John Canon, Gt.

Absent Thomas Freeman.

Ordered that Thomas Ashbrook be apointed Surveyor of the Road from Cat Fishes Camp half way to Pentecosts Mills and John McDowall the other half, and that the Tithables within three miles do work on and keep the sd. Road in repair.

Absent Wm. Harrison.

Ordered that Jno. Crawford be sum'd. to appear at the next Court to shew by what authority he detains James Crago as his Servant.

Colo. Wm. Crawford came before the Ct. and made Oath that Hugh Stephenson now decd. obtained a Warrant from Lord Dunmore while Governor of Virga. for three thousand Acres of Land & that the sd. Hugh Stephenson was an Inh't.

of Virginia & that he was a Captain of a Company actually raised in Virg'a. & and in the Service of Virg'a. in the year of Boquet's Campaign 1764, & the said Crawford further made
(195) oath that he was a witness to the sd. Hugh Stephenson's assigning to a certain Richd. Yeates one thousand Acres of the said Warrant.

William Crawford came before the Court & made Oath that Burton Lucas was a Subaltern Officer in the Service of Virg'a. in Colo. Wm. Byrds Regt. in the year 1758 or 59 in consequence of which he obtained a Warrant from Lord Dunmore while Gov. of Virg'a. for two thous'd. Acres of Land which was assigned by the sd. Lucas to Matthew Ritchie & Wm. Bruce.

Prest. Benja. Kuykendall & Joseph Beckett Gent.

Deed Labat to Chambers prov'd. by the Oath of Wm. Christy O. R. being formerly proved by the other subsc. Witnesses.

Andrew Swearengen gentleman Present.

Deed Edwd. Ward to Jacob Haymaker ackd. by sd. Ward. O. for R.

Two Deeds James McGoldrick to Edwd. Ward ack'd. O. R.

Deed Edwd. Ward to McGoldrick ackd. O. R.

William Crawford Gent. Sworn Surveyor.

Appraisement of the Goods Chattles and Credits of the Estate of Archibald Wilson deceased return'd order for Rec'd.

Deed Ed. Ward to James Freeman. Ackd. O. R.

(196) Manuel Gollehar being bound in Recognizance Ordered to be Discharged.

Administration of the Estate of Solomon Froman granted to Mary Froman, she having complied with the Law.

Ezekiel Hopkins, John Hopkins, Nicholas Devoir and Levengton Thomas, are appointed appraisers to sd. Estate.

Deed, John Johnston to John Hopkings prov'd. Or. for Record.

Ordered that James Chambers be bound in Recog'ze. L 500 and Samuel Irwin his Sec'ty. in L 25 for his appearance of the said James Chambers at the next G. Jury Court.

Aaron Williams took the Oath of Allegiance & fidelity. paid.

Samuel Beeler v Josiah Scott. Jno. Allen Spl. Bl.

Acquilla Whitaker took the oath of Allegiance and fidelity. paid.

Present Thomas Freeman Gent.

John Boley v Corn v Maning. Jno. Fife Sen. Spl. Bl.

Deed Ezekiah Applegate to Thomas Spencer acknowledged & O. R.

David Levesterton bound to the next Grand Jury Ct. held in L. 600, Benja. Collings & Saml. Irwin Secy's. held in L 300 Each.

(197) Ordered that Mary Guen the wife of Thos. Guen a poor Soldier in the Continental Service be Allowed 40 S. p. month for the support of herself and one child, to comm'ce the 28th of March Last, and to End the 28th of March Next.

Ordered that Joseph Pearce son of Elisha, be app'd. constable to serve the Ensuing year in the place of Benjaman Philips.

Decker v Jacobs, refered to James Wright, Joseph Perkerson & Saml. Devoir.

Ordered that Ct. be adjourned untill Tomorrow morning 9 oclock.

BENJA. KUYKENDALL.

Court met according to adjournment September 29th. 1779.

Present Edwd. Ward, William Crawford, Thomas Smallman William Harrison, and Thomas Freeman, Gent. Jus.

Licence is Granted to Robert McKindley to keep an Ordinary at his house for one year, he having complied with the Law.

Ordered that Josias Crawford Thomas Lapsley Jediah Ashcraft & Richd Crooks, to view a Road forom Pentecosts Mills to McKees Ferry near the mouth of Yough and make a return of the Convenience & Inconvenience to next Ct.

Licence is granted to John Farree to keep an Ordinary the Insuing Year he having Complied with the Law.

Ordered that the Sheriff Summon a Jury of twelve Men to condemn an Acre of Land the property of Wm. Black in fav'r. John Armstrong where he is now Building a Mill.

(198) Ordered that 40 S. pr. month be allowed the Wife of Francis Holland a poor Soldier in the Cont'l. Service for the support of

herself and one child to commence the 28th day of last March and to end the 28th day of March next.

Ward to Heth. Deed ackd. & O. R.

Present Benjamin Kuykendall, Gent.

Robert McKindley & James Fleming appointed Constables for the ensuing year.

Robt. McKindley sworn Const'l.

Ordered that John Goe be attached for not Swearing in as Constable.

Absent Wm. Harrison, Gent.

Geo. Berry v Andw. Crawford. Ord'd. that the Judgt. be set aside and Judgt. opened & Redocketed.

Ordered that Philip Whitsel be summoned to appear at the next Court to shew cause why he detains Patience York as a Servant and that she be committed to the care of Thomas Smallman till the next Court.

Inventory of Val. Crawfords Est. Retd. & O. R.

Wills v Quick Moses Holladay Spl. Bl.

Joshua Wright & Joseph Beckett, Gent. Prest.

(199) Henry v Slone, T. A. B. Then came a Jury Towit: Gabriel Cox, John Brown, Joseph Perkerson, David Andrews, Samuel Devoir, Moses Holliday, Uriah Johnston, Thomas Applegate James Wright Robt. McKey John Dean James McGee. Judgmt. for plaintiff L 15 & Costs.

Prest. Samuel Newell Gent.

Ordered that Susannah Harmon be bound to Samuel Newell Gent. according to Law.

Hugh Orra v Peter Branden. In Attachm't. Judgmt. for L 84.9.5 & Costs, & order of Sale.

Cox v Williams & Irwin. Then came a Jury towit. John Robertson, John Hopkins, Zekiel Hopkins, Michl. Humble, Jno. Quick Ezekl. Bernard, Adam Alex[r]. James Vannater Hezekiah Applegate Charles Records Jno. Collins Abraham Miller. Verd't. & Judgmt. for plaintiff L. 50. Costs.

Crow v Dye. Saml. Devoir Spl. Bail.

Marshall v Huff ag'd.

Deed Pentecost to Records. ackd. O. R.

Absent Thos. Freeman, Gent.

(200) Ordered that Colo. John Cannon have the publick salt

which now lies at Alexandria brought up to this County and Distribute it to the Persons Intitled to receive it, and that he be authorised to Contract for the Carriage on such Terms as he can, Taking care in the Distribution to Fix the price so as to raise the money due on sd. Salt for the Original Cost, Carriage, & other Contingencies.

Ordered that Benj. Kuykendal Esq. be authorised to have the Publick Salt now Lying at Israel Thompsons in Lowden County brought up on the same principals.

Ordered that Zacheriah Connell be Sommoned to appear at the next Court and render an acct. of the publick salt he has recv'd.

Thom's. Freeman Gent. Prest.

Samuel Thompson v John Hopkins. Ezekiel Hopkins Spl. Bail.

Ordered that Court be adjourned untill Tomorrow Morning 9 oClock. BENJA. KUYKENDALL.

(201) Present Isaac Cox, Joshua Wright, Samuel Newell, Joseph Beckett.

Attachments.

James Anderson v John McLean dis'd.
McMahan v Myers Discontd.
Campbell v Street Do.
Morgan &c v Connell Do.
Duncan & Wilson v Lyon Do.
Price v the same Do
Hull v Do Do.
Pelton v Smith Do.
Hammit v Hanks Do.
Douglas v Hill Do.
Virgin v Karr Do.
Parkeson v Douglas Do.
Decker v Hanks Do.
Boling v Rootes Do.
Oury v Castle Do.
Robertson v French Do.
Smallman v McConnel Do.
Thomas v Kilgore Do.

Parkison v Edwards Do.
Ormsby v Dunn Do.
Harrison v Wallace Do.
Ogle v McIwain Do.
Ohara v Brandon. Trial for 44L. 10s. 8d.
Cox, Admr. v Nelson discontd.
Ritchie v Hall Do.
Depue v Hardin. Judgt.
Lypolt v Lypolt agreed.

(202) Issues.

Cox, Trial. v Williams &c.
Lyda. Do. v Cox Judgt.
Wherry v White Contd
Miller v Humble Do
Johnson v Swearengen
Brownlee v Douglas Contd.
Shilling v Newkirk Do.
v the same Do.
Myers v Hooper Do.
Mitchel v same Do.
Shilling v Fortner Do.
v Myers Do.
Hooper v Geo. Myers Do.
Fullum v Johnson Do.
Springer v Kearsey referred.
Spears v Winemiller Contd.
Bousman v McGoldrick. Contd
Ward v Thorn &x
v Same contd.
Pentecost v Lynn
v Briscoe contd
Shilling v Taylor Do.
Hawkins, Asse. v Clarke Contd.
v Kuykendall Do.
Eaton v Kenon Discontd
v McLeland Do.
Bond v Mordecai. Judgt by default L 11.2 152 lbs. Tob'o. & 40s
v same Do. L 22.10. 152 Tob'o. 40 S.

Brodie, Asse. v French Discontd
Grubb v Douling Judgt. by default.
Vallandigham v Tigart Discontd
Cook, Asse. v McConnel Do.
McManamy v Robertson Do.
Semple v McKinzie contd.
Holladay, Asse. v Hawkins. Plea waved & Judgt.
Beal v Finn &x contd.
v McMahan Do.
John Nevill v Gist. Plea waved & Judgt. Inqu grant.
Hamilton, Asse. v Dunfield Discontd.
Cresop v Swearengen contd.
(203) Campbell v Bell contd
Fullum v Johnson &x }
v same } contd.
v McComish }
Andrew v Johnson &x Do.
v same Do.
Decker v Ruth
Clark v Again
Heth v Bruce contd.
Christy v Heth Do.
v same Do.
Froman v Boyce
Campbell v Thompson
Bruce v McMichael
Madison, Jun. v. Dunbarr
McLeland &x v Irwin
Hamilton v Norris
McAdams v Devore agd.
Innis v Scott
Brady v Williams &x
Washington v Pearsall.
Caldwell v Fry contd
Jones v Spears
Williams v Shane
v Protsman
v Carter
v Stocker

Stuart v Crawford
v Harrison

(204) Common Orders.

Innes v Sawins
v same
Morrison v Vannater N. G. & I'd.
Bousman v McGoldrick
Elliott v McIntosh W. E. Judgt.
v same Judgt & W. E.
Bradley v Boley N. G. with leave.
Curry v Wells Do.
Shirley v Thompson Non. Assr.
Atkinson v Matthews Judgt.
Smallman v Such W. E.
Bentley v Warren Agd.
Morton v Seaburn Agreed.
Innis, Ass'ee v Hougland
Day v Stansbury Judgt. W. E.
Johnson v Lindsey contd.
Do v Mills Do.
Waller v Springer N. G.
Nevill v Thompson
v Sharp
v Blackburn
Caldwell v Tygart &x Judgt.
Holladay v Matthews Judgt.
Henderson v Johnson
Reed v Springer Judgt L. 37.10 S. 170 L & 40 S.
Embly v Crowe N. G. w. Leave and Issued.
Hamilton v Swearengen

Writs of Enquiry.

Hawkins v Wheat contd
Nelson v Shilling discontd.
Shilling v Nelson Do.
McIlry v Templin } contd
v The same }
Hand v Whitaker Discontd.

Boley v Springer N. G. w. leave & I'd.
v Jno. Springer Do.
v same Do.
Ward v Wills N. G. w. Leave & I'd.
Cox v Williams
(205) Vance v Williams N. G. w. leave & I'd.
Ralston v Lowry contd.
Henry v Sloan Trial.
Fry v Filton contd
v Same Do.
White v Johnson Do.
Swigart v Murphy Do.
Brashears Admor. v Brashears Do.
Noble v Kuyd'l. discontd.
Whiteside v Girty Contd.
Riggle v Dye N. G. w. leave & I'd.
Richards v Boley contd.
Hawkins v Zane discontd.
v Hanks Do.
Froman v Dean contd.
Vance v McNew
Lyda v Richards Settled & discontd.
Clark v Parkeson contd.

References.

Briscoe v Todd Discontd.
Connel v Mounce Do.
Reasoner v Ruth. Judgt. 375 Tob'o & 40 S. paid.
Boling v Morrison discontd.
Wills v Newell Do.
Gist v Waller Judgt. W. E.
v Hall Judgt W. E.
v Boyles Do.
Burrows v Johnson Abates.
Sly v McKindley discontd.
Bradon v Vannator Do.
Richards v Ross Do.
Brownfield v Same Do.
Custard v Long Do.
Swassicks v Jones Do.

Pearse v Evans N. G. w. leave & I'd.
Murphy v Richards Discontd.
Hayes v Deal Do.
Ewalt v McCollister Do.
(206) Hougland v Laughlin N. G. w. Leave & I'd.
Swassicks v Swassicks discontd.
Newkirk v Shilling Do.
McFarlane v Beeler. Judgt. £ 22. S 11. 287 Tobo. & 40 S.
Andrew v Johnson
Matthews v Marshall &x. Judgt.
Cox v Breetsman. N. G. w. leave & I'd.
Vannator v Bradon Discontd.
v Parkeson N. G. w. leave & I'd.
Burrows v Williams. Abates.
Jones v McDonald discontd.
Dawson v Kirkpatrick N. G. w. leave & I'd.
Hall v Wells &x discontd.
Grimes v Logan Do.
Beeler v Walker Judgt. W. E.
Woods v McKee discontd.
Morrison v Swigart Do.
Froman v Boyce. N. G. w. leave & I'd.
Deal v Hays Discontd.
Crooks v Hougland. N. G. w. leave & I'd.
Pearse v Evans Do.
Wallace v Duncan discontd.
Tygart v Boley. N. G. w. leave & I'd.
Boyce v Froman &x Do.
Tigart v Chamberlain Judgt W. E.
McKy v Davison Do.
v Same Do.
v Same Do.
Mallocks v Brown discontd.
Brown v Mallocks Do.
Lyda v Collins Do.
Caldwell v Hougland N. G. W. leave & Issued.
Whitsel v McElwane Do.
Caldwell v Corn Do.
Chamberlain v Henthorn discontd.

Spears v Proctor Do.
v Gist I. W. C.
(207) Croghan v Waugh contd.
Newell v Robeson contd.
Shilling v Young discontd.
v Same Do.
v Demink Do
v Procter Do.
Nevill v Wiseman contd.
Shilling v Martin Discontd.
Sly v Smith Do.
Spear v McMahan N. G. w. leave & I'd.
Blackburn, Asse. v Peak Discontd.
Conrod v Carter Do.
Wood v Griffith Do.
Rogers v Proctor Do.
Clinton & Noble v Brashears. Judgt. by Default. L 4 19. & ¾ & 40 S.
Wagoner v Warner Discontd.
McGrew v McConnel Do.
v Phelps Do.
McMahan v Irwin Do.
McChandlis, Asse. v McComish Do.
Moor v Richmond Do.
Smallman v Slover Do.
Virgin v Moore Do
Barker v Jourdan Do.
Redford, Asse. v Hill Do.
Armstrong v Ramage Do.
Wilcox v Craighead Do
Barrackman v Shively Do
Reasoner v Shearer Do.
Ramsay v Chambers & Co. Do.
v The same Do.
Heth v Farree Do.
Perkin v Colloway Do.
Hughy v Thomas Do.
Stephens v Shilling Do.
Downer v Teagarden Do.

(208) Thomas v Lee Discontd.
Wilson v Croghan &x Do.
Brownfield v Cox Do
Bond v Long. Judgt. by default L 20 Costs 117 lb Tobo. & 40 S.
Tigart v Dunnavan Discontd.
Caldwell v Browster Do.
Sumral v Same Do
Shearer v Miller Do
Baker v Hendricks Do
Whitaker v Dixon Do
Witsel v Shearer Do
Gollihar v Dowlin Do
Stephens v Stout Do
McMullen & ux v Parkeson &x Do
v Same Do.
Moore v Virgin Do
Dodd v Virgin Do
v same Do
Moore v Virgin Do
Boyce v Philips Do
Campbell v Brownfield Do
Harrison v Karr Do
Jones v Clarke &x Do.
Phelps v McGrew Do.
McMichael v Frinch Do.
Purcel v Gibson Do
Halfpinny v Whitsel Do
Thomas v Merchant &x Do
Ireland v Wilson Do
Collins v Brady Do.
Black, Asse. v Dunlavy Do
Vaughan v McMahan Do
Stephenson v Reed &x Do.
Small v Gray Do
Holladay v Jones. Judgt. by default.
Tidball, Asse. v Shaner discontd.
Anderson, Asse. v Huey Do
(209) Stephenson v Barnett discontd.

McLeland v Grey Do
Sly v Smith Do
Young v Jackman Do
Lynn v Tilton Do
Martin v Johnson Do
Chambers v McLain Do
Ruse v Haymaker Do.
Martin v Glass &x Do
v Hamilton Do
Black v Chamberlain Do
Tigart v Burns Judgt. by default.
v Jeffery Discontd.
Winebiddel v Finch Do
Young v McCulloch &x Do
Morrison, Asse. v Ross Do
Brownfield v Smith. Judgt. by default. L 5. 10. 1 170 lb. Tob'o.
Hunter, Asse. v Jones discontd.
Carswell v Dunn Do.
Wallace v Murdoch Do
Fossett v Meek Judgt & W. E.
Campbell, Asse. v Dunn discontd.
Ridgly & Co. v Lynn. Judgt by default.
Morecroft v Douling Do
Fleming v Gibson discontd
Dunfield v Hickman Do
v Ross Do
v Lindsay Do
v Russell Do
v Fossett Do
v Pearcifull Do
Steel v Johnson Do
v Johnson Do
Downer v Morrison Do
Woods v McGachen Do
Steger v Smith Abates
Elliott & Co. v Martin discontd.
(210) Linch v McGlaughlin discontd
Semple v Kerns Do

Gray v Harrison Do

Croghan v Boley
v McCallister
v Bousman
v McKee
v Richmond
v Whitaker
v Abraham Whitaker
v Jas. Whitaker
v Kuykendall
v Frederick
v Roliter
v McLean
v Bousman
v Grimes
v McGrew
v Troop
v Swasicks
v Meek
v McManamy
v Drummond
v Campbell
v Myers &x.
v Gibson
v Weddell, Sen.
v Beard
v Mitchel
v Miller
v Ormsby
v Reno
v Elliott
v Price
v Loudon
v St. Clair
v Lowdon
} Do.

(211) St. Clair v Labatt Discontd.
Clark v Teabolt Do
Eyler v Adams Do.
Gahagan v Smith Do.

Enoch v Teagarden &x. Do.
Clinton v Mays Do
Hawkins v Humble Do
Fife v Churchill Do
Hite v Morgan Judgt. by default.
v White Do
v Evans Do
v Mynett Do
v Defebaugh Do
v Same Do Exn.
Bruin v Fife Do
v Same Do
v Same Do
v Same Do
Hales v Roatch Judgt. W. E.
Morgan v Nichols discontd.
v Bond Do
v Chamberlain Do
v Bever Do
Price v Lynn Judgt. by default.
v Weddel discontd.
v Hanks Judgt by default.
Gray v Peton discontd.
v Same Do.
Tigart v Dunavan Do
v Craven. Do
v Vannator Do
v Craven Do
v Oglin Do.
St. Clair v Sills Do.
Elliott v Girty Do.
Hawkins v Parkeson Do.
Robison v Crow Do.
(212) Shilling v Newkirk Discontd.
Rodgers v Williams &x Do.
v Parr Do.
v Tumbleson Do.
Zane, Asse. v Holman Do.
Castleman v Tabor Do

Lyon v Duncan Do
Hosier v Bruce Do
Glassell v Kizer Do
McGlassen v Young Do
Anderson v Rees Do
Dunlavy, Asse. v Ferrel Do
Armstrong v Ohara Do
Thomas v Stark Judgt. by default.
Ward v Springsteel discontd.
v Same Do.
Jones v Evans Do.
v Same Do.
v McGoldrick Do.
v same Do
Ogle v Wilson Do
v same Do.
Labat v Ramage Do.
Hamilton &x v Goe Do.
Clendening v Logan Do.
Nevill, Asse. v Holladay. Conditions perf'd. & contd.
Keiser v Jamison discontd
Kelso &x v Piggott Do.
Allison v Lyon Do.
Smith v Douglas Do
Martin v Elliott Do
Brecken v Cassat Do
Jones v Ormsback Do.
Wafords, Exrs. v Cox Do
Roots v Cook Do.
(213) Caldwell, Asse. v Lynn Agreed.
Kidd v McConnel Judgt & W. E.
Linch v Jones Do
v Bosnick Do.
Dunning v Bay Do.
Bradon v Elliott Do.
Crooks v Hilderbrand. Judgt. by default. L 4.5 160 lb. Tobo. 40 S.
Johnson v Steal discontd.
Hamilton v Martin Do

Berwick v Atkison Do.
Gilfillian Asse. v Tigart Do.
McInty v Gray Do
McCollister v Scott Do
Boley v Tigart Do
Robeson v McGoldrick Do
McElroy v McMahan Judgt. W. E.
Atkison v White discontd.
Price v Crawford Do
Wheat v Carmichael Do
Scott v Vallandigham Do
Campbell v Hanks Do
Holaday & Co. v Stout &x. Abates, D. D.
McCarty v Craighead discontd.
Lyon v Humblebearer. Judgt. by def't. L 37 10 160 lb. Tobo. & 140 S.
Frazier v Chambers discontd.
Miller v Hill Do.
Karnes v McQuin &x Do.
Boyd v Thomas Do
Wright v Springstone Do.
Davidson v Hanks Do
Walker v Dristnell Do.
Clark v Hawkins Do
Smith v Girty Do
Dillon v Perky Do.
McManamy v Ohara Do.
Richmond v Scott Do.
Ferrel v Dougherty Do.
Tharp v Collins Do
(214) Armstrong v Ohara Discontd.
Bousman v Ormsby Do.
Thomas v Elliott, Admr. Do.
Christy v White Do.
Brinkers, Exr's. v Hardin's Adm'ors. Judgt. by def't.
Davis & Co. v Young. Judgt. by def't.
Elvy v Dunn discontd.
Lyon v Downer Do.
Mitchel v Wade. Judgt. by def't. Process not served.

Wilson v McGinnis discontd.
Johnson v Stephens Do.
Wilson v Canon Do
Williams v Presser do
Croghan v Powel do
Hite v Dodson. Judgt. by def't. Process not served.
Ormsby v Bousman discontd.
Dunlavy v Robertson Do
Brashears, Admor. v Colvin Judgt. by def't.
Patterson v Tidball Judgt W. E.
Day v Dean N. G. w. leave & Joind.
Bever, Asse. v Cook &c. Admors. discontd.
Beeler v Ink N. G. w. leave & I.
Kersy v Springer ref'd.
Cox v Anderson agreed.
Crawford v Hamilton discontd.
Williams, Asse. v Anderson Do.
Wright v Hart. N. G. w. leave & I'd.
McCleland v Beeler discontd.
McMahan v Matthews Judgt. W. E.
Boyce v Froman N. G. w. leave & I'd.
Mooney v Records N. G. w. leave & I'd.
Boyce v Froman Non. Asst. & I'd.
v same Do
& ux v Graham
v same
v same } Discontd.
v same
v same
v Atkeson Judgt. W. E.
v Froman N. G. w. leave & I'd.
Protsman v Hill Judgt. W. E.
(215) Norris v Vineyard & Ux Judgt W E.
Fife v Tigart. &x Judgt. W E.
v same Do.
Bentley v Eaglen Do.
Clark v Boley Do
Hufman v Leatherman Do.
Munn v Crawford Do.
Boling v Norris N. G. w. leave & I'd.

Miller v Humble Cond's perform'd. & I'd.
Gilliland v Linn N. G. leave & I'd.
Shilling v Newkirk Do.
Dunagan v Boyce Agd.
McCollister v Corn Judgt. W. E.
Ward v Philps. Discontd.

Petitions

Sills v Irwin discontd.
Shilling v Blackman Do.
  v Delany Do.
Roatch v Shaner Do.
Christy, Asse. v Irwin Do.
  v Jackson Do.
Parker, Asse. v Davis Do.
Whitsel v Rybolt Do.
Sloan v Mitchel, Adm. Do
Hamilton v Hawkins Do.
Seaman v Miller &x Do.
  v same Do.
Cook v Berwick Do
  v Hart Do
  v Johnson Do
  v Dobbins Do
  v Parkerson Do
Vannater v Pelton Do.
McKenzie v Semple Do
Ryan v Park Do
McDonald v Grimes Do
Deal v Grove Do
Fennel, Asse. v Marshall Do
Colvin v Baily Do
(216) Wells v Johnson Discontd
Redford v Hill Do
  v Criswell Do.
Ryan v Shaner Do
Brent v Teagarden. Judgt. for L 2
Oury v Fisher }
  v Maurer } Judgt.
  v Miller }

Todd v Shearer discontd
Timmons v Gafney Do
Wright v Dunlavy Do.
Morgan v Saltsman Do.
Dunlavy v Fry Do
Swigart v Ross. Judgt. L 3. 15. 150 lb. Tobo & 20 S.
Baggs v Cumings Discontd.
Whitsel v Valentine Do.
Marshal v Brooks Do.
Spurgin v Patrick Do.
Pigman No. 2 v Layton Do.
Chriswell v Girty Do.
v same } Do.
v same }
Asse. v same } Do.
Asse. v Scott }
Clinton v Cuningham. Process not retnd.
v Donne Jud. L 2. 1. 2. Tobo. 150. & 20 S.
Wickwire v Douner Discontd.
Wills v Zane Discontd.
Hawkins v Bodkin Judgt.
v Coffee Judgt.
Virgin v Colvin discontd.
Paul v West Do.
Day v Christy Do
Taylor v Byerly Do
Humble v Clark Do
v Burns Do
Jones v McDowall Do
Fowler v Brown Do
Weddall, Asse. v Arle Do
McCleland v Small } Do.
v Same }
(217) Davis, Asse. v Downer Judgt.
v Warner Do. Process not served.
Dix v Groggs discontd.
Hardin, Jun. v Kincaid Do.
Miller v Custard Do
Ryan v Press Do

Fennel, Asse. v Mitchel Do
Maxwell v Ashcraft Do.
Cuningham v Bruce Do
Jolly v Barker Do
Moor No. 3 v Churchil Do.
Shaner, Asse. v Stephens Do
Jackson v Clark Do
Boley v Swigart Do.
v Russal Do
Green v Ward Do
Harrison v Armstrong Do.
Ross v Dunfield Do.
Dean v McMacmanomy Do.
Lestnett v Same Do
Roliter v Labatt Do
Steel v Merrick Do
Jackman v Clark Do
Hall v Redman Do
McCollister v Black Do
Savage v Teagarden Do
Fin v Williams Do
Adams v Horn Do
Lain v Peyton Do
Wallace v Meek Do
House v Mahon Do
Virgin v Moore Do
Adams v Shuster Do
Clendenin v Carmichael Do
Henthorn, Asse. v Martin Do
Semple v Owens Do
Hamilton v Hawkins Do
Ross v Fransway Do
Johnson v Wilson Do
(218) Morgan v Wooler Do
Steel v Thomas Do
McGlassen v Irwin Do
Pearse v Chery Do
Semple v Carol Do
Moore v Richmond Do

Dougherty v Black Do.
Tygart v Lindsay A. D. D.
v same
v same } Do. D. D.
Stewart v Scott discontd.
Campbell v Gahagan Do.
Vallandigham v Springer
v Clements
v Meeks
v Hartley
v Lindsay
v same } Do
Farree v Lynn Do
Maxwell v Thompson Do
Reed v Clarke Do
Dalton v Shaner Do.
Ross v Swift Do
v Black Do
Hawkins v Labat Do
Clarke, Asse. v Downer Do
Fin v Williams Do.
Kendal v Brownfield Do
Gary v McCulloch Do
McCullum v Edwards Do
Christy v Alexander Do
Spears v McDoran Do
Fitzgerald v Reiley Do
Cox v Boling Do
Halfpenny v Dennis Do
Wadel, Asse. v Brown Do
Asse. v Arnold Do
Shaner v Ross
v Plumber } Do
Flander v Marshall Do
(219) Elliott v Small
v Same
v Sinnett
v Winemiller } discontd.

Elliott v Dalton
v Frederick
v Armstrong
v Rodgers
v Same } Do.

Wills v Gohagan Do
Ewalt, Asse. v Armstrong &x Do
Brownfield v Hustage Do
McMichael v French Do
Baker v Knight Do
Tilton. Asse v Bell Do

Brintson, Exors. v Elvy
v Bruce
v Beeler
v Sayers
v Spencer
v Moyer } Do

Isaac Hite v Vantrees Judgt.
v Rich'd Postlethwait Do
v Wilson Do
v Carter Do
Hardin the Younger v Myers discontd.
Cook v Dobbins Do
Parkeson v Burns Do.
Russel v Gahagan Do
Collins v Dobson Do
Asse. v Clark Do.
Lyons v Butler Do.
Madison, Jun. v Sterling Do.
McMahan v Pritchett Do
Taylor v Hanks Do.
Isaac Cox v McMahan Do
Miller v Armstrong Do
Thomas v Lambert Do
Knight v Plumber Do
King v Hansel Do
McCashlin v Evans Do
(220) Holmes v Huston Do
McCollister v Corn Judgt.

Decker v Wilson discontd.
Stephenson v Nicholas Do
Beeler v Burns Do
Spears v same Do

New Pet'o.

Baggs v Cumins Judgt.
Day v Wilson agd.
Lewis v Byers Judgt.
Lypolt v Masterson agreed
Vinamon v Davis agreed
Johnson v Sly abates
Devores, Exors. v Scott discontd
v Tigart Judgt.
Crawford v Hanks discontd.
v Miller Judgt. L. 3.
Marshall v Brooks Exor. Judgt.

Alias's

Still & Ux v Williams P. C.
Crow v Pearse N. G. leave & I'd.
Henderson v Douglas Impl.
Wilson &x Exors. v Lynch &x C. O.
Evans v Russell P C
Stocker v Acklin Impl.
Bay v Jackson agd.
Riddick v Ross C. O.
Boley v Maning. Spl. Bl. Jno. Fife.
v same Do
Brewer & Ux v Stacy C. O.
Cook v Beckett agd.
Spears v Beckett &x Exors. Impl.
Dye v Allen Tharp C. O.
Nichold v Corn Dismd N. Apl.
Johnson v Allen Tharp Agd.
Matthews v Ellis Agd.
Say v Dean Spl. Bl. Imparl.
(221) Ward v Clark } C O
v McIlwane } P C
Crow v Glin agreed
McCullloch v Taylor Spl. Bl. Impl.

Whitsel v Wise Dis'd. N. Apl.

Pluries Cap.

McCormick v Holles Judgt. for Plt. & Ex.
McGlaughlin v Woods Judgt. W. E. L 8. 1. 4.
Bentley v Vittitoe agd.
Workman v Saltsman P C
Ritchie v Thornbury dismd
Reno v Walker agd.
v same agd.
Norris v Embly P C
Ross v Maning P C
Minor, Asse v Blazier P C
McComish v Springer P C
Anderson v Evans C. O.
Steel v Hamilton C. O
McMahan v Hauck No Impt. discontd.
Kearns v Logan P C
Springer v Waller agd.
Smith v Gibson Discontd.
How v Genoway ux. P. C
Burns v Loutherback C. O.
Whitsel v Crawford agreed
Beans v Johnson Judgt. for Plt Exn L 21. 10.
Harrison v Hall discontd.
Miller v Mitchel P C
v same Do
Barrackman v Harry C. O.
v Woods C. O.
Vallandigham v Walker P C
v Same C.O
Wills v Blackstone. dism'd. N. appl.
Lindsay v Smith } C O
v Hamilton }
Lintenbergher v Oldcraft. discontd.
(222) Labat v Smith discontd. N. Impl.
Pearse v Evans C.O
Laughlin v. Brown P C
McDonald v Slover agreed.

Colwell v Thorn N. Imp. discontd.

Kincaid v Henderson }
v Same } Spl. Impl.

Caldwell v Mills disd N. Apr.

Cumins v Patterson N. In dismd.
v Baggs disd. N. Apr.

Caldwell v Wray }
v Thorn } P C

Gibson v Meek P C

Gist v Alexander agd.

McGlaughlin v Piggot N. In discontd.

Hall v Lynch }
v Fossett }
v Shearer } dismd N. apce.
v Hatfield }

Heth v Stokes C. O

Chambers v Wallace Agreed

Gist v Cornwall C.O

Forrester v Murphy C.O.

Mitchel v Pelton Agd

Miller v Same }
v same } Discontd
v Humble } P. C

Appearances

Ferguson v Heth dismt.

Spears v Jones Richard Pauver Spl. Bl.

Ward v Clark C. O.

Postle v Greathouse. Als. Caps.

Boley v Folke A'gd.
v Orr S. B. & Impl.
v Fossitt

Stuart v Purdie Als Caps

Miller v Parkeson Als Caps.
v Gutridge Agd.
v Same agd.

Hugh Brodie v Samson Bever S. Impl.

(223) Crow v Watson agd.

Dunn v Stuart Als. Caps.

Johnson v McAdams Agd.

Sills v Burns discontd.
Loutherback v Same dismt.
Crow v Dye Spl. Bl. Impl.
Russel v Jackson agd.
Lypolt v Hall agd.
Maning v Slover Als. Caps.
Johnson v Evans Als. Caps.
Steel v Sellars agd
Decker v Jacobs retd.
Parkison v Megee } agd.
v same
Morrison, Sen. v Humble agd.
McGee v Parkeson } agd.
v same
Parkeson v Megee } agd.
v same
Douglas v James agd.
Moor v Richmond. discontd.
Dye v Brent als. Caps.
McMahan v Linsin agd.
Parkison v McGee } agd.
v same
Campbell v Blackman agd.
Steel v Stephens als.
Bever v Mayhal Co. Or.
v Miller, Sen. &x. agd.
Hopkins v Johnson dismd. no Inhabt.
Blackman v Pearse agd.
v Campbell agd.
Wilson v Blackman agd.
Blackman v Campbell agd.
(224) Bonum v Sappinton Als. C.
Boling v Wells A C
Johnson v Lindsay C O
Campbell v Tilton agd.
v Scott agd.
v Blackman N. I. discontd.
Ross v Blank Discontd.
Pearse v Hougland &x. agd.

Magee v Gambill als.
Bousman v Ormsby A. C.

v same
v same
v same
v same
v same
v same
v same
v same
v same
v same
v same
v same
v same
v same
v same
v same
v same } Als's. Caps.
v same
v same
v same
v same
v same
v same
v same
v same
v same
v same
v same
v same
v same
v same
v same
v same

(225) Bousman v Ormsby
v same
v same
v same

v same
v same
v same
v same
v same } A C
v same
v same
v same
v same
v same
v same
v same
Chambers v Ewalt A C
Chambers (Inft) v Same A C
Kuykendall v Colvin Imparl.
v Decker A C
Clark v Clark A C
v Clark A C
v Quin A C
Wright v Bever Impl
Cook v John McCashlin C. O.
Bousman v Ormsby Spl. Impl.
Conner v Slover agd.
Boley v Mitchel C. O.
Zachy Connell v Poe &x A C
Cresop's Exors. v Campbell C. O
Biddle v Good &x A C
Cresop v Plumber discontd.
Logan v Miller A C
Devore v Johnson agd.
Johnson &x v Cotes C O
Evans v Richards Als.
Mathew v McLain A C
Stockwell v A B agd.
(226) Thompson v Hopkins. Spl. Bl. Impl.
Kincaid v Henderson Impl.
Means v Graham Dismt. no appr.
Beeler v Scott Spl. Bl.
Bruce v Hougland agd.

Wills v Quick spl. Bl. Impl.
Nicholds v Day discontd.
Shaaf v Douner A C
Pentecost v Jones C. O
Fosset v Hall C. O
Lynch v Same C. O
Crow v Watson Agd.
Johnson v McAdam agd.
Sills v Burns S. Impl.
Crow v Dye Spl. Bl.
Dunn v Stuart Discontd.
Spivy v Records Impl.
Marshall v Huff Agd.

Recog'ce.

C. W. v Mounce discontd
v Springer discontd
v Steel disch'd.
v Black. Contd.
v Bradley contd
v the same Contd.
v Beall Discontd
v Winemiller. Ordered that his recogn. be prosecuted for want of appearance.

(227) Commonwealth v James Chambers, failing to appear, ordered to be prosecuted.

v David Duncan. Do.
v Moses Davidson Do.
v David Irwin Do.
v Susannah Schley Do
v Brawdy. Discontd.
v Dean Contd.
v John Carr. No. Appl. Ord. R. P.
v Hall Do.
v Ross Do
v. Smith & others Discontd.
v. Michl. Tygert. No appl. O. P. R.

Court met accord'g to adjrnt, Sept. 30, 1779.

Present, Thomas Freeman, Oliver Miller, Joshua Wright, Judge Beckett, Isaac Cox, Gent. Just.

Grand Jury Presentment.

v Johnston Campbell Discontd.
v John McDonald fined accd'g to Law
v Richd. McMahen Do No Guilty
v Christie agd.
v Henry Bowling fined according to Law.
v Roberts fined Do.
v McAdams fined accdg. to Law.
v Oharra fined accdg to Law.
v Johnston &x Discontd.
v Newkirk and others. Discontd.
v Labatt fine.
v McClellen N. Guilty
v Robertson fine
v Daviss Do
v Persons N. Guilty.
v McKendley fine.
v Irwin N. Guilty
v Duncan fine
v Flemming fined
v Bealle Do
v Lentenburger N. Guilty.
v Roberts fined
(228) Commonwealth v Devoir Abtes. D. Dead.
v Dodds fined
v Judy Do
v Henderson Do
v McKendley Do.
v Irwin Do.
v Castleman Discontd.
v Corn fined.

{ Informations agt Gray. Discontd. He adhering to the state of Penn'a. }

Indictments.

Lyda v Cox. Then came a Jury towit. James Wright, Gabl. Cox Benjamin Forster, Thos. Applegate Samson Bever Abraham Miller Ezekiel Bernard Andrew Pearse, Wm. Hawkins Hezekiah Applegate Robert McKie, John Alexander. Verdt. & Judgt. for Plt. L. 100.

Hopkins v Johnson. Att[a].

Judgt for L 80 & Ord. Sale and that the Sheriff pay to Abigail Johnson out of the money arising from the sale the sum of L 480 and the Bal[ce.] if any to be applied towards satisfaction of this Judgment.

Johnson v Johnson. Atta. Judgment & Order of Sale, except Six bushells of wheat and all the Keggs in the Shffs. return and the Bed Tick & one Ax & 1 pr. Geers being the property of Abighil Johnson, and the balance if any to be paid the plaintiff. Joshua Wright being sworn Garnishee sayeth he hath 130 l. flour in his Hands the property of the Defendt.

(229) James Boyce &x v James Grimes &x. N. G. & Joined. Then came a Jury, towit: James Wright, Abraham Miller Gabriel Cox, Ezekiel Barnett John Alexander, John Quick Uriah Johnston William Hawkins Thomas Applegate Hezekiah Applegate Samson Beavers Robert Macky Verdt. & Jugmt. for Plaintiff, L. 20.

James Boyce v James Grimes. Case.

Then came a Jury towit, James Wright, Gabriel Cox, John Alexander, Uriah Johnston, Thomas Applegate, Samson Beavers, Abraham Miller, Ezekiel Barnitt, John Quick, John Gabridge Hezekiah Applegate & Robert McKey. Verdt. Defd.

Ordered that Margaret the wife of Jeremiah McCarty a poor Soldier in the Continental Service from this State be allowed four pounds pr. month for the support of herself and three children, To Commence the first day of Apl. Last & Ending the first day of Apl. Next.

Anderson & Todd v Saml. Newell. W. Rep. Dismissed and a Writ of Restertution (on Returno Habondo) awarded.

Ordered that —— Matthews the wife of —— Matthews a poor Soldier in the Continental Service be allowed three pounds per month to commence from the first day of January last and to continue for nine months.

Thos. Freeman Gent. Abst.

(230) Ordered that George Wrey an Orphan of Sixteen years of age the first day of November next be bound to John Robertson according to Law the sd. John to give him a horse & Saddle at the expiration of his time.

Lewis Nicholas v David Day. Dismis'd for w't. of appearance.

Ordered that Benjaman Kuykendall Gent. be Impowered to Borrow five hundred pounds upon Interest, to be applied Towards Discharging the County Debt, and that the Court at the Laying the Next County Levy provide for the payment Thereof.

Ordered that Court be adjourned untill Tomorrow Morning 9 oClock. ISAAC COX.

Court met according to adjournment Oct. 1st, 1779.

Present Isaac Cox Joshua Wright Samuel Newell Joseph Beckett Oliver Miller Gent. Justices.

C. Wealth v Andrew Pearse. Then came a jury towit, Joseph Skelton James Wright Gabl. Cox Wm. Murley Isaack Custard Thos. Applegate John Wall Moses Holaday Saml. Lemin Elijah Rittenhouse Richd. McMahan Uriah Johnson. Verdt. for Defendant.

(231) Absent Saml. Newel Gent.

Wright v Kenneday. Atta. Judgt. L 41, and Ordered that 40 L be condemned in the hands of Edwd. Gather.

C. W. v Mary Boyce Sen. & Mary Boyce Junr. discontinued. Costs paid.

Golahar & ux v Bradly, Sen. Ordered that an Atta. do Issue.

Tacitus Gilyard v Isaac Ellis. Ordered to be redock'd.

Com Wealth v Douging. The Defendt. failing to appear Ordered that his Recogze be prosecuted.

Sciri Facias.

Martha Lapsly v John Reed contd.

Wm. Brashears v Thos. Hamilton Judgt.

Bazil Brown v The Same Judgt.

Com Wealth v James Smith &u. discontd.

Chancery.

Thomas Cresop v Willm. Shearer. contd.

Joseph Simon &u. v Alexander McKee contd.

Benjamin Wells v Thomas Rearden contd.

Ordered that the Sheriff do Summon a Grand Jury 24 good & Lawfull men, to attend at Nov. Court.

(232) Present Oliver Miller Gent.

Ordered that Richd. Noble be recommend to serve as an Ensign in Capt. Freeman Co. of militia in the room of Wm. Colvin who was broke by Verdt. of Ct. Martial.

Joshua Wright Sworn Capt. in the Militia. Com. read.

Ordered that Rebecca Davis Orpan & Infant of Lem'l. Davis be bound to Isaac Cox according to Law She being three years old the 16th Day of Augt. last.

Ordered that Court be adjourned till Court in Course.

ISAAC COX.

At a Court Continued and held for Yohogania County October 25th, 1779.

Present Edward Ward, Joshua Wright Benjaman Kuykendal Thomas Smallman Oliver Miller, Gent. Justices.

Colo. Isaac Cox having applied to us for a pasport to remove himself, family and attendance from this County to the County of Kentucky on the Ohio, It ordered that the sd. Isaac Cox have leave to remove himself and attendance as aforesd, he Deporting himself as a good Citizen and in amenity with the United States, having been long a Magistrate in this County, and Demeaned himself well therein. It is Expected that all good offices be done him by the Inhabitants of this Com. Wealth.

George Roots & Dolphin Drew, Sworn Atty's.

(233) Adm. of the Estate of Jacob Stelty dec'd, is granted to Anne his wife she having Complied with the Law. Wm. Frye, Zadock Wright, John Jones & John Trumbo or any three of them app's. sd. Estate.

Deed Poll James Bruce to George Bruce. Ackd. O. R.

Daniel Leet Sworn Deputy Surveyor having Produced a Commission for that Purpose.

Power of Att. Morris Brody to Gabriel Cox Ackd. O. R.

Ordered that Court be adjourned untill Tomorrow morning 9 o'Clock.

EDWD. WARD.

October the 26th, 1779, Court met according to Adjournment.

Present Edward Ward Thomas Smallman Isaac Cox Joshua Wright Samuel Newell, Gent. Justices.

Power of Atto. Daniel Swolevan to Geo. Roots. Ackd. O. R.

Thos. Reed v Evert Springer Impal. Granted, Money Deposited with the Court.

Benjamin Kuykendall Gent. Present.

(234) John Embly v John Crow. Then came a Jury Towit. Gabriel Cox John Kinkaid, John Duglass, James Wright, Henry Hogland, John Bowley, John Springer, Hugh Brawdy, Zadock Wright, Joseph Perkerson, Richd. Crooks, Isaac Newkirk.

Verdict for Defdt. & Ju.

Fife v Tygert. N. G. with leave & Issued. Then came the same Jury towit, Gabriel Cox, John Kinkaid, John Embly James Wright, Henry Hoagland, John Bowley, John Springer, Hugh Brawdy, Zadock Wright, Joseph Perkerson, Richd. Crooks & Isaac Newkirk. Verdict for Plaintiff & Jud. L 50.

Edward Ward Gent. came into Court and being Sworn on the Holy Evangelist of Almighty God Sayeth, That Thomas Smallman, Gent. was a Lieutenant and Quarter Master in the first Batalion in the Pennsylvania Redgment in Actual Service in the year 1758.

Oliver Miller Gent. Present.

Philip Gilliland v William Lynn. then came a Jury, towit, John Kinkaid, John Embly, James Wright, Henry Hogland, John Bowley, Wm. Crow, Hugh Brawdy, Zadock Wright, Joseph Perkerson, Richard Crooks, Isaac Newkirk, Jno. Crow. Verdt. for Plaintiff & Judmt. L 1000.

(235) Ordered that Jno. Springer be Sommoned to appear at the Next Court to shew Cause if any why he refused to Serve as a Jury man.

Van Swearengen v William Burris, David Williams S. B. & Impl.

Benjaman Kuykendall Gent. come into Court and being Sworn Sayeth, that in the Spring of the year 1754 he saw Maj. Edward Ward on his march to Virginia from what is now Fort Pitt, that the sd. Maj. Ward had the command of the party with him & that he understood that he was the commanding officer of the Post at the aforsd. place as an officer in the Virginia line & Surrendered to the French.

Todd v Gibson. Saml. Newell S. B. & Imp.

Ordered that Court be adjourned untill Tomorrow morning 9 oClock. EDWD. WARD.

October 27th, 1779 Court met according to adjournment.

Present William Crawford. Thomas Smallman, Isaac Cox Benjamin Kuykendall and Oliver Miller, Gent. Justices.

Certificate Adam Stephens to Isaac Cox On motion ordered to be record.

Colo. Crawford being Sworn Sayeth that The sd. Isaac Cox was a Subaltron Officer in the Virginia Service in the year 1764.

(236) Spears v Winemiller. then came a Jury, Towit. John Kinkaid, John Embley, James Wright, Henry Hogland, John Bowley, Hugh Brawdy, Zadock Wright, Joseph Perkerson, Richd. Crooks, Isaac Newkirk, John Crow & William Crow. Verdi't. for Plaintiff & Judmt for L 19.17.4.

Crow v Williams. Then came a Jury, towit, Enoch Springer, John Springer, Andrew Robertson, Thomas Spencer, Saml. Devoir, Saml. St. Clair, Samson Beavers, Saml. Hinch, Saml. Brice, Robert Johnston, Elisha Ritinghouse & Moses Holliday. Verdi't for plaintif & Jdm. L 300.

Joshua Wright Gent. Prest.

Spears v Gist. Then came a Jury towit. John Kinkaid, John Embly, James Wright, Uriah Johnston, John Bowley, Hugh Brawdy, Zadock Wright, Joseph Perkerson, Richd. Crooks, Isaac Newkirk, Thomas Bond, William Crow. Vedt. for plaintiff & Judm L 11. 16.

Crow v Dye Non asstn. & I'd.

Brawdy v Beavers. N. G. leave & Jo'nd

Wright v the same. N. Asst & Jo'nd

Ordered that the wife of John Overlin a poor soldier be allowed fifteen pounds pr. month for the support of herself and five Children commencing the first day of July Last and ending the first of January Next.

Ordered the wife of David Smith a poor soldier, be allowed twelve pounds pr. month for the suppurt of herself and four Children, Commencing & ending as afores'd.

Ordered that the wife of Thomas Dunn be allowed twelve pounds pr. month for the support of herself and four children Commencing the first of July Last & ending the first of January next.

Ordered that the States attorney Prefer a Bill of Indictmt. agt. David Williams for ass't on the Body of Elizabeth Crow.

Ordered that Ezuby Munn be allo'd. two Days attendance in the suit of Crow v Williams.

Ordered that Jacob Bouseman be allo'd. half a Dollar for a man & the same for a Horse for ferrying a Cross Monongahela.

(237) Berry v Crawford. Non Asst & Jo'nd.

Meers v Hooper Dis. Contd.

Same v Same. Do.

Hooper v Myers. Do.

Kinkaid v Henderson. N. G. leave & Jo'nd.

Same v Same Do.

Johnston v Springer Judmt W. Ey.

Bouseman v Ormsby. In Tresp. Dismd.

Ordered that John Lad serve his master Wm. Crawford, Eighteen month after the Expiration of his Time by Ind'tr. for Loss of Time in runing away and Expence in Taking him up.

James Hoge is app. Ensign & Joseph Kirkpatrick Liut. of Militia.

Ordered that Court be adjourned untill Court in Course.

THO. SMALLMAN.

(238)

At a Court Continued and held for Yohogania County, December 27th, 1779.

Present Edward Ward, Benjaman Kuykendal, Joshua Wright, Benjaman Frye & Joseph Beckett Gent. Present.

Deed of Surrender Pentecost to [——— ?] Ackd. O. R.

Indenture Elenor Frazer to James Mc.Mahen. Ackd. O. R.

Oliver Miller Gent. Present.

On motion of Michael Vonbuskkirk praying a Certificate of his Military Services, It appears to this Court (from Testimony) that the said Vonbuskkirk Served as an Insign under a Commission now produced in Court, from his Excellency Horatio Sharpe Governor of Maryland, dated the 2nd. of May, 1756, in a corps raised by Alexander Bealle for the Service of Maryland, and that the sd Vonbuskkirk hath for many years past and now is an Inhabitant of this State. Ord. to be Certif'd.

Ordered that James Wall, Walter Wall Richd. Sparks & Andrew Pearce Ju. do Review a road the nearest and best from the New Store on the Monaungohela River into the road near Andrew Dye's, and make return of the Conveniency and Inconveniences to next Ct.

Riddeck v Springer. John Springer Sp. bl.

Majr. Edward Ward having applied to this Court to Certifie his Gen'l. Character, It is ordered therefore to be Certified. That the sd. Maj. Edward Ward hath been a Justice of the Peace in this County since its Institution, and Demeaned himself wel therein, as also in the Ofice of Sheriff for sd. County, and that he has always deported himself as a Good Citizen of the Com. Wealth, & as an honest Man and a good Neighbour.

Ordered that Walter Wall and Joseph Warner[1] be app'd. Cons'b. and be sworn before the Next Majistrate to Qualify.

Ordered that Court be adjourned untill Tomorrow Morning 9 oClock.

EDWD. WARD.

(239) Court met according to adjournment Decemb. 28th, 1779.

Present Edward Ward, Benjaman Kuykendal Joshua Wright Oliver Miller, Gent. Justices.

License is granted to Cabriel Cox to keep an Ordinary at his House the Ensuing, he complying with the Law.

Dr. The County of Yohogania,

To the States attorney,		L 500.
To the Sheriff for Ex[?]. Services,	1200 To.	
To three called Courts,	600	
To the Clerk for Ex[?] Services,	1200. Do	
To three Called Courts,	600. Do.	

Ordered that the Sheriff collect forty Eight Shillings from each Tithable as a County Levy for the present year.

Ordered that Samuel Irwin Gent. be appointed attorney for the Com. Wealth in this County the ensuing year, in the room of Phil. Pendleton Gent. who has resigned.

Inventory of the Estate of James Devoir Deceas'd retd. Order to be recorded.

[1] Intended probably for Joseph Warne.

Ordered that Elizabeth Keyher, widow of Frederick Keyher a soldier from this State who died in the Service be allowed fifteen pounds pr. month for the support of herself and four children, commencg the 26th of Octob. and ending 26 Apr. next.

Ordered that Ruth Davis widow of James Daviss a soldier who died in the Service be allowed Twelve pounds pr. month for the support of herself and three children, commencing the 26th of Octob'r. Last and ending the 26 day Apl. next.

Ordered that Geo. McCormick and William Harrison Gent. the present and late Sheriffs, do bring in their accounts for settlement at the next Ct.

(240) Division and allotment of the one third of the Landed Estate of James Devoir, Deceased to his widow or Relict, returned and O. R.

At a Called Court held for the Trial of David Donee who stands charged with passing one eigh and one five Dollars. continental Counterfit Bills of Credit.

Prest. Edwd. Ward, Benj. Kuykendal, Joshua Wright, John Cannon, Saml. Newel, Joseph Becket, Benj. Frye & Oliver Miller.

The prisoner being set to the Bar, and being asked guilty or not Guilty pleads not guilty. the Court upon hearing the witnesses are of opinion that the prisoner is not Guilty of Forgery or counterfeiting but that he is Guilty of a high Misdemeaner, and fraudulent Imposition. Ordered that the said David Donee be bound over to the next Grand Jury Court and that the States Attorney prefer a Bill of Indictment. Whereupon the said David Donee with Hugh Brawdy and Stephen Hall his Security come into Court and entered into recogn. as aforesd. The sd Donee held in L 500 the sd sureties in L 250 Each.

Daniel Caugha & John Cannon come into Court and entered into recognizance for the appearance of the sd. Caugha, appearance at the next Grand Jury Court, and give testimony agt. David Donee, held in L 250 each.

Berry v Crawford Contd.

James Spear being bound in recognizance appeard. Ordered to be bound to the next G. Jury. James Spears with Andrew pearce Ju. his secr. held L 500 each.

John Brackenridge bound in recgn. appd. Ordered to be bound to Next G. Jury Ct. John Brackenridge with James Brackenridge his Sec. come into Cot. held in L 500 Each.

(241) Whereas John Campbell Esqr. Lieut. for this County, is now a Prisoner with the Indians, and it is uncertain when he may return to Take the Command of the Militia of this County, upon considering the same and the present situation of the Melitia of this County, it is the opinion of this Co't. that it is Necessary that some person should be appointed in the stead of the said Colo. Campbell, & it is therefore ordered that Dorsey Pentecost be recommended to his Excell. the Governor as a proper person to be appointed in the stead of the sd. Colo. Campbell.[1]

Ordered that Joseph Beeler be recommend as Colo. of the First Batalion of Militia in the stead of John Stephenson who hath resigned, the sd. Joseph being Colo. of the sd. Battalion.

William Harrison is recommd. to the Governor as a proper person to serve as Lieut. Colo. of sd. Battalion in the sd. of the sd. Joseph Beeler, the sd. William being Majr. of sd. Batta.

George Vallandingham is recomd. as Colo. of the 2nd. Battalion in the stead of Isaac Cox who hath res'd. the said George being Lut. Colo. of sd. Battalion.

Gabriel Cox is appointed Lieut. Colo. of the 2nd. Battalion he being Maj. Thereof.

Ordered that Colo. Joseph Beeler furnish the next Court with a List, Seniority and rank of the Caps. of the Militia of the first Battalion This County in order to Enable the Court to proceed to the choice of majors of the Melitia. and Colo. Vallandingham of the second Battalions.

Ordered that Benjaman Kuykendal be appointed to contract with some person to bring up two Hundred Bushels of Salt which now lies at Alexandria in the house of Joseph Watson, belonging to the County, and that John Cannon assign an Order relating thereto that he has in his hands to the sd. Benjaman Kirkendall.

[1] This was the John Campbell, one of the gentlemen justices of the court.

Ordered that Court be adjourned Til Court in Course.

JOHN CANON.

(242) At a Called Court held the 18th day of January 1780 for the Examination of David Lindsey and Thomas Pearcesal who stands charged with Perjury.

Present Edward Ward William Goe Benjaman Frye Joseph Beckett John Cannon, Joshua Wright Gent. Justices.

The Prisoners being set to the Bar pleads not Guilty, but they refusing to go through the Examination before the Examining Court, offered to Enter into Recognizance to appear before the next Genl. Court, Ordered that they Enter into recognizance accordingly. Whereupon the said David Lindsey with Henry Kersey & Tobias Mattocks his Securitys enter into recognize as aforesd, the sd. David held in L 1000 and his Secur'y. in L 500 Each. and the said Henry Kearsey enters securities for the personal appearance of the said Thomas as aforesaid held in L 1000. John Springer with Isaac Springer his Surety enter into recognizance for the Personal appearance of the sd. John at the next Gen. Ct. to Testify agt. the sd. David & Thomas.

John Springer Surety for Enoch Springer as afsd. held as aforesaid.

Joseph Ross with John Springer his Security held as afsd.

EDWD. WARD.

(243) At a Court held for Yohogania County January 24th 1780.

Present Edward Ward John Cannon Benj. Kuykendall, Joshua Wright Gent. Justices.

Ward v Broadhead. C. O.

Administn. of the Estate of Potter Smith dec. is granted to William Brown he having complied with the Law.

John Munn, John Hopkins, John Collings & Levingston Thomas appointed Appraisers to sd. Estate.

Ordered that Isaac Justin, John Chamberlain William Bruce & W$^{m.}$ Mayhall be allowed 175 lb of Tob'o. for 7 days attendance as a Guard on a prisoner, 84 dollars Each for finding their own provisions, and that the Sheriff pay the same.

Ordered that Joseph Perkerson be sommoned to Next Court

to Shew Cause why he detains James Drenning as a Servant who alleges he is a free person.

George Heart v Jacob Trowbough, the plaintiff failing to appear the Defd. prays not suit for want of security for Costs, which is accordingly granted.

Ordered that Court be adjourned until Court in Course.

EDWD. WARD.

(244) At a Court held for Yohogania County February the 28th, 1780.

(Present) John Cannon Benjaman Kuykendall Joshua Wright Samuel Newell Gentl. Justices.

Samuel McKay heir of AEneas McKay deceased proved to the satisfaction of this Court that his said Father was a Depy. Commissary under Genl. Commissary Leake in the Service of the King of Great Britain in the years 1771 and 1772, and that the said McKey has been a residenter in this State, and has never recv'd. any warrants for Lands under the sd. King's Proclamation of 1763, and Ord. to be Certified.

At the request of Ann Hammon Ordered that her son Isaac Hammon be bound to Isaac McMichael until he arrive at the age of 21 years being now 5 years of age, and that the sd. Mc-Michl. teach him to read wright & cipher as far as the rule of three, also trade and Mystery of Husbandry and give him one new suit of Cloth, a Bible, Grubing how and ax, at the expiration of sd Term.

Samuel Semple proved to the satisfaction of the Court that he served as a Captain in a Corps of rangers in the Pennsy'a. Service in the Last, and is Intitled under the Kings Proclamation of 1763.

Walker v McMahen. Order for Dedemus to Take Deppositions.

John Ormsby proved to the satisfaction of the Court that he served as Commissary in the Service of the Crown of Great Britain in the years 1758 & 1759 & 60, and that he has never obtained any warrant for lands under the sd. Kings Proclamation of 1763.

Philip Pendleton Asse. of John Ormsby prov'd. as afsd. that the said John Ormsby serv'd. as Paymaster in the service afsd.

On the application of Catherine Doblin who is afflicted with convulsive fits which render her Incapable of Procuring her Subsistence, Ordered that Richd. McMahen agree with some person to provide her with Necessary Subsistence untill the Next Court.

Andrew Heath Sworn Deputy Clerk.

(245) George McCarmick proved to the satisfaction of the Court that he served as an Ensign in a Company of rangers in the Virg'a. Service in 1764 and that he has never rec'd any premiums for sd. Service under the Procl. of 1763.

Thomas Smallman Gent. one of the Justices of the peace for this County, Proved to the satisfaction of the Court, that he was an Ensign Penna. redgment in the year 1756, and that he never receiv'd, any warrant or other Bennifeet under the Kings Proclamation of 1763.

Same as Lieut. in the first Penna. Redgmt. in 1756.

Same as Lieut. of Cavalry in the year 1757.

George Roots & Charls Wier Thruston, asse of sd. Smallman, pro'd. as Capt. in the first Pen'a. Redgmt. in the year 1760.

Same as Asse. of the same. Indian Agent at fort Charters in the year 1761.

Wm. McCarmick as Lieut. in a Virginia ranging Compy. in the year 1764.

Judy v Boyce. James Grayham Sl. B. & Impl.

Vannatree v Grimes. Wm. Boyce. Spl. B. & Iml.

Wm. Tully and Charles Records, his Sec'y, being bound in Recgn. and failing to appear Ordered to be prosecuted.

Thomas Smallman, John Cannon, George Vallandingham Gent. are recommended to the govern. to appoint one as Sheriff the Ensuing year.

Bargain & Sale. Dorsey Pentecost to John Hombler. ackd. & O. R.

Ordered that ferry keeps on the Monongahela River be allowed three dollars for ferrying a man & Horse.

Moore v Reddeck. Disctd. plaintiff.

Joseph Perkerson being Summoned to shew cause why he detains James Denning as a Servant appeared and after hearing the allegations of the parties the Court are of Opinion that the sd Drenning is a free person and is hereby Discharged from any farther Service.

(246) Alexander Fowler proved to the satisfaction of the Court that he serv'd. as Lieut. in the 74th. Redgmt. in the British Service in America in the Last War, and contd. therein to the end of sd. War, and that he never Recd. any Benefiet under the Kings procl. of 1763.

Alexd. Fowler assee. of Leut. George Brock proved as aforesd.

Alexd. Fowler Asse. of Leut. Anguish McNeill, p'd. as afsd.

Alexd. Fowler Assine of Leut. Henry Dolway. Prov'd. as afsd.

Alexd. Fowler, Asse. of Leut. Butler Stubbs. Provd. as afsd.

John Gibson Gent. one of the Justices of the peace for this County prov'd. to the Satisfaction of the Court that he s'd. as a Deputy Commissr. in the Service of Great Brittain at Fort Pitt in the year 1760, and that he has Never rec'd. any Benefiet under the kings procl. of 1763.

Bargain and Sale James Swolevan to Robert Campbell. ackd. O. R.

James Colvin prov'd to the satisfaction of the Court that he serv'd. as Ensign in a Company of Volunteers in the Virga. Service in the year 1764, and that he never recd. any Benefiet under the kings procl. of 1763.

Oliver Miller Gent. being bound in recognizance appeared in Court, and after hearing the Evidences are of Oppinion that the sd. Miller be discharge from his recogn.

Ordered that Court be adjourned untill Court in Course.

BENJA. KUYKENDALL.

At a Court held for Yohogania County March the 27th, 1780.

Present, Wm. Crawford, Joseph Beeler Edwd. Ward, Jos. Wright, Thos. Smallman Geo. Valandigham, Gentlemen Justices.

(247) On Motion Admn. is granted to Catherine Hull up. the Estate of Francis Hull dec'd.

Ordered that James Enis, James Shane, Wm. Ward & Wm Jenkins or any three of them being first sworn do appraise the same.

Ordered that she enter into Bond & security for the due administration thereof in a bond for thirty thousand pounds, which was entered into accordingly.

Present Richd. Yeates.

On the motion of Tobias Woods ordered that the Admrn. Bond of John Stephenson Admr. of Jeremiah Woods be put in Suit.

On Motion Admn. is granted Lewis Williams of the Estate of Wm. Wms. dec'd. & that he enter into bond with Security for the sum of ten thousand pounds, & that Wm. Dunn, Joseph Clem Thos. Mercer & Andw. Baker or any three first sworn do appraise the same.

Ordered that Jno. Cannon & Richd. Yeates Gentlemen do examine & settle the administrators acct. of the estate of Peter Smith decd.

Wm. Parkerson v Benj. Tomlinson. Thos. Edgington Spl. Bail.

Ordered that Joseph Cox be bound in the sum of ten thousand pounds with two securities to appear at the next Grand Jury Court to answer for stab'g. Jno. Elliott, himself in the sum of ten thousand pounds & the securities in the sum of five thousand each & that he Cox be of good behaviour in the meantime.

Ordered that Jno. Elliott be recognized to appear at the next Grand Jury Ct. to give evidence v Joseph Cox, in the sum of five thousand pounds w'ch is done accordingly &c.

Joseph Cox entered into Recognizance in the sum of ten thousand pounds & Jas. Innis & Hugh Scott his securities in
(248) the sum of five thousand pounds each, that the sd. Cox appear at the next Grand Jury Court to answer the Complain for stabing Jno. Elliott, & that he be of good behavior in the meantime.

Ordered that it be certified that Edwd. Ward Gentleman Acted as a Captn. in the 1st Pensylv. Battalian in the years 57 & 58, & as a Lieuten. 56 & 57 & as an indian agent in Service of the Crown in the years 60. 61. 62 & that he has had no satisfaction for the same from the K. of G. B. proclamation of 63.

Same that Andw. Vaughan served in the Virga Rejiments in the year 55 as a sirgeant & as above.

Same Andw. Rote served at the same time as a private &c.

Ordered that Thos. Miller be appointed a Constable in the room of Wm. Benwich for 1780.

Ordered that the Court adjourn untill tomorrow morning 10 oClock.

W. CRAWFORD.

At a Court Continued & held for the County of Yohogania March 28th, 1780.

Present Edwd. Ward William Goe Thos. Smallman Richd. Yeates, Gentlemen Justices.

(249) Ordered that Andrew Heth do agree by Auction to the lowest bidder with some person to repair the Court house and Jail likewise to errect a Pillory & Stocks as soon as possibly may be.

Bazil Brown v Robt. Hamilton, Thos. Hamilton Spl. bail & impl.

Ordered that Saml Wells be summoned to appear before the next Court to answer the Petition of Ann Wells his wife & that attachment Issue that he give security to appear & abide the order of Court & that he be of the peace toward the sd Ann and all other good subjects of this Commonwealth.

Upon the Complaint of James ODonald that Andrew Dun serjt. and John Shey soldier did grossly beat abuse & otherwise ill treat him the sd ODonald. Ordered that Col'o. Broadhead be requested to have the sd Soldiers delivered to the Civill Authority to be dealt with according to Law.

License granted to John Collins to keep a Tavern he complying with the law.

Ordered that Capt. Thomas Freeman be recommended to the Governour as a Majr. in the first Yohogania Battalion in the Room of Majr. Wm. Harrison promoted.

Ordered that Captn. Matthew Richie be recommended to the Governour to serve as Majr in the 2d battalion of Yohogania County in the Room of Majr Gabl. Cox promoted.

Ordered that Hezekiah McGruder be rec'd. as Captn in the 1st Batt'an. in the room of Captn. Freeman promoted.

(250) Ordered that George Redman be recommended as a Captn in the 2d Battalian in the room of Captn Philip Ross resigned.

Bazil Brown v Thos. Hamilton, Joseph Parkison Spl. Bail & imp.

Ordered that John Johnson be Recommended Capt in the room of Ct. John Crow.

Ordered that Andrew Dye be recommended first Lut. in the room of Elija Hart.

Ordered that Uriah Johnson be recommended 2d Lieut in the room of Wm. Crow.

Ordered that Samuel Devore be recommended as Ensgn in the room of John Johnson prom'td.

Jas. McClellin v Thos. Cummins, Gabriel Cox Spl. Bail & imp

Bawline v Norris. dismd.

On the Motion of James Richason that the Shf had attachd sundry goods in the hand of Garnishees upon the Supposition they were Wm. Lynn's, Ordered that the sd Goods be released.

Ordered that Jacob Bousman be allowed six dollars ferriage for a man and horse, three for each.

Ordered that all the Ferry keepers of this County, Jacob Bousman excepted, do receive four dollars ferriage for one man and one horse & no more.

Ordered that Peter Ellrod be allowed Sixty dollrs. pr. week for two months for boarding & Lodg Catherin Devilin.

(251) Wm. Christy proved his title to Military Service as ensign in the first Pensylv. Regement. &c &c. 1760.

Wm. Evans proved his title to military service as Artificer by warrant from the year 58 to 63 &c.

Hawkins v Clerk discontd.

Colwell v Lynn same.

Ordered that Nathaniel Brown be allowed Eighty pounds for maintaining Christopher Deklin four months past.

Brawdy v Beaver peremtory rule to try at next Court.

Jno. McClure proved his title to Military Service as an Ensign in the first Pennsylv. Regiment in the year 1760 & never has sold the same &c.

Whiteside v Girty. Then came a Jury towit, Gabl Cox Jno Johnson Jos. Wright, Jno Wall, Saml Devoir Stephen Hall, Elija Rittenhouse Wm. Crow, Andw. Dye, Henry Newkirk, James Spears, Andw. Pearce. Verdict for plf. 170 Damages & Judgmt.

Dedimus to take the deposition of Thos. Talbott to perpetuate his Testimony respecting a piece of Land on which Matthew Ritchie now lives.

Johnson v Springer W. I.

Day v Stanberry. Then came a Jury towit Zadock Wright, Jas. Brice, Robt. Johnson, Thos. Applegate, Tobias Mattocks, Tobias Deckart, Jas. Ferguson, Wm. Redick, Sampson Beavers, John Munn Antony Dunlavy Thos. Hambleton, find for the Plt. L 50 dam. & Judgmt.

(252) James Stevenson proved his Service as a Lieuten. in a ranging Compy &c. 74.

Wm. Harrison proved he Servd. as a Lieutnt. in the year 74 in a ranging Company &c.

Jno. Stephenson served as a Captn. in a Ranging Company in 74.

John Hinkston served as a Lieutn. in a Ranging Company in 74 &c.

Marcus Stevenson served as an Ensign in a Ranging Company in 74 &c.

William Crawford proved he served as a Lieut. of Light Horse in 1758 &c.

William Crawford proved his Services as a Majr of Rangers 1774 &c.

Administration granted to Wm. Park of the estate of James Park decd. he giving Security according to Law.

Joseph Vance Henry Graham, Thos. Stoms William Vanusan appointed to appraise the same being first sworn.

Ordered that Geog. Scott Orphant be bound to David Gaut to learn the art of Tanning trade &c.

Ordered that John Scott Orphant be Bound to John Cannon Gent.

George Valandigham Proved to the satisfaction of the Court that he Served as Lieut. under L. Dunmore 1774.

John Robinson as Capt. same.

(253) Thos. Warrin proved that he served as Insign under Capt. Cresop, in the year 1774.

John Lemon v Tobias Mattocks. John McComis Sp. Bl. & Impl.

Joseph Becket proved that he served as Lieut. in the year 1772 under Lord Dunmore.

John James Wood, same.

Ordered that John Wright be returned as Constable in David Andrews District in the room of Tobias Mattocks.

Ordered that Gersham Hull be appointed Constable in Capt. Thos. Bays district.

Zadock Wright proved to the satisfaction of the Court that he served as Lieut. under Ld. Dunmore 74.

The same as Serjt. in a Rangin Company in 64.

George Berry the sam. under Ld. Dunmore in 74.

Tater Elrod vs Elijah Hart. Atta. Isued.

Fantlyroy Seal vs Aquilla Whittaker. Atta. Isued.

Ordered that Isaac Israelos be appointed Overseer of half the road Leading from Pentecost's Mill to Cattfish Camp, in the room of Jno. McDonel.

Ordered that Richd. Johnson be appointed Overseer of the road from Devoirs Ferry to where the road Lead'g to the new Store strikes out of Fromans road & that the Tithables within three miles on each side work thereon.

Ordered the Court be adj'd. Till Tomorrow 8 oClock.

WILLIAM GOE.

At a Court held for Yohogania County March 29, 1780.

Present Edward Ward Thos. Smallman John McDonald Joseph Bealor Joshua Wright.

Crow v Dye. Then came a Jury towit, John Johnson John Robertson James Machen John Dean Thos. Spencer David Day Henry Newkirk Stephen Hall Samuel Devore Elija Rittenhouse David Williams, James Peirce. Vdt. for Plantf & Judgt.

(254) Ordered that the Atty do Indict Gersham Hull for assaulting John McDonald.

Ordered that Gersham Hull be recognized to appear at the next Grand Jury Court to ansr. the Complaint of Jno. McDonald, himself in the sum of five thousand pounds with two Securities of in two thousand five hundred each, Hugh Brady & Tobias Mattocks undertook for the sd Hull.

Ordered that Andrew Heth do furnish the Court with fire & water & make an acct. of the same.

Ward v Robertson, order that dedim's. Isue for either Party.

Connel v Wells. then came a Jury towit, Stephin Ashby, Andw. Dye, Wm. Crow, Joseph Warner, Andw. Pierce, Robt. Creghead, Mos. Hollyday, Hugh Brady Tobias Mattocks John McComis, Girsham Hull Danl. Apelgate. Verdt. for Plaintiff L 5000 & Judgment.

On Motion George Roots, Administn. is granted him on the estate of John Gabrial Jones deceased. Thos. Smallman, Robt. Campbell, Joseph Skelton, Samuel Sampel Appraisers of the same.

On motion Andw. Heth Administn. is granted him on the estate of Patrick McEllroy deceased. John Robertson, Gabl. Cox, Samuel Newil, Benjn. Keykindall, apprs. of the estate.

Braudy v Beever. then came a Jury towitt, John Johnson, John Robertson, James Spear, David Day, Henry Newkirk, Andw. Dye, Stephen Hall, Saml Devore, Elija Rittenhouse, Thos. Spencer, Joseph Warner, Jacheriah Connal. Verdt. for Plantff. & Damage L 2000.

Margaret Weever 12 days attendance on the above suit.

Katherin Unsetler 6 days, same.

John McComis 2 days, same.

Ward v Broadhead. N. Guilty with leave to put in what Plea he pleases.

(255) Andw. Dye v John Allintharp. Nt. Guilty & Join'd.

Ordered that Andw. Heth have the uper story of the Goal put into order for a Jury room.

James Spear v John Backingrig.

Ordered that a Ded'ms. Isue to take the depositn of Samuel McAdams & wife for Plantiff.

Richd. McMahen v Arnold Evins. Non assum'st join'd.

Ordered that the Sheriff summon a Grand Jury to May Court.

Ordered that the Sheriffs settle their accounts at the May Court.

Ordered that a Dedimus Isue to take the deposition of Martin Shundon in a suit between John McDonald & Gersham Hull.

Ordered that Court be adjurnd till Court in Course.

EDWD. WARD.

At a Court held for Yohogania County April 24th 1780.

Present Edward Ward, Joshua Wright William Harrison, Samuel Newil Joseph Beeler.

Admn. is granted to Jacob Beason of the Estate of Geo. Greaves he havg entd into Bond &c.

Ordered that Phil. Shute, Henry Beason, Jno. Collins, and Wm. Campbell or any three do appraise the sd Estate.

Ord'd that Benja. Die be summon'd. to appear at the next Court to show cause why John Frazer an Orphan should not be taken from him

(Pres[t.] Jos. Beeler, Gent)

Ordered that the Sherif do summon twenty four freeholders to attend as a Grand Jury against May Court.

John Brock, Thos. Bond, David Steel } produced their Commissions as Deputy Surveyors & took the Oath Accordingly.

(256) Ordered that Jacob Lancaster Orphan four years old be Bound apprentice to David McLean to Learn the Mistery of farming, to learn him to read write & Cipher as far as the Rule of three, two suits of Cloathing, sufficient shirts stockings & shoes or equivalent, ax Grubing hoe —— wedges.

Joseph Becket came into Court.

David Rice proved to the satisfaction of the Court that he served as a private in a Ranging Compa. commanded by Capt. Evan Shelby raised in Maryld. & in the Service of the Crown, in the year 1759 and that he was at the time of his enlistmt. an inhabt't of Virga.

Same, that he served as Pack hors drive in the year 1764 in the State of Virginia, & received No satisfaction for the same.

Joseph Bealor sworn Col. of Militia. Commission read.

Gabriel Cox sworn Lieut. Col. of Militia. Commission Read.

Inventory of the Estate with the settlement of Potter Smith returned. Ord. for R.

Ann Rolerson proved that John Robins was the father of a base born child begoten on her Body. Ordered that the sd Robins give Security for the maintenance of sd child. Whereupon the sd Robins with John Lemon his Security come into Court & entered into Recognizance of two Thousand pounds each &c. for the sufficient maintainence of sd. Child, so as to Indemnify the Parrish.

William Mitchell v John Bowlie. Disctd. plaintiff.

Joshua Wright v Sampson Beever, Disctd. plantiff.

Rolison v Robins. David Steel S. B.

James ODonald v John & Isaac Williams. Disctd. Plff.

James Sterit v Skinner Hutson. Andw. Dye. S. B.

Peter Ellrod v Elija Hart. Atta Judgt & W. E.

Benjaman Wells v Samuel Wells. Attmt. Judmt. & O. Sale.

(257) License is granted John Downer to keep an Ordinary at his House in Beeson's Town The ensuing year he having Complyed with the Law.

Van Swearengen proved to the Court that he servd. as a subaltron officer in the Last war in a corps raised in the Virginia Service, and continued therein until regular discharged, and that he never recd. any Satisfaction or advantage under the king of Great Britains Procl. of 1763.

Thomas Gist proved to the satisfaction of the Ct. that he served as a Cadet in the year 1757, and an Ensign in the year 1758, and a Lieut. in the year 1760 in a redgmt. raise in the Virginia Service and employed in the Last war, and continued therein until regularly disch'd., and in the year 1762 he again served as a Lieut. in another Regmt. raised and Imployed as afsd. and contd. therein until regularly discharged, and that he never recd. any satisfaction or advantage under the king's proclamation of 1763, except a warrant from Lord Dunmore for two thousand acres of land, and has ever since continued an Inhabitant of this State.

Admn. of the Estate of Philip Heath is granted to William Richman he having complid with the Law.

John Beal James Beal William Beal and Phil. Ross aptd appraisers.

Jacob Bowsman v John Ormsby. Injunction to stay waste.

Edwd. Ward v Daniel Broadhead. C. O.

Ed. Ward v Jno. Robertson. Bill & Time.

Ed. Ward v Dl. Broadhead. Plea Joind.

Indenture Mary Willson Samuel Semple proved ordered to be recorded.

(258) Benjamin Keykindall Sworn Sheriff for one month.

Ordered that Court be adjourned until Court in Course.

EDWD. WARD.

At a Court held for Yohogania County May 22, 1780.

Present Edward Ward, Oliver Miller Thomas Freeman Gent. Just's.

Colo. Joseph Beeler provd. that he served as a wagon Master from the State of Virginia in the late war between Great Britain and france and that he Contd. therein until regularly dischd. O. to be Certd.

Appraismt. and Sale of the Estate of Saml. Griffith decd. retd. Or. R.

Gabl. Green Sworn Depy. Survey. Com. Read.

Wm. Colvin appd. Constable in the place of Jacob Knap.

Thomas Patterson Assinee of Thomas Eaby produced a Disch'd signed Adam Steven Liet. Colo. of the first Virginia Redgmt, for the service of the sd Thomas Eaby as Artificer [?] for the Time of his Inlistment in the late war between Great Britain & France, which Ordered to be Certified.

(259) Joseph Beeler Jun. Sworn Lieut. of Militia. Com. Read.

Indenture Elizabeth Hazelton to Christopher Beeler prov'd. by Joseph Beeler Sen. and Joseph Beeler Jun. two of the subscribing witnesses. O. R.

Present Joseph Beeler Gent.

Abst. Edwd. Ward Gent.

David Duncan is appointed Gardian to John Farree Heir of Frederick deceasd. he having complied with the Law.

George Vallandingham Gent. Prest.

Edwd. Ward, Gent. Present.

Ordered that Thomas Fortner, And Vinson Fortner be bound to John Peters until they arrive to the age of twenty one, he learning them the Coopers Trade art and Mistery, and at the end afsd. Term give them the usual Freedom dues.

Deed of Surrender Jacob Knapp to William Chipley. Ackd. O. R.

The Last Will and Testiment of Stephen Richards deceas'd proved by the oaths of Charles Morgan and Samuel Park the two Subscribing Witnesses. O. R.

Ordered that Thomas Freeman and William Goe Gent settle with the Administratrix of the Estate of Saml. Griffith deceasd. and make return to the next Court.

Admn. of the Estate of Joseph Fortner deceas'd. is granted to John Peters he having complied with the Law.

Return of a Road from the new Store on Monongahala to the road Leading from Guests fort to Devores Ferry. Ordered to be confirm'd.

James Hodge Sworn Ensign. Commission Read.

(260) Then came a grand Inquest for the body of this County to-wit: John Wall, Stephen Hall, Walter Wall, Robert Craighead, Moses Holliday, James Sparks, John Robertson, Mabary Evins, John Taylor, Andrew Nigh, Stephen Richards, Henry Sawings, Samuel Devoir, Andrew Dye, John Johnston, who were Sworn, recd. their Charge and retired to their Chamber.

Thomas Smallman Gent. Sworn Sheriff. Commission Read.

Jeremiah Wright is recom'd. as Liut. of Militia in the stead of David Cox who has removed out of the County.

William McCarmick. recom'd. as Capt. in the stead of John Minter who has resigned.

Samuel Wilson recom'd. as Liut. in the stead of the said McCarmick, and William McKee ensign in the stead of the said Wilson.

Ordered that a former order of this Court recom'ding Hezekiah McGruder as Capt. of Militia in the stead of Capt. Freeman be set aside, and that Thomas Prother be recom'd. in the stead of the said Thomas Freeman.

Richd. Noble is recom'd. as Liut. in the stead of Thomas Prother, and Thomas Brown Jun. be recom'd. as Ensign. Rich'd. Beall Capt. in the stead of Capt. Joseph Ford who is removed, and Robert McGlaughlin, Liut.

Ordered that John Frazeer Orphan of John Frazier, decd. at the request of his mother be bound to James Wilson until he arrives to the age of twenty one years of age, he being at this time ten years old, and learn the sd John Orphan the Trade art and Mistery of a wheel wright and Teach or cause to be taught to read and Wright the English Language and to Cypher as far as the rule of three, and at the end of said Term give him two Suits of Cloathes one of which is to be New.

(261) Ordered that Court be adjourned until tomorrow morning 9 oClock.

EDWD. WARD.

Court met according to adjournment May 23d. 1780.

Present Edward Ward Joseph Beeler George Vallandingham Samuel Newell William Harrison, Thos. Freeman.

issues.
Wherry v White contd.
Brounles v Douglas. do.
Shilling v Newkirk. do.
Do. Do. Do.
same v Fortney Do.
Fullum v Johnson. Do
Bouseman v McGoldrick do.
Pentecost v Briscoe do.
Shilling v Taylor do
Hawkins vs Clarke do
same v Kuykendall do
Ward vs Thorn do
Sample v McKensie do
Beall v Finn do
same v McMahan do
Neville v Guest do.
Cresop v Swearengen do
Campbell v Beall. do
(262) Fullum v Johnson contd.
Same v Same contd.
Same v McComish contd.
Andrew v Johnson do
Same v Same do
Heth v Bruce do
Christie v Heth do
Same v Same do
Caldwell v Fry do
Boley v Springer do
Same v Same do
Ward v Wells do
Vance v Williams do
Riggle v Die do
Morroson v Vanater do
Bradley v Boly do
Curry v Wells do
Waller vs Springer do
Pierce v Evans do
Hogland v Laughlin do

Cox v Betsman do
Vanatre v Parkinson do
Dawson v Kirkpatrick do
Froman v Boyce do
Crooks v Hoagland do
Pierce v Evans do
Tyger v Boley do
Boyce vs Froman do
Caldwell v Hoagland do
Wetzell v McKelwaine do
Caldwell v Corn do
Spears v M[c]Mahan do
Day v Deane Do.
Beler v Inks do
Wright v Hart do.
Boyce v Froman contd
Mooney v Ricord do
Boyce v Froman do
Same v Same do
Same v Same do
Boling v Norris do
Miller v Humble discontd.
Shilling v Newkirk contd
Crow v Pierce do
Crow v Dye Do.

Presentments at issue.
State vs
Richard McMahan discharged defendt. paying Costs.
vs W[m.] Christy. do
vs Jno. McClellan do.
v — Parsons do.
vs Agnes Irwin do
vs Geo. Lintenberger do.

Common Orders.

Wilson Exrs. v Lynch &c. W. E.
Reddick v Ross W E.

Saml. Bruer & ux v Tacey W. E.
Dye v Tharp W E.
Henderson v Evans W E.
Steel v Hamilton W E.
Burns v Louderback W. E.
Barrickman v Harry W E
Same v Wood W. E.
Lindsey v Hamilton W E
Pierce v Evans W. E.
(263) Heth v Stokes W E
Guest v Cornwall W E.
Forrester v Murphy W E.
Ward v Clarke W E.
Boley v Orr W E.
Johnson v Springer W E.
Cooke v McCastlin W E.
Cresops, Exrs. v Campbell W E.
Johnson v Kates W E.
Pentecost v Jones W E.
Fossett v Hall W E.
Lynch v Hall W E.

Writs Enq'y.

Hawkins v Wheat contd
McIlroy v Templin abated by plaintiffs death.
Same v Same Same Order.
Roleson v Lowry contd.
Fry v Tilton contd
White, Jun. v Johnson do.
Fry v Tilton do
Swigart v Murphy do
Brashiers Admr. v Brashier Do.
Whitesides v Girty do
Froman v Dean discontd
Elliott v McIntosh contd
Same v Same do.
Smallman v Such do.
Day v Hansberry do
Richards v Boley do.

Gist v Waller do
Same v Hall do
Same v Boyles do
Beeler v Walker do
Tigart v Chamberlain contd
Same v Same do
McKee v Davison Do
Same v Same do
Fossett v Meeks do
Ells v Roach do
Kidd v McConnell do
Lynch v Jones do
Same v Berwick do
Drenning v Bay do
Braden v Elliott et als. do.
McElry v McMahan do
Ferguson v Heath do
Protsman v Hill do
Norris v Vineyard & ux do
Bentley v Eglin do
Clarke v Boley do
Hoffman v Leatherman do
Munn v Crawford do
McAllister v Corn do
McGlaughlin v Wood do
Newill v Robison Do
Nevill v Wiseman Do.
Neville v Holliday Do.
Wells v Quick Do.
Grubbs v Carter Do.
Taber v Applegate

Imparlances.

Spears v Beckett Admr. N. Guilty.
Kersey v Springer N. Guilty
Henderson v Douglas N. Guilty
Stocker v Aicklen N. Guilty
Boley v Manning Do.
Same v Same Do.

Day v Dean Do.
McCulloch v Taylor do.
Kinkaid v Henderson do.
Decker v Jacob contd
Kuykendall v Colvin N. Guilty.
(264) Thompson v Hopkins, paymt & sett off.
Beeler v Scott, Infancy.
Nolls v Quick N. Guilty
Sills v Burns, Do.
Spivy v Rickets, do.
Kinkead v Henderson, do.
same v same, do.
Spears v Jones, do.
Berry v Crawford, contd.
Bousman v Ormsby. N. Guilty &c.
Keykendall v Bogard, Non Assumpsit. Sp. Bail.

Plurias Capias.

Stewart v Purdie A P. Capias.
Miller v Parkison do.
Dun v Stewart, do.
Johnson v Evans, do.
Dye v Brent, do.
Steel v Stevens, Do.
Beavers v Mahal, do.
same v Miller, et als. do.
Chambers v Evalt Co
Chambers. Inft. v. Evalt C O.
Ward v Broadhead W. E.
Kuykendal v Decker, Imparlance.
Sheaff v Downer do.
Clarke v Clarke C O.
same v same C O.
same v Quinn P C.
Conell v Poe & others Exors. P. C.
Riddell v Goard P C.
Logan v Miller P C.
Mathews v McLean P C.

Boling v Wells, P C
Workman, Assee. v Saltsman P C.
Ross v Manning C O.
Miner v Blazier &c P C.

(265) Thomas Freeman proved to the Court That he served as Dept. Comissy in the Last war between Great Britian & France & was regularly discharged. O. to be Certified.

David Vance being bound in Recogn. being called came into Court which ordered to be discontd, also the witness Recogn. discd. said Vance giving security for his good behaviour for one year and one day in the sum of ten thousand Pounds with one Security in the like Sum whereon the sd. Vance with Moses Holladay his Security came into Court & entered into Recg. accordingly.

Ordered that John Bradly be bound over to his good Behavor for a year & a Day in the Sum of two Hundred five Hundred Pound & one Security in the like sum, whereon the sd. Bradly with Jacob Bousman his security came into Court & entered into Recognc. accordingly.

Jacob Bousman—John Ormsby. order'd. a writ to stay Waste. Isue.

James Boys v John Atkins. then came a Jury towit. Zadock Wright Hugh Stirling James Quick John Vanater, William Redick. Willm. Bruce Jacob Bousman John Springer Gabriel Cox Skiner Hutson Garsham Hull John Marshall. Verdt. for Plaintiff, Judt. L 30.

Enock Enis v William Hoglan. then came the same Jury as before. Verdit for pt. Judmt. for L 12.16.

Rich'd. McMahen v Paul Matthews. Then came the same Jury as before. Verdit. for pt. Judmt for L 73.10.

(266) Ordered that James Innis, Thomas Gist, Thomas Warren, Hezekiah McGruder, James Eager, David Ritchie, Henry Taylor, Benjaman Johnston, Samuel Semple, Charles Wheeler Jacob Bouseman, Joseph Scott James Ewing, Samuel Johnston, William Lea, Andrew Heath, John Robinson, Thomas Moore, Jacob Beeson, Reuben Kemp, and Walter Wall be recommended to the Governor as proper persons to be added to the Commission of the peace, and that the Clerk certify to the

Govenor of the Names of those persons now named in the Commission of the peace who refuses to serve.

Ordered that Joseph Bealor & John Canon be recommended as proper Person for Corenors for this County.

On the petition of Dorsey Pentecost siting forth that he is desirous of Building and compleating a water Mill on the Eastern branch of Churteers Creek, and that he owns the lands on both sides of the Creek so that no person will be Effected by the overflowing from his dam. Ordered that the sd Pentecost have leave to build and compleat a water mill at the place aforesaid according to law.

Administration of the Estate of William Fulks decd. is granted to his widow Anne Fulks she having complied with the Law, and that Samuel Beeler Joshua Meeks, Garshom Hull and John Hull or any three of them Appraise the sd Estate.

John Dean proved to the satisfaction that he served as a soldier in a ranging Company in the late war between Great Britain and France and continued in said Service until regularly discharged. Ordered to be Certified.

David Livingston being bound in recognizance and no prosecutor appearing ordered to be Discharged.

Ordered that Wm. Bruce Capt, James McMahon, Lieut., Joshua Carman, Ensign, be recomd. as proper persons to serve as Officers of Militia.

Ordered that Thos. Rigdon, Lieut Andw. Nigh proper person as Lieuts. of Militia.

(267) The Grand Jury found the following Bills Vizt. vs Joseph Cox, for an assault on the Body of John Eliot; one against John Reed for Forgery being called pleads not Guilty, Whereupon the said John Reed with Hugh Sterling and Zadock Wright, his securities, held, himself in Ten thousand pounds the securities five thousand pounds each, for the appearance of the sd. John and answer to a Bill of Indictment Exhibited agt. him. and the said Joseph Cox held in the like sum of Ten thousand pounds and Hugh Sterling and Alexandr Eady his securities in the like sum of five thousand pounds Each for the sd. Josephs appearance to answer as afores'd.

Jesse Beezon and Robert Davidson appointed Constables, som'ed before John McDaniel Gent. to be Qualified.

The Grand Jury present the following Bills. against Garsham Hull: for an assault on the body of John McDonald N. G.; against John Brackinrig an assault on Mary Spear, order a Capias Isue: against Do. assault on the Body of Jas. Spear, Cap.; against Joseph Parkeson assault on the Body of Sarah Jacob. Cap. Isue.

Garshom Hull with Richd. McMahen & John Dean his securities come into Court and entered into recognizance for his personal Appearance at the Next Court to answer a Bill of Indictment exhibited agt. him, held in Then thousand pounds his Securities in five thousand each.

The Grand Jury found a Bill agt. Garshom Hull for an assault on John McDonald Gent. Ordered that Capias Issue.

(268) Ordered that Court be adjourned to Court in Course.

SAMUEL NEWELL.

At a Court held for Yohogania County June 26th 1780.

Present Samuel Newil, Wm. Harrison Joseph Becket Oliver Miller Wm. Goe, Present.

Alias Capias

Keykendall v Deckart. Imparlance.
Boxton v Peas P. C.
Caldwell v Wray P. C.
Masters v Benet P. C.
Cresops, Exrs. v Power agred. G. Brant, Cost.
Keykendall v Creghead C O.
McDonald v Clerk P. C.
Johnson v Evins C O
McGee v Gambol P. C.
Taylor v Applegate C. O.
Sterling v Beevers. C O
Campbell v Quick P. C.
White v Williams P. C.
Crawford v Yates disctd.
Boxton v Norris, P. C
Enis v Spencer P. C
Leamon v Mattocks C. O.

Appearances.

Smallman v Irwin A. C
Same v same A. C
Applegate v Evins A. C.
Hutson v Whitacre A. C
Ward v Broadhead C O
Fleming v Cooper A. C
Holladay v Beever A. C
Moor v Taylor. A. C
(269) Eliot v Cox C. O
Steret v Hutson A. C
Leaman v Holladay A. C
Barrackman v Raymon A. C
Crow v Humble disctd.
McDonald v Hull A. C
Protsman v Lypolt A. C
McMachen v Bruce C. O
Ellrod v Hart A. C
Onsetler v Humble disctd.
Seal v Whitacre Do.
Spear v McIwain A. C
Nesbit v Harden A. C
Provines v Froman C. O
Gilfilin v Tygart A. C
Cuningham v. Louderback A. C
Keykendall v Matthews C. O Ms. Holaday. A Bail.
Warrin v McKenzey Disctd.
Hutson v Deckart C. O
Bradin v Vanater C. O
Roleston v Robins C. O
Keykendall v Fokes C. O
Walker v McMachen & Wife C. O
Farrin v Keykendall C. O Rt. McKee A. B.
Vanater v Braden C. O Vn. Swearengen A. B.
Smallman v Peterson A C
Brown v McCurdy A. C
Gambol v Beall A C.
Keneday v McCollolloige disctd.
Crow v Williams C. O Aw. Pierce A. B.

Smallman v Broadhead. C. O
Smallman v Duncan C. O
Same vs same C. O
Morry Boyd v Humble C. O leave to amend writ.
Ward v Broadhead C. O
Crawford v Sharp A. C
McMachen v Evins C. O
Brady v — & wife dismisd.
Williams, Asse. v Crow C. O Joshua Wright A. B.
Records v Thomas C. O
Williams, Asse. v Crow C. O
Williams, Asse. v Crow C. O J[a.] Wright A. B.
Boice v Workman. C. O
Cox v Campbell & wife
McAdams v Rarden A. C
(270) Cox & wife v Walker A. C
Jacobs v Parkison. disctd. P. for Cost.
Pentecost v McAdams disctd.
McIlhose v Colvan C. O
Paterson v Moor A. C
Sweringen v Fryer C. O
Sweringen v Brooks Imp.
Clerk v McDonald C. O
Pegg v Evins C. O
Appelgate v Evins C. O.
Cox v Davis & wife A. C
Cox v Thompson A. C
McMachen v Leamon discontd.
Campbell v Blackman A. C.
Beever v Mayhall A. C
Same v Miller Sen. &x. A. C
Hopkins v Johnson disctd.
Mathews v McClain A. C
Blackman v Peirce A. C
Same v Campbell A. C
Willson v Blackman A. C
Blackman v Willson A. C
Bonom v Sapington A. C
Boling v Wills A. C

Johnson v Lindsey A. C
Campbell v Totton A. C
Same v Scoot A. C
Campbell v Blackman A. C
Ross v Blunck A. C
Pierce v Hogland discontd. Cost pd.
Keykendall v Colvin A. C
Spivas v Record A. C
Sweringen v Burrace C. O
Harrison v Stuart A. C
Downer v Lawson. A. C
Anderson & Tod v Gibson C. O
Grahm v Boys agreed.
Mitchel v Downs. C. O
Fokes v Boley C. O
Fife v Holladay. C. O
McColley v Hogland agreed.
Newil v Irwin Imparlance.
Commonwealth v Lindsey. C. O
Corn v Elis A. C
Same v Pelton A. C
Anderson v Darby A. C
Vanater v Graham & wife C. O
(271) Jacobs v Workman & wife A. C
Clark v McDonald A. C.
Vanater Asse. v Creghead A. C
Masters v Benet A. C
McDonald v Clark A. C
White v Williams A. C
Little v Cherry C. O
Peters v Crow A. C
Peters Assne. v Same A. C
Same v Same A. C
Andrew v Singers A. C
Vance v Williams discontd.
Thomas v Egerton &c A. C
Gumbwill v Bell A. C
Downer v Waller A. C
Bruce v Mattocks A. C

Romine v McKinzey discontd.
Ward v Robertson. discontd
Records v Postelwait. Imparl. Jh. Alexr. S. B.
Miller v Vanater C. O
ODonald v Williams C O
McCleland v Beelor A. C
Redock v Irwin A. C
Humble v Crow A. C
Dunlavy v McAdams C. O
Campbell v Boley C. O
McDonald v Hull A. C.
Hall v Appelgate discontd.
Spencer v Cills A. C
Wallers v Hatfield A. C
Conal v Vanater C. O
Cook v Hardin A. C
Quick v Vanater C. O
Miller v Burns C. O
Kelly v Campbell A. C
Hammon v McClain A. C
Jacobs v Parkeson A. C
Justice v Frame Impalnce.
Springer v Tygart A. C
Richie v Parkeson A. C
Chamber v Evalt C. O
Fokes v Boley A. C
Duglas v Henderson Contd.
Frame v Justice C. O
Vanater v Stockwell contd.
Jacobs v Parkeson A. C.
(272) Edward Mills v Jackman A. C
Elis v Johnson A. C
Barnet v McDowel A. C
Hill v Lyday Contd.
Same v Same Contd.
Adams, Assne. v Richards C. O
Same v Same C. O
Thos. Cummin v Jas. Beggs, A. C
Paterson v Custer agreed

Nigh v Anderson A. C
Hurley v Pharlon C. O
Grubb v Carter A. C
Briscoe v Appelgate A. C

Attachment, Wm. Crawford v Benjn. Wells. Attcht two steers three Cows two mares two colts two two-year Olds two Hogs two Smooth guns one Shot Pouch & a Poder horn. Judmt. & O. Sold.

Chancery.

Bouseman v Ormsby. Injunction bill.

Indictments at issue.

C. W. vs Gresham Hull. Assault & Battery.
vs Jno. Reed. Misdemeanor.
vs Joseph Cox. Assault and Battery.

(273) Ordered that the Certificates Granted Alexr. Fowler, Assne. of Lieut. George Brooks, of Lieut. Butler Stubbs, of Anguish McNeil, of Henry Dolway, himself as Lieut., served in the Last war & Reduced upon halfe pay be properly certified.

Benjn. Johnson Produced a Commission of Depy. Surveyor. Commission Read & sworn in.

Wm. Johnson Produced a Commission as Depy Surveyor it being read & sworn to accordingly.

On the Petition of Joseph Saxton setting forth that he is infirm & not capable of git his living. Ordered that he be allowed one Hundred Dollars for one Month & that the Sheriff pay it out of the Money deposited in his hands.

The last will and Testement of John Blakley deceased proved by the Oath of John Wright one of the Subscribing witnesses. O. R.

Robert Blackley took the Oath of Executor of the Last will & Testement of John Blackley decd., he having Complied with the Law.

Ordered that John Bougher, Thomas Morehead, Samuel Holms & Thomas Fasithe or any other three of them being first Sworn do appraise the personal Estate and slaves if any of John Blackley dec'd, and make return to the next Court.

Peter Nesewanger being charge before the Court for wilfully exhibiting a melitious and Scandelous Lybell, Ordered that he give security to answer the next G. Jury, to be held in L 20,-000. and two suretys of L 10,000, Wm. Beagle held in L 1000, with Joseph Warner his securty L 1000, Matthew Beazle held in L 1000, with Wm. Beazle his secuity held in L 1000, Hugh Gundy with John Whiston his Security held L 1000, James Freeland held in L 1000, with Andrew White his security held

(274) L —— Andrew White held in L 1000 with James Freeland his Security held in L 1000. for their appearance at the next G. Jury Court to Testify against the aforesaid Peter Nesewanger.

Duglass v Henderson. Wm. Frye S. B. & Impl.

Mordaicai Richards and Stephen Richards took the oath of Executors to the Estate of Stephen Richards Deceas'd, they having Complied with the Law.

Ordered that John Fossit Chas. Morgan, Richd. Boyce and Jacob Long or any three appraise the sd. Estate and make return to next Court.

Ordered that Summons Isue for Benj. Pegg and Catherine his wife to attend at the next Court to give farther Security for the administration of the Estate of Francis Hull deceas'd. on the Complaint of David Williams one of the Securities for the sd. Administration.

Inventory and appraisement of the Estate of Francis Hull decd. returned. O. R.

Frome v Justis. Robt. Henderson Spl. B. & Imp.

On the petition of James McGoldrick seting forth that he is desirous of building a water Mill on Becks Run and that the land on each side belongs to himself so that no person will be effected by the overflowing from sd. Dam, Ordered that he have leave to build and Compleat a water mill on sd. Run according to Law.

Ordered that John Decker be summoned appear at the next Court to shew Cause why he Detains Elizabeth the Daughter of Jacob Kuykendall and that he bring the sd Elizabeth with him before the Court as aforesaid.

John Springer — Michael Tygert. Henry Kasey S. B & Imp.

Richd. Burns Sworn D. Sheriff.

(275) Ordered that Paul Mathews be allowed two Thousand Dollars for Erecting a Whiping post Stocks and Pillory.[1]

Gentleman deposetied

Wm. Goe, One hundred & fifty Dollars.

Oliver Miller Do. Do.

Joseph Becket One Hundred

Dorsey Penticost One Hundred

Samuel Newil One Hundred

to be Deducted out the money when Levied by the Sheriff.

Ordered that Court ajourn till Court in course

WILLIAM GOE.

At a Court held for Yohogania County on the 24 day of July, 1780.

present Saml. Newil, Joseph Becket, Joseph Beeler & Oliver Miller.

Appearances.

Jno. Ryan vs Peter Neiswanger. Trespass Case. C. O.

Samuel Cuningham v Conrod & Andrew Louderback, Benjn. Keykendall, S. B.

Ann Roleston appeared in Court in Consequence of a Summons & confest having a base born Child & paid the fine 50 s. Lodge in the hands of Saml. Newil, Esqr.

Alexr. Steel appeared in Consequence of a Summons & confest the Crime of swearing four profain oath. 20 s. Lodged in the hands of Samuel Newil, Esqr.

(276) Robert Sheerer bound in the sum of L 10000 & Philip Tabor in the sum of L 5000 his security to appear at the next G. Jury Court to testify for the State against Skiner Hutson, Minor Asterges.

Minor Asterges & Larince Roleston his Security bound in the sum of L 20,000 & his security in the Sum of L 10000 to appear at the next G. Jury Court to answer to what may be objected against him by the State.

Alexander McIntire bound in the sum of L 10000 & John Wall his security in the sum of L 5000 for his appearance at the next G. Jury Court to testify for the State against Skinner Hutson.

[1] See Introduction.

Philip Tabor v Thos. Applegate.

Then came a Jury, towit. Alexan. Steel, James Spear, Benjn. Pegg, Jacob Knight, Archibell Hull, John Boley, David Philips, Paul Mathews, Sampson Beever, David Richie, Robert Creghead, Edward King, W. Enqy, Judg. & Damage L 17, Plff.

Commonwealth v Ann Rardin, Nole proseque. fees paid.

Thos. Smallman Sheriff Protest against th Goal.

Ordered that Court adjourn till Court in Course.

SAMUEL NEWELL.

At a Court held for Yohogania County, Augt. 28, 1780.

Present Edwd. Ward, Joseph Beelor, Richd. Yates, George Valandigin, Oliver Miller.

Richd. McMachen v James Bruce. Judgt. Wrt. of Enqy.

Same v Arnold Evins. Judgt. Wrt. of Enqy.

George Valandigin produced a Commission of Col. of Militia & Sworn to accordingly.

The last will & Testament of Abington George Colvin proved in Court. O. R.

John Miller is exemted from paying any future County tax.

(277) At a Call Court held for the tryal of John Jackson for Passing Counterfeit Continental Money.

Com. Wealth v Jackson by Evidence of Daniel Appilgate & Joseph McCune the sd. Jackson is acquited.

23 forty Dollar Bills } Counterfeit lodged in the hands of
7 thirty Dollar Bills } Andrew Heth.

Ordered that Exn. Isue Hugh Brady agt. Sampson Beever David Steel & James McMullin on the Repleve. Bond given by them to replevy the effects of Sampson Beever on a Judgt. obtained by Hugh Brady & that it be indorsed no security or bail be taken.

Commonwealth v Garsham Hull. Jmdt. N. G. Joinder.

Commonwealth v John Brackenrig Indt. } N. G. & Joind.
same v same Indt }

Recognizance for John Brackenrig appearance at the Grand Jury Court, himself in two Thousand five Hundred Pounds upon each Inditiment & his Security Wm. Mayhall in the Same Sum.

Ordered that Summons Isue for Mordecai & Stephen Richard to give fresh security for the Estate of their Deceased father Stephen Richards.

Ordered that Summons Isue for Agness Stille to give fresh security for the Estate of of her deceased husband Jacob Stille.

Commonwealth v Joseph Parkeson, Ple'd. Guilty Jud't & dam'g. for Plf. L 300. David Richie security for fine & fees.

Commonwealth v Elizabeth Deckart Came into Court & Confest herself of haveing a base born Child & paid 50 s. fine. pd. to Richd. Yates, Gent.

Commonwealth v Sarah Jacobs, Came into Court & confest herself of haveing a base born Child & paid 50 s. fine. pd. to Richd. Yates Gent.

Commonwealth v Mary Boyd Came into Court & Confest herself of haveing a base born Child & paid 50 s. fine. pd. to Richd. Yates, Gentn.

Commonwealth v Catharin Develin failing to appear being sum'd. & return'd ex'd. Judgt. for 50 s. fine & the fees thereon accruing for haveing a base born Child.

Commonwealth v Ann Walker failing to appear being sum'd return'd Ex'd. Judgt. for 50s. fine & the fees thereon accruing for having a base born Child.

D'd. Richie v Jos. Parkeson } Imparlance.
same v same } Apearances John Wall S. B.

George Brown v Hugh McCrady. Apearnce, Nathaniel Blackmore S. B.

Jacob Knight v Tobias Wood Apearance. Mos. Holladay S. B.

(278) Michael Burk v Jacob Knight. Appearn. John Brotsman S. B.

Bill of Sale. Wm. Long to Morris Kaho. Acknowledged by Wm. Long and O. R.

Commonwealth vs. James Dornin, Recognizance for his appearance at next G. Jury Court, himself in L 5000 & Thos Timons & Joseph McKinnen in L 2500 Each.

Commonwealth v Mordecai Richards. Recognized in the sum of L 5000 to appear at the next G. Jury Court & his Securities John Leamon & Wm. Mayhall in L 2500 Each to prosecute Jas. Dornin.

Commonwealth v Jeremiah Morgan, Robt. Peat & Stephen Richards. Recognized to testify for the Commonwealth at the next G. Jury Court against James Dornin, each in L 3000.

Ordered that Court ajourn till Court in Course.

EDWD. WARD.

[Here six leaves have been cut from the end of the volume containing the foregoing records. But, as the entries last copied above, closing with the signature of EDWD. WARD, are at the top of the last page upon which there are any entries, most probably they are the last made in the volume, which, so far as we know, is the last record of a Court of Yohogania County, Virginia, held within the limits of Pennsylvania.

The EDWARD WARD whose name closes these records was the Ensign Edward Ward who surrendered the fort at the junction of the Monongahela and Allegheny rivers, to the French and Indians on April 17, 1754, and with his small command marched back and rejoined Washington at Fort Necessity.

MINUTE (OR ORDER) BOOK OF THE VIRGINIA COURT HELD FOR OHIO COUNTY, VIRGINIA, AT BLACK'S CABIN (NOW WEST LIBERTY, W. VA.), FROM JANUARY 6, 1777, UNTIL SEPTEMBER 4, 1780, WHEN ITS JURISDICTION OVER ANY PART OF PENNSYLVANIA HAD CEASED.

EDITED BY BOYD CRUMRINE, OF WASHINGTON, PA.

INTRODUCTION.

There have now been published the Minutes of the Virginia Court held for the District of West Augusta, first at old Fort Dunmore, now Pittsburgh, Pa., and for a while at Augusta Town, now Washington, Pa., 1775–1776 (Ann. Car. Mus., Vol. I, pp. 525–568) and also the Minutes of the Virginia Court held for Yohogania County, first at Augusta Town, and afterwards on the Andrew Heath farm, near West Elizabeth, 1778–1780 (*l. c.*, Vol. II, pp. 71–140, and pp. 205–429).

As stated in Vol. I, on p. 524, the Minute- or Order-books of the Court held for Monongalia County, at the house of Theophilus Phillips, on George's Creek, in the southern part of what is now Fayette County, Pennsylvania, were destroyed on the burning of the Court House at Morgantown in 1796. Therefore, the records of that Court, having jurisdiction over the southern part of what is now Fayette County, the southeastern part of the present Washington County, and more than half of the eastern part of the present Greene County, Pennsylvania, cannot now be reproduced. But, fortunately, when the Court for Ohio county, Virginia, was removed from Black's Cabin, on Short Creek, to Wheeling, in 1797, its records also were removed and are still to be found in the office of the Clerk of the County Court, in the Court House for Ohio County in that city.

These records of Ohio County, much used for over one hundred and twenty-five years, are in many places almost illegible, notwithstanding the great care that has been taken to preserve them; yet, because of the fact that, until the Virginia jurisdiction was entirely withdrawn from Pennsylvania, a large part of the territory in what is now Washington and Greene Counties, Pennsylvania, was within the jurisdiction of the Ohio County Court, of Virginia, it is proper that so much of these records as were made prior to August 28, 1780, when the last term of Court was held for Yohogania County, should also be published.

The Act of the Virginia Assembly of October, 1776, which divided the District of West Augusta into the three new counties, Ohio, Yohogania, and Monongalia, also established the boundary line between the County of Augusta and the District of West Augusta, which line had before that time been undefined. It was then defined as follows:

"Beginning on the Allegheny mountains between the heads of the Potowmack, Cheat, and Green Briar Rivers; thence along the ridge of mountains which divides the waters of Cheat river from those of Green Briar, and that branch of the Monongahela called Tygers Valley river, to the Monongahela river; thence up the said river and the west fork thereof to Bingeman's creek, on the northwest side of the said west fork; thence up the said creek to the head thereof; thence in a direct course to the head of the Middle Island creek, a branch of the Ohio, and thence to the Ohio, including all the waters of the said creek in the aforesaid District of West Augusta; all that territory lying to the northward of the aforesaid boundary, and to the westward of the States of Pennsylvania and Maryland, shall be deemed and is hereby declared to be within the District of West Augusta."

Then follow the provisions establishing out of the District of West Augusta the new counties of Ohio, Yohogania, and Monongalia, and the division lines between them, as quoted in Vol. II, p. 74 of these ANNALS.[1]

By reference to our map of the District of West Augusta, facing p. 518, Vol. I, of these ANNALS, studied in connection with the division lines of the three new counties made from said District, as shown in Vol. II, p. 74, it will be seen that the northern end of the present "Panhandle" of West Virginia, was put into Yohogania County. But on the settlement of the boundary controversy by the

[1] For the entire act and other interesting matters relating to the subject, see Crumrine's History of Washington County (1882), p. 183 and notes.

Baltimore Conference of 1779 (Vol. I, p. 522, of these ANNALS), the portion of Yohogania County north of Cross Creek was at first put into Ohio County, and subsequently became Brooke County.[1]

It will also be seen that Ohio County, as originally created, extended northward to the mouth of Cross Creek, southward to the mouth of Middle Island Creek, and from the Ohio River, eastward, so as to include the present townships of Hopewell, Independence, Buffalo, Blaine, Donegal, East Finley, and West Finley, and parts of Canton and Franklin in Washington County, as well as perhaps the western one-third of Greene County, Pennsylvania. Thus it was that a large part of the transactions of the early Ohio County Court of Virginia related to the business and protection of inhabitants of Washington and Greene counties, Pennsylvania.

Black's Cabin where the first courts of Ohio County were held, was on the north fork of Short Creek, about eleven miles northeast from Fort Henry, now Wheeling, and about six or eight miles northwest from West Alexander, in Washington County, Pennsylvania. There was Vanmeter's Fort, and not far away was Rice's Fort on Buffalo Creek in Washington County, Pennsylvania; and Beeman's and Ryerson's stations in Greene county, and Fort Jackson, now Waynesburg. And it will be remembered that in the days of this early court, before Washington, town or county, was thought of, the people who looked to it for protection to their lives and property were on the frontiers of civilization; across the Ohio was a wilderness of savages, the enemies of civilization. Our present knowledge of events in these times will be freshened and confirmed by entries made in the course of judicial business shown in these records.

Ohio county, Virginia, like Washington County, Pennsylvania, has been shorn of its magnificent proportions. Its southern part has been made into a number of new Virginian (now West Virginian) counties, and its northern part, above the mouth of Short Creek, has been divided into Brooke and Hancock counties, while, by the actual running of the western boundary of Pennsylvania, in 1784–5, it lost all its old possessions in Pennsylvania.

Following the records of the early Ohio County Court we shall later give the contents of a small manuscript volume containing the

[1] See History of Augusta County, Va., by J. Lewis Peyton, p. 177.

records of deeds, etc., proved before the court for the district of West Augusta, 1775–1776, and ordered to be recorded. The records referred to embrace conveyances made by many of the early settlers, and include permits by the commandant at Fort Pitt, for the occupancy and cultivation of portions of the "King's Orchards," etc., and will be very interesting to the student of the early history of Pittsburgh and its vicinity.

ORDER-BOOK NO. 1.

BLACK'S CABIN, OHIO COUNTY, Jan. 6th, 1777.

(1) In pursuance of an order of the General assembly of this Commonwealth for the division of the district of West Augusta into three distinct Counties, whereof the County of Ohio is one distinct & separate County, Agreeable to its Circumscribing Boundaries;

In Complyance with which & Certain other Instructions directed to John McColloch, Esq., directing him, the sd McColloch, to summon the several landholders within sd County to meet at the house of Ezekiel Dewits on Buffalo Creek, on the 27th of Decembr. last, as well for the purpose of Electing & Constituting a Committe in & for the s County, as for the making Choice of the seat for County Coart to be held at in future, within sd County, which was done accordingly; & a Majority determin'd in favour of a place known by the name of Black's Cabbin, on the waters of Short Creek, to be the place of holding Coarts in future.

Accordingly & in Complyance with a Certain writ of dedimus potestatom, directed to Willm Scott, James McMechen, & David Rodgers, Impowering eighther of them to administer unto Mesrs. David Sheepherd, Silus Hedges willm Scott & James Caldwell, theoath of Justice of the peace within sd County; therefore the Commission being red at Blacks Cabbin aforesd James McMechan there did on Monday the sixth of this Instant, did administer unto sd David Sheepherd, Silus Hedges, Wm Scott & James Caldwell the oaths of Justice of the peace, who being duly qualified the aforesaid Sheepherd did administer unto Messrs. Zachariah Sprigg, Thomas Waller & Danl McClain the said oath of Justice of the peace, who being duly qualified took their seats on the Bentch accordingly.

Whereupon, the Court Being sworn, Jn° McColloch, Esq. as high sheriff of said County, then did offer Messrs. John Mitchel & Sam! McColloch, Boath of this County, as sureties for the due executing the office of Sheriff within this County, who being accepted a Bond for that purpose was then accordingly executed in open Coart. Likewise another Bond of one thousand pounds Conditioned for his faithfully Collecting & duly accounting for all officers fees & Cetera & producing Mes^{rs} Jn'o Mitchel, Saml McColloch & James McMechen, as Sureties, who being likewise accepted & approved & a Bond for that purpose was likewise accordingly executed, & the s.^d McColloch took the oath of office in open Coart.

(2) The Coart then proceeded to the choise of a Clark, & James McMechen being approved of for that purpose & having taken the usual oath took his seat at the Clark's table accordingly

The Coart then adverting to the expediency that the Militia of this County should be under the best of Regulations and discipline, came to the following resolutions viz: that David Sheepherd, Esqr be recommended to his honour the Governour as County Lieutenant in and for this County, & Silas Hedges Esq as Colonel, & Mr David McClure as Lieutenant Colon.^l, & Mr Sam! McColloch as Major of Militia.

The Court then adjourned untill tomorrow at eight of the Clock. D. Sheepherd.

The Court met according to adjournment; present David Sheepherd, Silas Hedge, Willm Scott, James Caldwell, Zachariah Sprigg, Thos Waller & Daniel McClain, Gentlemen.

Furthermore it is ordered by the Court that Joseph Tumlinstone, Saml Mason, Jno Mitchel, Joseph Ogle, Saml Teter, David Williamson, Jacob Lefler, James Bochanen & Reasin Virgin be likewise Recommended to his honour the Governour as Captains of the Militia; & that Mes^{rs} Danl McClain, Thomas Ryan, John Biggs, Derick Hoaglin, Thos Clark, James Gillaspy, Charles Bonner, James Pattin & Jno Boggs be recommended as Lieutenants; and that Messrs Morgan Jones, Moses Williamson, Junr., William Biggs, Andrew Fouts, Isaac Tayler, Hinry Taylor, John Hanley, David English & Isaac Phillips be likewise recommended as Ensigns.

& Foreasmuch as the tract of land agreed upon for holding Coarts at in future doth of right appertain unto Abraham Vanmetre of Opechan Creek in the County of Bartley, Order.d, therefore, that Zachariah Sprigg, Silas Hedges, Esqr, be appointed to Contract & Covenant with s.d Vanmetre for not less than Two acres of s.d Tract Including the Cabbin & spring, In behalf of this County, for the purpose of erecting & Building thereon a Coart house, Prison and other necessary publick Buildings, for any sum not exceeding Twenty pounds, & Report make of their proceedings therein as soon as may be to this Coart.

& Whereas it may be expedient that Constables should be [appointed] within this County, Ordered therefore that John
(3) Caldwell, Stephen Parr, Tho.s Williamson, Eliazer Williamson, John Bodkin, Thos Clark, Dan.l Morgan be summoned to attend our next County Coart, then and there to be sworn in as Constables; But if any of the above Recited persons shall think it expedient to Qualify in as Constables before the next Justice of the peace, there attendance at Coart is hereby Remitted Respectively.

Ordered that Cap'tn Saml Mason, Lieu.t Ebenezar Zane, James McConnel, & Conrad Wheat, being first sworn, do view the best & most direct way for the laying out a Road from Fort Henery to the first fork of Wheeling, & thereupon due return make to our next County Court.

Ordered that this Coart be adjourned until Coart in Coarse.

DAVID SHEEPHERD

At a Court held in and for the County of Ohio on the third day of March 1777, present David Sheepherd, Silas Hedges, Zachariah Sprigg, William Scott, James Caldwell, Gentlemen.

David Rodgers took the oath of Justice of peace & took his seat on the Bentch According.

Mess.rs Ebenezar Zane, Conrad Wheat & Sam.l Mason, agreeable to a former order of this Coart for the purpose of laying out the best and most direct way for a Road from fort Henery to the first forks of Wheeling, Reported as follows viz: from Fort Henery over the Ridge to the lower end of Mason's Bottom; thence up the Creek Bank to wheet's Narrows; thence to the top & along the north side of Wills' [1] Nobb to a Blas'd white walnut on Will's old Road; thence to the upper end of Wills field on the Creek Bank; thence up the Creek Bank to Hawkins's old house; thence to a blas'd white oak on Williamson's Road; thence to the forks of Wheeling.

Ordered that Conrad Wheat be appointed an overseer of s[d] road & that the Tithables on three miles of each side be summoned to work thereon until the same be completed.

(4) Henry Nelson Came into Court and Complains that W[m] Sparks had in an illegal manner taken away his Child & unjustly detains the same without his consent. Ordered that the s[d] Sparks be summoned to attend our next Court & answer make to the above complaint

Ordered that James Fitspatrick, an orphan Child, be bound unto Sam[l] Bruce to learn the art and Mystery of a Taylor until he shall arrive to the age of Twenty one years.

Order'd that Isaac, Tade, & hannah, Melatto orphan Children, be bound unto David Rodgers, Esq[r]. until the boys shall be of the age of Twenty one years, & the girl untill she be of the age of Eighteen.

Ordered that Robert Henderson, a Retaken prisoner amongst the Indians, be bound unto David Rodgers, Esq[r]. until he be of the age of Twenty one years, to learn the art and Mystery of a weaver. But provided any parent or near Relative should appear, further ordered that said Rodgers yield up s[d] Child, the parent or Relative paying Reasonable Costs & Expenses.

Ordered that this Coart be adjourned untill Coart in Coarse.

DAVID SHEEPHERD

At a Court held in and for the County of Ohio on Monday 7th of Aprile, 1777; present Silas Hedges, William Scott, Daniel M[c]Clain, David Rodgers, Gentlemen.

This Coart is adjourned till Tomorrow at eight of the Clock.

SILAS HEDGES.

[1] It is hard to decide from chirography of the original whether this is *Mills'* or *Wills'*.

The Court met according to Adjournment; present Silas Hedges, David Rodgers, Zacharia Sprigg, Daniel McClain & Thos. Waller, Gentlemen.

Isaac Tayler took the oath of subsheriff in open Court.

William Hawkins acknowledged a Bill of sale made unto Jno. Wilson in open Court & ordered that the same be Recorded.

Wm. Sparks appeared before this Court, & having not had an opportunity of Convening his Evidence ordered that it lay over unto the next Coart & that the Child Continue in the Care of Wm. Sparks untill that time.

Jno. Walker appeared Before this Court & answer made to the Complaint Jno. O'Fin, with respect to the property of a Certain Bed; whereupon the Coart having duely Considered
(5) the matter & Evidence, ordered that the Sheriff be order'd to give up to Jno. Walker the Bed in dispute as his property, & that Judgment & execution be Issu'd against the sd. OFin for the Costs; & further that, whereas the aforesd. O'Fin has not produced to this Coart sufficient Evidence to support the Charge against sd. Walker, ordered that it be dismiss'd as Litigious.

Winney Price Came into Coart & made Complaint that she was unjustly detained in service by her Master Jno. Mitchel; the Court having Considered the matter agreeable to the Evidence that appeard orderd that the Case lay over till the next Court and that she Continue in the service of sd. Mitchel untill that time.

Jno. Mitchel appeard in support of his attachment & producd Benjamin Biggs as his surity Notwithstanding the Case is ordered to lye over untill the next Coart.

Ordered that this Court be adjourn'd untill three of the Clock in the afternoon.

SILAS HEDGES.

The Coart met according to adjournment, present as above.

Then came into Court Winey Price, & having Informed this Coart that she would Cheerfully Compromise matters with her Master Jn'o Mitchel, Beggs leave of this Court that she be Indulged the liberty of Indenting herself to her old Master

Jno. Mitchel for & during the Term of Eighteen months from the Twenty fifth day of may Insuing; therefore order'd that the s'd Winey Price be indulged that Liberty for & in Consideration of all her past offences & Misdemanours.

The Court taking unto their Consideration the Expediency of having a Courthouse Erected, ordered that a house for that purpose be erected of the following Dimentions & Conveniences, viz:

a Dimond Cornerd house of Dimentions Twenty Two by eighteen feet in the Clear; one Story & one half high; a floor above & below of hewd or sawn plank; Ten Joice in the upper floor, nine or ten feet high; in the Lower Story a Coart's Bentch & Clark's Table: Two windows of eight lights each eight by ten Inches; a pair of stairs & Cabbin Roof; a plain Door & hinges of Iron; likewise plain window Shutters, wth. Iron hinges.

(6) A Jail Twenty by sixteen feet on the outside, the Loggs of the walls to be round & Close laid the loft; floors & partitions to be of loggs squarid to eight inches thick; Two Rounds of Loggs above the Loft; Cabbin Roof'd; Doors & windows agreeable; A Stone Chimney with Iron Grates, the doors done with nails; Lock Sufficient; the Loft & floor to have each a Large Summur Supporting them in the middle.

& for the purpose of having the aforementioned Buildings Completed as soon as possible agreeable to the aforesaid Dimentions, ordered that Jno. McColloch, high sheriff, be ordered to put the same up at publick auction to the lowest undertaker.

Ordered that This Coart be adjourned untill Coart in Coarse

SILAS HEDGES.

The Court met according to adjournment on Monday the second day of June, 1777. Present David Sheepherd, Silas Hedges, Zacharia Sprigg, Daniel McClain, James Caldwell, William Scott, Gentlemen.

The last will & Testament of Thos. Newbury was proven in open Court. George McColloch made oath well and truly to Execute the last will & Testament of Thomas Newbury, Deceasd.; therefore order'd that Edward Robinson, Andrew

Boggs, James Miller & Isaac Meeks do appraise the s^{d} Estate of Thos Newbury dec^{d}.

Judgment is ordered against George Mc Colloch as Guarnishee for Jno McSwain, six pound Remaining in his hands attach by Joseph Ogle.

The following Militia officers took the oath of office in open Court (Viz): David Sheepherd as Colon^{l}, Saml McColloch as Major, Saml Mason, Jno Mitchel, Joseph Ogle & Saml Teter as Captains, Saml Tumlinston, Jno Biggs, Derick Hoaglin, & Thos Gillaland as Lieutenants, & William Sparks as Ensign of Militia.

(7) Jacob Lefler took the oath of Captain of Militia in open Coart.

Ordered that the Coart be adjourn^{d} until Coart in Coarse.

DAVID SHEPHERD.

At a Coart held for Ohio County on Monday the 6th of Aprile, 1778; present David Sheepherd, Silas Hedges, Zacharia Sprigg, Wm Scott & James Caldwell, Gentlemen Justices & Thos Waller.

John Williamson Came into Court and took the oath of Justice of the peace and took his seat accordingly.

Ordered that David Sheepherd, Esqr officiate In the office of high sheriff for this County, in the stead of Jno McColloch, Deceas^{d}, agreeable to an act of assembly in that case made & provided.

David Sheepherd came into Coart & Executed one Bond of office of five hundred pounds & produced Soloman Hedges, Saml Mason, Joseph Ogle & Andrew Fouts as sureties, who were Excepted by the Coart. Likewise one other Bond of three thousand pounds conditioned for his faithfully Collecting & duly accompting for all office fees by him Rec^{d} et cetra, & produced Saml Mason, Joseph Ogle, Soloman Hedges & andrew fouts as sureties, who were Likewise Excepted, Ordered that the same be recorded.

This Coart is adjourned untill tomorrow Morning at seven of the Clock.

SILAS HEDGES.

The Court met according to adjournment; present Silas Hedges, Jno. Williamson, Thos. Waller, Zacharia Sprigg & Jas. Caldwell, Gentlemen Justices.

David Sheepherd produced a Commission from his honour Jno. page, Esqr., Lieut. Governor of this state, appointing him Lieut. of Ohio County, was Red & sworn to in open Court.

Silas Hedges produced a Commission from his honour Jno. Page, Esqr., Lieut. Governor, appointing him Colonel of the Militia for this County which, was Red. & sworn to in open Court.

(8) Ordered that Rebekah Coons, wife of Adam Coon, Decd. be admitted to administer upon the Estate of her husband, she complying with the law.

Rebekeh Coons then produced James McMechen & George McColloch as Surities, who were excepted accordingly. Ordered that Ebenezer Zane Saml. McColloch Jacob Reager & Saml Mason, or any three of them being first sworn, do appraise the goods, Chattles & credits of the sd. Adam Coon, Deceas'd, & make report to the next Court

Ordered that Margret unsel, alias Margret Rentials, be admitted to administer upon the Estate of Henry Wall, Deceasd., She Complying with the Law. Margret then producd. Wm. hawkins & Jacob Lefler as surities, who were excepted accordingly.

Ordered that Thos. Waller, Jacob Miller, Barney Booner & Edward Geater, or any three of them, do appraise the goods and Chattles of the sd. Deceasd., they Being first sworn, and make return to next Court

Jno. handly producd. a note executed by Robt. walker, attested by Alexander Rice, whereupon Alexander Rice Came into Court to prove that he Testifi'd the sd note, & that the same was his handwriting & that he saw Robert walker execute the Same for Value Received.

Ordered that Jacob Reager be permitted to administer upon the estate of walter Colhoon, Deceas'd, he Complying with the law. Sd. Reager producd. Saml. Mason, Neil Galaspy, Conrad Stroup, & Jno. Mitchel as sureties, who were excepted accordingly. Ordered that Ebenezar Law, Saml. McColloch, David Sheepherd, & Wm. mcIntyre, do appraise the same, they being first sworn, & make Return to next Court.

2

Saml. Mason proved an accompt of 12.10 against the estate
of Rodgers McBride, Deceasd., therefore Ordered that Sam
(9) Mason be admitted to administer upon the Estate of Rodgers
McBride he complying with the law. Sd. Mason produced
Jacob Reager & Conrad Stroup & Neal Gillaspy as sureties,
who were accepted accordingly

Ordered that David Sheepherd, Wm. McLane, James Mc.Connel, and James Clark, or any three of them, being first sworn, do appraise the estate of sd. mcBride, deceasd, and Report the same to next Court.

Ordered that Neal Gillaspy be admitted to administer the estate of Mathew Atkinson, deceasd., he complying with the Law.

Sd. Gillaspy then produced an account against sd atkinson, whereupon sd Gillaspy produced Jacob Rearger & Saml. Mason as Sureties for his administering, who were accepted accordingly. Ordered that henry Sterniker, Jacob Links, James Martin & Jno. Williamson, they being sworn, do appraise the Estate, & make due Returns to our next Coart.

Conrad Stroup produced to this Court a Commission from his honour the Governor appointing him Lieutenant of Militia for this County, which was read & sworn to in open Coart.

Jerimiah Duns produc'd. to this Coart a Commission from his honour the Governour appointing him Ensign of Militia for this County, which being Red was sworn to in open Court

Charles Bonner produced to this Court a Commission from his honour the Governour appointing him Lieut. of the Militia for this County, which was red & sworn to accordingly

George McColloch produced the Inventory of the Estate of Thos. Newbury, Deceasd. ; ordered that the same be Recorded.

[Upon the motion of George McColloch to this Court, wherein he has Exhibited Certain Instances of David Sheepherds having acted out of the Line of his office as Commanding Officer of the Militia by commissioning certain officers of Militia without the recommendation of this Court ; whereupon this Court has thought that information thereof be made to his excellency the Governor, praying that he may take cognizance thereof as to him shall seem meet

Whereupon Colo. David Sheepherd came into Court and

produced sundry Commissions of Certain Gentlemen that he had Commissioned in the time of this Court's Recess, & pray[d] that the Court would regulate the sd Commissions as to them shall seem meet as he acknowledges that he had no Intention to detract from the prerogative of this Court as he Conceives that the urgent necessity of the times compell[d] him to act thus, and further prays that this Court would proceed to recommend suitable officers to fill up the sundry vacancies in the Militia.][1]

Jno. Hanly produc[d] an acknowledgment from Jacob Crow, attested by Jno Williamson & James Caldwell, Gentlemen Justices, and others; whereupon the sd Williamson & Caldwell, Two of the subscribing witnesses, Came into Coart & attested that the sd Crow had acknowledged the same before them, Two of the subscribing Witnesses; Ordered that the same be recorded.

Colo. David Sheepherd came into Court & prays the opinion of the Court as to whether he in the Case of his Commissioning Certain Militia officers of this County without the Recommendation of this Court for that purpose, was Intentionally to detract from the prerogative of this Coart in that Case or not, the Coart are of Opinion that he did not, Two members Ignoramus.[1]

(10) W[m] Scott enter[d] Special Bail in the Case wherein Jesse Martin is plaintiff & henry Martin def[t]; ordered that a didimus be issued to take the Evidence of Jn[o] Isral, as well in Behalf of Jesse Martin plaintiff & henry Martin defend[t], Before Jn[o] Williamson, Ja[s] Caldwell, Thos[s] Waller, Gentlemen Justices.

(11) W[l] Williams came into Coart & entered himself Defend[t] in the Case wherein Jesse Martin is plaintive, in a Case of Ejectment.

W[m] williams came into Court & entered himself defend[t] in the Case wherein Jesse Martin is plaintiff in Ejectment.

Henry martin enters Special Bail in the Case wherein Jesse Martin is plaintiff and W[m] Williams Def[t] in ejectment.

Ordered that Sam'l m[c]Colloch[2] be admitted to administer

[1] The portions above enclosed in [] are erased in the original; *Editor*.

[2] This was the famous Major McColloch, who, surrounded by Indians on the high hill in the rear of Wheeling, made the famous horse-back leap over into Wheeling Creek, and escaped unharmed.

upon the Estate of his father Jno. McColloch, Deceas'^{d}. he Complying with the Law; whereupon the s^{d} Saml produced Jno. Mitchel, George m^{c}Colloch, & Isaac Tayler as sureties, who were approved accordingly. Ordered that Ebenezer Zane, Jo^{sph}. Vanmetre, Benjamin Hammit, & Jno Wilson, or any three of them, being first sworn, do appraise the sam & make Return to next Court.

Ordered that a suppena be Issued to bring Joseph Wilson & Mathias Ault before our next Court, to give evidence relative to an orphan Child.

Thos. Waller produc^{d} an Indenture Executed by hercules Roony, & margret unsel. Binding a Certain henry unsel unto s^{d}. Roony, adjudged by this Coart sufficient to Bind s^{d}. henry agreeable to s^{d}. Indenture which was attested in open Court.

John Huff Enters Special Bail in the Case wherein hercules Roony is plaintiff & Margret unsel and W^{m}. Hawkins defendant.

Order'd that the Clerk issue summons for Thos. Peak, Letty Peak, Moses Sheepheard, Charles Bonner Francis Sharnick, Thomas hawkins, Thos. waller, to give evidence in the Case wherein Hercules Roony is plaintiff and Margret Unsel and Wm Hawkins defendant.

(12) agreeable to the Requisition of C^{l}. David Sheepherd this Coart ordered to recommend to his honour, the Governour, the following Gentlemen for Militia officers for this County, viz: Conrad Stroup & Isaac Micks, as Lieut^{s} & Jeremiah Dun, William Biggs & Hugh McConnel, as Ensigns of the Militia.

ordered that the Clerk issue Suppenas for Jno. Caldwell, Jno Smith, to give evidence in the Case between hercules Roony & margret unsel & W^{m}. hawkins Deft^{s}.

Jno. Bodkin vs Peter Rentials, Continued.

W^{m}. hawkins Enters special Bail in the Case wherein Jno. Bodkin is plaintiff & Peter Rentials Defen^{d}.

James Bochannon produced to this Coart a Commission from his honour the Governour appointing him Capt of Militia which was red and sworn to in open Coart.

William Caldwell enters special Bail wherein the Commonwealth is plaintiff & James Caldwell Defendant, viz the Grand Jury Court next.

Ordered that the Court be adjourned untill tomorrow at eight of the Clock. SILAS HEDGES.

Court met according to adjournment; present Silas Hedges, Thos Waller, Wm. Scott, & Zacharia Sprigg, Gentlemen Justices.

Isaac Tayler Came into Court, and on the motion of David Shipherd, high sheriff, sd. Tayler took the oath of deputy sheriff in open Court.

Whereas Jno. McColloch, Esq., late high sheriff for this County, having Deceasd., ordered therefore that David Sheep-herd, Silas Hedges & Wm Scott be recommended to his Excellency the Governour and the honorable Council as high sheriffs in his stead; & whereas this Court has never yet Recommended a Coroner, ordered therefore that Zachariah Sprig & Thos. Waller Esqrs. be Recommended as Coroners.

Ordered that the sheriff be directed to summons a Grand Jury against the next Court to be held in May next.

Ordered that Wm. Scott & James McMecken Esqrs. be appointed to meet Certain Gentlemen Commissioners from the County of Yohogany, for the settling the County line between this & the Counties of Yohogania & the County of Monongahala agreeable to act of Assembly, Return to our next Court.

(13) ordered that several Magistrates in this County do take the list of tithables agreeable to the following precincts. Viz:

That James Caldwell, Esq., take the list of all the Tithables on the waters of Wheeling Creek; & Zachariah Sprigg, Esq., take those on the waters of short Creek; Silas hedge, Esqr., all those on the waters of Buffalo Below Ezekiel Dewits; & Thos. waller, Esq., all the Tithables on the South side of Williamsons fork of Buffalo Creek & above Ezekeil Dewits; & Jno. Williamson, Esqr., all those on the north side of Buffalo above Andersons mill to the County line, south of and along the Road from Andersons mill past Isaack Taylors leading to Robt Cunninghams; & William Scott, Esq., all those remaining in the County.

Whereas Jno. McColloch & Dl. McClain, Esqr., are deceased, & Thos poak not within the limits of this county & Abraham . . . declines to qualify, Ordered that the following Gentlemen be Recommended to his excellency the Governour as proper persons to be added to the Commission of the peace in & for the County, viz: Edward Robinson, George McColloch, James Miller, Ebenezer Zane, David McClure, Saml. McColloch, Jos

Boggs, Jn° Dodridge, Charles Wells, Ja[s] Gillaspy, Jun[r]., & whereas, in the former Commission of the peace for this County, there must have been a Mistake in the Recommendation placing that of Silas prior to that of Soloman Hedges, s[d] Soloman having formerly acted as Jude in the Coart of hamshire, this Court therefore would pray that Soloman aforesaid be inserted the first in the List in the new Commission.

Ordered that Jn[o] Wrights, Jno Tilton, David English, Eliazer williamson, & Thos Williamson, be summoned to next Coart to be qalified as Constables, to serve the insuing year.

Dan[l] Glallaspy ver Conrad Wheat, Continued

William hawkins ver Thos oge, Continued.

Jn[o] Caldwell ver Catherine Neel, Continued.

Isaac Tayler ver William Caldwell, Continued.

Charles Stephenson ver Rob't. Lemmon, Continued.

(14) W[m] Caldwell ver Isaac Tayler, dismissed, not legally served.

Rob[t] M[c]kin ver James Clark, Continued.

Isaac Tayler ver Nathan Templeton, C. O. in Ejectment.

Jn[o] hanly ver Rod. Walker, S B, Continued.

Joseph Wells ver Jn[o] Carpenter, Continued.

W[m] Scott ver William Caldwell, Continued.

Ja[s] Gillaspy ver W[m] Caldwell. C. O.

Thos. Waller Esq. produced to this Court a recognisance against Murty Hanly & W[m] hawkins & James Patton as sureties, Wherein the Commonwealth is plaintiff, & the said Handly not appearing though solomly Called, nor either of the sureties, it is Considered by the Court that a Common order be Issued against s[d] Murty handly, W[m] Hawkins & James Patton, or either of them, to answer at our next Coart to the above Charge

Tho[s] Waller produc[d] to this Court a Recognisance, wherein the Commonwealth is plaintiff & Isaac Foglor Defen[d] & no evidence appearing, ordered that the s[d] Case be dissmissed,

Ordered that this Court be adjourn[d] until Coart in Coarse.

SILAS HEDGES.

At a Court Continued & held for Ohio County ; present Silas Hedges, Zachariah Sprigg, Jn[o] Williamson, & David Sheapherd, Gentlemen,

A Commission of the peace directed to David Sheepherd, Solomon Hedges, Silas Hedges, David Rodgers, Wm. Scott, James Mc.Mechen, James Caldwell, Jno. williamson, Zachariah Sprigg, Thomas waller, Edward Robinson, George McColloch, James Miller, Ebenezer Zane, David McClure, Saml. McColloch, Jno. Boggs, Jno. Dodridge, Charles Wells & James Gillaspy, Junr., wh. Being Red the following Gentlemen named therein took the oath of Justices of the peace & took their seats accordingly, viz: Silas Hedges, Zachariah Sprigg, James Gillaspy, Junr, Jno. williamson, Jno. Doldridge, Jno. Boggs, & George McColloch, Gentlemen.

A Commission from his Excellency the Governour, to David Sheepherd appointing him High Sheriff of the County of Ohio was red & swore to in open Court, whereupon sd. Sheepherd produsd. Resin virgin, Joseph ogle, & Andrew Fouts, sureties, & entered into Bond.

(15) Zacharia Sprigg, Gentlemen, took the oath of Coroner for this County, a Commission from his Excellency the Governour appointing him to that office being first red.

Letters of administration are granted to Margret alhauce on the Estate of George alhauce, Deceas'd., she Complying with the Law; whereupon the sd. Margret producd. Ezekiel Dewit & Thomas Waller as sureties.

Ordered that Barny Bonner, Alexander Douglas, Edward Geater, & Jacob Lifler, or any three of them, they being first sworn, do appraise the aforesd. Estate & make Report to next Court.

Administration is granted to Susannah Burn & James Car upon the Estate of Jonothan Burnn, Deceasd. they Complying with the Law; whereupon the sd. Susannah & James produsd. Frederick Lamb & John Doldridge as Sureties, & entered in to Bond and oath accordingly

Ordered that Thos. Clark, Arthor Mc.Connel, Andrew Scott & David Reynolds, or any three of them, they being first sworn, do appraise the good Chattle & Credits of sd. Deceasd. & make report to next Court.

Ordered that Allen Steward be Bound unto James Gillaspy agreeable to his acknowledgment & requisition before Wm Scott or any other Justice of the peace.

Resin Virgin produs^{d} to this Court a Commission from his Excellency the governour appointing him Captain of the Militia which was red & swore to accordingly.

Isaac Meeks produced to this Court a commission from his Excellency the governour apointing him a Lieutenant of the Militia which was Red & sworn to accordingly.

John Boggs produced to this Court a commission from his Excellency the governour apointing him Lieutenant of Militia which was Red & sworn to accordingly.

(16) Andrew Foutts produced to this Court a Commission from his Excellency the governour apointing him an Ensign of Militia which was Red & sworn to accordingly

ordered that Isaac Phillips & Wm List be recommended to his Excellency the governour as proper persons to serve as officers in the Militia, Phillips as Lieutenant and List as Ensign.

Jona Simmons took the oath of Deputy sheriff in open Court.

William Hawkins enters himself special for Peter Hildibrand at the suit of Jno Tilton

Bargain & sail from Alexander Douglas to Jesse Hollingsworth, for six hundred acres of Land, & ordered to be Recorded.

ordered that the Court be adjourned till tomorrow at eight of the Clock at the house of Andrew Ramsay

SILAS HEDGES.

The Court met according to adjournment on the 2^{d} day of June, 1778. present Jno Williamson, Zachariah Sprigg, Jno Boggs, James Gillaspy, George McColloch & Silas Hedges, Gentlemen Justices.

Ordered that James Henderson, an orphan Boy, be Bound unto Joseph ogle, to Learn the Shoemakers Trade & Mystery, Before any Justice of this County, aged ten years, Feb.^{ry}, 1778.

Solomon Hedges, Edward Robinson, & James McMechen, Gentlemen named in the Commission of the peace for this County, came into Court & took the oaths of Justice of the peace accordingly.

ordered that Mary ogle, wife of Jacob ogle, deceas^{d}, killed in the service of the United States, a Militia soldier of this

County, be allowed the sum of twenty five pounds to enable her to support herself & six small Children for the ensuing year, & to draw on the Treasurer for the same.

Ordered that Sarah Clark, wife of Hezekiah Clark, a Regular enlisted soldier in the thirteenth Virginia Regiment, be allowed for her own support & Two small Children for one year, the sum of fifteen pounds, & that a draft for the purpose issue to the treasurer.

(17) Zacharia Sprigg, with George McColloch Surety, Came in to Court and executed a Bond of £500 for the due Execution of the office of Coroner for the County of ohio.

Ordered that the sheriff apply to Mr Richard Yates for permission to make use of the district [1] Jail to Imprison Delinquents during these difficult times of danger & want of Jail at the Courthouse seat for this County, upon the most Reasonable Terms possible.

Ordered that David Sheepherd, sheriff for this County, advertise to the Lowest undertaker the Building of the publick Buildings for this County, agreeable to the Dimentions therein Containd.

James Bruce produced to this Court a Commission from his Excellency the Governour appointing him Ensign of the Militia, which was red and sworn to accordingly.

Upon the motion of Benjamin Biggs ordered that his ear mark an upper half-peny marck & slit in the right & Brand B B be recorded upon the near thigh.

Upon the motion of Nicholas Rodgers ordered that his mark a Swaller fork in the left ear & a crop in the right be recorded

Upon the motion of George McColloch, ordered that his mark a Crop off the left ear & slit in the same & under half peny in the right be Recorded.

Upon the motion of Zachariah Sprigg, order that his mark a Crop in each ear & hole in the right ear be Recorded.

Upon the motion of Isaac Tayler, orderd that his mark, a Crop in the left Ear be Recorded.

Upon the motion of Joseph ogle, ord that his mark a Crop in the left ear and under bit in the same be Recorded.

[1] This was the jail erected for the District of West Augusta, on the late Gabby farm, just west of Washington.

Upon the motion of Tho.[s] waller, orderd that his mark a Crop & Slitt in each ear be Recorded.

Upon motion of James Gillaspy, Jun.[r], orderd that his ear mark a Crop & Slitt in the near ear & two slits in the off ear be Recorded.

Jn.[o] warford mov'd that his ear mark a Crop in the left ear & under Bitt each be Recorded

(18) Upon the motion of Resin virgin ordered that his ear mark a swallow fork in the right ear be Recorded.

Upon the motion of Jn.[o] Boggs order'd that his ear mark a crop in each ear & hole in the right ear & Brand IB on the sholder & Buttock be Recorded.

Upon the motion of Edward Robinson, ordered that his ear mark an upper half-peny in the right ear & under half peny in the left be Recorded; also the Brand E on the sholder & R on the Buttock boath on the left side

Upon the motion of Jacob Newland, ordered that his mark a Crop in the left ear & hole in the right be Recorded

Upon the motion of Charles Hedges ordered that his ear mark an under half crop in the right & under bit in the same & under bit in the left ear be recorded

Upon the motion of Andrew Fouts orderd that his ear mark a Crop in the right ear & two under cross slits in the left ear be recorded

Upon the motion of Jno. Harris, ordered that his mark a crop and under slipe in each ear be Recorded

Upon the motion of James Andrews, ordered that his ear mark a Crop in the right ear & under bit out of each ear be Recorded.

Upon the motion of Derick hoaglin, ordered that his ear mark a swallow fork in the lift ear & under half peny in the right be recorded.

Upon the motion of James Newal, orderd that his ear mark a Crop off the right ear & under bit out of the left be Recorded

Upon the motion of Ebenezer Zane, ordered that his mark a Crop and slitt in the near ear & slitt in the off ear be Recorded

Upon the motion of Isaac Meeks, ordered that his mark a Crop off the right ear & slitt in each ear be Recorded

(19) upon the motion of David Sheepherd, ordered that his mark a Crop in the right & swallow fork in the left be Recorded.

A Recognisance against Saml Mason, for disposing of & exchanging some of the Continental Stores at Fort Henry, Exhibited by C^{l} David Sheepherd; whereupon the Defendant came in to Court & acknowledgd the Charge in part; whereupon this Court have Considered that Saml Mason afores^{d} be fined five pounds & Return into the hands of Co^{lo} Sheepherd an equally good gun, or the value thereof; valued by Raesin virgin & Joseph hoge, sworn for that purpose, valued at seventeen pounds; furthermore it appears to this Court that Saml Mason afores^{d} had exchangd his own property for the stores aforesd with a Certain V. Doulton, D. Q. master in the Continental service.

The Commonwealth v. Murty Hanly for Dissaffection to the State, the breach of a penal [statute] for the punishment of Certain offences; the Defend^{t} being Bound in Recognisance to this Court, the def'dt came in to Court & pleads not guilty; then came a Jury, viz: Resin Virgin, Jacob Newland, Benjamin Biggs, Charles Hedges, Isaac Tayler, Joseph ogle, Derick Hoaglin, Wm Biggs, Andrew Fouts, Oliver Gorrel, Jno warford & Jno Harris; who Bring a verdict for the Commonwealth. Mauty Hanly, guilty of speaking of offensive words against the Commonwealth, to suffer imprisonment from now to the first day of September next, then to pay a fine of ten pounds & to be discharged then upon taking the oath of fidelity or giving Security for his further Behavior.

Wm Hawkins v. Edward Mills, in attachment, the sheriff returns no goods found; orderd to be dismissed with Costs to plaintiff.

Upon the Motion of C^{l} David Sheepherd, ordered that Requisition be made to the worshipfull Justices of Yohogania County, to Call upon the Commissioners for adjusting the Boundary line Between the Coutny^{s} of Yohogania & Ohio as
(20) soon as possible & report their proceedings, so the Militia in the disputed Territory may forthwith be Called upon if Requir'd.

Absolam Sparks ver Jno. Carpenter, A Sum.

Joseph Wells ver Jno Carpenter, C. o, in Eject.

Wm. Scott ver William Caldwell, Continued.

Jno. Tilton v Jno. Bodkin, alias

James McMechen v Alexander Douglas; the Defendt Came in to Coart & acknowledged the debt in the plaintiffs Declaration alledg'd.. Wherefore, the Court have Considerd. that the sd. douglass pay the sum of Twenty pounds fifteen shillings Pen's money, of equal value to sixteen pounds twelve shillings Virginia money & Costs

George Corn ver Jona Simmons, Continued

Rob't walker v. Wm. Hawkins, C o

———— v. Jno. Hanly, alias

David McClure v Jeremiah Dunn, Dismiss'd

James Caldwell v Saml. Mason, Continued, the sd. Mason entering himself Defendant.

Orderd that Isaac Tayler be allowd for his service of going express to & Returning from Williamsbourgh, the sum of Twenty five pounds. Likewise 12 shillings he paid upon the Cards Consignd for this County, to be paid by the party that may draw the same agreeable to Certificate.

Ordered that Soloman Hedges & Jno. Williamson, Gentlemen, distribute the publick cards Consignd to this County upon proper & sufficient Certificates to them produc.d

Orderd that the sheriff Collect a publick Tax of four & Twenty shillings Poll upon all Tithables within this County, & pay the same to the Different orders from this Court, Excepting the proportion Levy to the treasurer.

Isaac Tayler v Nathan Templeton, S. B.

Andrew Robinson v Conrad Wheat, C o

James Gillaspy v Wm. Caldwell & Jane, in Slander; the Defend william failing to appear thoug Solomly Calld. by defend.t and on order from this Court, on Motion of the plaintiff, ordered that the same be forthwith tryd. Whereupon then Came a Jury as above, & bring a verdict for the plaintiff of three pounds & Costs, & Damage 1 peney.

(21) Sprig v. Jeremia Dunn C. O. against William Hawkins for Rescue.

Danl Gillaspy v Conrad Wheat, Continued.

Wm Hawkins v Conrad Wheat, Continued.
Wm Hawkins v Thos ogle, Continued.
Isaac Tayler v William Caldwell, C. O
Charles Stephenson v Robt Lemmon, Dissmissed.
Jno Bodkin v Peter Rentials, Cont.
Hercules Roany v Margret unsel, } Cont.
v William Hawkins, }
Jno Hanly v Rob't Walker, Continued.
Jesse Martin ve Henry Martin, Continued.
ver Wm William, Continued.
ver Elisabeth Cunningham, the same

David Sheepherd protests against the sufficiency of the Jail of this County.

James Gillaspy ver James Caldwell, C. O.

Ordered that David Martin, David Cox, John Ferguson, Henry Martin, be appointed Constables to serve the Ensuing year, & that they be summond to swair into said office before the nearest Magistrate Respectively.

Isaac Tayler v william Caldwell, in Case, came the parties, & the Defendant pleads the general Issue, whereupon there Came a Jury, viz: Resin virgin, Jacob Newel, Benjamin Biggs, Charles Hedges, John Harris, John Carpenter, Derrick Hoaglin, Wm Biggs, Andrew Fouts, oliver Gorril, Joseph ogle, Jno warford, who being sworn & impanel'^{d} find for the plantiff the sum of 1 shilling damage. It is considered by the Court that this Judgment be discharg^{d} by payment of one hundred and sixty pounds Current money of the State & Costs in that Behalf Expended.

(22) William Caldwell Enters special Bail for Nathan Templeton at the suit of Isaac Tayler

Ordered that it be a Rule in future in this Court to hold Courts for the trial of Jury Cases only in the months of Martch, May, august, and November.

Isaac Tayler took the oath of Deputy Clerk for this County

Ordered that this Court be adjourned till Court in Coars.

SOLOMON HEDGES.

At a Coart Continued and held by adjournment for Ohio

County July the 6th. 1778; Press'nt Solomon Hedges, Edward Robinson, Silas Hedges, George McColloch, Esqr. Gentlemen.

Jacob Wolf produced to this Court a comission from his Excellency appointing him Lieutenant of the Militia of this County, which was Read & sworn to accordingly.

Wm. Leet & David English produc'd to this Court Commissions from his Excellency appointing them Ensigns of Melitia, which was Read & sworn to Accordingly.

James Caldwell mentioned in the didimus came into Court and took the Oath of a Justice of the Peace & took his Seat.

David English being summoned as Constable to serve in that office, and took the oath agreeable thereto in open Court.

George McColloch Enters special bail for Wm. Hakins in a Case wherein James Smith is plaintiff & the sd. Hakins is Defendant.

At the motion of James Smith it is ordered that a Didimus to Thomas Freeman, Wm. Goe, & Joshue Wright, or any two of them, to take the Evidence of Johnston Campbell & Hugh Brison, in behalf of the Defendant & plaintiff, as also Benjd. Parkison &c.

John Carpenter enters himself Defendant in a Case wherein Joseph Wells is plaintiff in Ejectment, and Thomas Nichols Entrs himself Defendant at the suit of Rizon Virgin on an Ejectment.

(23) Jacob Wolf Enters himself Defendant at the suit of James McBride in Ejectment. Chrisly Wolf Enters himself Defendant in the suit wherein James Mcbride is plaintiff in Ejectmont.

ordered that this Court be adjourned to Court in Course.

SOLOMON HEDGES.

The Court met according to adjournment, August the 3d, 1778. Present Solomon Hedges, Silas Hedges, James Caldwell & James Gillespy, Gentlemen.

David McClure, Charles Wells, James Miller & Wm. Scott, being mentioned on the didimus, came into Court & took the oath of Justices of the Peace, & took their seats accordingly

David McClure produced to this Court a commission from his Excellency appointing him Lieutenant Colonel of Melitia for this County, which was red & sworn to accordingly

Ordered that a didimus Issue to take evidence of Capt Bohanar in behalf of Rob Walker against Wm Hakins & that David McClure & Wm Scott Do take this examination

Eloner Cox & Israel Cox Produced to this [Court] the Last will & testament of Gabrial Cox, Deceased, & the same was Proved in open Court & Ordered to be recorded.

Ordered that Jno Huff, Benjn Biggs, Jno Biggs & Derick Hogland, Do Appraise the Estate of gabrill Cox, Deceasd, and make report to next Court.

Whereupon Eleoner Cox produced to this Court Thomas McGuire & Francis McGuire as Secureties & entrd into bond & oath accordingly

Ordered that Eloner Cox & Israel Cox be admitted to administer on the afforsd Estate.

Ordered that Jemima Buckey be admitted to administer on the Estate of her husband she complying with the Law Whereupon the Last Will & Testament of sd Buckey was Producd in Court & Provd & ordered to be recorded.

Whereupon sd Eloner Product Levi Mills as a surety who was approved of accordingly & entered into bond

Ordered that Samuel Mccolloch, Jno Mitchel, Joseph Vanmetter & Jno Willson, they being first sworn, do aprais the sd
(24) Estate & make report to next Court.

Andrew moore enters himself Defendant in a case wherein Wm Haskins is plaintiff in Ejectment.

Robert Heger enters special bail for Andrew Moore in a case wherein Wm Hawkins is plaintiff & sd moore Defendnt, in an action of Trespass.

Wm Scott enters special bail for James Galaspy at the suit of Wm Caldwell, in a case of Tresspass & Detener.

John Tilton came into Court & took the oath of a Constable

Thomas Mcguire enters himself special Bail for Jno Carpenter at the suit of Nicholas Rogers, in a case of Trover & conversion

Joseph Hedges producd to this Court a Certificate from under the hand of Silas Hedges, Gent., of his taking up two stray Heifers with a Description of them, they being apraisd at £3 Each. Ordered that they be Advertised by the Clerk agreeable to Law & recorded.

Silas Hedges producd in Court a Certificate Certifid by Solo mon Hedges, Gen^{t}, of his being the taker up of a stray steer apraisd to £8. Ordered that the same be advertisd according to Law & recorded.

Ordered that Catherine Smith, wife of Samuel Smith, a regular Enlisted soldier in the 13th Virginia regiment, be alowed the sum of seven pounds Ten shillings to support herself and Three small Children for the Ensuing six months, and that a draught Issue to the Treasurer for that purpose.

Absolum Sparks vir Jno Carpenter, P S. Then cam the parties & the Defendant pleads the general Issue & the same is ordered to lye over till tomorrow until the defendant has the benefit of his evidence.

Ordered that this Court be adjourned until tomorrow morning at six o'clock.

SOLOMON HEDGES.

Court met according to adjournment, August 4th 1778, Present, Solomon Hedges, Silas Hedges, James Caldwell, James Gallespy, & James Miller.

Isaac Phillips producd to this Court a commission from his Excelency appointing him Second Lieutenant of Militia, which was red and sworn to accordingly

Upon the motion of Francis M^{c}guire, ordered that his ear mark two swallow forks & an under bit in the Left ear be recorded.

Upon the motion of Wm Harvey, it is orderd that his ear mark a crop in the Left ear a slit in the right and a half Crop be recorded.

(25) Upon the motion of Luke Seermehok (?), ordered that his ear mark a swallow fork in the right ear & a whole in the Left be recorded.

upon the motion of James Moore, it is ordered that his ear mark a slit in the Left ear & an uper bit out of the right be recorded.

Upon the motion of John Carpenter, it is ordered that his ear mark a swallow fork in the off ear two nicks, one on each side of the neer ear, and Brand I. C. on the neer shoulder be recorded.

Upon the motion of Andrew Ramsey it is orderd that his

ear mark a crop of the right ear and an under bitt under the same & a swallow fork in the Left be recorded

upon the motion of Jonas Simons, it is ordered that his ear mark a Crop of the neer ear & an under bitt under the off Do be recorded.

Ordered that David Inglish be recommended a Captain to his Excellency the governer, And Luke Enlow, a Lieutenant & Thomas Ryeres as Ensign.

David M[c]clure, Gent, absent.

An attachment David Mcclure on the goods & chattles of Alexander Dooglas, the sheriff returns that by virtue of sd attachment he hath attachd the following effects: two potts, one frying pan, 2 wheels, 1 bed stead, 1 Churn, 1 Barrel, Twelve sheep, four cows & calves, & one hefer, in the hands of Samuel Mason, Thomas Peak & W[m] Hawkins, and the said Alexander Douglas being solemnly called does not appear, Whereupon the said mason producs Hugh Siddwel an evidence, who being sworn saith he saw Samuel Mason Purchase the above articles of sd Dooglas, & the Coart is of opinion that the sale is good, & Thomas Peak & Samuel mason was sworn as garnishee, & nothing apers in their hands Except a side of Lether, in the hand of Mason, when taned.

Upon the motion of Samuel white, orderd that his ear mark a Under bitt out of each ear & a Slitt in the right be recorded.

On the motion of Jn[o] M[c]Cormick, orderd that his ear mark a Crop of the Left ear a Slit & under bitt in the right be recorded.

Upon the motion of Henry Levens ordered that his mark a crop and Slitt in the right ear & a hole & half crop in the Left be recorded.

On motion of Isaac Phillips, it is ordered that his mark a crop of the Left ear & a slitt & upper bitt in the right be recorded.

On the motion of Jn[o] Biggs, ordered that his mark a swallow fork in the Left & a hole in the right ear, Brand I B on the neer shoulder, be recorded.

David English product in this Court a commission from his Excellency apointing him a captain of the Melitia which was red & sworn to accordingly, recorded.

3.

(26) Luke Enlow producd a commission from his Excellency appointing him a Lieutenant of Melitia which was red & sworn to accordingly

The issue Absolum Sparks against John Carpenter, in case, by petition & summons, is ordered for a hearing. Then came the parties and Pleads upon the Issue joined as in Debt for one Deer skin, & the Court gives a Judgment for the plaintiff to have his account of £1.. 10.. & Costs in this behalf Expended.

Henry Nelson an Evidence, 2 days attendance allowed.

Jesse Martin vs Henry Martin. Trespass and Detiune. Dismissd at Pffs Request

It appearing to the Court Rowland Martin an Evidence be allowed two days attendance — ordered that he be allowed for the same

Jesse Martin vs Harry Martin { Ejectment. The Deft appears & enters himself Defendant in the Cause

Jesse Martin vs ——— Dement Ejectment. The sheriff returns that he served this ejectment on Dement, the Defendant; whereupon Rawly Martin, a Serjeant in Capt Scotts Company in the service of the United States, informs the Court on oath that he is materialy concerned in the ejectment, and if the same is tried when he may be ordered to some other state and consequent be not able to attend, the Court in pursuance of the Orders of the Honble the Continental Congress direct that no further proceedings be had thereon till the sd Martin is discharged.

James Gillespy Gent Absent.

James Gillespy Gent v William Caldwell & Jane Caldwell In Case

Then came the Ptff and the Defendant Jane Caldwell personally appeared in Court and prays that this Cause may be enquired of
(27) by the Country to which the Plff having signified and both parties being willing to have the same tried without the for-

mality of a Declaration, The Sheriff is commanded that he summon Twelve good and lawful men of his County to appear here in Court immediately; Whereupon Jesse Martin Wm. Buchannon, Joseph Wells, John Carpenter, Jacob Newland, Rezin Virgin, Derich Hogland, Jas Garrison, Samuel Mason, John Harris, Benjamin Biggs and James Clemons, who duly elected and sworn on their oaths do say they find for the Defendant one Penny damage and one penny Cost ——— Evidinces, 7.

Nicholas Maulson v John Donavan. Trepass & Detinue, Then came the parties and jointly prayed that the Differences between them may be enquired of by the Country without the form of a Declaration. Ordered that the Sheriff is commanded that he cause a jury to come before the Court immediately to enquire of the same; Whereupon David English, Wm. Hawkins, Wm. Caldwell, James Asby, Isaac Philips, Saml McBride, John Warford, Isaac Meek, Rawley Martin, Harvey Martin, Samuel Osburn & Wm Williamson, who being duly elected and sworn do say on their oaths that there is nothing for the plantif by his suit.

Ordered that the sherif do sumons a grand Jury to attend at November Coart.

Robt Walker vr. Wm. Hawkins, in Trepass & Detinue Continued.

Wm Hawkins enters special bail for Joseph Arnold at the suit of Nicholas Maulson.

Ordered that a didimus issue to take the Deposition of
(28) Rawley Martin before Zacharia Sprigg & Silas Hedge, at the suit of Jesse Martin and Harry Martin in Ejectment, and on behalf of Wm Williams likewise, he being a Soldier & of Consequence must be absent.

Ordered that the sheriff Collect Twenty shillings & six pence off of every Tithable within this County as a County Levy & the sum of Three shillings & six Pence as a proportion Levy, & Double that sum from all Who refuse to take the Oath of Allegiance, That is above sixteen years of age.

Orderd that David Mcclure's attachment against Dooglas be continued over to next Coart.

Ordered that the balance due on a bond attached in the hands of Samuel Mason after deducting £5 of discount, be paid to David M[c]clure on account of his attachment.

John Bodkins v. Peter Renchals, in Defamation, ordered that the cause be Dismist for non Prosecution.

Joseph Wells v. Jn[o] Carpenter, Ejectment, Dismist.

George Corn v John Seamons, Defraud, Continued to next Court at the Cost of the Plaintiff.

Joseph Tumbleston v Sam[l] Mason, in acc[t], the plantift not appearing tho solomly Called to Prosecut, Ordered that the s[d] suit be Dismist.

Upon the Evidence of David Shepherd Exhibited to this court upon oath of Jn[o] Huff's assaulting this court, order'd that the s[d] Huff be find the sum of Six Dollors & remain in Custody of the sheriff Until paid, & then Dismist wth Costs.

Ordered that this Court be adjourned untill Coart in Course.

SOLOMON HEDGES.

(28) At a Coart continued and held for Ohio County the 7th day of September 1778

Present, Silas Hedges, David M[c]Clure, James Gillespy, John Boggs, Ed[w] Robinson, John Williamson, Gentlemen Justices.

Mr James M[c]Mechen, Clerk of this Court, being down the Country, the Court proceeded to appoint James Berwick Clerk for the present Court who took the oath accordingly.

Absent David M[c]Clure, Gent.

David M[c]Clure Gent produced two Letters signed James M[c]Mecken, relative to his being appointed Clerk of this County. Ordered that the same be rejected and the said Letters filed among the records of this Court.

David M[c]Clure, Gent, Present

Isaac Taylor entered into Bond and Security to finish the Goal and Court house for this county the court house by the 1st March next, and the Prison by the 1st May next; Ordered that the sheriff do advance Mr Taylor the sum of fifty pounds and take Mr Taylors receipt for the same.

Isaac Taylor acknoweldged a Bill of Sale to George Corrothers for 200 acres of Land, which is ordered to be recorded.

Report of the Commissioners of the County Line between this County & County of Yohogania returned, & confirmed by the Court and ordered to be recorded.

Two Depositions of Raleigh Martin, a Soldier in the Continental service, ordered to be filed in the office

(29) Hugh Gillilan
v Jeremiah Dunn, S. B.
Annaniah Davis
Zephaniah Dunn.

Jeremiah Dunn enters himself Defendant in a Action of Ejectment at the suit of David Mc Clure.

Ordered that the Court be adjourned to the Court in Course

SILAS HEDGES

Summons to Sept^m 1778.

Hawkins v Kintelo, continued
Martin v Tuel, contnd
Flavin v Mason, contd

Appearance &c to Sept^m 1778.

Huff v Berwick, contd
Berwick v Huff, contd
Same v Same, contd
Tomlinson v Mason, contd
McClure v Dunn (Ejectment), contd
Virgin v Brounlee, contd.
Taylor v Caldwell, contd
Caldwell v Taylor, contd
Wells v Carpenter, contd Ejectm.
Hawkins v Kentielo, contd do
Walker v Handley, Plu Caps
Tilton v Bodkins, Al Caps
(30) Martin v Leet, Alias Capias
Drennin v Nemons, Al Caps
Markland v McBride, Al Caps

At a Court held for Ohio County on Monday, November 2^d, 1778; Present Solomon Hedge, Silas Hedge, Wm Scott, Geo. McColloch, James Caldwell, Charles Wall.

Philip Pendleton & Geo. Brent, Gent[m] took the oath of Attorney at Law and is admitted to practice as such in this Court.

Philip Pendleton Gent is appointed as a Deputy Commonwealth Atty for this County till some person is appointed by the Governor.

On the motion of John Moore seting forth his great age & Infirmits, It is Ord that he be for the future Exempted from the Payment of levy in this County James M[c]Machen the Clerk having removed himself out of this State and neglected to do his duty as such. It is ordered that a Complaint be Entered in the General Court against him for the same.

Admon of the Estate of Thomas Glenn, dec[d], is granted to his Widow Elizabeth Glenn, she having Complied with the Law

Ord that John Mitchell, Ebenezer Zanes, Levy Mills, Jos. Vanmeter, or any 3, app the Estate.

The Court having ordered a Complt to be lodged against James M[c]Mechan as Clerk of this county & he being out of this State the Court doth appoint David M[c]Clure Clerk until the same shall be determined, & thereupon the s[d] McClure took the Oath of a Clerk.

Grandjury for this County being called, James Clemons was sworn as foreman, and then Jacob Newland, Jacob Peat, James Moore, James Andrew, Samuel Mason, Jesse Dement, annaniah Davis, Ezekiel Biggs, Benjamin Biggs, Nicholas Rogders, James Newell, Thomas Gilliland, John Huff, John Mitchell, Jacob Drenning, & Ebenezer Martin was sworn

(31) David Williamson took the Oath of Captain of the Militia of the County which he produced in Court & O Certified

Samuel Williamson prod an Ensign Com of the Militia, took the Oath & Ordered to be Certified present, James Gillespie, Gent.

Upon examining Isaac Ellis, John Downing, W[m] Williams and John Baker, who was suspected of the murder of James Caldwell & Sam[l] Kennady, are of the opinion that they are not Guilty, & that they be discharged.

Ord that Jacob Lefler, Edward Gaither, James Brownlee & Sam[l] Mason, or any 3, app the Est of Geo Allhaunts, dec[d], & report the app, the former appraiser failing to return the appraisement.

On the Motion of Jacob Lefler seting forth that he was secy for Margt Unsel (who is since married to Peter Kintelo) for her admon of the Estate of Henry Wall, & that it app that he is Likely to suffer, It is ordered that the s[d] Margt & peter be summoned to appear at the next [Court] to deliver her up the Est or give him Counter Security.

The Grandjury having made several presentments, It is ord that the Several defts be Sum[d].

Orderd that the Court be adjd until tomorow morning 8 oclock SILAS HEDGE.

At a Court Continued and held for Ohio County November 3, 1778, Prest Solomon Hedge, Sila Hedge, James Caldwell, W[m] Scott, James Galespie, Geo M[c]Colloch.

Ord that William Price, a bastard child of Sarah Price, of the age of two years, be bound according to Law to John Waits on his motion.

Present Edward Robertson.

Ordered that the sheriff of this County pay Richard Yeats Six pounds it being this County's proportion of the district Goal out of the Money by him collected of the Tithables in this County.

Ordered that the sheriff pay Abraham Vanmetre Twenty pounds for the Lands which the County took to build a Court house and prison on, out of the Money by him collected of the Tithables in this County.

(32) Admons of the Estate of Frances Duke, dec[d], is granted to Col[o] David Shepherd, he having Complied with the Law.

Ord that Jacob Newland, Charles Headges, John Mitchell, & Joseph Vanmeter, or any 3, app the Estate.

Galespie v Wheat, Con[d]

Mitchell v Hamell, dis[d] by plt

Hawkins v Ogle, con[d]

v Wheat, con[d]

Caldwell v Neal, discon[d]

Delong v Flanagan, Cond.

Stephanson v Lemenon, descd.

M[c]Quire v Clark, Cond

Taylor v Templeton, a dedim to take the Dep[s] of Wit[s] in the State of Pennsylvania.

Handley v Walker, con[d].

Raaney v Unsel & Hawkins,

Handley v Walker, cond.

Martin v Williams, Cond.

Cunningham, Cond.

Scott v Caldwell, Sp. Imp. B.

Taylor v Caldwell,

Tilton v Bodkin, dis[d], no Inhab.

v Hillibrand, Cond.

Com v Lemons, Cond.

Walker v Hawkins & Handl, Cond

Caldwell vs Spindall, Saml Mason Enters himself def & Confesses the Lease Entry & ouster pleads N. G. A Demidmus to take the Dep[s] of Wits P.

Crow v Handley, Co.

Douglas v M[c]Guire, dis[d] no app.

Smith v Hawkins, Cond.

M[c]bride v Spindall; Jacob & Chrisley Wolf enter themselves deft, Confess the Lease Entry & ouster plead N. G. joined. P.

Virgin v Nichols, cond.

Maulson v Arnold, cond.

Gilliland v Dunner, agreed.

Caldwell v Zane, agreed.

English v Clark, Disd.

Martin v Martin, Ejec. Cond.

Galespie v Templeton, agd.

Hawkins v Moore, agd.

(33) Rodgers v Carpenter, Cond.

Jesse Martin v R. Martin, Cond.

McClure v Douglas, dis by plt.

McClure v Dunn, Ct.

Caldwell v Galespie, Emp. P.

Huff v Berwick, Cond.

Berwick v Huff, Cond.

Huff, Cond.

Drenen v Neinans, agd.

Hawkins v Kintole, Cond.

Wells v Carpenter, Cond.

Hawkins v Kintole, Cond.

Tomlinson v Mason, Cond.
Glenn v Douglas, discond.
Garrison v Shepherd, agd.
Martin v Tuell, agd
Martin v Leek, cond.
Hawkins v Mason, agd.
Hawkens v Kentoll, Cond.
Markland v Mcbride, NG, with leave Nomd. B
Virgin v Brownlee, Cond.
Caldwell v Taylor, Sp. Imp. P.
Taylor v Caldwell, Sp. Imp. B.
Kintolle & wife v Wall, Cond.
Clemans v Lane } John Waits, Spl in both suits & agreed
Lane } deft paying Costs
Drenin v Jolly, Ind.
Gillyard v Hawkins, Samuel Mason, Sp. Imp. B.
Caldwell v McMechen, dismd, no Inhab, Taylor, C.

Present Zachariah Sprigg, Gent.

The Last will & test of Samuel Wheat, dec'd, was proved by Zachariah Sprigg & Geo McColloch, two of the wit, & OR, & at the Motion of Jemima Wheat & Isaac Meek, the Est therein named Cert is granted them for Obtaining a probate, they having Compd with the Law: Ord that James Miller, Derick Hogland, Joseph Hedges & Andw Ramsey, or any 3, app
(34) the Est.

Then the Court proceeded to Lay the County Levy:

To John Biggs, by account £21	21– 0–0
To William Scott, by account, £	8– 0–0
To Philip Pendleton, Gent, as deputy Commonwealth atty £50–	
To Isaac Tayler, by account,	8
To David Shepherd, Gent, for extra services for 3 months 310 tob.	
To also 230 tob. for extra services, for 12 months,	9–12–
To James McMechin, by acc for extra services & for attending the running of the county line,	11– 2–6
To the sheriff for cclection,	12–15–0
To a deposition in the sheriff's hands,	81–18–0
By 352 tithables a 11 s. 6 p. each	202– 8–0

Ord that the sheriff Collect of every tithable person in the County 11/6, it being the County Levy for this County.

David Shepherd, Gent, with Secy, acknowledged their bond for his Collection of the County Levy.

Ord that Ezekiel Dewitt, Jeremiah Dunn, Edwd Smith, & Zachariah Sprigg, or any 3 of them, view the Most Convenient way for a road from the Court House to Annaniah Davis's Mill & mak report of the Conv. & Inconv thereof to the next Court.

Ordered that the Court be adjourned until the Court in Course. SOLOMON HEDGE.

(35) At a Court held for Ohio County on monday the 1st day of March, 1779.

Present, Solomon Hedges, Silas Hedges, James Caldwell, Edward Robinson, & Charles Wells, Gent.—Present James Miller.

McRobbin
v Attachment
Kerr, Frederich Lamp, Didimus issue to take evidence for Plt.

Ordered that Rawley Martin, an Orphan Child About 14 years of age, be bound to Henry Martin according to Law.

Crow v Hanley, Ordered that Didimus issue to examine plts evidences.

Ordered that David Hall, an orphan Child of three years of Age, be bound to Nathaniel Redford according to Law.

Bargain & Sale from Nathaniel Redford to James Caldwell for six hundred acres of Land & O R

Present, James Gillespie, Gent.

Henry Leven came into Court & took the Oath of Ensign of the Militia & O R to be Certified

Letters of Administration is Granted to Jacob Reager on the Estate of Thos. Worthington, he Complying with the Law.

Ordered that Ebenezer Zane, Conrad Stroup, Saml McColloch, & Yeates Conaor, or any three of them, being first sworn, do appas the Estate.

The Last will & Testament of Thos Worthington, deceased, was proved by Ebenezer Zane & Samuel Mason, two of the Witnesses & O R.

(36) Ordered that John Mitchell, John Willson, John Wiaths, & John McColloch, or any three of them, being first sworn, do app^{as} the Estate of John Bukey, Dec^{d}.

Ordered that the Adm of Henry Walls Estate Granted to Peter & Margarett Kintialo, alias Unsell, be revoked, Being Granted contrary to Law, & that the Same be Granted to Catherine Wall, Widow, who Entered into Bond

Certificate of a Stray rec^{d} and O R.

Orderd that Wm Peak, Thos Waller, Saml Mason, & James Clemens, or any three of them, being first sworn do app^{ns} the Estate.

Bargain & Sale from Wm Hawkins to James Caldwell for a tract of Land & OR.

Bargain & Sale from Jesse Martin to Thos Holbore & John Batsell for a tract of Land & O.R.

Bargain & Sale from Wm Hawkins to Thos Edgington for a tract of Land & O.R.

Bargain & Sale from John Boggs to James Clerk for 400 Acres of Land & OR

Certificate of Stray Hogs recd & O.R.

Appraismt of the Estate of Samuel White is returned to Court & OR.

Bargain & Sale from Walter Jerdon & Henry Moore for a tract of Land to John Mecombs & OR.

Bargain & Sale from Wm Caldwell to James Fisk for a tract of Land & O.R.

B & S from Wm Caldwell to Wm Williams ackd & O.R.

Steel v Dewitt } Case dam £ 250.
Wm Hawkins Enters S.B.

(37) Samuel Irwin took the Oath of An Atty at Law & is Admitted to Preach as Such in this Court.

The Last will & testament of James Leper was proved in Court by Arch^{d} Brownlee & John Gibby, & OR, and on the Motion of Margarett Leper, Certificate is granted her on the estate of James Leper, she having complyd with the Law. Ordered that John Brownlee Saml buyers, Chas Dodd, & John Allison, or any three of them being first sworn do app^{rs} the Same

B. & S. from Matthias Allto to Joseph Alixander ackw & O. R.

Ordered that Isaac Taylor, James Andrew Piter Killer & John Bess, or any three of them, being first sworn do view the the nearest & best way for a Road from the Court house to Annaniah Davis Mill & make report of the Conveniences & Inconveniences of the Same

B. & S. from John Carpenter to Francy Ryley Acknowledged & OR

Grand Jury Presentments

Commonwealth v Samuel Grahams ; Not Guilty
Thos McGuire,
Walter Jordon ; Not Guilty.
Peter Keller ; Fined.
Kenneth McClellend, Fined.
W^m. Biggs ; Fined

Ordered that the Court adjourn untill 8 OClock tomorrow

EDW. ROBINSON

The Court met according to Adjournment, 2nd. March

Present, Soloman Hedge, Silas Hedge, Chas. Wells, & James Gillespie, Gent.

B & S from Hercules Roney to Joseph Alexander, Acknowledged and O.R.

B & S from Isaac Taylor to W^m. Polk proved by one witness & orderd to Lie for further Proof

Present, Edward Robinson, Gent, John Boggs, & James Miller, Gent^m.

(38) Markland v McBride — Discontinued

Grand Jury presentments James Gillespie Gent Enters his Dissent

Markland v McBride — Ordered that Joseph Arnold & Jeremiah Arnold Each be allowed two days for attendance as witnesses in this Action

McClure v Douglas Attach^d. Judgment & Saml Mason Confesses he has Ten Shillings in his hands

On the motion of Matthias Alts Ordered that his mark the Left Ear a Crop & Slitt & the right Ear half Crop & O.R.

Commonwealth v. M^c^Guire Not guilty to which

B & S from Isaac Taylor to David Williamson acknowledged & OR.

Lamb v. Dewitt } Ejectment
Ordered that Didimus Issue to take witnesses Depositions for plt

M^c^Bride v Wolf } Eject
Ordered that Didimus Issue to take Witnesses Depositions

Ordered that the Sheriff Summons a Grand jury to attend next may Court

Commonwealth v. John Warford, the Atty for Deft objects to the validity of the Grand jury, Annanias Davis, one of them, being an occupier of a Mill; upon hearing the same the Court is of Opinion that the Same be quashed.

Ordered that the Sheriff pay the money for the Publick buildings as soon as collected to Isaac Taylor, Robt Taylor — (David Williamson Jacob Wolf Sarah Taylor David Williamson Jacob Wolf)

Ordered that Matthias Alt be allowed the Sum of fifteen pound for keeping Joseph Taylor a soldier For One Year past, that a Draft be drawn on the Treasurer for the same

(39) Appraisment of the Estate of Gabriel Cox, Deceased, is returned to Court & OR.

Wolf v Maulson, Acc^d^ proved & Judg

Clemens v Maulson, Judg for £21-17

Wm Caldwell v Gellespy, order for Ded^i^ to Examine Evidence

Ord, that the Court be Adjourned untill tomorrow 8 oclock.

SOLOMON HEDGES

The Court met according to adjournment 3^d^ March, Present, Solomon Hedgs, Silas Hedges, E^d^ Robinson & John Boggs, Gentlemen, present.

Williamson v Douglas Dismissd

Hedge v Dunbar, Dismissd.

Glen v Douglas, abates by Plt.s marriage.

Issues

McBride v Wolf, Eject Cond.
Taylor v. Caldwell, Cond.

References

Gillespie v Wheat, Disd.
Hawkens — Ogle, Cond.
— Wheat, Cond.
Delong — Flanagan, Disd.
Hanley — Walker, Discd.
Roney — Hawkins, Discd.
Martin — Williams, Cond.
— Cunningham, Cond.
— Dement, Cond.
— Martin — Henry Martin Deft by General Rule
Tilton — Hildebrand Dissd.
Com — Seamon Cond.
Scott — Caldwell
Walker — Hawkins Discond.
Crow — Handley, Not Guilty with Leave & Joined
Smith — Hawkins, Cond.
Virgin v Nichols, C O.
Taylor v Templeton, Cond. Plea Joined.
Maulson v Arnold, Discd.
McClure v Hildibrand, Dismd.
Rogers v Carpentor, Not Guilty, Joined.
McClure v Dunn, Judgment Finall.
(40) Caldwell v Gillispie, Not Guilty & Joined.
Huff v Berwick, Discond.
Berwick v Huff, Discd.
Huff, Decd.
Wells v Carpenter, John Carpenter Deft & General P L.
Hawkins v Kintialo, Cond.
Tumbleston v Mason, Payment, Joined.
Martin v Leet, Discd.
Virgin — Brownlee, Dismd.
Taylor v Caldwell, Not Guilty with Leave & Joined.

Caldwell v Taylor, Not Guilty with Leave & Joind.
Kintialo & wife — wall, Discd.
Gilliard — Hawkins, Pendleton Security for Cost conditions performed Cond.
Caldwell v. Taylor, not guilty with leave joined.
Sprigg v Dunn, Dismd.
Walker v Handley, Disd.
J. Handly — Crow, Dismd.
M. Handly — Crow, Dismd.
— Crow, Dismd.
Hannah — Johnston, CO.
Kelly — Douglas, Dismd.
Dickens — Flinn, Dismd.
Lyons — Caldwell, Dismd.
Dewitt — Dunn, Cond.
Robeson — Wheat, Agreed.
Grewes — Davis, Dismd.
Saunders — Smyth, Dismd.
Smyth & wife — Saunders, Dismd.
Kelly — Douglas, Dismd.
McClure — Lyons, Dismd.
Lloyd — Cole, Dismd.
Dewitt — Warford, Dismd.

Petitions

Hawkins — Kintialo, Cond.
Huston — Mason, Judgt.

Appearances

Stroup — Clerk, agreed.
Seamon — Carn, CO
Hawkins — Wheat, Agreed.
R. Taylor — Williamson, Sp Imp.
S. Taylor the same, Sp Imp.
Buchanan — Mason, Sp Imp.
Keller — Clerk, Dismd.
Steel — Dewitt, Sp Imp.

(41) Appearances

Bukanan — Mason, Sp Imp.
Harton — Hawkins, Sp Imp.

— Taylor, Sp Imp.

Madison — Stricker, Lawrence Stricker Enters Deft. Not Guilty Joined.

Lamb v. Dewitt, Ezekiel Dewitt Deft, Not Guilty & Joined.

Ordered that Charles Wells, David M[c]Clure, Isaac Taylor & Ebenezer Zane be and the same is hereby appointed to view & Give their Opinions to any money brought before them to know whether it be good or not.

Ordered that Isaac Meek, Derrick Hogland, Ed Robeson & John Shaw, or any three of them, being first Sworn, do view the nearest & best way For a Road from James Millers to the Court house, and make report of the Conveniences and Inconveniences of the same.

Ord that this Court be adjourned untill Court in Course

SOLOMON HEDGES

At a Court held for Ohio County April 5th 1779; Piesent Silas Hedges, Ed Robinson, James Miller, Charles Wells, & Solomon Hedges Gentm.

Ordered that David McClure Sind to Oldtown, Maryland, for the Books Left there by Doctor M[c]Mechen, for the use of this County, & that the Sheriff reimburse him what he pays for the same.

Patrick McGaughen v Spendall, Joseph Wells Enters himself Deft. O R

Keller v Clark, acct Proved £36. Jud[t] & O R

Ordered that Cha[s] Wells mark a crop & hole in the right Ear & brand C W & O R

Ordered that Joseph Wells mark a swallow fork in the Right Ear & under bitt & under bitt in the Left and his Brand I W & O. R.

Robert Woods came into Court & took the Oath of Surveyor for this County & gave bond

Ord: that this court be adjourned to Court in Course.

SOLOMON HEDGES.

At a Court held for Ohio County Monday, 3rd May, 1779.

Present Solomon Hedges, Silas Hedges, George McColloch, Ed Robison & Charles Wells, Gentlemen.

The appraisement of the Estate of John Buckey is returned to Court & O. R.

Ordered that Thos. Gardner be Exempted from paying any Further Levy in this County.

Present James Miller, Gent.

Bargain & Sale From Go. McColloch to Chas. Wells acknowledged and O. R.

Ordered that the Treasurer of this Commonwealth pay unto Andrew Robeson the sum of Twenty-five pounds, being allowed Ann Flemming for her support, her husband being in Continental Service.

Bargain & Sale from Dewit Hogland to Isaac Meek acknowledged & O. R.

James Miller v. Thomas Clerk attach't & ans Proved £ 12 judgm[t].

Bargain & Sale from Thomas Clark to John Chapman, acknowledged & O. R.

Bargain & Sale from Will[m] Bayley to Geo. Parker, acknowledged & O. R.

Ordered that the Treasurer of this Commonwealth pay unto Samuel McColloch the sum of Eighty pounds being allowed Mary Ogle for her support, her husband being killed in the Continental Service.

Bargain & Sale from Jonah Seaman to Geo. Stephenson, acknowledged & O. R. Jno. Mitchell, Security for pay.

Present John Boggs and James Gillespie, Gentleman.

Bargain & Sale from Robert Taylor to Ezekiel Boggs acknowledged & O. R.

On the motion of David McClure, ordered that his mark a crop in the right ear and hole in the same and crop in the left ear and hole in the same be recorded.

Bargain & Sale from Samuel McColloch to Moses Williamson, acknowledged & O. R. S. Mason pays Costs.

Bargain & Sale from James Richardson to John Chapman. Proved by Isaac Taylor one of the witnesses and ordered to lye for further Proof.

Bargain & Sale from Samuel Williamson to Joseph Arnold, acknowledged & O. R.

Bargain & Sale from Moses Williamson, Jun[r], to Samuel

Williamson. Proved by Murtey Handley one of the witnesses and ordered to Lye for further Proof.

Bargain and sale from Joseph Arnold to Samuel Mason, Proved by Murtey Handley and Samuel Williamson, two of the witnesses, and ordered to lye for further proof.

Ebenezer Zane and Samuel McColloch being mentioned in the Didimus, came into Court & took the oath of justices of the peace & took their seats accordingly.

Bargain & Sale from Patrick Magahan to Laurance McCarran acknowledged & O. R.

(42) At a court held for Ohio County 4th October, 1779 : Present Solomon Hedges, Silas Hedges, Zachariah Sprigg, James Miller, & Geo McColloch, Gentlemen.

The Commissioners for viewing the Clerks Office have made a return of the same Ordered that the same be Recorded.

Ordered that a License for Keeping an Ordinary be Granted unto Zachariah Sprigg he Complying with the Law; then sd Zachariah Sprigg Came into Court and Gave Dorrick Hogland for his Security

Kelly v Williamson, Dismist at Plts request.

Davis v French, Dismist at Plts request.

Commonwealth v Slidgegar, Dismised, Samuel Grahams Cost

Appraisment of a Hog returned to Court & OR

Hannah v Johnston, Dismist at Plts Request.

Ordered that the Clerk of this Court Certify Unto the Auditors of this Commonwealth that Mary Knox, Widow of Thos Knox, Deceased, was a serjant in Stephen Ashby's Compy in Colo. James Wood's Regiment and is Now Entitled to half pay Since March 177–.

B & Sale from Jonah Seaman to Wm. Harris, Acknowledged & OR.

Seaman v Corn, Dismised at Plts Request.

Corn v Seaman, Dismised at Plts Request.

Graham v Hill, Judgment for five pounds Equiv. to four pounds, Current Money of this State.

the Commissioners for Laying out a road from wells Mill, on Cross Creek, to the Court house, has Returned to Court their Report, ord that the Same be Recorded

Ordered that Francis McGuire do Act [overseer] of the Above Road, & that he summons all the tithables within three miles Each way.

(43) Samuel Graham v James Hannah then Came the Parties & Jointly Prayed that the Differences between them may be Enquired of by the Court without the Formality of a Declaration. Ordered that the Sheriff Cause a Jury to Come before the Court Imondiately to Enquire of the Same; Whereupon Ezekiel Dewitt, Annaniah Davis, Jacob Newland, John Carpenter, Jonah Seaman, Jeremiah Dunn, Christian Slidegar, Joseph Worley, Derrick Hogland, James McBride, Wm Harris & James Parks were Sworn.

The Jurors Agree that James Hannah, Deft, pay the Plt Samuel Graham ten Dollars and that the Plt Samuel Graham pay the Costs of Action and One Shilling Damage

EZEKIEL DEWITT.

McColloch v Sutherland, James Garrison S B.

Ordered that the Clerk Deliver Unto Robert Woods Surveyor of this County, four Blank Books & four Alphabets for said Books, for the Surveying Department of this County.

Moses Holliday v Henry Nelson, John Carpenter SB

Commonwealth v Jacob Drinnen, Fined.
v Joseph Paull, Cond.
v Kennith McClelland, Fined.
v McGinnis — Fined
v Huston — Fined
v Harris — Fined
v Wolf — Fined
v Graham — Fined
v Sprigg — Fined
v Altt — Fined
v Gillespy — Fined
v Miles — Fined
v Warford — Fined
v Dewitt — Not guilty
v Smith Fined
v Biggs Fined for Retailing Liquors.

(44) Common Wealth v Huff, Fined one Oath
v Huston, Find one Oath
v Harris, Find one Oath
v Williamson, Do Do
v Willson, Do Do
v Bowling, Do Do
v Dodd, Do Do
v Virgin, Do Do
v Taylor, Do Do
as Common Swearers

Ordered that the Sheriff Summons a Grand Jury to attend Next Month

Ordered that Susannah Fisher, an Orphan Child, be bound Unto Solomon Hedges according to Law. And that said Hedges pay unto sd Orphan the Sum of thirty Dollars Over & Above the Sum allowed by Law to Orphans at the Expiration of their time.

on the Motion of Joseph Worley Ordered that Samuel Teter, Wm. Sparks, Joseph Worley & John Ferguson, or any three of them, being first Sworn, do View the Nearest & best way for a Road from John Boggs Mill to Alexr. Wells, on Cross Creek, & make Report to Next Court.

Ordered that this Court be adjourned Untill Court in Course

SILAS HEDGES

(45) At a Court held for Ohio County Monday 1st November 1779; Present, Solomon Hedges, Silas Hedges, Wm. Scott, James Gillispy, Gents.

B & Sale from Isaac Taylor to William Polk, being formerly Proved by Thomas Gilliland & now Proved by Hugh Gilliland, OR

B & Sale from James Clemens to Robert Taylor, Acknowledged & OR

B & Sale from Edward Smyth to Isaac Smyth, acknowledged & OR.

Ordered that Andrew Ramsey do Act as Oveer from Wells' farm to Buffalo Creek, and Derrick Hogland From sd. Creek to the Court house, and that the Summons all the Tithables within three miles Each side the road to Work on sd Road

Administration of the Estate of Joseph Miller Deceased is Granted to James Clemens, he Complying with the Law; then sd Clemens gave Robt Taylor as his Surety. Ordered that Harry Martin, Wm Johnston, Robt Taylor, & Sammel Johnston, or any three of them, being first sworn, do appraise the Estate

Thomas Scott[1] Came into Court and took the Oath of an Attorney at Law and is Admitted to act as such

Present, Edward Robinson, Samuel McColloch, Gent.

Ordered that Robert Guthry be Summoned to Appear at Next Court to Declare what part of the Estate of Joseph Miller, Deceased, Remains in his hands

A Grand Jury for this County being Called, Samuel Mason was Sworn as Foreman, then Wm Sparks, James Garretson, John Carpenter, John Chapman, Joseph ogle, Joseph Wells, Charles Hedges, Thos Gilliland, Ezekiel Dewitt, Daniel Harris, Levy Mills, Thomas Chapman, Joseph Hedges, & Andrew Fouts was sworn

B & Sale from Joseph Wells to Isaac Miles, Ack & OR

(46) Appraisement of the Estate of John McColloch, Deceased, Returned to Court & OR

Gillespy v Dickeson } Ordered that the Defendant be Summoned to Next Court to Give sp. bail

Administration of the Estate of Samuel Kennedy is Granted to James Buchanan, he Complying with the Law; then s^{d} Buchanan Came into Court & Gave David McClure as his Surety

Ordered that Thomas Waller, Thos. Peek, David Hosack, & Neal Gillespy, or any three of them, being first Sworn, do appraise the Estate and make report to next Court.

B & Sale from Wm Hawkins to Peter Hildebrand, acknowledged & OR.

[1] Could this have been Thomas Scott, an adherent of the Pennsylvania jurisdiction, arrested by John Connolly's posse and taken before Lord Dunmore at Redstone Old Fort, in November 1774, just after the close of "Dunmore's War?" See Crumrine's History of Washington County, 178. That Thomas Scott resided on Dunlap's Creek near Redstone Old Fort, and on the organization of Washington County, Pennsylvania, became the first prothonotary of the new county, and was its representative in the First Congress of the United States.

Ordered that a Licence for keeping an ordinary be Granted unto Edward Smith, he Complying with the Law; then sd Smith Came into Court and Gave John Huff as his Surety.

Ordered that James Clemens take Care of the Real Estate of Joseph Miller Deceased, untill Further Orders.

Hawkins v Jacob & Mary Miller, Jacob Lefler SB.

Worley v Huff } Ordered that the Plt be Summoned to appear at next Court to Prosecute this Action or the same will be Dismist.

the Commissioners for Laying out a Road from Davis Mill to Court house Returned their Report to Court & OR.

Return of an Inquisition held by Chas. Wells & James Miller, Gent, Returned to Court & OR.

the Grand jury having made Severall presentments, Ordered that the Severall offenders be Summoned to next Court

B & Sale Isaac Miles to Joseph Smyth, ackd & OR. John Polk Security for Costs

(47) Buskirk v Barber } Ordered that a Didimus Issue to take the Examination of Elizabeth Ash for the Plt.

Rogers v Carpenter } Dismist

Ordered that this Court be adjourned untill tomorrow morning at 8 O'Clock

SOLOMON HEDGES

The Court Met According to Adjournment; Present, Solomon Hedges, Silas Hedges, Edward Robison, James Gillespie, Wm. Scott & Zachariah Sprigg, Gent.

Rogers v Carpenter } Ordered that Elijah Huff be allowed for four days attendance a Witness

Rogers v Carpenter } Ordered that Luke Scarmehorn be allowed For five days Attendance as a witness and Likewise ordered that Jacob Fokler be allowed For five days attendance in this Action as a witness

Robeson v Ashby } Attachment; the Sheriff returns he has Attached one hundred acres of Land or one half of a Survey and Summoned Isaac Taylor as a Garnishee

Isaac Taylor Came in, by Thos Scott his Atty, and moved that the s[d] Attachmt should be Quashed, Supposing the Same to be Improperly Brought; on Consideration the Court is of Opinion that the Same Shall Lye.

Ordered that the Court be adjourned to meet Immediately at Zachariah Spriggs Gent

SILAS HEDGES

(48) The Court met According to adjournment. Present, Solomon Hedges, Silas Hedges, W[m] Scott, Edward Robison & James Gillespy, Gent.

Then the Court Proceeded to Levy the County Levy

To James McMechen by acct	£80.17. 8
To David M[c]Clure for Extra Services	31.13. 2
To James Gillespy by acct	1. 0. 0
To Thomas M[c]Intosh by acct	36.12. 0
To W[m] Nimmons by Acct	6.12. 0
To David Shepherd for Extra Services for 1 year	28–14– 0
To David Shepherd for Express to Winchester or Ruther Zane's work	100 0 0
	£285– 8–10
To David Shepherd for Ball[n] of Last years acct	14– 6– 6
	£299–15– 4
To Sheriff for Collection	21 0 0
To a Depositum in the Sheriffs hands	31 14 8
	£352–10– 0
By 470 Tithables a 15s Each	£352 10 0

James Gillespy pd 5s, having recd that Sum for drunkenness

B & Sale from Robt Cwam to Charles M[c]Bride, Proved by James Gillespy one of the witnesses and Ordered to Lye for further proof.

M[c]Bride v Wolf, Cond.

Taylor v Caldwell, Cond.

Scott v Caldwell, Cond.

Caldwell v Mason, Cond.

Crow v Handly, Cond.
Taylor v templeton, Cond.
Caldwell v Gillespy, Dismist.
Wells v Carpenter, Agreed.
Tumbleston v Mason, Dismist.
Taylor v Caldwell, Cond.
Caldwell v Taylor, Dismist.
v the same, Dismist.

Ordered that the Sheriff Collect 15s from Each tithable Person within this County

(49) Hawkins v ogle, Cond.
v Wheat, Cond.
v Kintialo, Cond.
Jesse Martin v Williams, Cond.
v Cunningham, Cond.
v Dement, Cond.
v Martin, Cond.
Smith v Hawkins, Cond.
Hawkins v Kintialo, Cond.
Gilliard v Hawkins, Cond.
Virgin v Niccols, Cond.
Dewitt v Dunn, Cond.
Taylor v Williamson, Cond.
Sarah Taylor v Williamson, Cond.
Buchanan v Mason, Dismist.
v the same, Dismist.
Huston v Sayler, Cond.
Maddison v Stricker, Cond.
Lamb v Dewitt, Cond.
McGaughan v Wells, Con.
Miller v Cox, Cond.
v Geo & Mary Sparks, Cond.
Clerk v Huff, Cond.
Williamson v McBride, Cond.
Lamb v Wells, Agreed.
Mason v. McBride & Wilson, Cond.
Gillespy v Dukeson, Cond.
Buskirk v Barber, Cond.
Cox v Cane, Cond.

Barber v Spencer, Cond.
Worley v Huff, Cond.
M[c]Entire v Carpenter, Dismist.
Huff v Ryley, Agreed.
Flahavin v Huston, Cond.
English v Curry, Cond.
Holliday v Nelson, Cond.
M[c]Colloch v Sutherland, Cond.

Appearances

Hawkins v Miller, Cond.
v Guther, Agreed.
Moore, agreed.
(50) Huff v Boner, Agreed.
French v Graham, Cond.
Commonwealth v Paul, Judgn[t] for £10 & Costs

Petition and Summons

Hawkins v Kintialo, Con[d].

Attachment

Robeson v Ashby, Cond.

Ordered that Ezekial Dewitt do act as overseer for the Opening the Road from Boggs Mill to the Court house & that he Summons the tithables within one mile to North of sd Road & the tithables within three miles of the South of sd Road to work thereon.

Ordered that Samuel Mason do act as an oveer to make a Road from Jacob Wolfs to Thomas Wallers, and that he Summons the tithables within Three Miles Each side said Road to work thereon.

Ordered that David Shepherd, Brice Virgin, Rich[d] Dickerson, & Daniel Leet, or any three of them, being First Sworn, do View the Nearest & best way for a Road from Jacob Wolfs to the County Line Leading towards Redstone, & make Report to Next Court.

Ordered that a Review be made for a Road from W[m] Hawkins to the Forks of Whelan, & that W[m] Hawkins W[m] M[c]Entire, David Shepherd, & Samuel Mason, or any three of them, being first Sworn, do view the Same and make Report to next Court.

Ordered that Thomas Waller, Cha[s] Boner, David English, and Andrew Robinson, or any three of them, being first Sworn, do view the nearest and best way for a Road from Wallers fort to the County Line, Leading Towards Crawfords ferry, & make Report to next Court

Commonwealth v Isaac Taylor; a Number of Depositions being returned to Court against the Deft. the Court on Consider are of Opinion that the s[d] Taylor Be Dismissed

(51) Ordered that this Court be adjourned Until Court in Course

SILAS HEDGES

At a Court held for Ohio County, on Monday the 6th Day of March, 1780, Present.

Solomon Hedges, W[m] Scott, James Caldwell, & George M[c]Colloch, Gent.

Ordered that a License be Granted unto John Biggs to keep an ordinary at his house, he Complying with the Law; Whereupon sd John Came into Court and Gave Charles Hedges as his Surety. Present, Ebener Zane & Charles Wells, Gent.

Admn of the Estate of Thos Ryan, dec[d], is Granted to Silas Zane, he Complying with the Law.

Ordered that John Mitchell, Benjamin Hammitt, Joseph Vanmeter, & Jacob Reager, or any three of them, Being first Sworn, do appraise the Estate of Tho[s] Ryan.

Joseph Beeler came into Court And Proved his Service as a Captain in the Virginy Service in Col[o] Brocodes [Bouquet's] Campaign; he Likewise proved his being a Waggon master in General Forbes Campaign.

Present, James Miller, James Gillespy, Gen[t].

Carpenter v Rogers, Benjamin Biggs Enters S Bail.

Cox v Cane, slander. Ordered that a Didimus Issue to take the Deposition of Sarah Barber for the Plt

Wheat v Conner, slander. Ordered that a Didimus Issue to take the Deposition of James Beagham for Plt.

(52) William Flavhavin
v } debt
William Huston

Then Came the Parties and Jointly Prayed that the Differences Between them may be Enquired of by the Country without the form of a Declaration. Ordered that the Sheriff summons a Jury to attend Immediately to Enquire of the same: Whereupon James Clemmens, Jesse Martin, James Parks, James Moore, John Warford, James Andrews, Jacob Newland, James Garretson, Jacob Reager, Benjamin Biggs, Nicholas Rogers, & Samuel Mason, who being duly Elected and Sworn do say: [1]

Ordered that William Scott, Silas Hedges, Gent, be recommended to his Excellency to appoint One of them to Serve as a Sheriff in the Room of David Shepherd.

Joh̃n Carpenter fully proved to this Court that he served as a Soldier in the Old Virginy Regiment before 1763.

Matthew Fowler fully proved to this Court that he served as a Corporall in the Old Virginy Regiment before 1763

that [2] the Assess the Plts damage to Seventy pounds sixteen shillings; but it is Considered by the Court that this Judgment be Discharged by the payment of thirty Five pounds Eight Shillings, & Costs.

Ordered that a Licence be Granted Unto James Gillespy, Jun.r, to keep an Ordinary at his house, he Complying with the Law; Whereupon sd James Came into Court & Gave William Scott as his Surety.

Jesse Martin Came into Court & Fully proved his Service as an Ensign in the State of Virginy in the year 1758.

Jesse Martin Came into Court and proved his Serving as an Artificer in the Virginy Service in the year 1760.

(53) Joseph Worley v. Elijah Huff, Ordered that the Same Be Dismissed

Ordered that Andrew Scott be Appointed Constable For the Ensuing year in the Room of Jacob Reager.

James Parkes Proved to this Court that he Served as an artificer in the Virginy Service in the year 1760, and Ordered to be Certified.

John Carpenter
v
James Karr } Attachment, the Sheriff Returns he Could find no

[1] See verdict, infra.

[2] See beginning of entry, supra.

Goods, but has Summoned Arthur McConnell as Guarnishee. Ordered that the same Lye Over Untill to Morrow.

Wheat v Conner, Slander. On the Motion of the Deft that he should only be held to Common Bail, the Court Ordered it so.

Ordered that this Court be adjourned to meet at Zachariah Spriggs tomorrow at 8 o'clock.

WILLIAM SCOTT

The Court Met according to adjournment: Present, James Caldwell, George McColloch, Ebenezer Zane, & James Gillespy, Gents.

Certificate of a Stray Heifer is returned to Court by James Gillespy, Gent, & O.R.

Certificate of a mare is Returned to Court by John Boggs, Gent, & O.R.

(54) Certificate of a Stray Sow returned to Court by James Gillespy, Gent, & OR.

Certificate of a Stray Heifer is returned to Court by Charles Wells, Gent, & O.R.

Certificate of a Stray mare is returned to Court by Charles Wells, Gent, & OR.

Certificate of a Stray Colt is returned to Court by Wm. Scott, Gent, returned to Court & OR.

Certificate of a Stray Hogg is returned to Court by James Gillespy, Gent, & OR.

Certificate of five Stray Hogs is Returned to Court by Wm. Scott, Gent, & O R.

Certificate of a Bay mare is returned to Court by Wm. Scott, Gent, & O R.

Ordered that Edward Geither be summoned to attend at Next Court to answer the Complaint of his Late Servant John Rower.

Present Wm. Scott, Silas Hedges, Jas. Miller, Gent.

John Carpenter
v
James Kerr } Attachment. Ordered that John Doldridge, Arthur McConnell, John Huff, William Sparks, & Thomas Uri, be and they are hereby appointed to Settle all Disputes in this Action Between the parties and make report to next Court.

Davis v French, Jeremiah Dunn Enters himself Special Bail.

Worley v Huff; Ordered that Michael Huff Be allowed For three days attendance Before November, & three days Since Nov as a Witness in this Action.

Hedges v Tilton, Ordered that the same be Dismissed at Plt request.

(55) Certificate of a Stray Steer is returned to Court by James Miller, Gent, & OR.

Sarah Taylor
v
David Williamson Dismissed at Plts Request.

Robert Taylor
v
David Williamson Dismissed at Plts Request.

Appearances

Wheat v Kerr, Allias
Conner, Continued.
Beagham, Allias
Hawkins v Miller, Continued,
Wall v Miller, Allias.
Carpenter v Rogers, Continued & Set to Sept for tryall
Smyth v Curry Allias.
Garretson v Robinson, Settled & Costs paid.
Stroup v Williamson, Continued.
Hawkins v Rower, Continued.
State & Gillespy, v Virgin, Alias.
Gillespy v Virgin, Allias.
Tombleston v Mason, Allias.
Snowden v Alexander, Allias.
Lutes v Miller, Continued.
Roany v Smyth, Allias.
Mills v Stroup, Allias.
Wheat, Allias.
Tule Fitzgerald, Allias.
McGee Russell, Allias.
Davis v French, Continued.
Hedges v Tilton, Discontinued at Plts request, Costs paid.

Parks v Cox, Discontinued at Plts request Costs paid.
Miller v Lutes, Continued.
Ryley v Rogers, Continued.
(56) McBride Wolf, Continued.
Taylor v Caldwell, Continued.
Scott v Caldwell, Issue for tryal next Sept Court
Caldwell v Mason, Discontinued.
Crow v Handly, Continued.
Taylor v Templeton, Continued.
v Caldwell, Continued.
Hawkins v Ogle, Continued.
v Wheat Continued.
Kintialo, Eject. Judgment
Martin v Williams, Continued.
v Cunningham, Continued.
Dement, Continued.
Martin, Continued.
Smyth v Hawkins, Discontinued.
Hawkins v Kintialo, Trespass, Judgt & Writt of Enquirey.
Gilliard v Hawkins, Discontinued.
Virgin v Nichols, Continued.
Dewitt v Dunn, Discontinued.
Huston v Saylor, Discontinued.
Maddison v Stricker, Continued.
Lamb v Dewitt, Continued.
McGaughan v Wells, Continued.
Miller v Cox, Continued, set for tryal.
v Geo & Mary Sparks, Issue for tryal to Septr.
Clerk v Huff, Continued.
Williamson v McBride, Discontinued.
Mason v McBride & Wilson, Discontinued.
Gillespy v Dickeson, Discontinued.
Buskirk v Barber, Continued & Set Sepr for tryal.
Cox v Cane, Continued.
Barber v Spencer, Continued.
English v Curry, McKnight & Blackburn, Continued to Sept next for tryall.
Holliday v Nelson, Continued.
McColloch v Sutherland, Continued.

Hawkins v Miller, Discontinued.
French v Graham, Continued.

Appearances

(57) Davis v Tilton, Continued.
Cox v Mummey, Continued.
Delong v Snitiker, Allias.

Petition & Summons.

Hawkins v Kintialo, Judgmt, Fa Fie.

Attachments.

Robinson v Ashby, Discontinued at Plt[s] request.
Carpenter v Kerr, Continued.
Bolin v Dowlin, Continued.

Presentments

Commonwealth v Smyth, Continued
v Keller, Continued
v Moore, Continued
v Biggs Senr, Continued.
v Harris, Continued.
v Paul, Continued.
v Zane, Continued.
v Rogers, Continued.
v Graham, Continued.

Taylor v Williamson — Ordered that Eleazer Williamson be allowed for two days attendance as a witness in this action. And Likewise Ordered that David Frame be allowed for two days attendance in this Action.

Bargain & Sale from Patrick M[c]Gaughan to Joseph Scott, proved by W[m] Scott, one of the Witnesses, & Ordered to Lye for further Proof.

Bargain & Sale from Fulton to Dunlap, proved by Ed Robinson & And[w] Robinson, two of the Witnesses, & OR.

Bargain & Sale from Kidd to Fulton, proved by Edward Robinson & And[w] Robinson, two of the Witnesses, & O.R.,

Ordered that the Court be adjourned Until Court in Course

SILAS HEDGES

(58) At a Court held for Ohio County on Monday 3d day of April. Present, Salomon Hedges, Silas Hedges, Wm Scott, & Edward Robeson, Gent.

Appraisment of the Estate of Samuel Kennedy, Deceased, is Returned to Court, & O.R.

Bargain & Sale from Patrick M^c^Gaughan to Joseph Scott, Being formerly Proved by Wm Scott & now Proved by Andw. Scott, sd Lands Adjoin the Land of sd McGaughan on the south James Marshall on the North Andrew Scott on the West, & OR

Stroup v Williamson, Dismist for Non Prost. Ordered that Thomas Wiliiamson Be allowed for one days attendance in this action

M^c^Colloch v Sutherland; Judgment for One hundred & Sixty Pounds with Costs upon Nihell Dicitt. Ordered that this Court be adjourned Untill tomorrow 8 Oclock

SOLOMON HEDGES.

The Court Mett According to Adjournment; Present, Solomon Hedges, Silas Hedges, Edwd Robeson, & Zachariah Sprigg, Gentlemen.

On the motion of Wm Hawkins, Ordered that his mark a Cropp of the Left Ear & Slitt in the Right be Recorded.

On the motion of Henry Green, Ordered that his mark a Cropp of the Left Ear & hole in the same & slitt in the Right Be Recorded. Wm Hawkins Security for Costs.

Ordered that the Sheriff Summons a Grand jury to attend the Next Court

Ordered that Samuel Hill, an Orphan Child about 3 years Old; be bound unto David Caldwell according to Law, if the mother of sd Child will give her Consent to the Same.

(59) Common Wealth v E^d^ Smyth for Retailing of Spiritious Liquors; Judgment for Ten pounds & Costs.

v Peter Keller, Judgment for Ten pounds & Costs.

v James Moore, Judgment for Ten pounds & Costs.

v Benj^m^ Biggs senr. Judgment for Ten pounds & Costs.

v John Harris, Judgment for £10 & Costs.

v Jacob Paul, Judgmt for £10 & Costs.

v Nicholas Rogers, for prophane Swearing.

Judgment for 5 s. and Costs

v Samuel Graham Judgmt for 5 s & Costs.

Bethsheba Randle, Heiress at Law to David Randle who was killed on the field of Battle, Proved to this Court Sd. David Randle Served a Lieut in the Regular Service in the Year 1763, & O.R. that the Same be Certified.

James Park Proved to this Court that he Served as a Serjant in the Regular Service in the Year 1763, & OR that the same be Certified

Wheat v. Kerr, Plu Capias.

v. Beaghm, Plu Capias.

Wall v Miller, Plu Capias.

Smyth v Curry, Plu Capias.

State & Gillespy v Virgin, Plu Capias.

Gillespy v Virgin, Plu Capias.

Tomlinson v Mason, Plu Capias.

Snowden v Alexander, Dismist at Plts Request.

Berry v Smyth, Plu Capias.

Mills v Stroup, Plu Capias.

v Wheat, Plu Capias.

———v Fitzgerald, Plu Capias.

McGee v. Russell, Plu Capias,

Delong v Snidiker, Plu Capias.

Carey v Robinson, Cond.

Taylor v Williamson, Cond.

Caldwell v Martin, Condd.

(60) Carpenter v Bailey, All Capias.

Caldwell v Taylor, All Capias.

Graham v McDonald, All Capias.

v the Same, All Capias.

Zane v Reagan, Dismist.

Dunn v Snidiker, All Capias.

Huston v Sayler, All Capias.

Dewitt v Hupp, Dismist at Plts Request.

Hannah v Spencer, All Capias.

v the Same, All Capias.

Hawkins v Wheat, All Capias.

v Boney, All Capias.

Dunn v Taylor, Cond.

On the Motion of James Hannah Ordered that his mark a Crop of the Right Ear & hole in the Left Ear be Recorded

Ordered that this Court be adjourned Untill Court in Course

SOLOMON HEDGES

At a Court held for Ohio County on monday the 1st. day of May.

Present, Solomon Hedges, Silas Hedges, Zachariah Sprigg, & Geo. McColloch, Gent.

John Mitchell Came Into Court and Entered himself Security for the Good Behavior of Joseph Wilson Untill Next Court.

Ordered that this Court be adjourned Untill Seven OClock tomorrow Morning. SOLOMON HEDGES

(61) The Court met according to Adjournment. Present, Solomon Hedges, Silas Hedges, Geo. McColloch, & Saml. McColloch, Gent.

Certificate of a Stray Steer taken up by Andw. Roany, Before Solomon Hedges, Gent, is returned to Court & O R.

Bargain & Sale from Zephania Dunn to Wm. Johnston, Acknowledged & O R

Bargain & Sale from Zephania Dunn to Kennith McClelland, Acknowledged & OR.

Bargain & Sale from Zephania Dunn to Thomas Gilliland, Acknowledge O.R.

Wheat v Conner } Dismist at Plaintiffs Request.

On the motion of Silas Zane, Ordered that his mark a Slope of the Under side of Each Ear & his Brand S. Z. be Recorded.

DeLong v Snidiker } Zephania Dunn Enters himself S B

Dunn v Snidiker Zephania Dunn enters himself S. B.

Mills v Stroup } Jacob Reager Enters himself S B. Ordered that a Didimus Issue to take the Deposition of Conrad Wheat, Junr., for Defendant

(62) Dewitt v Garrison } Frederick Lamb Enters himself S. B.

Issues

M^c^Bride v Wolf, Dismist.
Taylor v Caldwell, Dismist.
Scott v Caldwell, Con^d^ to Sepr for tryal.
Crow v Handly, Con^d^.
Taylor v Caldwell, Dismist.
v Templeton, Dismist.

References

Hawkins v Ogle, Cond to Next Court for tryal.
v Wheat, Cond to Next Court for tryal.
Martin v Williams, Dismist.
v Cunningham, Dismist.
v Dement, Dismist.
v Martin, Dismist.
Virgin v Niccols, Con^d^ to Next Court for tryal.
Maddison v Stricker, Dismist.
Lamb v Dewitt, Dismist.
McGaughan v Wells, Continued to Next Court for tryal.
Miller v Cox, Con^d^ to Sepr for tryal.
v Geo & Mary Sparks, Con^d^ to Sepr for tryall.
Clerk v Huff, Contd to Next Court for tryall.
Buskirk v Barber, Cond to Sepr for tryall.
Cox v Cane, Cond to Next Court for tryall.
Barber v Spencer, Cond to Next Court for tryall.
English v Curry, Cond to Sepr for tryall.
Halliday v Nelson, Cond to Next Court for tryall.
McColloch v Sutherland, Cond on a Nihell Dicitt, Judgment.
French v Graham, Dismist at Plt^s^ Request.
Hawkins v Miller, Cond to Next Court for tryall.
Carpenter v Rogers, Cond to Sepr for tryall.
Hawkins v Bower, Cond to Next Court for tryall.
Lutes v Miller, Dismist.
(63) Taylor v Williamson, Cond to Sepr for tryall.
Davis v French, Cond.
Miller v Lutes, Dismissed at Plt^s^ Request.

Ryley v Rogers, Dismist at Plt[s] Request.
Davis v Tilton, Dismist.
Caldwell v Martin, Cond.
Cox v Mummy, Cond.
Dunn v Taylor, Cond.

Appearances

Wheat v Kerr, Dismissed at Pl[ts] Request.
Wall v Beagham, Dismist.
v Miller, a 2[d] Pl Capias.
Smyth v Curry, Cond.
State & Gillespy v Virgin, Attachm[t].
Gillespy v Virgin, Attachmt.
Tomlinson v Mason, 2[d] Pl Capias.
Berry v Smith, 2[d] Pl Capias
Mills v Stroup, Cond.
v Wheat, Cond.
Tuel v Fitzgerald, Dismissed.
McGee v Russell, 2[d] Pl Capias.
Delong v Snidiker, Cond.
Carpenter v Bailey, Cond.
Caldwell v Taylor, Cond.
Graham v M[c]Donald, Cond.
v The same, Cond.
Dunn v Snidiker, Cond.
Huston v Sayler, Cond.
Hannah v Spencer, Dismist.
v The same, Dismist.
Hawkins v Wheat, Pl Capias.
v Roney, Pl Capias.

(64) Bargain & sale from Benj[m] Biggs to James M[c]Kay, Acknowledged & O R

Appearances.

Manly v Rogers, cond.
Dewitt v Garrison, Cond Plea Not Guilty with Leave & Joinder.
Davidson v Wolf, allias.
Lamb v Bailey, Cond.
Huff v Bailey, Cond.

Cary v Robinson, capias.

Manly v Rogers } Frederick Lamb Enters himself S.B.

Carpenter v Kerr, Dismist.

On the motion of Ezekiel Dewitt, Ordered that his mark a Crop of the Near Ear be Recorded.

On the Motion of Yeates Conner, Ordered that his mark two Swallow Forks in Each Ear be Recorded.

On the Motion of Christian Snidiker, Ordered that his mark a Swallow Fork in the right Ear and Slitt in the Left Each be recorded.

On the motion of Matthew Kerr, Ordered that his mark a Crop & two Slitts in the Left Ear and upper bitt in the Right Ear be recorded.

A Bond Given to Ezekiel Dewitt by Frederick Lamb is OR

Ordered that Joseph Ogle, David English, David Williamson, Isaac Meek, Thomas Chapman, Samuel Glass, George Humprys, Thomas Gilliland, John Carpenter, Andrew Fouts, Daniel Harris, John Huff & George Dement, Each be Find in the Amount of two Hundred pounds of Tobacco for not Appearing agreeable to Summons as Grandjurymen.

(65) Ordered that Silas Zane, Conrod Stroup, Yeates Conner & And[w] zane, or any three of them, being first Sworn, do appraise the Estate of Walter Calhoon, Deceased, the former app[rs] being moved from that part of the County where the Estate Lyes so as the Cannott Attend.

Frederick Lamb applied this day to Ezekiel Dewitt For a rehearing of the plantation whereon Dewitt now Lives but said Dewitt positively refused.

Bolin v Dolin } Attachm no Goods found but Summoned sd Dolin as Garnishee & Ordered to be Continued.

Ordered that this Court be Adjourned Until Court in Course

SOLOMON HEDGES

At a Court held for Ohio County on Monday the 5th day of June, 1780.

Present, Solomon Hedges, E[d] Robeson, James Miller, & Zachariah Sprigg, Gent.

Joseph Vanmeter Fully Proved to this Court that he Served as a Soldier in a Ranging Compy in 1758 & 1759, Commanded by Rob[t] Rutherford, Cap[t] & Comandante & ordered to be Certified

Carey v Robinson, Dismist at Plts request.

Holliday v Nelson, Dismist for Non Prosecution.

Present, James Gillespy, & W[m] Scott, Gent.

Delong v Snidiker, debt; Tne parties appeared & prayed that their Cause may be Enquired of by their Country without the Formality of a Declaration, Ordered that the Sheriff Summons a Jury to appear Immediately to Inquire of the same. Whereupon Thomas Mills, George Dement, Ezekial Dewitt, Jacob Keller, John Wilson, Tho[s] Chapman, James Moore, Joseph Vanmeter, Conrod Stroup, John Mitchell, Daniel Harris & Joshua Russell, who being duly Elected & Sworn, do say that the Assess the Pltf damage to one Shilling & Costs. It is Considered by the Court that this Judgment be Discharged by the Payment of Six pounds twelve Shillings & Costs.

Ordered that Luke Scurmehorn, Sen[r], & Luke Scurmehorn, Jun[r] be allowed for One days attendance as Witness in this Action

(66) The award of an arbitration held between Ezekial Dewitt & Frederich Lamb is proved in Court & OR

On the Motion of William Carson Ordered that his mark a hole in the Left Ear & swallow fork in the Right Ear be Recorded.

Ordered that Jennet Clark, Daughter of Kiah Clark, now two Years of Age, be bound Unto William Carson According to Law, Agreeable to her Father & Mothers Request by Letter.

Jeremiah Dun v Christian Snidiker; Case, Dam £700, then Came the parties & Jointly Prayed that their Difference may be Enquired of by their Country without the Formality of a Declaration. Ordered that the Sheriff Summons a Jury to Appear Immediately to Enquire of the same. Whereupon Thomas Mills, George Dement, Ezekial Dewitt, Jacob Keller, John Wilson, Tho[s] Chapman, James Moore, Joseph Vanmeter, Conrod Stroup, John Mitchel, Daniel Harris & Joshua Russell, who being duly Elected and sworn, do say that the Find for the Def[t] THOMAS MILLS, FORMAN.

Ordered that Edward Geither Deliver unto John Bower in one month from this Date Clothing to the Value of two Hundred and Ten pounds to be adjudged by Wm. Hawkins & James Clemens to be worth that sum or that sum in money.

(67) Ezikeal Dewitt v James Garrison; Case. Then Came the parties & Jointly Pray that their Differences may be Enquired off by their Country without the Formality of a Declaration. Ordered that the Sheriff Summons a Jury to appear Immediately to Enquire of the same, whereupon George Dement, Derrick Hogland, Annaniah Davis, Samuel Glass, James Clemens, Joseph Ogle, Saml. Mason, Andw Fout, Isaac Meek, John Whitsel, Edward Geither & Daniel Harris.

Ordered that Luke Scarmehorn be Allowed for one Days Attendance in this Action.

State & Gillispie v Virgin, in Attachment; the sheriff returns there is nothing to be found.

Gillispie v Virgin, in attachmnt; the sheriff returns there is nothing to be found.

Wall v Miller, Ed Geither, S.B.

Hawkins v Geither, Jacob Miller, S.B.

Bower v Geither, Jacob Miller, S.B.

Davidson v Wolf, Jacob Wolf S.B.

Mc.Gee v Russell, James Clemens, S.B.

Miller v Wheat; Ordered that a Didymus Issue to take the Deposition of James Beagham.

Ordered that Thos. Gilliland, Isaac Phillips, & Isaac Ellis be recommended to his Excellency the Governour as Capts., & Timothy Downing, John Carpenter, Henry Nelson, James Brownlee, & John Bean, as Leuts.

(68) Thomas Holburt, Matthew Mackland, & Joseph Worley, as Ensigns of the Militia

Wm. Scott Came into Court & took the Oath of Sheriff of this County & Entered into Bond Accordingly.

Ordered that a Licence for Keeping an Ordinary be Granted unto Ezekial Dewitt at his house, he Complying with the Law. Whereupon sd Ezekial Came into Court & Gave John Carpenter as his Surety.

Assignment on a Bill of sale Dunn to Gilliland is acknowledged by Tho[s] Gilliland to Hugh Gilliland & O R.

Virgin v Niccols, Dismist at Plt[s] Request.

Ordered that this Court be Adjourned Until Eight OClock tomorrow morning.

E ROBINSON

(69) The Court Met According to Adjournment. Present, Solomon Hedges, Edward Robinson, James Miller & James Gillispie, Gentlemen.

Ordered that a Licence be Granted unto Jacob Wolf for Keeping an Ordinary at his house, he he Complying with the Law. Whereupon s[d] Jacob came into Court & Gave James Clemence as his Surety.

Then the Court Proceeded to Settle the Rates For ordinary Keepers.

Ordered that the Ordinary Keepers in this County sell at the following rates:

For half a pint of whiskey,	6 dollars.
For a breakfast or Supper,	4 ditto.
For 1 dinner,	6 ditto.
For Lodging with clean sheets,	3 ditto.
For 1 horse to hay one Night,	6 ditto.
For pasturage one Night,	3 do.
For 1 Gallon of Corn,	5 do.
For 1 Gallon of Oats,	4 do.
For half pint whiskey with negas,	8 do.
For 1 Quart strong Beer,	4 do.

Present Zachariah Sprigg Gent

Scott v Caldwell, Con[d] to Sep[r].

Crow v Handly, Cond.

Hawkins v Ogle, Judgmt confesed for Six pounds & Costs.

v Wheat Judgnt for Deft.

M[c]Gaughan v Wells, dismissed.

Miller v Cox, Cond to Sept.

v Geo & mary Sparks, Cond to Sept.

Clerk v Huff, Judgmt confessed for £11–4 & Costs.

Buskirk v Barber, Cond to Sep[r].

Cox v Cane, Cond.
Barber v Spencer, Dismissed.
English v Curry, Cond to Sep[r].
M[c]Colloch v Sutherland, Cond.
(70) Taylor v Williamson, Cond to Sep[r].
Hawkins v Miller, Dismissed at Plts request.
Carpenter v Rogers, Cond to Sep[r].
Hawkins v Bower, Dismissed at Plt[s] request.
Davis v French, Cond to next Court for Tryall.
Caldwell v Martin, Cond to next Court for Tryall.
Cox v Mummy, Cond to next Court for Tryall.
Dunn v Taylor, Dismist.
Smyth v Curry, Cond to next Court for Tryall.
Mills v Stroup, Cond to next Court for Tryall.
v Wheat, Cond to next Court for Tryall.
Carpenter v Bailey, Cond to next Court & Frederick Lamb Enters S B.
Caldwell v Taylor, Dismissed.
Graham v M[c]Donald, Cond to next Court for Tryall.
v the same, Contind to next Court for Tryall.
Huston v Saylor, Cond to Sep[r] for Tryall.
Manly v Rodgers, Cond.
Lamb v Bailey, Dismissed at Plts request.
Huff v Bailey, Dismissed at Plts request.
Wall v Miller, Cond.
Tomlinson v Mason, Dismissed at Plts request.
Roney v Smyth Attachment,
M[c]Gee v Russell, Cond.
Hawkins v Wheat, Cond.
v Roney, Attachment.
Davidson v Wolf, Cond.

(71) Ordered that Ebenezer Zane Take a List of the tithables from the Mouth of Whelan to the forks of said Creek; that Silas Hedges take a List of Capt Mitchells Compy; That James Miller take a List of Capt Ogles Compy; that George McColloch take a List of Leflers Compy. That Zachariah Spriggs take a List of Englishes Compy; That James Gillispie take a List of Ellis Compy; That James Caldwell take a List of Wil-

liamsons Compy; That John Williamson take a List of Philips Compy: That Charles Wells take a List of Gillilands Compy;

Appearances.

Graham v Hannah, Con[d].

Whitsell v Biggs, Dismist at Plts request.

Ward v Waller, Dismissed at Plts request.

v The Same, Dismist at Plts request.

v the same, dismissed at Plts request.

v the same, dismissed at Plts request.

Hawkins v Geither, Cond.

Bower v Geither, Cond.

Sharp v Summers, Allias.

Russell v Gillespie, Cond.

Russell v Gillespie, Cond.

Lamb v Barr, Dismissed at Plts request.

Attachments.

Bolin v Dolan, Dismissed.

State & Gillespie v Virgin, Dismissed.

Gillespie v Virgin, Dismissed.

(72) Ordered that Ann Brickell, Daughter of George Brickell, be Bound Unto Edward Robinson According to Law.

The Court is of Opinion that the Court house is Compleated by Isaac Taylor, & that his Bond for that purpose be Made Void.

On the Motion of Peter Keller, Ordered that his mark a Crop of the Right Ear & Slitt in the Left Ear be recorded.

On the Motion of Aron Delong, ordered that his Mark a Cropp off the Right Ear and an Under Slope in the Left Ear be recorded.

On the Motion of W[m] Scott, Ordered that his mark a Crop off the Near Ear and a Swallow Fork in the off Ear be recorded.

On the Motion of Jacob Keller, Ordered that his mark a swallow fork in the near Ear & a half Crop in the Upper side of the Off Ear.

Dewitt v Garrison, Ordered that this Action Lie Over Untill Next Court & that the Jury already Sworn do appear at the Court House the first day of Next Court to try the same Cause.

(73) Hawkins v Wheat. The Plt Appeared, the Deft failing to Appear though Solemnly Called, Ordered that the Sheriff Summons a Jury Immediately to appear to Enquire the same. Whereupon James Hannah, Aron Delong, Benjamin Biggs, Junr., James Garrison, W^{m}. Lamb, Ezekiel Dewitt, Robert French, James Moore, Isaac Taylor, James Andrew, Zephaniah Dunn & Andrew Moore, who being duly Elected and Sworn do say that they Find for the Deft

BENJ^{N} BIGGS, FORMAN

Ordered that this Court be Adjourned Untill Court in Course

SOLOMON HEDGES

(74) At a Call Court held for the Examination of Edward Chapman for Passing Money Supposed to be Counterfeit:

Present, Solomon Hedges, Silas Hedges, Zachariah Sprigg, James Caldwell, George McColloch, James Miller, & James Gillespie, Gent,

it is the Opinion of this Court that the said Edward Chapman, Now a Prisoner at the Barr, be Delivered to the Sheriff to Go to Goal, Unless he Can Give Security to appear at Next Grand jury Court

SOLOMON HEDGES

(76) at a Court held for Ohio County on Monday the 7th. day of August 1780.

Present, Solomon Hedges, Charles Wells, Zachariah Sprigg, James Miller, James Gillispie & John Williamson, Gent.

Commonwealth v Samuel Bruce; the Constable returns a Mitimus with the Body of sd Samuel; it appears by the Mitimus he was Committed on Supposition of stealing of a Bell, the property of James Dornan, of the Value of Nine pounds. The Court after hearing the Witnesses Examined is of Opinion that the sd Bruce is guilty of stealing sd bell & that the Sheriff take the sd Samuel Bruce and Give him Twenty-five Lashes on his Bare Back.

Certificate of a stray Horse taken up by Samuel Buskirk returned to Court & O.R.

Taylor v Williamson } Ordered that a Didimus Issue to take the Examination of David Frame, For Plt.

English v Curry } Ordered that a Didimus Issue to take the Examination of John Dickeson, for Plt.

Crow v Handly } Ordered that a Didimus Issue to Examine the Plts Evidence.

Wall v Miller, Debt; Judm[t] Confessed for Nineteen Pounds Four Shillings & Costs.

Miller v Hawkins, Dismissed at Plts request.

Hawkins v Miller, Dismissed at Plts request.

Ordered that Alexander Bowling do Act as Constable for the Ensuing year in the room of Harry Martin.

(77) James Gillespie, Gent, has returned his List of Tithables.

James Caldwell, Gent, has returned his List of Tithables.

Present Ebenezer Zane, Gent.

Whereas Rawley Martin, an Orphan Boy, being Formerly Bound to Harry Martin, is Brought to Court, it being supposed that the sd boy was Ill Used. After hearing the Evidence the Court is of opinion that the Boy be taken from sd Martin and Bound Unto Jacob Reager, to Learn the Art & Mistery of a Blacksmith, to be Bound According to Law. the Boy is Sixteen years of Age the First day of Last April.

Certificate of a Stray mare taken up by Thomas Stephenson is returned to Court & O.R.

Carpenter v Bailey, Dismissed at Plt[s] Request.

Ordered that this Court be adjourned For three Quarters of an hour.

The Court Met According to Adjournment.

Present, Solomon Hedges, E[d] Robeson, John Williamson, Samuel McColloch, James Gillespie, James Miller, Gent.

Admn is Granted Unto Geo Dement on the Estate of Joseph Black, Deceased, he Complying with the Law; whereupon sd Geo: Came into Court and Gave Jesse Dement his Surety.

(78) Ordered that John Williamson, Robt Taylor, James Caldwell & John Lane, or any of them, being First Sworn, do appraise the Estate of Joseph Black, Deceased, & make return to Next Court.

Isaac Taylor Came into Court & took the Oath of Deputy Sheriff.

Chas. Wells, Gent, returned his List of Tithables. Caldwell v Martin, Slander; the Defendant says the Plt is Perjured and he Can Prove it; therefore he Pleads Justification. Ordered that the Sheriff Summons a Jury to Attend Immediately, whereupon Annaniah Davis, Fred Lamb, James McCoy, John Harris, James Hannah, Aaron Delong, Senr, Derrick Hogland, Wm. Logan, Chas Hedges, Andw Zane, Andrew Fouts & John Nichols, Being Duly Elected & Sworn, do say that the Find the Plaintiff Guilty of False Swearing and Judgment on motion.

ANNANIAH DAVIS, Forman.

Ordered that James Gillespie Junr, Harry Martin, John Baker, Charles Tuel, Each be Allowed for One Days Attendance in this Action.

Ordered that Thos Pritchard be Allowed For Forty Miles traveling to Court & the same home & for one Days attendance at Court.

(79) Ordered that a Licence be Granted Unto David English to Keep an Ordinary at his house, he Complying with the Law. Whereupon sd David Came into Court & Gave Wm. Hawkins as his Surety.

Sharp v Summers, Jas. Caldwell, S.B.

Dewitt v Garrison, Dismissed at Plts request, it being agreed by the Parties.

Scott v Caldwell, Ordered that James Marshall & Thos. Urie do Act as Arbitrators in this Action & their Judgment to be Finall.

Ordered that Isaac Taylor & John Nichols Each be Allowed for four days Attendance as witnesses in this Action.

Ordered that this Court be Adjourned Untill Eight OClock tomorrow Morning

Ed. ROBINSON

(80) The Court Met According to adjournment. Present, Ed Robinson, James Miller, James Gillespie & John Williamson, Gent. Present Solomon Hedges, Gent.

Scott v Caldwell, Cond.

Miller v Cox, Do.

v Geo & Mary Sparks, Cond.

Buskirk v Barber, Cond.
English v Curry, Do.
Taylor v Williamson, Do.
Carpenter v Rogers, Do.
Huston v Sayler, Do.
Crow v Handly, Do.
Cox v Cane, Do.
M[c]Colloch v Sutherland, Do.
Davis v French, Do.
Cox v Mummy, Do.
Smyth v Curry, Dismissed.
Mills v Wheat, Cond to Oct[r].
v Stroup, Cond.
Carpenter v Bailey, Dismissed.
Graham v M[c]Donald, Cond.
v the same, Cond.

References

Manly v Rogers, Cond.
M[c]Gee v Russell, Cond.
Hawkins v Wheat, Dismissed.
Davidson v Wolf, Judgment for £56 & Costs.
Hawkins v Geither, Con[d].
Bower v Geither, Cond.
Russell v Gillespie, Cond.

Appearances.

Hawkins v Miller, Agreed.
Miller v Hawkins, Agreed.
Dunn v Taylor, Cond.
Bailey v Grooms, Allias.
Bailey v Bailey, Agreed.
Sprigg v Taylor, Agreed.
Bailey v Bailey, Agreed.
Gilliland v Gilliland, Allias.
Lutes v Miller, Allias.
v the Same, Allias.
Nichols v M[c]Caley, Cond.
Scott v Ryley, Allias.

Allias Capias

Sharp v Summers, Cond.

Attachments.

Roney v Smyth, Cond.

Hawkins v Roney, Cond.

Caldwell v Martin, Ordered that Joseph Wells & Isaac Ellis be Allowed Each 1 Days Attendance as Witness in this Action.

(81) Caldwell v Martin, Ordered that this Action be Continued to next Court for a Rehearing.

Ordered that David M^c^Clure be Appointed Full Clerk of this Court in the Room of James McMechen, who we Understand is out of this State this two Years, he was Sworn in Accordingly.

Ordered that the Sheriff Advertise the Goods taken in possession of Edward Chapman, a Late Prisoner, for sale the first Day of Next Court, in Order to Defray the Expenses incured on acct of Trying and securing s^d^ Chapman

Ordered that the Sheriff advertise the Goods taken in possession of David Gamble, a Late prisoner, For Sale on Monday the first Day of Next Court toward Defraying the Expenses incurred by said Gamble.

Certificate of a stray Horse taken up by Robert M^c^Guire is returned to Court & O R.

Andrew Lane Produced a Certificate that he had killed three wolves, to be Allowed him at the Laying of Next County Levy.

(82) Graham v Hanna, Case: dam. £300. Ordered that the Sheriff Summons a Jury to Enquire of this Cause Immediately. Whereupon Jesse Dement, John Nichols, Joseph Wells, George Dement, David Inglish, Charles Tuel, And^w^ Robinson, James Parks, Andrew Zane, Cornelius M^c^Entire, John Caldwell & Charles Hedges, who being Duly Elected & Sworn, do say the assess the Plt Damage to One hundred Dollars & Costs.

Ordered that Nicholas Rogers be allowed for two Days attendance in this Action.

(83) Ordered that the Ordinary Keepers in this County Sell at the Following Rates — viz:

	Dollars[1]
For Half pint whiskey,	6 do.
For Do with Sugar,	8 do.
For Breakfast or Supper,	6 do.
For Dinner,	10 do.
For Lodging with Clean sheets,	3 do.
For 1 Horse to hay 24 Hours	6 do.
For pasturage, Do,	3 do.
For 1 Gallon of Corn,	5 do.
For 1 Do Oats,	4 do.
For 1 Qt Strong Beer,	4 do.

Ordered that this Court be adjourned Untill Court in Course

JOHN WILLIAMSON

[The next term of this Court was held on September 4, 1780, but as Yohogania County had held its last term of court on August 28 of that year, and no Virginia Court was ever held afterward within the limits of Pennsylvania, our transcript of these court records will here end. Yet the Ohio County Court, removed from Black's Cabin to Wheeling in 1797, continues in existence to this day, and its ancient records are now in the custody of Mr. RICHARD ROBERTSON, the present Clerk of that Court, by whose kind permission we have been enabled to make our copy. This series of papers disclosing the transactions of these old Virginia Courts within the limits of Pennsylvania, will be followed in the next issue of the ANNALS OF THE CARNEGIE MUSEUM by a transcript of the Deed Book of the old court held for the District of West Augusta at Fort Dunmore, 1775–1776, before the division of that district into the three counties, Ohio, Yohogania, and Monongalia.— B. C.]

[1] For the depreciation of the currency of this date, see Vol. II, p. 210, of these ANNALS.

THE RECORDS OF DEEDS FOR THE DISTRICT OF WEST AUGUSTA, VIRGINIA, FOR THE COURT HELD AT FORT DUNMORE (PITTSBURGH, PA.), 1775–1776; COPIED CONSECUTIVELY AS RECORDED.

EDITED BY BOYD CRUMRINE, OF WASHINGTON, PA.

INTRODUCTION.

The following pages present a literal transcript of the original manuscript volume, in paste-board covers, in which were recorded by John Madison, the Clerk of the Court held for the District of West Augusta at Fort Dunmore, in 1775 and 1776, the contracts, deeds, and mortgages, proved, or acknowledged, before said Court and ordered to be recorded.

The record of the first deed recorded was "examined" and the deed delivered to Bernard Gratz, the grantee thereof, on May 28, 1775. Towards the end of the book, however, are found copied a number of instruments relating to real estate, the records of which are not shown to have been "examined" and attested by the Clerk. Why this was is not known.

No similar book, containing the records of deeds, etc., proved or acknowledged before the Court for Yohogania County, has been found. When that Court was organized and held its first day's session, to wit, on December 23, 1776, Virginia as well as Pennsylvania had become an independent State in the newly-formed United States of America; and one of the matters of business done on that day was to choose and appoint unanimously Dorsey Pentecost as the Clerk of Court, and to demand "the Records and Papers from John Madison, Junior, Deputy Clerk of East Augusta, in whose custody they are, which he peremptorily refused, notwithstanding he confessed he had seen an act of assembly directing him so to do," and to order "that a Process be issued to apprehend the said John Madison, and forthwith bring him before the Court to answer the above misdemeanor" (See Vol. II. of these ANNALS, pp. 79, 81).

This John Madison, Jr., was the son and deputy of John Madison, who had been appointed Clerk of the County Court of Augusta County when that court was first organized at Staunton, Va., to wit, on December 9, 1745, (Peyton's History of Augusta County, p. 32), and he had been sworn in as Deputy Clerk at the last term of the Court held at Fort Dunmore, to wit, on August 20, 1776, the next session being held at Augusta Town (now Washington, Pa.), on September 17, 1776, (Vol. I. of these ANNALS, p. 565). John Madison, the Clerk, was a cousin of the father of James Madison, who became President of the United States, and was the father of Rev. James Madison, long the distinguished head of William and Mary College, and the first Bishop of the Protestant Episcopal Church of Virginia. (Peyton's History of Augusta County, p. 345).

INDIAN TITLES.

To make the transcripts of the conveyances by George Croghan and others contained in the records following more intelligible, as well as to throw light upon entries made of transactions before the Court for the District of West Augusta, copies are presented of two old Indian conveyances made at the great Treaty with the Six Nations held at Fort Stanwix, now Rome, Oneida County, New York.

The French and Indian War had terminated in 1763, resulting in the ending of the French Occupation of the Monongahela and Ohio Valleys. The same year had occurred and ended Pontiac's Conspiracy, and a general peace with the Indians followed until Dunmore's War in 1774, the pioneers being disturbed only by sporadic Indian raids and depredations. The Indians, however, still claimed the lands upon the waters of the Monongahela, Allegheny, and Ohio Rivers as their own. These Indians, called by the French the Iroquois, formed a confederacy, named by the English "the Six Nations," composed of the Mohawks, Oneidas, Senecas, Onondagas, Cayugas, and Tuscaroras, and had their Council House, or seat of government, in the valleys of western New York. It was chiefly to establish certain boundaries limiting their exclusive rights on the East, that the Treaty at Fort Stanwix had been brought about.

The congress was opened on October 24, 1768. There were present Sir William Johnson, Baronet, his Majesty's Superintendent of Indian Affairs; William Franklin, Esq., Governor of New Jersey; Frederick Smith, Chief Justice of New Jersey; Thomas Walker,

Esq., Commissioner for the Colony of Virginia; Richard Peters and James Tilghman, Esqrs., for the Provincial Council of Pennsylvania; George Croghan, Daniel Claus, and Guy Johnson, Esqrs., Deputy Indian Agents, as well as many others of the whites, attracted by interest or curiosity; and on November 5, 1768, after full conference and extended discussion, at least three grants by the Six Nations already executed were delivered; one to Thomas Penn and Richard Penn, the proprietaries of Pennsylvania; one to William Trent, in trust for the Indian Traders whose goods had been carried off by the Indians from Logstown (below Pittsburgh) in 1763, and one to George Croghan, for himself absolutely.

By the cession to the proprietaries of Pennsylvania, the Six Nations granted a large tract of country lying within the general boundary of Pennsylvania and contained within the following limits, to wit:

"Beginning in the said Boundary Line, on the East side of the East Branch of the River Susquehanna, at a place called Owegy, and running with the said Boundary Line down the said Branch on the East side thereof, till it comes opposite the mouth of a Creek called by the Indians Awandae, and across the River and up the said Creek on the South side thereof, and along the Range of Hills called Burnett's Hills by the English, and by the Indians ———, on the north side of them, to the head of a Creek which runs into the West Branch of Susquehanna, which Creek is by the Indians called Tiadaghton, and down the said Creek on the south side thereof, to the said West Branch of Susquehanna; then, crossing the said River and running up the same on the south side thereof, the several Courses thereof, to the Fork of the same River, which lies nearest to a place on the River Ohio [Allegheny] called Kittanning, and from the said Fork, by a strait line to Kittanning aforesaid, and then down the said River Ohio [Allegheny], by the several Courses thereof, to where the western Bounds of the said Province of Pennsylvania crosses the same River; and then, with the said Western Bounds to the South Boundary thereof; and with the south Boundary aforesaid, to the East side of the Allegheny Hills, and with the same Hills, on the East side of them, to the West Line of a Tract of Land purchased by the said Proprietaries from the Six Nation Indians, and confirmed by their Deed bearing date the twenty-third Day of October, one thousand seven hundred and fifty-eight; and then with the Northern Bounds of that Tract to the River Susquehanna, and crossing the River Susquehanna, to the Northern Boundary line of another Tract of Land purchased from the Indians by Deed bearing Date the twenty-second Day of August, one thousand seven hundred and forty-nine; and then, with that Northern Boundary Line to the River Delaware, at the North Side of the mouth of a Creek called Lechawacsein; then up the said River Delaware, on the West Side thereof, to the Intersection of it by an East Line, to be drawn from Owegy aforesaid, to the said River Delaware; and then, with that East Line to the Beginning, at Owegy aforesaid."

The grant from which this quotation is made seems to have been dated November 5, 1768: See I Olden Time, p. 401; also, IX Col. Records, p. 554. But two other grants had already been executed, the first being that to William Trent, in trust for the Indian traders, dated November 3, 1768, here given in full, our copy having been made from the dupicate original parchment deed now or lately hanging in the State House at Philadelphia.

THE SIX NATIONS TO WILLIAM TRENT, IN TRUST.

TO ALL PEOPLE To whom these Presents shall come, Greeting: Know ye That We, Abraham, a Mohawk Chief; Sennghois, a Oneida Chief; Saguarisera, a Tuscarora Chief; Chenaugheata, Chief of the Onondaga Council; Tagaaia a Cayuga Chief, & Gaustarax a Seneca Chief; Chiefs and Sachems of the Six United Nations, and being and effectually representing all the Tribes of the Six United Nations, send Greeting:

WHEREAS, Robert Callender, David Franks, Joseph Simon, Levy Andrew Levy, Philip Boyle, John Baynton, Samuel Wharton, George Morgan, Joseph Spear, Thomas Smallman, Samuel Wharton, Administrator of John Welch, deceased, Edmund Moran, Evan Shelby, Samuel Postlethwait, John Gibson, Richard Winston, Dennis Crohon, William Thompson, Abraham Mitchel, James Dundas, Thomas Dundas, and John Ormsby, in and by their several and respective letters or Powers of Attorney duly signed, sealed, and delivered by them and now produced, interpreted and explained to us, have constituted, nominated and appointed William Trent, of the County of Cumberland and Province of Pennsylvania, Merchant, their lawful Attorney and Agent to ask, Sollicit, demand and receive from the Sachems, Councellors, and Warriors of the said Six United Nations, a Grant of a Tract of Land as a Compensation, Satisfaction, or Retribution for the Goods Merchandise and Effects of the said William Trent and the Traders aforesaid, Which the Shawanese, Delaware and Huron Tribes, Tributaries of the said Six Nations, (Contrary to all good faith, and in Violation of their repeated Promises of Safety and Protection to their Persons, Servants and Effects whilst Trading in their Country), did, in the Spring of the year one thousand seven hundred and sixty three, Violently seise Upon and unjustly appropriate to their own Use ;

AND WHEREAS, we are now convened in full Council by Order of our Father the King of Great Britain, France and Ireland, Defender of the Faith, &c., at Fort Stanwix, in the province of New York, in order to agree for, ascertain and finally fix and settle a permanent and lasting Boundary Line between the Hunting Country which we, at the Conference aforesaid, shall and will reserve for ourselves, our Children and our Tributaries, and the Territories of the said King of Great Britain.

AND WHEREAS application was formerly made to the Six United Nations by Sir William Johnson, Baronet, at the Requisition of the aforesaid Traders who had sustained and suffered the losses aforesaid, for a Retribution for the same, which the Six United Nations promised and agreed to, whensoever He the said Sir William Johnson, Baronet, should be empowered by his said majesty, the King of Great Britain, to establish the Boundary Line aforesaid ;

AND WHEREAS, the said Sir William Johnson, Baronet, has now at this present Congress reminded the said Six United Nations of their said Promise, and at the earnest desire of aforesaid Traders, by their Attorney, Strongly recommended to the Six United Nations to make them a Restitution by a Grant of a Tract of Land to his said Majesty the King of Great Britain, his Heirs and Successors, to and for the Only Use Benefit and Behoof of the said William Trent, in his own Right and as Attorney as aforesaid :

ALL WHICH the said Six United Nations, having taken into their Consideration and being heartily disposed to agree thereunto as an Instance of their Justice and Concern in the said losses, do therefore, by these Presents, signify publish and declare that notwithstanding the Grant and Gift hereby made and given by them Unto his said Majesty the King of Great Britain, and So forth, To and for the Only use Benefit and Behoof of the said William Trent, in his own Right and as Attorney as aforesaid, will be included within the Cession, Sale and Boundary Line which the said Six United Nations shall and will make, sell and grant to the said King of Great Britain, at the Conference aforesaid, holden at Fort Stanwix aforesaid, by the said Sir William Johnson, Baronet, yet nevertheless the said Six United Nations have neither asked, demanded, nor received from Him the said Sir William Johnson, Baronet, nor from any other Person or Persons in Behalf of the said King of Great Britain, any Consideration for the hereby given and granted Premises, neither shall nor will the said Six United Nations, nor their Heirs nor Descendants, (and by these presents They the Six United Nations wholly and intirely interdict and prohibit them from so doing), demand nor receive from the said King of Great Britain, nor from his Successors, nor from his or their Ministers or Servants, any Consideration whatsoever or howsoever for the hereby granted, bargained or now given premises, or any part, purpart, or parcel thereof, the same being their own Voluntary Act and Deed Solely and bona fide designed and intended by Them as a Compensation, Satisfaction and Retribution for the Losses sustained by the said William Trent and the Indian Traders aforesaid by the Depredations of the Shawnesse, Delaware and Huron Tribes of Indians aforesaid In the aforesaid Year one thousand seven hundred and sixty three:

NOW THIS INDENTURE WITNESSETH That we the said Abraham, Sennghois, Saguarisera, Chenaugheata, Tagaaia, and Gaustarax (Chiefs and Sachems of the said Six United Nations, and being and effectually as aforesaid representing all the Tribes of the said Six United Nations), for and in the consideration of the Sum of Eighty Five Thousand Nine Hundred and Sixteen Pounds, Ten Shillings and Eight Pence, lawfull Money of the Province of New York, (the same being the amount of the Goods and Merchandise which were unjustly seized and taken as aforesaid by the Shawnesse, Delaware and Huron Tribes of Indians aforesaid, from the said William Trent, Robert Callender, David Franks, Joseph Simon, Levy Andrew Levy, Philip Boyle, John Baynton, Samuel Wharton, George Morgan, Joseph Spear, Thomas Smallman, Samuel Wharton, Administrator of John Welch, deceased, Edmund Moran, Evan Shelby, Samuel Postlethwait, John Gibson, Richard Winston, Dennis Crohon, William Thompson, Abraham Mitchel, James Dundas, Thomas Dundas, and John Ormsby, in the aforesaid year one thousand seven hundred and sixty three, Whereof just and fair Accounts have on Oath anp

Affirmation been produced, interpreted and explained to Us and which at our Desire are now lodged and deposited with the said Sir William Johnson Baronet; And for and in Consideration of the Sum of Five Shillings, lawfull Money aforesaid, to Us in hand paid by the said William Trent, the Receipt whereof We do hereby acknowledge, Do give, grant, bargain and Sell Unto his said Majesty, his Heirs and Successors, to and for the only use Benefit and Behoof of the said William Trent, in his own right and as Attorney aforesaid:

All that Tract or parcel of Land BEGINNING At the Southerly side of the Mouth of little Kanawha Creek, where it empties itself into the River Ohio, and Running from thence South East to the Laurel Hill; Thence along the Laurel Hill until it strikes the river Monongahela; Thence down the Stream of the said River Monongahela, according to the several Courses Thereof, To the Southern Boundary Line of the province of Pennsylvania; Thence Westerly along the Course of the said Province Boundary Line as far as the same shall extend, and from Thence by the same Course to the River Ohio; Thence down the said River Ohio according to the several Courses thereof to the place of Beginning,

TOGETHER with all and Singular the Trees, Woods, under-Woods, Mines, Minerals, Oars, Waters, Water-Courses, Fishings, Fowlings, Huntings, Profits, Commodities, Advantages, Rights, Liberties, Passages, Hereditaments, and Appurtenances, whatsoever, to the said Tract or Parcel of Land belonging or in any wise appertaining, or which now are or formerly have been accepted, reputed, taken, known, and Occupied, or enjoyed, to or with the same or as part, parcel or Member Thereof; and the Reversion and Reversions, Remainder and Remainders, Rents, Issues, and Profits of all and singular the said premises above mentioned and every part and parcel thereof, with The Appurtenances; and also all the Estate, Right, Title, Interest, property, claim and demand, whatsoever, whether Native, legal or equitable, of Us the said Indians and Each and Every of Us and of all and every other person and persons whatsoever of or belonging to the said Nations, of, in, to and out of all and singular the Premises above mentioned and of, in, to, and out of Every part and parcell thereof, with the appurtenances,

TO HAVE AND TO HOLD all and singular the said Tract, Parcel and parcells of Land, given, granted and bargained Premises, with their Appurtenances, Unto his said Majesty King George the

Third, his Heirs and Successors, but to and for the Only use Benefit and Behoof of the said William Trent, in his own Right and as Attorney aforesaid, his Heirs and assigns, forever;

AND the said Abraham, Sennghois, Saguarisera, Chenaugheata, Tagaaia, and Gaustarax, for themselves and for the said Six United Nations and all and Every Other Nation and Nations, Tribes, Tributaries, and Descendants of the said Six United Nations, and their and Every of their posteritys, the said Tract and Parcell of Land and Premises and Every Part thereof, against them the said Abraham, Sennghois, Saguarisera, Chenaugheata, Tagaaia, and Gaustarax, And against the said Six United Nations and their Tributaries and Descendants, and all and Every of their posteritys, to his said Majesty, his Heirs and Successors, but to and for the Only Use Benefit and behoof of the said William Trent, in his own Right and as Attorney aforesaid, his Heirs and Assigns, Shall and will Warrant and forever defend by these Presents.

IN WITNESS Whereof, we, the said Chiefs and Sachems, in behalf of Ourselves respectively and in behalf of the whole Six United Nations aforesaid, have hereunto set Our hands and seals, In the presence of the persons Subscribing as Witnesses hereunto, at the Congress held at Fort Stanwix aforesaid, this the Third day of November, in the Ninth year of his Majesty's Reign, and In the Year of our Lord One thousand seven Hundred and Sixty Eight.

ABRAHAM, or TYCHAURISERA (Seal),
Chief of [*Totem*] *the Mohawks.*
WILLIAM, or SENNGHOIS (Seal),
Chief of [*Totem*] *the Oneidas.*
HENDRICK, or SAGUARISERA (Seal),
Chief of [*Totem*] *the Tascaroras.*
BUNT, or CHENAUGHEATA (Seal),
Chief of [*Totem*] *the Oonondagas.*
TAGAAIA (Seal),
Chief of [*Totem*] *the Cayuagas,*
GAUSTERAX (Seal),
Chief of [*Totem*] *the Senecas.*

Sealed and delivered in the presence of us — The letters (d n and the words to said) being first interlined; the words Sennghois, Saguarisera, Chenaugheata wrote in a Razure.

WM. FRANKLIN,
Governor of New Jersey.

FRE. SMYTH,
Chief Justice of New Jersey.
THOMAS WALKER,
Commissioner for Virginia.
RICHARD PETERS and JAMES TILGHMAN,
Of the Council of Pennsylvania.
JOHN SKINNER,
Captain of the 70th Regt.
JOSEPH CHEW,
of Connecticut.
JOHN WITHERHEAD,
of New York.
JOHN WALKER,
of Virginia.
E. FITCH,
of Connecticut.
THOMAS WALKER, Jun.,
of Virginia.
JOHN BUTLER,
Interpreter for the Crown.

Recorded in the office for recording of Deeds for the City and County of Philadelphia, in Book J., vol. 5, page 243, etc.

Certified under my Hand & Seal of my Office aforesaid, This 12th day of January, 1769.

[Seal] Will Parr, Recd.

[ON MARGIN.]

This is the Copy of the Grant mentioned in The annexed Affidavit of John Skinner, Esquire, SWORN before me this Day.

Dated the Third Day of February, One Thousand Seven Hundred and Seventy Six.

WILLIAM ATKINSON,
MAYOR,
of New Castle upon
Tyne in the Kingdom
of Great Britain.

William Trent, the grantee of the foregoing deed, was the Captain Wm. Trent, under whom Ensign Edward Ward, with his small force of men, was constructing the fort at the Forks of the Ohio, when, on April 17, 1754, he surrendered to the French and Indians, who completed the fort and called it Fort Duquesne. Subsequently Trent must have executed a sufficient conveyance to his beneficiaries for their interests in this grant, for at a session of the Court for the District of West Augusta held on April 17, 1776, there were proved and ordered to be recorded a "Deed of Lease and Release of Trust from William Trent," to the many persons named, and a "Deed of Partition from and between the same Persons," showing how very many individuals had by that time become interested in this celebrated grant: Vol. I of these ANNALS, page 562.

On November 4, 1768, the day after the above-mentioned grant to William Trent, in trust, and the day before the delivery of the cession to the proprietaries of Pennsylvania, there was made a grant to George Croghan, which is presented here because of the many grants made under it of lands lying on the south side of the Monongahela and Ohio, extending southward to the neighborhood of the present Bridgeville, or beyond, which grants are recorded in the records to be presented.

THE SIX NATIONS TO GEORGE CROGHAN.

TO ALL PEOPLE to whom these presents shall come, Greeting: Know ye, that we, Abraham, a Mohawk chief; Sennghois, an Oneida chief; Chenaugheata, an Onondaga chief; Tagaaia, a Cayuga chief, and Gaustarax, a Seneca chief, chiefs and sachems of the Six United Nations, and being and effectually representing all the tribes of the Six United Nations, send greeting.

WHEREAS, Iohonerissa, Scaroyadia, Cosswentanica, chiefs or sachems of the Six United Nations, did, by their deed duly executed bearing date the 2nd day of August, 1749, for and in consideration of the following goods and merchandise being paid and delivered to them at a full council of the Six United Nations, Delawares and Shawanese, held at Logstown, on the river Ohio, on the 2nd of August, 1749, that is to say: 240 strouds, 400 Duffield blankets, 460 pairs of half thick stockings, 200 shirts, 20 pieces of calico, 20 pieces of callimancœ, 20 pieces of embossed serge, fifty pounds of vermillion, 50 gross of gartering, 50 pieces of ribbon, 50 dozen of knives, 500 pounds of gunpowder, 1000 of bar lead, 3000 gun flints, 50 pounds of brass kettles, 4 pounds of thread, 1000 needles, ten dozen jews-harps, 20 dozen tobacco tongs, and 100 pounds of tobacco: grant and sell unto George Croghan, of the Province of Pennsylvania, Esquire, in fee, a certain tract or parcel of land, situate, lying and being on the southernly side of the river Monongehela: BEGINNING at the mouth of a run nearly opposite to Turtle Creek, and then down the river Monongehela to its junction with the river Ohio, computed to be ten miles; then running down the eastern bank and sides of and unto the said river Ohio to where Raccoon creek empties itself into the said river; thence up the said creek ten miles, and from thence on a straight or direct line to the place of beginning on the aforesaid river Monongehela, CONTAINING, by estimation, one hundred thousand acres of land, be the same more or less.

AND WHEREAS, the said Iohonerissa, Scaroyadia and Cosswentanica, chiefs or sachems, as aforesaid, for the consideration hereinafter mentioned to them in full council, as aforesaid, paid and delivered, that is to say: 140 strouds, 240 Duffield blankets, 275 pair of half thick stockings, 120 shirts, 12 pieces of calico, 12 pieces of callimancœ, 12 pieces of embossed serge, 30 pounds of vermillion, 12 gross of gartering, 30 pieces of ribbon, 30 dozen knives, 300 pounds of gunpowder, 600 of bar lead, 1000 gun flints, 30 pounds of brass kettles, 4 pounds of thread, 500 needles, six dozen of jews-harps, six dozen tobacco tongs, and 50 pounds of tobacco: did, by one other deed bearing date the same day and year last aforesaid, grant, bargain and sell unto the said George Croghan, in fee, one other tract or parcel of land, situate, lying and being on the river Yoxhiogeni, including the Indian village called the Seurchly[1] old town; the same tract or parcel of land containing 15 miles in length, on the said river, and ten miles in breadth, and including the lands on both sides of the said river Yoxhiogeni, which 15 miles in length and ten miles in breadth, he, the said George Croghan, has liberty to locate either upon or down the said Yoxhiogeni, but nevertheless in such manner so as to include and locate the said Indian village and land called the Seurchly[1] old town, which said tract or parcel of land contains, by estimation, 60,000 acres, be the same more or less.

AND WHEREAS, the said Iohonerissa, Scaroyadia and Cosswentanica did, by one other deed, bearing date the day and year last aforesaid, for the consideration herein mentioned to them in full council paid and delivered, as aforesaid, that is to say: 96 strouds, 160 Duffield blankets, 184 pair of half thick stockings, 80 shirts, 8 pieces of calico, 8 pieces of embossed serge, 20 pounds of vermillion, 20 gross of gartering, 20 pieces of ribbon, 20 dozen of knives, 200

[1] Perhaps Sewickley.

pounds of gunpowder, 400 of bar lead, 1000 gun flints, 20 pounds of brass kettle, 2 pounds of thread, 500 needles, 4 dozen jews-harps, 4 dozen tobacco tongs, 50 pounds of tobacco: Grant, bargain and sell unto the said George Croghan, in fee, one other tract or parcel of land, situate, lying and being, and BEGINNING on the east side of the river Ohio, to the northward of an old Indian village, called Shanopinstown, at the mouth of a run called the two mile run; then up the said two mile run where it interlocks with the heads of the two mile spring, which empties into the river Monongahela; then down the said two mile spring to the several courses thereof unto the sd. Monongehela; then up the said river Monongehela to where Turtle Creek empties itself into the same river; then up the said Turtle creek to the first forks thereof; then up the north or northerly branch of the said creek to the head of the same; thence a north or northerly course until it strikes Plum creek; then down said Plum creek until it empties itself into the river Ohio, and then down the said river Ohio to the place of beginning, where, as aforesaid, the two mile run discharges itself into the said river Ohio; CONTAINING by estimation 40,000 acres, be the same more or less,

Which said several grants, bargains and sales, [were] duly made and executed, by the last mentioned chiefs or sachems, in pursuance of certain powers and authorities delegated to and vested in them for the purpose aforesaid by the chiefs or sachems of the Onondaga Council, in full council assembled;

AND, WHEREAS, the said first-mentioned chiefs or sachems of the Six United Nations, parties to these presents, are not only truly and sensible and convinced that the said George Croghan hath faithfully and justly paid and delivered unto Iohonerissa, Scaroyadia and Cosswentanica, chiefs or sachems as aforesaid, all and several the goods and merchandize herein particularly recited and mentioned, but of the great justice and integrity of the said George Croghan, used and reserved by him towards the said Six Nations and their allies in all his public and private conduct and transactions, wherein they have been concerned:

NOW, KNOW YE THEREFORE, that we, the said chiefs or sachems of the Six United Nations, in full council assembled at Fort Stanwix, for and in consideration of the sum of five shillings to them in hand paid by the said George Croghan, the receipt whereof they do hereby acknowledge, and for and in consideration of the aforesaid goods and merchandize paid and delivered by him unto Iohonerissa, Scaroyadia, Cosswentanica, chiefs as aforesaid, have granted, bargained, sold and aliened, released, enfeoffed, ratified and fully confirmed, and by these presents do grant, bargain, sell, alien, release, enfeoffe, ratify and fully confirm unto his Most Sacred Majesty George III., King of Great Britain, France and Ireland, Defender of the Faith, &c., his heirs and successors, for the use, benefit and behoof of the said George Croghan, his heirs and assigns, all those the above described or mentioned tracts or parcels of land, granted or intended to be granted by the said several recited deeds as aforesaid, and also all mines, mineral ores, trees, woods, underwoods, waters and water courses, profits, commodities, advantages, rights, liberties, privileges, hereditaments and appurtenances whatsoever unto the said several tracts or parcels of land belonging or any way appertaining; and also the reversion and reversions, remainder and remainders, rents, issues and profits thereof, and of every part or parcel thereof, and all the estate, right, title, interest, use, property, possessions, claim and demand of them, the said Abraham, Sennghois, Saguarisera, Chenaugheata, Tagaaia, Gaustarax, chiefs or sachems aforesaid, and of all and every other person and persons whatsoever, or belonging to said nations, of, in, to and out of the premises, and every part and parcel, thereof,

TO HAVE AND TO HOLD the said several tracts and parcels of land, and all and singular the said granted or bargained premises, with the appurtenances, unto his said Majesty, his heirs and successors, to and for the only use, benefit and behoof of the said George Croghan, his heirs and assigns forever;

AND the said Abraham, Sennghois, Saguarisera, Chenaugheata, Tagaaia and Gaustarax for themselves and for the Six Nations, and all and every other nation and nations, tributaries and dependents on the said Six United Nations, and their and every of their posterity, the said several tracts of land and premises and every part thereof, against them, the said Abraham, Sennghois, Saguarisera, Chenaugheata, Tagaaia and Gaustarax, and against the said Six United Nations, and their tributaries and dependents, and all and every of their posteritys, unto his said Majesty, his heirs and successors, to and for the only use, benefit and behoof of the said George Croghan, his heirs and assigns, shall and will warrant and forever defend, by these presents;

PROVIDED, always, nevertheless, and it is the true intent and meaning of these presents, and the said Abraham, Sennghois, Saguarisera, Chenaugheata, Tagaaia and Gaustarax, do hereby covenant and agree to and with his said Majesty and his heirs and successors, to for the only use, benefit and behoof of the said George Croghan, his heirs and assigns, that if any or all of the said several tracts of land or any part thereof, shall hereafter be found to be within the bounds and limits of a certain grant bearing date the 4th of March, 1681, made by Charles II., King of Great Britain, &c., to William Penn, Esq., for the tract of country called and known by the name of Pennsylvania, that then and in such case, his said Majesty, his heirs and successors, to and for the only use, benefit and behoof of the said George Croghan, his heirs and assigns, shall be permitted and shall have and enjoy full right, power and authority to survey and locate the said several quantities of 100,000 acres, 60,000 and 40,000 acres of land, be the same more or less, as contained within the limits and bounds of the said several and respective tracts or parcels of land mentioned and described as aforesaid, in such quantities and in such parts and places of, in and within the cession or grant of land or territory, which shall be ceded and granted at the conference aforesaid, to the said King of Great Britain by the chiefs or sachems of the said Six United Nations, anything herein contained to the contrary thereof in any wise notwithstanding.

In witness whereof the said chiefs and sachems, in behalf of ourselves, respectively, and in behalf of the whole Six United Nations aforesaid, have hereunto set our hands and seals, in the presence of the persons subscribing as witnesses hereunto, at a Congress held at Fort Stanwix, aforesaid, this, the 4th day of November, in the year 9th of his Majesty's reign, and in the year of our Lord 1768.

ABRAHAM, OR TYCHAUESERA, *a chief of the Mohawks.*	The mark [The Steel] (l. s.) of his nation.
WILLIAM, OR SENNGHOIS, *a chief of the Oneidas.*	The mark [The Stone] (l. s.) of his nation.
HENDRICK, OR SAGUARISERA, *a chief of the Tuscaroras.*	The mark [The Cross] (l. s.) of his nation.
BURT, OR CHENAUGHEATA, *a chief of the Onondagas.*	The mark [The Mountain] (l s.) of his nation.
TAGAAIA, *a chief of the Cayugas.*	The mark [The Pipe] (l s) of his nation.
GAUSTERAX, *a chief of the Senecas.*	The mark [The High Hill] (l. s) of his nation.

Sealed and delivered in the presence of us: The word "Croghan" being first written on Rasures eleven times, and the words "and, or down tract," being first interlined. Sealed and delivered in presence of us all, the foregoing interlineations, Rasures and writings on Rasures being first made.

WM. FRANKLIN, Governor of New Jersey.
FRE. SMYTH, Chief Justice of New Jersey.
THOMAS WALKER, Commissioner for Virginia.
RICHARD PETERS, } of the Council of Pennsylvania.
JAMES TILGHMAN, }
JOHN SKINNER, Capt. in the 70th Regiment.
JOSEPH CHEW, of Connecticut.
JOHN WEATHERHEAD, of N. Y.
JOHN WALKER, of Virginia.
E. FITCH, of Connecticut.
THOMAS WALKER, JUNIOR, Virginia.
JOHN BUTLER, Interpretor for the Crown.

The foregoing deed to George Croghan is copied here from Peyton's History of Augusta County, page 74. It was recorded in the Recorder's office at Philadelphia, and on September 23, 1775, it was offered for proof and record before the Court for the District of West Augusta held at Fort Dunmore on that date, but objection being made it was ordered to lie over for further proof. (See Vol. I of these ANNALS, page 554.)

It will be remembered that in 1768, the year of the treaty at Fort Stanwix when all these Indian grants were made, the boundary controversy between Pennsylvania and Virginia was not yet ended, and it was still unknown how far the province of Pennsylvania extended to the westward. Mason and Dixon, when extending the southern boundary line in 1767, had been stopped by the Indian chiefs composing their watchful escort, at the second crossing of Dunkard Creek, in the southern part of Greene County, at a point thirty six miles short of Pennsylvania's five degrees of longitude from the Delaware; "it was the will of the Six Nations that the survey should be stayed:" Latrobe's Address. But, when it was settled by the Baltimore Conference of 1779 that the southern boundary of Pennsylvania should be extended to its full length, and that from the southwest corner thus reached the western boundary should be a line drawn due north from that corner, then it became known to a certainty that the grants to William Trent, in trust, and to George Croghan, had both become worthless as to lands within the boundaries of Pennsylvania.

The southwest corner and the western boundary of Pennsylvania were actually marked out on the ground in 1784–5; and Croghan's grant, which had been fruitlessly relied upon to protect the settlers upon George Washington's lands in what is now Mt. Pleasant Township, Washington County, Pennsylvania, became extinct; it is still in evidence, however, by marks upon trees occasionally confusing the surveyors of the present day. And by the beneficiaries under the deed to William Trent, in trust, there was formed the Indiana Company, which had quite an interesting history. Pushed out of Pennsylvania, as it eventually was, Lieutenant Thomas Hutchins, an engineer with Bouquet's expedition, made a survey of its lands in what is now West Virginia, about the southwestern corner of Pennsylvania. The company called its immense tract "Indiana," and pressed a recognition of its title successively before the Legislature of Virginia, the Congress of the United States, and the United States Supreme Court, and failed in all its efforts; so that for a hundred years that celebrated grant, also, has been a matter of ancient history only.

It is manifest, however, that at the time all these Indian grants were made it was believed that the western boundary of Pennsylvania would fall on a line parallel with the meanders of the Delaware River, and would eventually lie somewhere east of the Monongahela River at Pittsburgh.

TRANSCRIPT OF THE RECORD OF DEEDS.

(1)[1] EXAMINED AND DELIVERED
Bernard Gratz, May 28, 1775.

This indenture made the tenth day of July in the year One Thousand Seven Hundred and seventy two Between George Croghan Esquire on the one part and Bernardus Gratz of the City of Philadelphia Merchant on the other part: Whereas Iohonorissa Scaraydia and Cosowantinecea, Cheifs or Sachems of the Six United Nations of Indians, did by their deed duly Executed Bearing date the Second day of August One Thousand Seven Hundred and forty nine for the Consideration therein Specified Grant Bargain and Sell unto the

[1] The marginal figures represent the pages of the original record.

said George Corghan in Fee a Certain Tract or Parcel of Land Situate lying and being on the South side the Monongahela River Beginning at the Mouth of a Run nearly Opposite to Turtle Creek and then down the said Monongahela River to its Junction with the River Ohio Computed to be ten Miles, then Running down the Eastern bank or side of the said River Ohio to where Racoon Creek empties itself into the said River. Thence up the said Creek ten miles, and from thence on a direct line to the place of beginning; Containing by Estimation One hundred thousand Acres be the same more or less as by the said Deed may more fully appear; And Whereas certain chiefs or Sachems fully representing the Six united Nations aforesaid in full Council at Fort Stanwix Assembled did by their deed duly executed bearing date the fourth day of November One thousand seven hundred and sixty eight for the Consideration therein mentioned grant ratify and confirm unto his most Sacred Majesty George the third by the Grace of God King of Great Britain france and Ireland &c his heirs and successors for the Use benefit and behoof of the said George Croghan all the above bounded and described tract or parcel of Land and premises as by the said Deed Poll Recorded in the Office for recording of Deeds in the City and County of Philadelphia in Book J Volume the fifth Page the two hundred and thirty ninth &c may more fully and at large appear Now this Indenture Witnesseth that the said George Croghan for and in Consideration of the sum of Six hundred pounds lawful money of Great Britain to him the aforesaid George Croghan by Him the aforesaid Bernard Gratz in hand paid the
(2) receipt whereof the said George Croghan doth hereby acknowledge And by these Presents doth freely and absolutely grant bargain and sell alien release and confirm unto the said Bernard Gratz (in his actual possession now being by virtue of a Bargain and Sale thereof to him made for one whole year by Indenture bearing date the day next before the day of the date of these presents and by force of the Statute for transferring of Uses into possession) and to his heirs and Assigns for ever A Certain tract or parcell of Land being part of the aforesaid tract of Land situate lying and being on the West branch of Racoon Creek, Beginning at a White Oak tree marked on two

sides with three Notches and a Blaze above them being the most South Westerly Corner of the aforesaid tract of Land granted by the United Nations of Indians as aforesaid North forty three Degrees and thirty Minutes East, three hundred Chains to a stone, thence South fifty-Six Degrees and twenty one minutes East three hundred and fifty Chains to a Stone Corner of Joseph Simons's Land, thence by the said Simons's Land South fifty Degrees and thirty minutes West three hundred and seventy two Chains and ninety links to a Stone Corner of said Simons's Land standing in the South West bounds of the aforesaid original tract of land thence along the Bounds of the said Original tract North forty four degrees and thirty minutes West to the place of beginning containing Ten thousand one hundred and twenty nine acres two Quarters and thirty Perches with the allowance of Six Acres Pr Cent for Roads &c — Together with all and singular the members Appurtanances and advantages thereunto belonging And all the Estate Right Title and Interest Claim and demand whatsoever or both at Law and in Equity of him the said George Croghan of in and to all and singular the said premises above mentoned and of in and to every part thereof with the Appurtenances To have and to hold the said tract of Land Heriditaments and premises above mentioned and every part thereof with the Appurtenances unto the said Bernard Gratz his heirs and Assigns to the only Use benefit and behoof of Him the said Bernard Gratz his heirs and Assigns forever Subject Nevertheless to the Quit Rents to grow and become due to his Majesty his heirs and successors & to no other Incumbrance whatsoever And further that the said George Croghan and his heirs and every
(3) other person and persons and his and their heirs anything having or claiming in the said premises above mentioned or any part thereof by from or under him them or any of them shall and will from time to time and at all times upon the reasonable Request and at the proper Costs and charges of him the said Bernard Gratz his heirs and Assigns make do and execute or cause to be made done and executed all and singular such other lawful and reasonable Act and Acts, Thing and things, Device and Devices Conveyance and Conveyances in the Law whatsoever for the further better and more perfect granting and con-

veying of all and singular the said premises and every part thereof unto the said Bernard Gratz his heirs and Assigns to the only proper Use and Behoof of him the said Bernard Gratz his heirs and Assigns forever As by the said Bernard Gratz his heirs or asigns or his or their Council learned in the Law shall be reasonably advised devised and required

In Witness whereof the said George Croghan hath hereunto set his hand and affixed his seal the day and year first above written. — Geo. Croghan [L S] Signed Sealed & delivered in the presence of us, Joseph Simon Robt Lettis Hooper Junr.

Received the day of the date of the within written Indenture Six hundred pounds Sterling money of Great Britain being the full Consideration mentioned in this Deed.

Geo Croghan

Witness
Joseph Simon
Robt Lettis Hooper Junr.

Bedford ss

Personally appeared before me Alex[r]. McKee one of his Majestys Justices of the peace for said County Joseph Simon and Robert Lettis Hooper Junr. subscribing Witnesses to this Instrument in writing and being duly sworn according to Law did say that they personally knew the said George Croghan and saw him sign seal and deliver this Instrument in writing and acknowledge it to be his Act and Deed and desired it might be recorded as such Witness my hand and Seal July the tenth one thousand seven hundred and seventy two

Alex. McKee [L S]

At a Court Continued and held for Augusta County at Fort Dunmore May 18th 1775.

(4) George Croghan Gent acknowledged this his deed of Bargain and Sale with a receipt thereon Endorsed to Bernard Gratz Gent which is Ordered to be Recorded

Test JOHN MADISON Cl Cu

EXAMINED AND DELIVERED
Bernard Gratz, May 28, 1775.

This Indenture made the Sixteenth day of May in the year of our Lord One Thousand seven Hundred and seventy five Between George Croghan of Pittsburg Esquire of one part and Bernard Gratz of Philadelphia Merchant of the other part: Whereas Iohonorissa Scarayadya and Cosswantinicea Cheifs or Sachems of the six United Nations of Indians did by their deed duly Executed bearing date the Second day of August in the Year of our Lord One thousand seven hundred and forty nine for the Consideration therein specified grant bargain and sell unto the said George Croghan in fee a certain Tract or Parcel of Land situate lying and being on the South side the Monongahela River, beginning at the mouth of a Run nearly opposite Turtle Creek and then down the said Monongahela River to its Junction with the River Ohio computed to be ten miles then running down the Eastern Bank and sides of and unto the said River Ohio to where Racoon Creek empties itself into the said River thence up the said Creek ten miles and from thence on a Direct line to the place of beginning containing by Estimation One hundred thousand acres be the same more or less as by the said Deed may more fully appear. —— And Whereas certain Chiefs or Sachems fully representing the six united nations aforesaid in full Council at Fort Stanwix Assembled did by their Deed Poll duly executed bearing date the fourth day of November One thousand seven hundred and sixty eight for the Consideration therein mentioned Grant ratifie and confirm unto his most sacred Majesty George the third by the Grace of God King of Great Britain France and Ireland &c his heirs and successors for the Use benefit and behoof of the said George Croghan all the above bounded and described tract or parcel of Land and premises as by the said Deed Poll Recorded in the Office for recording of Deeds in the City and County of Philadelphia in Book J Volume the fifth page the two hundred and thirty ninth &c may more fully and at large appear Now This Indenture Witnesseth that the said George Croghan for and in Consideration of the sum of Two thousand One hundred and one pounds nineteen shillings lawful money of Great Britain to him the said George Croghan by him the aforesaid Bernard Gratz in hand paid the receipt whereof he the said George Croghan doth hereby acknowledge hath granted bargained sold aliened released and confirmed and by these presents doth fully freely and absolutely

grant bargain sell alien release and confirm unto the said Bernard Gratz and to his heirs and assigns for ever A certain Tract or parcel of Land being a part or parcel of the aforesaid described tract of Land situate lying and being on the Western side of Chartiers Creek beginning at a stake corner to James Innis and running thence with the said Innis's line S 83 E 680 Rod to a Stake on a line of Lot No 18 thence with the said line N 7 E 186 Rod to a Stake Corner to said Lot and to Lot No. 22 thence No 63 15 West 47 Rod to a Stake Corner to said Lott thence N 7 E 160 Rod to a white Oak Corner to said Lot, thence N 52 E 130 Rod to a Stake on a line of the said Lott Corner to Lot No 27 thence with a line of the said Lot N 46 45 W 157 Rod to a Stake corner to said Lot, thence N 52 30 East 347 Rod to a Stake Corner to said Lott and to Lot No 32 thence N 72 E 331 Rod to a stake on a line of Lot No 31 Corner to said Lot No 32 thence North 315 Rod to a Stake Corner to said Lot No 31 and the Lot No 41 thence N 47 W 36 Rod to a Stake Corner to said Lot N 41 thence N 4 W 224 Rod to a Stake Corner to said Lot No 41 thence N 86 E 126 1/2 Rod to a Stake corner to said Lot and to Lot No 42 thence N 27 East 101 3/4 Rod to a Stake Corner to said Lot No 42 and to Lot No 46 thence N 7 E 354 Rod to a Stake Corner to said Lot No 46 thence S 67 30 E 59 1/2 Rod to a Stake Corner to said Lot and to Lot No 55 thence N 17 E 186 Rod to a stake corner to said Lot No 55 and to Lot No 13 thence North 56 Rod to a White Oak on the Western bank of Chartiers Creek Corner to said Lot No 13 thence down the Western side of said Creek with the meanders thereof to a White Oak on the said Western Bank thereof Corner to said Lot thence with the line of the said Lot N 28 W 120 Rod to an Elm on the said Western Bank of the said Creek Corner to said Lot thence down the Western side of the said Creek with the meanders thereof to a hickory on the said Western Bank of the said Creek corner to John Mainard thence with the said Mainard Line S 84 W 280 Rod to a stake Corner to the said Mainard and to Lotts No 64 and 62 thence S 7 W 205 Rod to a Stake corner to said Lot No 62 thence N 83 W 304 Rod to a Stake corner to said Lot thence N 7 E 158 Rod to a stake
(6) Corner to said Lot and to Lots No 64 & 65 thence N 83 W

240 Rod to a stake Corner to said Lot No 65 thence with a line of said Lot N 7 E 116 Rod to a Stake on the said line Corner to Edward Ward, thence with the said Wards line N 63 45 W 247 Rod to a Stake on the said Line and thence S 7 W 2697 Rod to the place of beginning including the Lots No 19, 20, 21, 23, 24, 25, 26, 28, 29, 33, 34, 35, 36, 37, 38, 39, 40, 43, 44, 45, 47, 48, 49, 50, 51, 52, 53, 54, 56, 57, 58, 59, 60, 61, and 75 containing fourteen thousand and thirteen Acres with the Allowance of 6 Acres Pr Cent for Roads and highways with the Rights Members and appurtenances thereof and all houses Edifices, Buildings Orchards Gardens Lands Meadows Pastures feedings Commons Trees Woods under woods Way Paths Waters Watercourses Easements Profits Commodities Advantages Hereditaments and Appurtenances whatsoever unto the said tract of land belonging or in any wise appertaining also the reversion and Reversions Remainder and Remainders Rents and Services of all and Singular the said premises above mentioned and every part and parcel thereof with the Appurtenances And also all the Estate Right Title Interest Claim and demand whatsoever both at Law and in Equity of him the said George Croghan of in and to every Part and parcel thereof with the Appurtenances. To have and to hold the said tract of Land hereditaments and premises above mentioned and every part and parcel thereof with the appurtenances unto the said Bernard Gratz his heirs and Assigns to the only proper Use Benefit and Behoof of him the said Bernard Gratz his heirs and Assigns forever Subject nevertheless to the Quit Rents to grow and become due to his majesty his heirs and Successors and to no other Incumbrance whatsoever And farther that he the said George Croghan and his heirs and every other person and persons and his and their heirs any thing having or claiming in the said premises above mentioned or any part thereof by from or under him them or any of them shall and will from time to time and at all times hereafter upon the reasonable request and at the Cost and charges of the said Bernard Gratz his heirs and Assigns make do and execute or cause to be made done and executed all and every such further and other lawful and reasonable Act and Acts, thing and
(7) Things Device and Devices, Conveyance and Conveyances in

the Law whatsoever for the further better and more perfect granting Conveying and Assuring of all and Singular the said premises above mentioned unto the said Bernard Gratz his heirs and Assigns to the only proper Use and behoof of him the said Bernard Gratz his heirs and Assigns for ever as by the said Bernard Gratz his heirs and Assigns or his or their Council learned in the Law shall be reasonably devised or advised and required In Witness whereof the said George Croghan hath hereto set his hand and Seal the day and year first above written

Sealed and Delivered Geo Croghan [L S]
In the presence of us
John Campbell
Joseph Simon
John Campbell

Memorandum Liviry and Seisin made by the said George Croghan to the said Bernard Gratz of all and singular the premises hereby conveyed or intended to be conveyed according to the true Intent and meaning of the within Indenture of Bargain and Sale, before the Signing Sealing and Delivery thereof Witness my hand the date within written

Geo Croghan

Received the day of the date of the within written Indenture of the within named Bernard Gratz Two thousand one hundred and one pounds nineteen Shillings lawful money of Great Britain being the full Consideration money in this written Indenture mentioned.

Witness Geo Croghan
John Campbell
Joseph Simon
John Campbell

At a Court Continued and held for Augusta County at Fort Dunmore May the 18th 1775.

George Croghan Gent Acknowledged this his deed of Bargain and Sale with Livery and seisen and a Receipt thereon Endorsed to Bernard Gratz which is Ordered to be Recorded

Test JOHN MADISON Cl Cu

[457]

(8) EXAMINED AND DELIVERED
Bernard Gratz May 28th 1775

This Indenture made the Sixteenth day of May in the year of our Lord One thousand seven hundred and seventy five Between George Croghan of Pittsburgh Esquire of the one part and Bernard Gratz of Philadelphia Merchant of the other part Whereas Iohonorissa, Scarayadia and Coswantinecea chiefs or Sachems of the six united Nations of Indians did by their deed duly executed bearing date the second day of August in the year of our Lord One thousand and Seven hundred and forty nine for the Consideration therein specified grant bargain and sell unto the said George Croghan in fee a certain tract or parcel of land situate lying and being on the South side of the Monongahela River Beginning at the mouth of a Run nearly opposite Turtle Creek and then down the said Monongahela River to its Junction with the River Ohio computed to be ten miles then running down the Eastern Bank and sides of and unto the said River Ohio to where Racoon Creek empties itself into the said River thence up the said Creek ten miles and from thence on a direct line to the place of beginning containing by Estimation One hundred thousand Acres be the same more or less as by the said Deed may more fully appear And Whereas certain chiefs or sachems fully representing the six united nations aforesaid in full Council at Fort Stanwix assembled did by their deed Poll duly executed bearing date the fourth day of November One thousand seven hundred and sixty eight for the Consideration therein mentioned grant ratify and confirm unto his most sacred Majesty George the third by the Grace of God King of Great Britain France and Ireland & his heirs and Successors for the use benefit and behoof of the said George Croghan all the above bounded and described tract or parcel of land and premises as by the said Deed Poll recorded in the Office for recording of Deeds in the City and County of Philadelphia in Book J Volume the fifth page the two hundred and thirty ninth &c may more fully and at large appear Now this Indenture witnesseth that the said George Croghan for and in
(9) Consideration of the sum of four thousand seven hundred and twenty two pounds sixteen shillings and sixpence lawful money of Great Britain to him the said George Croghan by him the

said Bernard Gratz in hand paid the receipt whereof he the said George Croghan doth hereby acknowledge hath granted bargained sold aliened released and confirmed and by these presents doth fully freely and absolutely grant bargain sell alien release and confirm unto the said Bernard Gratz and to his heirs and Assigns forever a certain Tract or Parcel of Land being a part or parcel of the aforesaid described tract of Land situate lying and being on the Waters of Robinson Run and Racoon Creek Beginning at a Stone on the said Croghan Boundary Line Corner to William Christy and running thence with the said Line S 44. 30 E 3065 Rod to a Stake on the said Line corner to James Innis thence with the said Innis's Line N 45 E 360 Rod to a Stake corner to said Innis, thence N 7 E (along the lines of Lots 21–25. 29. 36–39–45–50–54–60 and 75) 2697 Rod to a Stake on the Line of Edward Ward thence with the said Wards said Line N 63–45 W 1488 Rod to a Stake Corner to said Ward thence S 45. 45. W 976 Rod to a Stone corner to David Rogers and thence along said Rogers and said Christys Lines S 44 W. 854 Rod to the place of beginning containing thirty one thousand four hundred and eighty five and a half Acres with the Allowance of Six Acres pr Cent for Roads and high Ways with the Rights Members and appurtenances thereof and all Houses Edifices Buildings Orchards Gardens Lands Meadows Pastures Feedings Commons Trees Woods Underwoods Ways Paths Waters Water Courses Easement Profits Commodities Advantages heriditaments and appurtenances whatsoever unto the said tract of Land belonging or in any wise appertaining And also the Reversion and Reversions Remainder and Remainders Rents and Services of all and singular the said premises above mentioned and of every part and parcel thereof with the appurtenances And also all the Estate Right Title Interest Claim and Demand whatsoever both at Law and in equity of him the said George Croghan of in and to every part and parcel thereof with the Appurtenances To have and to hold the said Tract of Land Hereditaments and premises above mentioned and every part and parcel thereof
(10) with the appurtenances unto the said Bernard Gratz his heirs and Assigns to the only proper Use benefit and behoof of him the said Bernard Gratz his heirs and Assigns for ever Subject

Nevertheless to the Quit Rents to grow and become due to his Majesty his heirs and Successors and to no other Incumbrance whatsoever And farther that he the said George Croghan and his heirs and every other person and persons and his and their heirs any-thing having or claiming in the said premises above mentioned or any part thereof by from or under him them or any of them shall and will from time to time and at all times hereafter upon the reasonable Request and at the Cost and Charges of the said Bernard Gratz his heirs and Assigns make do and execute or cause to be made done executed all and every such further and other lawful and reasonable Act and Acts Thing and Things Device and Devices Conveyance and Conveyances in the Law whatsoever for the further better and more perfect granting conveying and Assuring of all and singular the said premises above mentioned unto the said Bernard Gratz his heirs and Assigns to the only proper Use and behoof of him the said Bernard Gratz his heirs and Assigns for ever as by the said Bernard Gratz his heirs and Assigns or his or their Council learned in the Law shall be reasonably devised or advised and required In Witness whereof the said George Croghan hath hereunto set his hand and seal the day and year first above written

Geo Croghan [L S]

Sealed and delivered
In the presence of us
John Campbell
Joseph Simon
John Campbell

Memorandum Livery and Seisin made by the said George Croghan to the said Bernard Gratz of all and singular the premises hereby conveyed or intended to be conveyed accord-
(11) ing to the true Intent and meaning of the within Indenture of Bargain and Seal before the Signing Sealing and delivery thereof Witness my hand the date within written

Geo Croghan

Received the day of the date of the within written Indenture of the within named Bernard Gratz four thousand seven hundred and twenty two pounds sixteen shillings and six pence lawful money of Great Britain being the full Consideration money in this written Indenture mentioned

Witness Geo Croghan
John Campbell
Joseph Simon
John Campbell

At a Court continued and held for Augusta County at Fort Dunmore May the 18th 1775

George Croghan Gent acknowledged this his Deed of Bargain and Sale with Livery and Seisen and a receipt thereon endorsed to Bernard Gratz which is ordered to be recorded

Test JOHN MADISON Cl Cu

EXAMINED AND DELIVERED
Joseph Simon, May 28th, 1775

This Indenture made the 9th day of July in the year of our Lord One thousand seven hundred and seventy two Between George Croghan of Fort Pitt Esquire on the one part and Joseph Simons of Lancaster in the province of Pennsylvania Merchant on the other part Whereas Iohonorissa Scayaradia and Caswantiecea chiefs or Sachems of the six united Nations of Indians did by their deed duly executed bearing date the Second day of August One thousand seven hundred and forty nine for the Consideration therein specified grant bargain and sell unto the said George Croghan in fee a certain tract or Parcel of Land sytuate lying and being on the south side of the Monongahela River beginning at a Run nearly opposite to Turtle Creek and then down the said Monongahela
(12) River to its Junction with the River Ohio computed to be ten Miles then running down the Eastern Bank or side of the said River Ohio to where Racoon Creek empties itself into the said River thence up the said Creek ten miles and from thence on a direct line to the place of beginning containing by estimation One hundred thousand Acres be the same more or less as by the said Deed may more fully appear And Whereas certain Chiefs or Sachems fully representing the six united nations aforesaid in full Council at Fort Stanwix assembled did by their Deed poll duly executed bearing date the fourth day of Novem-

ber One thousand seven hundred and sixty eight for the Consideration therein mentioned grant ratify and confirm unto his most sacred Majesty George the third by the Grace of God King of Great Britain france and Ireland &c his heirs and Successors for the Use benefit and behoof of the said George Croghan all the above bounded and described tract or parcel of Land and premises as by the said Deed poll Recorded in the Office for recording of Deeds in the City and County of Philadelphia in Book J Volume the fifth page the two hundred and thirty ninth &c may more fully and at large Appear, Now this Indenture witnesseth that the said George Croghan for and in Consideration of the Sum of Six hundred and thirty pounds lawful Money of Great Britain to him the said George Croghan by him the said Joseph Symonds in hand paid he the said George Croghan doth hereby acknowledge And by these presents doth fully freely and absolutely grant bargain sell alien release and confirm unto the said Joseph Symonds (in his Actual possession now being by Virtue of a Bargain and Sale thereof to him made for one whole year by Indenture bearing date the day next before the date of these presents and by force of the Statute for transferring of Uses into possession) and to his heirs and assigns for ever a certain Tract or parcel of Land being a part or parcel of the aforesaid described tract of Land situate lying and being on Racoon Creek Beginning at a Stone being the most South West Corner of Eight thousand Acres of Land granted to Alexander Ross and others thence by the same Land and Lands of the said George Croghan South twelve Degrees East three hundred and Sixty five Chains to a Stone
(13) thence South forty four Degrees West One hundred and eighty Six Chains to where the Original bounds of the aforesaid tract Granted to the said George Croghan by the united Nations aforesaid cuts or intersects Racoon Creek at the South West side or Bank thereof thence by the said Original Bounds North forty four Degrees and thirty minutes West three hundred and ninety four Chains to a Stone Corner of one other tract of Land granted to Bernard Gratz thence by the same Land North fifty Degrees and thirty minutes East three hundred and seventy two Chains and ninety Links to another stone Corner of the said Gratz's Land, thence South fifty six Degrees and twenty

one Minutes East forty nine Chains and eighty Links to the place of beginning Containing ten thousand five hundred and eighty Acres with the Allowance of Six Acres pr Cent for Roads and highways with the rights Members and Appurtenances thereof and all the Advantages unto the Same belonging or in anywise appertaining And also all and Singular the Estate Right Title Interest Claim and Demand whatsoever both at Law and in equity of him the said George Croghan of in and to all and singular the said premises above mentioned and of in and to every part and parcel thereof with the appurtenances To have and to hold the said tract of Land Hereditaments and premises above mentioned with the Appurtenances and every part and parcel thereof unto the said Joseph Simons his heirs and assigns to the only proper Use and behoof of him the said Joseph Simons his heirs and assigns for ever, Subject nevertheless to the Quit Rents to grow and become due to his Majesty his heirs and Successors and to no other incumbrance whatsoever And further that the said George Croghan and his heirs and every other person and persons and his and their heirs any thing having or claiming in the said premises above mentioned or any part thereof by from or under him them or any of them shall and will at all times hereafter upon the Reasonable request and at the Cost and Charges of him the aforesaid Joseph Simonds his heirs and Assigns make do and execute or cause to be made done and executed all and singular every such
(14) other lawful and reasonable Act and Acts thing and things, Device and Devices, Conveyance and Conveyances in the Law whatsoever for the further better and more perfect granting of all and singular the said premises above mentioned unto the said Joseph Symonds his heirs and assigns to the only proper Use and behoof of the said Joseph Symons his heirs and assigns for ever As by the said Joseph Symons his heirs and Assigns or his or their Council Learned in the Law shall be reasonably advised devised and required In Witness whereof he the said George Croghan hath hereunto set his hand and affixed his Seal the day and year first above written being the 9th day of July 1772

Sealed and Delivered Geo Croghan [L S]
In the presence of us
Bernard Gratz
Robt Lettis Hooper Junr

Received the day of the date of the written Indenture of Joseph Simons Six hundred and thirty pounds lawful money of Great Britain being the full Consideration in this deed mentioned

Witness Geo Croghan

Robt Lettis Hooper Junr

Bernard Gratz

Bedford ss

Personally appeared before me Alexander McKee Esquire one of his Majestys Justices of the peace for said County Robert Lettis Hooper Junr and Bernard Gratz subscribing witnesses to this Instrument in writing and being duly sworn according to Law did say that they personally knew the said George Croghan and saw him sighn seal and deliver this Instrument in writing as his Act and Deed and as such desired it might be recorded Witness my hand and Seal this tenth day of July 1772 Alex.r McKee [L S]

At a Court Continued and held for Augusta County at Fort Drumore May the 18th 1775

George Croghan Gent acknowledged this his deed of Bargain and Sale with a receipt thereon indorsed to Joseph Simons Gent which is ordered to be recorded

Test JOHN MADISON Cl Cu

---

(15) EXAMD & DELIVERED
Edward Ward, May 30th 1775.

This indenture made the eighteenth day of November in the year of our Lord One thousand seven hundred and seventy three between George Croghan of Fort Pitt Esquire of the one part and Edward Ward of the same place Gent on the other part Whereas Iohonorissa Scarayadia and Cawantinecea Chiefs or Sachems of the Six united Nations of Indians did by their Deed duly executed bearing date the second day of August in the year of our Lord One thousand seven hundred and forty nine for the Consideration therein specified grant bargain and sell unto the said George Croghan in fee a certain tract or parcel of Land situate lying and being on the South side of the Monongahela River beginning ten

Miles up the said River above the mouth of a Run nearly opposite Turtle Creek and then down the said Monongahela River to its Junction with the River Ohio computed to be ten miles then running down the Eastern Bank and sides of and unto the said River Ohio to where Racoon Creek empties itself into the said River thence up the said Creek ten miles and from thence on a direct line to the Place of beginning containing by Estimation One hundred thousand Acres be the same more or less as by the said Deed may more fully appear And Whereas certain Chiefs or Sachems fully representing the six united Nations aforesaid in full council at Fort Stanwix assembled did by their Deed Poll duly executed bearing date the fourth day of November One thousand seven hundred and sixty eight for the Consideration therein mentioned grant ratify and confirm unto his most sacred Majesty George the third by the Grace of God King of Great Britain France and Ireland &c his heirs and successors for the Use benefit and behoof of the said George Croghan all the above bounded & described Tract or parcel of Land and premises as by the said Deed Poll recorded in the Office for recording of Deeds in the City and County of Philadelphia in Book J Volume the fifth Page the two hundred and thirty ninth &c may more fully and at large appear Now this indenture witnesseth that the said George Croghan for and in consideration of the sum of four hundred and Eighty five pounds two Shillings lawful money of Great Britain to him the said George Croghan by him the aforesaid Edward Ward in hand paid the receipt whereof he the said George Croghan doth hereby acknowledge hath granted bargained sold aliened released and confirmed and by these presents doth fully freely and absolutely grant bar-
(16) gain sell alien release and confirm unto the said Edward Ward (in his actual possession now being by virture of a bargain and Sale thereof to him made for one whole year by Indenture bearing date the day next before the day of the date of these presents and by force of the Statute for transferring of Uses into possession) and to his heirs and Assigns for ever A certain tract or parcel of Land being a part or parcel of the aforesaid described tract of Land situate lying and being on the Branches of Montures or the half moon Run Beginning at a Stake on

Westfalls Line corner to David Price and running along the said Price's Line South 7° West 216 Rod to a Stake Corner to said Price and Thomas Joist and thence continuing the said Course along the said Joists Line 124 Rod in all 340 Rod to a Stake on the said Joists said Line thence North 63.45 West 1735 Rod to a Stake thence North 32.15 East 323 Rod to a Stake thence South 63.45 East 160 Rod to a Stake Corner to the said Edward Ward thence continuing the said course along the said Wards Line 814 Rod in all 974 Rod to a Stake Corner to the said Ward and John Westfall and thence continuing the said Course along the said Westfalls line 612 Rod in all 1586 Rod to the place of beginning containing three thousand two hundred and thirty four acres with the Allowance of Six Acres pr cent for Roads and Highways with the Rights Members and Appurtenances thereof and all houses Edifices Buildings Orchards Gardens Lands Meadows Pastures Feedings Commons Trees Woods Underwoods Ways Paths Waters Watercourses Easements Profits Commodities Advantages Heriditaments and appurtenances whatsoever unto the said tract of Land belonging or in anywise appertaining And also the Reversion and Reversions Remainder and Remainders Rents and Services of all and singular the said premises above mentioned and of every part and parcel thereof with the appurtenances And also all the Estate Right Title Interest Claim and Demand whatsoever both at Law and in Equity of him the said George Croghan of in and to all and singular the said premises above mentioned and of in and to every part and parcel thereof with the Ap-
(17) purtenances To have and to hold the said Tract of Land Hereditaments & premises above mentioned and every part and parcel thereof with the appertenances unto the said Edward Ward his heirs and Assigns to the only proper Use benefit and behoof of him the said Edward Ward his heirs and Assigns for ever Subject nevertheless to the Quit Rents to grow and become Due to his Majesty his heirs and Successors and to no other Incumbrance whatsoever And farther that he the said George Croghan and his heirs and every other person and persons and his and their heirs anything having and Claiming in the said premises above mentioned or any part thereof by from or under

him them or any of them shall and will from time to time and at all times hereafter upon the Reasonable request and at the Cost and Charges of the said Edward Ward his heirs and Assigns make do and execute or cause to be made done and executed all and every such further and other lawful and reasonable Act and Acts thing and things Device and Devices, Conveyance and Conveyances in the Law whatsoever for the further better and more perfect granting conveying and assuring of all and singular the said Premises above mentioned unto the said Edward Ward his heirs and Assigns to the only proper Use of him the said Edward Ward his heirs and Assigns for ever As by the said Edward Ward his heirs or Assigns or his or their Council learned in the Law Shall be reasonably devised or Advised and required in Witness Whereof the said George Croghan hath hereto set his hand and Seal the day and year first above written

Sealed and Delivered Geo: Croghan (Seal)
In the presence of us
N. B. The words on the other part in
the fourth line of the first page and the
word Ward in the Sixteenth line of the
Second page were interlined before signing.
James Innis
John Campbell

Received the day of the date of the within indenture of the therein named Edward Ward the full and just sum of four hundred and eighty five pounds two Shillings Sterling or eight hundred pounds eight Shillings and three pence three fifths
(18) Currt lawful money of Pennsylvania being the full Consideration money in the within written Indenture mentioned

Witness Geo Croghan
James Innis
John Campbell

At a Court continued and held for Augusta County at Fort Dunmore May the 20th, 1775

George Croghan Gent acknowledged this his Deed of Bargain and Sale with a receipt thereon Endorsed to Edward Ward Gent which is ordered to be recorded

Test JOHN MADISON Cl Cur

EXAMINED AND DELIVERED
Edward Ward, May 30th, 1775

This Indenture made the eighteenth day of November in the year of our Lord One thousand seven hundred and seventy three between George Croghan of Fort Pitt Esquire of the one part and Edward Ward of the sd place Gent on the other part Whereas Iohonorissa Scarayadia and Coswantinecea Chiefs or Sachems of the Six United Nations of Indians did by their deed duly executed bearing date the second day of August in the year of our Lord One thousand Seven hundred and forty nine for the Consideration therein specified grant bargain and sell unto the said George Croghan in fee a certain tract or parcel of Land situate lying and being on the South Side of the Monongahela River beginning ten miles up the said River above the mouth of a Run nearly opposite Turtle Creek and then down the said Monongahela River to its Junction with the River Ohio computed to be ten miles then running down the eastern Bank and sides of and unto the said River Ohio to where Racoon Creek empties itself into the said River thence up the said Creek ten miles and from thence on a direct line to the place of beginning by Estimation One hundred thousand Acres be the same more or less as by the said Deed may more fully appear And whereas certain chiefs or Sachems fully representing the Six United Nations aforesaid in full Council at Fort Stanwix Assembled did by their Deed Poll duly executed bearing date the fourth day
(19) of November One thousand seven hundred and Sixty eight for the Consideration therein mentioned grant ratify and confirm unto his most Sacred Majesty George the third by the Grace of God King of Great Britain France and Ireland &c his heirs and Successors for the Use benefit and behoof of the said George Croghan all the above bounded and described tract or parcell of Land and premises as by the said Deed poll recorded in the Office for Recording of Deeds in the City and County of Philadelphia in Book J Volume the fifth Page the Two hundred and thirty ninth &c may more fully and at large appear. Now this Indenture witnesseth that the said George Croghan for and in Consideration of the sum of Five hundred and seventy seven pounds nineteen Shillings lawful money of Great

Britain to him the said George Croghan by him the aforesaid Edward Ward in hand paid the receipt whereof he the said George Croghan doth hereby acknowledge hath granted bargained sold aliened released and confirmed and by these presents doth fully freely and absolutely grant bargain Sell alien release & confirm unto the said Edward Ward (in his Actual possession now being by Virtue of a Bargain and Sale thereof made to him for one whole year by Indenture bearing date the day next before the date of these presents and by force of the Statute for transferring of Uses into possession) and to his heirs and assigns for ever a certain tract or parcel of Land being a part or parcel of the aforesaid described tract of Land situate lying and being on the Northern Bank of the Ohio River Beginning at a White Oak on the said Southern Bank of the said River and nearly opposite to the Lower end of the Long Island and likewise beginning to John Westfall and running with the said Westfalls Line South 32°. 15′ West 760 Rod to a Stake Corner to said Westfall thence North 63.45 West 814 Rod to a Stake Thence North 32.15 East 928 Rod to an Elm on the said Southern Bank of the Ohio River and thence up the said Southern Side of the said River with the Meanders thereof South 46.30 East 24 Rod thence South 33.45 East 22 Rod thence South 25.15 East 54 Rod thence South 19.30 East 48 Rod Thence South 27 East 38 Rod thence South 22.45 East 4 Rod, thence South 47.15 East 54 Rod thence South 31.15 East 20 Rod thence South 44.30 East 48 Rod thence South 59.30 East 56 Rod thence South 71.15 East 112 Rod thence South
(20) 62 East 56 Rod thence South 60.30 East 40 Rod thence South 79 East 14 Rod thence South 69.15 East 12 Rod thence South 61 East 32 Rod thence South 65.30 East 22 Rod Thence South 44 East 26 Rod thence South 56.45 East 88 Rod thence South 74 East 22 Rod and thence South 52.30 East 54 Rod to the place of beginning containing Three thousand eight hundred and sixty-three Acres with the Allowance of Six Acres Pr Cent for Roads and highways with the Rights Members and appurtenances thereof and all houses Edifices Buildings Orchards Gardens Lands Meadows Pastures Feedings Commons Trees Woods Underwoods Ways Paths Waters Watercourses Easement Profits Commodities Advantages Hereditaments and

Appurtenances whatsoever unto the said tract of Land belonging or in any wise appertaining and also the Reversion & Reversions Remainder and Remainders Rents and Services of all and singular the said premises above mentioned and of every part and parcel therof with the appurtenances And also all the Estate Right Title Interest Claim and demand whatsoever both at Law and in Equity of him the said George Croghan of in and to all and singular the said premises above mentioned and of in and to every part and parcel thereof with the appurtenances To have and to hold the said Tract of Land heriditaments and premises above mentioned and every part and parcel thereof with the Appurtenances unto the said Edward Ward his heirs and Assigns to the only proper Use benefit and behoof of him the said Edward Ward his heirs and Assigns for ever. Subject nevertheless to the Quit Rents to grow and become due to his Majesty his heirs & Successors and to no other incumbrance whatsoever And farther that he the said George Croghan and his heirs and every other person and persons and his or their heirs any thing having or claiming in the said premises above mentioned or any part thereof by from or under him them or any of them shall and will from time to time and at all times hereafter upon the reasonable request and at the Cost and Charges of the said Edward Ward his heirs and Assigns make do and execute or cause to be made done and
(21) executed all and every such further and other lawful and reasonable Act and Acts Thing and Things Device and Devices Conveyance and Conveyances in the Law whatsoever for the further Better and more perfect granting conveying and assuring of all and Singular the said premises above mentioned unto the said Edward Ward his heirs and Assigns to the only proper Use and Behoof of him the said Edward Ward his heirs and Assigns for ever As by the said Edward Ward his heirs or Assigns or his or their Council Learned in the Law shall be reasonably devised or Advised and required In Witness whereof the said George Croghan hath hereto set his hand and Seal the day and year first above written

Sealed and Delivered Geo: Croghan (Seal)

In the presence of us

N. B. The words, Ten Miles up

the said River above at the
beginning of the Ninth line
of the first page were inserted
before signing —
James Innis
John Campbell

Received the day of the date of the within Indenture of the therein named Edward Ward the full & just sum of five hundred and seventy seven pounds nineteen Shillings Sterling or nine hundred and fifty three pounds one penny and four fifths Currt lawful money of Pennsylvania being the Consideration Money in full in the within written Indenture Mentioned
Witness Geo Croghan
James Innis
John Campbell

At a Court continued and held for Augusta County at Fort Dunmore May the 20th 1775

George Croghan Gent acknowledged this his Deed of Bargain and Sale with a Receipt thereon endorsed to Edward Ward Gent which is Ordered to be recorded

Test JOHN MADISON Cl Cur.

(22) EXAMINED AND DELIVERED
John McNess by your Order
October 15th 1776

This Indenture made the eighteenth day of November in the year of our Lord one thousand seven hundred and seventy four Between Michael & George Kintner of the County of Augusta of ye one part and Francis McBride of the County aforesaid of ye other part Witnesseth that the said Michael & George Kintner for and in Consideration of the sum of Five Shills current money of Virginia to him in hand paid by ye said Francis McBride at or before ye sealing and delivery of these presents the receipt whereof is hereby acknowledged hath granted bargained and sold and by these presents doth grant bargain and sell unto ye said Francis McBride and his heirs a part of two tracts the one of one hundred of One hundred and sixty acres first granted to

Jonathan Douglass and was by him conveyed to Nicholas Mace by Lease and release and was by him conveyed to said Kintners and 97 Acres a part of a tract of 200 Acres first granted by Pattent to said Kintners and Bounded as followeth viz Beginning at a 2 Black Oaks on Poages Line and thence North Sixty five degrees West Seventy Poles to a White Oak said Poages Corner and with his Line North 30 Degr East 176 Poles to a forked Black Oak & Th No 56 West 35 Pole to a White Oak and No 70 Degr West 50 Pole to Nicholas Maces Corner of said tract & So 29 West 174 Po to the line of that tract & thence So 39 West 150 Pole to a White Oak and Locust Saplin & So 62 East 124 poles to 3 hiccorey Grubs & thence and North East One hundred and twenty two poles to a White Oak and Locust and thence the same Course 20 po. to ye. beginning Corner Containing Two hundred and fifteen Acres and all houses Buildings Ways Waters Watercourses profits commodities Herediatments and appurtenances whatsoever to the said premises hereby granted or in any part thereof belonging or in anywise apertaining & the Reversion and Reversions Remainder and Remainders Rents Issues and Profits thereof To have and to hold ye. said tract of Land and all and singular other the premises hereby granted with ye. appurtenances unto the said Francis McBride his Executors Administrators and assigns from the day before the date hereof for and
(23) during the full term and time of One whole year thence next ensuing fully to be compleat and Ended Yeelding and Paying therefore the Rent of One Pepper Corn on Laddy Day next if the same shall lawfully be demanded to the Intent and purpose that by Virtue of these presents & of ye. Statute for transferring Uses into possession on the said Francis McBride may be in Actual possession of the premises and be thereby enabled to accept and take a grant and release of ye. Reversion & inheritance thereof to them and their heirs In Witness whereof the said Michael & George Kintner hath hereunto set their hands and Seals ye. day and year first above written

Sealed and Delivered	Michael x Gindner [L S]
In the presence of	George GG Gindner [L S]

John Dunbar
John B Bailey
John Thomas

At a Court held for Augusta County at Fort Drumore May 16th 1775

Michael Ginder and George Ginder acknowledged this their lease for Land to Francis McBride and Ordered to be recorded

Test JOHN MADISON

This Indenture made the nineteenth day of November in the year of our Lord One thousand seven hundred and seventy four Between Michael Kintner and Catherine & George Kintner and Susanna his wife of the one part and Francis McBride of the other part Witnesseth That for and in Consideration of the sum of fifty six pounds fourteen Shillings and nine pence current money of Virginia to the said Michael & Catherine Kintner and George Kintner and Susanna in hand paid by the said Francis McBride at or before the Sealing and Delivery of these presents the Receipt whereof they do hereby acknowledge and thereof doth release acquit and discharge the said Francis McBride his Executors and Administrators by these presents them the said Michael and Catherine George Kintner & Susanna hath granted bargained sold aliened and confirmed and by these presents doth grant bargain sell alien and confirm to the said Francis McBride a part of two tracts of Land y.e one of one hundred and Sixty Acres first granted to Jonathan Douglass and was by him conveyed to Nicholas Mace by lease and release and was by him conveyed to said Kintners and 97 Acres a part of tract of 200 Acres first granted by Pattent bearing date to said Kintners and Bounded as followeth viz: — Beginning
(24) at 2 Black Oaks on Poages Line and thence North Sixty five Degrees West seventy poles to a White Oak said Poages Corner and with his line No. 30 Degr East 176 poles to a forked Black Oak and thence No. 56 West 35 pole to a White Oak and No. 70 Degr West 50 poles to Nicholas Maces Corner of said tract & So 39 West 174 to the line of that tract & thence So 39 West 150 poles to a White Oak and Locust Saplin & So 62 Degr East 124 poles to 3 Hickory Grubs and then North East 122 Poles to a White Oak and Locust & thence y.e same Course 20 pole to the beginning containing two hundred and fifteen Acres and all houses Buildings Orchards Ways Waters Water Courses Profits Comodities Hereditaments & Appur-

tenances whatsoever to the said premises hereby granted or any part thereof belonging or in anywise appertaining and the reversion and reversions Remainder and Remainders Rents Issues and profits thereof And also all the Estate Right Title Interest Use trust Property Claim and Demand whatsoever of the said Michael & Catherine Kintner George Kintner and Susanna of in and to the said premises and all Deeds Evidences and Wrightings touching or in any wise concerning the same To have and to hold the Lands hereby conveyed and all and singular other the premises hereby granted and sold and every part and parcel thereof with their and every of their appurtenances to ye said Francis McBride his heirs and Assigns for ever to ye only proper Use & behoof of him the said Francis McBride & for his heirs their Executors and Administrators doth covenant promise & grant to and with the said Francis McBride his heirs and Assigns by these presents that the said Michael Kintner and Catherine George Kinter and Susanna now at the time of the Sealing and Delivery of these presents is seized of a good sure perfect and indefesible Estate of inheritance in fee Simple of and in the premises hereby bargained and sold and that they have good power and lawful absolute Authority to grant and convey the same to the said Francis McBride in Manner and form aforesaid and that the said premises now are and so for ever hereafter shall remain and be free of and from all former and other Gifts Grants Bargain Sales Dower Right and Title of Dower Judgments Executions Titles Troubles Charges and Incumbrances whatsoever made done and Committed by the said Michael & G. Kintner or any other person or persons whatsoever (the Quit Rents hereafter to grow due and payable to our Sovereign Lord the King his heirs and Successors for and in respect of the premises only
(25) excepted and foreprised. And that the said Michael & Catherine Kintner George Kintner and Susannan and their heirs all and singular the premises hereby bargained and sold with the Appurtenances unto the said Francis McBride his heirs and Assigns against them the said Michael and Catherine George and Susannah and their heirs and all and every other person and persons whatsoever shall warrant and forever defend by these presents And lastly that them ye said Michael Kintner

& wife and George Kintner and wife and their heirs and all and every other person and persons and their and their heirs anything having or claiming in the premises hereinbefore mentioned or intended to be hereby bargained and sold shall and will from time to time and at all times hereafter at the reasonable Request and at the proper Cost and Charges in Law of him the said Francis McBride his heirs and Assigns make do & execute or cause or procure to be made done and executed all and every such further & other lawful and reasonable Act and Acts, thing and things Conveyance and Assurances for the furthur better and more perfect conveying and Assuring the premises aforesaid with their and every of their appurtenances to the said Francis McBride heirs and Assigns as by the said Francis McBride his heirs & Assigns or their Council learned in the Law shall be reasonably devised advised or required In Witness whereof the said Michael Kintner & Catherine and George Kintner and Susannah hath hereunto set their hands and Seals the day and year first above written

Sealed & Delivered	George x Gindner (Seal)
In the presence of	George GG Gindner (Seal)
John Dunbar	Cathrine C. Gindner (Seal)
John B. Baily	Susannah S Gindner (S L)
John Thomas	

At a Court held for Augusta County May 16 1775

Michael Ginder & George Ginder acknowledged this their release for Land to Francis McBride and Ordered to be recorded Test JOHN MADISON.

Augusta County to wit

George the third by the Grace of God of Great Britain
(26) France and Ireland King Defender of the faith &c To Thomas Smallman and John Gibson Gentlemen Greeting Whereas Michael Kintner & Catherine and George Kintner and Susanna his wife by their certain Deeds of Lease and Release bearing date the 18 & 19th day of November 1774 for the consideration therein mentioned did give grant bargain and sell Alien release and Confirm unto Francis McBride two tracts of Land one Containing 160 Acres first granted to Jonathan Duglass and the other containing 97 Acres part of a tract granted the said

Kintners by Patent And Whereas Catharine and Susannah the wives of the said Michael and George are unable to travel to our said County Court of Augusta to be privately examined apart from their said husbands and whether they voluntarily without the force threats or compulsion of their said husbands are willing to relinquish their Right of Dower to the said Lands in the said Deed mentioned as the Law in that Case directs — Therefore Know ye that We give Power and Authority to you the said Thomas Smallman and John Gibson to go to the houses of the said Michael and George and there to examine the said Catherine and Susannah privately and apart from their said husbands whether they are willing to relinquish their Right of Dower to the said Land in the said Deed mentioned and whether they do the same of their free will without any force threats or Compulsion of their said husbands and whether they are willing that their Acknowledgement shall be recorded with the said Deeds and that you certify the same distinctly to our Justices of our said County Court of Augusta and that you have then there the said Deeds together with this writ which we send you Witness John Madison Clerk of our said Court the 21st day of February 1775 in the 15 year of our Reign JOHN MADISON

The Execution of this Writ appears by a Schedule hereunto annexed

By Virtue of the within writ to us Thomas Smallman and
(27) John Gibson directed We did personally on the 21st day of February 1775 privately and apart from their said husbands examine Catherine & Susannah Ginder whether they are willing to relinquish their Right of Dower to the Lands sold by their said husbands to Francis McBride who declared and acknowledged that they freely and voluntary relinquished the same without the force threats or Compulsion of their said husbands and that they desired that the said Deeds together with this relinquishment of Dower by them made should be recorded in the County Court of Augusta all of which we do hereby certify to the Justices of our said Lord the King given under our hand and Seals this 21st day of February 1775 —

Tho Smallman (L S)
John Gibson (L S)

At a Court held for Augusta County at Fort Dunmore May the 16th 1775

This Commission for the private Examination of Catherine the wife of Michael Gender & of Susanna the wife of George Gender to a tract of Land sold by their said Husbands to Francis McBride being returned is Ordered to be recorded

Test JOHN MADISON

EXAMINED AND DELIVERED
John McNess October 15th 1776 with
Private Examination by Order

This Indenture made the eighteenth day of November in the year of our Lord God one thousand seven hundred & Seventy four Between Michael & George Kintner of the County of Augusta of the one part and Nicholas Mace of the County aforesaid of the other part Witnesseth that for and in Consideration of the sum of five Shillings Current money of Virginia in hand paid by the said Nicholas Mace at or before the sealing and delivery of these presents the receipt whereof is hereby acknowledged hath granted bargained and sold and by these presents doth grant bargain and sell unto the said Nicholas Mace & to his heirs One certain tract or parcel of Land containing fifty Acres lying and being in the County of Augusta
(28) on the Branches of Brocks Creek being a part of two tracts the one of Two hundred Acres granted to said Michael and George Kintner by Pattent bearing date the Twenty sixth day of July One thousand seven hundred and sixty five And a part of a tract of thirty four Acres made over to said Kintners by Jonathan Douglass by Deeds of Lease & Release Dated ye 14th & 15th days of November 1762 being all on the North side of a Ridge joining to said Maces other Lands and Bounded as followeth viz & Beginning at a Black Oak on a Ridge and thence No 29 Degrees East One hundred and ninety four poles to crossing both tracts to 2 Black Oaks on the Pattent Line & with the same North seventy West twenty poles to 2 White Oaks and hickory & So 41 Degrees West One hundred and eighty pole to a White Oak thence North Sixty five degrees West Thirty two poles to a Locust near a Branch and thence South Twenty eight West Twenty four poles to some White

Oak Grubs on a Ridge and thence South Sixty five East ninety four poles to the Beginning And all houses Buildings Orchards Ways Waters Water Courses Profits Commodities Hereditaments and Appurtenances whatsoever to the said premises hereby granted or any part thereof belonging or in any wise appertaining and the Reversion and Reversions Remainder and remainders Rents Issues and profits thereof To have and to hold the said tract of Land and all and Singular other the premises hereby granted with the appurtenances unto the said Nicholas Mace his Executors Administrators and Assigns from the day before the date hereof for and during and unto the end & term of one whole year from thence next ensuing fully to be compleat and ended yielding and paying therefore the Rent of One Ear of Indian Corn on the last day of the said Term if the same shall be lawfully demanded to the Intent and purpose that by Virtue of these presents and of the Statute for transferring Uses into possession the said Nicholas Mace may be in the more full and Actual possession of the said premises and be thereby the better enabled to accept and take a Grant and Release of the Reversion and Inheritance thereof to him and to his heirs In Witness Whereof the said Michael & George Kintner hath hereunto set their hands and Seals the day and year above written

Sealed and Delivered
in the presence of us
John Dunbar
his
John B Bayley
mark
John Thomas

his
Michal × Gindner (L S)
mark
his
George GG Gindner (L S)
mark

(29) At a Court held for Augusta County at Fort Dunmore May 16th 1775

Michael Ginder & George Ginder acknowledged this their Lease for Land to Nicholas Mace which is Ordered to be recorded

Test JOHN MADISON

This Indenture made the nineteenth day of November in the year of our Lord God One thousand seven hundred & Seventy

four Between Michael Kintner & Kaithrine his wife & George Kintner and Susannah his wife of the County of Augusta of the one part and Nicholas Mace of the County aforesaid of the other part Witnesseth that for and in Consideration of Twenty pounds Current Money of Virginia to the said Michael & Catherine Kintner and George Kintner & Susannah his wife in hand paid by the said Nicholas Mace at or before the Sealing and delivery of these presents the receipt whereof he doth hereby acknowledge and thereof doth release acquit and discharge the said Nocholas Mace his heirs and Assigns by these presents Them the said Michael Kintner & Catherine his wife and George Kintner and Susannah hath granted Bargained and Sold aliened released and confirmed And by these presents doth grant bargain Sell Alien release and confirm unto the said Nicholas Mace (in his Actual possession now being by Virtue of a Bargain and sale to him thereof made by the said Michael and George Kintner for one whole year by Indenture bearing date the day next before the day of the date of these presents and by force of the Statute for transferring Uses into possession) and his heirs One certain tract or parcel of Land containing fifty Acres lying and being in the County of Augusta on the Branches of Brocks Creek being a part of two tracts the one of Two Hundred Acres granted to the said Michael and George Kintner by Pattent bearing date the twenty sixth day of July One thousand seven hundred and sixty five and a part of a tract of thirty four Acres made over to said Kinters by Jonathan Douglass by Lease and Release dated the 14th and 15th days of November 1762 being all on the North side of a Ridge joining to said Maces other Land and bounded as followeth viz: Beginning at a Black Oak on a Ridge and thence North Twenty nine Degrees East One hundred and ninety four poles crossing both tracts to two Black Oaks on the
(30) Patent line & with the same North Seventy Degrees West Twenty poles to Two White Oaks & a hickory and South forty one Degrees West One hundred and eighty poles to a White Oak and thence North Sixty five Degrees West thirty two poles to a Locust near a Branch and South Twenty eight West twenty four poles to some White Oak Grubs on a Ridge & thence South Sixty five East Ninety four poles to the beginning

and all houses Buildings Orchards Ways Waters Water Courses Profits Commodities Hereditaments and Appurtenances whatsoever to the said premises hereby granted or any part & parcel thereof with their and every of their appurtenances And the Reversion and Reversions Remainder and Remainders Rents Issues and Proffits thereof And also all the Estate Right Title Interest Use trust property claim and demand whatsoever of them the said Michael and Catherine Kintner & George Kintner of in and to the said premises and all Deeds Evidences & writings touching or in any wise concerning the same To have and to hold the said tract of and all and singular other the premises hereby granted and released and every part and parcel thereof with their and every of their appurtenances to the said Nicholas Mace his heirs and Assigns forever to the only proper Use and behoof of him the said Nicholas Mace his heirs and Assigns forever. And the said Michael & Catherine & George and Susannah Kintner for themselves their heirs Executors & Administrators Doth covenant promise and grant to and with the said Nicholas Mace his heirs and Assigns by these presents That the said Michael & George Kintner now at the time of the Sealing and Delivery of these presents is seized of a good sure perfect and indefeisable Estate of Inheritance in fee Simple of in and to the said premises hereby granted and that he hath good power & lawful and absolute Authority to grant and convey the same to the said Nicholas Mace in manner & form aforesaid and that the said premises now are and so forever shall remain and be free and clear of and from all form and other Gifts Grants Bargains Sales Dower Right and Title of Dower Judgments Executions Titles Troubles Charges & Incumbrances whatsoever made done committed or suffered by the said Michael & Catherine Kintner
(31) and George & Susannah Kintner or any other person or persons whatsoever (the Quit Rents hereafter to grow due & payable to our sovereign Lord the King his heirs and Successors for and in respect of the said premises only excepted and foreprised) And lastly that the said Michael and George all and singular the premises with the appurtenances unto the said Nicholas Mace his heirs and Assigns against them the said Michael and Catherine Kintner & George Kintner & Susannah

& their heirs & all and every other person & persons whatsoever shall & will warrant and forever defend by these presents In Witness whereof the said Michael Kintner and Catherine his wife and George Kintner & Susannah his wife hath hereunto set their hands & Seals the day and year first above written

Sealed & Delivered
In presence of
John Dunbar
John B Baily (his mark)
John Thomas

Michael × Gindner [L S] (his mark)
George GG Gindner [L S] (his mark)
Catherine C Gindner [L S] (her mark)
Susannah S Gindner [L S] (her mark)

At a Court held for Augusta County at Fort Dunmore May the 16th 1775

Michael Ginder & George Ginder acknowledged this their Release for Land to Nicholas Mace which is Ordered to be recorded

Test JOHN MADISON

Augusta County to wit

George the third by the Grace of God of Great Britain France and Ireland King Defender of the faith &c To Thomas Smallman and John Gibson Gentlemen Greeting Whereas Michael Kintner and Catharine his wife and George Kintner & Sussannah his wife by their certain Deed of Lease & Release bearing date the 18th & 19th day of November 1774 for the Consideration therein mentioned did give grant bargain sell alien and confirm unto Nicholas Mace fifty Acres of Land on the branches of Brocks Creek And Whereas Catherine & Susannah the wives of the said Michael and George are unable
(32) to travel to our said County Court of Augusta to be privately examined apart from their said husbands and whether they voluntarily and without the force threats or Compulsion of their said Husbands are willing to relinquish their Right of Dower to the said Lands in the said Deed mentioned as the Law in that Case directs Therefore Know ye that we give power & authority to you the said Thomas Smallman & John

Gibson to go to the house of the said Michael & George and thereto examine the said Catherine & Susannah privately and apart from their said Husbands whether they are willing to relinquish their Right of Dower to the said Land in the said Deeds mentioned and whether they do the same of their own free will without any force threats or compulsion of their said Husbands & whether they be willing that their Acknowledgement shall be recorded with the said Deeds and that you certify the same distinctly to our Justice of our said County Court of Augusta and that you have then there the said Deed together with this writ which we send you Witness John Madison Clerk of our said Court the 21st day of Feby. 1775 in the 15 year of our reign

JOHN MADISON

The Execution of this Writ appears by a Schedule hereunto annexed:

By Virtue of the within Writ to us Thomas Smallman & John Gibson directed we did personally on the 21st day of Feby 1775 privately and apart from their said Husbands examine Catharine & Susannah Kintner the Wives of Michael & George Kintner whether they are willing to relinquish their Right of Dower to the Land sold by their said Husbands to Nicholas Mace who declared and acknowledged that they freely and voluntarily relinquished the same without the force threats or Compulsion of their said husbands and that they desired that the said Deeds together with this relinquishment of dower by them made should be recorded in the County Court of Augusta all which We do hereby certify to the Justices of our said Lord the King Given under our hands & Seals this 21st day of Feby. 1775:

Tho Smallman [L S]
Jno Gibson [L S]

At a Court held for Augusta County at Fort Dunmore May 16th 1775

This Commission for the private Examination of Catherine the wife of Michael Ginder and of Susannah the wife of George Ginder to a tract of Land sold by their husbands to Nicholas Mace being returned is ordered to be recorded

Test JOHN MADISON

(33) EXAMD & DELIVERED Major Edward Ward June 6th 1775 By Captn Charles Edmonstone commanding his Majestys Forces on the Communication to Fort Pitt Permission is hereby granted to Mr. Alexander Ross Agent for the Contractors for Victualling his Majestys forces in North America to use and improve a certain piece of Ground adjoining his Majestys fields at Fort on which he purposes to cultivate and raise Corn & Meadow and at some considerable expense therefrom supply this Garrison with fresh provisions Under this restriction Nevertheless that he is to give free and immediate possession to the Commanding officer at this Garrison whenever and at whatever time it shall be demanded he repaying the said Alexander Ross all the Costs and Charges accruing on & by the Cultivation and Improvement of said piece of Ground Given under my hand this Nineteenth day of September 1768

Chas Edmonstone Capt
Commanding

I Alexander Ross do by this Indenture for and in Consideration of one hundred pounds to me pd the receipt whereof I do hereby acknowledge bargain sell make over and Assign my right Title and claim to all the Estate mentioned in the within permit to Maj. Edward Ward his heirs & assigns for ever To have and to hold the same together with all the issues profits immunities and hereditaments whatsoever thereunto belonging hereby binding myself my heirs Exors & Admtrs to warrant and defend the same against the Claim or Claims of any person or persons claiming under me Witness my hand and Seal this 15th day of December Anno Dom 1774

Signed Seal'd & Delivered Alexander Ross [L S]
In the presence of
"My Right Title & Claim to"
being first interlined between
the third & Fourth lines
A McKee C. Graydon
John Free

At a Court Continued and held for Augusta County at Fort Dunmore May 20th 1775 Alexr Ross Gen't acknowledged this

his Deed of Bargain and Sale to Edward Ward Gen't which is ordered to be recorded

Test JOHN MADISON

(34) EXAMINED & DELIVERED Majr Edward Ward June 6th 1775

By Capt Charles Edmonstone Commanding his Majestys Forces in the district of Fort Pitt Permission is hereby granted to Mrs Susanna Edmonstone to occupy and improve upon a piece of Ground containing ——— joining to what is commonly called the Kings Garden & Orchard, In Consideration of which she or her Assigns is to pay Twenty Shillings yearly if demanded and also to be subject to such regulations as may be ordered by the Commander in Chief or by the Commanding Officer of the District for the Good of his Majestys Service Given under my hand at Fort Pitt the 25th October 1767

Chas Edmonstone
Commanding

Know all Men by these presents That I Susannah Edmonstone now at Fort Pitt for and in Consideration of Twelve pounds Pennsylv Currency to me in hand paid by Alexander Ross the Receipt whereof I do hereby acknowledge have granted bargained sold and assigned and by these presents do grant bargain and sell and assign over unto the aforesaid Alexander Ross his heirs and Assigns all my Right Title and Interest to the within permit or Instrument of Writing for the piece of Ground therein mentioned In Witness whereof I have hereunto set my hand and seal this third day of November in the year of our Lord One thousand seven hundred & Seventy two

Signed Sealed and Delivered in the presence of
Edw Hand

Susanna Edmonstone [L S]

I Alexander Ross do by this Indenture for and in Consideration of Thirty pounds to me in hand paid the receipt whereof I do hereby acknowledge bargain sell & deliver make over and Assign my Right Title & Claim to all the Estate mentioned in the annexed permit from Charles Edmonstone to Susannah

Edmonstone and by her Assigned to me to Majr Edward Ward his heirs and assigns for ever To have and to hold the same together with the immunities & heriditaments thereunto in anywise belonging Hereby binding myself my heirs Exors & Admrs to warrant and forever defend the same against the Claim or claims of any person or persons whatsoever claiming under me Witness my hand and seal the 15th day of Dec. 1774.

Sign'd Seal'd & Delivered Alexander Ross [L S]
in presence of us
"my Right Title & Claim to"
being first interlined between
the Second & third lines
A McKee C Graydon
John Feree

At a Court continued and held for Augusta County at Fort Dunmore May 20th 1775

Alexander Ross Gent acknowledged this his Deed of Bargain and Sale to Edward Ward Gent which is ordered to be recorded

Test JOHN MADISON

EXAMINED & DELIVERED
Majr Edward Ward June 6th 1775

By Captain Charles Edmonstone Commanding his Majestys Forces in the District of Fort Pitt— Permission is hereby granted to Edmund Prideux to possess Till and Occupy a certain piece of Ground containing Seven Acres and eight chains Bounded and adjoining a piece of Ground called the Kings Orchard & Brick Pounds In Consideration of which he or his Assigns is to pay twenty Shillings yearly if demanded and also to be subject to such regulation as may be ordered by the Commander in chief or by the Commanding Officer of the district for the Good of his Majestys Service—— Given under my hand at Fort Pitt the 8th of May 1771

Chas. Edmonstone
Commanding

Know all Men by these presents That I Edmund Prideaux Ensign in the 18th Regiment now at Fort Pitt for and in Consideration of the sum of Fourteen pounds Pensylvania Cur-

(36) rency to me in hand paid by John Campbell the receipt whereof I do hereby acknowledge have granted bargained sold and Assigned and by these presents do grant bargain sell and assign over unto the aforesaid John Campbell his heirs and Assigns all my Right Title and Interest to the within Permit or Instrument of writing for the piece of Ground therein mentioned In Witness whereof I have hereunto set my hand and seal this Sixteenth day of November in the year of our Lord One thousand seven hundred and seventy two

Signed Sealed & Delivered Edmd Prideaux [L S]
in the presence of
Alexander Ross

I assign over all my Right and Title of the above Permit or Instrument of writing unto Alexander Ross for the piece of Ground therein mentioned as Witness my hand & Seal this twenty Seventh day of Augt One thousand seven hundred and seventy three

Witness John Campbell [L S]
William Richmond

I Alexander Ross do by this Indenture for & in Consideration of thirty pounds to me paid the receipt whereof I do hereby acknowledge bargain sell make over & assign my Right Title & Claim to all the Estate mentioned in the annex'd permit granted by Charles Edmonstone to Edmund Prideaux by him assigned to John Campbell and by him to me to Majr Edward Ward his heirs and Assigns for ever To have and to hold the same together with all the issues profits and immunities & Hereditaments thereunto in anywise belonging Hereby binding myself my heirs Ex[or] & Adm to warrant and for ever defend the same against the Claim or Claims of any person claiming under me Witness my hand and seal this 15th day of Decr 1774

Sign'd Seal'd & Deliver'd Alexander Ross [L S]
in the presence of
"my Right Title & Claim to"
being first interlined between
the second & third lines
A McKee C Graydon
John Free

(37) At a Court Continued and held for Augusta County at Fort Dunmore May the 20th 1775

Alexander Ross Gent acknowledged this his Deed of Bargain & Sale to Edward Ward Gent which is ordered to be recorded

Test JOHN MADISON

EXAMINED & DELIVERED
Majr Edward Ward June 6th 1775

By Major Charles Edmonstone Commanding his Majestys Forces in the District of Fort Pitt—Permission is hereby granted to William Thompson and Alexander Ross to possess till and occupy a certain piece of Ground containing bounded and adjoining a piece of Ground claimed by John Campbell and John Donne including what is called the Kings and Artillery Gardens with the Orchards &c and the Brick ponds In Consideration of which they or their Assigns is to pay Twenty Shillings yearly if demanded And also to be subject to such Regulations as may be ordered by the Commander in chief or by the Commanding Officer of the District for the good of his Majestys Service—

Given under my hand at Fort Pitt the 28th of October 1772

Charles Edmonstone
Commanding

Know all men by these presents that We Charles Edmonstone Esqr Major, Edmund Prideux and Edward Hand Ens[ns] in the 18th Regiment now at Fort Pitt for and in Consideration of the sum of Thirty five pounds Pensylva Currency to Us in hand paid by William Thompson & Alexander Ross the receipt whereof we do hereby acknowledge have granted bargained sold and assigned and by these presents do grant bargain sell and assign over unto the said Thompson and Ross their heirs and assigns all our Right Title & Interest to what is commonly called the Kings fields Gardens and Orchard together with all other Improvements made by us and in our possession As Witness our hands and seals this 28th day of October 1773

Charles Edmonstone [L S]
for myself & Ensign Prideaux
Edwd Hand [L S]

(38) Know all whom it may concern That I Alexander Ross have for and in Consideration of Forty pounds to me pd the Rect whereof I hereby acknowledge bargained sold granted and made over and by these presents do bargain sell grant and make over and assign Thompson and Ross Right Title and Claim to all and singular the Estate mentioned in the within permit granted to William Thompson and Alexander Ross unto Major Edward Ward his heirs and Assigns for ever together with all the issues profits immunities & Hereditaments thereunto belonging of whatsoever kind And I do hereby warrant and forever defend the above mentioned Major Edward Ward his heirs and assigns the above named premises from the Claim or Claims of the aforesaid William Thompson or any other person or persons claiming under him or me, for the true performance of which I bind myself my heirs Exr & Admr by this Indenture Witness my hand and seal this 15th day of Dec Ann Dom. 1774

Sign'd Seal'd & Deliver'd "Thompson & Ross's Right Title and Claim to" being first interlined between the fifth & Sixth lines.

Alexander Ross
for self & [L S]
William Thompson

A McKee
C Graydon
John Free

At a Court continued and held for Augusta County at Fort Dunmore May 20th 1775

Alexander Ross Gent acknowledged this his Deed of Bargain and Sale to Edward Ward Gent which is ordered to be recorded

Test JOHN MADISON

EXAMINED & DELIVERED
Jacob Bousman the 19th June 1775

This indenture made this Thirty first day of December in the year of our Lord One thousand seven hundred and seventy Between George Croghan of Fort Pitt Esquire on the one part and Jacob Bousman of said place of the other

part Whereas Iohonorissa Scarayadia & Coswantinicea Chiefs or Sachems of the Six United Nations of Indians did by their Deed duly executed bearing date the Second day of August in the year of our Lord one thousand seven hundred and forty nine for the Consideration therein specified grant bargain and sell unto the said George Croghan in fee a certain tract or parcel of Land situate lying and being on the South side of the Monongahela River beginning at the mouth of a Run nearly opposite the mouth of Turtle Creek and then down the said Monongahela River to its Junction with the River Ohio
(39) computed to be ten miles, then running down the Eastern Bank and sides of and unto the said River Ohio to where Racoon Creek empties itself into the said River Ohio thence up the said Creek ten Miles and from thence on a direct line to the place of beginning containing by Estimation one hundred thousand Acres be the same more or less as by the said deed may more fully appear And Whereas certain Chiefs or Sachems fully representing the Six United Nations aforesaid in full Council Assembled at Fort Stanwix did by their Deed poll duly executed bearing date the fourth day of November one thousand seven hundred and Sixty eight for the Consideration therein mentioned Grant bargain ratify and confirm unto his most sacred Majesty George the third by the Grace of God King of Great Britain France and Ireland &c his heirs and Successors for the Use benefit and behoof of the said George Croghan his heirs and assigns for ever all the above bounded and described tract or parcel of Land and premises as by the said Deed Recorded in the Office for Recording of Deeds in the City and County of Philadelphia in Book J Volume the Fifth Page the two hundred and thirty ninth &c may more fully and at large appear Now this Indenture witnesseth that the said George Croghan for and in Consideration of the sum of thirty pound sixteen Shillings lawful money of Great Britain to him the said George Croghan by him the said Jacob Bousman in hand paid the receipt whereof he the said George Croghan doth hereby acknowledge hath granted bargained sold aliened released and confirmed and by these presents doth fully freely and absolutely grant bargain sell alien release and confirm unto the said Jacob Bousman (in his actual

possession now being by Virtue of a bargain and sale thereof made to him for one whole year by Indenture bearing date the day next before the day of the date of these presents and by force of the Statute for transferring Uses into possession) and to his heirs and Assigns for ever a certain tract or parcel of Land being a part or parcel of the aforesaid described tract or parcel of Land situate lying and being on the West side of Shirtees Creek beginning at a Maple tree on the West side of said Creek thence North Eighty Six degrees West Seventy four perches to a Marked White Oak thence South sixty five degrees West forty seven and an half perches to a post set up on the West Bank of said Creek thence down the said Bank and side of the said Creek One thousand and four and three Quarter perches to the place of beginning Three hundred and eight
(40) Acres and an half Acre with the Allowance of Six Acres pr Cent for Roads and highways with the Right Members and Appurtenances thereof and all houses Edifices Buildings Orchards Gardens Lands Meadows Commons Pastures feedings Trees Woods Underwoods Waters Water Courses Easements Profits Commodities Advantages Hereditaments and Appurtenances whatsoever unto the said tract of Land belonging or in anywise appertaining and also the reversion and Reversions Remainder and Remainders Rents and Services of all and Singular the said premises of every part and parcel thereof with the Appurtenances And also all the Estate Right Title Interest Claim and Demand whatsoever both at Law and in Equity of him the said George Croghan of in and to all and singular the said premises above mentioned and of in and to every part and parcel thereof with the appurtenances To have and to hold the said tract of Land Hereditaments & premises above mentioned and every part and parcel thereof with the Appurtenances unto the said Jacob Bousman his heirs and Assigns to the only proper Use Benefit and behoof of him the said Jacob Bousman his heirs and Assigns for ever Subject nevertheless to the full Quit Rents to grow and become due to his Majesty his heirs and Successors and to no other Incumbrance whatsoever And further that he the said George Croghan and his heirs and every other person or persons and his and their heirs anything having or claiming in the said premises above mentioned or

any part thereof by from or under him them or any of them shall and will from time to time and at all times hereafter upon the reasonable Request and at the Cost and Charges of the said Jacob Bousman his heirs and Assigns make do and execute or cause to be made done and executed all and every such further and other lawful and reasonable Act and Acts thing and things Device and Devices Conveyance & Conveyances in the Law whatsoever for the further better and more perfect granting conveying and assuring of all and Singular the said premises above mentioned unto the said Jacob Bousman his heirs and Assigns to the only proper Use and behoof of him the said Jacob Bousman his heirs and Assigns for ever as by
(41) the said Jacob Bousman his heirs or Assigns or his or their Council learned in the Law shall be reasonably devised advised and required In Witness whereof the said parties to these presents that is to say the said George Croghan hath hereunto set his hand and seal the day and year first above written

Sealed and Delivered Geo: Croghan [L S]
In the presence of us
William Sells
Ann Girty

Received the day of the date of the within Indenture of the within named Jacob Bousman the sum of Thirty pounds and Sixteen shillings lawful money of Great Britain being the full Consideration Money in the said within written Indenture mentioned

Witness Geo: Croghan.
William Sells
Ann Girty

At A Court held for Augusta County at Fort Dunmore May the 16 1775

George Crogan Gent acknowledged this his Deed of Bargain and Sale and a receipt thereon endorsed to Jacob Bousman which is ordered to be recorded

Test JOHN MADISON

This Indenture
made the thirty
first day of De-
cember in the year of our Lord One thousand seven hundred
and seventy Between George Croghan of Fort Pitt Esquire of
the one part and Benjamin Tate now of the same place Sergeant
in his Majestys Eighteenth Regiment of foot of the other part
Whereas Iohonorissa Scarayadia & Coswentinicea chiefs or
Sachems of the six united Nations of Indians did by their Deed
duly executed bearing date the second day of August in the
year of our Lord One thousand seven hundred and forty nine
for the Consideration therein specified grant bargain and sell
unto the said George Croghan in fee a certain tract or parcel of
Land situate lying and being on the south side the Monon-
(42) gahela River beginning at the Mouth of a Run nearly opposite
to Turtle Creek and then down the said River Monongahela
to its Junction with the River Ohio computed to be ten Miles
then running down the Eastern Bank and sides of and unto the
said River Ohio to where Racoon Creek Empties itself into
the said River thence up the said Creek ten miles and from
thence on a direct line to the place of beginning containing
by estimation One hundred thousand Acres be the same more
or less as by the said Deed may more fully appear And Whereas
certain Chiefs or sachems fully representing the Six united
Nations aforesaid in full council at Fort Stanwix Assembled
did by their deed poll duly executed bearing date the fourth
day of November One thousand seven hundred and sixty eight
for the Consideration therein mentioned grant ratify and confirm unto his most Sacred Majesty George the third by the
Grace of God King of Great Britain France & Ireland &c his
heirs and Successors for the Use benefit and behoof of the said
George Croghan all the above bounded and described tract or
parcel of Land and premises as by the said Deed Recorded in
the Office for recording of Deeds in the City and County of
Philadelphia in Book J Volume the fifth Page the Two hundred
and thirty nine &c. may more fully and at large appear Now
this Indenture witnesseth that the said George Croghan for and
in Consideration of the sum of Thirty eight pounds eight
shillings lawful money of Great Britain To him the said

George Croghan by him the said Benjamin Tate in hand paid the receipt whereof he the said George Croghan doth hereby acknowledge hath granted bargained sold aliened released & confirmed and by these presents doth fully freely and absolutely grant bargain sell alien release and confirm unto the said Benjamin Tate (in his actual possession now being by Virtue of a bargain and sale thereof made to him for one whole year by Indenture bearing date the day next before the day of the date of these presents and by force of the Statute for transferring of Uses into Possession) and to his heirs and assigns for ever a certain tract or parcel of Land being a part
(43) or parcel of the aforesaid tract or parcel of the aforesaid described Tract of Land situate lying and being on the East side of Shirtees Creek beginning at a marked White Oak Tree on the East Bank of said Creek a Corner of William Lees Land thence by said William Lees Land South forty three Degrees East One hundred and seventy six perches to another marked White Oak tree another Corner of said William Lees Land thence South fifty degrees East One hundred and fifty five perches to a marked black Oak tree thence South Sixteen Degrees West One hundred and seventeen perches to a marked White Oak tree thence North eighty four degrees West One hundred and thirty eight perches to another marked White Oak tree thence South Twenty Seven degrees West forty Six perches to another marked White Oak Tree, thence West Sixty three perches to a marked Lyn Tree thence North fifty Degrees West thirty One perches to a marked Sugar Tree thence North eight degrees West eighteen perches to a post set up and marked on the East bank of said Creek thence down the East Bank and side of said Creek the different Courses thereof three hundred and ninety perches to the place of beginning containing three hundred and eighty four Acres with the Allowance of Six Acres Pr Cent for Roads & Highways with the Rights Members and appurtenances thereof and all Houses Edifices Buildings Orchards Gardens Lands Meadows Commons Pastures feedings Trees Woods Underwoods Ways Paths Waters Water Courses Easements Profits Commodities Advantages Heriditaments and Appurtenances whatsoever unto the said Tract of Land belonging or in any wise appertaining and also the Re-

version and Reversions Remainder and Remainders Rents and Services of all and Singular the said premises above mentioned and of every part and parcel thereof with the appurtenances And also all the Estate Right Title Interest Claim and Demand whatsoever both at Law and in Equity of him the said George Croghan of in and to all and singular the said premises above mentioned and of in and to every part and parcel thereof with the appurtenances To have and to hold the said tract of Land Heriditaments and premises above mentioned and every part and parcel thereof with the Appurtenances unto the said Ben-
(44) jamin Tate his heirs and Assigns to the only proper Use benefit and behoof of him the Benjamin Tate his heirs and Assigns forever Subject nevertheless to the Quit Rents to grow and become due to his Majesty his heirs & Successors and to no other Incumbrance whatsoever And further he the said George Croghan and his heirs and every other person & persons and his and their heirs anything having or claiming in the said premises above mentioned or any part thereof by from or under him them or either of them shall and will from time to time and at all times hereafter upon the reasonable Request and at the Cost and Charges of the said Benjamin Tate his heirs and Assigns make do and execute or cause to be made done and executed all and every such further and other lawful and reasonable Acts and Acts thing and Device and devices Conveyance and Conveyances in the Law whatsoever for the further better and more perfect granting conveying and Assuring of all and Singular the said premises above mentioned unto the said Benjamin Tate his heirs and Assigns to the only proper Use and behoof of him the said Benjamin Tate his heirs and Assigns for ever as by the said Benjamin Tate his heirs or Assigns or his or their Council learned in the Law shall be reasonably Devised or advised and required In Witness whereof the said Parties to these presents have hereunto set their hands and Seals the day and year first above written

Sealed and Delivered Geo: Croghan [L S]
in the presence of Us before signing the words "Eighteen Perches" in the twentieth line of the Second page being inter-

lined and the words "Benjamin
Tate" being wrote on Erasures
in the Second, third, Eleventh
Seventeenth Nineteenth and
Twentieth lines of the third page
John Campbell
Jacob Bousman

Received the day of the date of the within Indenture of the within named Benjamin Tate Thirty eight pounds eight Shil-
(45) lings lawful money of Great Britain being the full consideration Money in the said within Written Indenture mentioned

Geo Croghan

Witness
John Campbell

Be it remembered that on the thirty first day of December Anno Domini 1770 Before me Charles Edmonstone Esquire Captain in his Majestys 18th Regiment of foot commanding the Garrison of Fort Pitt personally appeared the within named George Croghan Esq who acknowledged the within written Indenture to be his Act and Deed and desired the same may be recorded as such Witness my hand and seal at Fort Pitt the day and year above said

Chas Edmonstone [L S]

At a Court held for Augusta County at Fort Dunmore May the 16th 1775

George Croghan Gent acknowledged this his Deed of Bargain and Sale with a receipt thereon endorsed to Benjamin Tate which is Ordered to be recorded

Test.

This Indenture made the ninth day of October in the year of our Lord One thousand Seven hundred and seventy two Between Benjamin Taite Sergt in his Majestys eighteenth or Royal Regiment of Ireland of the one part and John Campbell of the town of Pittsburgh County of Bedford and province of Pensylvania of the other part Witnesseth that the said

Benjamin Taite for and in Consideration of the sum of Sixty Six pounds ten Shillings Pensylvania Currency to him in hand paid by the said John Campbell the receipt whereof the said Benjamin Taite doth hereby confess and acknowledge he the said Benjamin Taite hath granted bargained and sold and by these presents doth grant bargain and sell unto the said John Campbell all that Plantation or tract of Land situate lying and being on the East side of Shirtees Creek opposite to Lands of Jacob
(46) Bousman about eight miles from Fort Pitt with all the Improvements thereon and also the Reversion & Reversions Remainder and Remainders Rents and services of all and Singular the said premises above mentioned and of every part and parcel thereof with the appurtenances To have and to hold the said Lands and premises above mentioned and every part and parcel thereof with the appurtenances unto the said John Campbell his Executors Administrators and assigns for the only proper Use benefit and behoof of Joseph Simon James Milligan and John Campbell Merchants of Pittsburgh aforesaid their Executors Administrators & Assigns for ever Provided always and upon Condition That if the said Benjamin Taite his heirs and assigns do and shall well and truly pay or cause to be paid unto the said John Campbell his Executors Administrators or Assigns the full sum of Sixty six pounds ten shillings lawful Pensylvania Money in and upon the first day of October next which will be in the year of our Lord One thousand seven huudred and seventy three without any Deduction or Abatement of Taxes Assessments or any other Impositions whatsoever either Ordinary or extraordinary that then and from thence forth these presents and everything herein contained shall cease determine and be void anything herein contained to the Contrary notwithstanding In Witness whereof both parties have hereunto interchangably set their hands & Seals the day and year first above written

Sealed and Delivered Benj: Tate Sergt [L S]
In the presence of
James Heron
Robert Elliott

Bedford County ss

Before me John Fraser Esquire one of his Majestys Justices of the peace & for the County aforesaid personally appeared
(47) the above named Benjamin Tate and acknowledged the above Indenture to be his Act and Deed and desired the same may be recorded as such In Witness whereof I have hereunto set my hand and seal this thirteenth day of October 1772

John Fraser [L S]

Entered in the Office for Recording of Deeds in and for the County of Bedford in Book A Page 35 the twenty fourth day of December Anno Dom 1772 Witness my hand and seal of my office aforesaid

A^r St Clair.

At a Court Continued and held for Augusta County at Fort Dunmore May 20th 1775.

This Mortage from Benjamin Tate to John Campbell Gent was produced and Ordered to be recorded

Test.

EXAMINED AND DELIVERED
John Campbell Oct 1775

I do hereby certify that Peter McGachney is intituled to fifty Acres of Land agreeable to his Majestys Proclamation in the year 1763. And being desirous to locate the same in the County of Augusta if he can lay it on any Vacant Lands that has not been Surveyed by Order of Council & patented since the above proclamation you are hereby Authorised and required to survey the same — Given under my hand and seal this 24th day of September 1774

DUNMORE [L S]

To the Surveyor of Augusta County

Entered in the Surveyors Office the 17th May 1775 and requested to be located by the Assignee on his Improvements at ye fort of Grants hill Pittsburg

To Major Crawford[1] to Execute THOS LEWIS, S A C[2]

[1] This was Col. Wm. Crawford, burned at the stake by the Indians in 1782.

[2] Surveyor of Augusta County, Virginia.

I do hereby Assign all my Right and Title of the within
(48) Warrant of fifty Acres of Land to which I am intituled as a disbanded Soldier of the forty Second Regiment residing in America under his Majestys Proclamation of 1763 unto John Campbell Esq of Pittsburg he having paid me a valuable Consideration for the same therefore desire the same may be surveyed for him & a Patent issued out in his Name

Given under my hand this 17th May 1775

Witness — Peter P M McCachney (his mark)

John Gibson
Andrew Robertson
Thomas Russell

At a Court continued and held for Augusta County at Fort Dunmore May the 17th 1775.

Peter McCachney acknowledged this Claim of Land to John Campbell Gent which is ordered to be recorded

Test JOHN MADISON

Know all Men by these presents That I John Ormsby of the Town of Pittsburgh Gentleman for and in Consideration of the sum of twenty four pounds lawful money of the Colony of Virginia to me in hand paid by Benjamin Johnston of Fredericksburgh in the said Colony the receipt whereof I do hereby acknowledge have granted bargained and sold and by these presents do grant bargain and sell unto the said Benjamin Johnston his heirs and Assigns Two certain Lotts in the said town of Pittsburgh situate within a Square of Ground in the Occupation of and being the property of the said John Ormsby viz the first to contain Sixty feet fronting the River Monongahela to begin at the Eastermost or South Eastermost Corner of the said Square and to extend back as far as the West side of the Second Street of the said Town, the other Lott containing Sixty feet front on said Second Street and opposite to the Lott now in the Occupation of Samuel
(49) Evalt it being the Corner Lott and to extend back as far as the Eastermost side of Third Street together with the appurtenances

thereto belonging To have and to hold the aforesaid described Lots of Grounds with the Appurtenances to the said Benjamin Johnston his heirs and Assigns to the only proper Use and behoof of the said Benjamin Johnston his heirs and Assigns for ever hereby warranting and defending the same hereby granted premises against all manner of Persons whatsoever Subject only to the Lord of the fee for Quit Rents that may become due for the said Lots and the expences of Pattenting the same when requested the said John Ormsby shall and will make all and every Deed or Deeds for the Conveying the said Lots in fee simple subject as aforesaid unto the said Benjamin Johnston his heirs and Assigns for the true performance hereof I do hereby bind myself my heirs Executors and Administrators to the said Benjamin Johnston his heirs and Assigns in the penal sum of five hundred pounds like money firmly by these presents Witness my hand and seal the seventh day of May Anno Domini One thousand seven hundred and seventy four

Sealed and Delivered John Ormsby [L. S.]
In the presence of us
Tho: Smallman
John Boyd
James Berwick

Received the day of the date of the within Deed the sum of twenty four pounds Virginia Currency being the Consideration therein mentioned

Witness John Ormsby

At a Court continued and held for Augusta County at Fort Dunmore May 20th 1775

John Ormsby acknowledged this his deed of Bargain and Sale to Benjamin Johnston which is ordered to be recorded.

Test JOHN MADISON Cl Cu

EXAM AND DELIVERED
Wm Elliott Nov 15, 1776

Know all Men by these presents that I Robert Elliott of Pittsburgh for and in consideration of the sum of One hundred and fifty pounds lawful money of Pensylvania to me in

hand paid by William Elliott of the County of Augusta the receipt whereof I do hereby Acknowledge have granted bargained and sold and by these presents do grant bargain and
(50) sell unto the said William Elliott a certain Improvement Plantation and tract of Land situate of Forbes old Road and about twelve miles from Pittsburgh adjoining Lands now or late the property of Ephraim Douglas containing Nine hundred Acres with all my right and Title of in and to the same To have and to hold the said premises with the appurtenances to the said William Elliott his heirs and Assigns to the only proper Use and behoof of the said William Elliott his heirs and Assigns for ever Subject to the purchase money Interest and Quit Rent due to the Lord or the Lords of the fee thereof And I the said Robert Elliott against me or my heirs and against all manner of Persons whatsoever the Lord of the fee aforesaid only excepted the hereby granted premises to the said William Elliott his heirs and Assigns shall and will warrant and for ever defend by these Presents In Witness whereof I have hereunto set my hand and seal the twentieth day of May One thousand seven hundred and seventy five

Sealed and Delivered in the presence of us
John Irwin
Jno Gibson
Jas Berwick

Robt Elliott (Seal)

At a Court Continued and held for Augusta County at Fort Dunmore May 20th 1775

Robert Elliott acknowledged this his deed of Bargain and Sale to William Elliott which is ordered to be recorded

Test JOHN MADISON

EXAMINED & DELIVERED
Hannah Aston December 7th 1775

Know all men by these presents that I James Cumberford for and in Consideration of the sum of Sixty pounds v. c. to me in hand well and truly paid by George Aston the receipt whereof I do hereby acknowledge have bargained and sold and by these presents do grant bargain sell & assign and make

over to him all my Right Title Interest Claim and Demand of two tracts one on Mill Creek & other Tract Land situate lying
(51) and being on the Waters of Mountours Run with the appurtenances thereunto belonging or any wise appertaining To have and to hold the same tract aforesaid unto the said George Aston his heirs and Assigns to the only proper Use Benefit and behoof of the said Aston his heirs and assigns and every part thereof against all Manner of Persons (the Lord of Soil only excepted) shall and will warrant the said. As Witness my hand and Seal this 3d day of January in the year of our Lord One thousand seven hundred and seventy five 1775

Sealed & Deliver'd In the presence of
Valentine Tho D'Alton

his
James O Cumberford [L S]
mark

At a Court Continued and held for Augusta County at Fort Dunmore February 23d 1775

This Deed of Bargain and Seal from James Cumberford to George Aston was proved by Valentine Thomas D'Alton the witness thereto and ordered to be recorded

Test JOHN MADISON

EXAMINED & DELIVERED
Hannah Aston 7th December 1775

Know all Men by these presents That I Simon Butler for and in Consideration of the sum of One hundred and fifty pounds v. c. to me in hand well and truly paid by George Aston the receipt whereof I do hereby acknowledge have bargained and sold and by these presents do grant bargain sell assign and make over to the said Aston four Improvements or tracts of Land situate lying and being on the Waters of Mill Creek one of the Branches of the Ohio with the appurtenances thereunto belonging or anywise appurtenaning To have and to hold the said Improvements to said Aston his heirs and Assigns to the only proper Use Benefit and behoof of the said Aston his heirs and Assigns and every part and parcel thereof against all manner of Persons (the Lord of the Soil only excepted) shall and will warrant & Defend the said from all Manner of Persons As Witness my hand and seal this third day of January in the year of our Lord One thousand seven hundred and seventy five 1775

Witness present — Simon his X mark Butler [L S]
Valentine Thos D'Alton
Jacob Bousman

(52) At a Court Continued and held for Augusta County at Fort Dunmore February 23d 1775

This Deed of Bargain and Sale from Simon Butler to George Aston was proved by Valentine Tho D'alton one of the Witnesses thereto and ordered to be recorded

Test JOHN MADISON

EXAMINED & DELIVERED
Hannah Aston 7th December 1775

Articles of Agreement made and concluded on by and between Cornelius Doherty of the one part and George Aston of the other part Witnesseth that the said Cornelius Doherty doth covenant grant and agree with Georgc Aston his heirs and Assigns, my heirs hereby doth covenant grant agree with the said George Aston to let him have a certain Quantity or parcel of Land the said Doherty having one third of the said Lands Aston hereby obtaining securing and getting for me a patent or lawful Right for the said Lands being about 3000 Acres more or less which the said Aston is to be at the expences attending the securing the said Lands and surveying &c which land I do hereby Warrant and Defend from all manner of Persons lawfully claiming the same (the Lord of the soil only accepted) said Lands lying on the Waters of Lower Traverse Creek joining Bostian Frederick on the one part and Abraham Kuykendal on the other part said Lands being now improved In Witness whereof I have hereunto set my hand and seal this 30th day of Jany 1775

Witness present — Cornelius his A. mark Doherty [L S]
Valentine Tho D'Alton
Joseph his J mark Kerswell

At a Court Continued and held for Augusta County at Fort Dunmore February 23d 1775

This Agreement between Cornelius Doherty and George Aston was proved by Valentine Thomas D'Alton one of the Witnesses thereto and Ordered to be Recorded

Test JOHN MADISON [L S]

---

(53) EXAMINED & DELIVERED Geo Morgan September the 29th 1775

This Indenture made the Nineteenth day of September in the year of our Lord One thousand seven hundred and Seventy five Between George Croghan Esquire of Pittsburgh of the one part and Thomas Lawrence of the City of Philadelphia Esquire of the other part Whereas Iohonorissa Scarayadia and Cosswantinecea Cheifs or Sachems of the Six United Nations of Indians did by their deed duly Executed bearing date the Second day of August in the Year of our Lord One Thousand Seven Hundred and forty nine for the Consideration therein Specified Grant Bargain and Sell unto the said George Croghan in Fee a Certain Tract or Parcel of Land situate lying and being on the South side of the Monongahela River Beginning at the mouth of a Run nearly Opposite Turtle Creek and then down the said Monongahela River to its Junction with the River OHio computed to be ten Miles then running down the Eastern Bank and sides of and unto the said River OHio to where Racoon Creek empties itself into the said River thence up the said Creek ten Miles and from thence on a direct line to the Place of beginning Containing by Estimation One hundred Thousand Acres be the same more or less as by the said Deed may more fully appear And Whereas certain chiefs or Sachems fully representing the Six United Nations aforesaid in full Council at Fort Stanwix assembled did by their deed duly Executed bearing date the fourth day of November One Thousand Seven hundred and Sixty Eight for the Consideration therein Mentioned Grant Ratifie and Confirm unto his Most sacred Majesty George the Third by the Grace of God King of Great Britain France and Ireland &c his Heirs and Successors for the Use Benefit and Behoof of the said George Croghan all the above bounded and described Tract or Parcel
(54) of Land and Premises as by the said Deed Poll recorded in the

Office for recording of Deeds in the City and County of Philadelphia in Book J Volume the fifth page the two hundred and thirty ninth & may more fully and at large appear Now This Indenture Witnesseth that the said George Croghan for and in Consideration of the Sum of Two Thousand seven hundred & Eighty seven Pounds lawful Money of Great Britain to him the said George Croghan by him the aforesaid Thomas Lawrance in hand paid the receipt whereof he the said George Croghan doth hereby Acknowledge hath Granted Bargained Sold Aliened Released and Confirmed and by these Presents doth fully freely and absolutely Grant Bargain Sell Alien Release and Confirm unto the said Thomas Lawrance (in his Actual Possession now being by Virtue of a bargain and Sale thereof made to him for one Whole Year by Indenture bearing date the day next before the day of the date of these Presents and by force of the Statute for transferring of Uses into Possession) and to his Heirs and assigns forever a Certain Tract or Parcel of Land being a part or parcel of the aforesaid described Tract of Land situate lying and being on the southwestern side of the River OHio and bounded to the Northward by the Logs Town Tract and the Lands of Alexander Ross Esquire to the Westward by the Land of Joseph Simons, George Croghan Esquire and David Rodgers to the Southward by the Lands of Barnard Gratz and Major Edward Ward and to the Eastward by the River OHio Beginning at a Sassafras on the Southwestern Bank of the said River and Running S 78° W 320 perches to a Spanish Oak Corner to Alexander Ross Esquire thence with the said Ross's line S 12° E 820 Perches to a White Oak Corner to said Ross thence with the said Ross's line S 78 W 1748 perches to a Stake Corner to said Ross and Joseph Simons thence with the said Simons's line S 12° E 640 perches to a Stone Corner to said Simons and George Croghan Esquire thence with the said Croghans Line S 44° 30 E 964 perches and 20 links to a Stake
(55) Corner to a Stake Corner to said Croghan and David Rodgers thence continuing the said Cource with the said Rodgers's 336 perches Making in the whole 1300 Perches and 20 links to a Stone Corner to the said Rogers and Barnard Gratz thence with the said Gratz's line N 43° 15 E 977 Perches to a Stake Corner to Major Edward Ward thence with the said Wards line N

32° 15 E 323 perches to a Stake corner to said Ward thence with the said Wards Line S 63° 45 E 160 perches to a Stake Corner to said Ward thence with the said Wards line N 32° 15 E 928 Perches to an Elm on the said Southwestern Bank of the said River OHio Corner to the said Ward and thence down the said River on the said Southwestern side with the Various Courses thereof 1347 Perches to the Place of Beginning Containing Eighteen Thousand five hundred and Eighty Acres with the Allowance of six acres pr Cent for Roads and Highways with the Rights Manners and Appurtenances thereof and all Houses Edifices Buildings Orchards Gardens Lands Meadows Pastures Feedings Commons Trees Woods Underwoods Ways Paths Waters Watercourses Easements Profits Commodities Advantages Hereditaments and appurtenances whatsoever unto the said Tract of Land belonging or in anywise Appertaining and also the Reversion & Reversions Remainder and Remainders Rents and Services of all and Singular the said Premises above Mentioned and of every part and parcel thereof with the Appurtenances and also all the Estate Right Title Interest Claim and Demand whatsoever both at Law and in Equity of him the said George Croghan of in and to all and Singular the said Premises above Mentioned and of in and to every part and parcel thereof with the Appurtenances To have and to hold the said Tract of Land Hereditaments and Premises above Mentioned and every part and parcel thereof with the Appurtenances unto the said Thomas Lawrance his heirs and Assigns to the only proper use
(56) Benefit and Behoof of him the said Thomas Lawrance his heirs and Assigns forever Subject Nevertheless to the Quit Rents to grow and become due to his Majesty his Heirs and Successors and to no other incumbrance whatsoever And farther that he the said George Croghan and his Heirs and every other Person and Persons and his and their Heirs any thing having or Claiming in the said Premises above Mentioned or any part thereof by from or under him them or any of them shall and will from time to time and at all Times hereafter upon the Reasonable Request and at the Cost and Charges of the said Thomas Lawrance his heirs and Assigns make do and Execute or Cause to be made done and Executed all and every such further and other Lawful and Reasonable Act and Acts thing and things

Device and Devices Conveyance and Conveyances in the Law Whatsoever for the further better and more perfect Granting Conveying and assuring of all and Singular the said Premises above Mentioned unto the said Thomas Lawrance his heirs and assigns to the only proper use and Behoof of him the said Thomas Lawrance his Heirs and assigns forever as by the said Thomas Lawrance his Heirs and assigns or his or their Council learned in the Law shall be Reasonably devised or advised and Required In Witness whereof the said George Croghan hath hereto set his hand and seal the day and year first above Written

Sealed and Delivered Geo: Croghan [L S]
in the Presence of us
William Trent[1]
Geo Morgan[2]

Pittsburg September the Nineteenth One Thousand Seven hundred and Seventy five Received of Mr. Thomas Lawrance the sum of Two Thousand Seven hundred and Eighty seven pounds Sterlg Money of Great Brittain being the full Consideration Expressed in the above Deed as Witness my Hand

Witnesses Geo: Croghan
William Tren
Geo Morgan

(57) At a Court Continued & held for Augusta County at Pittsburgh September the twenty third day of September 1775

George Croghan Esquire Acknowledged this his deed of Bargain and Sale to Thomas Lawrance which is Ordered to be Recorded

Test JOHN MADISON

EXAMD & DELIVERED
John Gabriel Jones Sept 25th 1775

This Indenture made the nineteenth day of September One Thousand Seven Hundred and Seventy five Between William Parkyson of the County of Augusta in the Colony of Virginia of the one part and John *Mitchell*[1] of the said County and Colony aforesaid of the other part being of

[1] See Introductory, ante p. 13.

[2] Colonel Geo. Morgan, Princeton, N. J., the Indian agent at Pittsburgh, subsequently (1796) removing to "Morganza," in Washington County, Pennsylvania.

lawful Age that for and in Consideration of the sum of Twenty Pounds in hand paid hath put and placed himself Voluntary for the Space of Three years and three Quarters from the date of these presents and him the said William Parkyson to serve for the aforesaid term in the Capacity of a Servant and as such to demean himself According to his Wit Power and Ability and Agreeable to the Laws of this Colony and the said William Parkyson for himself his heirs or Executors doth Promise and agree to find the said Servant in Competent and Sufficient Meat Drink and Apparal Washing and Lodging and all other things fit and Necessary for a Servant and at the Expiration of the said Term to pay the Customary dues In Witness whereof both Parties have hereunto set their Hands and Seals the day and year above Written

Sign'd Sealed and Delivered John × McMullin[1] [L S]
his mark
in the presence of William Parkison [L S]
J G Jones
Benjn Davis
Silas Zane

(58) At a Court Continued and held for Augusta County at Pittsburg the 20th day of September 1775

This Indenture from John McMullin to William Parkyson was Proved by the Oaths of John Gabriel Jones and Benjamin Davis two of the Witnesses thereto and Ordered to be recorded

Test JOHN MADISON

EXAMINED & DELIVERED
John Jeremiah Jacobs October 8th 1775

Know all men by these Presents that I Robert Denbow of the County of Westmoreland in the Province of Pennsylvania for and in Consideration of the Sum of fifteen Pounds to me in hand paid by Michael Cresap the receipt whereof I do hereby Acknowledge Have Bargained and Sold and by these presents do bargain and sell unto the sd Michael Cresap[2] one Tract or Parcel of Land Situate Lying and being in Westmore-

[1] So recorded; was it John Mitchell or John McMullin who thus became an "indented servant"?

[2] Charged by Logan with having killed his relatives in the spring of 1774.

land County in the Province of Pens[a] af[d] adjoining the Lands of David Rogers and Joseph Brenton on the Monongahaly being part of a Larger tract of Land I purchased of James Brenton and Containing by Estimation two hundred and fifty acres To have and to hold the said Tract or Parcels of Land with all and Singular the Appurtenances thereto belonging unto the said Michael Cresap and his heirs forever and Whereas the said Michael Cresap hath allowed me the use and Occupation of the said Land for the Space of Six Months from the date hereof I do hereby further Covenant and agree with the sd Michael that I my heirs Executors or Administrators shall and will deliver up Possession of the said Land to the said Michael Cresap at or before the Expiration of the said Six Months from the date hereof In Witness whereof I have hereunto set my hand and Seal this twenty eighth day of September 1773

Signed Sealed and Delivered in the Presence of
Geo Brent
Jo[s] Dorsey
Henry Brenton

Robert (his D mark) Denbow [L S]

At a Court Continued and held for Augusta County at Pittsburgh September the 21st 1775

(59) This Deed of Bargain and Sale from Robert Denbow to Michael Cresap Gent was proved by George Brent Gent one of the Witnesses thereto and Ordered to be recorded

Test JOHN MADISON

EXAMINED AND DELIVERED
John Jeremiah Jacobs October 8th 1775

Know all men by these presents that I James Brenton of Augusta County Virginia Monongahela Settlement for and in Consideration of the Sum of Fifty Pounds Pennsylvania Currency to me in hand paid by Michael Cresap Senr the Receipt whereof I do hereby Acknowledge and my self fully Sattisfyd have Bargained & sold and delivered and by these Presents do Bargain Sell and deliver a Certain Tract or Parcel of Land lying about one Mile distant from Monongahela River and Bounded by the following persons John Adams on the North East Edward Dorsey on the East Thomas Brown West and Edward White on the North with all and singular the appurtenances thereunto belonging or in any ways appertaining Containing by Estimation about two hundred and fifty Acres be the same more or less To have and to hold the said Tract or Parcel of Land to him the said Cresap his heirs and assigns forever from and against me my heirs Executors Admr or Assigns and from and against all Manner of Person or Persons the Lord of the Soile Excepted only and shall and will forever Warrant and defend the said Land with the appurtenances In Witness whereof I have hereunto set my hand this 5th day of September 1775

Witness James Brenton

the D mark of Robert Denbow

Jno Jer^{h} Jacobs

Interlined (the Lord of the Soil Excepted only) before the sealing and Delivery of these Presents

At a Court Continued and held for Augusta County at Pittsburgh September 21st 1775

This Deed of Bargain and Sale from James Brenton to Michael Cresap was proved by the Oath of John Jeremiah Jacobs one of the Witnesses thereto and Ordered to be Recorded

Test JOHN MADISON

---

(60) EXAMINED & DELIVERED
John Jeremiah Jacobs October 8th 1775

Know all men by these presents that I Josiah Little of Mannilling Township Westmoreland County in Pennsylvania for the Valuable Consideration of Seven Pounds ten Shillings Pennsylvania to me in hand paid by John Corey of Springhill Township in said County the Receipt whereof I do hereby Acknowledge and myself therewith fully Sattisfied Contented and paid have bargained Sold set over Released Conveyed and Confirmed and by these presents do bargain Sell Set over and Confirm and deliver unto the said John Corey his Attorney heirs Executrs Admrs and Assigns a Certain tract or parcel of Land Containing two hundred Acres be it more or

less as it is butted and bounded Easterly on the Lands of Andrew Rob &c Westerly on the Land of Isaac Willson and the Watters of the Middle run Northerly on the lands of sd Willson and Rob & Southerly on the Land of Hugh Gilmore at the Lick Called the Buffaloo Lick To have and to hold the above bargained and Mentioned Peice of land together with all its Improvements fences buildings timber Watter and Watter Courses with all the other priveledges and Appurtainnances Whatsoever thereunto belonging or in anywise appertaining against any Lawfull Claims or demand of myself my heirs Executrs Admintrs or Assigns or any other person or persons Whatsoever Claiming the same (the Rites and Services belonging to his Lordship the proprietor herein only Excepted) and further I do hereby Certifie that at the time and untill the Execution of these presents I am Justly and lawfully seized of the said Premises by Virtue of a purchase made of the same (by me) from a Certain James Willson of this place which said
(61) peice of Land together with all the above said Priviledges and appurtenances I do hereby bind myself my heirs Executors Administrs and every of them to the said John Corey his heirs Exctr Admr and assignes to warrant and forever defend against the Claime or demand of the said Willson his heirs or assigns or any other person or persons whatsoever Claiming the same in testimony whereof I have hereunto set my hand and Seal this 18th day of March in the year of our Lord Christ One Thousand Seven hundred and seventy four 1774

Signed Sealed and deliv- ered in presence of us Josiah Littel [Seal]

his
John × Pettijohn
mark

Know all men by these presents that I John Corey of Dunlaps Creek Settlem't for and in Consideration of the sum of Fifty Pounds Pennsylvania Curry to me in hand paid by Michael Cresap Senr the Rect whereof I do hereby Acknowledge have Bargained and by these Presents do Bargain and Sell unto the sd Cresap all the Tract or Parcel of Land Contained in the within Bill of sale from Josias Little to me dated the 18th of March 1774 together with all the appurtenances there-

unto Belonging or anyway appertaining but Nevertheless if the said John Corey can and do pay the said Michael Cresap his Certain Attorney heirs or Assigns within the space of twelve Months from the date hereof a Certain sum of Money Contained in a Bond from him to said Cresap of the 19th of Dec 1772 together with all Interest and Costs &c then this Bill of Sale to be Void and the Property of the within Mentioned Land to revert to me the said Corey as if such Bill of Sale had never been given but on the Contrary I do Promise to deliver to the said Michael Cresap or his Attorney Peaceable Possession when required by him or them and do and will forever Warrant and defend the said Land to him the said Cresap his heirs or Assigns against myself my heirs Executors or any other Person or Persons Whatsoever According to the true Intent and Meaning of these presents In Witness whereof I have
(62) hereunto set my hand and Seal this 1st day of September 1775

Witness John Corey

Jno Jerh Jacobs[1]

At a Court Continued and held for Augusta County at Pittsburgh September 21st 1775

This deed of Bargain and Sale from John Corey to Michael Cresap Gent was proved by John Jeremiah Jacobs the Witness thereto and Ordered to be Recorded

Test JOHN MADISON

EXAMD & DELIVERED
Jacob Saylor

This Indenture made the Eleventh day of September in the year of our Lord One Thousand Seven hundred and Seventy five Between Andrew Robinson of Pittsburgh Taylor of the one part and Jacob Saylor of the same place Gunsmith of the other part Witnesseth that the said Andrew Robinson in Consideration of the sum of five Shillings lawful Money of Pennsylvania and also for the securing of the sum of forty Pounds seven Shillings and one penny like lawful Money due to a Certain Benjamin Elliott for which said sum the said

[1] Michael Cresap's clerk in the Old Redstone storehouse; subsequently married Cresap's widow.

Jacob Saylor stands bound by Recognizance for the said Andrew Robinson in the County Court of Bedford County in the Province of Pennsylvania he the said Andrew Robinson hath granted bargained and Sold and by these Presents doth grant bargain and sell unto the said Jacob Saylor a Messuage a Stable and four Lotts of Ground situate in the Town of Pittsburgh aforesaid whereon the said Andrew Robinson now lives with all the Improvements and Appurtenances thereunto belonging and all the right Title and property of him the said Andrew Robinson of in and to the same To have and to hold the aforesaid hereby granted Premises with the Appurtenances unto the said Jacob Saylor his heirs and assigns to the only proper Use and behoof of the said Jacob Saylor his heirs and assigns forever Subject only to the Purchase Money due and to become due to the Cheif Lord of Lords of the fee thereof and the aforesaid Andrew Robinson against him and his heirs and against all Manner of Persons claiming by from or Under him
(63) the aforesaid Premises unto the said Jacob Saylor his heirs and assigns shall and will Warrant and forever defend by these Presents Provided Nevertheless and it is hereby declared to be the true Intent and Meaning of these Presents that if the said Andrew Robinson shall and do on or before the tenth day of November next ensuing the date of these Presents well and truly pay and Satisfy the afore mentioned Sum of forty Pounds Seven Shillings and one penny together with all lawful Interest and Charges of Court and all Incident Expences accruing on the same and shall also indemnify and forever save harmless the said Jacob Saylor his heirs Executors and Administrators of and from the Payment of the said Judgment then this present Indenture to cease and be Void to all Intents and purposes as if the same had never been made in Witness Whereof the said Parties have hereunto set their hands and Seals the day and year afore written

Sealed and Delivered Andrew Robrtson [L S]
in the Presence of us
Jas Berwick
John Rossan
Jno McCallister

At a Court held for Augusta County at Pittsburgh January 16th 1776

This Mortgage from Andrew Robinson to Jacob Saylor was proved by the Oaths of James Berwick and John McCallister two of the Witnesses thereto and Ordered to be certified.

Test JOHN MADISON

Know all men by these presents that I Mordecai Moses Mordecai of Pittsburg for and in Consideration of the Sum of Three Hundred Pounds Current Money of Pennsylvania to me in hand paid the Receipt whereof I do hereby Acknowledge Have Granted Bargained sold and delivered by these Presents Doth Grant Bargain Sell and deliver unto Joseph Simon one plantation and Improvement, situate lying and being on Sucks run near Pittsburg, and all houses buildings and appurtenances thereunto belonging and also two Copper Stills with all the utensils thereunto belonging and all the household furniture now in my Possession or belonging to me To have and to hold the said Plantation and Improvement with all the appurtenances
(64) thereunto belonging, and all and Singular other the premises hereinbefore mentioned unto the said Joseph Simons his heirs and assigns to the only proper use and behoof of the said Joseph Simon his heirs and assigns forever And I the said Mordecai Moses Mordecai for myself my heirs Exors and Administrators the said Plantation and Improvement with the Appurtenances thereunto belonging with all and Singular other the Premises herein before mentioned, unto the said Joseph Simon his heirs and assigns Will Warrant and forever defend — In Witness whereof I have hereunto set my hand and Seal this 19th day of July 1775

Mordecai M Mordecai [L S]

Testes
Jno Anderson
John Campbell
Robert Campbell

At a Court Continued and held for Augusta County at Fort Dunmore September the 20th 1775

This Deed of Bargain and Sale from Mordecai Moses Mordecai to Joseph Simon was proved by the Oaths of John Anderson and Robert Campbell two of the Witnesses thereto and Ordered to be Certified

Test.

This Indenture made this twenty sixth day of August in the Year of our Lord One Thousand Seven Hundred and Seventy five Between William Dunbar of Manchac Settlement on the Missippi of the one part and Charles Simms of Pittsburgh Attorney at Law of the other part Witnesseth that the said William Dunbar for and in Consideration of the Sum of Ninety three Pounds Sterling to him in hand paid by the said Charles Simms the Receipt whereof he doth hereby acknowledge, Hath Granted Bargained and Sold aliened and Confirmed and by these Presents doth Grant Bargain Sell Alien and Confirm unto the said Charles Simms his heirs and assigns one third part of a Certain Tract of Land situate lying and being on Raccoon Creek on the West side of the Laurel Hill in the County of Augusta Beginning at the most South Easterly corner of two thousand Eight hundred and Seventeen Acres of Land Granted to Alexander Ross by George Croghan Gent thence South twelve degrees East Sixty Eight Chains and thirty three links to a Corner of a Certain Tract of Land granted as aforesaid to Robert Lettis Hoopers Land South Seventy Eight degrees West four hundred and thirty seven Chains to another Corner of the said Hoopers Land thence North twelve degrees West Sixty eight Chains and thirty three links to a Corner of Alexander Ross's Land aforesaid thence
(65) by the said Alexander Ross's Land North Seventy eight Degrees East four hundred and thirty seven Chains to the place of Beginning containing two thousand Eight hundred and Seventeen Acres which said Tract of Land was sold Conveyed to the said William Dunbar by George Croghan Gent by deed bearing date the Ninth day of January in the year of our Lord One Thousand Seven hundred and Seventy two and all Houses Buildings Yards Gardens Orchards Ways Woods

Waters Water Courses Profits Commodities Hereditaments and Appurtenances whatsoever to the same belonging or in anywise Appertaining and the Reversion and Reversions Remainder and Remainders Rents Issues and profits thereof and also all the Estate Right Title Interest property Claim and demand of the said William Dunbar of in and to one third part of the aforesaid Tract of Land To have and to hold one third part of the above Mentioned Tract of Land and premises unto the said Charles Simms his heirs and assigns to the only proper use and behoof of the said Charles Simms his heirs and assigns forever And the said William Dunbar doth Covenant promise and Grant to and with the said Charles Simms that he the said William Dunbar his heirs and Assigns and all and every person or persons claiming by from or under him or them shall and will from time to time and at all times forever hereafter upon the request and at the Cost and Charges in the law make do and execute or cause or procure to be make done and Executed all and every such further and other lawfull and reasonable Act and Acts thing and things Conveyances and assurances in the Law for the better and more perfect granting conveying and assuring the hereby Granted Land and premises unto the said Charles Simms his heirs and assigns as by the said Charles Simms his heirs and assigns his or their Council Learned in the Law shall be reasonably advised devised and required In Witness whereof Alexander Ross Attorney for the said William Dunbar by Virtue of a power of Attorney from the said William Dunbar bearing date the twenty eighth day of February in the year of our Lord 1772 hath hereunto set the hand and affixed the Seal of the said William Dunbar the day and Year first above written

Signed Seald and Delivered
In presence of
C Graydon
James M[c] Kee
Dan[l] Brown

At a Court Continued and held for Augusta County at Pittsburgh April the 17th 1776

(66) This deed of Bargain and Sale from William Dunbar by his

Attorney Ross to Charles Sims was proved by the Oaths of Caleb Graydon and Daniel Brown two of the Witnesses thereto and Ordered to be Certified

At a Court Continued and held for Augusta County at Pittsburgh April the 18th 1776

This deed of Bargain and Sale from William Dunbar by his Attorney Alexander Ross to Charles Simms being formerly proved by the Oaths of Caleb Graydon and Daniel Brown two of the Witnesses thereto was this day further proved by the Oath of James McKee the other Witness thereto and Ordered to be recorded

Test

This Indenture made this twenty sixth day of August in the Year of our Lord one thousand seven hundred and Seventy five Between Alexander Ross Esq of Pittsburgh in the County of Augusta and Colony of Virginia of the one part and Charles Simms Esq Attorney at Law of the same place of the other part Witnesseth that the said Alexander Ross for and in Consideration of the Sum of two hundred and two Pounds Sterling Money of Great Britain to him in hand paid by the said Charles Sims the receipt whereof he doth hereby Acknowledge Hath Granted bargained and sold aliened and Confirmed and by these presents Doth Grant Bargain and sell alien and Confirm unto the said Charles Simms his heirs and Assigns the following Lands that is to say, one half or equal Moiety of a Tract of Land situate on the Southwest side of the River Ohio above the Mouth of Raccoon Creek being part of the Bottom commonly called the long Bottom, beginning at a Swamp Maple Tree standing on the lower Bank of a Small run where it emptys into the River Ohio being the first run below Ryleys run which Run emptys itself into the river at the head the aforesaid long Bottom, then from the said Swamp Maple tree up the several Courses of the river Ohio to a Swamp'd Maple tree Marked on two sides With three notches on each side and a blaze above them for a Corner thence South forty five degrees West One hundred and forty three chains to a stone,

thence North forty five degrees West One hundred and fifty three Chains to a Stake, (South Seventeen degrees East distant 17 links stands a white Oak tree mark'd A R) then from said
(67) stake, North forty five degrees East forty one Chains and fifty links to a stone thence along the bounds of a Tract of Land granted to Rob[t] Lettis Hooper Junr South forty five degrees East thirty five Chains to a Stone corner of said Hoopers Land thence North forty five degrees East one hundred and Seventy Chains along the bounds of said Hoopers Land to the place of Beginning containing two thousand One hundred and Sixty seven Acres be the same more or less which said Tract of Land was sold and Convey'd unto the said Alexander Ross by George Croghan Gent by deed bearing date the ninth day of January in the year of our Lord One Thousand Seven hundred and Seventy two also one third part of a Certain Tract or parcel of Land situate lying and being on Raccoon Creek Bounded as followeth Beginning at a Stake from which stake south three degrees West distant hereby four links stands a Spanish Oak tree Mark'd with the letter A and a blaze above, thence from said stake South twelve degrees East sixty eight chains and thirty three links to a Corner of William Dunbars Land thence South Seventy eight degrees West four hundred and thirty seven Chains to another Corner of William Dunbars Land; thence North twelve degrees West Sixty eight Chains and thirty three links to a Stone from which stone North Eighty three degrees East distant Seventy six links stands a White Oak tree Mark'd with the Letter A and a blaze above, then from said stone North Seventy eight degrees East by Lands of the aforesaid George Croghan and Nathaniel Kerkendall four hundred and thirty seven Chains to the Place of Beginning containing two thousand Eight hundred and Seventeen Acres be the same more or less which said Land was sold and Conveyed by George Croghan to the said Alexander Ross by deed bearing date the Ninth day of January in the Year of our Lord One Thousand Seven Hundred and Seventy two and all Houses buildings Yards Gardens Orchards Ways Waters Water Courses profits Commodities Hereditaments and Appurtances whatsoever to the same belonging or in anywise Appertaining and the Reversion and Reversions Remainder and Remainders

Rents Issues and Profits thereof and also all the Estate Right Title Interest property Claim and demand either in Law or equity of him the said Alexander Ross of in and to the Moiety of the first Mentioned Tract and to one third of the last Mentioned Tract of Land To have and to hold the hereby Granted Land and premises unto the said Charles Simms his heirs and Assigns to the only proper use and behoof of the said Charles Simms his heirs and assigns forever and the said Alexander Ross doth hereby covenant promise and Grant to and with the said Charles Simms that he the said Alexander Ross and his heirs and all and every person or persons claiming by from or
(68) under him or them shall and will from time to time and at all times hereafter upon the request and at the Cost and Charges of the said Charles Simms his heirs or assigns make do and Execute or cause or procure to be made done and Executed all and every such further and other Lawfull and reasonable Act and Acts thing and things Conveyances and Assurances in the Law for the better and more perfect Granting conveying and assuring the before Mentioned Land and premises unto the said Charles Simms his heirs and assigns forever as by the said Charles Simms his or their Council learned in the Law shall be reasonably advised devised and required In Witness whereof the said Charles Simms hath hereunto set his hand and affixed his seal the day and year first before written

Sign'd Seal'd & Deliver'd — Alexr Ross [L S]
In presence of
C Graydon
James McKee

Received of the within named Charles Simms the within Mentioned Sum of two hundred and two Pounds Sterling Money of Great Britain being the Consideration within Mentioned Witness my hand this twenty sixth day of

Witness — Alexr Ross
C Graydon
James McKee
Danl Brown

At a Court Continued and held for Augusta County at Pittsburgh April the 17th 1776

This deed of Bargain and Sale from Alexander Ross to Charles Simms was proved by the Oaths of Caleb Graydon and Daniel Brown two of the Witnesses thereto and Ordered to be Certified

At a Court Continued and held for Augusta County at Pittsburg April the 18th 1776

This deed of Bargain and Sale from Alexander Ross to Charles Simms being formerly proved by the Oaths of Caleb Graydon and Daniel Brown two of the Witnesses thereto was this day further proved by the Oath of James McKee the other Witness thereto and Ordered to be recorded

Test

This Indenture made this twenty sixth day of August in the Year of our Lord One Thousand Seven Hundred and Seventy five Between Alexander Ross Esq of the Town of Pittsburg of the first part and Charles Simms of the same place Attorney at Law of the other part Witnesseth that the said Alexander Ross for and in Consideration of the Sum of Fifteen Pounds Current Money of the Province of Pennsylvania to him in hand paid by the said Charles Simms the receipt whereof
(69) he doth hereby acknowledge Hath granted Bargained and Sold and by these presents Doth Grant Bargain and Sell unto the said Charles Simms his heirs and assigns one equal half or Moiety of a Certain Quantity or parcell of Land situate in the Town of Pittsburg on the Bank of the Allegheny River and is the same Lott or parcell of Land whereon the said Alexander Ross formerly had a house, and all houses buildings yards Gardens Orchards Ways Waters Water Courses profits Commodities Hereditaments and appurtenances whatsoever to the same belonging or in any wise appertaining and the Reversion and Reversions Remainder and Remainders Rents Issues and profits thereof and also all the Estate Right Title Interest use trust property Claim and demand of the said Alexander Ross of in and to the said Moiety of the said Lott or parcel of Land, To have and to hold the said half or Moiety of the

said Lott of Land with the appurtenances unto the said Charles Simms his heirs and assigns to the only proper use and behoof of the said Charles Simms his heirs and assigns forever In Witness whereof the said Alexander Ross hath hereunto set his hand and affixed his seal the day and year first above written

Signed Sealed and delivered Alexr Ross [L S]

In presence of

the Words "one equal half or Moiety of"

being interlined before Signed

C Graydon

James McKee

Danl Brown

At a Court Continued and held for Augusta County at Pittsburgh April the 17th 1776

This deed of Bargain and Sale from Alexander Ross to Charles Simms was proved by the Oaths of Caleb Graydon and Daniel Brown two of the Witnesses thereto and Ordered to be Certified.

At a Court Court Continued and held for Augusta County at Pittsburgh April the 18th 1776

This deed of Bargain and Sale from Alexander Ross to Charles Simms being formerly proved by Oaths of Caleb Graydon and Daniel Brown two of the Witnesses thereto was this day further proved by the Oath of James McKee the other Witness thereto and Ordered to be recorded

Test

Know all men by these presents that I William Dunbar of Manchac Settlement on the Mississippi for divers good Causes and Considerations me hereunto moving have made ordained Constituted and Appointed and by these Presents do make ordain Constitute and Appoint Charles Simms of Pittsburg Attorney at Law my True and Lawfull Attorney for me and in my name to sell transfer and Convey or otherwise dispose of all my Right Title Estate and Interest of in and to a Certain Tract or parcel of Land situate on the Waters of Raccoon Creek which Land I purchased from George Croghan

Gent in what manner and to such person or persons as to him
(70) shall appear best and most conducive to my Interest and for me and in my name to make and Execute such Deeds and Conveyances as may be necessary for transferring and Conveying my Right and Title to said Lands to any person or persons that may become Purchasers thereof or any part thereof hereby ratifying and Confirming whatever my said Attorney shall lawfully and legally do relative thereto In Witness whereof Alexander Ross Attorney for the said William Dunbar by Virtue of a Power of Attorney bearing date the 28th day of February 1772 hath hereunto set the hand and Affixed the Seal of the said William Dunbar

Signed Sealed & delivered Will Dunbar [L S]
in presence of
C Graydon
James McKee
Danl Brown

At a Court Continued and held for Augusta County at Pittsburgh April 17th 1776

This Power of Attorney from William Dunbar by his Attorney Alexander Ross to Charles Simms was proved by the Oaths of Caleb Graydon and Daniel Brown two of the Witnesses thereto and Ordered to be Certified

At a Court Continued and held for Augusta County at Pittsburgh April the 18th 1776

This Power of Attorney from William Dunbar by his Attorney Alexander Ross to Charles Simms being formerly proved by the Oaths of Caleb Graydon and Daniel Brown two of the Witnesses thereto was this day further proved by the Oath of James McKee the other Witness thereto and Ordered to be recorded

Test

Know all men by these presents that I Alexander Ross for divers good Causes and Considerations me hereunto moving have made ordained Constituted and Appointed Charles Simms of Pittsburg Attorney at Law, my true and Lawfull at-

torney for me and in my name to sell transfer and Convey or otherwise dispose of all my right Title and Interest of in and to Two Tracts of Land the one situate on the Ohio River the other on Raccoon Creek also one Lott or parcel of Land on the banks of the Allgany River whereon the said Alexander Ross formerly had a house in the Town of Pittsburg in what manner and to such person or persons, as to him shall appear best and most conducive to my Interest, and for me and in my name to make and Execute such deeds and Conveyances as may be necessary for transferring and Conveying my Right and Title to said Lands to any person or persons that may become purchasers thereof or any part thereof hereby ratifying and Confirming whatever my said Attorney lawfully and legally
(71) shall do relative thereto In Witness whereof I have hereunto set my hand and seal this twenty sixth day of August 1775

Signed Sealed and delivered Alexr Ross [L S]
In presence of
C Graydon
James McKee
Danl Brown

At a Court Continued and held for Augusta County at Pittsburgh April the 17th 1776

This Power of Attorney from Alexander Ross to Charles Simms was proved by the Oaths of Caleb Graydon and Daniel Brown two of the Witnesses thereto and Ordered to be Certified

At a Court Continued and held for Augusta County at Pittsburgh April 18th 1776

This Power of Attorney from Alexander Ross to Charles Simms being formerly proved by the Oaths of Caleb Graydon and Daniel Brown two of the Witnesses thereto was this day further proved by the Oath of James McKee the other Witness thereto and Ordered to be recorded

Test

CONCLUSION.

The publication of the records of these old Virginia Courts, exercising jurisdiction over the valleys of the Monongahela and Ohio more than a century ago, has now been completed. Communications received by the editor have disclosed that these records have excited much interest both north and south of Mason and Dixon's Line. Their existence seems to have hitherto been wholly unknown to many of the historians of old Virginia. Our work, however, should be supplemented by a small addition.

It is only of late that the full significance of a portion of the contents of one of the deed books in the recorder's office for Washington County, Pennsylvania, has been understood. It is apparent that when Col. James Marshel, the first recorder of deeds for Washington County, had filled his first volume, marked Deed Book A, vol. 1, with deeds acknowledged before Washington County officials and recorded from January 1, 1782, to November 20, 1784, utilized for his next volume a book in which had been recorded a number of last wills that had been admitted to probate before the County courts of the District of West Augusta and Yohogania County, Virginia. These wills, with their probate, were first recorded in a manuscript volume, and the balance remaining blank was utilized by Colonel Marshel as his second volume, marked Deed Book B, vol. 1, by simply beginning his Washington County records with a deed recorded on November 20, 1784, and proceeding 410 pages until his last deed was recorded on April 25, 1786, when he struck the wills which had been recorded by Dorsey Pentecost, the Clerk of the old Virglnia Courts, many years before.

It will be remembered that at the session of the County Court for the District of West Augusta, held on September 18, 1776, at Augusta Town (now Washington, Pa.), Dorsey Pentecost, who then lived on the East Branch of Chartiers Creek, in what is now North Strabane Township, Washington County, Pennsylvania, was appointed Clerk of Court in the stead of John Madison, and on December 23, 1776, he was reappointed, and a demand was made by the Court upon John Madison, Jr., Deputy of John Madison, to turn over to his successor the records then in his possession, which demand was refused, and process awarded to compel compliance: Vol. I of these ANNALS, pp. 567, 568; Vol. II, pp. 79, 81. On the organization of Washington County, Pennsylvania, Dorsey Pentecost, theretofore an ardent Virginian, became an ardent Pennsylvanian and a prominent official of that jurisdiction.

On account of the genealogical interest in the old wills referred to, brief abstracts of them will now be presented as a final instalment of these papers.

ABSTRACTS OF OLD VIRGINIA WILLS.

1. Ellis Ellis, of Redstone Settlement; dated July 13, 1776; attested by Thomas Freeman, Thomas Prather and Leven Green; proved November 20, 1776, at a court for the District of West Augusta: Beneficiaries, wife, Ann; sons, Isaac, Thomas, Jonathan; daughter, Ann.

2. Jacob Lamb, of Pigeon Creek in West Augusta County; dated November 4, 1776; attested by John Crow, Andrew McClean, John Wright, Abraham Westfall, Archevil White; proved[1] June 24, 1777: Beneficiaries, brothers Peter, John; brother-in-law George Kintner; sisters Catharine, Susannah.

3. Job Robins; dated August 10, 1777; attested by Joseph Brown, Francis Sprouse; proved on August 25, 1777: Beneficiaries, wife Rebecca; sons Amos, James, John; daughter Anne.

4. Jonathan Reed, of West Augusta, Colony of Virginia; dated November 4, 1776; attested by Hugh McCreedy, Noah Fleaharty; appoints Edward Cook and Dorsey Pentecost and Joseph Beckett, to settle and have adjusted all his late public accounts in regard to his vitualing the Troops stationed on the Ohio; proved September 23, 1777: Beneficiaries, wife Sarah; sons John, Jonathan; daughters Mary, Sarah, Martha, Ruth; executors Edward Cook, wife Sarah, and Joseph Beckett.

5. Joseph Kirkwood, of Yohogania County, State of Virginia; dated April 24, 1777; attested by Nicholas Little, George Gallaspie, Robert Meek; proved October 29, 1777: Beneficiaries, wife Margaret; son David; unborn child, "the old woman," and Martha and Mary.

6. James Pearce, Yohogania County, State of Virginia; dated February 15, 1778; attested by James Wall, Joseph Warne, Walter Wall; proved March 24, 1778: Beneficiaries, wife Sarah; sons Andrew, Lewis, James, Stephen, Jonathan.

7. William Chaplin, of West Augusta, Colony of Virginia; attested by Charles Bilderback, Elizabeth Swearingen, William Nation; proved on March 23, 1778: Beneficiaries, Abraham Chaplin, Isaac Chaplin, Elizabeth Swearingen, Mary Chaplin, William Chaplin, Vance Chaplin, —devises "one place at Cain Tuck."

8. John Vance, of Yohogania County in Virginia; dated December 10, 1777; attested by William Crawford, Benjamin Wells, Samuel Hecks; proved March 23, 1778: Beneficiaries, wife Margaret, sons

[1] This and the wills following were all proved before the Yohogania County Court.

David, William (land on waters of Raccoon Creek joining Crohan's line), Moses; daughters Elizabeth, Mary.

9. James Freeman, Schoolmaster, in the County of Yohogania; dated July 3, 1778; attested by John Thompson, Gilbert Cameron; proved August 26, 1778: Sole beneficiary John McDonald, of the said county, farmer.

10. Abranam Vaughan, of Yohogania County, State of Virginia; dated September 8, 1778; attested by Edward Hatfield, Christopher Brice, Thomas Gist; proved September —, 1778: Beneficiaries, son Richard, daughters Isabel and Hannah Comly; devises a tract on "Harmon's Run, it being the place whereon I now reside."

11. Will of John Pearce, Senr., of Augusta County, Colony of Virginia; dated March 19, 1776; attested by Dorsey Pentecost, Moses Coe, John Peters; proved September —, 1778: Beneficiaries, grandson Daniel, son of son Daniel; sons Isaac, Elisha, Joseph, John, Jonathan, Andrew; daughters Mary Smith, Sarah Watkins.

12. Catharine Lamb, of Yohogania County; dated January 22, 1779; attested by Peter Swath, Henry Devore, Jeremia Washburn; proved March —, 1779: Beneficiaries, Catharine Kintner, Susannah Kintner; executor, George Kintner, husband of daughter Susannah.

13. James Devoor, of Yohogania County, Virginia; dated November 14, 1778; attested by Nicholas Depue, Tobias Decker, Daniel Depue, Jr.; proved March —, 1779: Beneficiaries, children Jacob, Andrew, Henry, John, Sarah Pearshal, Samuel; children under age David, Moses, Catharine, Francis, James; all his real estate, except the Ferry to sons David and Moses.

14. John Bleakly, of Frederick County, Virginia; dated November 20, 1779; attested by John Wright, Samuel Burns; proved March —, 1779: Beneficiaries, mother Margaret Megill, Henry Megill, each £100 if they come to America; Robert Bleakly, William Alexander.

15. Stephen Richards, of Yohogania County, Virginia; dated March 1, 1780: Beneficiaries, wife Elizabeth; sons Mordecai, Stephen, Thomas. [Will not all copied, and no probate entered.]

16. James Ross, Gentleman, "of Racune Settlement in Yohogania County, Virginia"; dated January 6, 1781; attested by James McClellan, James Ross; proved March —, 1781: Beneficiaries, wife Mary; sons James, Moses, Robert, Andrew, John; daughters, Hannah Andrews, Margaret Ross, Isabel Ross, Febee Ross.

INDEX

-A-

-B-

-C-

-G-

-H-

-Mc-

-Q-

-R-

-U-

-V-

-W-